THE ART OF NEEDLECRAFT

THE
ART OF
NEEDLECRAFT

BY
R. K. POLKINGHORNE, B.A.(Lond.)
AND
M. I. R. POLKINGHORNE, B.A.(Lond.)

WITH
THIRTY-TWO ART PLATES
AND
THREE HUNDRED AND TWENTY-EIGHT
DIAGRAMS IN THE TEXT

ASSOCIATED NEWSPAPERS LTD.
NORTHCLIFFE HOUSE   LONDON, E.C.4

PRINTED IN GREAT BRITAIN BY
MORRISON AND GIBB LTD., LONDON AND EDINBURGH

CONTENTS

PLATES

THE
ART OF NEEDLECRAFT

CHAPTER I

EMBROIDERY—INTRODUCTION

Introduction. Materials and Tools. Use of the Embroidery Frame.
Valuable Hints on Embroidery. Transferring Designs upon
Materials. Using Bought Transfer Designs, etc. Finishing and
Pressing Embroideries. Washing Embroidery.

OF all the crafts practised by women, embroidery remains
the most popular. In olden days it was, however,
still more popular perhaps because life was more leisurely and
" ready-made " garments not so easy to buy. To-day there
seems to be a revival of interest in needlecraft, especially in
embroidery. Beautiful work is being done, no longer depending
for its charm on the closely packed stitches or the tedious nature
of the work involved, but upon bold and intelligent designs.

Women of to-day have, too, a wonderful variety of materials
from which to select, and these materials inspire new methods and
new ideas.

But however modern the embroideress is, she must know
her stitches. Stitches are the language of her craft, they must
express the characteristic spirit of embroidery and no other
craft. In other words, her technique must be good if she wants
to make successful use of new ideas.

MATERIALS AND TOOLS

More detailed advice about materials will be given in the
different chapters on embroidery. Different kinds of embroidery

need of course slightly different materials. Here we are going to deal with materials in a general way. They are very simple :

(1) *Embroidery Silks or Threads and Fabrics.*—There is an endless variety of real and artificial silk, cotton, and wool-working threads. Most of the makers of silk, woollen, and cotton threads are willing to sell shade cards of their stock, and these prove invaluable for reference when an embroideress is starting a piece of work.

The embroidery itself can be done on linen, casement cloth, unbleached calico, glass-towelling, or some other strong cottons or silks. Canvas of different kinds is needed for some embroideries (see chapter on Embroideries done on Counted Threads), such as cross stitch and tapestry, and the right type is obtainable at any good art-needlework shop. It is useful to have bunches of patterns of linens, silks, woollens, and jute fabrics of all textures and colours that you think might form suitable backgrounds for your work. These should be kept up to date and renewed from time to time, because new fabrics are continually being put on the market.

(2) *A Pair of Small, Sharp Scissors.*—It is wise to have a cork in your embroidery basket, so that when you have finished your work, you can stick the points of your scissors into it. They get blunted easily.

(3) *Crewel or Embroidery Needles.*—Needles are so very important that they need a whole section to themselves. By degrees you will learn the importance of the right needles.

Embroidery needles have a long narrow eye, and their points are exceedingly fine. Experience soon shows one that the eye must be just big enough to take the silk or thread *easily* ; if a strand has to be pushed or coaxed through the eye with difficulty, it gets rubbed and roughened. The needle must also make a hole big enough for the following thread to pass through without catching or rubbing.

On the other hand, if the eye is too big, it easily becomes unthreaded, and the stitches do not look neat if the needle makes holes larger than the threads will fill. It pays to buy needles of the best quality. Always look at the eye when you buy needles. Inferior needles often have eyes imperfectly drilled ; the hole may be rough and this roughens the thread.

If by any chance your needle bends (it should not bend if it is a good needle) get rid of it at once, because you cannot make a straight stitch with a crooked needle. You will soon collect a good selection of needles, for experience and common sense will tell you that a twisted thread (round like a small cord) will fit best into round holes, while thin strands easily pass through flat ones. You can get needles with round and flat holes.

(4) *Wool Needles.*—If you begin with wool embroideries (and many people do because they are so quickly worked) you will need wool and wool needles. You will want these needles for wool cross-stitch, tapestry, and the various wool stitches. These are described in the chapters on Embroidery done on Counted Threads, and Tapestry.

Wool needles have blunted points and are thickish.

(5) *Other Equipments.*—When you come to certain special embroideries which need large holes for the thread to pass through, you can get *punch needles*, but at first you can manage quite well with the ordinary ones.

In some embroidery, for example in *broderie anglaise* and eyelet work, you will want to make holes—neat little round holes. At first, perhaps, you will use the points of your little sharp scissors, but this is not very satisfactory. You will find it pays to buy a *stiletto* ; this only costs a few pence, and you will be constantly finding a use for it.

USE OF THE EMBROIDERY FRAME

It looks very expert and workmanlike to have your work stretched tautly in one of these hoop-like embroidery frames, but apart from looks a great many embroideries are much easier to work when your material is well stretched.

Hoop Frames.—Hoop frames consist of two rings of wood, one of which fits closely within the other. The material is laid on the smaller hoop, then the larger one is pressed over it, holding the stuff stretched. It is useful to have two hoop frames, one of medium size and one small, but the medium one will do very well alone. The best hoop is one that has some kind of screw or tension arrangement to keep the material from slipping. A steel frame with a spring is preferable to one made of wood. It does not damage the material.

A medium-sized frame can be rested on the table or the back of a chair. A similar kind, mounted on a stand, can be obtained, but this type is more expensive. It must be remembered that a frame is not essential. Some embroideresses are inclined to work too much in a frame, whilst others who have become so skilful through constant practice scarcely ever use a frame.

On the whole, perfection of technique is perhaps more easily attained in a frame, for the work does not pucker, and greater precision can be obtained in working out the design.

Frame work is of course a slower process in which both hands are used, the left hand on the top of the frame passing the needle through the material to the right hand underneath. For large work (tapestry work, etc.) ordinary stretchers supported on trestles are the most usual. (See Tapestry Work.)

VALUABLE HINTS ON EMBROIDERY

1. Take care that your needle does not get rusty. This often happens if you work out of doors. It is wise to have an emery cushion in your embroidery outfit : this is most useful for keeping your needles smooth and shining. All needles work better for an occasional polish.

2. Sometimes it is really necessary to knot your thread when you begin your embroidery, as when you make gathers for smocking, but the general rule for embroidery is—*don't make knots*. Begin by making a few running-stitches at the wrong side of the material, just where your embroidery will cover them. Some people make a couple of tiny back stitches one over the other.

3. Don't thread your needle with too long a strand of silk or wool, for it begins to roughen and lose its freshness through passing so often through the material. When you have finished one needleful take care to bring the needle through on the wrong side, and leave enough thread to be able to run it in and out of a few stitches at the back, that will hold the end neatly hidden.

4. Never break your silk or thread, cut it. Directly it begins to look the worse for wear, get rid of it and have a new thread. It is better to waste your embroidery silk than to spoil your finished work.

5. Use a neatly made thimble that is quite plain, one with

a fancy surface may catch your silk as you work. Some people prick their left forefinger a good deal as they sew, and have to wear a little shield that can be bought at an embroidery shop. A simpler remedy is to stick a bit of stamp paper round your finger, renewing this as required. A forefinger roughened with needle-pricks is a very serious handicap if you are working with silks.

6. Make sure that your hands are clean. Some people are naturally clean workers, but others find it difficult to keep their work clean. Your hands may sometimes look perfectly spotless and yet they seem to soil your work ! This is because your hands tend to get sticky ; to remedy this, soak your hands in tepid water with a little alum dissolved in it, then let this dry on. This is a very wise precaution when doing white work.

7. Have a cotton bag that is dustproof to keep your work in, and either wear a sewing-apron or keep a large handkerchief (man's size) to spread over your lap. If your work is very delicate, keep the part already worked covered with tissue paper.

Transferring Designs upon Materials

In many forms of embroidery it is necessary to transfer designs upon the material.

Suitable designs will be suggested in the coming pages in connection with the different types of embroidery. Here we are dealing mainly with the transferring of designs. Designs will vary not only with the type of embroidery used, but also with the use to which the finished article is to be put ; for example, a design for a tablecloth should always allow for the fact that the article must be frequently washed, and so on. Suitability of design will be discussed again in connection with the various stitches.

Now there are many ways of tracing a design on to the material ; these vary according to the colour or the texture of the stuff. Before we begin a detailed description of these ways, one or two general principles should be remembered about placing the design.

Placing the Design.—(1) The design must be placed accurately on the material. Certain precautions must be taken to ensure that the edges of a border agree with the thread of the material.

or that a panel is placed in the centre of the material to be embroidered.

That this shall be so, the edge of each side of the material should be made straight according to the thread, and if the material is likely to fray, it should be overcast. In the case of a border, when the distance from the edges has been decided, it is wise to make a line of tacking in a contrasting colour accurately round the margins in conformity with the thread of the material. The corresponding edges of the border design can then be pinned on to the tacked line while the tracing is being made.

(2) In the case of a design that entirely covers the whole surface of the material, or in the case of a central panel, use the following method for placing the design : First draw a line down the middle of the design from top to bottom and then draw another line across the middle from left centre to right centre. Next tack similar lines on the material, taking care to follow the warp and weft (*i.e.* thread directions) of the material. If these two sets of lines are now carefully pinned over each other, there should be no difficulties, and the design as a whole will be found to be placed correctly with regard to the thread direction of the material.

Transferring Designs.—Better results can often be obtained by making one's own designs, but for those who have little leisure bought transfers are very convenient. The danger of using bought transfers is that one is apt to choose unsuitable designs. Many designs that look pretty and are chosen for their prettiness are most unsuited for the article that they have to decorate. However, with care and thought good and suitable transfers can be found, and these save a great deal of trouble. We will begin by describing how to deal with bought transfers.

Using Bought Transfer Designs

It is a great advantage sometimes to buy transfer designs which are ready to be ironed off on the fabric. These are quite inexpensive and there is a wide choice available. It is important, as we have said before, when choosing a design to pick out one which is suited both to the fabric and to the type of embroidery you wish to do.

Two Kinds of Transfers.—Transfer designs are printed in two colours, blue and yellow. It is best to use the blue wherever possible as it is less trying to the eyes, and there are a greater variety of designs printed in this colour.

If you are working on dark colours and on blue and mauve, yellow transfers must be used, as a blue design will not show up.

On any dark green or brown materials, especially browns that have a yellow tinge, yellow transfers are best, but the design should be worked by daylight, as it does not show up too clearly.

Ironing the Transfer correctly.—A clear outline is most important, so the transfer must be correctly ironed on the material. Use a smooth padded surface, such as an ironing-board, and see that the material lies evenly upon it, as any hollows, however slight, will spoil the outline of the design. Lay the material on, right side up.

Different materials require slightly different heating of the iron, so that it is wise to experiment by stamping on to an odd piece of material any part of the design that is not wanted. If the iron is too cold the transfer does not mark at all or only very faintly ; if the iron is too hot the outline is blurred, heavy, and thick.

An iron rightly heated gives a clear firm outline. An irregular outline is caused by an uneven surface under the material or by faulty heating.

Take care to arrange the transfer face downwards on the right side of the material and in the correct position ; fasten by pins well away from the design, so that there is no danger of the iron going over the pins and so making marks on the stuff. Before removing the transfer lift a corner to see that the design has come off clearly.

Blue transfers require more heat to mark well than yellow transfers, while the yellow need slower and more even pressure. To absorb part of the heat when ironing put two thicknesses of newspaper over the transfer. If the transfer does not come off well, press again with only one sheet of newspaper under the iron. If you have much pressing to do, it is necessary to heat the iron several times, for as the iron cools the outline becomes faint.

Remember : it is most important *to press* the iron down on the paper, then lift it to move it to another part, and press again. You must not move it backwards and forwards as in ordinary ironing. You are really *stamping* the transfer pattern on to the material.

Be careful not to unpin the transfer until you have looked underneath one corner to see if it is coming off clearly ; if not, press again. Once the transfer is shifted, ever so slightly, it cannot be put back into the right place again.

Transferring Designs on Different Materials.—All smooth fabrics, as a rule, take transfers well. Some fabrics need special treatment. *Organdie* and *voile* should have the design stamped on the *wrong* side. The outline can be seen quite clearly, and is not so heavy as if stamped on the right side.

It is better not to stamp thin transparent stuff such as georgette, chiffon, and net. Tack the transfer underneath the material so that the design shows through ; work through fabric and transfer and then tear the paper away.

Velvet and other pile materials will not take transfers unless the nap is flattened first by pressing it on the right side. Then when it is cool, stamp off the transfer. When the design is embroidered the nap can be raised again by steaming it from the wrong side.

Another method is to tack the transfer over the right side of the velvet and work through the transfer and the material as already described.

Removing Outlines stamped on by Mistake.—This cannot be done from white and pastel satins. If the material is washable, the lines can be removed by washing and well rubbing with good soap flakes. If the material cannot be washed or if washing is unsuccessful, the outlines should be rubbed hard with benzine With some materials methylated spirits is best.

Transferring Original Designs

1. *Using Transfer Ink.*—First draw the design on cartridge paper. Make a clean line tracing of it on thin transparent paper (not tracing paper) ; now ink over the lines of the design with a fine brush or pen, using transfer ink, but on the side of the paper opposite to that on which the pencil tracing was made

(otherwise the design would be reversed). Now iron the tracing on the material.

2. *Pricking and Pumicing Method.*—If this method is used the design must be traced on tracing paper. Then with a fairly fine needle prick the lines of the design with little holes, taking care to space them evenly and closely together. Fix the eye of the needle into a fold of strong paper, so that the needle can be held more easily. Now place the pricked tracing over the material and pin firmly to a drawing-board, then rub powdered pumice (obtainable from any chemist) evenly through the holes with a soft pouncing pad. If the design has to be transferred to white material, then powdered charcoal must be mixed with the pumice powder, until the mixture is dark enough to show up.

The tracing paper must be secured firmly, as the slightest movement causes the outline to be somewhat blurred. If this should happen, shake off the powder from the material and try again. When the design has been clearly marked on the material, blow away any surplus pumice. Now paint over the lines with a fine brush in suitable water-colour paint. On very dark material the lines must be painted in Chinese white, to which a little gum arabic is added to prevent the paint crumbling off when the material is being embroidered.

One advantage of this method is that the transfers may be used over and over again, and this is very desirable when the design has to be repeated.

3. *Carbon Paper Method.*—The carbon paper used must be an *embroidery* carbon, not a typewriter one. Any surplus carbon should be rubbed off the paper before using it, otherwise it might soil the material.

Place the material on a drawing-board, then the carbon paper, carbon side downwards, and over this the design. Pin the design firmly, taking care that the drawing-pins do not go through the carbon paper. Go over the outlines of the design with a hard pencil, or a leather tracer, pressing firmly and evenly, but the impression should be delicate and faint—not heavy and dark. For dark materials a white carbon must be used. When the transfer is finished, go over the lines with a fine brush in water-colours, if necessary.

The disadvantage of this method is that unless every care is taken, the carbon paper makes unwanted marks on the material. These marks have a tendency to spread over the surface when the material is being embroidered, and give it a soiled appearance.

In the case of very fine materials or materials such as velvet, the method of transferring the design has already been described when dealing with Bought Transfers.

FINISHING AND PRESSING EMBROIDERIES

Finish off all thread ends tidily on the wrong side, and cut off any that stick out. In taking out the tack-threads use a small pair of tweezers, as it is sometimes difficult to get at the threads with fingers only.

All embroidery, when finished, must be pressed on the wrong side, on a blanket spread evenly over a deal table. Two or more blankets should be used when pressing enbroideries with a raised surface such as broderie anglaise, satin-stitch and button-holed outlines, so that the design has something soft to press into. Bead-work needs two or three layers of blankets. Spread over the blanket a piece of clean muslin.

If the work is large, the blanket should be spread on the floor so that the whole piece can be laid out at once, and smoothed and coaxed until the edges are square and the sides straight. It is wise to fasten in place by pinning it at the centre of each edge and then at the corners.

Damping the Work.—Dip a clean sponge in tepid water, wring it until no more water can be squeezed out, and then pass it gently and evenly over the back of the work. Cover the work with a piece of muslin and press with a hot iron.

The Iron.—How hot the iron should be depends upon the type of embroidery. A fairly hot iron is necessary for white work, especially on linen ; a warm iron for taffetas and other silks ; a cool iron for artificial silk and organdie, as heat hardens the silk and tends to take out the colour.

How to get rid of Puckers.—Broderie Anglaise, Richelieu, and some other embroideries tend to pucker in working. To get rid of these puckers spread out the embroidery on a board, smooth it, and pin it to shape. Then damp the wrong side with a sponge, and leave it stretched until it is dry.   If necessary sponge again and let it dry, now lay a piece of damp muslin over it, and press the wrong side with a fairly hot iron.

Tapestry and large pieces of cross stitch must always be carefully stretched. First make the back of the work thoroughly damp by sponging ; then spread it out right side downwards on a drawing-board and pin it in position, taking care that the edges are perfectly straight ; they will probably need a little stretching and adjusting. Leave it to dry. Then unpin it and lay it face downwards on two thicknesses of blanket and press with a fairly warm iron.

Appliqué and wool embroideries must be pressed on a very thick blanket.

WASHING EMBROIDERY

Dissolve the best soap flakes procurable in very hot water to make a lather. When the lather is not too hot for your hand, squeeze the work in it very gently, then place it in clean water of the same temperature and squeeze again ; then put it into fresh water for a last squeezing.

Now spread an absorbent towel on the table, place the embroidery on it, smooth it out and cover with another towel. Take out as much moisture as you can by patting the work all over.

If the embroidery is on linen or cotton, iron it while it is damp ; silk and georgette embroideries must not be ironed until the work is *just* dry. Place the work face downwards and cover with a piece of dry cambric or muslin. It is best to press a little at a time and lift up a part to see how it is getting on. Embroideries must always be pressed at once ; they should not be left damped and rolled up for a future pressing.

CHAPTER II

SIMPLE MODERN EMBROIDERY

Useful Stitches—Buttonhole Stitch, Tailor's Buttonhole, Buttonhole Stitch (Linked), Long-and-Short Buttonhole Stitch, Buttonhole Stem Stitch, Surface Buttonholing, Cretan Stitch, Chain Stitches, Back Stitch, Satin Stitch, Stem Stitch, Outline Stitch, Seed Stitch, Rice Stitch.

White Embroideries of Long Ago—Swiss, Renaissance, Richelieu, Madeira, Venetian, Hebeo.

Embroidery upon White Material

FORMERLY the kind of embroidery we are now going to describe was only known by the name of " White Embroidery." This term is no longer correct, because it is done in colours quite as often as in white, so we have headed this section " Embroidery upon White Material."

Once it was exclusively used for trimming underlinen and articles of dress, and the different kinds of white embroidery are distinguished by the different modes of working. It includes embroidery in which the pattern is wholly or partly cut away, as in broderie Anglaise and Madeira work ; embroidery in which the background is cut away, as in cut-work, Richelieu, and Venetian ; and surface embroidery which involves no cutting, such as much initial and monogram stitchery.

We will begin by describing the stitches most useful in modern days, and the forms of white embroidery still popular. The stitches we shall describe are probably the most important in modern embroidery. Then we will say just a few words about the old form of white embroidery—Swiss, Madeira, Renaissance, Richelieu, etc.

Method of Work.—Embroidery, as we have said before, is often done on an embroidery-frame called " tambour-frame."

Only skilful workers can altogether dispense with this aid, for an untrained hand can hardly avoid puckering. If you work without a foundation, the material must be held quite smoothly over the forefinger so that the threads lie perfectly straight, otherwise the pattern is very apt to get pulled out of shape in the working. With the three other fingers you hold the material fast, the thumb resting on the work itself, beyond the outline of the pattern, which must be turned towards the worker. It is always the outside edge of a pattern that should be turned towards the palm of the hand.

Transferring the Design.—This has already been dealt with in Chapter I.

USEFUL STITCHES

As we have said before, the first need of the embroideress is to know her stitches well. Never begin a piece of embroidery until you have practised all the stitches that you are going to use.

It is an excellent plan to make a " sampler " of a dozen or so of the most used stitches. It gives practice in making the stitches and you can easily carry it about with you and consult it when you want to choose a stitch. Linen is the best material for a sampler. To keep the edges from fraying, practise the various buttonhole stitches that are now going to be described around it, and then add rows of the rest of the stitches across it. Work your stitches in different colours so that they show up well.

Buttonhole Stitch (Fig. 1).—Buttonhole stitch is to embroidery very much what hemming stitch is to plain sewing. It has a host of uses and is both practical and decorative. It is used to neaten all kinds of edges—scalloping is simple buttonhole stitch—it outlines many types of embroidery, it holds down the edges of appliqué (see section on Appliqué), and it may be used to carry out a complete design. It is very much used in the type of embroidery that we are now describing, and is especially useful in cut-work. You will notice how useful it is in broderie anglaise and Hardanger where it finishes cut edges firmly and prettily. Many small flowers in outline embroidery are quickly worked in open buttonhole stitch. It also, or with other stitches, makes countless pretty borders for dress purposes.

The open variety of buttonhole stitch, in which the stitches are well separated, is often referred to as blanket stitch. (See Blanket Stitch.) Really, blanket stitch is one variety of open buttonhole stitch—the kind used to edge blankets.

Every type of buttonhole stitch is best worked with a twisted thread.

To work the Buttonhole Stitch.—Fig. 1 shows how to work the buttonhole stitch. It is worked from left to right. Hold the thread down with the thumb, and place the needle through the material at right angles to the direction of this thread. Draw the needle through over the thread still held in position by the thumb, as in Fig. 1. Pull up the thread, and it will form a bar along the edge, known as the *purl*—continuous yet starting afresh with every stitch. This purl is the distinguishing mark of every type of buttonhole stitch.

There are many varieties of buttonhole stitch.

Tailor's Buttonhole (Fig. 2) is begun in a similar way, but before the needle is drawn through the material, the thread

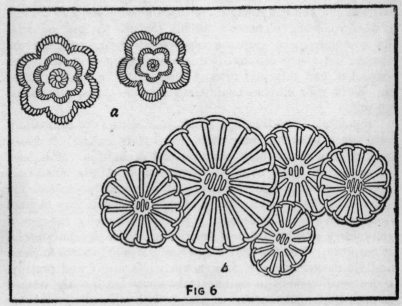

FIG 6

FIG. 6.—(*a*) Surface Buttonholing.   (*b*) Buttonhole Flowers.

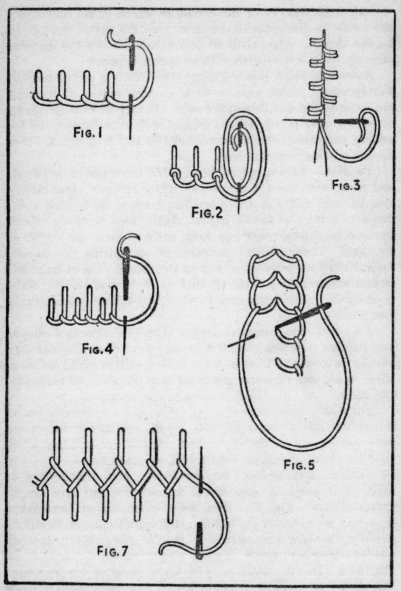

FIG. 1.—Buttonhole Stitch. FIG. 2.—Tailor's Buttonhole. FIG. 3.—Linked Buttonhole Stitch. FIG. 4.—Long-Short Buttonhole Stitch. FIG. 5.—Buttonhole Stem Stitch. FIG. 7.—Cretan Stitch.

coming from the eye of the needle is placed round and under
the needle in the opposite direction from the thread held down
by the thumb.   The needle is then drawn through the material
(Fig. 2).   Work this stitch with *no* spaces between.

Buttonhole Stitch (Linked) (Fig. 3).—This is a pretty form of
buttonholing, useful when a seam or two widths of material
are to be joined in a decorative way.   It may be used for seams
of bedspreads, two-material cushion covers, underwear, or for
adding contrasting hems to tablecloths and tray-cloths.   (See
section on Insertion Stitches.)

To work.—Fold in narrow hems along the edges to be joined,
and tack them down if necessary.   Place the two edges closely
side by side, either in an embroidery-hoop or by tacking them
down to a strip of brown paper.   Take three narrowly spaced
buttonhole stitches over one hem, making them the depth of
the hem.   Then, without fastening off or cutting the thread,
take three more just below, but in the second edge of material.
Continue alternating three stitches in each edge till the seam
is complete.   The stitch may be varied by taking two each side
(see Fig. 3).

Long-and-Short Buttonhole Stitch (Fig. 4).—This is a simple
and popular edge finish suitable for any piece of work.   Another
version is to use stitches of three heights, either going up from
short to tall and then starting again with the short, or gradually
descending from the tall through medium, to short.

Buttonhole Stem Stitch (Fig. 5).—This is a useful variation of
buttonhole stitch useful for bold stems, veinings of leaves, or
as a border on children's clothes.   Buttonhole stitches when
used for stems, leaves, or flowers, etc., are known as—

Surface Buttonholing or *Buttonhole-Stitch Embroidery.*—
Buttonhole stitch is very useful for carrying out any simple
flower design.   Fig. 6 shows some examples of buttonhole
flowers.   Work round the outline with spaced buttonhole stitch,
making the long stitches about ⅛ inch long.   Work another
row of buttonhole stitch, slightly smaller inside the first, as in
Fig. 6, *a*.   In the centre work a small circle of buttonholing.
The flower in Fig. 6, *b*, is worked with long buttonhole stitches
and can have a centre of satin stitch.   For buttonhole rings,
see Chapter IV.

Buttonhole Stem Stitch (Fig. 5)

To work.—Rule two parallel lines half an inch to three-quarters of an inch apart, to keep the stitches perfectly even. Rule a third line down the middle. Make a line of slanting buttonhole stitches, well spaced out, outwards from this middle line, with their purl edge along one of the outer lines. Work a second row on the other side, with its spikes meeting those of the first in the middle. When this stitch is used as a border it looks very effective if the spikes are more widely spaced and a French knot is placed between every two.

Cretan Stitch. Another Variation of the Buttonhole Stitch (Fig. 7).—This stitch consists of buttonhole stitches placed back to back, as in Fig. 7, the narrow space between the two rows causing the heading to form a plait down the middle of the stitch. It is a bold stitch and useful for borders and as an insertion stitch. It is usually worked on white linen in red or blue.

Chain Stitches.—This group of stitches is a most interesting and extensive one. For bold outlining or for filling the double outline of stems quickly and effectively, this stitch is excellent. It is said that chain stitch can be used in more ways than any other stitch. As an outline stitch or as a solid filling it is equally successful. It can be used in coloured embroidery worked on silk or linen, or executed solely in white. In both cases it is successful. The decorative possibilities of its varieties when arranged in bands and worked spontaneously are very attractive, and chain stitch itself, used on large shapes, gives texture and meaning to the embroidery.

Chain stitch is also a good padding stitch to use under scalloping or satin stitch. (See sections on Scalloping and Satin Stitch.)

Chain stitch uses up a good deal of thread, and this must be remembered when buying thread for the chain stitch.

To work.—Ordinary chain stitch is simple to work (see Fig. 8). Work downwards or towards yourself. Bring the needle up from the wrong side at the top of the line or design. Put the needle in close to where it came up, holding the thread down under the needle with the left thumb to form a loop. Pull up the thread. Now insert the needle inside the loop, bringing it out again a little lower down the line. Pull up the thread to

form a small loop, as before ; this will give the series of links
from which the stitch is named.

Work chain stitch a little loosely or it will pucker the stuff.
Keep the loops of even size (see Fig. 8).

Chain Stitch (Twisted).—This is a striking variation of chain
stitch, and it can be used for decorating hems of household
embroidered articles or as a dress decoration.

To work.—Work as for ordinary chain stitch, with this
difference. Instead of starting each stitch (after the first)
within the loop already formed, place the needle to the left of
the last loop. It may also be worked much more closely together,
so that the links do not show up separately, and the effect is
of a rope rather than a chain. It is then called *Rope Chain
Stitch*.

Zigzag Chain Stitch or Diagonal Chain Stitch (Fig. 9).—
This makes a pretty border. Draw two threads to show the
width of the border, or pencil two lines. Take the first chain
stitch slantwise from bottom to top, the second down again to
the bottom, and repeat, as in Fig. 9. Care should be taken that
the needle splits the thread of the preceding stitch in order to
keep the stitch in position.

Back Stitch (Fig. 10).—This is an elementary and important
stitch both in embroidery and plain sewing. In embroidery it
is used for outlines where a broken rather than a smooth look
is required. It is specially suitable for very indented outlines,
as it goes easily round even sharp curves. It is a favourite
stitch for quilting. (See section on Quilting.) In plain sewing
it is used where a very strong join is needed.

To work.—Work from right to left, holding your material
so that the line you are to stitch is across your fingers. The
needle itself is actually moved from left to right. Bring the
needle through to the right side of the material, and put it in
again to the right of where it came out. Bring it out to the
left of where it first came through. Each time the needle passes
back to fill the gap making stitches of equal length, as in Fig. 10.
Continue alternating a short back stitch on the surface with a
double-length one underneath. All the back stitches should
connect neatly, be the same length, and be worked loosely
enough not to pucker the material. If short back stitches are

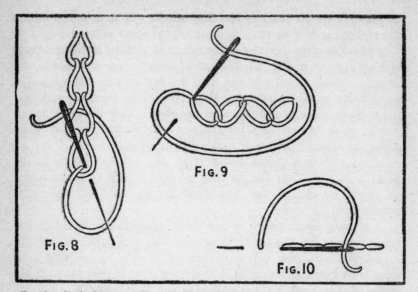

FIG. 8.—Chain Stitch.   FIG. 9.—Zigzag Chain Stitch.   FIG. 10.—Back Stitch.

worked in coarse thread, not quite touching each other, almost a beaded effect will result.

Satin Stitch (Fig. 11).—This is merely top sewing laid out flat and the stitches set close together. It is perhaps the most commonly used stitch in embroidery and is suited for practically all materials. If a certain modelled or raised effect is desired (as often in white embroidery), it is advisable to pad the surface which is to be satin-stitched with several long stitches of coarse thread, which may then be covered over. (See section on Couching and Laid Work.)

Since satin stitch is the most important of all filling stitches, it should be practised until it can be worked to look as smooth and satiny as its name. It is much used for leaves and in flower embroidery.

To work.—Satin stitch is a series of stroke stitches lying side by side so closely that none of the fabric shows between them (see Fig. 11). Bring the needle through to the right side on one edge of the outline to be filled, and put it in again exactly opposite on the other edge of the outline, making a straight line of thread across the space. Bring the needle up again as close as possible to the start of the first stitch, put it in again beside the end of the first stitch, and so on till the space is filled (Fig. 11). The effect is often prettier if the stitch is worked slanting across the outline, as in Fig. 11, instead of directly up and down and across. Slanting stitches are used for leaves, etc. If veins are needed, the worker may define these by making them the junction between one set of stitches and another. Care must be taken not to work one set of satin stitches into another, as this gives a ragged or indefinite appearance to the work.

Long-and-Short Satin Stitch (Fig. 12).—If the space to be filled is so wide that the stitches would be very long and liable to catch in things, the variation known as Long-and-Short Stitch must be used.

Long-and-short stitch is also best adapted for working one colour gradually into another, as in the shaded petals of flowers.

Stem Stitch, also called *Crewel Stitch* (Fig. 13).—This is a very favourite outline stitch, and is used a great deal for working stems and leaf-veins when embroidering flower motifs. Fig. 13 shows how it is worked. Work from the bottom of your line upwards, keeping the thread always to the *right of your* needle, as in Fig. 13. Bring the needle through from the wrong side, and put it through again on the line or stitch-space above. Bring your needle out at your starting-point, and repeat, always bringing your needle out at the top of the previous stitch. At the wrong side of your work this gives a line of perfectly even back stitch.

Strictly speaking, in stem stitch the stitches are overlapped more than in *crewel* stitch, but in practice the two are slightly different varieties of the same stitch. Stem stitch is also worked from left to right.

There are two variations of the stem stitch :

(1) Work as before, but bring your needle out each time just to the left, a thread or so lower than the top of the previous stitch. This gives a much thicker line and a corded effect.

(2) As before, but this time bring out your needle well above the top of your previous stitch. This has a looser, lighter effect, but is decorative and very quickly worked. At the wrong side you get the effect of a line of running stitches.

Outline Stitch.—Practically the same as stem stitch but the

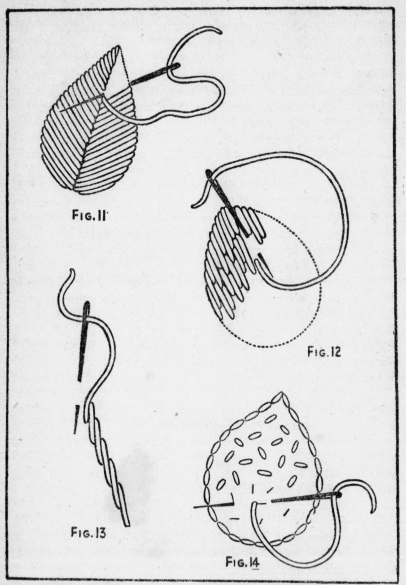

FIG. 11

FIG. 12

FIG. 13

FIG. 14

FIG. 11.—Satin Stitch.   FIG. 12.—Long-and-Short Satin Stitch.
FIG. 13.—Stem Stitch or Crewel Stitch.   FIG. 14.—Seed Stitch.

thread is kept to the left of the needle. A popular outlining stitch easily confused with stem stitch, but the position of the thread and stitches varies in the two.

To work.—It can be worked upwards or from left to right. To work upwards, start at the bottom of the outline to be covered. Bring the needle through from the wrong side, and take a stitch a little higher up, the needle pointing downwards. Keep the thread to the left of, and underneath, the needle. Pull up the thread. Pick up a second stitch from above downwards, making the bottom of this come out just at the top of the first stitch. Continue in the same way until the line is covered.

Seed Stitch (Fig. 14).—This is a light and dainty filling stitch. It is really a small back stitch, or, to be more correct, a number of small back stitches scattered over the surface to be filled. Some embroideresses insist that these stitches should be worked in regular rows, and evenly spaced, the spaces in one line below the stitches in its neighbour.

The seed stitch is also known as Dot or Mignonette Stitch. It is generally used when a broken filling is more effective than a solid one. Also when surfaces are large or backgrounds are large, seed stitch can be worked much more quickly than satin stitch. Some workers make very tiny stitches or running stitches at intervals all over the surface instead of the back stitch. These do not stand up so much nor are they so noticeable as the back stitches.

Rice Stitch.—This is another very simple stitch for backgrounds or filling other large spaces, such as big flower petals. It is really a larger edition of seed stitch.

To work.—Simply make, as for seed stitch, a number of stroke stitches each the size of a grain of rice, scattering them irregularly over the surface to be filled ; they can be worked as running stitches ; or, for a more raised and pleasing effect, as back stitches.

WHITE EMBROIDERY OF LONG AGO

Those interested in the history of needlework will like to know a little about the different kinds of embroidery once known as " White Embroidery."

Swiss Embroidery.—This kind of embroidery is worked in satin stitch with open-worked centres. (See broderie anglaise.) Madeira work is very similar.

Renaissance Embroidery. — This is the term applied to embroidery worked entirely in buttonholing and connected by buttonhole bars without picots. The buttonholing is done over a single tracing thread and of the same width throughout, excepting on the outside edge, where it may be made a little wider. The flowers and leaves on the outside edge are often ornamented with picots in dot stitch. The designs used are of the type known as Renaissance, and consist largely of scrolls and arabesques. (See coming chapters for Picots.)

Richelieu Embroidery.—A beautifully bold form of cut-work in which the design is outlined in buttonhole stitch and the background cut away, twisted or woven bars with picots connect the various parts of the design. The designs used are less conventional and more varied than in Renaissance embroidery and include figures, animals, and flowers.

Madeira Embroidery is practically a variation of broderie anglaise, worked by the women of the island of Madeira. It is also called stiletto work, because the whole of the pattern, except for satin-stitched dots, is pierced with a stiletto, or cut. In this it differs from broderie anglaise, in which much of the design (leaves, etc.) is satin-stitched. (See Chapter IV. for Broderie Anglaise.)

Venetian Embroidery is very like Richelieu embroidery (see this heading), but differs from it in having the buttonholed outlines well padded, so that they stand out in relief. Inside the buttonholed outline the linen is not left plain, as in Richelieu, but is embellished with fancy filling or open-work stitches.

Hebeo Embroidery is of Danish origin. It dates from the sixteenth century, and is a special form of white embroidery worked for centuries by the women of a certain Danish *hede* (heath) on the linen they spun and wove from their home-grown flax. Old Hebeo work was at its best about 1840, but afterwards it declined. Some of its former beauty has been revived by a Danish art school in modern times. It is used for table and house linen, and combines chain-stitch embroidery in graceful designs with open-work patterns and satin-stitched flowers.

It is very interesting to visit antique shops and museums, such as the South Kensington Museum in London, and examine specimens of beautiful old embroidery ; from them one often gets good ideas for designs and pattern-making.

CHAPTER III

SOME MORE SIMPLE STITCHES AND USEFUL IDEAS FOR EMBROIDERY

Feather Stitches of different kinds, Fly Stitch, Lazy-Daisy Stitch, Wheat-ear Stitch, Stroke Stitch, Split Stitch, Wave Stitch, Ladder Stitch, Roumanian Stitch, Coral Stitch, French Knot, Rose Stitch, Bullion Stitch, Pekinese Stitch, Gradation in Embroidery, the Irish Stitch. The Herringbone Group of Stitches.

BESIDES the useful stitches already described in Chapter II., there are a great many more simple, pretty stitches that one must know both for *plain needlework* and fancy work. The ones we are now going to describe include the very popular and necessary Feather Stitches and Herringbone group of stitches. These stitches you will meet with over and over again in different parts of this book. You will also find in this chapter some stitches that are new to you and that you will like because they are so simple and decorative. You will like to decorate a tea-cloth with the Irish stitch, and try your hand at gradation in embroidery.

Feather Stitch (Fig. 15).—This is quick and dainty when a bordering effect is wanted, giving a lacy and open effect. It can be used to finish the hems or edges of embroidered articles, and is especially used for decorating in a simple way children's frocks and underwear. It can also be worked inside a leaf outline when you want a natural veined look.

To work.—The beauty of this stitch depends upon its even-ness, so at first pencil-lines to work along will prove a help. If you study a line of feather-stitching by holding it upright you will see that it is really a simple form of buttonhole stitch, with the stitches below each other instead of alongside.

32

Rule two lines as far apart as you wish the width of your feather stitch to be. (With practice you will soon get the knack of keeping the stitches regular.) Bring your needle through at the top of the left-hand line, hold down the thread with your left thumb, and put the needle through in the right-hand line lower down. Make a little straight stitch down the line (or a little slanting one, as in Fig. 15), bringing the needle out *over* the thread. Pull down your thread to make the feather-loop, as in buttonholing, then cross to the left-hand line, and make a similar downward stitch in that. Repeat as in Fig. 15.

Feather Stitch (Triangular).—This is only a slight variation of ordinary feather stitch, but it has a more formal look. It is especially suited to embroideries with straight-line effects, and is perhaps one of the best types of feather stitch for crazy patchwork.

To work.—Use, as before, two parallel pencil-lines about ¼ inch apart as guides. Bring the needle up from the wrong side. Take a stitch *exactly* along the left-hand line, pointing towards you, and keeping the thread *under* the needle. Take the next

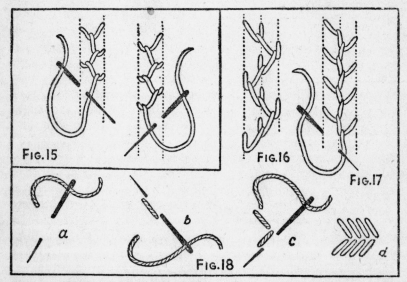

FIG. 15.—Feather-stitching (Simple). FIG. 16.—Double Feather Stitch. FIG. 17.—Fishbone Feather Stitch. FIG. 18.—Fishbone Stitch.

2

stitch in the same way down the right-hand line, making its top level with the bottom of the first stitch. Remember as in buttonhole stitch to keep the thread always beneath the needle.

Feather Stitch (Double and Treble) (Fig. 16).—For this rule three parallel lines, ⅜ inch apart for Double and ½ inch apart for Treble.

Begin at the top of the left-hand line, come across to the middle line and make the second stitch, then down to the third line (the right-hand line) for the third stitch. Go back to the middle line, then to the left-hand line, and repeat.

Work treble feather stitch just as double, but with one more stitch on each side.

These stitches are, of course, only more elaborate variations of feather stitch, and they are useful for making wider borders or as trimmings for children's frocks.

Feather Stitch (Closed).—Work as for simple feather stitch, but take rather longer stitches down each side. Then, instead of leaving spaces between the stitches, put your needle back at the lower end of the previous stitch at the side on which you are working. This gives an effect of two lines of back stitch, with a zigzag line down the middle. It shows up along a hem.

Feather Stitch (Fishbone) (Fig. 17).—Rule three lines as for double feather stitch. Bring your thread through at the top of the left line and put it back through the middle line lower down. Bring it out again in the middle line, farther down, over the thread. Put your needle through in the right-hand line, level with the point you came through in the middle, then make an oblique stitch, bringing your needle out in the middle line. Put it back in the left-hand line, level with the point it came through on the right-hand line, and make another oblique stitch to the middle. Continue in the same way (Fig. 17). Feather stitch (fishbone) must not be confused with fishbone stitch that we will now describe here for convenience, although it does not belong to the Feather Stitch family.

Fishbone Stitch (Fig. 18).—This stitch is often used for filling leaves. It is worked from left to right. Bring the thread through to the right side of the material. Put in the needle ⅛ inch to the right and ¼ inch down. Bring it out ⅛ inch to the left and ¼ inch down (Fig. 18). (Again a line ruled down the middle

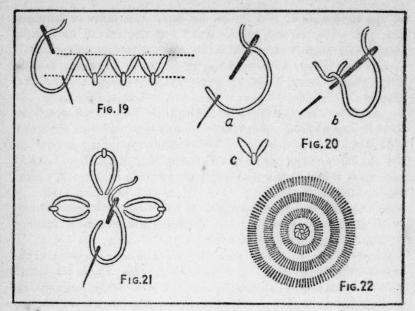

FIG. 19.—Fly Stitch.   FIG. 20.—Another form of Fly Stitch.   FIG. 21.—Lazy
Daisy.   FIG. 22.—The Stroke Stitch.

will help the beginner.) Pull the thread through. Now, pointing the needle the opposite way, put it in $\frac{1}{8}$ inch to the right and
$\frac{1}{4}$ inch up, and bring it out $\frac{1}{8}$ inch to the left and $\frac{1}{4}$ inch up (Fig. 18).
Pull the thread through. Continue in this way, putting the
needle in first up and then down, as shown in Fig. 18.

Fly Stitch (Fig. 19).—This stitch has many uses as a simple
hem or edge finish, or to build up borders in conjunction with other
stitches. It may be considered as half a lazy-daisy stitch (see
Lazy-Daisy Stitch) or as a form of open buttonhole stitch. (See
section on Buttonhole Stitch, Chapter II.) As with most
stitches, its beauty lies in its regularity. Begin by using guide
lines—these can be easily pencilled on to the material. The
stitch is worked from right to left. It is also called Y stitch.

To work.—Bring out the needle from the wrong side at the
right-hand end of the work, and on the upper of the two ruled
lines. Along the same line, a little further to the left, insert
the needle on a downward slant, so that it will emerge again

to the right side at a point on the lower line midway between the two points on the upper line. Put the thread under the needle and keep it there while the stitch is drawn up into a V, secure with a tiny downward bar stitch, as in lazy-daisy (which see) ; start the next V touching the first at its upper corner. Be careful to work loosely so as to keep the material unpuckered.

Another Variation of Fly Stitch (Fig. 20).—This stitch is worked downwards. Bring out the needle at the top left-hand side of the V to be worked. Then, holding the thread down with the thumb, put the needle in at the top right-hand side of the V and bring it out in the centre below (with the thread still under the needle, as in Fig. 20). Put the needle in again, taking it over the thread just below where it came out (Fig. 20). Bring it out at the top of the next V, and continue in the same way.

Lazy-Daisy Stitch, or *Cat's Paw Stitch* (Fig. 21).—This is a quick stitch, for each stitch makes the entire petal of a flower or a small leaf. It is a very popular stitch for small flowers or leaves in designs that are embroidered in outline. It is well suited to many-petalled daisy-like flowers—hence its name, though it is also called the *Picot Stitch*.

To work.—Lazy-daisy is really a form of chain stitch (see Chapter II.) in which each link in the chain is detached from the others and held down with a small extra stitch. (See also Wheatear Stitch and Fly Stitch.)

Begin at the centre of a flower or the stem end of a leaf, bring the needle through from the wrong side. Hold down the cotton with the left thumb, and put the needle back into the stuff where it came out, bringing it up to the right side again at the upper end of the petal or leaf, as in Fig. 21. Keep the needle over the loop of thread thus formed, and pull up the loop fairly loosely to cover the petal or leaf outline. Secure the loop down by making a little bar stitch across its outer end, which takes the needle back to the wrong side of the material ready to start the next stitch.

Lazy-Daisy (Double).—First work the outer ring of lazy-daisy loops in white. Then work a pink loop inside each of the first loops, taking the little stitch (which holds the tip of the loop down) over the tip of the first loop as well.

Wheatear Stitch (see Fly Stitch, Lazy-Daisy, and Buttonhole

Stitch).—This is useful for the elaborate veining of large leaves or for working ears of corn if they occur in a design. It also makes a good border. It is much used in white embroidery (see Chapter II.) and the more complicated kinds of cut-work.

To work.—It is a simple combination of lazy-daisy and buttonhole stitch, the two being worked alternately. First make a lazy-daisy stitch on the outline to be worked. After taking the needle through to the wrong side to complete the holding stitch of this, bring it up again ¼ inch to the left of the lazy-daisy. Put it in again ¼ inch to the right, and bring it out at the bottom of the lazy-daisy (the end with the holding-down stitch). Keep the thread under the needle while drawing through, and the buttonhole loop is formed, thus giving the grain of corn its ears. Work another lazy-daisy immediately below, touching the loop. Continue in the same way.

Stroke Stitch, or *Millefleurs* (a thousand flowers) (Fig 22).—This is much used for clusters of many-petalled small flowers with a ray effect, such as daisies. It is, of course, the simplest of all stitches, and it is especially useful for embroidering stars and for short, straight lines anywhere in a design. As it has only the single thickness of the thread, the thread used should be a fairly thick one for effective work.

Split Stitch.—A neat and close stitch for fine work. In appearance it is like a slim version of chain stitch but much flatter.

To work.—Work upwards or away from you. Bring the needle up from the wrong side. A little distance higher up take a short stitch, with the needle pointing towards you. As you pull the thread tight, the needle must pierce or split it, instead of passing to one side. As the thread has to be divided, it must not be too fine. Instead of a somewhat thick thread, two strands of stranded cotton may be used, and the needle passed between them, thus giving an elongated chain-stitch effect.

Wave Stitch.—This is simply a variation of running stitch, using two separate threads, which look best when of different colours. It is used (1) for borders for household linen or curtains and makes quite an imposing decoration ; (2) if worked all in one colour it gives a realistic effect of waves in a ship design or seascape ; (3) it is useful for making tucks in children's frocks, for it is decorative, and the tuck can very easily be let down if desired.

To work.—Make a row of running stitches (for running stitches, see the chapters on Plain Sewing), with the distance between the stitches about twice as great as the length of the stitches, which should be short.

With a second thread (preferably of a contrasting colour) take the needle under each running stitch but without catching the fabric. Go under the stitches alternately from the upper and the under side. Bring the needle up from the wrong side at the inner or centre end of the line to be covered (that is, if a flower is being worked). Insert the needle again at the other end of the line and bring it up again from the wrong side (in the same operation) at the start of the next stitch, unless this is too far away.

Be careful that each stitch exactly covers its stamped line, and is neither loose nor tight enough to pucker the material.

Ladder Stitch, also known as *Roman Stitch* (Fig. 23).—This is another stitch belonging to the very large buttonhole-stitch group. It looks well as a simple border on household linen or children's clothes. To make it more decorative a French knot may be added to the centre of each square. It also forms a useful way of joining lace to underwear, or borders to traycloths or runners, etc. Owing to its square formation it is a good stitch to serve as a basis on which to build wide borders composed of several combined stitches (see Chapter IX., " Plain Sewing ").

To work.—Work as for ordinary open buttonhole stitch (see section on Buttonhole Stitch, Chapter II.), but place the needle *slanting* instead of upright to form each stitch, and start that stitch from *inside* the previous loop. When the thread is drawn up, a triangle is first formed, and this should be left rather loose, so that there is slack enough for the next stitch taken to draw it into a square, as in Fig. 23, and leave the thread loose enough to give the wave effect.

Roumanian Stitch, or *Oriental Stitch* (Fig. 24).—This is a good and quick filling stitch. It takes less time and thread than satin stitch.

To work.—Rule two parallel lines as guides. Bring out

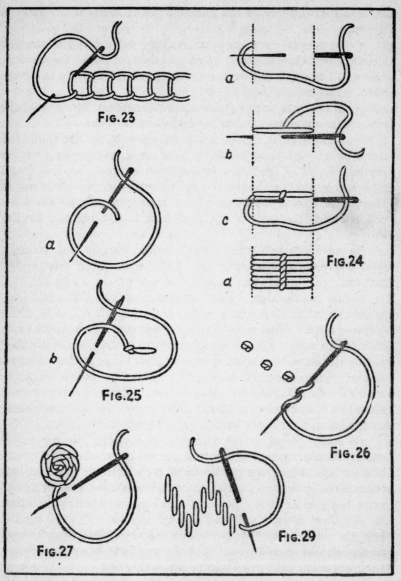

FIG. 23.

a

b

c

d

FIG.24

a

b

FIG.25

FIG. 26

FIG.27

FIG.29

FIG. 23.—Ladder Stitch.   FIG. 24.—Roumanian Stitch.   FIG. 25.—Coral
Stitch.   FIG. 26.—French Knot.   FIG. 27.—Rose Stitch.   FIG. 29.—
Irish Stitch.

39

the needle at the top on the left and put it in again at the top right-hand side, bringing it out again to the middle, with the tip of the needle over the thread (Fig. 24). Put the needle in again just below where it came out last, but over the thread (Fig. 24). Bring it out on the extreme left, just under the first stitch. Proceed as before. The stitches may be worked close enough to touch or with narrow spaces between. When veining leaves, take diagonal stitches instead of vertical ones.

Coral Stitch (Fig. 25).—This stitch is effective for outlines, especially curved ones, or when a knotted, broken-up look is wanted. It gives the effect of beads at intervals on a thread. It is much used in Teneriffe embroidery. It can be worked downwards, that is towards the worker, or from right to left.

To work.—To work it from right to left, bring the needle through to the right side of the fabric, then ¼ inch to the left put the needle in and bring it out slanting slightly, and picking up a tiny piece of material. Twist the thread over the needle and round to the left and back under the needle, as in Fig. 25. Pull the thread through. Put in the needle ¼ inch to the left, and proceed as before (Fig. 25).

French Knot (Fig. 26).—This is a popular stitch and has a great many uses. French knots, varying in number, make the best of all centres for small flowers. Sometimes outline designs are carried out in French knots, giving a beaded effect. French knots can also be used for small berries. They make a simple decoration for children's frocks, and they can be used with advantage to hold hems which are to be let down later, as they do not mark the material. They look well, as we have said before, worked inside ladder stitch, herringbone stitch, etc.

To work.—Bring the needle up to the right side and pick up a tiny piece of the material at the point where the knot is to be. Twist the thread once, twice, or three times (according to the size required) around the needle, as in Fig. 26. Pull the needle through, holding the thread down with the left thumb, and the thread will form a knot. Put the needle in again, and bring it out where the next French knot is to be.

Another way to work is to bring the needle up to the right side, twist the thread as before once or twice around the needle, at the same time holding down the slack of the thread above the part twisted. Push the needle through to the wrong side as close as possible to where it emerged, holding the thread down until it is all drawn through.

Should this knot be inclined to " topple," put a tiny extra stitch over the loose side of the knot in this way : bring the needle up close to the loose side and put it down through the centre of the knot. This extra stitch is particularly useful when making berries.

For ordinary crewel work, the only stitches needed are stem stitch or crewel stitch, satin stitch, and the useful French knot already described.

Rose Stitch or *Rambler Rose Stitch* (Fig. 27).—This is an easy way of making simple little rose forms in a pattern. If roses are worked in twos and threes, with a few lazy-daisy leaves, they make a pretty scattered decoration for a little child's dress.

To work.—Make a French knot in the centre and then work a series of stem stitches (or outline stitches) round and round it, beginning in the middle and proceeding outwards till the rose is of the required size. If an oval is required, begin with two French knots side by side, and work round these. It is a good plan to make the French knot and inner coils of stem stitch a deeper shade than those outside.

Bullion Stitch (Fig. 28).—Sometimes called long French knots from the similarity in working of the two stitches. Bullion stitch is used when an elongated French knot is needed. Grouped or wrapped closely round each other, as in Fig 28, several bullion stitches make an effective small raised rosebud, and are much used this way in Italian coloured embroidery on linen. If several stitches are placed radiating outwards from a French-knot centre, a daisylike flower in relief is easily made.

To work.—Bring the needle through from the back where you want your stitch to be. Put it in where the other end of the stitch is to be ($\frac{1}{4}$ inch or more away), and bring it out where the thread first came out, as in Fig. 28, No. 1. Twist the thread round and round the needle from seven to twelve times (according to the length the finished stitch is to be), as in Fig. 28, No. 2. Hold the twisted cotton down with the left thumb and pull the

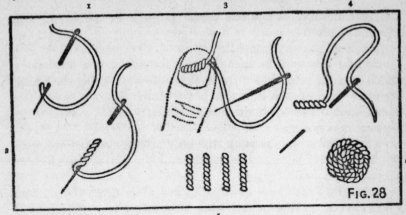

FIG. 28.—Bullion Stitch.

cotton through, as in Fig. 28, No. 3. Pull the thread tight, and
put in the needle at the end of the stitch (where you put it in
before (Fig. 28, No. 4), and bring it out where one end of the next
stitch is to be. Continue in this way. A line of stitches can
be made (Fig. 28, No. 5). To work a raised rosebud, work
bullion stitch round and round a French-knot or satin-stitch
centre, as in Fig. 28, No. 6.

Pekinese Stitch (Fig. 30).—This is a very effective stitch. If
Chinese embroidery is studied, this stitch will be found worked
with great precision in fine silks to give a lovely graded effect.
Many workers will like it, for it has a bold appearance, especially if
wools or coarse silks are used. It is essentially a broad stitch
and therefore does not lend itself to the working of angular
corners.

The design may be worked in outline in this stitch or filled
in solidly by working round the edges until the shape is covered.
Both graded effects and strong contrasts can be obtained by the
use of this stitch.

Fig. 30, *a* and *b*, shows the working. Be careful not to leave
the second stage of the stitch too loose. It must form a tight
loop round the foundation stitch. Be careful not to pucker
the ground. As the Pekinese stitch is a heavy one, the ground
material should also be heavy. Care must be taken in all
embroidery to adjust the weight of the thread to the material.

The second stage of the stitch can be worked in a contrasting colour, if desired.

Braid Stitch (Fig. 31).—This is an excellent stitch for making raised lines or stems in wool or linen threads. A long diagonal stitch is made from left to right downwards, the needle is then directed through the material horizontally from right to left, coming out below the beginning of the first stitch. The thread is then taken upwards diagonally rather above the end of the first diagonal stitch, making a slightly less sloping stitch than the first and in the opposite direction. By repeating this process a braid of a beautiful plaited appearance is made, which may be from ⅛ to ½ inch wide (Fig. 31).

Gradation in Embroidery and *Shaded Flower Embroidery.*— There are many ways of obtaining a graded effect in embroidery, some tending towards realism and others to a more decorative and conventional effect. By gradation in embroidery we mean the colours shading from light to dark, or *vice versa*.

The best known stitch for graded effects is the long-and-short stitch. This, when worked in a radiated direction in various tones, shades, tints, or colours, can produce wonderful effects. The direction of the stitch is all important ; then the colours must be arranged so that they blend and graduate in a gentle way.

Other stitches that are useful for graded work are—tent

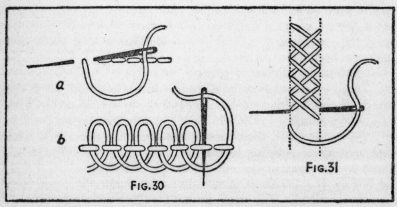

FIG. 30.—Pekinese Stitch.   FIG. 31.—Braid Stitch.

stitch (see chapter on Tapestry) and cross stitch (see Chapter VI.). These stitches when worked on fine materials with carefully arranged colours give a fine effect of gradation.

Irish stitch (Fig. 29), Roumanian stitch (Fig. 24), and satin stitch can also be used, and an almost imperceptible but decorative effect of gradation can be obtained, as line after line of stitches is arranged. Buttonhole stitch, chain, stem, double back stitch, Pekinese, worked round and round the contour of a shape in various tones, also give a decorative treatment in gradation.

The careful matching and shading of colours to produce embroidered flowers, fruits, and birds, that are really like those seen in Nature, is a beautiful form of embroidery, and by means of exquisite stitchery wonderful effects can be obtained. A large number of shades of one colour are needed for successful shading ; it is wise to have one skein of every tone in each particular range. It is, therefore, not an economical form of embroidery, and it is no use trying to do it cheaply, since all the beauty depends on careful gradation, and this means many skeins of wool.

More hints and stitches suitable for graded-colour work will be found in the chapters on Tapestry.

THE HERRINGBONE GROUP OF STITCHES

(1) *Ordinary Herringbone* (Fig. 32).—This stitch is very useful both in embroidery and in plain sewing. It can be used as a border or as an all-over pattern when several rows are worked side by side. It is also useful for joining hems and pieces of material to each other in a decorative way. It combines well with other stitches.

To work.—Draw two parallel lines on the material, bring the needle through at the left-hand side of the lower line ; then with the needle pointing to the left, take a small stitch on the top line a little to the right, then pass to the lower line again, and with the needle still pointing to the left, take another small stitch a little to the right of the one previously taken on the top line, as in Fig. 32. Continue to take the stitches alternately on each line as described. The stitch should give an open zigzag effect.

(2) *Double Back Stitch* (Fig. 33, *a* and *b*).—This is a different

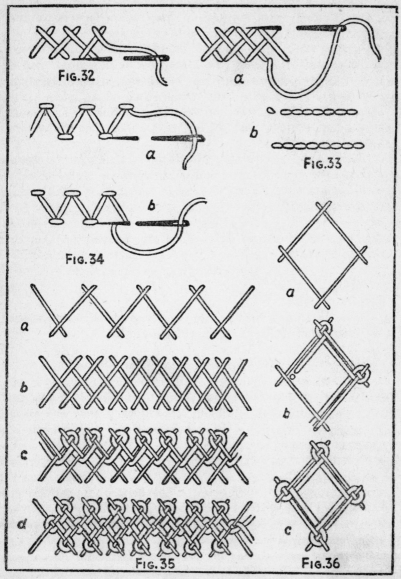

FIG. 32.—Herringbone.
FIG. 34.—Chevron Stitch.
FIG. 33.—Double Back Stitch Herringbone.
FIG. 35.—Interlacing Stitch on Herringbone.
FIG. 36.—Variation of the Interlacing Stitch.

and useful variety of the herringbone stitch. It is made by working it closely so as to form a close row of zigzags on one side and a double row of back stitches on the wrong side, as in Fig. 33, *a* ; hence its name " double back stitch." It is sometimes used with the close row of zigzags on the front of the material, and sometimes with the double row of back-stitching on the front. It is a reversible stitch.

It can be used on fine silk, organdie, or linen lawn. It is then worked from the back of the material, so that the double row of back stitches outlines the design on the right side, whilst the crossings of the coloured thread at the back of the work shows through the material in an interesting way. If the material is very transparent, a white thread on a white ground is quite effective. This " shadow " work, as it is called (see Chapter VII., section on Shadow Work), can be used on collars, cuffs, and other small articles. Double back stitch can also be used for filling in leaves and flowers.

(3) *Chevron Stitch* (Fig. 34).—This is another useful variation of the herringbone stitch.

To work.—Draw two parallel lines on the material as before, bring the needle to the front of the material on the top left-hand side, take the needle to the bottom line a little to the right of the starting-point on the top line, and with the needle pointing to the left, take a small stitch along the line. Draw the thread through, and holding this down with the thumb, take a small stitch immediately to the right of the one just made, as in Fig. 34. Draw the thread through the material, and repeat the same process on the top line, a little to the right of the last stitch. This is a very useful stitch in borders and all-over patterns, but its chief use is in connection with smocking. (See Chapter X. on Smocking.)

(4) *Interlacing Stitch* (Fig. 35).—The herringbone stitch can be interlaced with another thread of contrasting colour, or by placing one row between another. The latter method gives a more complicated pattern effect.

The interlacing of two or more rows has been developed into an interlacing stitch which has wonderful possibilities as a unit of design. It makes a very strong insertion stitch and has a pleasing lace-like effect.

To get the best effect, use a coarse thread of either wool, cotton, or silk. The stitch looks well whether worked with a thread that matches the fabric or with one that forms a pleasing contrast to it. As the interlacing stitch is rather complicated for the beginner to work—complicated, that is, until each stage has been understood—it is wise to begin working with wool on some coarse material. Although the stitch is based on herring-bone, some variation is necessary.

To work.—The first row (*a*, in Fig. 35) is an openly spaced line of herringbone in which the needle, after the top stitch is taken, is always slipped under the thread. It is essential to remember to do this, as it is impossible to work the rest of the stitch unless this method is carefully followed. The second row (*b*, in Fig. 35) is placed between the first row, and not only is the needle slipped under the top thread, but it must also be slipped under the bar made just before the top stitch, as in *b*, in Fig. 35. The work should be carefully examined when these two rows are completed, and if the threads do not interlace perfectly there is some mistake in working. It is easy to see a mistake, because the threads appear loose, instead of being well held together.

In the third row (*c*, in Fig. 35) the thread does not enter the material except at the beginning and the end of the row, but it is *interlaced* into the foundation strands formed by the two rows of herringbone. Work this row as before from left to right. *c*, in Fig. 35 shows how the thread is interlaced. It must not be pulled tightly, but allowed to lie loosely in position.

In the fourth row (*d*, in Fig. 35) the thread is interlaced into the three preceding rows, and again does not enter the material except at the beginning and the end of the row, or where a fresh thread is begun. When interlacing this thread the work should, if possible, be turned around and the fourth row begun from the *end* of the third row. Fig. 35, *d*, shows the working, but care must be taken to follow the diagram so that the interlacing is correct. The final effect of the stitch should be compact. The height of the stitch varies with the thickness of the thread used. It is wise before beginning a piece of work to make trial stitches. It is most important that the first row of stitches should be well spaced out, because the final result is not so good if the first row is too closely sewn. Another point : the stitches of the second row should be taken exactly opposite those of the first ; this makes the complete stitch correct and pleasing.

The work looks best in one colour, though some people use two : one colour for the two foundation threads and another for the two final rows.

Various interesting arrangements of this stitch can be thought out, and it has been used a great deal in Germany and the East in the past.

A small diamond-shaped spot, useful for covering a surface, can be made on a herringbone basis and interlaced, as shown in Fig. 36, *a*, *b*, and *c*.

CHAPTER IV

EDGINGS, EYELETS, AND INITIALS

Edgings, Different Kinds of Scallops, Cut-Work, Picots. Eyelet Holes,
Eyelet Stitch, Buttonhole-Ring, Eye Stitch, Broderie Anglaise.
Initials and Monograms, Marking Linen.

EDGINGS

I T is very useful to know a few pretty edgings, and there
are many narrow ones that give interest to a finished
article, especially to embroidered articles. Crochet edgings are
often suitable and wear well. (See section on Crochet Work.)
The most popular stitch for edgings is the buttonhole stitch,
as I expect you have found out. Besides the buttonhole stitch
we shall describe a few other interesting edgings that give interest
and variety to needlework.

Antwerp Edge (Fig. 37) is a useful stitch. The diagram shows
clearly how it is done.

Armenian Edge (Fig. 38) is a loop formed by working braid
stitch to the edge of the material, as shown in Fig. 38. The
method of working buttonhole picot edge is described further
on in this chapter.

A narrow edging can also be formed with beads. (See the
chapter on Tassels, Cords, and Fringes.) But nothing gives
such a firm edge as scalloping.

Different Kinds of Scallops.—This is perhaps the only embroidery stitch which will give such a firm finish to raw edges
that no hem or other turning in is necessary. It is in reality
a close, padded buttonhole stitch which, when used on edges,
is called scalloping. Scalloping is a great feature of broderie
anglaise (see section on Broderie Anglaise) and other forms of
cut-work (see section on Cut-Work). This is a very favourite

edging for children's clothes, lingerie, and household linen, being simple to work and very hard wearing. It used to be looked upon as a trimming principally for flannel and similar materials, but to-day it is used practically on all types of fabric except the very thin.

It is generally embroidered from a transfer, but if you have no transfer handy you can make your own scallops with the help of a button or a coin. Rule a straight line or draw a thread so that the lower edges of your scallops are quite even. Outline the lower edge first, then mark the inner with a smaller round.

Now outline your scalloping with running stitch, working the outside edge first. Pad thickly with darning stitch, taking this backwards and forwards until the surface is completely covered. The padding can also be done with a line of chain stitch—this is much quicker. Darning cotton makes the best padding. Efficient padding is essential if the edge is to wear well. *Never cut your scallops out before working them,*

After padding, work the scallops with close buttonhole stitch, purl edge to the outside. Here are the different stages of scalloping—outlining, padding, working, cutting out.

There are many variations of the ordinary crescent shape that are well worth trying if one wants a decorative border, but whatever the shape of the edge they are all worked in the same way. (See Fig. 48.)

When buttonholing is completed, with very sharp embroidery scissors cut away the material as close as possible to the buttonhole edge, taking great care not to cut the stitches.

It is well to allow ¾-inch turnings on edges that are to be scalloped.

Cut-Work.—As we have said before, the buttonhole stitch is much used in cut-work. Cut-work is an interesting style of work which may be carried out in white thread on white material, or in coloured silks with the use of metal thread.

The design must be very carefully planned and in such a manner that no portion of it will hang loose when the background is cut away. The shapes of the background portions to be cut away should also be carefully considered ; they must not be long and narrow, nor too large. The use of embroidered bars to hold the design together is not always considered good

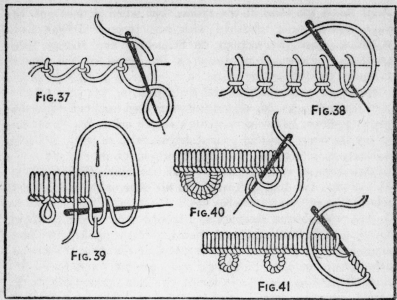

FIG. 37.—Antwerp Edge.   FIG. 38.—Armenian Edge.   FIG. 39.—Simple
form of Picot.   FIG. 40.—Bolder type of Picot.   FIG. 41.—Picot: another
form.

by the best workers; in many designs these should not be
necessary. The design itself must be bold and no part so narrow
that there is not room for a row of buttonholing to be placed
along each side. Before buttonholing the edges of the pattern,
it is a wise plan to run a strong thread just inside the lines of
the design. This gives a firmer ground for the buttonholing
and makes the edges stronger.

One can get exquisitely pretty lace-like effects in cut-work,
especially if neither background nor design is completely cut
away, but small parts of each are removed as a pleasant contrast
to the solid remainder.

Although cut-work looks complicated, like most one-stitch
embroideries, it is really very easy. Special cut-work transfers
can be bought by those who cannot make their own designs.
It washes well and wears well. It is particularly suited to household linens, such as sheet shams, pillow-slips, tray-cloths, lunch-
mats, duchesse sets, and chairbacks. Often the embroidery

itself forms the edge of the article, but when it does not, the edges are generally finished with scalloping or Italian hem-stitching. (See the sections on Scalloping and Italian Hem-stitching.) Examples of cut-work are given in the coming chapters in conjunction with bars. This is a little different from the cut-work we have just described.

Picots (Figs. 39, 40, 41).—Picots are often used in conjunction with cut-work. They give variety to the somewhat hard edge of the buttonhole stitch. The simplest form of picot is a loop worked as part of the buttonhole stitch, as in Fig. 39. The thread is looped round a pin and then buttonholed firmly across. This gives a lace-like appearance to the edge of the work if it is repeated at regular intervals.

Fig. 40 shows a stronger and bolder type of picot. Work a length of buttonholing and then take the thread back about an eighth of an inch and catch it into the heading of the button-hole, as in Fig. 40. Pass the thread forwards and backwards three times and buttonhole together. This method brings the needle into the original position, and the line of buttonhole stitch can be continued.

Fig. 41 shows another kind of picot; the diagram clearly shows the working.

EYELETS

Eyelet Holes.—Eyelet holes are pierced and embroidered holes, round, oval, or leaf-shaped. They form the basis of broderie anglaise, and are also much used in embroidery initials and monograms, and in Madeira and Venetian embroideries. They are employed both in dressmaking and fancy needlework, as slots through which cords or ribbons may be run.

To work.—Use a firm fabric for good results. To make a round eyelet, pencil a small circle or use a transfer. Run closely round the outline with the working thread to give a firm founda-tion. Pierce the circle inside the running stitches with a stiletto for a small hole ; for a large hole, snip a tiny cross in the centre. This must not go right to the outline. Do not cut any material away, but overcast closely and tightly round the hole, over the running stitches, thus catching in the pierced ends of the material. Round eyelets may be buttonhole-stitched instead of overcast, if preferred, and this method is usual in Venetian embroidery.

Sometimes several holes are placed touching each other. In this case, to prevent the work from tearing when in use, it is wise to take the running stitches along the lower edge of the first hole, crossing to the upper edge of the second, and so on, alternately. When the circles are to be thicker on the top than elsewhere, pad the top with several rows of running stitch and overcast them all.

A stiletto should not be used for oval or leaf-shaped eyelets, instead cut down their centres with sharp, small scissors, catching in the cut edges tightly when overcasting.

Remember when working eyelets to keep the stitches quite close together without overlapping, and pull them firmly. The edge should be like a fine, very stiff cord when finished, with no fray-ends showing anywhere.

When working a slot to take a wide ribbon on thin material, such as muslin or nainsook, mark the slot and work all round it before cutting the opening ; otherwise it is almost impossible to avoid pulling the slender slot into a shapeless hole. *Always work eyelets from right to left.* If you do it the other way about, you will find your cotton twisting all the time.

When you can make firm, nicely shaped eyelets you have mastered a very important bit of embroidery.

Eyelet Stitch (Fig. 42).—This makes a good background stitch for a bold and simple pattern. The eyelet stitch is begun by bringing the needle through the fabric on the edge of the circle, and taking two small back stitches (as shown in Fig. 42), then bringing the needle up through the starting-place, and proceeding by taking another two back stitches into the centre of the circle, bring the needle out on the edge of the circle a little farther along in such a position that it is possible to work two back stitches on the edge again. The circle can have about 12 back stitches on its circumference ; notice that adjoining circles each share two back stitches. The stitches should be drawn tightly together so that little holes appear round the edges of the circles and large ones in the centre.

The ordinary buttonhole wheel with its variations can be dealt with here. This can be worked around a small hole very much in the same way as the eyelet stitch. The buttonhole-ring described below is also very useful for decorations. It has no hole in the middle.

The Buttonhole-Ring (Fig. 43).—Make the stitches in the same way as for buttonhole stitch, but let them radiate from one centre. They will of course be nearer together at the centre than the circumference. Buttonhole-rings worked across a cosy look very effective. They can be made to look like a lovely line of hollyhock flowers. In this case, don't let the stitches radiate from one centre, but from the edge of a small circle. Inside this small circle work some French knots.

Buttonhole-Ring (Double) (Fig. 44).—This is worked in the same way as a buttonhole-ring, but the smaller ring is worked over the centre of the first larger ring, giving a raised effect to the centre (see Chapter II. for " Buttonhole Stitch ").

Eye Stitch (Fig. 45).—Eye stitch gives a pretty effect. It is formed by sixteen stitches going into a single hole in the centre, but these stitches are spread into a square on the outside edge. Pull the stitches tightly. A line of back stitch is then worked round the edge, as in Fig. 45. This stitch is very useful when working out check patterns. It also forms an alternative to cross-stitch lettering. (See coming section on this.)

Algerian Eye Stitch (Fig. 46).—This can be used as an all-over pattern for large designs. It is worked over a square. Work from the centre outwards, two stitches being taken into the middle of each side and two into the corners.

Broderie Anglaise (Fig. 47).—This is a very popular form of white embroidery. It combines pierced work with outlined or solid surface stitches. It really dates back as far as the sixteenth century, and was probably introduced into England from France or Italy.

Patterns worked in broderie anglaise are found on both household linen and articles of dress. In the loan collection of the late Sir Robert Filmer at the Victoria and Albert Museum are some beautiful examples applied to collars and cuffs of fine linen embroidered during the first half of the seventeenth century.

At times it is much in vogue for decorating underwear, especially when it is fashionable for lingerie to be made of fairly substantial cotton or linen material which will take pierced work

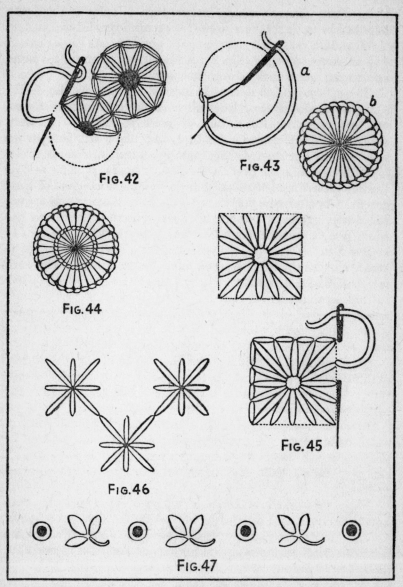

FIG. 42.—Eyelet Stitch.   FIG. 43.—Buttonhole-Ring.   FIG. 44.—Double
Buttonhole-Ring.   FIG. 45.—Eye Stitch.   FIG. 46.—Algerian Eye Stitch.
FIG. 47.—Broderie Anglaise.

well. Many dainty dress accessories such as collar and cuff sets, handkerchiefs, etc., may also be decorated in this way.

The best materials for broderie anglaise are firm, closely woven ones—sheeting, linen, madapolam, tarantulle, piqué, and real silk such as jap and shantung varieties.

It needs more skill to work it successfully on flimsy fabrics.

Eyelets, already described, either round, oval, or leaf-shaped, are the characteristic feature of broderie anglaise. In fact, many designs are carried out entirely in eyelets, with perhaps the addition of a few stem-stitched stems and satin-stitched dots.

Although a great deal of broderie anglaise is done to-day, the results are not often good from the point of view of good design. As a rule the holes pierced or cut in the material are not sufficiently grouped, but are spotted indiscriminately over the whole design, and the white leaves and flowers which are usually embroidered as a setting to the cut-work grow on weak, vague stems, and the result is a graceful but *formless* pattern. The work is worth a good design.

Fig. 47 shows a very simple border.

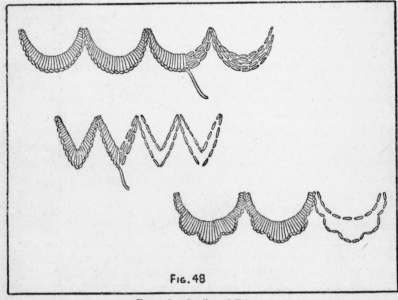

Fig. 48

FIG. 48.—Scalloped Edges.

The edges of work adorned with broderie anglaise are generally finished with scalloping, as this suits the type of work beautifully (Fig. 48). However, hemstitching is often more convenient for dress items and is much used.

As with all white work, broderie anglaise is somewhat trying to the eyes. It is wise, therefore, to adopt the plan used by embroideresses in Madeira (their work very much resembles broderie anglaise). They dip their working thread in a little blue before using it. The contrast of colours makes all the difference to the eyesight, and the blue tint disappears at the first washing. Small bits of broderie anglaise, especially eyelets, are much used in working monograms and initials. (See section on Monograms and Initials.)

An excellent book is published by the French firm, Cartier-Bresson, entitled *Les Points de Broderie*, which fully explains the technique of this type of work and also gives a few good designs suited to it.

INITIALS AND MONOGRAMS

With the introduction of an indelible ink for marking purposes, the practice of embroidering the initials of the owner on household linen and under-garments has fallen very much into disuse. But beautiful things need a more dignified treatment. From time to time, too, embroidered initials or monograms are in fashion for decorating dresses and appear on pockets, hand-bags, and so on.

Initial transfers are obtainable in a great variety of styles and sizes, suitable for anything from sheets to handkerchiefs. Choose letters that are not too ornamental in form. It is better taste to have clear, rather plain letters, and to add any decoration needed in the form of surrounding eyelets, flower sprays, or prettily shaped shields.

Many different forms of embroidery may be used for the working of the letters.

Cross stitch is a favourite on material with threads that can be counted easily, while a mixture of this and darning makes a quick, simple marking for huckaback towels. (See chapter on Embroidery on Counted Threads.)

Padded satin-stitch letters, surrounded by a simple decora-

tion of eyelets, always look well. Sometimes a whole letter is
made in touching eyelets. Chain stitch and ladder stitch both
make quick and not too heavy filling stitches for initials. Again,
the outline may be back-stitched or outline-stitched, and the
interior of the letters filled with seed stitch or lace stitch. (See
Chapter II., Fig. 14.)

Cross-Stitch Letters (Fig. 49).—For more about the cross
stitch you must read the next chapter ; here we are dealing with
cross stitch only from the point of view of making letters.

Cross-stitch letters are often built up on the threads of the
material. They are usually seven squares in height and can be
worked so that the lettering is legible on both sides of the material.
By working the cross stitch as in Fig. 49, a square is made on
the back of the material and a cross on the front. In order to
get this arrangement it is necessary to cross one of the sides
of the stitch twice. Cross stitch is both decorative and legible.

Eye-Stitch letters are constructed in the same way, but this
stitch (see Fig. 45) forms a larger and bolder letter.

Both cross stitch and eye stitch are suitable methods for
fine or coarse work. They can be worked from a diagram drawn
on squared paper. Chapter VI. deals with Embroidery on
Counted Squares and the use of squared paper.

A skeleton Roman " non-serif " letter makes a good but
severe basis for embroidered letters. This may be worked
solidly or in outline. Overcast, satin, back stitch, knotted
stitches, chain, Pekinese, appliqué, and rope stitch or twisted
chain are all suitable for working this type of letter.

Sometimes a letter is given added interest by placing it in
a shape and treating the background with a decorative arrangement of drawn threads or reticella (see Chapter V.), or some
pretty background stitch. A floral or geometric knotwork border
can also surround a letter which is not enclosed in any particular
shape.

It may help those who have a good deal of household linen
to mark if we add here a useful summary of some of the quickest
methods.

(1) Bought name-tapes especially made. These are hemmed
on.

(2) Marking-ink used directly on the garments or on tape.

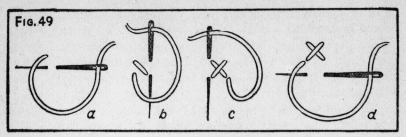

FIG. 49.—Cross-Stitch.

(3) Chain stitch. Write the name faintly in pencil and then work over with a very fine thread.

(4) Cross stitch. One method of using the cross stitch for letters has already been described. Another easy method for names is to work the names over canvas (use bead canvas with penelope weave). Make the stitches all cross the same way and stab stitch over canvas (but if you are using a transfer, pick up the stitches). When the name is finished cut away the canvas, but leave sufficient length of thread to hold when drawing the threads from under the cross stitches.

(5) For monograms and initials the following stitches are most useful : cross stitch, satin stitch, chain stitch. For satin stitch, first outline in fine sewing silk, pad between, then work the stitch. Many workers like to use a frame when doing monograms in satin stitch in this way.

CHAPTER V

DRAWN-THREAD WORK, INSERTION STITCHES, BARS, AND FILET EMBROIDERY

Drawn-Thread Work. Hemstitching. Italian Hemstitching. Insertion Stitches or Faggoting Stitches—all the most useful and beautiful. Bars, Bars and Cut-Work. Some simple and interesting Embroideries involving Drawn-Thread Work, Cut-Work, and Bars.

WE now come to some very important needlework. Many of the simple stitches we have already described could have been invented by the clever needlewoman without the help of a book, and are probably known to her in practice if not by name. However, names make things more interesting.

DRAWN-THREAD WORK

Drawn-thread work is a slightly more difficult form of needlework, but it comes into a great variety of fancy work, and you will meet it again in Chapter VI. under the title of Needle-Weaving or Swedish Weaving. There are, indeed, many more or less definite types of drawn-thread work, but most types intermingle and are therefore difficult to classify.

But perhaps what will be of most interest in this chapter or section are the Insertion Stitches ; these are so valuable for joining. It is real economy often if several strips of material can be joined together in a decorative manner to make curtains. These insertion stitches are also invaluable in dressmaking. (See the section on Home Dressmaking.)

We will begin, however, by describing some of the most well-known and useful forms of drawn-thread work.

Drawn-in Drawn-Thread Work (Fig. 50).—This variety is used by itself and in tendril embroidery. (See section on Tendril

Embroidery.) In this work lines of colour are inserted into the fabric so that they look as though they might have been woven in when the stuff was made.

It is best to use stranded cotton in one or more strands, according to the weave of the material being decorated. The process is simple. Where the line of colour is wanted, draw out one thread completely. Begin at one end to draw out the next thread to the one drawn out, but only pull this one out one inch, or two. Take a strand of stranded cotton twice as long, plus one inch, as the thread of the material that has been drawn out. Double it, and tie the linen thread partly drawn out to the loop thus formed.

Now pick up the same linen thread *at the other end* of the line and pull it out gently and cautiously. As it comes out, it will pull through in its place the double coloured strand of cotton tied to it, weaving it perfectly into the material. You must draw carefully, constantly putting the pull on a different place, or the thread you are drawing out will break. If it does, pull it right out and start again by tying the cotton to the next thread in the material.

When the coloured thread is completely in, trim off the ends. By varying the numbers, colours, widths apart, and length of the threads drawn in, a great variety of different borders may be thought out. But this method of decoration is suited only for comparatively short lines of trimming. Short lines not going from edge to edge may be finished off with a triangle worked in satin stitch, as in Fig. 50. This is a very strong form of decoration and wears as long as the material itself, for it never gets out of order. It can be used on linen, handkerchief linen, shantung, silk, and voile.

Household linen such as small mats, etc., underwear, babies' frocks, handkerchiefs, and modesty fronts can be decorated in this way.

Hemstitch (Fig. 51).—This is the most popular of all drawn-thread stitches, and is much used as a fancy hem on linen embroideries. It is also used to decorate fine underwear, linen frocks, etc. It is an interesting form of white work. (See Chapter II.)

To work.—If it is being used as a hem, you must first turn in and tack the hem ; then from the hem inwards draw out consecutive horizontal threads to a width of about $\frac{3}{16}$ of an inch or $\frac{1}{8}$ of an inch. Some workers like to draw out the threads first and then turn down and tack the hem to meet the drawn threads.

Hints on Drawing Threads.—Pick out a single thread near the selvedge with a pin and break the thread. Now gently ease the material on it so as to get out as long a thread as possible without a break. If the thread breaks, hold the material up to the light to find the end. Draw out all the rest of the threads on the side away from the hem, or its width will be altered. Keep and count the threads, if necessary, so as to be sure to draw the same number from all parts of the garment. Some people find it helpful to draw the first two or three threads under a magnifying glass. This applies especially to fine material. If the hemstitching is to come in the interior of the stuff where there is no hem, simply draw the thread at the right place.

Hold the stuff with the edge away from you and the hem upside down and work from left to right. With a fine thread in the needle, bring it through the inner edge of the hem, hiding the knot in the hem. Pointing the needle to the left, take up on it four vertical strands in the drawn part, as in Fig. 51, then insert it again diagonally behind the four strands, as in Fig. 51, emerging in the edge of the hem. Thus the thread in order to pass behind the strands a second time will first pass in front of them, completely encircling them. Pull the thread and the part round the strands will pull them tightly together. Make a little stitch into the solid edge just beyond the four strands to hold the pulling thread firmly. Then put the needle behind the next four strands, and continue in the same way. Fig. 51 should make the method of working quite clear.

Hemstitch Bar or *Double Hemstitching* (Fig. 52).—This stitch is an interesting variety of hemstitching. It is sometimes known as double hemstitch because of the double line of working.

To work.—Proceed exactly as described for the hemstitch. When the hemstitch is completed along the hem edge, turn the stuff, and hemstitch the other edge in the same way, taking up just the same groups of four threads. These threads, instead of forming triangles as in ordinary hemstitch (Fig. 51), are turned

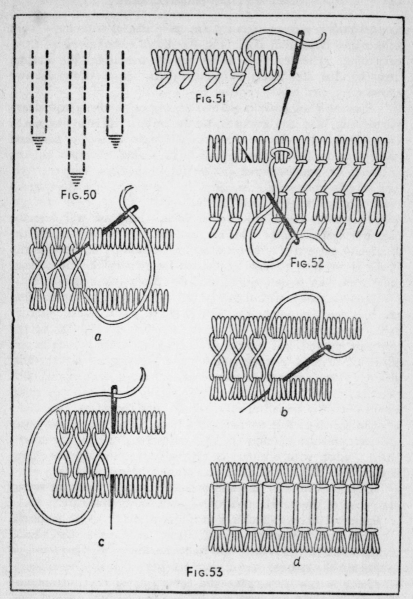

FIG. 50.—Drawn-in Drawn-Thread Work.   FIG. 51.—Simple Hemstitching.
FIG 52.—Double Hemstitching and Bar Hemstitch.   FIG. 53.—Four stages
in Italian Hemstitching.

into straight, narrow bars by the extra line of stitching—hence the name Hemstitch Bar. Fig. 52 shows a *double row* of hemstitching. The top row shows simple hemstitch, the bottom row bar hemstitch or double hemstitch. Notice how the two rows are joined in a decorative way.

Hemstitch (*Diamond*).—This is a pretty diamond-pattern hemstitch that can be used to decorate a surface but not a single row. It must be worked on a material that is firm and has threads that draw readily. It makes effective square, oblong, or wedge-shaped panels for chairbacks, runners, etc. Be sure to work on a firm, close linen or tweed, else the pattern will drag and tend to look untidy.

To work.—There are two methods. First we will describe the quickest method. This can only be used in cases where the diamond pattern is *to be lined*, as for cushions, etc., because the back is not neat enough to be used for articles like table linen. Mark out the shape and size of the panel required and draw threads both ways within this space, cutting them at the marking so that they do not pull away outside it. The number of consecutive threads drawn will vary according to the size of the pattern wanted, but always *twice* as many must be left as are drawn. A good average rule for linen is to draw six threads, leave twelve untouched, then draw six more, and so on, both vertically and horizontally. This gives a check effect of small open squares alternating with bars of linen threads.

Do all the work on the wrong side. The spaces form the pattern and the stitches are only to shape and hold the spaces firm. Work with ordinary sewing cotton matching the fabric exactly, so that the stitches are practically invisible.

Begin by working a small open buttonhole stitch all round the edge of the panel. With the same continuous thread make a single buttonhole stitch round the nearest bar of the material, another over the next bar, and so on all along a row. Each stitch pulls the preceding one tight, narrowing the bars and so enlarging the spaces.

Reverse the work, take the thread along the buttonholed margin to where the next row of bars can be buttonholed, and continue so back and forth until the panel is finished. It tends to pucker up rather, but it will flatten out when damped and well pressed. For a cushion or chairback, line the openwork with a contrasting shade.

A second method is to prepare the panel edges as already described, but working from the *right* side, whip over each bar twice, the second time catching up the first whipping thread and so centering the stitch neatly. Pull the thread very taut. Whip every row both vertically and horizontally. (See section on Bars.) This method of work makes the back look neater.

Hemstitch (Single Crossing). — This is a pretty twisted hemstitch that can be used for decorating the hems of clothes and embroidered linen articles. On the whole it is quickly and easily finished.

To work.—Begin by drawing consecutive threads to a depth of $\frac{1}{4}$ inch. Bring the needle through from the wrong side at one end. Pass over six vertical strands (any number may of course be chosen), but pick up the next six on the needle and double it backwards under not only these six but the other six missed previously. This gives a twisted or crossed look. Take the needle forward under the twisted strands, draw up the thread, and continue to repeat the passing over and doubling backwards with the next six strands.

Italian Hemstitching (Fig. 53).—This is used on a great deal of Italian embroidery and in tendril embroidery (see the section on Tendril Embroidery.) This is always eight threads in width. Draw two threads, leave in four, then draw two more, thus making up the eight. Just a single row of Italian hemstitching makes a very pretty border.

To work with, choose a contrasting coloured cotton and an even, single-strand thread, such as Coton à broder or Convent embroidery cotton.

Italian hemstitching is worked on the wrong side, and from left to right, the stitches crossing over like an S on the wrong side (see *a*, *b*, and *c* in Fig. 53) but making a single straight bar stitch on the right, as in *d* in Fig. 53. The diagrams show clearly how the stitch is worked.

Hemstitching in Squares.—Hemstitched squares are often used as a trimming on frocks or in the corners of tablecloths, etc. Mark your square, cut threads at the end of each line to be drawn before you pull the threads. At each corner there will

3

be an open square, because here the threads are drawn both ways. Hemstitch your threads each side in the usual way, at the wrong side of the work, but when you come to the corners take your needle through to the right side and buttonhole-stitch the cut edges firmly. Go through to the wrong side to hemstitch the next side of the square.

To apply a contrasting colour, prepare your drawn threads as for an ordinary hemstitched square. Cut your contrasting square to a thread along each edge (allow ⅛-inch turnings). Tack the square in the centre of the drawn lines, its edge exactly touching the inner edge of these lines. Catch in the edges of this square as you hemstitch this inner edge.

Insertion Stitches, or Faggoting Stitches

By using insertion stitches, two edges, whether curved or straight, can be joined in a decorative way.

Faggoting is a joining of two seams or other edges by an openwork stitch. It is a pretty way of attaching a hem, or of connecting seam edges when it is necessary to make a trimming of the seam, or setting the skirt to the yoke on a child's dress, and so on.

This is the method for adding a hem, or faggoting strips together for a collar, vest, or yoke : Use bias strips of material, double them lengthwise, turn in the raw edges to face each other, and tack them firmly. (To join edges of single material, make a very tiny hem along each side.)

It is usual to tack the two edges of material on to brown paper or some stiff material whilst working these stitches, as this prevents one from puckering one edge against the other. The space between the two edges of material varies according to the stitch chosen, and should be carefully gauged, because some stitches need more space than others ; the usual distance is ¼ inch. Some insertion stitches are also stronger than others, and this fact must be considered.

(1) *Diagonal Faggoting* (Fig. 54).—This is the most quickly worked stitch of this type. (It is sometimes called twisted insertion stitch, but this name is better applied to the next stitch we shall describe.) Faggoting stitches are worked through the two edges but not through the foundation. Bring up the needle in the lower edge and take a stitch diagonally across

in the other edge, inserting the needle from the wrong side upwards. Put the needle under the stitch just made ; then make a second diagonal stitch across to the lower edge, and so on. This stitch has almost a herringbone effect.

(2) *Twisted Faggoting*, or *Bar Stitch* (Fig. 55).—For this bar stitch, work from right to left. Begin at the top right-hand edge and put your needle through from front to back in the lower edge exactly opposite your starting-point. Twist your needle point over and under the bar stitch two or three times in an upward direction ; the number of twists depends on the length of your stitch, which should be covered to get a corded effect. Then put the needle back close to the hole through which it first came out and to the left of it. Slip it along inside the fold, and bring it out again ready to begin the next stitch. Repeat.

This stitch is a favourite for lingerie. It gives the effect of hemstitch. It should be very narrow when used on fine material. It is sometimes used for fringing on a lace edging. It is also known as *veining*.

(3) *Knotted Insertion* or *Knotted Seam Stitch* (Fig. 56).— This, as can be seen, is a zigzag knotted stitch. It is very useful for attaching borders to runners and pillows ; it can also be used to join the separate lengths of window curtains. It looks attractive when it joins the yoke and the main part of a child's dress, and the cuffs and sleeves. As it is such a definite stitch it has decorative possibilities.

The stitch is really composed of two successive buttonhole stitches. Tack the two edges to be joined to smooth wrapping-paper, as already described. Insert the needle in the upper edge of the right-hand piece, as in Fig. 56, *a*. Carry thread across to the left-hand piece, insert the needle about $\frac{3}{16}$ of an inch from the edge, and bring it out above the thread, as shown in Fig. 56, *a*. Now take a little buttonhole stitch into the loop just made, as shown in Fig. 56, *b*, bring the needle out above the thread, and tighten into a knot. For the next stitch on the other side, put the thread under the needle and take a stitch similar to that shown in Fig. 56 about a quarter of an inch or half an inch below the stitch just made in *b*. Finish the stitch with a knot as before. Continue these knot stitches, alternating from side to side.

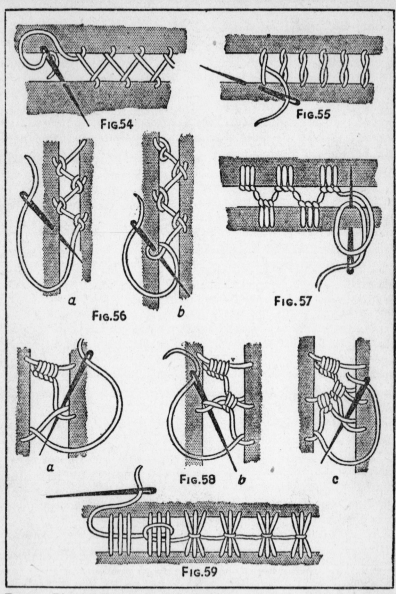

FIG. 54.—Diagonal Faggoting or Open-Work Seam Stitch.   FIG. 55.—Twisted Faggoting or Bar Stitch.   FIG. 56.—Knotted Seam Stitch.   FIG. 57.—Tailor's Buttonhole Insertion.   FIG. 58.—Italian Buttonhole Insertion Stitch.   FIG. 59.—Stack Stitch.

(4) Buttonhole stitch adapts itself well as an insertion stitch, as has been shown. (See Chapter II. for the Buttonhole Stitch and Linked Buttonhole Stitch.) The linked buttonhole stitch is a specially decorative way of joining seams. The tailor's variety, as shown in Fig. 57, is stronger than ordinary button-holing and gives more space between the two materials being joined. Blanket stitch (see Chapter II.) is effective and is quickly worked. There are quite a number of buttonhole insertions, as can be seen, but the most complicated is the one we are now going to describe, known as :

Italian Buttonhole Insertion Stitch (Fig. 58).—To work this stitch, the two edges of the pieces of material to be joined should be about ½ inch apart. It is best to rule lines on the foundation paper or canvas to which the edges are to be tacked in order to ensure an even distance all along.

The needle is brought through at the top corner of the material on the right, and a horizontal bar made to connect the opposite edge of the left-hand material, as in Fig. 58. Over this bar from left to right work five buttonhole stitches. The needle then picks up the edge of the right-hand material about ¼ inch below the first stitch ; it is then brought across to the opposite side and a stitch made, not directly opposite to the last right-hand stitch, but slightly lower, thus forming a second bar. Three buttonhole stitches are now worked from the centre of the last bar outward towards the right. The needle next picks up the material on the right-hand side about ¼ inch lower down, and then three buttonhole stitches are worked from the middle outwards to the left-hand side on the double thread, and then, picking up a piece of material on the same side about ¼ inch lower down, con-tinue from the middle outwards to the right-hand side to work three buttonhole stitches on the double thread, and so on till the row is finished.

(5) *Herringbone Insertion.*—Herringbone stitch (see Chapter III.) also forms a most useful basis for insertion stitch, and inter-lacing stitch (see Chapter III.) is one of its most attractive varieties. Interlacing stitch forms a strong but lace-like band between two pieces of material.

(6) Various other insertion stitches may be made by working an edging stitch, as braid edging or Antwerp edging (Fig. 37),

along the edges of the two materials to be joined, then joining these edgings by means of a row of knotted insertion or some other suitable stitch.

(7) *Stack Stitch* (Fig. 59) gets its name from its likeness to piled stacks of corn. Press a narrow hem on each of the edges to be joined, and tack them on to stiff paper, as described before, ¼ in. apart. Take a straight bar stitch across the space from one edge to the other. Make two more bars close to the first and each other from each edge alternately. Leave a space equal to the width of the group of three bars, then work another three bars, and so on all along, as in Fig 59.

Begin again with a matching or contrasting thread. Take it under the set of three bars, over backwards, under again forwards, pulling the thread tight to give it the stacked effect. Work in the same way all along, carrying the thread on, unbroken, from one group to the next.

Crochet Insertion.—For this decorative form of insertion, especially adapted to wool and long curtains, see the Chapters on Crochet Work and on Wool Craft.

BARS

Bars play quite an important part in many forms of embroidery, especially open-work embroidery and some forms of cutwork, so a section on them will prove useful.

Bars may be twisted, buttonholed, overcast, or needle-woven (darned), according to choice and the nature of the embroidery on which they appear. They are often necessary in cut-work. (See section on Cut-Work, Chapter IV.)

Twisted Bars, or *Overcast Bars.*—To work these, take a thread from the main outline across the space to the other edge. Then return to the starting-point by overcasting loosely over this thread with the remainder of the working thread ; you then have a loose spiral twist.

Buttonholed Bars.—These are very useful in cut-work. Take a thread three times across the space at the correct spot. Still with the same thread, closely buttonhole the triple bar all across, placing the purl of the buttonhole along the edge that is to be cut away. If the material is to be cut away from both sides of the bar, as sometimes happens, buttonhole with the purl along one edge first, leaving spaces between the stitches. Afterwards buttonhole again along the second edge, fitting this row of stitches into the spaces.

Needle-woven Bars.—Work these just as for needle-weaving (see Chapter VI.), but working on a made bar two or four threads thick instead of using the threads of the fabrics. Bars like these are not so strong.

Examples of these bars will be seen in Fig. 60, which shows an example of filet embroidery, and in Fig. 62, which shows Italian cut-work with a hemstitched hem and crocheted edge. (See section on Crochet Work.)

Some Interesting Embroideries involving Drawn-Thread Work and Cut-Work

It will interest the home worker to have a list of well-known and historic types of embroidery based on drawn-thread work and cut-work, especially if we select from each the patterns or ideas most suitable for the busy housewife. This list will be found useful for reference and it will make visits to Art-Needlework Shops more interesting. Remember we have only picked out characteristic features that can be copied quickly if desired.

(1) *Tendril Embroidery*, sometimes called *Florentine Work.*— This work combines Italian hemstitching with characteristic conventional motifs that always end in formal-looking tendrils, and little squares or diamonds in a form of cut-work. It is generally worked on natural linen with a mercerised-cotton thread. The following stitches are generally used—satin stitch for the solid parts of the design, cord stitch for the tendrils (for cord stitch, see chapter on Raised Work) ; the little cut squares or diamonds are whipped round.

Suitable transfers for this work can be bought, but it is more interesting to buy an actual specimen of the work (the work is much sold in this country, and it is not expensive), and then make one's own design based on this.

(2) *Rosebud Embroidery*, another form of *Italian Embroidery.*— This consists of small rosebud motifs enclosed or linked up by coloured lines in drawn-in drawn-thread work (see this heading) or, less frequently, by running or some other simple outline stitch. The embroidery is very simple. The roses are always made of

bullion stitch in two shades of one colour, and they are surrounded by little pointed leaves worked either in lazy-daisy or stroke stitches.   Bullion stitch is described in Chapter III.

(3) *Sicilian Work.*—This is more elaborate than other Italian embroideries.   It is worked in bright, pleasant colours, in a mixture of needle-weaving, hemstitch, cut-work, bars, and a special Sicilian openwork stitch called trellis stitch, which we will now describe.

Trellis Stitch.—This is an an easy stitch, because it is the coral stitch worked in rows across a " run " of drawn threads instead of on solid material.   Draw a " run " of threads ½ inch wide.   Along the run work four parallel rows of coral stitch, picking up four to six linen strands (always the same number) at each stitch. Finish each edge of the run with bar hemstitch.

In the corner of Sicilian work there is often, as in Teneriffe work, a needle-woven " windmill."

Windmill Corner.—Begin by padding with running stitch and then closely buttonholing over the outer right angle of the corner, or if making the windmill to fill an isolated square, run and buttonhole round the entire square.   Now lay single threads (as when making bars) across the corners diagonally both ways, then again across twice, once vertical, and once horizontal.   Take these threads into the buttonholed edge of the material or into the darned sets bounding the corner on two sides.   For the windmill, twelve laid threads are needed, three for each of the four arms.

Take one of the diagonal corner threads as the middle thread of each set of three, darn these in the usual needle-woven way, starting at the centre where they cross, and ending the darning about three-quarters of the way along the threads.

A *fan corner* is simpler for beginners and is suitable for a corner where the border design is quite narrow.   Buttonhole the corner as described for the windmill, lay five diagonal threads, coming respectively from the corner itself and from two points along the sides that make the corner, and *all* going into the point of the inner corner of the border.   Darn the fan thus made, darning a little further along the three centre threads than along the outside two.

(4) *Teneriffe Work.*—This is also known in America as Mexican drawn-thread work, but it is Spanish in origin.   It uses the

woven fans and windmills described above, which indeed are also used in Swedish embroidery, and also the ordinary hemstitch for hems and for edging corners and borders.

Some of the stitches used in this work give it a beautiful lace-like appearance, but they are too complicated for the worker at home. Some of the easier ones are given below, and they are well worth trying.

The work can be done either on a rather fine linen or a smooth cotton, such as casement cloth. All white is usual, but blue working threads give a note of colour and make the work less trying for the eyes.

The chief stitch used is coral stitch. The work is arranged in borders and corners. The following border is an effective one ; some prefer to use the embroidery hoop when working this border, because it keeps the added threads stretched all at the same tension.

Four-legged Stitch.—This is a wide, effective border. Draw threads to make a " run " $\frac{3}{4}$ inch deep. Work ordinary hemstitch along each edge, taking up four threads each time.

Now work single crossing along the middle of the run, taking up sixteen threads, that is, " four legs " of the ordinary hemstitch. With a fresh long thread begin again along the middle ; work a coral-stitch knot over the single crossing thread half-way between two crossings, take the thread up to half-way between crossing and top edge, and coral-stitch across each of the four legs. Knot again over the next single crossing thread, then take the working thread down, and coral-stitch across the lower four legs of the next crossing. Continue up and down in this way to the end, then return, doing the legs missed the first time, and re-knotting over the middle thread. This working makes a delicate hexagonal pattern superimposed on the single crossing —a very popular Teneriffe device.

Stars.—These are another feature of Teneriffe work. These are quick and easy to work. An inner border can consist of two rows of them, with extra ones at each corner.

The number of threads drawn must vary somewhat with the texture of the stuff. Experiment first, drawing enough to give the proper pull on the square without puckering it. These stars should be worked on a frame.

Divide the space to be covered into ¾-inch squares by drawing threads both ways, the squares to be solid fabric divided by " runs " from two to four threads wide. Now use a thin, strong thread (for example one strand of stranded cotton), stitch over from each corner into the centre of the square, and from two points along each side, also into the centre. Pull the thread up rather sharply each time, so that the edges of the square are drawn into star-like points. Do not fasten off, but carry the thread to the next square. Work a line of coral stitches between the stars both ways.

(5) *Reticella.*—This work is on the border between embroidery and lace-making. Reticella is a lace made by embroidery methods. It is usually in square motifs showing star-like or diamond patterns and using the bars (see section on Bars) of cut-work, which are called, in reticella, brides or barrettes. Buttonhole stitch is the chief stitch employed.

Reticella is based on cut or drawn threads. Sometimes threads are left as a basis for the work, and at other times the material is cut entirely away, the space being filled with a lace-like pattern. The edges of the shape are, of course, made secure by (1) overcast stitch, or (2) buttonholing (blanket or tailor). If the linen is cut away before the reticella is worked, it is wise to sew the linen to a piece of strong material, so that the worker can adjust the length of threads that form the bars more easily.

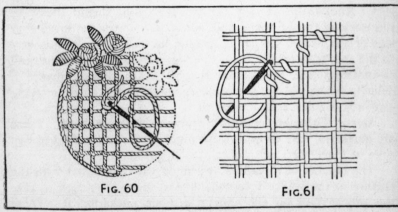

FIG. 60.　　　　FIG. 61.

FIG. 60.—Filet Embroidery.　　FIG. 61.—Overcasting Drawn Threads.

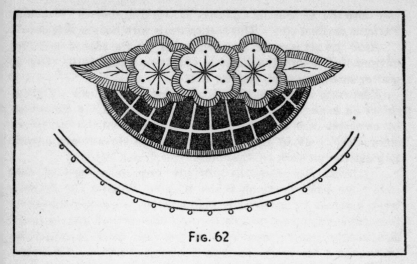

FIG. 62

FIG. 62.—Italian Cut-Work with a Hemstitched Hem and a Crocheted Edge.

The bars are worked as already described. They may be woven, buttonholed, or overcast bars. Surface buttonholing, tailor's buttonholing, and picots are all used in this form of embroidery. It is generally worked in white or natural coloured linen thread on a background of a similar colour.

(6) *Filet Embroidery* (Fig. 60).—This is very similar to Reticella.

Filet embroidery can be used to very good effect in almost any punched-work design (see Chapter VII.) or in spaces intended for medallions or lace insertions. Fig. 60 shows clearly how the work is done and how the knot is made. First mark out the shape to be covered with filet embroidery. Use a medium-size linen thread for strength, and carry this across the space in parallel lines about $\frac{3}{16}$ inch apart, fastening the threads on the line of the design with back stitches. After the space is filled with threads running in one direction, they are carried across at right angles, knotting the thread at each crossing in the manner shown in Fig. 60. These knots hold firmly, and a pretty filet net is the result.

This net can be used as a background for darning, weaving, or embroidery, or it is decorative in its simplest form, as shown.

(See also the section in Chapter VI. on Darning or Weaving Patterns on Filet Net. This section deals with bought filet net.)

After the net is made, as shown in Fig. 60, the edge is carefully buttonholed before the linen is cut from underneath. Use a pair of small, sharp scissors for this.

Filet embroidery looks very dainty on a baby's cap. Fig. 62 shows an example of Italian work that can be easily simplified by using one rose and two leaves. It is very similar to Hebeo embroidery, only in Hebeo embroidery the threads are drawn to make the network background. This brings us to :

(7) *Hebeo embroidery* has already been mentioned in the chapter on Embroidery on White Material, Chapter II. In this work a square of material is first buttonholed round the edge, then alternately two threads left and two threads drawn both horizontally and vertically. The network thus produced is overcast in a fine cotton so as to be almost invisible. The overcasting is done diagonally, as in Fig. 61. Upon this network a pattern can be worked solidly with a coarser thread, so that the effect is that of a solid pattern worked on a net basis. This network can also be decorated with numerous patterns in weaving, etc., and this is often, in Hebeo work, used as a contrast with parts that are richly embroidered. This kind of work is mostly executed in white.

(8) *Russian Drawn-Thread Work.*—Russian drawn-thread work is also partly dependent on the network effect described above. A bold design is planned which is enriched with bands of stepped satin stitch and faggoting stitches and outlined with heavy chain. The outer borders of the design are secured by buttonholing. The background network is then formed by drawing the threads and overcasting them as described.

CHAPTER VI

EMBROIDERIES DONE UPON COUNTED THREADS

The Cross-Stitch Group. Darning. Needle-Weaving or Swedish Weaving. The Tacking Stitch and its Varieties—Holbein Stitch and Basket Stitch, Diamond Pattern. Roumanian Embroidery. Darning or Weaving on Net. Darning Patterns on Filet Net. Darning on Huckaback. Darned Wheels. Hardanger Work.

WE now come to some very simple and interesting work, and what is perhaps more important to the busy housewife, quick work and inexpensive work. The materials used are coarse linen, burlap, hessian, crash, huckaback, loosely woven dishcloths, nets, or any mesh materials. The greater number of these, as you can see, are not expensive materials.

First, we will talk about some of the very simple yet delightful stitches that can be used on these coarse materials, then we will take particular materials and their use. Some stitches are of course more suited to some materials than others, but we will begin with a stitch that is almost universally used on every material—the famous cross stitch and its varieties.

The worker will find it interesting to make a " sampler " of these stitches to see their effect and their variations.

THE CROSS-STITCH GROUP (Figs. 63, 65, *a*, *b*)

Cross stitch is a very useful form of decoration. The design is usually fairly geometric and formal, and it is often applied to tablecloths, aprons, dresses, etc.

It is usual to work it directly on to the material by counting the threads, and by following a diagram drawn on squared paper. In order to do this, the threads should be clear and distinct and the linen fairly loosely woven, but if the fabric

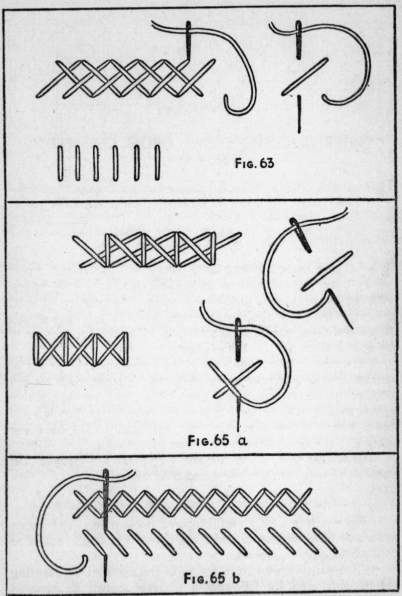

FIG. 63.—Cross Stitch, Long Arm.   FIG. 65.—(a) Cross Stitch, Montenegrin.
(b) Cross Stitch, oblong.

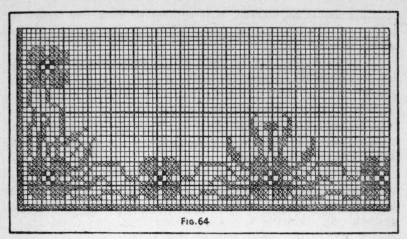

FIG. 64.

FIG. 64.—Pattern for Cross Stitch.

be fine or of velvet or silk (where the threads are not sufficiently marked), canvas may be tacked over it very carefully and the design embroidered through the two materials. With this method, the cross stitch should be tightly worked, otherwise when the canvas is drawn away, the threads of the cross stitch will lie loosely on the surface of the material. Transfers with all the crosses marked on them can also be used. There are few materials that cannot be cross-stitched if a suitable transfer is used.

Cross stitch is so simple that it never loses its popularity, and almost any type of design may be translated into terms of cross stitch with good results.

Owing, as we have said before, to the geometrical construction of the stitch, cross-stitch work really looks best if the design is rather formal and of a patterned and " repeat " kind. Colour charts should be carefully worked out before beginning.

Most tapestry and cross-stitch designs are interchangeable, as the working stitches are so similar. (See section on Tapestry.)

To work.—Simply place two stroke stitches of equal length one over the other at right angles, so that a cross or multiplication sign (X) is formed. All cross stitches in a given piece of work should cross over the same way, and when a number close together are being worked, it is simpler to work one stroke of each cross all along the line, and then return crossing each stroke with a second.

A pretty cushion can be made with a Java canvas cover. It has a cross-stitch design made with silk embroidery thread of dull green, rose, and black. Fig. 64 shows details of the design. In making a cushion like this, first decide upon the size that you wish to make the stitches. Near one edge of the canvas count threads, and with pins mark along the edge the spaces required for groups of 5 stitches each.

On cross-stitch paper which is laid off with similar groups of squares, plan one-fourth of the design for the pillow. This is a sure method of obtaining good margins and a well-spaced pattern. In planning a design, study the background shape that is left in the centre and be sure that it forms a pleasing outline. If you wish to make a cross-stitch design on a finely woven material, remember that you will need to use cross-stitch canvas basted on the cloth. When the embroidery is completed the threads of the canvas are pulled out, as already mentioned. Embroidery wools may be used instead of wash silks; mercerised thread may also be used. A useful bag can be made of crass and decorated with cross stitch. The edges are turned in and tacked down. Rows of cross stitches (in black wool) are worked over the edges at each side and at the top, and a row of red cross stitches are worked inside the black ones. A pattern is worked each side of the bag in red and black cross stitch. Any simple pattern can be chosen, and of course any two colours that go well together. The squares shown in Fig. 64 can be adapted to this bag.

Cross Stitch Overcast, also called Criss-cross Overcasting.— This is a simple and very useful adaptation of cross stitch to a hem or to double edges. It makes a bold and effective trimming for the joins of cushion covers or to finish the hems of runners and tray-cloths.

To work.—Keep the right side of the material towards you, and start working from right to left. Make a row of slanting overcast stitches right over the hem or edge. Make them ¼ inch deep, or a little more (except on handkerchiefs and underwear), and keep the stitches an even distance apart. When the line is finished, return in the reverse direction, slanting the stitches the other way and working into the same holes as in the first row. Thus a series of cross stitches over the edge is formed. This stitch is very effective *if evenly* worked. A good way to ensure evenness is first to stitch the hem by machine with fine cotton, loose tension, and a long stitch. This takes the place of tacking and has the additional advantage of giving even spaces for the overcasting. Work the first slanting row through *alternate* machine stitches; when returning, use the stitches missed before. This makes the work both quick and regular. The machine stitches may afterwards be pulled out, though they will hardly show.

Two-sided Italian Cross Stitch (Fig. 66).—This stitch is really a cross stitch surrounded by a square, each corner of which is emphasised by a small hole, formed by drawing the working thread tightly. This stitch must be worked on a fairly coarse and loosely woven linen, otherwise the appearance is stodgy and laboured. In some Italian work the background is embroidered with this stitch, whilst the pattern is left in the plain fabric. But this stitch can be used in various ways, in

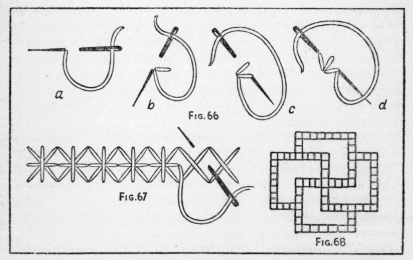

FIG. 66.—Two-sided Italian Cross Stitch.   FIG. 67.—Devil Stitch.   FIG. 68.—
Squared Cross Stitch.

conjunction with other kinds of stitches ; it is useful for borders
and the filling of many large shapes.

No tracing on to the material is required when the design
is entirely composed of two-sided Italian stitch (or indeed of
ordinary cross stitch) ; the design follows the threads from a
diagram drawn on squared paper.

To work.—In order to work the stitch successfully, study the
diagram, Fig. 66, carefully. First make a short stroke to the
left, then a slanting one as in diagram, then a straight one to
form another side, then a slanting one crossing the first slanting
stroke. The whole stitch is not complete until *two* rows are
worked. The thread must be drawn tightly in order to get
the right effect.

Devil Stitch (Fig. 67).—This is a variation of cross stitch.
Work a line of cross stitch, then work over it so that each cross is
turned into an asterisk. Begin at the left end of the row of
cross stitches, and at the left side of the last stitch. Bring your
thread through from the back, level with the centre, take it
across the centre of the cross, and put your needle through
opposite your starting-point, as in Fig. 67. Slant your needle
backwards, and bring it out between the two upper corners of
the cross, then bring your thread down over the centre of the
cross again and put your needle through on the lower line exactly
opposite the spot it came out at the top. Bring it out again
at the right end of your horizontal stitch and repeat (Fig. 67).

Squared Cross Stitch (Fig. 68).—By working your crosses on
the wrong side you can outline squares on the right side. You
must work from the right side. (See Fig. 49, Chapter IV., for
method of working this stitch.)

Assisi embroidery is a simple and attractive Italian embroidery
worked mainly in cross stitch. Unlike ordinary cross-stitch
embroidery the design is left unworked and the background filled
with cross stitch. Formal designs suit this embroidery best.
It is used a great deal for household articles—mats, cloths,
runners, cushion covers, pyjama cases, and so on.

The pattern or design is first outlined in double running
stitch or in back stitch. The former stitch is worked by taking
a line of running stitch round the outline, each stitch the length
of a cross-stitch square, and then coming back, putting a stitch

where you left a space the time before, and the other way about. The outlining is often done in black. The cross stitch is usually worked in rows ; first you make the half-stitches slanting one way, then come back along the line crossing these. Make sure that the first stitches in each cross, over the whole background, *slant* the *same* way.

DARNING (Fig. 69)

In embroidery this quick stitch is simpler and varies more than when used for mending. (See section on Darning in Chapter X.) In embroidery it consists of rows of running stitches, the in-and-out of the stitches alternating in each row. The term " darning stitch " also denotes sometimes a single row of running stitches used to outline a design.

The chief use of darning in embroidery is to fill backgrounds or fairly large parts of the design.

Pattern darning, since it consists of the regular picking up of threads, will vary according to the way in which the threads are picked up. The darning may be horizontal or vertical. Sometimes a colour contrast is introduced into the background, thus producing a striped effect. Darning is often spoken of as weaving.

To work.—Make rows of straight stitches with spaces between the same length as the stitches. In alternate rows go under where the previous row shows a surface stitch, and *vice versa*. Keep the lines very even. If a much-filled-up effect is wanted, pick up only a thread or two each time, leaving long stitches lying on the stuff. Thus almost continuous lines are formed with the minimum of thread and work.

When a background is to be darned, this should be done before the design is embroidered, and the darning should be close enough for the rows to touch and strictly alternated. The design superimposed on the pattern darning must be bold, so that the background effect does not confuse with the main design. It is usual to outline the main design in a chain stitch or stem stitch (see Chapter II.) or whipped-run stitch (described further on in this chapter), whilst the design itself is left in the plain material.

It is essential to leave the threads of the pattern darning

fairly slack, as, unless this is done, the material becomes very puckered.

Material suitable for pattern darning is a loosely woven linen or jute fabric ; if a fine material be chosen, the work becomes tedious and looks less decorative.

Other uses of darning :

(1) To make simple borders (Fig. 70).

These are specially suited to the needs of the beginner, and only require care in counting the threads. They give practice in pattern-making ; good colour effects can be obtained and they lead to more beautiful work later.

(2) As a filling for large leaves, flowers, and other forms, it may also be used for working broad bands without any super-imposed design. This treatment is very effective when worked in wool on coarse material.

(3) *Surface Darning.*—This, as its name implies, is a darn worked on the surface of the material. It is most useful when working both geometric and floral forms. It combines well with other stitches as chain, whipped-run, and those that give light effects to the solidity of the surface darning. In working this stitch, as we have said before, the needle enters the material at each end only. The thread must be laid loosely on the material or else, when the darn is completed, the material will tend to pucker. This is a useful stitch to use when making loops through which cords are to be passed. In such case the needle first enters the material at each end only ; but in going across it is taken backwards and forwards through the laid threads *without* entering the material at each side. This method is much used for the draw-strings of small bags, or for the tops of aprons through which braid has to be threaded.

NEEDLE-WEAVING OR SWEDISH WEAVING (Figs. 71 and 72)

This bold, handsome stitch is also known as Swedish darning stitch. It is one of the most effective of the drawn-thread stitches, and makes an excellent decoration worked in thick threads on crash or other coarse materials (tweed or linen in dress material) for runners, chairbacks, cushions, scarves, pochettes. Bright colours suit it best.

It is a form of embroidery worked on the threads of the

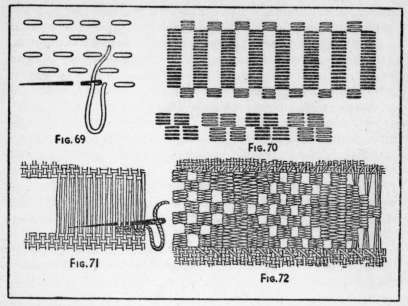

FIG. 69.—Darning Stitch.   FIG. 70.—Patterns in Darning Stitch.   FIG. 71.—
Swedish Weaving.   FIG. 72.—Pattern in Swedish Weaving.

material when the threads in the opposite direction (*i.e.* either
the warp or the weft) have been withdrawn. The weaving can be
done in cotton, silk, or wool, but the choice of ground material
is limited, as it can only be worked on material from which it is
possible to draw the threads.

To work.—Draw consecutive threads across the material to a
depth of from ¼ inch to ¾ inch, according to the weave desired
and the thickness of the working thread. Leave a few strands
of stuff untouched at one end, then at the top of the drawn strip
bring your thread through to the right side. Avoid starting
with a knot, securing it instead with a short end and a back
stitch.

Pass the thread over a suitable number of threads—say four
in a thick material—then under the next four. Turning back,
pass over the group you have just gone under, and under the first
group. Continue darning back and forth in this way until the
bar is filled. Fasten off by running the thread as invisibly as

possible under the stitches of the bar. Wider bars may be made by darning twice over and under a larger number of strands before turning the needle. Fig. 71 shows a pattern being woven. A great number of patterns can easily be thought out, all of course geometrical and made up of straight lines. Various diamond and triangular repeat patterns may be formed by taking up more or fewer sets in each row. A *set* is the number of threads (generally from three to eight) which the needle goes over or under each time, and the set must be kept the same throughout a pattern.

Patterns can be thought out by experimenting on odd pieces of material, or they can be worked out first on a piece of squared paper, blacking in the squares which represent the pattern. To vary the design, bars may be interspersed among the darned sets; these bars are made by overcasting the threads instead of darning them.

It may interest those who like technical terms to know that a " run " is the name given to that part of the material from which the threads have been drawn.

A beginner should not draw, at one time, so many threads as to make a " run " deeper than one inch, because the exposed loose threads are rather difficult to manage. Some workers even use a tambour-frame in order to hold these threads tightly and in a good position for working. Many find it advisable to work from the centre of the run outwards so that the ends will be alike in pattern. It is then necessary to estimate the number of threads to pick up in the needle when weaving; the number should not be too great, or the weaving threads will be loose and the material will pucker on each side of the woven band. The number of times the thread passes over and under each group of threads must be constant, otherwise the pattern effect will not be even.

A broad band is easier to work if divided into narrow sections; a band 4 inches broad should be divided into two or three sections, each part being separated by a narrow band of three threads, which prevents the exposed threads from becoming too long and detached.

The thread should not be drawn tightly when a coloured band is worked, but when embroidering with a white thread on white material, the only means of obtaining a pattern is by pulling the weaving thread tight so that open spaces are left, as in Fig. 72. (See section on Open-Work.)

Needle-weaving combines well with cross stitch.

Besides being worked on the upright threads of a material when the horizontal ones have been pulled out, it may be worked on loose bars made with the needle and thread. The woven bars then serve as ornamental slots or casings through which bag strings or belts may be run.

Fig. 72 shows a pattern in Swedish weaving. This is an elaborate pattern sometimes called Persian open-work with squares. For this twenty threads must be drawn out. It can also be worked in three different colours or three different shades. Each figure of this pattern takes eighteen clusters of three threads.

The Tacking Stitch and its Varieties

Pattern darning is really a development of the tacking stitch. (For the tacking stitch, see the chapters on Plain Needlework.) Here we are going to describe a few interesting varieties of the tacking stitch. We have already seen how useful the simple stitch itself is in making patterns and how it serves as an intro-duction to pattern-making in embroidery. We have dealt with this in the paragraphs on darning. Now here are two useful developments of the tacking stitch :

(1) *Whipped-run Stitch* (Fig. 73).—This is a useful variety of tacking stitch, especially when working lines in a spontaneous way. Run a small tacking stitch into the material, taking up as much material as the space left, then wrap a thread through the stitch that lies on the surface of the material, and do not go through the material except at the beginning and end of the row, or when a fresh thread is begun, as in Fig. 73. This wrapping thread may be the same colour as the one run into the material, or it may be of some contrasting colour. This stitch is very useful for line work and it makes a pleasing solid filling for large forms. In the latter case it is worked by following the outline of the form until a solid effect is obtained.

It is an economical method of embroidery, as most of the thread lies on the surface, but care must be taken not to pull the thread too tightly or the material puckers badly.

(2) *Holbein Stitch* (Fig. 74).—Another line effect produced by

tacking stitch is known as " Holbein stitch." This is worked
by running a small, even stitch into the material and then returning by using another tacking stitch to fill in the spaces left.
This stitch has the advantage of being alike on both sides, and is
used for making small patterns in outline in a thread of one
colour.

Basket Stitch (Fig. 75).—This is quite an effective filling stitch
and will also do for simple borders (see also section on Darning).
It is so called because it suggests the weave of a basket. When
used as a border the upright lines should be in a different colour
from the horizontal ones.

To work.—Work short horizontal strokes or tacking stitches
in pairs and in rows, leaving spaces between them rather shorter
than their own length. Next fill the spaces with pairs of vertical
stitches the same length and distance apart.

Diamond Pattern (Fig. 76).—Small and large diamond
patterns form a good background stitch and are easily worked
on huckaback.

To work.—Insert the needle under one raised thread in one
row, and under a raised thread in another row, slanting. Come
back again slanting to the raised threads in the first row. The
second row is the same as the first, but begin on an entirely
different line of raised threads, and slanting the thread upwards
instead of downwards, as in previous row, so putting the thread
in the same stitch as the row above.

Roumanian Embroidery (Fig. 77)

This is a pleasant form of work based on the embroidery
done by peasants. The design can be followed out directly
on the canvas. It is often worked on hand-woven white material.
See that the material is perfectly straight as to the edges, and
then tack canvas (twenty threads to the inch) over the surface
very carefully. It is essential that the edges of the canvas and the
fabric correspond and that the tacking is very thorough.

The original work was generally done in black with red, or
blue with red, or in blue thread only. It is very effective indeed
in these colours.

The stitch is a back stitch formed by going over two threads
of the canvas at once. The stitches at the back should be as

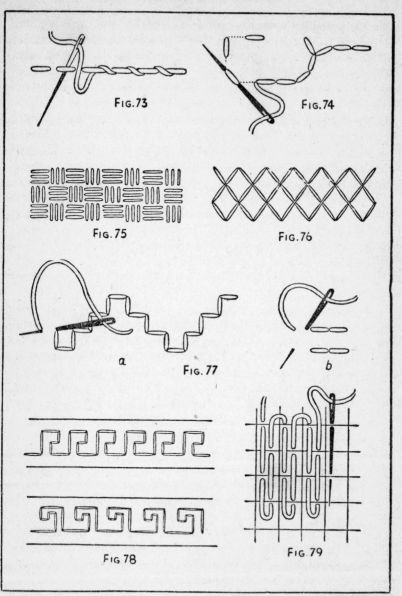

FIG. 73.—Whipped-run Stitch.   FIG. 74.—Holbein Stitch.   FIG. 75.—Basket
Stitch.   FIG. 76.—Large Diamond Pattern.   FIG. 77.—Roumanian Embroidery.   FIG. 78.—Greek Frets.   FIG. 79.—The Filet Weaving Stitch.

far as possible horizontal, and in working out a single line, ordinary back stitch is used, but when embroidering a pattern often a double stitch must be used, as in the pattern shown in Fig. 77.

A *double line* is worked together by crossing the needle over alternately at the back from one line to the other, as in Fig. 77. When working a border, begin to embroider from the middle so that the two edges may be alike. This is of great importance when a square mat or tablecloth is being decorated. If care is not taken, great trouble will be experienced in fitting the design in the corners. Take care also not to put the needle through the threads of the canvas.

This form of embroidery washes well and so is well suited for tablecloths, etc.

Needle-weaving and cross stitch combine beautifully with this form of embroidery.

DARNING OR WEAVING ON NET

This form of darned embroidery is also called weaving on net. It is done with embroidery wool on coarse-mesh curtain net. It is very easy because of the nature of the materials. All one needs to know is a stitch or two with which to fill the squares, and with these stitches a variety of designs can be worked out. Patterns drawn on checked paper (they can also be bought) and any filet patterns can be used. Almost any kind of open net can be woven or darned and made up into attractive articles. You will find a great number of different nets for sale in the shops, coarse-mesh net, lace net, and strong fibrous net. The strong nets make durable articles such as stool covers, cushion covers, rugs (see sections on Rugs), etc. From coarse-mesh curtain net, short curtains, bedspreads, jumpers, etc., can be made.

In all darning on net, a thread should be used which is thick enough to fill the mesh well without distending or dragging it. It is sometimes necessary to use double wool when darning a large-mesh curtain. For dress net stranded cotton is excellent, as the right number of strands can be chosen to fit the mesh.

Before beginning to darn in a border pattern, turn up the raw edge, several meshes deep, to the wrong side. Make only a *single* turn. Darn the bottom few rows through the double net, thus making a neat hem and giving extra strength to the edge of the work.

Darn continuously up one row and down the next. When taking a new thread, do not start with a knot, but lose the end among the last stitches taken with the old thread. Do not cut wool, break it—the broken frayed end is easily lost in the stitches.

Conventional borders, for example frets like the Grecian fret shown in Fig. 78, are usually chosen, and these run along the bottoms of the curtains and perhaps up the sides, or around the edges of a bedspread. In the centre is a conventional motif of some kind.

Transfers will not, of course, iron off on net. But if a repeat pattern is chosen it can first be drawn out on squared arithmetic paper and used as a chart for copying. As the pattern repeats frequently, it can soon be learned, and then the work can go on without the chart.

If a floral design has to be darned on fine dress net for a veil, lay a transfer under the net and tack transfer and net together. Then darn through both net and the tissue paper of the transfer, afterwards tearing the paper away.

Besides the darning stitch the simplest stitch to use on net is a straight over-and-over stitch. Another good stitch is the long-and-short stitch. In this stitch the long and short stitches of adjacent rows alternate and fit into each other.

Those who cannot afford to buy net will find that they can do wonderful things with loosely woven dishcloths and coloured wool. Pretty little woollen garments for small children can be woven—two dishcloths make a small tunic. In the last chapter among the novelties you will find out how to work a pretty work-bag from these same dishcloths. They can be joined together to make beautiful colourful cushion covers, small bedspreads, etc.

Darning Patterns on Filet Net

This is also spoken of as weaving on filet net. This is another method of work on a network basis. The filet net is bought, the pattern is darned or woven on it, and then it is inserted into a piece of linen.

In working patterns on filet net, each square of the net is crossed twice in each direction by the linen thread. Pretty lacy tray-cloths can be made from fine darned ecru curtain net. Buttonhole around the edge and work flowers or some pretty motif in each corner.

A very pretty and dainty type of embroidery can be worked on a hexagonal net background. The design must be drawn on tracing cloth and the net tacked to this so that the design can be seen through and worked on to the net. Muslin appliqué on a hexagonal net background is another form of embroidery on net.

We might say a word here about the filet-weaving stitch. This is the same as that used for making real filet lace when filling in the squares, and it has already been mentioned. The wool moves in and out, passing back and forth twice in each line of squares, as in Fig. 79. The stitch is the same on both sides and it is therefore excellent for making curtain ornaments, runners, etc. The wool enters the net at square 1, and goes in and out of the squares as far as this portion of the design requires, say to 2. Here it turns, goes around a thread, and then travels back through the same squares, but this time under where before it went over, and over where before it went under, as shown in Fig. 79.

Any ends left by a change of colour or by starting are concealed in the weaving.

Filet-weaving can be continued for any number of squares.

In filet-weaving the background can be filled in, using a different coloured wool to set off the design, or it may be left unwoven; lines or patches of empty squares give a lace-like appearance to the work, and a prettier effect is often obtained. Some workers line the open net with silk of a contrasting colour, but this makes the work more expensive.

Underarm purses of all patterns can be made of net and embroidered with net-weaving stitches. They make delightful gifts and are very quick to work.

Really strong market bags can be made of strong burlap and ornamented with a few rows of interwoven stitches in bright wools, but perhaps the cheapest, quickest, and most effective work is :

DARNING ON HUCKABACK

Huckaback, with its very definite weave and its surface threads just waiting to be picked up, is ideal for darned embroidery. We have already mentioned its use in the short section on the Diamond pattern.

Towels, duchesse sets, lunch mats, washstand mats, etc., may be made from huckaback, which can be bought either in white or colours.

The designs used on it can be more varied than those used on net.

Huckaback darning is almost all on the surface, thus giving a good effect for very little work. Pick up only the definite surface threads, these hold the stitches without hiding them, and as they occur at regular intervals on the material they keep the pattern uniform.

Put in conventional borders by counting the threads and working from a chart or from the pattern which you have drawn out yourself on squared paper. Stranded cotton can be used for the embroidery, and it washes well. Use clear, decided colours, either one, two, or three.

Border patterns are always effective in two well-contrasted shades or tints of the same colour.

Geometrical patterns, house and tree designs, are easy to darn if they consist almost entirely of straight lines.

DARNED WHEELS

These wheels, with their slightly more elaborate variation, overcast wheels, are used in many kinds of embroidery to fill effectively either round or square spaces. They used to be even more popular than they are to-day. As they can vary greatly in size, they are very useful.

Make a large cross stitch by placing a horizontal stitch over a vertical one. Work over these two diagonal stitches, so that you have eight spokes of a wheel. With the same thread or a contrasting thread, start at the centre where the long stitches intersect, and darn round and round, over one spoke and under the next alternately. The darning may be continued to only half the depth of the spokes or right up to their ends, according to the effect desired.

Overcast wheels have the same uses and are much the same in appearance as darned wheels, but they take a little longer to work and look more like real wheels. This stitch is a realistic way of working spiders' webs also.

To work.—Make the spokes just as for darned wheels, but instead of darning them, go under two spokes and then overcast back over the last spoke ; continue round and round till the spokes are half or completely filled. Pretty borders can be made of half-wheels, with five spokes.

These " spiders' webs " were very popular in the early years of the twentieth century, especially on a background material of a special soft canvas with alternate checks of white and a colour. The spiders' webs were worked either on all the white squares or on all the coloured squares in thick mercerised cotton. This work was then made up into cushion covers and tablecloths, etc.

HARDANGER WORK

This is a Norwegian embroidery which takes its name from the Hardanger Fjord in Norway.

It is handsome, bold work, done on an open-mesh canvas, and combines simple cut-work and drawn-thread work with blocks of satin stitch. Geometrical patterns are used which can be counted out on the canvas mesh. These are usually worked in white or natural canvas. The effect of Hardanger work is rather that of bold and heavy lace. It is therefore most often used for household linen.

CHAPTER VII

SOME EASY AND INTERESTING DECORATIVE EMBROIDERY

Couching and Laid-Work, Snail Trail, Cord Stitch. Punch-Work or Punched Embroidery. Bermuda Faggoting. Beading for Hem. Shadow Embroidery. French Shadow Embroidery. Shadow Quilting. Outline Embroideries. Landscape and Map Embroidery.

SOME of the work we are now going to describe will be found very interesting and some of it quite new. Those who like quick effective work should notice carefully what is said about French Shadow Embroidery and the new Outline Embroideries. In the section on Shadow Quilting they will find new ideas for presents and bazaars.

We will begin with Couching, which may already be familiar to some readers.

COUCHING AND LAID-WORK

Couching is the name given to the method of attaching a group of threads to a ground material by means of stitching. For this purpose the suitable stitches are varied and numerous, and include satin, herringbone, Cretan, open chain, etc. ; by their use many pretty borders can be thought out.

Simple couching (Fig. 80) is one of the simplest and quickest stitches. It is very useful for emphasising a hem, outlining a bold design, or covering the edges of appliqués. It consists in laying a thick thread or cord on the material and holding it down with bar stitches worked across it at intervals with a thinner thread. This may match or contrast with the laid thread. Two or more thicknesses of thread may be laid, to give additional breadth to the couching.

Besides forming an outline to a design, simple couching may

be placed side by side to form a mass. When the tying-down stitch is made to form slanting lines over the surface of the form embroidered, it is called *Bokhara couching*.

To work Simple Couching (Fig. 80).—Bring the laid thread, in a large-eyed needle, up from the wrong side at one edge of the line to be worked. Remove the needle and let the thread lie loose. With the working thread in a smaller needle, work very short bar stitches at right angles across the laid thread, holding the latter in position with the left thumb. The bar stitches, or tying-down stitches, should be regular distances apart, usually $\frac{1}{4}$ to $\frac{1}{2}$ inch. At the end re-thread the laid thread, take it down to the wrong side, and there fasten off both threads. If the laid thread is too thick to go through a needle, poke a hole for it with a stiletto at the beginning and end of the work.

Snail Trail is an excellent stitch for the rapid working of lines and is suitable for any firm material. It also makes a good filling for large spaces worked close together in lines. It is equivalent to couching worked with one thread (Fig. 81).

To work.—Hold the thread down about one inch from where it comes out with the left thumb. Place the needle vertically close above the thread and bring it out again through the loop immediately below the thread, thus forming a knot—the knots to be placed from $\frac{1}{4}$ to $\frac{1}{2}$ inch apart, according to the thickness of the thread used.

Couching (*Twisted*).—This gives a more striking outline than ordinary couching. It is a good way to introduce several colours. Twist two or three thin threads together into a cord and use this as the laid thread, couching it down in the manner already described.

Cord Stitch.—This stitch is useful when a *fine* but prominent and raised outline is needed. It belongs specially to the various types of white embroidery (see Chapter II.), such as broderie anglaise and filette or punched work, but it is very effective, too, in coloured stitchery. It is sometimes called *fine satin stitch* or *roll stitch*.

To work.—First make the padding by covering the outline with closely set, small running stitches (see chapters on Dressmaking for the running stitch). Then work very short satin stitches across the running stitches, entirely hiding them.

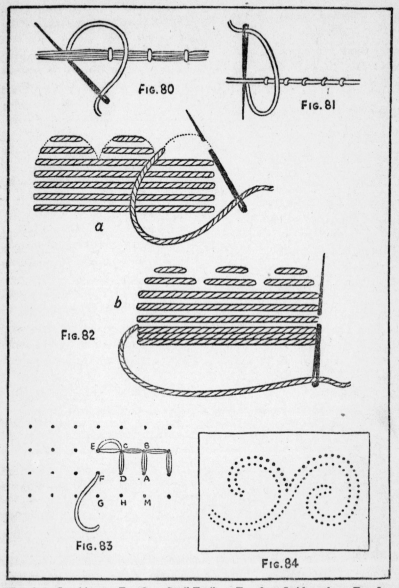

FIG. 80.—Couching.   FIG. 81.—Snail Trail.   FIG. 82.—Laid-work.   FIG. 83. —Punch Stitch or Lace Stitch.   FIG. 84.—Bermuda Faggoting.

The Use of Metal Threads.—Small purses and bags can be decorated with a form of couching called " Or nué." This is a method of couching down gold or aluminium threads with various coloured silks. A double line of metal thread is worked over at the same time, small silk stitches being taken at right angles. The rows of gold threads are placed side by side, and the portion of the design that occurs along the line is worked in various coloured silks. The design grows as each row is completed. The gold threads must be stitched over with very fine silk, used in very small stitches, or else the metal threads will be pushed apart and they will not form a pleasing background to the silk embroidery. The background must be a strong one—linen covered with silk. Most people do this kind of work on a frame. It should be pasted at the back before it is released in order that the gold may not wrinkle on the surface.

Laid-Work (Fig. 82).—Laid-work is a development of couching. It is very useful for filling large forms. It may be worked in silk or wool, but silk is much more usual ; nevertheless charming results can be obtained in wool. The laid threads may be of one colour, arranged in stripes or in gradation. They are fastened down at frequent intervals and in various patterns, according to the direction of the laid thread.

Care must be taken to apply laid-work to suitable articles, as it is not so durable as a more tightly stitched type of work. Most people use a tambour or table frame when embroidering laid-work.

To work.—Thread a needle with the thread to be laid. Then lay the threads across the shape to be covered, holding them down by a small stitch entering the material at each side, as in Fig. 82. Because of the stitch made each side it is difficult to bring the laid threads absolutely close together. However, the spaces left can be filled by passing over the shape a second time. In this way a more regular spacing of the threads is obtained, as in Fig. 82, 2nd step.

The tying-down stitches are then worked in an opposite direction to the laid threads. These stitches can be simple couching as already described, back stitch, chain stitch, etc., and they can be arranged to form patterns over the surface.

An outline to laid-work is often a great improvement. This

may be of couching, stem or chain stitch, worked in silk or wool, or consisting of metal threads couched doubly round the edge.

Punch-Work or Punched Embroidery

This is also sometimes called Filette Embroidery or Rhodes Embroidery. In America it is known as punched work or punched embroidery, because the openwork stitch characteristic of it is worked with a punch needle. Special punch needles are sold in embroidery shops. They have very large heads that make large holes.

Punch-work is becoming very popular at the present moment, for it is a quiet and dignified style of embroidery. Very often the chief characteristic of punch-work is the background, which is patterned all over with little holes, the design standing out in plain linen.

Punch Stitch, also known as Lace Stitch (Fig. 83).—This is much used as a background stitch and worked in continuous rows. It is a good method of joining lace to material in fine underwear—hence the name lace stitch. Thread the punch needle with fine cotton (stranded cotton is used, and two strands is suitable for background work), but always choose a cotton similar in texture and colour to the background for the punch stitch. If a contrasting colour is used, the stitches between the holes will attract the attention before the holes, which will rather spoil the effect. If you really want a contrasting shade, introduce it into the outline of your design. (It is sometimes necessary to tie the thread into the eye of the needle. See Turkey Stitch.)

To work the Punch Stitch or Lace Stitch.—Remember it is a double back stitch worked with a large needle which makes holes in the material, and it is worked in a certain definite order to give a double line of holes in one operation. The stitch is generally worked from right to left (sometimes downwards). As a guide make a double row of pencil-dots on the material, about ⅛ of an inch apart both ways and mentally letter them, as shown in Fig. 83.

You can buy designs already traced on materials and then the dots are all made for you.

To work this stitch, take the needle *twice* through each pair of dots in the order as follows, drawing the thread tightly to emphasise the holes thus made.

When working the first row the order of the stitches is : AB, CD, EC, FE, and so on to the end of the row.

Coming back the order of the stitches is GF, DF, HD, AD, MA, and so on. The work soon becomes automatic and if it is done correctly the threads will always cross on the wrong side.

When a background is decorated with this stitch it is effective to outline the design in stem stitch. When joining lace in this way, stitches taken into the upper row of holes go through both lace and material, those in the lower row through the material only just below the bottom of the lace.

The process is the same whether you work from right to left or downwards.

BERMUDA FAGGOTING (Fig. 84)

A single line is drawn with a pencil on the wrong side of a sheer fabric, the work is also done on the wrong side and is a single bottonhole stitch taken across the drawn (or stamped) line from side to side. A punch needle is used as before for the fine cotton to form the holes.

Turkish Stitch (sometimes called *Turkey Stitch*).—This is a well-known punch stitch. It is often used in elaborate broderie anglaise and to trim fine underwear. Work with a punch needle and a fine thread such as No. 80 cotton, or a single strand of stranded cotton. You must tie the fine thread into the giant eye. Work downwards. Pick up a short stitch at the top of the line to be worked, then make another stitch over it, pulling up the working thread very firmly so that a small hole is made in the material. This second time bring out the needle lower down, ready to begin the next stitch. In fact, what you really do is to work a line of back stitches with a very large needle, but working over each stitch twice instead of once.

So far the work may look rather disappointing because the holes seem shapeless and confused. But now put a fine thread in a fine needle, and go along one side of the line of holes, over-casting each hole twice and pulling the thread tight each time. Overcast in the back-stitching thread when doing this, so that it is not visible across the holes.

Return along the other side of the line, again overcasting twice into each hole, and you will be delighted with the dainty and delicate pierced effect. It looks a little like hemstitching, but as it is not dependent on the thread of the material, it can be worked around a curve.

BEADING FOR HEM (Fig. 85)

This is perhaps one of the most useful stitches known to the needle-woman. The hem is turned down and basted. The work is then done on the wrong side through the two thicknesses. When it is completed the fabric above it on the wrong side is cut away. It is an easy stitch, because it is simply a double hemstitch (see Chapter V.) worked over a cord. An outline can be drawn and the stitch is worked each side of this and over the cord. This stitch can be used where plain hemstitching with drawn threads could not. It is, however, only suitable for fine materials. This beading may be used as an edging on a garment where lace is to be whipped on.

It is worked in cotton over a thread of coarse cotton.

SHADOW EMBROIDERY

This is a novel form of embroidery. Shadow embroidery is the name given to work that consists of covering the design with a filling stitch worked on the wrong side of transparent material, so that the colour of the working thread shows through to the right side in a rather shadowy tint. It is used on sheer materials such as voile, organdie, and georgette, and looks very dainty and fairylike. It is especially suited to small articles such as pin-cushions, mats, tuck-in cushion covers, handkerchief sachets, etc. It is sometimes used for trimming fine babies' frocks.

It is quick and easy to work. Choose a pattern that is well broken up into small (especially narrow) spaces. Daisies and long narrow leaves look effective. Transfer the design on the wrong side of the material as faintly as possible.

For working, choose a flat thread that fills well, such as stranded cotton. Choose dark colours that will show well through the material.

Work entirely on the wrong side ; only one stitch is used—

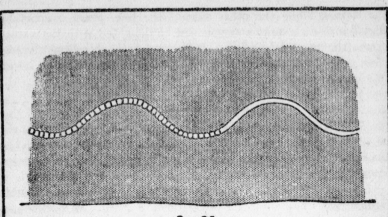

FIG.85

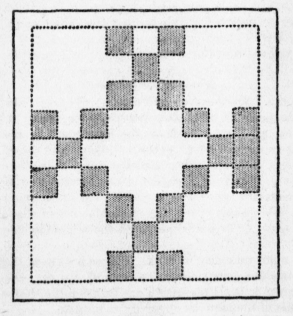

FIG.86

FIG. 85.—Beading for Hem. FIG. 86.—French Shadow Work—simple and effective.

the herringbone (see chapter on the Herringbone Group of Stitches and also the section on Dressmaking). Work this across the narrow petals and other spaces of the design. Work closely so that the stitch will show on the right side in a series of almost continuous short stitches marking the outlines. If this is done the colour filling will look solid from a short distance and the effect is almost that of a very soft appliqué. As the material is transparent, you must take great care to dispose of the beginnings and ends of threads. Tuck them neatly in the herringbone stitches to avoid the use of conspicuous knots.

French Shadow Work. — This is easy and very pretty. Squares are often used in French work. These squares are not stamped on the fabric, but a thread is drawn from each side to ensure accuracy of outline. The squares are first worked across one way and then the other, taking up an equal number of threads each time, so that the effect is pretty on the right side. Many good arrangements of squares can be thought out, and the Greek fret design looks well. In this case the corners of the design are worked double. In French shadow work, the threads must be carefully counted as for drawn work, in order that the blocks may be perfectly even.

The use of small, simple squares in this kind of shadow embroidery makes it particularly suitable for dresses and blouses of fine material. It is also simple and pretty for children's frocks. Fig. 86 shows a good example.

The addition of a few eyelet holes often adds to the beauty of shadow embroidery.

SHADOW QUILTING (see Section on Quilting)

Pretty handkerchief sachets, needle-cases, and dressing-gowns for little children can be made in this way. Crêpe de Chine, white or a very pale tint, can be used, and muslin. If a dressing-gown is being made, it must be padded with flannel.

Transfer the design required on to the muslin. Embroider it in long-and-short stitch and satin stitch. Use embroidery wool in the most vivid colours. Take the stitches close together so as to make the design thick. If it is a sachet, couch four lengths of wool round the outline of the sachet. Now tack the

piece of crêpe de Chine over the muslin so that the edges fit
nicely. Then with white sewing-silk outline the design with
small neat running stitches, through both muslin and silk. The
thick wool beneath will give the work a padded quilted look.
Finally, line the case with another piece of crêpe de Chine and
take the line of running stitches just inside the wool edge.

OUTLINE EMBROIDERIES

Outline embroideries are very quick and therefore very
modern. They are particularly suited to the beginner and
for children who are just learning fancy stitches. Outline
embroideries can be done on almost any material and with
almost any thread, their characteristic feature is that the designs
are worked in outline only and no filling stitches are used. It
follows from this that the designs used must be good in silhouette
and well distributed over the surface to be covered, otherwise
they look mean and scrappy. Beautiful outlines, however, look
very charming and give a light effect which is well suited for
children's dresses or clothing and for small articles such as tea-
cloths, shoe-bags, covers for hot-water bottles, etc.

For outline embroidery, because there is no light or shade
effects, use plenty of clear, vivid colours both in the material in
the working thread or both. Pastel shades should not be used,
they make too weak an outline. Touches of black, especially
round the edge of the work, help to hold it together. Here and
there, to make the design bolder, a small detail can be worked
in satin stitch.

Good results are generally obtained by using patterns of the
picture type containing animals, figures, houses, trees, etc.
The following stitches are recommended, the outline ones of
course, namely : outline stitch itself, split stitch, crewel stitch,
running stitch, back stitch, and coral stitch ; these can be
supplemented by the open buttonhole stitch (for edges and round
flowers), lazy-daisy, couching, and French knots.

LANDSCAPE AND MAP EMBROIDERY

These are suitable for small framed pictures or unframed wall
hangings. Many beautiful needle pictures were made in the
olden days, especially in the sixteenth and seventeenth centuries.

To-day they seem to be becoming popular again, especially picture maps.

Any of the stitches already described are suitable, for it is not a new kind of embroidery, it only suggests new patterns for the worker.

Really large hangings with bold designs can be lovely things. Some of the modern posters can be copied to advantage, and embroidered (or blind appliqué ; see section on Appliqué Work). Natural crash makes a good background. It must be bound or hemmed with a contrasting colour. Linen or satin can be used for the appliqués.

The embroidery must be a mixture of outline and filling stitches, so that it is neither too heavy or too light ; this especially applies to garden scenes, which are very popular. Sometimes landscapes and maps are carried out in fine cross stitch all through, but this is trying to the eyes and some workers find the use of the same stitch tedious.

Landscape and garden transfers can be bought, but it is more interesting to embroider one's own house or garden or a friend's house. First make a sketch from life or from a photograph. Begin with a small picture of the house or a pretty part of the house, and then if it is successful try a more elaborate needle picture. For a small scene, outline the house, railings, and trees in outline stitch, use stroke stitches for filling in the roof and trees, French knots for any flowers on the walls or railings, open buttonhole stitch can be used for the clouds, and so on. The embroideress who has a good many stitches at her command will be able to accomplish some delightful work. Aim at a vivid impression.

Maps, again, should aim at boldness and simplicity. They are generally decorated with ships or with tiny pictures characteristic of each place shown. It is difficult to obtain a map transfer, but a map can be copied from an atlas or a large-scale walker's map. The places can be marked in letters if pictures cannot be drawn. The letters should be worked in outline stitch, but use back stitch for very small letters. Coast-lines can be made with narrow satin stitches, running stitches will do for country boundaries and lakes, outline stitches will do for rivers, and so on.

CHAPTER VIII

APPLIQUÉ, PATCHWORK, AND INLAY EMBROIDERY

Appliqué, Embroidered Appliqué, Chinese Appliqué, Blind Appliqué, Ribbon or Tape Appliqué, Lacy Effects in Appliqué, The Three-Sided Stitch. Patchwork, Crazy Patchwork, American Block Patchwork. Inlay Embroidery.

APPLIQUÉ

APPLIQUÉ is a very bold, decorative form of embroidery in which a great variety of effects is possible. It is simply cutting out pretty shapes in one material and applying them to another which serves as the background. All sorts of pretty pieces of odd material can be used up, so it is not an expensive form of embroidery.

The colour effect and the design depend upon the materials used, the actual stitchery or embroidery is to hold the two materials together and not for decoration ; appliqué is therefore a very quick form of embroidery.

There are many different forms of appliqué work, and a great number of different materials can be used, so that it is a suitable form of decoration for all sorts of household articles, such as cushion covers, bedspreads, fire-screens, runners, bags, mats, etc. It has only a very limited use for dress trimmings, because it tends to be too bold in effect.

Perhaps it is most useful of all as a trimming for garments or coverlets used by little children.

It gives little ones great delight to find a bunny or a chicken on their bib, ducks or gay flowers on their rompers, and animals and flowers on their coverlets.

Fig. 90 shows an appliqué pattern of a rabbit that is very

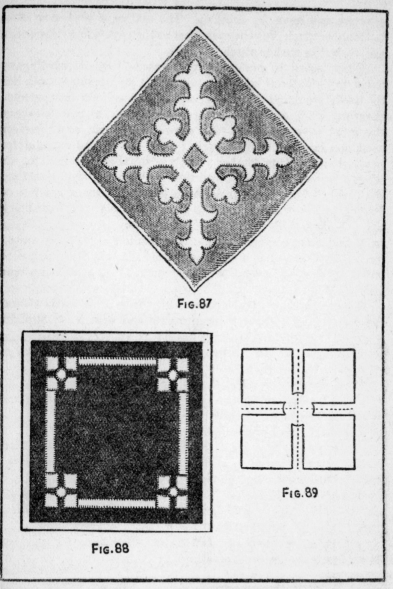

Fig.87

Fig.88

Fig.89

FIG. 87.—Cushion in Appliqué-work—pattern cut in one piece.   FIG. 88.—Boat Cushion of oilcloth Appliqué.   FIG. 89.—Unit of design for corner of Boat Cushion.

effective and loved by children. The outline is worked in close buttonhole stitch, but the eyes, part of the ears, whiskers, cheeks, are worked in outline stitch.

With regard to materials to be used—there is hardly any fairly firm material which is not suited to appliqué, both for the background and the applied pieces, such as linen, firm cottons, shantung silks, etc. Oil baize (American cloth) and felt have this great advantage that their edges do not fray, and therefore need not be completely covered; they are specially useful for small shapes. Thin leather is also a suitable material, for its edges also need no special protection. A very interesting method is to cut the appliqué forms in various small shapes of felt or leather and then stitch them to the ground material with black silk. These small shapes can be arranged in many different ways and look very effective. This method is specially suited for cushions, and it is a good way of using up odds and ends of felt or leather left over from other work. (See section on Soft Leather Work.)

When appliqué work is being done with thin material and the design is suitable (not too intricate and with many straight

FIG. 90.—An Appliqué design.

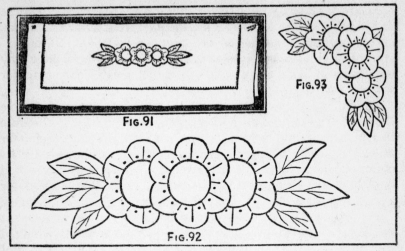

FIG. 91.—Tablecover decorated with Appliqué.   FIG. 92.—Pattern for
Appliqué.   FIG. 93.—Pattern for Appliqué.

lines) all the edges of the applied pieces can be turned down
and hemmed to the background.

A very simple but bold effect can be obtained by the use of
linen of contrasting colours, one coloured linen being used for
the background and the other for a pattern cut *in one piece* with
no detached parts, as in Fig. 87, which shows a cushion cover
in two colours. Old cushions can often be decorated in this
way and odd pieces of material used.

We will now describe in detail some different kinds of appliqué
work, all simple and inexpensive.

Embroidered Appliqué (Figs. 90 and 91).—In this kind the
applied portions are held down to the background with embroidery
stitches, and these applied portions or appliqués have their
details embroidered upon them ; for example, leaves have veins,
flowers have their stamens added, and so on.

There are two methods of sewing on the cut portions : (1)
In the first method, cut out the applied pieces roughly, that is, leave
a margin of material around the outline, then buttonhole-stitch
them in the right places, working of course carefully round the
outline ; the rough edges can now be cut away close to the
purl of the buttonhole stitch, as in scalloping. This is a good

method for materials that fray easily, but it requires two copies of the transfer, one for ironing on the background, the other for cutting up and stamping on the appliqué material. No other stitch can be used but the buttonhole stitch, for it is the only one that will allow the material to be cut away right up to it without fraying further.

(2) In the second method, which is perhaps more popular, the applied pieces are cut out exact to their outlines. Each is then laid exactly in its right place on the background and pinned or tacked down; whichever method is used, the applied pieces must be perfectly flat and unwrinkled. To help in getting this, especially in the case of a large appliqué, put a thin coating of a good dry paste like Grip-Fix over the *centre* of the *background*. Do not paste the appliqué itself, as this may wrinkle it, and do not paste anywhere near the edges as the paste makes it hard later for the needle to go through. If pins are used for fastening down oil-baize appliqués or leather appliqués, remember that they leave permanent holes in these materials, so they must be inserted near the edges where the holes can be covered by the buttonhole or other stitching.

A twisted embroidery thread is best for the buttonholing; this can be the same colour as the appliqué or a shade or two darker. Close buttonholing is needed for all fabrics that fray, as we have said before; but oil baize, felt, and leather (velvet persian) can be appliquéd down with a well-spaced stitch which is more quickly worked and gives a lighter effect.

In machine-made appliqués chain stitch is sometimes used to hold down the applied pieces, but in hand work, although the chain stitch can be used for some materials, it is not very satisfactory, as it does not hide the edges well. Couching is good for fastening appliqués, and it is much quicker to work than buttonholing, but care must be taken to see that the laid thread is really thick and broad enough to cover and protect the edges properly. Several thicknesses of a moderate thread laid side by side look better and make a flatter covering than a single very thick one. Embroidery wool used double is useful and eight-ply or rug wool can be used for bold appliqué.

In many designs there are lines and small details both on the background and on the appliqués which cannot be expressed in appliqué work ; these must be worked in ordinary embroidery, using the stitches already described in the different sections on embroidery work.

Interesting scenes or pictures can be built up in appliqué. In this case it often happens that parts of the design are two or three appliqués thick, as portions of one have to be laid over the other in the building-up process. Be careful to lay these appliqués on in a definite order or the sense of perspective will be spoilt. Begin with the portions that represent the background—for example, the sky, distant hills, or trees—so working up to the foreground objects.

We will now take the making of some useful articles in appliqué.

(1) *Boat Cushions or Garden Cushions* (Fig. 88).—Oilcloth is very useful for making cushions for the boat or garden. They are not damaged by the damp weather, and a little water coming in contact with oilcloth boat cushions will not ruin them. They can be easily cleaned. Black oilcloth can be used as in Fig. 88, or grey or dull ochre or any neutral colour. The appliqué designs can be of contrasting lines of plain material, such as pliable oilcloth, gingham, or linen. Figures (flowers or leaves) cut from runfast cretonne may also be appliquéd to the oilcloth.

If you wish to emphasise the form or edge of the appliqué, use embroidery thread or raffia of harmonious colours for the stitches which hold down the edge of the design. Buttonhole, blanket, or couching stitches are effective.

If the accent of the form is not desired, then the edges of the appliqué should be turned in and basted. Sew with fine cotton thread, taking the same small stitches that you would in felling a seam. Some sewing books call this stitch " fell stitch."

In planning oilcloth appliqué designs, keep the forms very simple, as in Fig. 88. Fig. 89 shows the shape of the appliqué pattern used in the corners.

After the design is cut from the oilcloth, put a small touch of paste on the centre of each portion, and put each portion in its right place on the cover. Do not turn in the edges of the material, but cover them with blanket stitches, using washable embroidery thread or raffia.

The edges of the cushion may be bound with braid. Fig. 91 shows a tablecover of unbleached muslin with some flowers and leaves appliquéd to it. Fig. 92 shows the design that has been used, but many people will probably prefer the design in the corner as shown in Fig. 93. This has the same units as in Fig. 94, but they are rearranged.

The flowers are cut from fine rose gingham. Around the cloth is also a band of fine rose gingham, appliquéd with short basting stitches made with thin strands of black embroidery thread.

Use very short, uneven basting stitches of three strands of black embroidery thread to appliqué the gingham. Outline the rosettes and make the single long stitches that radiate from the centres. The dots in the drawing represent French knots, made with four strands of dull, light-yellow embroidery thread. The leaves are outlined with light green thread, using short, uneven basting stitches.

We have only given a few suggestions for colours, as they must suit individual taste, and they should match their surroundings as far as possible.

Chinese Appliqué.—This is a special type of embroidered appliqué and is combined with a little simple cut-work. As a rule a neutral beige background is used, with the appliqué flowers and leaves in a number of bright shades. Fine linen is used both for the background and the appliqués.

As only an open buttonhole stitch is used, although all outside edges are scalloped, it follows that a special process must be used to prevent the linen edges from fraying. It is this process that makes the work rather slow.

Here is the process : Stamp or draw the appliqué design on a piece of material (it is best to deal with only one or two appliqués at a time, completing them as far as possible before starting on others), but before cutting it out, paste it on a rather larger piece of tissue paper. Be sure to paste the paper, not the stuff. Press the two smoothly together all over (the paper pasted on the back keeps the appliqué itself from fraying) then cut it out to the exact outlines of the pattern. Place the appliqué, paper side downwards, in its correct position on the background, pasting its centre down to the background and pinning the edges with tiny pins. At once buttonhole down the appliqué, leave unstitched for the time any small portions of the appliqué under which the raw edges of an adjoining leaf or stem has to be tucked. When the appliqué comes against an edge of the background that has to be cut or an outside edge of the article to be made, cut away the background to the exact outline of the appliqué. At once buttonhole-stitch down the appliqué, catching in the cut edge of the background with it before it has time to fray.

As appliqués are not reversible once the paper is pasted to them, take careful thought, before pasting this on, whether the appliqué is to face right or left, up or down, and choose the right side for pasting the paper accordingly.

All markings on leaves and flowers must be worked in outline stitch, but centres of " full-faced " flowers can be worked in satin stitch.

Appliqué border designs look well in this method. Be careful to choose a pattern that has few odd details to be embroidered, for this alters the style. It is essentially edge, not interior, work. It is very suitable for runners, chairbacks, table-centres, mats. Fig. 92 might be worked out in Chinese appliqué.

Blind Appliqué.—This is a very popular and common type of appliqué. It is the name given to appliqué that is not embroidered (except perhaps in very small details), but is secured to the background with slip stitch or blind stitch (hence the name " blind appliqué ").

Blind appliqué is said to have come from the United States. It is best suited to designs in plain materials which are so excellent in line and colouring that they need no added embroidery. It is also used for designs carried out wholly or partly in patterned materials, on which decorative embroidery stitches would be lost.

It is the simplest and easiest kind of appliqué and is therefore suitable for very large pieces of work, such as wall hangings and bedspreads (see section on Patchwork Quilting).

To make it, cut out each piece of appliqué with narrow turnings. Pin or tack the pieces in place, keeping pins or tackings away from the edge. Slip-stitch down all around to the background, turning under the surplus edges with finger and thumb, or with the needle-point as you go along. It is best to use sewing cotton that matches the appliqué. Afterwards the work must be well pressed.

Ribbon Appliqué or Tape Appliqué.—Small patterns that consist of long narrow pieces may be appliquéd in narrow ribbon or tape. As ribbon or tape has a ready-made edge there is no fear of fraying, so it can be stitched on with simple hemming. This method is well suited to small designs for underwear, needle-books, book-markers, etc. Where the narrow parts of a design are curved, bias tape doubled lengthwise can be substituted for straight tape. Small details of the design can be worked as in ordinary embroidery.

Simple amusing designs can be made for children's rompers, etc., from black tape. Match-stick figures are easy to draw. Plan a row of little black children; their bodies are pieces of black tape, drawn in near one end to form the neck. Lively arms and legs can be added in back stitch, using black thread; eyes, mouth, and other details can be added if desired.

Strips of any material can of course be used in appliqué work, and attached to the background by overcasting or hemming. These have much the same appearance as ribbon appliqué.

Embroidered patterns are generally worked on the ribbons or strips of material; some may be left plain according to the fancy of the worker. The final effect need not be one of stripes, but a pleasantly broken surface pattern and varied colours.

Lacy Effects in Appliqué.—Appliqué is often thought of as strong, bold work; but lace-like and dainty effects can be obtained by the application of muslin or net. There are various forms of this appliqué, such as linen applied to linen lawn by means of drawn threads and hemstitching. There is also the application of one thin material to another where the threads are not drawn round the shapes, but the three-sided stitch is used to attach the two materials together. This stitch gives the appearance of a hemstitched edge. Fig. 94 shows clearly how the stitch is worked. It is a very useful stitch.

PATCHWORK

Patchwork and appliqué are very closely related. It is often difficult to say where one ends and the other begins.

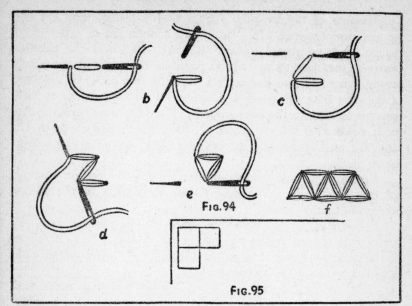

FIG. 94.—The Three-Sided Stitch.   FIG. 95.—Corner of Runner decorated with
Patchwork.

Generally speaking, appliqué is done with embroidery stitches
and patchwork with plain sewing ones.

Modern patchwork is used for a great variety of things, not
only quilts, as in olden days, but cushions, tea-cosies, border
trimmings for chairbacks, etc.

There are three kinds of patchwork—(1) Crazy, in which the
pieces are put together higgledy-piggledy, according to their
shape, without any attempt at design. (2) All-over geometrical
patchwork. (3) American block patchwork, made in a series of
small squares, each with the same design, and then joined
together. (See Chapter IX., section on Patchwork Quilting.)

Crazy Patchwork. — This is the most economical kind,
because no material is wasted by cutting it to shape, but each
piece is fitted together in the manner of a crazy pavement.
Silk, velvet, linen, and cotton patches can be used. Silk and
velvet can be used together, and so can linen and cotton, but
on the whole it is wise to keep to one type of material for each
article.

Because of the irregular shapes of the pieces, they are not joined directly together. Instead, a foundation of unbleached calico or some cheap material is used. On these the patches must be arranged as prettily as possible, the edges of one patch being turned in and overlapped over the raw edges of another. Take care that the patches lie smoothly and secure them with careful tacking to the background. They are then permanently held down with feather stitch or chain stitch (see Chapters II. and III. on Embroidery Stitches) worked in a contrasting colour or in black.

Crazy patchwork looks most effective if only a certain number of the pieces are patterned. About two-thirds of the pieces should be plain material.

Sometimes definite colour-schemes can be worked out. If patchwork is used as the border of a tray-cloth, it looks effective if the inner hemmed-down edges of the patches are covered with a line of couching in a deeper colour.

All-Over Geometrical Patchwork.—Most Victorian patchwork was of this type. Geometrical shapes were always used because they are the only kind that will join endlessly to each other without leaving gaps. But while the shapes are regular, plain and pattern pieces of every colour are mixed together. In these forms of patchwork the pieces themselves are sewn together and not on to a background as in crazy patchwork.

In modern work four squares of material, each of a different bright colour, are often seamed together to make a cushion cover, each square sometimes having an appliqué pattern on it. (Appliqué and patchwork, as we have said before, shade into each other.) Squares of felt make good cushions, or squares or oblongs of leather (velvet persian), but as a rule far smaller pieces are used. It is easy and interesting to build up simple all-over patterns with small squares, oblongs, hexagons, diamonds, and triangles. Metal templates of these shapes can be bought (some workers make their own from cardboard) ; these only need be pencilled around to make a pattern. A paper pattern should be made for each patch. This is the only way to make geometrical patchwork really correct.

Here is the method for making a cushion of diamond-shaped pieces, a very simple geometrical pattern :

Cut for each patch a pattern from brown paper or other stiff paper. Be sure to cut each pattern from the same template, so that the size does not vary in the least. Pin the paper pattern on to the material and cut it round, allowing ¼-inch turnings. Fold these turnings back over the paper pattern to the wrong side, and tack securely all round through patch, paper, and turnings. As soon as sufficient patches have been prepared, arrange them according to the pattern and oversew their folded edges together from the wrong side. Do not remove the tackings and release the patterns until the whole of the patchwork is done. Beautiful leather cushions can be made in this way. (See the section on Leather Work.)

A quilt or any single-thickness article made in this way must be lined to cover the raw edges of the patches. Patchwork of this kind is very strong and lasting.

This form of patchwork combines very well with appliqué. First build up a good shape with geometrical patches made as just described, and then hem the shape down on to a plain background.

Table runners can be decorated with arrangements of three squares or four triangles at each corner, and a diamond shape composed of triangles in the centre. Fig. 95 shows a corner decorated in this way. Good colours must be used for these patterns.

When only a few triangles are needed, good ones can be very simply obtained by cutting squares of the material and then dividing them in half diagonally.

The best effects are generally obtained from unpatterned linen.

American Block Patchwork.—This type of patchwork is made from a series of squares of unbleached calico. These squares are called blocks and they are joined together (with or without intermediate strips) to form a quilt. Each block is made up separately first with a definite pieced patchwork design (or appliqué patchwork design). The design is the same for all the blocks although the colour may vary according to the pieces available.

For more details about American Block Patchwork, see Chapter XII. on The Quilting of Patchwork.

INLAY EMBROIDERY

This work is simple to do, and it wears and washes well. Inlay work is just the opposite to appliqué ; instead of contrasting pieces being added to form a pattern, squares of material are cut away so that the coloured fabric beneath shows through with an inlaid effect.

The materials needed for this work are cheap—(1) glasscloth towelling checked in red or blue ; (2) casement cloth or other cotton material matching the colour of the check ; (3) a cotton thread also matching the check (coton à border is a good thread).

This work is suitable for a great variety of purposes—traycloths, mats, runners, tablecloths (for informal purposes), napkins, shoe-bags, etc.

Make up the article in the usual way, but line it completely with coloured casement cloth. Next plan your pattern—that is, decide which squares from the glasscloth you will cut away. It is a good plan to work your pattern out first on squared arithmetic paper. Fig. 86 in Chapter VII. shows a suitable pattern for this work, but unlike shadow embroidery, the alternate squares are cut away to form crosses. Having decided on the squares to be cut away, begin to cut each carefully, but do not cut right up to the checked lines, leave tiny turnings inside each square instead. Now secure each square to the coloured lining beneath with open buttonhole stitch, the purl coming along the turning edge. Instead of the simple way of using the squares of glass-towelling, inlay work may also be done with a design. It is then known as Découpé (Cut-Out) Embroidery. Any design suitable for appliqué will do. Cut away and buttonhole down to the lining the appliqué parts of the design. Stems or fine portions that cannot be cut out must be worked with suitable embroidery stitches.

Very handsome table centres may be made in this way.

Some of these methods of appliqué and découpé are suitable for leather work. (See the chapters on different ways of decorating leather.)

CHAPTER IX

PLAIN SEWING AND TRIMMINGS FOR PLAIN SEWING

The Work-Basket and its Contents. Hints. Tacking, Hemming, A Run Hem, Slip-stitched Hem, Felling, Running, Seaming or Top Sewing, Overcasting.

Seams—Run and Fell Seams, French Seams, Counter Hem Seam, Mantua Maker's Seam, Flannel Seams, Herringboning, Catch Stitch, Seaming Lace.

Trimmings for Plain Sewing—Binding, Joining a Bias Bind, A French Hem, A False Hem, A Straight Bind, A Piping Cord, Shell Binding, Tuck Running, Whipping, Gathering, Gauging, Lace-trimmed Lingerie.

IN the chapters on embroidery we mentioned the few tools necessary, but as time goes on one enlarges one's equipment. For plain sewing and for dressmaking (see section on Dressmaking) one needs really a greater variety of things than for embroidery.

Plain sewing is a serious business, and we will now describe a well-stocked work-basket. Notice how it has grown from the few articles described in Chapter I. Choose for your work-basket a roomy one. Many people like a wicker basket on a stand, as it is light and easy to carry about. They can be bought ready lined with pockets for cottons, etc., but it is an easy matter and very much cheaper to buy a plain basket and pad and line it yourself, making all the little pockets before attaching the lining to the basket.

Your work-basket should contain :

Three pairs of *scissors*—a cutting-out pair, a medium-sized pair, and embroidery scissors.

A *thimble*. (See that it fits comfortably.)

Needles. (1) Short needles (betweens, as they are called), sizes 7, 8, and 9. (2) Darning needles, numbers 5, 6, and 7. (3) Crewel needles for embroidery work. (4) A wool needle.

A *bodkin* and *stiletto*.

Pins. Small ones and some large.

Buttons. Unpierced linen and pearl buttons in various sizes.

Cottons. White and black, number 60 for ordinary sewing purposes and number 30 or 40 for sewing on buttons, etc. Various coloured cottons can be bought as they are required to match different materials.

Tacking cotton.

A *tape measure*. It is worth while to buy a good one. The cheap ones wear out very soon and are often inaccurate.

Black and white tape.

Hooks and eyes ; press fasteners.

Darning cottons ; silks and wool for mending.

A *penny notebook* for embroidery silks. Keep the skeins between the leaves. This prevents them from getting entangled, and so wasted.

Some Hints worth Remembering

It seems superfluous to mention such a little thing as a pin ; but the use of a long thick pin will produce holes that are apparent until the article is washed, and will even stain the threads of thin materials to such an extent as to break them.

Steel pins can be bought for 3d. or 4d. an ounce, and are always used by good dressmakers and milliners when cutting out piled material such as velvet. Brass pins would leave permanent marks.

Lillikin pins are very thin and only half an inch in length and are useful for fine dainty work.

These can be bought by the ounce loose, or stuck on a paper. They have only to be used to be appreciated.

Never allow any one to cut string, paper, or the stalks of flowers with your scissors. The edges may become blunt, or you will find a " kink " in the blade the next time you use them— that is, a spot where they do not cut cleanly and evenly.

When cutting out it is a good plan to wind a little cotton-wool round the handles of your scissors if you are not used to the work. This will prevent your fingers from becoming sore.

Remember to thread your needle from the end which hangs from the reel to prevent knots forming in your cotton as you sew. This is very important when whipping or gathering, as a knot might mean beginning the work all over again.

" Between " needles are not used by many people, but you will find that fine sewing is infinitely easier and quicker when a " between " needle is used. It may probably take some time to get used to them, but it will be worth the trouble in the long-run.

Small fancy buttons, hooks and eyes, and press fasteners can be kept in a small screw-top bottle. They will not get lost in the work-basket and they can be seen quite easily.

Always sit in a good light when sewing, and try not to stoop over your work or you will get tired very quickly.

PLAIN SEWING

Tacking.—" A garment well tacked is half made." There is a great deal of truth in this saying, and yet so many people think tacking quite unworthy of their consideration and use pins for fixing seams and for putting together a garment ready for fitting.

Work the tacking carefully and you will find all the rest of the sewing so very much easier; and you will have no puckered seams and other signs of bad workmanship to discourage you and damp your enthusiasm.

Use fine soft cotton of pale blue, pink, or any colour that will not soil the material and that can be easily seen.

Make a knot in the end of a long piece of cotton so that the tacking threads can be more easily pulled out when the sewing is finished. Begin at the right-hand side, put the needle straight through the material, and bring it out about $\frac{1}{4}$ inch farther on. Pass over $\frac{1}{4}$ inch and put the needle in and out again in the same way as the last stitch. This is a small tacking stitch. The stitches should be the same size on both sides and should be worked just above where the line of hemming or running stitches will be worked. For long seams tacking stitches should be $\frac{1}{2}$ inch or even 1 inch longer. Fasten off the cotton strongly, so that the stitches will not work loose. Do this by working the last stitch twice into the same hole. This is known as a back stitch. If you are tacking up a garment to be tried on, it is better to use one long and two quite small stitches alternately ; this is firmer. Remember to keep your tacking stitches exactly parallel to the edges. Tacking is not only used to keep together two layers while they are being joined, but often as a guide to stitchery. (For more about Tacking, see Chapter XXV.)

Hemming.—Good hemming is really harder to do than many of the embroidery stitches we described in Chapters II. and III. The secret of good hemming is not *tiny* stitches, but stitches regular in size and spacing.

Hemming is used to fasten down material which has been turned down and folded over to protect a raw edge. It makes a neat and firm edge.

To make a hem, hold the wrong side of the material towards you and turn down a narrow piece along the edge to be hemmed, using the thumb and finger of the left hand, press the fold with the right thumb and finger, pleating it under the thumb if it is a curved edge. This first turn must not be deep—a deep turn does not add strength but only bulkiness, and makes a hem clumsy. Only when the material is transparent should the first turn be as deep as the second, such as the hem of lace or net curtains. Fold over the hem a second time as wide as you require the hem to be. This must be kept exactly the same width throughout the length of the hem. A small piece of paper cut the width of the hem is a great help to most workers.

If you are turning the hems of a square or an oblong such as a table runner or a chairback, always turn the opposite sides first and then the other edges. The hem must now be tacked.

To begin the hemming, point the needle away from you and catch up a small piece of the upper fold, draw the needle through, leaving $\frac{1}{2}$ inch of cotton ; tuck this under the hem with the needle—hold the hem with the left thumb and begin to hem. Put the needle into the single material just below the fold to the left of where the cotton comes out, and bring it out on the fold, slanting the needle to the left. As you proceed with the work hold the hem over the first two fingers of the left hand, keeping it quite firm with the thumb in front and the third finger behind. The middle of the thumb should be on the edge of the hem.

To join on a new length of cotton draw out the old cotton from the fold of the hem, and put the needle with the new thread into the same hole ; hold down the hem firmly and go on with the hemming as before. Then the join will not show at all.

Do not forget that the stitches you are working must hold down the hem securely. The size of the stitch must be the same on both sides of the material.

Fasten the cotton off by making another stitch over the last one and then slip the needle back between the folds of the material for about one inch before cutting the cotton. Take out the tackings.

When hemming an oblong or square such as a chairback, etc., start in the middle of a side and then the joins in the cotton will not come in the corners.

If the corners are mitred work as far as the corner, then slip the needle to the extreme edge of the second fold, hem along the mitred corner, and proceed with the next side. Never use a separate cotton to hem down the mitred corner.

A Run Hem.—This is useful for plain work. Its name tells you what it is. It is quite simple and as the stitches are parallel with the weave of the material they often show less than the ordinary hemming stitch does. Prepare your hem in the ordinary way and then work along the folded edge with tiny running stitches. This hem is often used for babies' frocks.

Slip-stitched Hem.—You use this when you want a hem to be invisible. Slip-stitching is used a good deal in dressmaking for catching down linings, facings, etc. It will not stand very much strain. The hem should be turned in in the usual way, and tacked down not too close to the edge. Pick up just *part* of a thread or threads in the single material (so that your stitch will not show through on the right side), then slip your needle into the fold of the hem and along inside it to make a long stitch, say about a quarter of an inch. Bring it out through the inner layer of the fold, near the edge but not quite on it, so that it does not show. Pick up a bit of a thread or threads as before, and repeat. Be careful not to pull the stitches too tight or the hem will pucker.

Flannel Hem.—A single turning is used, its raw edges herring boned in place.

Felling.—The same stitch as hemming. The word is used in connection with seams where two pieces of material are joined together, one edge is folded in and hemmed down as in a " run and fell " seam.

Running.—Running is a stitch used for making tucks or gathers (see section on Gathers) or for joining material together as in a French seam.

It is just like tacking, only the stitches are generally made smaller. Start at the right-hand side of the work with a back stitch. If the material is thin, like georgette, several stitches can be taken up on the needle at a time, but each stitch must come through on to the other side.

To make a join in the cotton—fasten off the old cotton with a back stitch, and then run the needle backwards between the folds. Put the needle with the new thread in the stitch before the last, work a back stitch, and then proceed with the running. Fasten off with a back stitch.

Seaming or Top Sewing.—This is used for joining selvedges together as in making a pillow-case, and also joining two pieces of material together when the raw edges have been turned in, as in the end of a band or a cuff or a belt. Put the wrong sides of both pieces together, with the edges quite level and pin into position with a few pins at right angles to the edge. Tack firmly and then begin to sew from right to left. Hold the work firmly between the left thumb and finger, and fasten on by taking up the edge nearest you, leaving $\frac{1}{2}$ inch of cotton as in hemming, but this time it must be worked over by the first six or seven stitches. Only the extreme edge of the material must be taken up, and the needle must always be pointed straight towards the worker.

Make a strong neat join in the cotton by unpicking half of the last stitches made with the old cotton and then put the needle with the new thread into the hole thus left. Work over both threads for six or seven stitches. Fasten off by working backwards over three stitches, thus making three little crosses, and slip the needle under several more stitches before cutting off the cotton.

Towels and other articles made of strong, thick materials are often tacked ready for hemming, and then the hem is turned back and the edges are top-sewn instead of hemmed. This is very much stronger.

Overcasting.—This is a stitch worked in the same way as top sewing but from left to right instead of from right to left. It is used for neatening raw edges such as those on the turnings of sleeves. Great care must be taken not to pull the cotton tightly, or the edge will be rolled under and cause bulkiness.

SEAMS

These are used to join together two pieces of material. They should be strong, neat, and flat, and the same width along the entire length.

Most seams are in pairs—one for right and one for left side, and the fells must always fall towards the back of the garment. This can be done quite easily if the right-hand side seam is turned down from the top of the garment, and the left-hand seam from the bottom of the garment.

Run and Fell Seam.—A quick and easy way of joining material, but more suitable for thin material than thick. It is the seam most in use for general sewing. It is strong and flat and looks very neat when carefully made.

Here is a simple way to work it. Pin the two pieces to be joined right sides together, the edge of the one nearest you being about ⅛ inch below the other. Turn this projecting edge down over the other so that the fold or bend touches the raw edge of the inner layer and tack as you go. Take care to keep the edge quite straight. Now run the two layers together just below the raw edge of the turning, your stitches exactly parallel with it. Then press the tacked fold flat on to the material, tack it down and fell it in place—you use, of course, an ordinary hemming stitch for this. Some workers press the tacked fold down so carefully that there is no need to tack it. This tacked fold is the fell.

French Seam.—This is used to join thin materials, where as little as possible must be seen of the stitches, or for such garments as overalls or cotton frocks.

To make the seam, pin the two wrong sides of the material

together edge to edge. Tack and then run with an occasional back stitch ⅛ inch from the raw edges. Then cut off the turnings to ⅛ inch, take out the tackings and open out the seam, flattening it with the fingers. Now fold the work so that the right sides are together and the join comes exactly on the fold. Tack ⅛ inch from the top, and then run along just below the tacking, working a back stitch every inch or so, so that you make a neat little case for the enclosed turnings.

Take care not to leave any frayed or ravelled cottons showing on the right side below the second tacking stitches.

Counter Hem Seam.—This is useful when the material is thick and the machine is going to be used.

Turn down about ⅛ inch on the wrong side of one of the pieces to be joined, and ⅛ inch on the right side of the other. Place the folds one over the other, and then tack together. The folds can be either hemmed down or stitched by a machine.

Mantua Maker's Seam.—This is only suited for thin material. When finished it looks very much like a French seam.

Put the two right sides of the material together with the edges level. Turn down a narrow hem with both pieces. Tack and then hem, taking care that all stitches go well through the double material.

Flannel Seams.—Seams on flannel have to be worked differently from seams on cotton materials as the double folds would be very thick and clumsy.

There are two ways of joining flannel : *First way.* Put the right sides of the material together, the back edge ¼ inch above the front, and tack. Join the two pieces together by running about ¼ inch below the raw edges. Take out the tackings and flatten out the seam. Fold the wide turning over the narrow one and tack, keeping it as flat as possible. This is not easy, and a good deal of care is needed. Herringbone down the fell, and remove the tackings.

Second way. This is a flatter seam, but it is not so strong, and should only be used where there will not be very much strain on the material, such as on a baby's flannel.

Again put the right sides of the material together but with the edges level. Tack and then run them together ¼ inch from the raw edges. Take out the tackings. Open the seam and press out the turnings, herringbone down both edges. If the edges happen to be selvedges, then one line of herringbone stitch is sometimes worked over the join. This method is not considered so good as the first, or as the flannel seam described under the heading " Herringboning " below.

Herringboning (see also Flannel Seams).—This stitch has already been described in the section on Embroidery (Chapter III.). In plain sewing this stitch is used for flannel, also for many woollen materials that do not fray easily and are rather thick for an ordinary flat-felled seam.

Place your two layers together with raw edges even and join them with running stitch. Trim away the turning nearest to you, leaving just sufficient material to prevent the stitching pulling away. Then press the other turning over flatly, and catch down its edge to the material with herringbone stitch.

As the stitch is worked from left to right, begin at the left-hand side with a back stitch on the double material, now make a stitch to the right exactly under and parallel with the raw edge, another on the fold, and so on alternately. The needle is usually brought out just opposite where the needle was put in for the last stitch.

A join in the cotton should be made on the double material in the same way as when working the running stitch.

This is a very useful stitch for filling spaces in conventional embroidery designs. It is worked in exactly the same way as described above, but no spaces are left between the stitches.

Catch Stitch.—This is worked in just the same way as herring-boning, but from right to left, so that no crosses are made, but merely a series of threads slanting downwards and upwards. It is not so strong as herringboning, but much more quickly worked. (See Chapter XIV.)

We might end this section with a word about seaming lace.

Seaming Lace.—For lace a single seam is best, and if possible a machined seam. Press the seam open very flat, trim the turn-ings, and overcast the raw edges with small stitches. (Metal fabrics can be treated in the same way.) Another good method for metallic tissues is to machine with a very small stitch as a single seam, then roll the turnings and overcast the roll with small neat stitches. Small running stitches (with an occasional back stitch) can be used instead of machine-stitching, but it is not quite as good. The joins, of course, must be made with great care. Press them well afterwards.

TRIMMINGS FOR PLAIN SEWING

There are a number of different ways of neatening edges in simple sewing and dressmaking—binds, piping, additional pieces, facings, hems (flat and rolled), whipping, embroidery, and other trimmings (see chapters on Embroidery), appliqué, lace, etc.

We will describe some of the most useful and practical ways.

Binding.—All the material used for binding should be *bias* strips (=crossway cutting). Material cut on the cross (bias) stretches and is slightly elastic. Strips of such material, *i.e.* with both edges on the bias, are applied to many purposes where these qualities are an advantage.

These strips must be cut on the direct cross if they are to set evenly. When material is folded so that the crease is on the direct cross, every selvedge thread (warp thread) of one layer lies in exact line with the weft thread of the other layer. An edge on the direct cross is a fold like this cut through. This may sound difficult, but we will now describe the process of binding very simply.

Binding is a very attractive and strong method of neatening raw edges, such as the neck and sleeves of a nightgown or the edges of a collar. The binding, as we have said before, must be cut on the cross, thus it will be quite flat even on a curved edge. To do this, fold over a corner of the material so that the crease made is the diagonal of a square. Open out the material and draw a straight line with a ruler along the crease. Now draw lines parallel to this first line as far apart as the width of the strips required. Their width will depend on the width you wish the bind to be when it is finished. Cut carefully along the pencil-lines.

Joining a Bias Bind (Fig. 96).—To join the strips together place the right sides touching each other, cross the ends so that the blunt pointed end goes to the sharp pointed end, and leave the sharp ends of both strips projecting about $\frac{1}{8}$ inch beyond the sides (as in Fig. 96), otherwise the two pieces will not be level when the seam is flattened out. Run the edges together

Set of collar and cuffs worked in simple broderie anglaise on white appliqué.

[To face p. 128

Head cushion embroidered in buttonhole stitch.

Embroidered initial in coral stitch.

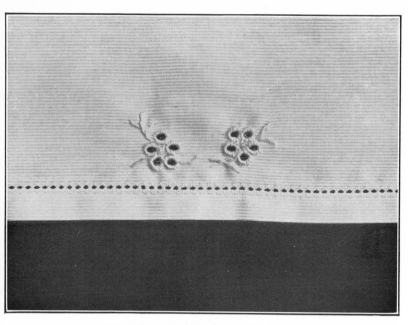

Detail of broderie anglaise.

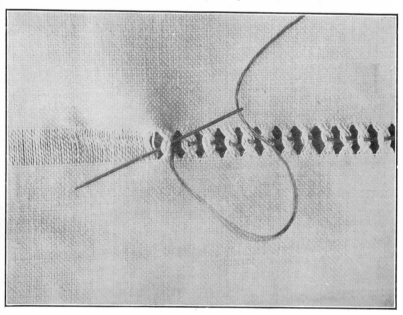

Single crossing hemstitch.

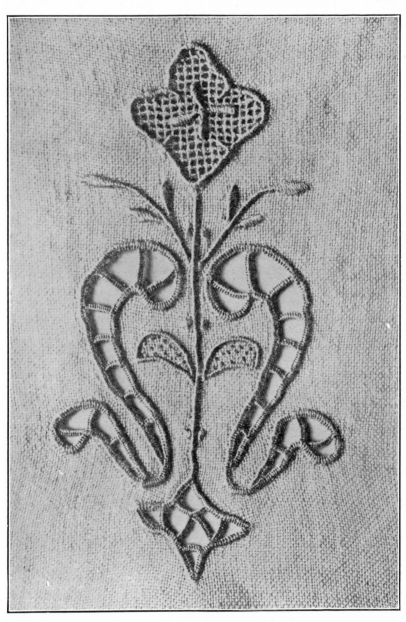

Cut-work embroidery.

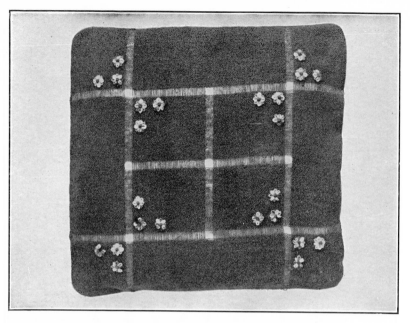

Cushion in woollen material with drawn threads and lazy-daisy embroidery.

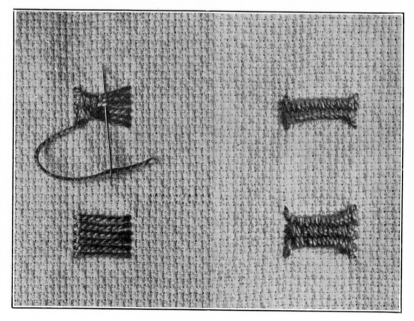

Swedish or needle weaving.

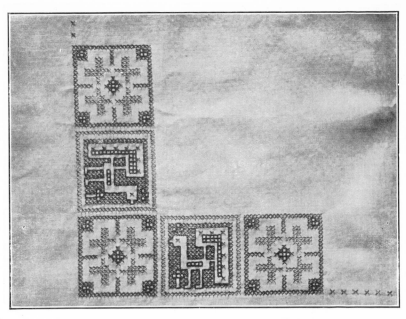

Detail of tablecloth in back stitch, with cross-stitch background.

Simple embroidery in lazy-daisy, cross stitch, and outline stitch.

Darning in gay wools on a net curtain.

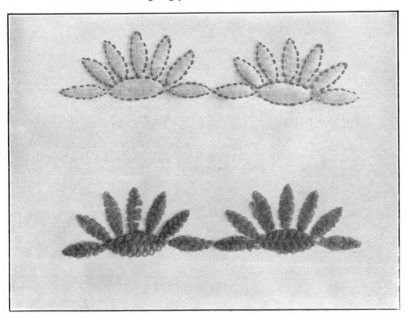

Shadow embroidery : *Above,* right side.　　*Below,* wrong side.

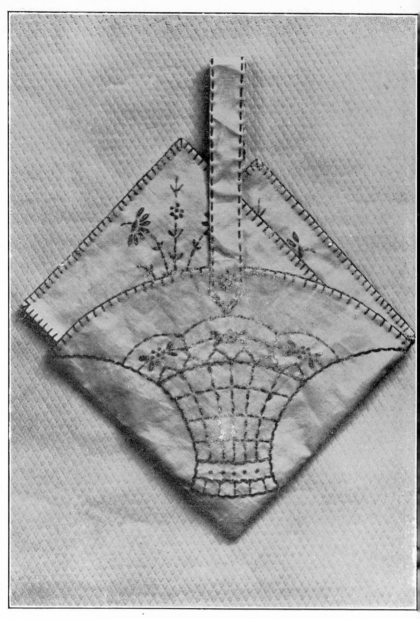

Outline embroidery: Two pot-holders in a hanging case.

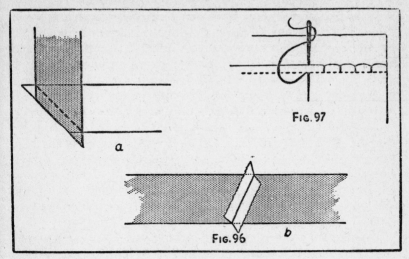

FIG. 96.—Joining a Bias Bind.   FIG. 97.—Shell Binding.

very strongly, flatten out the turnings left and right, and cut off the projecting points. Take care that all the joins come on the wrong side. It is very easy to make a mistake. Fig. 96 shows exactly how the joins are made.

If the material has a diagonal twill, the lines must run along it.

A French Hem.—Stretch the strip lengthways ; it will set better. Place the right side of the strip to the right side of the garment with the edges level. Tack and run it into place, ¼ inch from the top. Press the seam flat with the fingers, and then snip the turnings here and there. This will make all the difference to the set of the hem.

Now fold over the strip, turn in the edge and fell it down exactly on top of the running stitches.

When a French hem is needed on a long straight length, such as a frill, it can be worked more quickly in this way : Make a tuck ⅛ inch wide on the wrong side and 1 inch from the bottom, then hem the raw edge on to this tuck.

To bind very thin materials such as organdie or georgette, the strip may be used double. In this way it is possible to make a finer hem, and the thin material is very much more easily handled. The strip must be cut twice the usual width, and

5

then folded in half and stretched lengthways under a warm iron. Place the raw edges level with the edge to be bound on the right side. Run into position, then fold over the bind and hem the edge exactly on the running stitches as before.

A False Hem.—Use a false hem when it would be impossible to turn down an ordinary hem in a satisfactory manner. This is the case at the wrist of a pyjama sleeve and many other places.

Cut strips of material on the cross, the required width. Put the right side of the strips to the right side of the garment, edge to edge. Run or stitch about $\frac{1}{4}$ inch down from the top. Snip the turnings, and fold over the strip to the wrong side, making the join come exactly along the edge. Turn under the raw edge, and tack down the hem, making it set quite flatly. Then hem down in the usual way.

Sometimes a false hem is used for a trimming, and a very good and neat one it makes, especially if the material used is of contrasting colour to the garment. When fixing a hem of this kind, put the right side of the strip to the wrong side of the garment, run it into place, and then turn it over on to the right side. The hem can then be fixed with any fancy stitch, such as chain stitch or French knots, or, in the more usual manner, by machine-stitching. Many undergarments, babies' blankets, etc., are trimmed in this way.

A Straight Bind.—A straight edge can be bound with a straight strip of material just as described for a bias bind. Prussian binding or braid is often used for this. Materials that are too thick to be turned down and hemmed are often bound. It is also used as a trimming. Ribbon can be used as well as braid. You must take great care in putting on a straight bind that you do not stretch the binding or the edge of the garment will be puckered.

In the case of ribbon, simply press your ribbon in half, lengthwise, slip it over the raw edge, tack and stitch. If you are machining your bind, one stitching should catch both edges.

On a baby's flannel the binding is usually run on one side and then turned over and hemmed on the other; but if it is a thick household article to be bound, the braid is generally folded in half as described for the ribbon, tacked over the raw edges and stitched by machine. The corners of the binding in each case must be mitred and felled down neatly.

A Piping Cord.—This is another way of finishing off a curved or straight edge. A baby's bonnet or coat is often piped. Seams of cushions and loose covers, or the edge of a yoke or waist line, are often decorated with a piping cord.

It is quite a simple thing to fix, but gives a very professional air to an article when it is well done.

A crossway strip is required to cover the cord, and the width of it depends on the thickness of the cord. Cut the strip wide enough to cover the cord, making allowance for turnings on each side, and $\frac{1}{2}$ inch more, if the piping is to be used for neatening an edge.

Place the piping cord that is to be used for a seam in the middle of the wrong side of the crossway strip. Fold the material over the cord, and tack close up to the roll. Put this between the two pieces to be joined, the raw edges must be quite level. Then stitch the four thicknesses together. This can be done more neatly, and closer to the cord, if it is worked by hand rather than by machine. Of course it is not practical for loose covers and long seams, but it is well worth the time and trouble for cushions and small articles.

When the cord is used for piping and neatening an edge, fold the crossway piece over the cord, so that one edge is deeper than the other, and then tack close up under the roll. Now put the narrower edge level with the edge to be piped, right sides together. Tack and stitch the piping into position. Turn under the wider edge and fell it down, so that the piping is exactly at the top.

Piping can be carried out in self material, but it is a good way of introducing a contrasting colour.

Shell Binding (Fig. 97). — This is a very pretty way of finishing the edges of a collar, a jabot, a bow in the front of a blouse or dress, or any part of a garment that needs trimming as well as neatening.

Cut a crossway strip of material $1\frac{1}{2}$ inches wide. Place one raw edge to the edge to be neatened, right sides facing. Run the two together, and then fold the bind over and fell on the running stitches as described for a French Hem.

Use embroidery silk to match the material or in contrasting colour. Fasten on with a back stitch on the wrong side, and work from right to left. Now, holding the right side toward you, make two tight stitches over the bind, slip the needle along about ½ inch through the folds and make two more stitches, and so on.

Diagram No. 97 will help you to work this simple trimming quite easily.

Tuck Running.—Tucks are generally used at the present day for ornamentation. On thin materials nothing can be prettier than groups of fine tucks, especially on dainty blouses, jabots, crêpe de Chine handkerchiefs, and baby's gowns. Only a running stitch is employed, so that any one with even no knowledge of embroidery can use this form of ornamentation.

When arranging for tucks always remember that a tuck takes up three times its width, *i.e.* (1) the right side of the tuck, (2) the under side of the tuck, (3) the width of the material that the tuck lies on; so that for a tuck ¼ inch wide you must allow ¾ inch of material. It is a good plan to work the tucks in the piece of material before cutting out the garment, especially in the yoke of a baby's frock or on a blouse front.

When the tuck is a narrow one, it is quite a simple matter to keep it straight, but if any difficulty is found take a piece of paper or thin cardboard and make a notch the width of the tuck from the top edge of the paper, and use this as a gauge.

Fold each tuck quite flat before creasing the material for the next one, otherwise you may find that the space between the tucks is uneven and the whole effect of the tucking is spoilt.

Whipping.—This is a very useful stitch for neatening the edges of fine materials such as georgette, crêpe de Chine, or organdie. If it is worked carefully it is almost invisible. The edges of frills, handkerchiefs to hold your powder puff, silk scarves, etc., can all be successfully neatened by whipping.

Always cut frills from the width of the material so that the selvedge threads run down the depth of the frill, otherwise they will set very badly.

To work the stitch, hold the material with the wrong side towards you, and start at the right-hand side by running a few stitches backwards close to the raw edge and then make a back stitch.

With the left thumb roll over the raw edge to make a neat

tight roll, the tighter and smaller the roll the better. Breathing on the left finger and thumb and holding the material as firmly as possible will help you to do this.

Now work over the roll with oversewing, taking care that the needle comes out each time under the roll and not through it.

Sometimes a raw edge is gathered up with whipping stitch. Work it in just the same way, but use a stronger cotton, and then draw it up gently when you have finished and fasten the end round a pin.

A frill is usually made twice the length that it is required to be when finished. To join a frill to any edge, place the two right sides together and pin at each end. Loosen the whipping cotton and arrange the gathers. Hold the whipped edge towards you and join by taking up the extreme edge of the article and bringing the needle each time inside the curl of the whip, in very much the same way as top sewing is worked.

It is not usually necessary to gather lace by whipping. A thread at the top of the lace can generally be found that will gather it quite satisfactorily. Pull it very carefully, and a little at a time.

Gathering.—This is not so much used now as most of our garments are either flat or the fullness gathered in by an elastic. It is still used on babies' and children's frocks.

Use a strong needle for gathering, and fasten the thread securely about $\frac{1}{4}$ inch down from the raw edges. Work from right to left and pick up half as much as you pass over. Draw up the cotton and wind the end round a pin put in at the end of the gathers.

Stroke the gathers before putting them into a band or yoke, so that they will be quite regular along the length of it.

Begin at the left-hand side, and using the eye of a strong needle lift up each gather and then push it under the left thumb and press it firmly.

Loosen the gathering thread and place the edge of the yoke or band exactly to this thread. Put pins in at the beginning and end, arrange the gathers evenly. Put in more pins, and then tack carefully.

To set the gathers into the band, begin at the right-hand side as for hemming. Then take up each gather in turn and a small piece of the fold for each stitch. The wrong side of the yoke is finished in the same way, every gather having its own stitch.

Gauging.—Rows of gathers are often used as trimming, when they are known as gauging or shirring. Chapter XI. describes Italian Shirring or Smocking ; see also what is said in this chapter about English Smocking. See that the rows are accurately spaced, and stitch below stitch all the way down, so that you have really neat columns of stitches and spaces. It is best when drawing up these gathers to pull all the threads at once, instead of finishing them one at a time. In the case where there is a good deal of fullness to be drawn up, as in a child's full-skirted dress, many dressmakers do the gathering with a long stitch and short space alternately.

Sometimes in dressmaking, when gathering is done to draw up shoulder fullness or for some other purpose, two gathering threads are often employed about a quarter of an inch apart (this distance depends on the material used). These gathers of course are not stroked.

Lace-trimmed Lingerie. — The quickest and perhaps the clumsiest way of trimming a garment with lace is to machine it on to the underwear you desire to trim. But the prettiest and daintiest methods are the following (these methods are equally applicable to net edgings or hems) five ways of joining lace edging to underwear :

(1) *Whipping.* This has already been described. It needs practice.

(2) *Overcasting.* Quick and easy, but not so neat as the other four methods.

(3) *Satin Stitch.* For this stitch, see Chapter II. This is slow, but strong and very decorative. It is useful for lace that has not a very pronounced pattern. Slightly lap the plain edge of the lace over the raw edge of the stuff, both lace and stuff having right sides uppermost. Tack them together. With two or three strands of stranded embroidery cotton work a line of chain stitch over the tackings. Cover this with close satin stitch, taken into the lace on one side and into the stuff below it on the other. Finally, cut away any surplus material on the wrong side close to the stitches, being careful not to cut the stitches themselves.

(4) *Lace Stitch*. This stitch is clearly described in Chapter VII. It is not quick, but it always looks lovely and dainty. Tack the lace to the right side of the stuff ½ inch below the raw edge. Work the lace stitch along the edge of the lace, where it will form a series of dainty little squares. When you have finished, cut away any surplus stuff close to the stitches on the wrong side.

(5) *Roman Stitch*. This, too, forms a series of delicate little squares along the edge of the lace. Tack on the lace as for lace stitch. If the material is fragile, crease a single narrow turn on the right side before tacking. Roman stitch is a series of buttonhole stitches taken with a *slanting* needle (see Chapter III.). The square effect is a result of taking each slanting stitch through the loop of the previous stitch, working rather loosely. Trim away the raw edge afterwards close to the stitches.

Here are a few useful hints when turning corners with a lace edging :

If the lace is gathered on, gather it more fully at the corners. This will prevent any dragging. But if you are putting the lace on flat, then it must be neatly mitred at each corner. To do this, fold the lace at right angles and pin it. Seam diagonally from the corner of the lace to the corner of the article you are trimming, and press the seams open.

You may wish to insert a lace motif into the material, as this is a pretty decoration. First tack the motif on the material in the right position. Use fine embroidery silk and buttonhole the lace edges to the material with close stitches. The material at the back of the lace must be now cut away with sharp embroidery scissors. Cut carefully up to the stitches, so that the lace is now transparent.

CHAPTER X

MENDING AND PATCHING

M ENDING is not always interesting but it is very necessary. In this chapter you will find help in mending almost every kind of hole and tear, and best of all some advice as to how to prolong the life of some garments and household linen. A good deal of mending can be done by the machine, and this is worth remembering. The book of instructions that goes with your machine will give you many useful hints as to how to use your machine to help you to mend.

It is a good habit to do each week's mending as soon as it comes from the wash ; in this way holes and worn places are prevented from getting too bad. If one forms this regular habit of mending every week it is surprising what time it saves in the end. We will begin with perhaps the commonest form of mending—

DARNING

Darning Thin Places in Woollen Garments.—You have already met with darning in a pretty and attractive guise in Chapter VI. Darning consists of filling a hole or drawing together a tear by *re-weaving* the fabric with a thread of a similar colour and material. This re-weaving is done with a needle in darning stitch.

136

Darning is used for mending small holes in most fabrics, and for practically every type of hole in woven articles such as stockings, socks, vests, combinations, and so on.

A great number of people (perhaps the greater number) use the left hand, as described below, when darning, but some find this tiring. In this case buy a wooden darning ball or egg to put under the hole to hold it while it is being darned. The danger of using these balls is that one tends, unless one is very careful, to strain the hole over it, so that the result, when the ball is taken away, is a bulging darn.

Here is some advice about darning worth remembering. Darn the thin places in woollen garments before any of the threads break and make a hole, and thus save yourself time and trouble later on. To do this, turn the garment on to the wrong side and begin to darn about ½ inch to the left of the worn part. Hold the garment over the left hand and put the needle in, pointing it away from you. Pick up two loops of material and pass over the same number, until you have as many stitches on your needle as it will hold. Pull the needle through, and darn on again until you come to the top of the thin place. Now point the needle towards you and work downwards, picking up the threads you missed in the last row of darning, and *vice versa*.

Work to and fro in this way, making each line of darning one stitch longer at each end until the middle of the thin patch is reached, then make each row one stitch shorter at each end, so that the darn is the same shape on each side of it.

Always remember to do this when working any kind of darn, so that the pull of the darning wool does not come on the same line of threads each time.

A loop of wool is usually left at the end of each row of darning, to prevent the work being puckered.

New Stockings.—" A stitch in time saves nine." It is a good plan to darn new stockings in the places most likely to wear into holes. Toes, heels, and, in children's stockings, the knees as well.

Sometimes a card of wool is sold with new socks and stockings ; use this for strengthening them before wearing.

Work on the wrong side from left to right and pick up not more than one thread, and pass over about three, according to the thickness of the stocking. In the next row pick up the middle thread of those you have passed over, and pass over the next three, and so on.

After each row has been worked, pass the finger of the left hand down the length of the row. This will loosen the darning and so prevent the worker from puckering.

If this darning is carefully worked with matching wool, it will not show on the right side. After the stocking has been worn some time, the darning threads will begin to wear. Pull them out carefully and redarn the stocking. If you do this, your stockings will last twice as long as they usually do.

Some people prefer to sew a piece of fine net on to the wrong side of the heels of new stockings. Fine silk net is necessary for silk stockings. This method is quicker than the darning, but there is the possibility of the net rubbing the heel and causing a blister.

Darning a Hole in a Woven Garment.—Cut off any fluffy edges round the hole, and if it is very large, tack a piece of stiff paper or cardboard behind it, so that the garment will not be pulled out of shape while being darned.

It is a good idea to draw the edges of the hole together with ordinary sewing cotton before working the darn, taking great care not to pucker the material. The sewing cotton must be removed when the darn is finished.

Begin at the left-hand side and darn the worn part round the hole, as described before. When you come to the hole, carry the thread straight across, picking up one edge and passing over the next alternately. Then finish darning over the worn part round the hole. Unless the hole is very small, the darning should always extend ½ inch beyond it.

Now turn the stocking round and darn in the opposite direction. Begin about ¼ inch to the left of the hole, and pick up and miss the threads of the first darning only, carrying the work ¼ inch above and below the hole. A lattice-work of threads is formed over the hole. Continue working a ¼ inch beyond the hole.

A Hedge Tear.—When the tear occurs on a very thick material, draw the edges together with "fishbone" stitch (see Fig. 181 in Chapter XXV.), using a selvedge thread of the material. If this is not possible, use strong, fine thread to match the cloth.

Take the stitches $\frac{1}{8}$ inch in from the cut and work several stitches into the corner.

Damp and press the mend, and it should be practically invisible. Brush up the nap of the material.

A Hedge Tear on Thinner Materials.—When the hedge tear is in thinner materials, it is more difficult to mend, as the edges are usually frayed.

First draw the edges together, as previously described for thick materials. Use fine sewing cotton to do this, or a hair from your head if it is the right colour. Hair is strong and yet fine.

If the threads of the material are very fine, it is better to draw the edges of the tear together so that they are kept on the wrong side of the garment. To do this, put the needle in $\frac{1}{8}$ inch from the edge, pass it under the cut, and bring it out $\frac{1}{8}$ inch on the opposite edge—hold the thumb over the tear while drawing the cotton through—put the needle in a short distance from where it came out, and bring it out on the opposite side, and so on.

For the darning, use threads from the selvedge of the material, as these are stronger than the weft, or thread as much like the material as possible.

Begin at the left-hand side about $\frac{1}{4}$ inch outside the tear and $\frac{1}{2}$ inch above it. Take up two threads and miss two, exactly in a line with the threads of the material, for about $\frac{1}{2}$ inch below the tear. Begin the second row two threads to the right, picking up those missed in the last row.

Make each row of darning the same length, and continue working in this way for three-quarters of the tear, keeping the raw edges as much as possible on the wrong side.

Unthread the needle and turn the work round so that the undarned end of the tear is to the left. Now darn this side in just the same way as the other side, but continue darning to the end of the cut and $\frac{1}{4}$ inch beyond it.

Re-thread the needle with the cotton from the first rows of darning, and continue right across the cut and $\frac{1}{4}$ inch beyond it. In this way the corner of the tear is strengthened by two rows of darning.

A Hedge Tear in Muslin or Organdie.—Use one or two threads of stranded cotton for mending muslin or organdie. Draw the edges together, carefully holding the thumb over the tear when pulling through the cotton. Then darn in exactly the same way as described before, but carry the darning beyond the tear to the extreme edge of the darning, for about ⅛ inch on each side of it.

A Cross-Cut Darn.—A cross-cut is so called because it cuts across both selvedge and weft threads. It needs to be very carefully darned to prevent the material from being pulled out of shape.

A cut in a tablecloth should be mended before it goes to the wash, so that the cut will not become a hole.

Draw the edges together with linen thread—"flourishing thread" as it is called. Make a crease ¼ inch from one end of the cut and another ¼ inch from the other end, at right angles to the first crease. You may pencil the lines if you prefer to do so.

Begin the darn on the wrong side of the cloth, just where the two lines or creases meet. Pick up two threads and pass over two, and make as many stitches beyond the end of the cut as there are in the line before reaching the end of it. This is done so that there shall be as many stitches to strengthen the cut above as there are below it. Work parallel to one crease.

Work to and fro over the cut as described for a hedge-tear darn, always keeping the same amount of strengthening each side of the cut. Leave short loops at the end of each line to keep the cloth flat, as linen thread always shrinks, and keep each line of darning as straight as possible with the thread of the material.

Now darn across, beginning at the same place as before but working parallel to the other crease. Take great care to keep the raw edges of the cut on the wrong side and to prevent them from fraying. Work the same amount of strengthening each side of the cut, and make each stitch go well through on to the right side.

If the darn has been worked properly, it will be six-sided, with a square of crossed darning in the middle.

PATCHING

Use a patch for covering a hole or a thin place too large to darn. A large darn is more conspicuous than a patch.

Do not throw away the whole of an old garment or household article. Keep the best parts in a bag ready for patching. New materials are not good for this purpose, but when there is no other material available, it must be washed first. This must not be forgotten, or when the article is washed, the new patch will shrink and pull the old material and probably make fresh holes.

Always cut the patch a little larger than is necessary to cover the hole or worn part. Then fray out the edges until you can pull one thread straight off each side. Cut off the uneven threads, and you will have a patch cut quite straight to a thread. This will be a great help in getting the patch to set well.

The stitches used in patching are all very simple, the only difficult part is the fixing, so take time over this and you will be rewarded with a neat, strong patch.

To patch Flannel or Woven Garments.—Cut an oblong or square of material large enough to cover the worn part of the garment, and $\frac{1}{4}$ inch extra for turnings.

If there is a hem or a seam near the hole, it must be unpicked, and then when the patch is quite finished, the hem must be resewn and the seam rejoined on the new material.

Tack the patch over the hole on the wrong side of the garment. Make sure that the threads, or, in the case of a woven material, the ridges of the loops, run in the same direction on the patch and garment.

Begin at a corner on the double material, and fasten down the edges of the patch with herringboning, using fine silk or wool. Be careful to take the upper stitches through both thicknesses of material and the lower stitch just under the raw edge.

Turn the garment on to the right side and cut away the worn part to within $\frac{1}{4}$ inch of the herringboning. Now herringbone the edge of the garment on to the patch.

A piece of net or thin woven material can be put under the hole or worn part and then darned down, instead of inserting a patch.

A Dress Patch.—*First method :* This is a strong, neat way of mending serge or tweed coats and cotton frocks.

Children's cotton frocks often become badly torn. The best and quickest way of mending them is to put on a " dress " patch, which should hardly show if the pattern is matched carefully.

Put the garment on the table right side uppermost. Take a piece of material, exactly like the frock and very much bigger than the patch is to be—especially if the pattern is large and so difficult to match—and put it over the hole.

Turn under the edges of the material until you have a patch which covers the hole and exactly matches the design or weave in the garment. This sometimes takes a long time ; it must be done very accurately.

Cut down the turnings of the patch to $\frac{1}{4}$ inch, and then tack it over the hole. Hold the patch towards you and sew the edges of patch and garment, using cotton of the same colour or threads taken from the selvedge of the garment.

Cut the turnings on the wrong side to $\frac{1}{4}$ inch and oversew or loop-stitch them to make them neat. Flatten out the sewing stitches and press with a warm iron. Woollen materials should be pressed under a damp cloth.

Second method : This way is more difficult, but if it is carefully worked with threads from the material and pressed well, it hardly shows at all.

Prepare the patch in just the same way as before, but tack it on to the wrong side instead of the right.

Turn to the right side and cut carefully from the hole towards two corners on a selvedge side. Cut just to the corner of the patch and not a thread beyond.

Now unpick the tacking on this side, so that the torn part of the garment can be turned under to match the edges of the patch. Sew the edges of the patch and garment together, and unthread the needle.

Cut from the hole towards the other two corners on the selvedge side, and finish in the same way. Last of all, work the top and bottom of the patch, using up the cotton left on the selvedge sides.

Press the turnings open on the wrong side—you will need to snip the material at the corners to do this—and then oversew or blanket-stitch the raw edges.

The corners of this patch are not so strong, but very much flatter than the first method.

A Patch for Thick Cloth.—Cut the edges of the hole quite even, either oblong or square. Using this worn piece of material as a pattern, cut out a patch with the edges cut straight to a thread.

Put the garment wrong side up on the table and drop the patch in place, watching the nap and selvedge threads on garment and patch. Fix the patch with a few large stitches on each side.

Now, with fine needle and silk or ravellings of the material, join the edges together with what is really a small darning stitch. Work on the wrong side. Bring the needle through the thickness of the cloth to $\frac{1}{8}$ inch from the edge of the garment. Put the needle in close to where the cotton came out, press it through the thickness of garment and patch to $\frac{1}{8}$ inch from the edge of the patch. Work backwards and forwards in this way, drawing the edges together so that they just meet and no more.

Take out the fixing threads and press carefully. Brush the nap of the cloth on the right side, and then the patch should not be detected.

This way of patching is only suitable for thick materials that do not fray. The working of it is very tedious, but it is worth while, as no stitches show on the right side and only a small one, where the needle is put in, on the wrong side.

To mend Leather Gloves

A Split.—Use very fine silk the colour of the glove and buttonhole both edges of the split. When you have finished, do not fasten off the cotton, but hold the two rows of knots together with the left thumb and finger, and oversew them.

In this way the glove is not pulled out of shape and the mend lies quite flat.

To patch Leather Gloves

Cut away the worn part round the hole in the glove into a round or oval shape. Use this as a pattern and cut out a patch from an old glove.

Buttonhole round the edge of the hole and the patch. Drop the patch into place and sew the buttonhole knots together.

There is no strain on either the glove or the patch and, after washing chamois gloves, this method of mending hardly shows.

To patch Table Linen

Cut away the worn part round the hole into a square or oblong. Cut out a piece of damask ¾ inch bigger all round than the hole.

Draw out threads from each side of the patch until it is just the right size to fit the hole.

Pin the patch to a piece of paper, with the right side up. Slip the paper under the hole and then tack the cloth to the paper, keeping the sides close up to the patch. Always putting your needle between the cloth and the patch, take up first about four threads on one side and then four on the other. Make the stitches as close together as possible.

The frayed edges on the wrong side may be cut off or left on.

To mend Bed Linen

Thin Places.—Darn with stranded cotton or flourishing thread if the sheets are made of linen.

Sheets generally wear thin down the middle. Before holes or slits occur, turn the sides to the middle, and the sheet has a new lease of life.

To do this, sew the selvedges together, cut the sheet down the middle, and then turn down and hem the new outside edges.

Holes.—When the hole occurs in the corner or hem of a pillow-case, unpick the sewing, patch the article, and then re-work the hem or seam.

If a buttonhole tears badly, sew it up neatly, darn the tear, and work another one about an inch away. Move the button.

Directions for working the patches on cotton and linen is found under the heading of " Calico Patch."

A Machine-stitched Patch.—This is a quickly worked patch, and when it is finished no stitches show on the right side.

Cut the edges of the hole quite even into an oblong or square. Using this worn part of the material as a pattern, cut out a patch with ¼-inch turnings all round. Make a snip at the corners of the hole. Put the garment wrong side up on the table and pin the patch into place. Turn to the right side and make sure that the patch is flat. Then tack and stitch the edges of the patch and garment together. Press and neaten the edges on the wrong side, as described under the heading " A Dress Patch."

An Emergency Patch.—This is said to be the method used by sailors ! Cut the edge of the hole quite even to a thread, and then cut out a patch to fit exactly into the hole. Put the garment right side down and drop the patch into place. Put pieces of surgical plaster on the wrong side to secure the patch to the garment. Using threads of the material, lightly darn across patch and garment with invisible stitches. Brush the nap across the edges of the patch.

Calico or Linen Patch.—This patch is used to mend sheets, pillow-cases, etc. Cut out a piece of material large enough to cover the hole and the worn part. Turn down $\frac{1}{4}$ inch on the right side of the patch. Tack the patch on to the wrong side of the garment, taking care that the selvedge threads of the patch and the garment run in the same direction. Fell all round the patch and take out the tackings. Turn to the right side and cut the worn material diagonally to within $\frac{1}{2}$ inch of each corner, then cut it away evenly to a thread. Snip the corners and fold the edges under. Hold the patch towards you and sew all round the inner square.

When the article to be patched is very thin, the patch may be felled on both sides.

CHAPTER XI

SMOCKING

Honeycombing. Surface Honeycombing. Stitches and Patterns used in Smocking. Decorating Flat Pleats. Italian Smocking or Shirring.

SMOCKING is never out of fashion. It is a lovely decorative way of holding gathers together. It gets its name from the fact that it was originally used for the smock-frocks or overalls worn by English farm labourers long ago. The word " smock " means properly a garment one creeps into or slips over one's head.

Smocking is especially used for children's clothing; it is simple and childlike, like so many crafts of long ago. It has, too, the advantage of being to a great extent elastic, and smocked garments stretch as a child grows. It is always a popular and suitable decoration for grown-up blouses and overalls of fine linen or silk.

The best materials for smocking are cotton and silk fabrics which are firm but not too thick. As much fullness is needed, woollen materials are not so suitable, as they tend to look bulky. If smocking is used on woollens, it should be confined to narrow panels here and there.

It must be remembered that this form of decoration requires plenty of material before it will give a satisfactory effect. The lines of the gathers should have a tube-like effect ; any skimpiness of material spoils the decorative qualities of smocking. But thin woollen materials can be used, especially if the material has been previously pleated with $\frac{1}{4}$ or $\frac{1}{8}$ inch accordion pleats. This method prevents any bulkiness at the foot of the smocking. It is useful for the decoration of the tops of skirts.

To carry out smocking successfully, the following directions should be carefully followed :

First, the gathering must be done with great evenness and regularity, for the beauty of the smocking depends almost entirely on this.

It is wise not to trust to the eye for keeping the rows level and equal distances apart ; either mark out a series of dots on the material, measuring them with a ruler, or iron off on the wrong side of the material a smocking transfer which consists of rows of dots already spaced out.

Transfers may be bought with the dots at various distances for different kinds of smocking. An average space between the dots is $\frac{3}{16}$ or $\frac{1}{4}$ inch. You must allow from two to four times as much width for smocking as the width it is to be when finished, according to the distance apart of the dots. Naturally the farther apart the dots are, the greater the width required.

To mark the material with dots, whether in pencil or with a transfer, it must be stretched quite taut on a board (a drawing-board or pastry-board will do) and held down with drawing-pins. If you are not using a transfer, you must prepare a long strip of cardboard with two complete rows of dots very accurately marked on it. Pierce each dot with a stiletto so as to make a hole through which the point of a pencil will go. Lay the card on the material and make a pencil-mark through each hole in the two rows, then shift it to mark the next two rows. The card can be kept after use and it will form a permanent marker.

Some workers mark out the first line with tape-measure and pencil, following the grain of the material exactly. In coarse linen the first line may be run by counting the threads. In olden days this was always the method, for the labourers' overalls were made of coarse material. The running stitches that are to gather the material together should be small, about $\frac{1}{8}$ inch (with stitch and space the same) if you mark out your own dots, but if you buy a bought transfer, have $\frac{1}{4}$-inch spacing. Bought transfers are often not sufficiently accurate.

The marking and the gathering should be done on the wrong side of the material—that is, with the wrong side of the material uppermost, to keep the right side spotless and clean.

When the material has been marked, begin gathering with a long thread and a good knot, make a back stitch in addition, in case the knot pulls through. Begin by inserting the needle in the top dot on the right-hand side, bring the point up half-way between this dot and the second dot in the same line, then in through the second dot and out half-way between this and the third dot, and so on, till the gathering thread goes the whole way along, covering the row of dots. Again thread the needle, and now run along the second row of dots in the same manner, stitch under stitch. When as many rows are gathered as you require, draw up the threads to the width required, and keep the gathers in place by twisting the ends of the cotton round pins stuck in the material. Remember to gather each row on a separate thread, and wind each thread on a separate pin. Some people measure and mark the thread to the finished size so that the gatherings will be all alike. Honeycombing (see coming section) may be drawn up tightly for working the embroidery stitches, because it will expand when the threads are withdrawn, but other smocking can only be worked a very little narrower than required finally.

The material when gathered should look as though it had been well pleated, and there will be no need of stroking the gathers down, they will lie in folds perfectly flat and even. Before beginning any pattern, find out how many rows and how many gathers will be required to bring the pattern in accurately, and mark the material to allow for just so many of each; this is especially necessary with regard to Open Diamond, Feather Stitch, and Chevron, and other wide patterns. However, some workers run one extra row above and one or two below the first and last lines of embroidery; this prevents the embroidery from being uneven.

All gathering threads are pulled out when the work is complete.

The fundamental smocking stitch is stem stitch or outline stitch. The modern introduction of feather-stitching, herring-boning, etc., must not be too often copied or admired, because these stitches tend to mask the pleated background. The whole point of smocking is the utilisation of this background; it is because honeycombing does this, that it is rightly the most popular form of smocking.

We will now describe some of the stitches used in smocking.

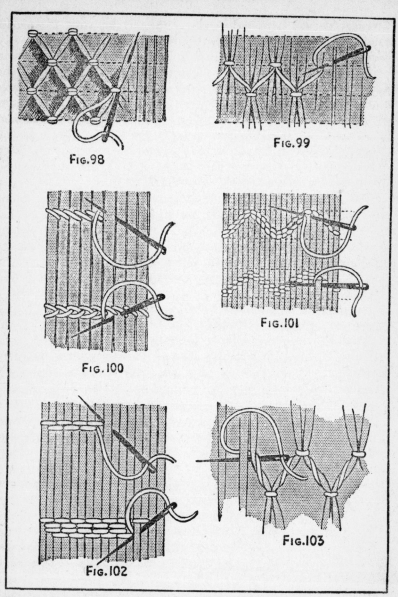

FIG. 98.—Honeycomb Stitch.   FIG. 99.—Surface Honeycomb.   FIG. 100.—
Outline Stitch.   FIG. 101.—Outline Stitch making curves and vandykes.
FIG. 102.—Cable Stitch.   FIG. 103.—Surface Honeycomb from right to left.

The threads will be found a good guide for the work, and it is as well to work over the gathering threads as far as possible, to ensure the evenness of the rows.

The stitches used are very much the same as those of bygone days, but a great variety of designs can be effected by the combination of two or three stitches. It is helpful to know that, with the exception of feather stitch and some varieties of surface honeycomb, all the stitches used in smocking *are worked from left to right.*

HONEYCOMB PATTERN (Fig. 98)

Fig. 98 shows the real English Honeycomb pattern of hollow cells caught together at the four angles by stitching. The stitch for honeycombing, like all smocking stitches, is worked on rows of gathers instead of the usual flat surface ; but it is a little different from other smocking stitches, because most of it is invisible and hidden in the folds, whereas the other smocking stitches are simply ordinary embroidery stitches that are not only worked on the surface but show on the surface of the gathers as the feather stitch, outline stitch, etc.

The honeycomb pattern is worked in the following way : Have the gathers arranged and drawn up in the manner already described, hold the material with the right side towards you, thread the needle with silk, and bring it up from the back to the front at the left-hand top corner in the first pleat and exactly over the gathering thread ; catch the next pleat to this by a stitch from right to left through each, work another stitch through both pleats, then insert the needle in the same place but in the second pleat only (Fig. 98), and bring it out in the same pleat over the second gathering thread ; catch the third pleat to this by a stitch through each, work another stitch through both pleats, then insert the needle in the same place but in the third pleat only, and bring it out in the same pleat over the first gathering thread, and proceed in this way all along, working a stitch alternately in each row ; two pleats are taken together in every stitch, and the last pleat of one stitch becomes the first pleat of the next. In going from one line of gathers to the other, be careful always to slip the needle lengthways up and down, never across. Work the third and fourth lines as you have already worked the first and second, and continue until the requisite depth is attained.

When you have completed the first two rows, it is wise to turn the work upside down and work back over the third and fourth rows, and so on.

Remember that this method of smocking simply consists of back-stitching together two pleats alternately in a lower and upper row, the second pleat in one stitch always becoming the first in the next (though higher or lower), so that a diamond or honeycomb pattern is formed. It is wise to begin this form of smocking with a knot. It is so easy that you will like to make a child's frock in this way or a nice loose overall for yourself.

Another Variety of Honeycomb.—This variety of honeycomb is very pretty for working round the necks of little children's dresses. It is done in the form of scallops. First of all, work a double line of honeycomb as already described. Then begin in the same pleat on the left-hand side, do four stitches in one line and three stitches in the other, and fasten off. Begin again on the third pleat, and do two stitches in one line, and only one stitch intermediate in the second line, so bringing the scallop to a point. You must, of course, arrange the size of the scallops so as to bring them in evenly upon the material. Larger scallops can be made by beginning with six stitches instead of four, and reducing them from six to one only.

It will be seen at once that honeycombing may be combined with other stitches (see the coming paragraphs for these) to form straight bands, diamonds, squares, or points. We have described the simplest form.

AMERICAN HONEYCOMBING OR SURFACE HONEYCOMBING
(Fig. 99)

Surface honeycombing is shown in Fig. 99. This is a variety of ordinary honeycombing with the thread between the stitches taken on the *right* side of the material instead of the wrong, so that they show, and *two fresh pleats* are taken at each stitch.

Work from left to right.

(1) *First row.* Begin as in ordinary honeycombing; in the first row pick up pleat 1 with the thread below, then pleat 2 at

the same level with the thread above, as in Fig. 99. Draw the
two pleats together very firmly.

(2) *Second row.* Carry the thread down to lower row over
two pleats ; in the second row pick up pleat 3 with the thread
below, and pleat 4 at the same level with the thread above.
Draw together pleats 3 and 4. Be very careful not to drag the
rows together. The needle is always brought up between the
two pleats, as in Fig. 99.

Now carry the thread back to the first row again in the
same way, each stitch advancing over two pleats to the
right.

There are many variations of surface honeycombing. Another
way of varying the method above is to take up one new pleat
at each stitch instead of two.

There are other simple variations of surface honeycombing
that are worked from right to left, as in Fig. 103. Begin on
the second pleat at the right-hand side with a back stitch over
the second and first pleats, bringing the needle out at the same
place as before. Then the second and third pleats are picked
up over the next gathering thread and a back stitch made (as
in Fig. 103) over the two pleats. The next stitch is taken on
the lower row over the third and fourth pleats, and the work
goes on thus, with one stitch up and one down, to the end of
the row. This is an easy stitch.

Many variations may be thought out by picking up stitches
on the pleats between the main rows—for example, vandykes
and diamond shapes can be made. (Vandyke and Diamond
pattern will be found worked out fully further on.)

We will now describe some of the most useful stitches used
in smocking and show how patterns are worked. Coloured silks
are generally used in all smocking ; the colours either match
the material or form a contrast.

OUTLINE STITCH (AND STEM STITCH) (Fig. 100)

You remember reading in Chapter II. about the outline stitch
and the stem stitch and noticing how much alike they are.
You must not be confused, therefore, if some books or papers
on Smocking say the stem stitch is the most important stitch,
and other papers say the outline stitch is most important.   They

are really slight variations of exactly the same stitch, and their use is clearly seen in smocking.

We will begin with the use of the outline stitch.

The fundamental smocking stitch is the outline stitch. It is worked in single, double, or treble rows. It is a very useful border stitch, as it is often worked on the top of the gathers and holds them together. It forms a decorative narrow band across them, as in Fig. 100. It is also used to separate more elaborate stitches.

To work.—Hold the work with the pleats vertical. Begin in the pleat on the extreme left. One pleat is taken up at each stitch. In working a single outline, as in Fig. 100, the needle is brought up above the thread each time. When working a second row, the stitch is often reversed by taking the needle under the thread, as in the lower work in Fig. 100, instead of on top. This gives the stitch the appearance of a chain stitch. (You remember from Chapter II. that in outline stitch the thread must be kept to the left or working across underneath the needle. In stem stitch the thread is kept to the right or above the needle. These two stitches are clearly seen in smocking.)

Many pretty patterns can be worked in outline stitch and stem stitch. Two or three rows may be worked close together, in straight rows, waves, or vandykes, as in Fig. 101.

CABLE STITCH (Fig. 102, upper part)

This stitch can also be worked in single or double rows.

Single Cable Stitch.—This is very similar to outline stitch, but the needle is taken alternately above and below the thread, one extra pleat being taken up at each stitch. Thus, first stitch, thread above needle ; second stitch, thread below needle, and so on.

Double Cable Stitch (Fig. 102, lower part).—Work a row of single cable stitch just above the gathering thread, then a second row just below it, reversing the thread in the second row, so that where it comes above the needle in the first row, it will come below it in the second row, and so on. A pretty effect, something like a linked chain, is produced by this stitch.

Another method of working the double stitch is to work two rows of the single stitch instead of reversing the second row.

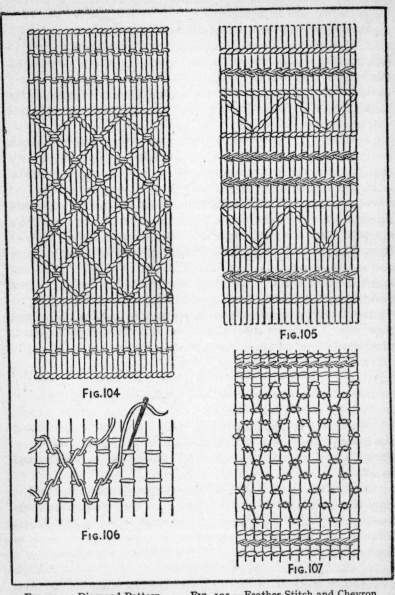

FIG. 104.—Diamond Pattern.
FIG. 105.—Feather Stitch and Chevron.
FIG. 106.—Decorated Flat Pleats.
FIG. 107.—Decorated Flat Pleats.

Diamond Pattern (Fig. 104)

Draw four lines from right to left three-eighths of an unch apart for the top and bottom of the pattern, as in Fig. 104. The lines in the middle are for the working of the diamonds, and these are a quarter of an inch apart.

The heading is of outline stitch and rope stitch (see Cable Stitch), as already explained.

For the diamonds, begin with a stitch on the first pleat just below the heading (the stitches are all outline stitches or stem stitches), next a stitch consecutively on the second, third, fourth, and fifth pleat, each stitch a little lower than the stitch previous, so that the fifth stitch comes directly upon the next gathering thread; then work a stitch on each of the next four gathers in an upward direction, and you again come just under the heading; continue thus up and down to the end of the row. Begin again on the first pleat of the next gathering thread, and work successively upwards a stitch on each pleat till you come to the next gathering thread already worked upon, when you make a second stitch under the stitch already there—this is where the diamonds meet; go four stitches successively downwards and you will again be at the point of a diamond; again work upwards, then downwards, and so on for the width of the embroidery. Always remember that the double stitches which form the points of the diamonds are to come upon a gathering thread, and that *three* stitches, and three stitches only, are to be on each side of every diamond.

Diamond Pattern in Scallops.—This is a pretty variation of the diamond pattern. It is especially suitable for embroidering round the necks of children's dresses and overalls. It is worked in the form of scallops. Begin with two lines worked according to the diamond pattern given already, then work three whole diamonds under five in the top line, two under the three, then one under the two, so bringing the scallop to a point of one diamond. This trimming can be worked wider or narrower as desired.

Diamond Lattice Pattern.—This is a very effective pattern and is generally worked in double silk. It looks a little like Honeycomb, but is more decorative because of the stitches; for

in the middle or " Lattice" part of the pattern the silk is
kept entirely in front of the work and passes across and across
diagonally from one line to the next.

Fifteen gathering threads are generally used, and these
are a quarter of an inch apart, except that from the heading to
the line where the pattern begins a half an inch is left.

For the heading, have the silk double, bring the needle up
in the first pleat at the left-hand top corner, insert it in the
second pleat on the same line, and bring it out in the same pleat
on the second line (or row) ; insert it in the same line of the
third pleat, and bring it out in the same pleat on the top line ;
insert it on the same line in the fourth pleat, and bring it out
in the same pleat on the second line ; insert it on the same line in
the fifth pleat, and bring it out in the same pleat on the top line ;
and so on, up and down the two lines, to the end of the row.
Then work in the same manner from the third line to the second,
which, as you will see, brings a double set of stitches in the
middle row and completes the heading.

The Lattice.—Now to work the lattice. This is worked on the
nine middle gathering threads, taking only one pleat at a time.
Bring the needle up in the second pleat of the first line (a stitch is
to be formed below the stitch in the middle line of the heading),
insert it on the same line to take up the third pleat only, and
draw the third and second pleats together, with the silk below
the stitch ; insert the needle on the second line to take up the
fourth pleat only, then on the same line to take up the fifth
pleat only, and draw the fifth and fourth together with the silk
above the stitch ; insert needle on the top thread to take up
the sixth pleat only, then on the same line to take up the seventh
pleat only, and draw the seventh and sixth pleats together, with
the silk below the stitch ; continue to the end of the row.

Then begin on the second pleat of the third row. Take up
the third pleat only and draw the third and second pleats
together, with the silk above the stitch ; take up the fourth
pleat on the second line, take up the fifth pleat on the same
line, and draw these two pleats together in a stitch just close
below the stitch that is there already and, with the silk below
the stitch, insert needle on the third line to take up the sixth pleat
only, then on the same line take up the seventh pleat only, and

draw these two pleats together, with the silk above the stitch, and so on. Next, bring up the needle to work a stitch close under the first stitch of the last row, and go on in the same way till you complete the depth required. The pattern is finished with another like that with which it began.

BASKET PATTERN

This is a surface pattern. It is easily worked. Have ten lines of gathers three-eighths of an inch apart. Run the gathers as already described. Then bring up the needle in the first pleat on the top line on the left-hand side, take up the second and first pleats together on the needle ; take up the second pleat only on the needle in the same place, and, bringing out the needle below the stitch, take up the third and second pleats together on the needle ; take up the third pleat only on the needle in the same place, bringing out the needle above the stitch ; then work the fourth and third pleats similarly, then the fifth and fourth, and so on, bringing the needle out below the stitch and above the stitch alternately. On the space occupied by the three top lines of thread you get in five lines of this basket smocking. The stitches are packed close together but overlap like the weaves of a basket. Work four single lines of basket smocking in the middle of the pattern—and finish with five lines close together to match the beginning.

FEATHER STITCH

This is the well-known stitch described in Chapter III. as used in plain needlework. It is worked from right to left. One pleat is taken up with each stitch. A pretty diamond pattern can be made by working two rows of feather stitch, so that the top points of the second row touch the lower points of the first row.

Smocked garments are often decorated in feather stitch— straight lines, waves, geometrical patterns, all being worked in this stitch.

Feather Stitch and Zigzag.—We will describe this in detail so that you will understand how to work feather stitch on smocking. Having the gathers in order, hold the material so that the pleats run from right to left instead of up and down. Begin in the second pleat a little above the gathering thread, and take up the first and second pleats with the silk round the point of the needle as if going to make a buttonhole stitch, then insert the needle to take up the second and third pleats a trifle below the gathering thread, and place the silk around the point of the needle for another buttonhole stitch, and continue working alternately a stitch on each side of the gathering thread.   Work the centre of the pattern in the same way, only you do five stitches consecutively to the right and five stitches consecutively to the left, closely together and in zigzag fashion.

Feather Stitch and Chevron (Chevron is like Vandyke) (Fig. 105). —Draw lines at distances suitable for the pattern, and gather in the usual way.   Then begin by working the six straight lines of outline stitch shown in Fig. 105.   Next do the four lines of feather stitch (for method of working, see above).   The intermediate lines of Chevron are worked by taking up the pleats one by one in a slanting direction, doing first six outline stitches down and then six stitches up, as already described for the side stitches of the diamonds.

CHAIN STITCH

This again is a stitch often used in plain embroidery and described in Chapter II.   Two pleats are taken up with every stitch, advancing one pleat each time.   It can be worked in straight lines or in vandykes.

HERRINGBONE PATTERN

This pattern requires nine lines drawn from right to left, three-eighths of an inch apart, and crossed by other lines half an inch apart for the width of the stitches.   When the gathering is done, work a row of outline stitch along the top and bottom lines.   (This, as we have said before, keeps the gathers together and makes the working of a pattern easy.   The rows of outline stitches also look decorative.)   On the six middle threads work three rows of herringbone stitches.   Bring the needle out on the first of these threads in the first pleat, come down to the second thread and insert the needle from right to left through the third and second pleats, go up to the first thread and insert the needle from right to left through the fourth and third pleats, then down and through the fifth and fourth, and up and through the sixth and fifth, and proceed thus, working a stitch on each line alternately to the end of the row. Work the other two rows of herringbone in the same manner.

We have now taken all the chief stitches and patterns—like diamonds, waves, vandykes, etc.—used in smocking. From these it is possible to make one's own designs.

The home worker has a well-selected number to choose from, and she can build up very handsome patterns or confine herself to simple ones that are quickly worked. Simple geometric bands running across the gathers give the best effect; any attempt to make floral designs or other free forms is against the nature of this kind of work.

It is often advisable, as we have said before, to begin at the top of the smocking with a line or lines of stem stitch—this regulates and holds the gathers in position—and to finish with a line of stitching which gives a broken edge; otherwise the fullness springs away from the stitching in a way that is not always pleasing. Sometimes the fullness at the top can be disposed into pleats which can be fixed into a yoke.

There are, of course, a number of good ways of arranging the designs in smocking, some giving lighter and more dainty effects than others. Bear in mind the purpose of smocking when choosing a design, as some stitches are much more elastic than others. The most elastic of all is the honeycomb pattern, whilst the one that is the tightest or " gives " the least is a broad zigzag formed by stem stitch.

Smocking looks interesting and dignified when worked in self-coloured threads on a similar coloured background. It is not dependent on colour for its effect, but should colour be used, it ought to be simple. Very pretty effects can be obtained, however, by working in two (at the most three) contrasting colours, especially on a light-coloured material. On a dark-coloured ground a lighter shade or tint of the same colour is often particularly effective.

Smocking in the olden days was often very elaborate. Each country had a distinct and characteristic style; this style as a rule took its character from the embroidery which always trimmed the garment.

In modern times the style of smocking varies with the fashion in vogue, but as a general rule wherever fullness is required smocking can be used. Simple smocking is, of course, never out of fashion for children's dresses or overalls.

When choosing materials, remember that Viyella (especially fine Tropical Viyella) will make a lovely frock for a baby's first dress, if it is smocked in honeycomb. Japanese silks, tussore, crêpe de Chine, linen, and muslin are all easy to work. Choose a thread for the working that is in keeping with the material— for example, on velvet use a thick thread; on cashmere, silk, or muslin use twisted embroidery silk; and on linen or similar material use linen or mercerised thread.

Do not forget that smocking is useful for bed-jackets, tea-jackets, and dressing-gowns.

THE DECORATION OF FLAT PLEATS AND TUCKS
(Figs. 106, 107)

Another kind of work closely related to smocking is the decoration of flat pleats. While smocking is based on accordion pleats, this is based on *flat* pleats or tucks.

If the tucks are made by running, using the hand, much tedious work must be done before the actual decoration can be commenced.

A quicker method is to lay the material out in flat pleats, as shown in Fig. 106, and begin the embroidery at once. The material used may be silk, linen, or wool. The size of the flat pleats will vary with the weight of the material, but about ¼ of an inch broad is the usual size for most purposes.

In Fig. 107, first running-stitches are taken in rows across the pleats. These look very decorative. The running-stitches are then linked together, as in Fig. 107, to form diamonds. Pretty borders can be added in chain stitch and feather-stitching.

This method of decoration is useful for articles of dress as well as for articles of household use.

ITALIAN SMOCKING OR PATTERN SHIRRING

If you want to decorate your little one's frock in an out-of-the-common way, or make a warm dressing-gown or jacket for yourself, read this.

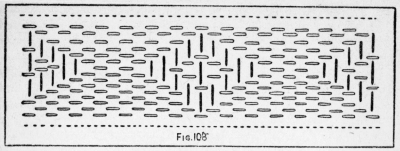

FIG. 108.—Italian Smocking.

The peasants of Italy have always been clever with their needles, and though the younger folk to-day in Italy have not the time or patience to spend long hours over fine work as in former days, they still remember and work some pretty patterns of long ago. Here is one. Pattern shirring, or Italian gathering, is a pretty variety of smocking.

No transfers are needed or marking out of dots. The pattern is made in the gatherings, which in this case are worked closely together and complete the design. The gathering threads are, of course, not pulled out afterwards, as in English smocking.

The gathering threads, since they are part of the pattern, can be of the same colour as the material or of a contrasting colour or shade.

Material in narrow stripes (say ⅛ inch wide) is very easy to work, as the stitches can then be regulated to the width of each stripe. Silk or muslin is very suitable for this kind of work.

The patterns that can be made in this kind of smocking are limited. Diamond and vandyke shapes must form the basis of all designs for shirring, because it is quite impossible to make any other shapes than those composed of slanting lines.

The gathering is done in rows from right to left across the material ; every two rows are worked with one piece of thread.

Thread the needle with a piece of thread twice as long as the pattern, begin on the right side of the material, at the right-hand top corner of the place where the band of shirring is to be worked. Make a line of small, even running-stitches across to the left-hand top corner of the band, leaving half the thread at the right side. Unthread the needle, rethread it with the piece

6

left on the right-hand side ; insert the needle directly under, and about $\frac{1}{8}$ inch below the point where it first entered the material, then work a line of longer even running-stitches, as in Fig. 108, across to the left-hand side again.   With another thread work a third line of gathering $\frac{1}{16}$ inch below, picking up every alternate pleat, as in the chart, Fig. 108.   Work a fourth row like the second, and repeat the third and fourth rows to the end of the work, *leaving the right number of pleats free* to form the pattern.   The stitches in the last row (when the pattern is completed) should be the same length as those in the first row, so as to regulate the fullness.

The threads are taken to the back of the work as each row is completed and, where necessary, a half-stitch is made to make the ends of the rows even.   When all the gatherings are finished, draw up the threads and overcast them to the material.

When making patterns in this form of smocking, it is much easier to draw a chart, as shown in Fig. 108.   This shows a very simple diamond pattern.   It will look delightful on a frock in silk or muslin made for a tiny child.   This chart clearly shows the arrangement of the stitches we have just described.   The horizontal lines show the gathering threads, the upright ones the pleats that are left free to form the pattern.   The pattern can be repeated any number of times if a deeper band is needed, but the narrow band looks simpler for a child.   Double diamonds and vandykes can easily be worked out on charts.

Remember the beauty of this work lies in the evenness of the pleats.

The same material as already described for ordinary smocking is suitable for Italian smocking, and the same silks and cottons.

CHAPTER XII

QUILTING

Quilting. Designs used in Quilting. Italian Quilting. The Quilting of
Patchwork. Some Easily Done Quilting.

THIS is one of the oldest forms of embroidery. It can be
traced back to very ancient times. At first it was a
way of adding warmth to bed-coverings by stitching a warm
interlining firmly between a top ornamental cover and a lining,
so that the stitches themselves made a pattern. The use of
a thick padding gave a pretty relief effect to the pattern, and
this is so decorative that in modern quilting it is used for many
articles which do not require the warmth of the padding.

After being forgotten for some time it is again becoming
popular and has taken on some interesting modern forms. It
is an effective, quickly made, and strong decoration for tea-
cosies, cushions, hot-water-bottle covers, kettle-holders, and
chair-seats for the home. For dress purposes it is useful for
wadded kimonos and padded dress-hangers.

In quilting, as we have said before, three layers of material
are stitched together in a design or pattern. The top layer is
pretty and fairly thin ; silk, taffeta, or soft linen, cotton, or
organdie are all suitable for this. The lining should be a soft,
cheap cotton—cheesecloth is often used. The padding between
may be a layer of cotton-wool if a good deal of warmth and a
high relief effect are wanted. If warmth is unnecessary, or
less light and shade is desired, a fluffy material such as wincey,
flannel, or flannelette.

The quilting transfer is often stamped on the lining material
and the quilting stitches worked from the under side ; this is
so that the transfer lines will not show. However, as the transfer

lines generally wear away during working, it is safe and much more interesting to quilt on the upper surface.

Quilting on a large scale is generally done on a frame, but probably the home-worker will only undertake small pieces of quilting, and they can be held in the hand quite well.

When the pattern has been transferred, lay the three thicknesses together and tack them very firmly together. This tacking is very important, for the work is spoilt if a layer shifts. Many workers machine-stitch all round the edges through the three thicknesses. Then hand-tack across and across the surfaces both ways and diagonally, so that the tackings are never very far apart anywhere.

Several stitches can be used for quilting a design. The most common is a running-stitch, but back stitch and chain stitch are quite suitable. Chain stitch was a favourite in olden days, but it is not often seen to-day. Running-stitch is quick and satisfactory, but back stitch gives a more solid effect.

Most workers begin in the centre and embroider outwards. Unless the materials are very thin, it is generally best to stab back and forth when quilting, rather than to take two or three stitches at once. In this way one is sure that every stitch goes through all three layers.

Most quilting is done in one colour only. Match the top surface but choose a shade or tint of the colour. Some workers use a definitely contrasting colour, and if desired, each portion of the design may be a definite colour. Ordinary sewing cotton or silk or a thin, firm embroidery thread can be used ; but, unlike ordinary embroidery, the thread is not intended to show much, for the charm of quilting lies not so much in the very simple stitches used but in the relief effects obtained by padding.

DESIGNS USED IN QUILTING (Fig. 109)

The type of design is important ; try to arrange it so that whilst some parts of the work are closely stitched, other parts are left to " bubble up." In this way that variety of surface is obtained that makes the charm of quilting. A flowing type of design with geometric forms is very suitable, but whatever forms are expressed, the design must be planned in the first place to hold the three materials firmly together.

Sometimes no design is used, the quilting being done in a geometrical pattern made by ruling diagonal lines across the surface both ways at regular intervals to form a diamond pattern, or a series of circles or semicircles can be used.

Quilting may be used as a background to other coloured embroidery. A pretty effect can be obtained by embroidering sprigs on the top surface and then quilt by enclosing each in a circle; these circles can be connected with diagonal lines. Another quite effective plan is to use a sprigged material and quilt in some simple pattern suggested by the arrangement of the sprigs.

Sometimes it is possible to quilt the floral pattern of a fabric itself, where this is large and bold enough. The fabric must be padded and lined, then the quilting is done all round the outlines. Patterned handkerchiefs can be used in this way, and they make very effective little handkerchief or glove sachets or cases for safety-pins, etc.

When a quilted article is flat and not seamed round the edges—for example, the cover of a perambulator—the best way of finishing the edges is to bind them with bias tape or bias strips of silk. (See section on Home Dressmaking.)

Eyelet holes are often a valuable addition to a bedcover. They assist ventilation and also form extra units of design.

Cord is sometimes run between parallel lines of running, and thus ridge-like patterns are formed; but one should be careful about introducing methods of work that are not legitimate padding. This brings us to Italian Quilting.

ITALIAN QUILTING

Italian quilting is *corded quilting*. Instead of padding all over like ordinary quilting, Italian quilting pads the outline of the design only. The design is worked in double lines for the purpose, and the padding is inserted between these double lines, thus giving a raised or corded effect to the outlines. No warmth, or little warmth, is added by this method, but the effect is very delicate and attractive.

The work is quick and can be used for cushion covers, perambulator covers, cot covers, chair seats, pin-cushions, hand-bags, etc. Silk, voile, and soft cottons are all suitable for Italian quilting.

Tack carefully together at various points the top surface
and the silk or cotton lining when you have transferred the design
on either the top surface or the lining.   (It is best, on the whole,
to transfer the design to the lining.)   The transfer must, of course,
be one specially designed for Italian quilting.   Bold appliqué
designs can often be used ; in this case, draw in double outlines
½ inch or less inside the original ones.

Having got your pattern transferred and the two materials
tacked together, next run or back-stitch along both outlines in
a matching or contrasting colour, using sewing cotton or fine
silk.   To pad these double outlines, thread a large, blunt needle
with 8-ply wool.   (Oddments of rug wool can be used, or embroidery wool in four thicknesses.)   Now turn the quilting so
that the lining is uppermost, and with a pair of fine scissors
carefully poke a hole, through the *lining only* (be careful not to
go through the top surface), between the two rows of stitching
that forms the double outline.   Run the needle into this hole
and carry it along the passage made by the double outline as
far as possible.   Soon a turn in the design will make further
advance impossible, poke another hole to let the needle out, and
start again with a fresh length of padding.   Continue to pad all
the outlines in this way.

The padding should be done with wool the same colour as
the top surface.   When the top surface is transparent and white,
or pale in colour, a pleasing effect can be obtained by using
vividly coloured wool for padding, so that it shows through the
transparent top.   (See section on Shadow Embroidery.)

In Italian quilting of this kind the stitching should match
the padding in colour.   Any small details unsuited for padding
can be worked in ordinary embroidery stitches through both
thicknesses of material.

If the wrong side of the quilting shows, it must have an
additional lining to hide the ends of wool.

If suitable designs are chosen, based upon enclosed *spaces* of
various shapes (a common pattern for Italian quilting), the
cording can be done in the following tidy way without poking
holes.   Tack the top and lining together *only* in the very centre,
pin them at the corners.   Run a back stitch all round the *inside*
outline of a space.   Take out the pins, slip the padding wool

Fig.109

FIG. 109.—Designs used in Quilting.

between the two layers of stuff close up to the stitched outline, and then make the outside line of stitching, thus enclosing the wool neatly.   Continue in this way, outlining the spaces, padding and outlining again.   A little experience will soon suggest suitable patterns that can be treated in this way—concentric squares, diamonds, etc., are all possible.

THE QUILTING OF PATCHWORK (see also Chapter VIII.
on Patchwork)

Such large things as quilts should properly be quilted in a frame ; a modern substitute is to quilt each block separately and then join them together afterwards.   It is a long job, whether a frame is used or not.   The quilt frame is quite simple, but it takes up a good deal of room in a small house.

In the old days in America (the land of beautiful patchwork quilts) quilting parties were given.   Eight women often sat all day at a frame, four along each side.   In this way the quilting was finished by the evening, and there was time for rest and amusement.

Those who have the courage to embark on a patchwork quilt will find it very interesting work.   Don't machine all the patches together in one day, but build the quilt up in blocks as they did in the olden days—for example, divide your quilt into 9-inch squares or blocks, each of which is patched separately. In this way it will become pleasant light work that you can pick up at odd moments and as you find the patches you want.   It is interesting to watch your squares growing.

Block patchwork may be either pieced (that is all the patches seamed together) or laid (appliqué).   It can also be a mixture of both, the patches being first joined into a pattern and then appliquéd down to the background.   (Runners and tray-cloths are made in this way. See section on Appliqué Work.)   Piecing is the most economical, as no background is needed.   Appliqué has this advantage that complicated and curved outlines can be used and so one gets more variety and charm.

Now supposing all one's patchwork blocks or sections are ready, a lining must be chosen—this can be a white cotton material or unbleached calico ; then a padding—the padding

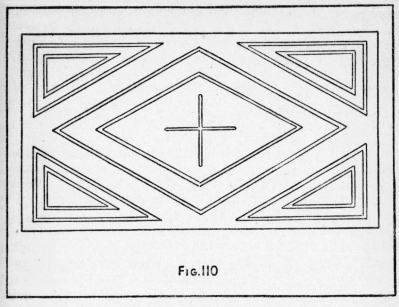

FiG.110

FIG. 110.—Design for Italian Quilting.

can be two layers of flannelette or an old blanket worn very thin and smooth ; over this will come the patchwork top, with all its seams carefully ironed out flat and its right side uppermost.

Now what quilting pattern shall be chosen ? Suitable patterns can sometimes be bought or some simple arrangement of ruled diagonal lines used, or of overlapping circles (these circles can easily be made by marking round a teacup). These latter patterns are especially useful where plain squares (white or coloured) alternate with patchwork blocks are being quilted.

If every block or section is made of patchwork, the best plan is to quilt along the lines of the patchwork pattern ; this saves all marking or the transferring of designs. For the home-worker the quilting can be done in sections by using the panel of a clothes-horse as a frame. This has the advantage of standing upright and not needing any support. A quilt frame, which is four very strong pieces of wood fastened together at each corner by iron clamps and having narrow strips of heavy material such as ticking nailed along each edge, needs to be supported on something, say the backs of four chairs of equal height. The various layers of the quilt are pinned or tacked to the strips of ticking to keep them stretched and immovable during quilting. The clamps can be adjusted tightly so that nothing can slip.

SOME EASILY DONE QUILTING

Quilted Cushion Covers.—The most practical things to make at home and the most useful are perhaps quilted cushion covers.

To make a quilted cushion top, first decide upon the size and shape you wish it to be. It is wise to cut a full-sized pattern for the top on plain paper, on this you can plan your design. If you are not good at planning designs, try to find a suitable transfer. Study the background spaces and see that they are a pleasing shape.

When the design is satisfactory, transfer it to very thin, soft muslin—this is to be used for the lining of the pillow top or cushion top. Old material may be used. Place a thin sheet of cotton wadding between the lining and the top material—the top material can be unbleached muslin. Pin, then tack, the three layers together. Use buttonhole twist or wash embroidery thread about the size of the twist to make the quilting. Do the quilting with short, *even* running-stitches made on the lining side.

If you like, practise some quilting on scraps of cloth that have been padded with cotton of the same weight as that used in your cushion top, before you begin. The unbleached muslin will look pretty quilted with rose thread. As the cushion you are quilting is not thick, but is really just a pad, no side pieces are necessary. A double ruffle can be made of a straight strip of cloth folded through the middle lengthwise, gathered and sewed in the seam that joins the top and the bottom of the cushion together. You have now made something pretty, useful, and inexpensive for your room.

Round or square flat cushions can be made to fit your chairs or window-seats, etc.

When you have made the above cushion cover successfully you may like to try your hand at Italian quilting.

Fig. 110 shows a pretty and easy design, as all the lines

are *straight* lines, and it is so easy to pull the wool through. This same pattern can also be worked out in ordinary quilting.

If it matches your room, this cushion looks charming in two tones of rose.

Pretty iron-holders, kettle-holders, etc., can be made in quilting. These make charming gifts, and are useful for bazaars if made in gay colours. Gingham, cotton prints, satin, are all useful materials. For quick work choose muslin or checked gingham woven with ¼-inch squares; small brass rings will be needed for hanging up the holder, and some sheet wadding, also some embroidery threads.

Cut two squares of gingham or muslin and allow ½-inch turning, and a square of cotton wadding. Pin the wadding between the two pieces of gingham. If desired, the squares of gingham can have borders of cross stitch to make it more decorative. Work the cross stitch before pinning the three pieces together. Then pin and bast them. Many pretty patterns can be quilted on the muslin holders, either by using a short running-stitch or adjusting the sewing-machine to a long stitch. Use contrasting colours for quilting. Oversew the edges. The edges can also be decorated with rows of running-stitches. The charm of these simple things depends upon the design and colour.

The advantage of using gingham is that cross-stitch patterns can easily be worked on it. Designs in quilting look best on plain muslin, so that the embroidery threads show up well as they run around the designs.

Some pretty ideas for shadow quilting and quilting will be found in Chapter VIII. on Appliqué and Patchwork.

CHAPTER XIII

CORDS, TASSELS, AND FRINGES

A Simple but Uncommon Necklace, A Spiral Knotted Cord, A Square
Knotted Cord of Four Strings, A Wide Flat Cord with Diagonal
Stripes, Serbian Cord, A Twisted Cord. Tassels. Pompons.
Fringes of Different Kinds, A Fringe for the Border of a Curtain,
A Tasselled Fringe, How to cut Fringes, Bead Edging.

A *SIMPLE but Uncommon Necklace.*—There are many
allusions in this book to cords, tassels, pompons, and
fringes, and they are so useful that they deserve a chapter to
themselves.

It will perhaps hardly be believed that a beautiful necklace
can be made from old-fashioned reel knitting—a necklace that
will rival in uniqueness and beauty a bead necklace !

Smooth the opening of a reel with No. oo sand-paper (a
smooth block of wood can be used if desired with a hole in the
centre about $\frac{5}{16}$ of an inch in diameter). Four brads with small
heads are driven at regular intervals around the opening. They
make the four corners of a square.

Now choose the embroidery silks for the cord or necklace.
Choose colours that will match your blouse or form a contrast
to it. A pretty cord can be made from a reel of golden thread
and four skeins of brown embroidery silk, or if your blouse is
blue or white, choose silver thread and blue embroidery silk.

Wind the skeins of silk on to a card, and knot the ends
together, because a long strand is needed.

Tie the ends of the brown and golden threads together and
push them through the hole in the reel where the nails are.
Hold these ends and the reel in the left hand, and make a loop
around each nail with the double threads. Then wind the
threads round, always keeping the gold thread on top ; hold

them in position with the thumb of the left hand, and with a bodkin lift the underneath loops over the top of the nails ; this is like casting off stitches in knitting.

Go on winding the threads round and slipping the underneath loops over the nails until the cord is about 36 inches long.

Cut off the threads. Thread the ends through the bodkin, lift the loops off the nails with the bodkin, and secure them together with a knot or two. Now make a cord of all gold in the same way. Twist the finished cords together and tie them at the ends.

Tassels for the Necklace.—Wind the two coloured threads round the first three fingers of the left hand twelve times. Hold the loops with the thumb, cut the ends and thread them through the bodkin. Now pass the bodkin under the loops between the thumb and first finger, and knot the loops together. Slip off the bodkin and tie the ends to the ends of the cords.

To make a neat finish wind a single gold thread over and over the joins and ends of cords and tassels until they are covered. Cut and thread the gold thread through the bodkin, push it down the centre and draw it out among the tassel ends. Now cut through the loops of the tassel at the other end, and knot the necklace just above. If desired, an ornamental ring can be slipped over the necklace and rest on the knotted part.

When you have made these gold or silver necklaces, give the reel to your little girl or some other little girl to make a pair of reins.

Pretty mats can be made by sewing the cord made in this way round and round, using overhand stitches. Round or oval mats can also be made in this way, and if good colour-schemes are used they are most useful on polished tables.

A Spiral Knotted Cord of Two Colours.—This is a very pretty and simple cord with a spiral effect. It may be worked quite well in the hands only, although some people as the work increases find it convenient to have some support to hold it. The cord may be fixed in the hole of a reel, or the end may have a weight attached to it. Two embroidery threads of different colours, for example red and white, about one yard in length are needed.

Place the two threads at right angles to each other, white across red. Now take the bottom red thread and tie it across

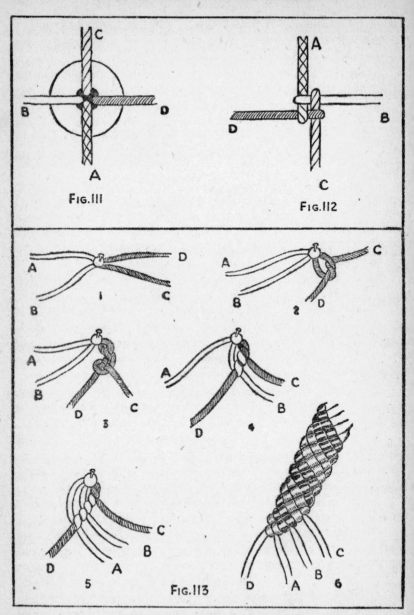

the upper white one by a *single* tie knot ; pull back both the ends to the same position as before.   Next take the white thread and tie it across the knot just made by the red thread, and place ends in their former position ; now take the red again and tie, and so on.   In the process of working, the cord twists itself and when finished will appear as a spiral of red and white.   The advantage of having two colours is obvious, as it is so much easier to see which two threads must be tied, besides being more effective.   The thicker the thread used the thicker is the cord made.

A Square Knotted Cord of Four Strings (Figs. 111, 112).— To begin with, it is best to have the four threads of different colours.   The cord when finished is square or four-sided, and is made by crossing every thread at right angles to the last. A large reel or ribbon-roller with a hole in the centre is useful to put the threads in to begin with.   Knot the four ends of the threads together and insert the knot into the hole of the reel ; place the threads outward opposite each other, as in Fig. 111.

Take A and carry it across B to lie parallel with C. Take B and carry it across A and C to lie parallel with D.   Bring C across B to where A was at first.   Bring D over C and thread it through the loop formed by A at starting (Fig. 112).   It will be noticed now that the position of each thread is shifted from left to right.   To regain the first position, the threads are again crossed as before, only they start from the right-hand side, as it were, working backward.   That is, each thread goes straight across to the opposite side in turn, and the last one is threaded through the loop made by the first.   The threads must be held down between the fingers of the left hand while working, but at first the reel can be placed on the table and both hands left free to work.

A Wide Flat Cord with Diagonal Stripes (Fig. 113).—This is a somewhat different type of cord, and as it is flat it is especially useful for girdles, and for draw-strings when these have to be flat.   It can also be sewn on curtains as a decorative edge, or on cushions.   (See Chapter XIV.)

To make it you need four strands, two each of two colours. Knot them together and pin them securely to a drawing-board or deal table.

Arrange the strands A, B, C, D as in Fig. 113 (1), where A and B of the same colour are on one side and C and D of the other colour on the other side.

Bring D to the left, then bring C *under* and over D, and knot them as in Fig. 113 (2). Make the knot firm and knot them together again, as in Fig. 113 (3).

Bring B *under* and over D, and knot them as in Fig. 113 (4). Now knot B once again round D. Bring A across and knot it twice round D, as in Fig. 113 (5). When C, B, and A have each been knotted twice round D, the beginning of the cord will appear as in Fig. 113 (6).

Now make C the diagonal bar across the cord by bringing it into the position shown by the dotted lines in Fig. 113 (6). Then knot B, A, D each in turn twice round C.

Then make B the diagonal bar and finally A ; then begin again with D and repeat the process.

If each strand is knotted three or more times around the strand forming the diagonal, wider stripes of colour will result. Be careful to make firm, even knots, and you will get a very attractive and successful cord.

A Serbian Cord (Fig. 114).—This pretty cord can be made on the fingers and is really a form of hand crochet (see section on Crochet Work). When once you understand the method you can make this cord very quickly. Work it in two colours. It will form a circular cord with three stripes of each colour.

Choose two strands of contrasting colours and knot them together. Hold the knot in the right hand, between the thumb and second finger, catching up strand B on the first finger as in Fig. 114 (1), and holding its length in place by pressing it against the palm with the little finger. Bring strand A round the loop and hold it in the left hand (Fig. 114 (1)).

Now pass the first finger of the left hand through the loop B as shown in Fig. 114 (2) ; with this finger catch hold of the strand A and pull it up through the loop. As this is done, pass the knot to the left hand. The loop is now on the left finger. With the right hand pull the strand B firmly as in Fig. 114 (3).

Now pass the first finger of the right hand through the loop and catch up the strand B and pull it through (Fig. 114 (4)). Hold the knot with the right again, and pull the strand A tightly

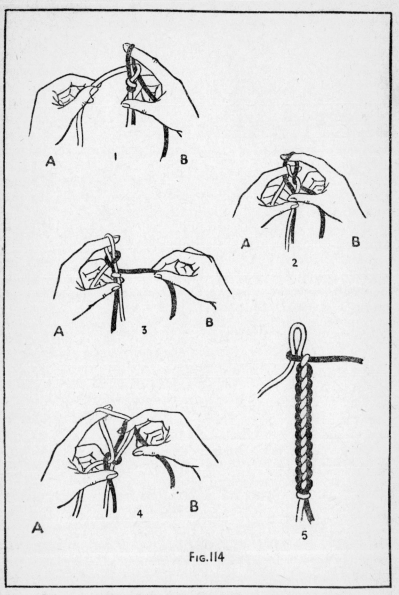

Fig. 114

FIG. 114.—Serbian Cord or Crochet Cord; (5) The finished cord.

with the left hand. Your hands are now again in the same position as in Fig. 114 (1).

Continue in this way. Fig. 114 (5) shows the finished cord.

Notice the following points in making this cord : (1) How the knot changes from one hand to the other each time. (2) Make the loop large enough for the finger to " crochet " through it easily. (3) The loop knot and strand forming the knot are all held in one hand. The other hand is only used to hold the cord which is to be pulled through the loop.

A Twisted Cord.—Here is a simple way of making a twisted cord. Having decided upon the length of cord required, take three times this length of thread. For a cord of average thickness six strands of embroidery cotton are required. Tie a knot at each end and insert a pencil through each loop. These pencils must be twisted in opposite directions by two people standing facing each other. They must stand as far apart as the length of the thread and see that the thread does not hang loosely between them, as otherwise knots are apt to form as the thread is twisted. When the cord shows a tendency to curl, a small weight should be hung at the exact centre, then when the two pencils are brought together the two halves of the cord will automatically twist together.

By using threads of different colours, for example, three of one colour and three of another, a very pleasing variety will be obtained in the twisted cord.

Each end may be knotted and ravelled out, so producing primitive tassels.

Twisted cords are most suitable for trimming cushions and tea-cosies, and they can be more easily made to match the colour-scheme than bought ones.

TASSELS

There are many different ways of decorating tassels, but the main foundation of all tassels is the same, and consists of a cardboard gauge cut to the size of the tassel required. The silk or wool is wound round this foundation until a suitable thickness is obtained. Knot the threads together at the top and slip them off the card. If the tassel is wanted for the end of a cord, the cord should now be inserted at the top. Wind thread round the tassel at a suitable distance from the top to form the head of the tassel.

Two ways of decorating the head are :

(*a*) *Surface Buttonholing* (see Chapter II.).—This is begun round the base of the head and worked towards the top of the tassel.

(*b*) *Ball Stitch*.—A loose knot is tied round the top of the ball and the stitch worked on to this : not through the ball of the tassel. Draw the knot tight and secure the end in the ball. Having completed the first row of ball stitch, begin the next row by placing the stitch exactly between the stitches of the preceding row. Although the head of the tassel becomes wider, there are still the same number of stitches, because each stitch is placed farther apart as the size of the ball increases.

There are many ways of adding variety and interest to tassels. Beads may be used for this purpose, while pieces of felt are most suitable for the enrichment of work of a bolder type.

To make decorative balls cut a piece of soft material $\frac{1}{2}$ inch wide and tapering gradually to a point. Roll this up, starting from the wide end, and secure with a few stitches. Then cover it with ball stitch or surface buttonholing.

Pompons

These are most suitable for decorating little caps for babies or young children. They can also be used to finish off the ends of a neck or waist string. They can be made in two ways :

(1) Cut two circles of cardboard. Place them together and cut out a circle in the middle. Wind wool or silk round both until they are well covered. Slip the sharp point of the scissors under the wool and cut round the edge. Separate the cardboard discs slightly and tie round the strands firmly between the discs. Slip off the discs and fluff up the threads.

(2) Wind the wool over a piece of cardboard as in making a tassel. The cardboard should be about $1\frac{3}{4}$ inch wide. When there are enough strands on the cardboard, slip a bodkin threaded with wool along one edge and tie the wool together firmly. Cut along the other end, fluff out the wool, and trim the edges.

FRINGES

It is very useful to be able to make a fringe, as it forms an effective finish to a variety of articles, such as scarfs, curtains, mats, towels, etc. There are many different ways of making fringes, a few of which are given here :

A Self Fringe or a fringe made by fraying the material.

Linen is most suitable for fraying. A few threads must be drawn from the edge of the material to the required depth, and the top of the loose portion is hemstitched or over-sewn to prevent the threads from unravelling further. Buttonholing or a herringbone stitch will serve the same purpose. The loose threads can now be frayed out to form a fringe, which may be knotted into a pattern or left plain.

A Wool Fringe for a Scarf.—This makes a very pretty finish to a scarf, and is an effective way of introducing a touch of colour if needed. It is not a difficult fringe to make.

Fringe the edge of the material to the required depth. Cut strands of wool a little more than twice the depth of the fringe. Each strand must be doubled, and the doubled end threaded through a large-eyed crewel needle. Pass the needle through the material from the wrong side about a quarter of an inch above the fringing ; pass it back again just below the point it came through first. Now unthread the needle and put the two ends of the strand through the loop. Pull the ends even, so that the loop lies close to the edge of the material. Do this all along the edge of the scarf, using two or more different colours. This fringe is now at the back of the fringe made of the material. If you wish the material fringe to form the background you must put in the needle from the right side first.

A Fringe of Silk and Wool for a Scarf.—Fringe the material to the right depth. Choose some skeins of flossy silk that matches the scarf and cut them into strands a little over twice the depth of the fringe. Pass each strand through the edge of the material at intervals of about half an inch, using an embroidery needle. Draw them through so that they hang evenly. Now tie two strands of silk with an equal number of threads from each side of the silk into a simple knot. Pull the knot up to the edge

FIGS. 115, 116, and 117.—A Fringe for the Border of a Curtain.

of the material. Knot the whole fringe in this way, smooth it
out, and cut the edge evenly.

A Fringe for the Border of a Curtain (Figs. 115, 116, 117).—
First work a buttonhole stitch (spaced along the edge. Fig. 115
shows how they are spaced). Thread the needle with four
threads of embroidery twists or embroidery wool. (You need
a large-eyed blunt-pointed needle.) Have the threads a little
over twice the length you want your fringe to be. Begin at
the left-hand side. Pass the needle downwards under the first
long buttonhole loop, and pull through, leaving half the length
above. Now pull this length left above down over the buttonhole edging and hold it in the left hand. Now pass the needle
from right to left over and under the length that is being held
down, then insert the needle in the next buttonhole stitch (this
time the needle will go upwards), pull it through leaving a little
loop below the edging ; this time pass the needle under and
over the *loop* from right to left. You now have the two ends
coming from the loop as in Fig. 115. Make both the ends even
and draw up fairly tightly to the edge. Begin the next knot in
the second loop of the buttonhole stitch and finish it in the third
loop. Go on in this way until the fringe is complete. Now begin
at the left again, take half the first group of threads and half
the second group and knot them together about half an inch
from the edging (a cardboard gauge can be used to keep the
meshes even) leaving long ends as in Fig. 116. When this row

is completed, begin again at the left and halve the strands and knot in the same way. This second knotting makes a diamond pattern as in Fig. 117.

A Tasselled Fringe.—Each tassel requires about ten to twelve strands of silk, (depending on the fineness of the silk), about 6 inches long for short tassels.

Fold each bundle of strands in half. If the tassels are to be fixed to loose material, pierce the material as close to the edge as possible with a steel crochet hook or stiletto. With the crochet hook draw the doubled end of the strands through the material. Now put the ends of the strands through the loop and pull the knot tightly. The tassels look better if they are put fairly close together.

If the material is a firm one, it is better to secure the hem with a knotted loop stitch, leaving the thread slack between each knot, and attach the tassels to the loop stitch instead of to the edge of the material.

How to cut Fringes.—Wind the wool or silk quite evenly around a cardboard gauge which should be a little wider than the depth of the fringe. Slip the point of the scissors under the top and cut the threads. The strands will now be all of an even length.

Bead Edging.—A pretty edging can be made of beads in the following way : Pick up two small beads on the needle and take a stitch into the edge of the material ; go back through one of the beads and pick up two more beads on the needle and repeat the process.

All these cords and fringes will be found very useful in connection with the simple upholstery and curtains and cushions described in Chapter XIV., " Making the Home Beautiful."

CHAPTER XIV

MAKING THE HOME BEAUTIFUL

Simple Upholstery, Special Stitches—Catch Stitch, Napery Hem. Loose
Covers. Cushions. Curtains. Pelmets.

IF you like making large, simple, beautiful things you will
enjoy trying to make your house pleasant and comfortable
with new loose covers, cushions, and curtains. A little home
upholstery indeed forms a pleasant change from ordinary plain
needlework and embroidery. No difficult cutting-out is needed,
for so many things are just plain squares or oblongs. Nearly
all the stitches are those you use for plain sewing. Your machine
will help you a great deal in this work. Here are two stitches
that prove helpful in this kind of work.

Catch Stitch.—This is used chiefly in pelmets to catch down
raw edges to interlinings. It is worked over a raw edge. Very
often single-turn hems are made with it on bulky materials such
as velvet and velours. These would not turn in twice flatly.
It is worked by bringing the needle up from the wrong side of
the edge to be caught down, well inside the edge. From these
pick up horizontally a thread or two of the interlining, just
below the raw edge of material ; move diagonally forward again,
this time upwards, pick up a short horizontal stitch in the
material—remember, well inside the edge. Go on alternately
picking up a horizontal stitch in the interlining and in the material
and pulling the thread taut, so that the material and interlining are firmly held by a continuous series of open V stitches
(see also Catch Stitch, Chapter IX., " Plain Sewing ").

Napery Hem.—This, as its name tells you, is used for hemming
household linens. It is sometimes called the French hem—
top sewing and upright hemming. Its stitches go exceedingly

well with the coarse weaves of household linen. It is without doubt the best hand hem for table linen, linen runners, cretonne and printed linen curtains, and handkerchiefs.

To work it, you must double-fold the material for a hem. Then crease the whole hem backwards to lie along the right side of the material. Now overcast finely along this new crease, through all three thicknesses (the two of the hem and one of the main part of the material). Remember that the needle must always be inserted right *across* the crease, so that on the right side the stitches are very tiny vertical ones and on the wrong side they are slanting.

Piping plays a large part in simple upholstery; we have already dealt a little with piping in Chapter IX., " Plain Sewing and Trimmings for Plain Sewing." Piping in upholstery is a little different from piping in plain sewing. Cord, sold in hanks of several yards, is always used in upholstery.

It is wise to shrink piping cord before you use it by boiling it, because it sometimes causes puckering when the article containing it is washed.

To cover the cord use either ready-made bias tape (first iron the prepared creases out of it) or bias-cut strips of self or contrasting material. The cutting and joining of bias strips has already been described in Chapter IX.

We will begin by describing how to make loose covers. Some people find these somewhat difficult compared with cushions and curtains.

Loose Covers

Loose covers can serve many purposes. Firstly, they can be used to protect the delicate fabrics of settees and chairs; and secondly, to brighten up a room where the furniture is shabby, or to make a room look uniform when all the furniture is not covered with the same material.

Whichever is your object in wanting to make loose covers, you must make them with great care so that they fit well. Badly fitting covers, however beautiful the material of which they are made, will make a room look untidy and ill-cared-for.

Choice of Material.—As with curtains, the choice of material will depend on the wallpaper, and the same rule holds good—

never have patterned materials if the wallpaper is patterned, although some conventional designs will match quite well with patterned wallpaper.

Cretonne was the popular material for covers years ago, but since covers are now being used more for decorative purposes, artificial silk slubs and repps and printed linens are the vogue.

The artificial silks can be bought in a wonderful range of colours, both plain and shot, but they are more expensive than the linen or cretonne, and should not be used if the covers are likely to have a great deal of hard wear and require washing very often.

Large-patterned materials are always wasteful. If the material has a large spray of flowers, that spray would have to be placed in the middle of the back of the chair, on the seat, and on the sides or top of each arm ; this means that the rest of the material, unless it can be used for insets or frills or pipings, is wasted.

Plain or striped materials are more economical and more easy to handle than patterned ones.

Quantity of Material Required.—The chair or settee must be measured carefully. As a general rule the seams of a loose cover must correspond with the seams on the furniture covering —so the measurements must be taken from the seams.

The Back of the Chair.—Measure the outside of the back from the roll or seam to the bottom of the chair, then add on 2 inches for turnings. Write down each measurement as you take it. Now measure over the roll and down to the seat in front, and add on 2 inches for turnings and 3 inches for tucking down the cover. If a linen cover is being made, add 6 inches.

The Seat.—Measure from the back of the seat to the front, add the same amount for tucking in and turnings. Add to this the depth of the straight piece in front of the chair from the seat to the bottom of the chair, and again add turnings.

The Arms.—Take the measure for these in the same way as for the back of the chair—and remember to double the measure for the two arms.

Add these measurements together to find how many yards you will require, then allow one yard extra for the front pieces of the arms and for piping.

A settee is measured in exactly the same way, but you must multiply the seat measurement and the front and outside of the settee back by two or three, according to the number of widths of material the settee will take to cover it.

Buy, at the same time as the material, some cotton to match, a box of steel pins, piping cord, and needles.

Points to remember while cutting the Covers :

1. The selvedge threads must run from the top to the bottom of each piece and from the back to the front of the seat.

2. If the material is likely to shrink—cotton and linen goods usually do—fit the covers loosely, that is, do not pin the cover close to the chair.

3. One pattern on the material must run down the middle of each large piece of the cover. If there is a pattern reaching from one side of the material to the other, be sure to place one of these patterns exactly in the middle of the inside of the back and in the middle of the seat. A great deal of material is bound to be wasted in doing this, but the result would be disastrous if it is neglected.

4. Pin each piece of material in place exactly as is described in detail later on for the outside of the back of a chair cover.

Cutting out the Covers.—This is done on the chair or settee.

Begin at the outside of the back of the chair, at the seam under the roll. Put the right side of the material to the chair and pin it down the middle of the back, allowing turnings of $1\frac{1}{2}$ inch to project above the seam and down one side. Smooth the material with the hands outwards from the pins and put in a row of pins down each side, smooth upwards and put the pins along the seam, then downwards and pin along the bottom edge. Now press the material over the edges of the chair, and cut it off $1\frac{1}{2}$ inch beyond this crease.

For the front of the back, pin the material right side to the chair, all down the middle, allowing it to project, as before, $1\frac{1}{2}$ inch beyond the seam and on one side. Cut off the extra material on the other side to within $1\frac{1}{2}$ inch as far as the arm.

Run the fingers across the material just where the back meets the seat, measure from this crease the allowance for turnings and " tuck in," then cut off the material. Run the fingers down the material where the arms meet the back—cut the material off

1½ inch beyond this crease. Start at the back of the seat and pin the material to the piece covering the back—edge to edge —then push the material well down at the back of the seat. At the sides allow for turnings and " tuck in," and in the front of the seat allow for turnings only.

The Front of the Seat.—Pin the material to the front of the seat covering, making the join come exactly over the seam on the chair. Smooth the material over the edges of the chair and then cut it off 1½ inch beyond the crease.

The Arms and Sides.—Cover the outside of the arms and sides of the chair in the same way as the outside of the back, and the inside of the arms in the same way as the inside of the back. Pin the outside of the arms to the outside of the chair-back and the inside part to the inside of the chair-back—the material must not be pulled tightly over the chair when pinning this latter seam, push it well into the joins of the back and arm and then pin the seam.

The Front of the Arms.—Cut two pieces of material roughly to fit this part of the chair. Pin them into position, starting at the top of the arm and making the join come exactly over the seam of the chair. You may find the material over the top of the arm will not set quite flat into the front-arm piece. If you do find this, then pin little darts in the over-arm piece until it does set quite flat—remember that two or three small darts are always better than one large one. Pin the " tuck in " at the sides of the seat to the " tuck in " of the inside-arm pieces, then push them well down into the crevice.

The chair is now covered. Go over every seam, adjusting pins where necessary. Make quite sure that the seams of the cover are over the seams of the chair and that they are quite straight—an uneven seam is very ugly. Sit on the chair and get some one to tell you if there is any pull on any of the seams—look especially at the seam between the inside back and inside arm.

When you are quite certain that the cover fits well but not tightly, cut down all the turnings to within 1 inch. Unpin one of the back seams until it is possible to take off the chair cover. Be sure to remove all the pins that were used to pin the material to the chair, otherwise they may tear the chair covering.

Tacking up the Cover.—Tack the seams under the roll of the arm and the roll of the back of the chair—also the seams at the sides and back of the seat, and any darts that have been made.

Prepare a piping cord for all the other seams and for the bottom of the chair cover. Unpin about 6 inches of a seam at a time and tack the piping between the seam.

Stitching the Cover.—Stitch all the seams that are not piped, and then the ones that are, as close up to the roll as possible. Neaten the lower edge of the cover with a piping cord—the method of preparing the cord and fixing it will be found in the Plain Needlework section, Chapter IX.

The Opening.—Cut a piece of material $2\frac{1}{2}$ inches wide and twice the length of the opening.   Put the right side of this strip to the right side of the cover and run the two edges together, so that the running stitches are in a continuous line with the seam ; carry the piece up one side of the opening and down the other. Cut the turnings level and fold the bind over them, turn down the inner edge, and fell exactly on top of the running stitches.

Turn the binding thus made under at the join on the right-hand side and allow it to project out on the left-hand side—work a bar at the top of the opening. Sew hooks and eyes on this bind about 1 inch apart—not more, or the opening will bulge. Press-fasteners can be used, but unless they are strong they will spring open.

A Frilled Cover.—Make the cover in just the same way as described above, but instead of neatening the bottom edge with the piping cord, tack it into position with the raw edges level.

Now make the frill. Measure from the piping cord to the ground, add the amount required to make a hem at the bottom and $\frac{1}{2}$ inch for turnings at the top of the frill—this will give you the width of the strip. Measure all round the cover—half as much again or twice as much, according to how full you wish the frill to be, will give you the length of the strip.

Cut the strip out, with the selvedge threads running across the width of the strip ; make all the necessary joins in the strip, and then turn down and hem the lower edge and ends of the strip. Boxpleat the frill and tack it to the lower edge of the cover, with the raw edges level and the right sides together. Stitch close to the piping cord.

The frill may be gathered instead of boxpleated if you prefer it that way. The chair cover with the frill is not so fashionable as the plainer, more severe type described above.

To cover a Settee.—This is just the same as making a chair cover, except that the outside and inside of the back and the seat of the settee will require more than one piece of material to cover them, and so joins must be made.

Place a piece of material, as described in making a loose cover for a chair, exactly in the middle of the outside of the back of the settee, pin securely, and then cut it off at the lower edge. Now place a second and a third piece, one each side of the first, in just the same way and pin them together, matching the pattern exactly. Cut the two side pieces down to within $1\frac{1}{2}$ inch of the chair edges.

Cover the inside of the settee back and the seat, covering first the middle and then the sides of each, and proceeding in the same way as in covering the chair. The arms and sides will be exactly the same as the chair.

When the settee is quite covered, pin all the seams together, push the " tuck in " well down into the crevices, and allow several people to sit down on it, to see if there is any pull on the seams ; make any adjustments necessary, and proceed with the finishing as described before under the " Chair Cover."

Other Types of Settees and Chairs.—Many of the modern types of settees and chairs are flat on the top of the arms and back. Making covers for this type of suite is just as easy as any other, and the procedure is the same. Start at the top of the large pieces, pinning the material to the chair at the seam, and work downwards. When all the big pieces are in position, cut out the strips to cover the tops and fronts of the arms, and the top and back of the suite. The seams of the chair will help you. Then cut down the turning to within $1\frac{1}{2}$ inch, and proceed as before.

Another way of finishing the Lower Edge.—A quick and neat way of finishing the lower edge of covers is to cut the back, sides, and front about 4 inches longer than necessary. When the cover is finished, with the exception of the lower edge, turn down and stitch a hem on all four sides. Sew tapes on to each corner and fasten them under the chair. On a settee several tapes will be necessary along its length.

CUSHIONS

For comfort one cannot have too many cushions in a room ; they add, moreover, to its charm if they are attractive in shape and colour.

A shabby room can generally be brightened up by the addition of a few wisely-chosen new cushions. This can be done at very little expense if small remnants of material are used, for these can often be bought cheaply and are very suitable.

In the chapters on Wool Craft and Felt Work and Leather Work we have said a little about cushion covers in felt, oil baize, and leather ; in the chapter on Quilting we have described quilted cushions ; but here we want to explain exactly how cushions are made—and not only their covers.

Many people only make cushion *covers*, because they say the cushions themselves can be bought so cheaply. But if you want a cushion of a certain size or a distinctive or odd-shaped cushion, you must make your own.

Almost any kind of material can be used, either furnishing fabrics or dress materials of silk, cotton, or linen. The good parts of a velvet cloak or silk frock or a pair of curtains can often be adapted to make excellent cushion covers.

For hard wear, choose linen or crash, either plain or ornamented with appliqué or embroidery. Slub repps wear well, and can be bought in a variety of beautiful colours, which are usually fadeless.

Cushions for the car can be made from dyed hessian, thick cloth, or suède. A bundle of scraps can often be bought cheaply, and, when sewn together, make a very attractive, strong cushion. (See chapter on Leather Work.)

For dainty, decorative cushions, taffeta, Japanese silk, or satin should be used.

Square Cushions.—Cut two squares of material the size you want your cushion to be, making an allowance for turnings. If your cushion is to be trimmed or embroidered, it must be done now, before starting to make up the cover. If remnants are to be used, join them together with fancy stitches or ribbon or braid to hide the joins. Of course the pieces must be arranged symmetrically and the colours must harmonise.

A plain silk cushion can be trimmed by stitching a piece of wide ribbon, or an odd piece of silver or gold tissue, across one corner of the square, or straight down the middle of the cushion. Tassels sewn to the corners make a very elegant finish to a square cushion.

Put the two squares together, right sides facing, tack and stitch the edges together along three sides and just round the corners of the fourth side. Press the seams open and turn the case on to the right side. Sew a cord over the seam, making a loop or loops at the corners—at the open end the cord must be sewn to one side of the cushion, in a continuous line with the seam. Slip the cushion in the case, and slip-stitch the open end. (For Slip Stitch, see Chapter IX.)

Piping cords are used more often than cords. Prepare the cord by covering it with a crossway strip of material, either the same or in contrast to the cover. Tack and sew it between the two squares, as described in the Plain Needlework Section under the heading of " Piping." At the opening, sew the piping to one square, and slip-stitch the other into position, after the cushion is in the case.

Sometimes an opening is wanted on a washable cover. Instead of working the slip-stitching as described above, run a strip of material, 2½ inches wide, all round the opening—right sides together. Join the ends of the strips together and then fold over the strip, turn in the inner edge and fell it down exactly on the previous running stitches. This false piece is tucked inside the cushion and press-fasteners sewn on at regular intervals. Soft buttons and buttonholes may be used instead.

Bolster Cushions.—These are more suitable for settees or couches. They are usually about 26 inches long and 24 inches round. This is an easy way of covering a bolster cushion. Cut a piece of material wide enough to go loosely round and 1 inch extra for turnings and about 16 inches longer than the cushion. Join the strip lengthways and add any trimming. A panel or panels of ruched material or a strip of ribbon or material of contrasting colour is quite effective. Turn down a 2-inch hem at both ends of the tube and slip-stitch them.

Put the cushion in the case, then gather and draw up the ends of the tube close up to the cushion. Cover the gathering thread with a braid or cord. This will make a little frill at each end of the cushion, but, if you like, the frill could be made of the same material as the panel of trimming.

Second Method of making a Bolster Cushion.—Cut a strip of material the exact length of the cushion and wide enough to go round it. Stitch it lengthways to form a tube shape. Cut two rounds of material the size of the ends of the bolster and pipe the edges. Now stitch the " rounds " to the two ends of the tube-shaped piece, leaving as small an opening as possible for putting in the cushion. Slip-stitch the opening strongly. A small motif of silk embroidery can be appliquéd on to the middle of each " round," or two tassels make a very good finish.

Ruched Cushions.—These are usually made of fine silk material such as taffeta, plain and shot, or Japanese silk. Soft artificial silks can also be used.

Cut out two rounds of material, one for each side—the size depends on your own personal taste. It is a good idea to look at some in a shop and then you will know which you like the better—a large or small " round." If the material used is very soft and likely to pull out of shape easily, line it with a piece of strong calico. Now pipe the edges of the " round." A small piece of embroidery worked on these rounds is very effective. If you decide to embroider your cushion, it must be done now, before proceeding with the making up.

Pin the " rounds " on to the cushion, and measure from one to the other, over the edge of the cushion. Cut a strip of material as wide as this measurement, and allow 1 inch for turnings. The length of the strip will depend on how full you want the ruching to be.

Join the strip along the short sides, and gather it on each long side—pull up the gathering threads to fit the " rounds." Stitch one end to one piped edge, as described in the Plain Needlework Section, but only stitch about half of the other side. Slip the cover over the cushion, then pin, and tack the rest of the seam. This must be slip-stitched very neatly and strongly.

The cushion can be made more elaborate by working gauging or gathered tucks in the strip before it is joined to the " rounds."

Tucks, in groups of three, can be worked in the middle of the strip and again half towards the raw edges. Piping cords, or a fine white string, should be run in the tucks, to draw them up to the size of the cushion.

Directions for working these trimmings will be found under the heading of " Trimmings " in Chapter IX.

Box Cushions.—These are very fashionable just now. They can be made any shape—square, triangular, round, or oblong. If you prefer any other shape, take a piece of paper and cut out different shapes until you find the one that pleases you. Then make it up in the same way as described below for a triangular cushion.

Fold a square of material in half, to form a triangle. Cut it along the fold to make the two sides of the cushion. Whatever shape your cushion is to be, cut out two pieces from the pattern you have made. Now work any embroidery or appliqué. Join on an inset 2 inches wide right round the triangle by machining the edges together on the wrong side and then on the right side, machine a row $\frac{1}{4}$ inch from the edge—this makes a French seam standing out on the right side. Oversew this edge with a thick embroidery cotton, first one way and then the other—this will make a cross stitch over the edge. This method is particularly suitable for thick materials. The edges of a suède cushion should be stitched on the right side only.

Leave the middle of one side unstitched, put the cushion inside, then slip-stitch the edges together and finish the line of stitching by hand to complete the French seam—then finish the cross stitch.

The seams may be piped in the same way as has been described before.

Box Cushions with Ruched Insets.—Some box cushions look well when made up in velvet, with ruched insets of taffeta or any other silk.

Cut out two pieces of material the shape the cushion is required, for the top and bottom of the cushion. Pipe round the edges, using a thick piping cord, and cover it with material the same as the top, or, if the cushion is not to be embroidered, in a contrasting colour. Measure round each side of the cushion and cut out the silk for the gathered insets one and a half times or twice this length, joining it as many times as may be necessary.

Divide the strip into divisions and mark with pins—three

7

divisions for a triangular cushion, four for a square, and so on. Mark the divisions on the top and bottom of the cushion in the same way. Gather each side of the strip, draw up the thread to fit the cushion, and then tack it to the piped edge, placing the division marks together and distributing the fullness evenly. Stitch as close to the piping cord as possible, leaving open part of one side. Turn the cover right side out and put the cushion in. Slip-stitch the remainder of the seam which has been left open.

When you have made one of the cushions described above, you will probably be able to copy any other kind that you may see in a shop or friend's house.

To make a Tassel.—Wind the silk or wool over a card, the length the tassel is needed, then tie the strands together very tightly. Take the silk off the card and tie the double row of strands again, 1 inch below the first tie. Put a knob of cotton-wool between these two ties and this will form a head for the tassel—this can be as large or as small as you like. Now make a crochet chain and wind it round and round the head, securing it with invisible stitches here and there. Leave an end of chain by which to attach it to the cushion.

Cut the loops at the other end of the tassel, and if the threads are at all crinkled or do not hang quite straight, hold the tassel in the steam from the kettle and shake it. (See also Cords, Tassels, and Fringes, Chapter XIII.)

The Filling for the Cushion

This makes all the difference to the comfort of the cushion.

Down.—This makes a beautifully soft cushion, but it is very expensive.

Feathers.—These are good and make a soft cushion, and they are cheaper than a down filling. A bolster that is no longer wanted in the home would make the filling for a number of cushions.

If you live in the country it is generally possible to buy feathers quite cheaply, and it is a simple matter to prepare them.

Put half a pound of lime into half a gallon of water, and allow it to stand for a day or two. Pour the water into a bath, leaving the lime behind. Soak the feathers in the lime water for a few hours, then strain the water off by pouring lime water and feathers into a pillow-case or bag. Sew up the bag so that the feathers cannot come out.

Wash the feathers in the bag in just the same way as you would wash woollens—in warm soapy water, and rinsing in warm water. While the feathers are drying, keep shaking them from one end of the bag to the other.

Kapok.—This is a vegetable down and it is very cheap. It has one disadvantage that it is inclined to become bumpy and hard when the cushion has been used for some time. Before filling a case with kapok, pull each little piece thoroughly and work over it more than once, then the cushion will probably last for years without getting bumpy.

To make a Cushion Case.—Use ticking if the cushion is to be covered with a thick fabric, and something strong but not so stiff, such as unbleached calico, if the cushion is to be covered with a dainty material.

Whatever is used must first be soaped with yellow soap to prevent the feathers from working through the material. Machine the case together and soap the seams to fill up the holes made by the machine needle.

Fill the case with whatever filling you have chosen, turn in the edges of the open end, and oversew strongly.

When filling the case, spread a sheet over the floor, and when the work is finished, gather it up, and little or no mess will be made.

If the cushion is to be an oblong or a bolster shape, or any of the newer shapes for cushions, the case must be made into the same shape, but square cushions can very often be put into a round or triangular-shaped case quite satisfactorily.

CURTAINS

Curtains reflect the personality of the mistress of a house even more than furniture—for whereas there are only a few designs of furniture from which to choose, there are literally hundreds of materials from which to choose curtains, and many ways in which to make them and arrange them. So before deciding on your curtains, give the matter plenty of thought and consideration.

The colour of the curtains will depend on the colour of the

furniture and carpet and on the aspect of the room. If the furniture is old or shabby, be very careful that the new curtains do not emphasise their drabness. Warm colours, such as red and yellow, are best for a north or east aspect, while cool greens and mauves are more suitable for sunny rooms.

If the wall paper or the furniture is patterned with flowers, especially if they are large ones, it would not be advisable to have patterned curtains. Choose the predominating colour of the furniture and buy a plain material to match.

The amount of money one has to spend will largely determine the kind of material bought, but if the right material is chosen for the curtains and they are well made, and especially if a little hand embroidery is added, curtains of distinction and charm will be the result.

Appliqué work or stencilling are quick ways of getting a striking result.

Many curtain materials are absolutely fadeless, and it pays one to buy this kind, even if the initial cost is more.

Bedroom Curtains.—These are usually made of the same material as the bedspread.

A cheap and effective set can be made by using cretonne for the middle of the bedspread—one width of material for a single bed, with a border (half the width of the material) of plain material the colour of the background or predominating colour of the cretonne. The curtains are made in the same way, but with a narrower border of the plain material.

Sometimes the flowers or birds can be cut out of the cretonne and appliquéd on to a plain material to form a border at the bottom of the curtains and round the sides of the bedspread. Another way is to arrange the flowers just here and there, as your fancy dictates.

Nursery Curtains.—Materials on which there is printed nursery rhymes, animals, etc., are very pleasing for this purpose. It is a very simple matter to cut out animals from advertisements or other pictures and use them as patterns for cutting out the shapes in material to be appliquéd on to plain curtains and bedspreads.

Cotton materials of fast colours that will withstand the washtub over and over again are the best for nursery use.

Dining-Room or Lounge Curtains.—Printed linen curtains, lined or unlined, are charming for summer curtains. For the winter, damask of silk or wool or artificial silk slub repps are suitable materials.

Plain coloured serge, velour, velvet, or linen, with a stencilled design for a border, is very effective and quickly worked. All instructions are given with the stencilling outfit, and good stencils can be bought already cut from art dealers.

Bold designs should be chosen for appliqué or stencilling work. (See the chapters in this book on Appliqué Work and Stencilling.)

Kitchen Curtains and Bathroom.—Baize cloth or American cloth is often used, and this is very economical. (For baize-cloth curtains, see Chapter XVI., " Wool Craft and Felt Work.")

Some people use rubber sheeting for the bathroom, as this, like baize cloth, is not affected by the constant steam.

Drawing-Room Curtains.—A patterned silk or plain velvets to match the suite are best for the drawing-room.

If you are going to embroider your curtains, you must choose a somewhat elaborate design and be prepared to spend a good deal of time and trouble in the working of it, as a drawing-room does not, as a rule, require the bold effects which are generally achieved by quickly worked designs.

Curtain Fittings.—The next point to be decided is the manner in which the curtain is to be hung. Rings on a rod was the old way of fixing curtains, but metal runners and wheels, which are rustless, are mostly used nowadays.

If you have poles fixed in your house and you do not want to go to the expense of new fittings, a pelmet is a good way of bringing the appearance of the curtains up to date. A board, like a narrow shelf, is fixed by brackets above the window-frame, and the pelmet is attached to the sides and front, thus covering the old poles and rings.

It is as well to buy the stronger and more expensive type of curtain fixtures, as there is the possibility of the cheaper makes giving trouble, and it costs as much to have the cheap makes fixed as it does the more expensive.

Amount of Material Required.—Curtains are usually made one and a half times the width of the window. When the two widths of the material is not sufficient to do this, a half-width must be added to the outside of each curtain—the pattern on the material being matched very carefully so that the join does not show.

Measure the window from the top down to where the curtain is wanted, add to this measurement the amount needed for the heading at the top and the hems at the foot. Multiply this by the number of widths of material required to cover the windows, and you have the amount of material that is required for your curtains.

If the material is thin and the curtain is to be unlined, allow for a wide hem at the foot, in order to make the curtain heavier and so hang more gracefully.

When there is a large design on the material and a join has to be made in the curtain, a certain amount of material is bound to be wasted in matching the design on both widths, so a little extra material must be bought to allow for this.

Short Net Curtains.—Curtain net shrinks in the wash, so cut them out generously.

When measuring for the amount of material required, allow twice the amount required for the hems and heading at the top and for the hem at the bottom.

Turn down a solid hem—the first and second turning the same width—at the top and the bottom. This makes the heading a little stiffer so that it will not fall over; also the curtain will hang more gracefully for having a heavier hem. Moreover, unless you make the first and second turnings of your hem the same, the hem looks unsightly on net or lace curtains, because the first turning shows through and makes the hem thicker in one place than the other. Tack the hems carefully, keeping them quite straight to a thread.

It is a great mistake to stitch the curtains by machine; but if this must be done, stitch through a piece of paper at the same time as the net, and then the curtain will not be pulled out of shape.

Fasten down the top hem by ordinary hemming stitches. Measure up quarter inch, or the amount required for the rod, and work a row of running stitches. Fasten down the bottom hem in the same way as the top hem, or one or several rows of running stitches may be worked in the same, or contrasting, colour to the curtain.

It is not advisable to use a wire expanding curtain-rod for net curtains, as it will be found that the springs get entangled with the open mesh, and it is not easy to remove them without tearing the curtain.

To make Unlined Curtains.—First cut the material into lengths, being careful that the same pattern is at the top of each length. Make the necessary joins by top sewing the selvedges together if possible, taking care to match the pattern. Neaten the sides with slip-stitched hems or with galon or braid.

Turn down and stitch or fell by hand the hems at the top and bottom of the curtain. The top hem is best secured by one of the patent tapes, such as " Rufflette," then the fullness can be pulled up by the cords provided ; hooks or rings slipped under the cords ready to hang on to the cornice pole, patent runway, or any other kind of support to be used.

The lower hem is sometimes weighted with lead weights, to make the curtain hang more straight.

To make Lined Curtains.—When curtains are intended to keep out the draught or the pattern on the wrong side is some-what ugly, then the curtains must be lined. Choose a fadeless plain material of the predominating shade of the curtains or one in complete contrast to the curtains.

Any embroidery or appliqué work must be done before the lining is stitched in. If there is a fold in the material it must be pressed out.

Cut the lining 1 inch smaller all round than the curtain. Turn down the curtain 1½ inch on to the wrong side. Tack and catch-stitch down, taking up the top threads only, on the single material, so that no stitches show on the right side. The corners must be mitred. Press on the wrong side under a thin cloth.

Now turn down the edges of the lining and pin over the raw edges of the curtain. This is best done flat on the table, so that the lining does not pucker the curtain. Top-hem the lining into place. (For Top-hemming, see Chapter XXV.)

PELMETS

A pelmet should only be used if the ceiling of the room is high—if it is low, a pelmet will make it look still lower.

It should be borne in mind that a pelmet always adds rather a dignified air to a room, so that if this is not required, fit a pleated or gathered frill above the curtains instead of a pelmet.

To make a Pelmet.—Cut a piece of paper the length of the sides and front of the pelmet board and a little wider than you have decided to have the pelmet. Now cut the lower edge of the paper the shape that you wish. You will find this quite easy, if you look in any furniture catalogue or showroom to give you ideas. The edge may be left straight.

Cut this shape in quite stiff material, such as tailor's canvas or buckrum. Using the same pattern, cut out the pelmet with 1-inch turnings all round and a lining with ½-inch turnings.

To make up the pelmet, put the material on the table with the wrong side up—pin the canvas to the material, starting from the middle and working out to the sides. Fold the turnings over the canvas and catch-stitch them, being careful not to allow any stitches to show through on the right side. If there is a curved edge on the pelmet, the turnings must be snipped to make it set quite flat, and all corners should be carefully mitred.

Any embroidery should now be worked, unless buckrum has been used, when embroidery or appliqué work must be done before mounting.

Very pretty motifs can be bought to give a good effect—geometrical designs worked in braid or galon is another way of trimming a pelmet. Press carefully on the wrong side.

Now turn in the edges of the lining, and fell over the raw edges of the pelmet.

More ideas for making the home beautiful will be found in Chapter XVI., " Wool Craft and Felt Work " ; Chapter XV., " Tapestry and Needlework Rugs " ; and Chapter XVII., " Stencilling." Indeed, you will be able to find ideas in almost every chapter.

TAPESTRY AND NEEDLEWORK RUGS

What *Tapestry* is. Materials. Stitches : Tent Stitch or Petit Point, Cross Stitch Again, Gobelin Stitch, Rice Stitch, Oriental Stitch, Jacquard Stitch and Byzantine Stitch. Tapestry Chain Stitch. Jacobean Embroidery. Step Stitch Weaving. Florentine Embroidery, Stool Tops. Finishing Stool Tops.
NEEDLEWORK RUGS—Cross Stitch Rugs. Straight Gobelin Stitch, Hungarian Stitches, Knitting Stitch.

NOTHING perhaps makes the home so pleasant as a cheerful fireside, and you can make your fireside cheerful with pretty rugs and gaily embroidered cushions and stools. The kind of embroidery you need for the cover of your stool or chair-back or cushions is called :

TAPESTRY

This is a very old form of embroidery. It is also known as needlepoint. Tapestry, strictly speaking, is a fabric woven on a loom. Hand-made tapestry is an all-over embroidery worked closely on canvas. It often depicts pictorial subjects like the Bayeux Tapestry, which is really embroidered work of the time of William the Conqueror. In these days we generally include under the name " tapestry " every kind of embroidery done on counted threads, and in which the stitches *entirely cover the stuff* on which the work is done.

As tapestry is firm, heavy, and strong, but will not wash, it is mainly used for furnishing such as chairseats, footstools, firescreens, wall hangings, cushion covers, etc., and sometimes smaller articles like handbags. It is slow work, but it is interesting.

Very elaborate work, especially pictorial tapestry, is best done on a frame ; an upright frame of course is necessary, not the hoop frame described in Chapter I. But large frames are fairly expensive and moreover take up a great deal of room, so many people manage their tapestry in the hand. In this case it may be helpful to weight the end of the work with dressmakers' weights to keep it from puckering. This of course only applies to large work.

We will begin a more detailed account of tapestry by first describing the materials used and then the most useful stitches, and finally designs and useful articles.

Materials—(1) *Canvas.*—Tapestry is worked on canvas. Two kinds of canvas are generally used—(i) plain or single-thread canvas, and (ii) double-thread or Penelope canvas. The latter is the most popular because its threads are more easily counted.

Different makers make different varieties of tapestry canvas, and the mesh varies. In tapestry work it is most important for the mesh of the canvas to match the wool or thread used. Large mesh canvas is no good for fine wool, and thick wool is no use on a fine mesh. So choose your canvas and your wool carefully. Special tapestry wool can be bought in very lovely colours that make tapestry work a joy.

One should not hurry over one's tapestry work, but keep it for a pleasant pastime.

When choosing canvas, remember it is a great help to have easily counted threads, because the usual method of working a design is to count it out on the threads from a chart, as in cross stitch. At the present day many designs can be bought already printed on the canvas, so that it is only necessary for the worker to cover each portion with its appropriate colour. This is not so interesting as working out one's own design.

(2) *Needles.*—The proper tapestry needles are long, strong, and blunt, with eyes that can be easily threaded.

(3) *Thread.*—For a long time silk and wool were the only materials used for tapestry, but within the last few years great progress has been made in the manufacture and dyeing of cotton threads, and these have begun to play a great part in tapestry work. All the stitches that are described here can also be carried out with *raffia* on canvas. (See Chapter XXI., on Raffia Work.)

THE MOST USEFUL STITCHES FOR TAPESTRY

(1) *Tent Stitch*, or *Petit Point* (Fig. 118).—This stitch has a confusing number of names for it is also known as needlepoint,

half-cross stitch, and tapestry work. It is the best known of all
the many stitches used in tapestry work or needlepoint, and many
pieces of work are carried out entirely in tent stitch or petit point.

The name half-cross stitch is a good working description.
Simply make the first slanting half of a cross stitch (see Chapter
VI.), working over either one or two threads of the canvas
according to the size of the stitch desired. These slanting
stitches must be worked closely side by side so that they cover
the surface completely. It is best to put the needle in upright.
Couched tent stitch is used in tapestry when, owing to the large
size of the canvas mesh or the comparative fineness of the working
thread, tent stitch does not cover the surface well. Work it
exactly as for tent stitch, but couch down with your stitches
another thread, which lies under the stitches and pads them,
thus giving greater solidity to the result.

(2) *Cross Stitch* (see Chapter VI.).—This is also strictly
speaking a tapestry stitch, but it is used in many different forms
of embroidery. It fills up more than tent stitch, so it can be worked
on a more open-mesh canvas or with a finer thread than tent stitch.

(3) *Gobelin Stitch.*—This is a variation of tent stitch. It is worked
so that it covers two vertical threads, but, like tent stitch, only one
horizontal one, giving slightly diagonal lines which are rather deep.

(4) *Rice Stitch* (Fig. 119).—Begin by filling in the whole with
big cross stitches, covering four threads each way ; then over
these work the so-called " rice " stitch. These cross the four
points of the big cross stitches and meet in the space between
them where they form another cross. This stitch is very decorative
and may be done in two colours. The big cross stitches should
be done in rather coarse cotton, the " rice " stitches in finer
cotton of a different colour.

(5) *Oriental Stitch* (Fig. 120).—In this stitch you make four
diagonal stitches, over one, two, three, and four crossings of
the threads of the canvas respectively, these four stitches form
triangles one above the other. The empty spaces between the rows
are filled with gobelin stitches covering two threads, as in Fig. 120.

(6) *Jacquard Stitch and Byzantine Stitch* (Fig. 121).—If you
have a large plain surface to cover you should choose a stitch
that is itself a pattern, Jacquard stitch and Byzantine stitch and
many others will be found to produce the effect of brocaded stuff.

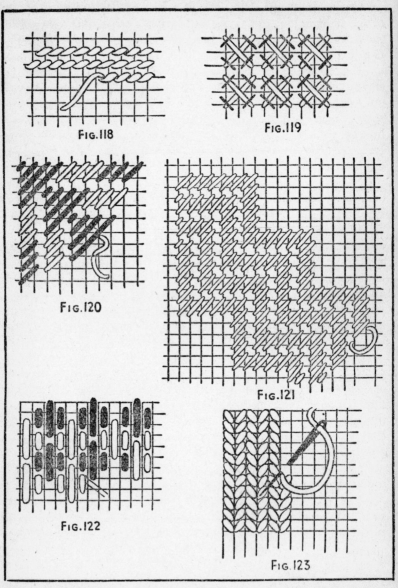

FIG. 118.—Tent Stitch.   FIG. 119.—Rice Stitch.   FIG. 120.—Oriental Stitch.
FIG. 121.—Byzantine Stitch.   FIG. 122.—Hungarian Stitch.   FIG. 123.—
Knitting Stitch.

In the Jacquard stitch the first row of stitches is composed of six slanting stitches underneath one another over two double threads, and six beside one another, from left to right, also over two double threads.

The second row consists of the same number of stitches similarly worked downwards and from left to right, only over one double thread, and so on. It is very like the Byzantine stitch shown in Fig. 121 ; in the Byzantine stitch you make the same number of stitches as in the Jacquard stitch, but with this difference that the two rows of stitches are made either over two double threads or four single ones.

(7) *Tapestry Chain Stitch.*—Ordinary chain stitch worked on canvas was used for many old pieces of needlework. It is softer than many of the other stitches, so it is suitable for indefinite borders, it is also a good blending stitch. Work it just as for ordinary chain stitch (see Chapter II.), but picking up a thread of the canvas at each stitch. It cannot be worked to and fro like most tapestry stitches. Begin each row separately and keep a different needle for each colour. This saves constant re-threading. Many stitches already described in Chapters II. and III. can be used in tapestry work, for example, the long-and-short stitch, stem stitch, fishbone stitch, etc.

Designs.—It is a great help to study old designs ; geometrical patterns always look well, and there are countless ways of arranging these and other conventional designs. Naturalistic designs, landscapes, flowers, etc., need perhaps more thought, but they can be of great interest and beauty. Sometimes the design occupies the whole area. More often it is surrounded by a dark or neutral-coloured background.

There are many more tapestry stitches than these we have described here, but very few of these are used by modern workers. Most of the modern work to-day is done in tent stitch or petit point—tea-cosies, bags, cushion covers, handkerchief sachets, or other sachets, footstool covers, etc., all look well in this stitch.

JACOBEAN EMBROIDERY

This work, that has lately been revived, is an imitation of the kind of embroidery done in England in the seventeenth century. The embroidery is done in fine coloured wools on twilled linen or Bolton sheeting of natural tint. Special wools are now sold for Jacobean embroidery of the correct colour and texture—for example, Penelope Crewel Wool. The Jacobean designs and colourings are particularly beautiful : trees, birds, fruits, and flowers are all intertwined and balanced in a large sweeping symmetry of curves and a soft, rich harmony of tones, the whole effect of grace and strength being greatly aided by the skilful combination of stitches—one of the most frequently used stitches being long-and-short stitch.

STEP-STITCH WEAVING OR EMBROIDERY (Fig. 124)

This is really a form of old Norwegian embroidery. It finds a ready welcome among the new art handicrafts. It is very useful for handbags, purses, runners, chair seats, stool seats, etc. The process is well adapted to modern geometric patterns as the stitch is applied to a stiff net foundation with a mesh of eight squares to the inch.

If medium weight wool yarn is used only one stitch is required to a net mesh, thus making quick progress possible in weaving by this method.

Under-arm purses about 4 inches by $7\frac{1}{2}$ can be made in about two or three hours, and they are both strong and beautiful.

The best needles for the work are $2\frac{1}{2}$-inch blunt tapestry needles.

As the stitches are all laid perpendicularly, the process is very simple. Starting with a large stitch, the stitches get smaller and smaller, thus making *the steps.* Plan the pattern carefully first. All working threads begin and end in the back of the canvas and are carried under the canvas to the nearest motif of the same colour, and each motif may be worked individually, just as the worker chooses. All the motifs around the outside of the design should be woven first, working all the time from the outside to the centre of the design.

Before starting, fold over three meshes of the net on right-hand along side and bottom. Begin weaving five meshes in diagonally from folded corner. Most designs require two stitches of each height, but larger articles like shopping bags should have three stitches of each height in order to give the pattern the proper size and accent.

The characteristic steps must be seen. Step-stitch weaving on chair tapestries gives a decorative effect similar to needle- point.

FLORENTINE EMBROIDERY (Fig. 125)

Florentine embroidery can be considered under two headings : the old and the modern. There is a great difference between the old designs, some of which date back two or three hundred years, and those of to-day. The latter are bolder and more striking in effect and more monotonous, the former are more subtle, more carefully thought out and arranged. All Florentine work is done with the canvas, not diagonally. The stitches may be long or short, or the patterns may be a mixture of both, but one of the chief features of this particular work is the way that these stitches always overlap. The stitches invariably start one hole *behind* the finish of the preceding stitch ; there is never an interval in the continuous line of colour. Sometimes the stitches start half-way beside the next stitch ; or in other words, if the first stitch is six holes in length, then the stitch next it will start immediately beside the centre hole of the first thread. Perhaps a word of explanation ought to be given as to what is exactly meant by the length of stitches : a stitch of six implies that the needle comes up through a hole in the canvas (not counted) and, passing over five, goes down through the sixth. The first hole is never counted because it is common to *two* stitches, the stitch just made and the one directly beneath it ; for this reason it is best to ignore that first hole when counting for the length of stitch. When the work is done on fine canvas and with fine thread, a stitch of seven holes in length may sometimes be employed, but as a rule it is wisest not to go beyond a stitch of six, especially if the thread is coarse, as it tends to pull out of shape after the work is completed. Most patterns have alternate short and long stitches arranged according to the design, and these short stitches are generally two holes in length : that is, the thread passes over one hole and goes down through the following one.

One of the very oldest patterns in existence is the Bargello design, shown in a museum of that name in Florence. Many variations have been built up on this ancient piece of work. At the present day many shops in Florence show modern pieces of work founded on that old design, but there is not much variety to be seen. In England it is still more difficult to purchase or see a fresh idea in the way of Florentine Embroidery. Most people are content with a simple " thunder-and-lightning " pattern, conventional zigzags across the strip of canvas. Yet there are possibilities of varying the work without departing from its characteristic feature. Beautiful colour effects can be obtained, for it is a form of shaded embroidery (see Gradation in Embroidery, Chapter III.). The design can have waved and blended stripes ; twisted lines ; points that melt in the background. Much depends on the skilful blending of colours, shades, and tints.

Fig. 125 shows one of the best designs that Florence produces to-day. Five shades or tints of any colour are needed. The shades or tints should be close enough in tone to melt almost imperceptibly into one another, for the whole beauty of the design depends, as we have said before, on gradation. The darkest shade or tint is first worked, and every stitch is the same length, namely, a long one of seven, so use fine canvas and fine embroidery silk. Fig. 125 shows clearly the pattern that can be thus described : 4 stitches down, 1 stitch up, 1 stitch down (beginning near the base of the last stitch) ; then, still continuing downwards, 1 double stitch (that is, 2 threads side by side), 1 treble stitch (3 threads side by side), 1 quadruple stitch, 1 treble stitch, 1 double stitch, 2 single stitches. This

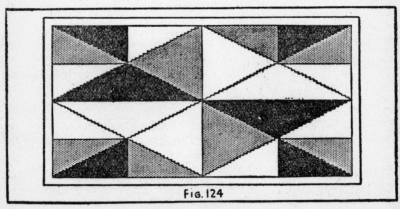

FIG. 124.

FIG. 124.—Example of Step-Stitch Weaving.

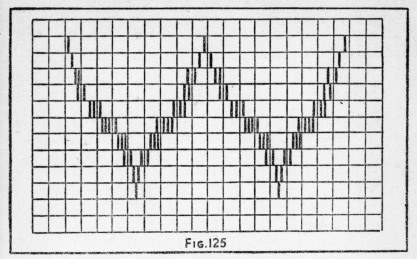

FIG. 125.—Diagram for working Florentine Design.

last stitch is the last one of the side of the pyramid ; the work then ascends in reverse order, beginning just above this particular stitch. Every row in this pattern is worked in the same way, so there is no trouble in learning the design ; once the first row is correct it only has to be repeated below in ever lighter tints. Florentine work is very useful for decorating sofa cushions or designing loose book-covers.

COVERING STOOL TOPS WITH TAPESTRY

From a wise use of the stitches we have described delightful stool tops or chair tops can be made that wear well. If you choose good designs you are almost sure to get a rich antique effect.

Old chairs can often be made beautiful by having backs and seats embroidered for them.

If you have a stool you wish to cover, you proceed in this way :

Work your design on the canvas so as to leave at least an inch margin all round. If the work is at all distorted when finished, stretch it out to the right shape on a kitchen table covered with white blotting-paper. Fasten it with drawing-pins and press under a damp cloth. Leave it until perfectly dry.

Mitre the corners by bringing together the sides of the unworked squares and oversewing, cutting away the surplus canvas. Put the tapestry right side down on the table, fit the pad inside (you must make a pad for your chair or stool top), then the loose top, if the chair or stool has a loose top. Now pull the margins of canvas evenly over, fastening them with tacks. Lastly, cut a piece of backing material, either hessian or sateen, slightly larger all round than the seat, turn in the surplus edges and press, and slip-stitch or catch-stitch into position. (See Chapters IX. and XIV. for these stitches.)

If the chair or stool has no loose top you must proceed a little differently. Put the pad in and sew the margins of canvas over it, line with sateen, leave strips of sateen or hessian on each side to nail under the chair or stool. In the case of a chair tapes can often be used with which to tie the tapestry, or tags to pin under the stool.

Embroidered Rugs or Needlework Rugs

Wool plays an important part in the making of beautiful rugs, and in the chapters on " The Craft of Home-made Rugs " a great variety of ways of making rugs will be described, but here we are only going to deal with embroidered rugs.

A large number of stitches can be used for these, practically any of the shorter tapestry stitches, provided they are short and compact and will not rub with wear. The main objection to these pretty rugs is that they lack solidity and are not heavy enough. However, there is now a new canvas called Helvellyn that makes a good foundation for the tapestry stitches we have described and the new ones that we are about to describe.

Cross Stitch is suitable for embroidered rugs and can be worked on Helvellyn canvas. To give added thickness to the rug the cross stitch can be worked or couched over a length of wool. A cross-stitch rug is very interesting to make and can be very lovely, but it takes a long time to do. It is an excellent plan to share the work of making this rug, because it lends itself to co-operative work. It can quite well be made in sections, and if these are carefully joined the whole appearance is very effective.

If a firm canvas is used suited to the size of the wool the simple cross stitch is quite sufficient, but if coarse rug canvas is used it is sometimes necessary to do a double cross stitch so as to make a firm material. When working out the design in cross stitch on your rug it is best to outline the design in cross stitch first and then do all the filling in. Take great care to make all the crosses the same way and of the same tension, as the mat must be flat and even. Cross-stitch flat rugs are specially useful in small houses where some of the furniture is almost sure to be placed on them at some time or the other, because they do not crush or spoil from being under a weight.

The Tent Stitch (Fig. 118).—This stitch makes good rugs and can be worked on Helvellyn canvas, or an excellent cheap jute canvas called " Panmure " cloth (this cloth also makes very lasting rugs in cross stitch), or coarse canvas. When using this stitch on coarse canvas bring the wool up from the back of the canvas, carry it along on the surface to the left for a certain number of holes (for example, five or seven), then pass the needle in an upward direction through the fifth hole and out through the hole just above the fifth hole. Now carry the wool back and pass the needle in a downward direction through the hole above where the wool started, bring it up in the hole where the wool started, and begin to couch down the two strands of wool by passing the needle through the holes above and below the lines of wool, working the tent stitch. When the end of the strands is reached, lay down two more strands parallel to the covered ones and in the same way. If the work is done correctly the stitches should now slant in the opposite direction. A square can be made by working the tent stitches in alternate rows. A pretty mat may be made in squares of alternate colours. If desired, the corner squares can be worked so that the stitches appear vertical and the rest of the squares with the stitches running horizontally. The tent stitch when worked over one or two strands of wool is sometimes called the *couched stitch*. Two strands of wool makes a softer mat, but it uses more wool.

The Straight Gobelin Stitch is another stitch that can be worked over a strand of wool to make a softer rug. This is a vertical stitch taken over two parallel threads of canvas, a stitch being made between each warp thread of the canvas. This gives a pleasing ribbed or corded surface to the rug.

Hungarian Stitches (Fig. 122).—These are excellent stitches for filling in the canvas and give gently shaded effects. On Helvellyn canvas they can be used for chair and stool seats as well as rugs. There are several grounding stitches known as Hungarian. Fig. 122 shows one. It is worked in horizontal lines, one encroaching upon the other so as to cover the stuff completely. Begin by a vertical stitch over two threads of the canvas, then make a stitch over four threads, which projects one thread beyond the first stitch, above and below, then end with a vertical stitch over two threads, and after skipping two vertical threads of the canvas, make a second group of stitches and so on. The diagram (Fig. 122) shows exactly how; in the second row the long stitches are set in the middle between two groups of stitches, so that all the stitches touch each other.

Another way of working the Hungarian stitch is to make vertical stitches, each crossing two threads of canvas, and each stitch one thread apart, but the second stitch must begin opposite the middle of the first stitch. This gives a smooth brickwork effect.

Again, one can have an alternate long-and-short stitch, the first passing over four threads of canvas and the second over two threads, or over one thread and two threads alternately.

Knitting Stitch (Fig. 123).—This is also called Sumac or Kelim stitch. It gives an interesting surface effect. The stitch is simple, being merely a long diagonal stitch passing over one horizontal or weft thread—from left upward to the right, and over two vertical warp threads. A second row is taken, returning from right to left of the line with the stitch sloping in the opposite direction. This is quite a beautiful stitch, and it is best suited to formal geometric designs.

Chain stitch can be used as an alternative to knitting stitch, but it is not so compact or even. It must be spaced according to the thickness of the thread used.

All stitched rugs must be either blanket-stitched or crocheted over the edges. Some people hem two or three rows of Axminster chenille round the mats instead of finishing as described above. Axminster chenille gives a pretty, furry effect as a border.

Many of the beautiful patterns found on rugs woven on a loom can be copied in needlework rugs. See the chapter on Needle-Woven Rugs.

CHAPTER XVI

WOOL CRAFT, OIL BAIZE, AND FELT WORK

Wool Embroideries of To-day. Woollen Edges—the Battlement Stitch,
the Paling Stitch. Rolled Edges. The Carpet-Slipper Stitch.
Cut-Wool Work. Rug-Wool Couching. Appliqué and Wool
Work. Wool Work on Oil Baize, Curtains, Cushions, etc.
Felt Work and Wool.—Tools, Ways of working on Felt. Bags.
Cosies. Slippers. Purses. Tea-pot Holder. Felt Flowers.

WOOL at the present day has a great variety of uses. It
is soft and pleasant to handle, it is easy to work, and
it can be bought in delightful colours, shades, and tints. A great
number of chapters in this book refer to wool and show the
different uses of wool, but even so it deserves a chapter to itself.

You have seen how it can be used for tapestry work, and
embroidered rugs, and in Chapter XIX. you will see how it can be
used for hooked rugs of different kinds. It is very useful for
darning on net and gauze, for weaving (see the chapter on
Weaving), and for knitting and crochet. In this chapter we are
going to say something about wool embroideries of the present
day, woollen edges and some other uses of wool not mentioned
in the other chapters, especially the use of wool and felt, including
some novel suggestions for the uses of odds and ends of felt.

Wool Embroideries of To-day

Stitchery or embroidery in wool is best done on soft woollen
fabrics, cotton crêpe, meshes or nets, coarse linens ; some loosely
woven silks or mercerised cloths can also be used, but perhaps
wool embroidery looks best on coarse linen, burlap, crass, etc.
The great advantage of wool embroidery is that the most ordinary
materials like burlap, unbleached muslin, or even oil cloth (oil
baize or American cloth) become gay and pleasing with a few
stitches.

Wool embroidery has two other advantages. It is not expensive, and it does not try the eyesight like fine embroidery.

So many people love embroidery and love the beautiful stitches we have shown in the first chapters of this book, but they often dare not attempt a piece of embroidery because it takes *so long*. If they use wool this difficulty disappears, because modern wool embroidery is very quick, it is not like modern tapestry or old-fashioned tapestry and Berlin wool work of long ago ; it is gay-coloured, bold and simple in outline, and very quick to work.

Wool embroideries at the present day are becoming very popular, perhaps because such good qualities of wool can be bought that stand constant washing.

Whatever type of wool embroidery you are doing, the fact that you are using a thick definite working thread like wool gives a bold effect with the minimum of stitchery.

Fortunately for the too-busy housewife elaborate and complicated stitches are not suited to wool work ; that is perhaps why beginners and children find it such pleasing work.

Simple geometrical borders look well in wool, for example, two rows of running stitch or stem stitch, with the space between filled with alternate squares of straight stitches, four stitches in each square.

The Devil stitch makes a pretty border, if you space the " stars " at equal intervals.

A rosette made of small, straight stitches, all having a common centre, makes a pretty decoration for common use. Another simple effective border consists of opposite diagonal stitches half an inch long, meeting each other at the base (see the Fishbone Stitch, Chapter III.) ; the fly stitch (Chapter III.) is another very effective stitch in wool work.

Simple borders can be made of little stitches about $\frac{1}{4}$ inch long taken at an angle and meeting at a point so that they form a zigzag.

Outline squares and diamonds can be repeated in border form.

Chain stitch (Chapter II.) is excellent for borders and for outlining rounded forms.

Simple motifs can be worked in cross stitch. Simple stitches worked in horizontal borders and zigzags give charm to the simplest table runner. Indeed all runners and table centres in wool embroideries should have simple borders—a line of couching in fly stitch or perhaps a right-side hem held down with a running stitch.

Flower designs are also popular for wool work because they lend themselves to elementary stitches. As the stitches are simple you must rely on design and colour for your effect. Work the flowers in stroke stitch, spaced buttonhole stitch, satin stitch or lazy-daisy, whichever seems most suitable ; leaves can be worked in lazy-daisy or satin stitch. Sometimes a good flower effect is obtained by carrying out the whole design in outline or chain stitch. Sometimes a simple flower design looks rather empty. In this case it is a good plan to add a black or brown trellis work in darning stitch to hold the flowers together and cover the blank spaces. The trellis work can easily be ruled out on the material with pencil, either in squares or diagonals. All the above work should be done, as we have said before, as far as possible on loosely woven wool material such as tandelaine, but the favourite materials are linen, linen crash, or one of the heavier cottons. Silk is not always a very suitable background.

A great many useful articles are very effective and very hard-wearing when worked in wool embroidery, for example, cushion covers, runners, covers for chairs, bags of all kinds, shoe-bags and work-bags, table centres, bedspreads, etc.

Remember when embroidering with wool these three things —Never pull the stitches too tight. Use a needle with a large eye so that the wool will not get frayed by being dragged through it. Cut the wool, do not break it as in weaving.

Woollen Edges

Every one probably knows how valuable wool is for finishing edges. Think how quickly blanket stitch can be worked and what a fine edge it makes ! Every one knows this. Woollen edges are not only colourful and pleasing, but they save the frayed edges of things—curtains, cushions, even rugs.

We have shown in the section on Crochet how useful and decorative crocheted woollen edges and seams are. Here we will describe one or two new edgings that are very decorative. These edges are made simply with needle and wool.

Fig. 126 shows a pretty decorative border suitable for cushions, curtains, and tablecloths. It is very quickly worked. It is buttonhole stitch worked in rays, because the needle is taken three or five times into the same hole, as shown in Fig. 126. At the fourth or sixth stitch start in the next hole about half an inch to the right. The spacing of the holes is a matter of choice.

Bright borders like this are very effective. This pattern can be made even more effective by having stitches of darker or contrasting coloured wool worked each side of each group. These outline stitches can be made afterwards.

Fig. 127 shows another stitch suitable for laying down hems or for borders in conventional designs. It is called the *Battlement Stitch*.

It looks very effective when worked in several shades of the same colour, but it can be worked in the same colour or in contrasting colours. Begin by working a row of blanket stitch, the stitches to be half an inch in height and half an inch apart. This proportion is for coarse wool on thick material; for finer material the stitches should be worked in suitable proportion.

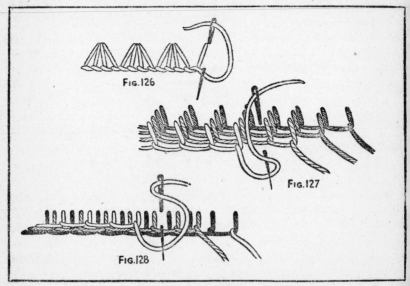

Fig. 126.
Fig. 127.
Fig. 128.

FIG. 126.—Wool Edging.   FIG. 127.—Battlement Stitch : Wool Edging.
FIG. 128.—Paling Stitch : Wool Edging.

The first row of blanket stitch should be very carefully worked, for upon its evenness depends the regularity of the following rows, and consequently the effect of the completed work. When the first row is finished, begin again at the left-hand side, and work a second row of blanket stitch on the top of the first, but a little to the left of it, and a little below it. Then work a third row a little to the left and a little below the second row. Work a fourth row in the same way. In the last row the tops of the stitches should touch the horizontal threads of the first row, as in Fig. 127.

The *Paling Stitch* (Fig. 128) makes a strong border. Both these stitches are useful for the bottoms of curtains to add weight to them.

Paling stitch, like battlement stitch, is begun with a row of blanketing ; but in it a second and third row of blanketing are worked a little above and a little to the right of each preceding row. Care should be taken to work the tops of all the stitches in every row on the same level ; thus the stitches in the last row will be taken much shorter than those in the first row. This stitch can be worked in several shades or colours.

Barb stitch makes pretty decorative bars, especially where a raised effect is desired.

Barb stitch is principally composed of two rows of blanketing placed back to back, and not too coarsely worked. First make one row of blanketing along a line, and then turn the work and make a second row, stitch for stitch along the first, so that the two rows lie exactly side by side, and make a pattern something like a fishbone. Then take a thread of wool or silk of a contrasting shade or colour and unite the two rows of blanketing by working an overcasting stitch into each couple of horizontal threads along the middle. When working the overcasting, do not take up any of the material upon the needle, but only the two threads.

ROLLED EDGES

Rolled edges are very new and attractive, and they are among the most useful of borders. They are so firm and durable. The woollen stitches in this type of border are taken over closely rolled edges ; tacking, as a rule, is unnecessary, as the edges can be rolled over with the left hand, while the right hand does the stitching.

To work : roll over the edges to make a roll $\frac{3}{16}$ inch (or more) thick. Take slanting over-and-over stitches along the roll, then return crossing these, thus forming cross stitches. The rolled edge may be turned to the right side or left.

Instead of taking slanting over-and-over stitches, straight ones can be taken and worked in blocks. Well spaced, these blocks look very effective.

You will surely want to decorate the edges of your table runners or curtains with these attractive borders.

Now we will turn from something quite new to something old, namely :

The Carpet-Slipper Stitch

This is a wool-work stitch from France. It is very old indeed, but it never gets forgotten. It is useful for handbags if worked in rather rich but soft colours. In appearance it is like ribbed velvet, thick and of a soft pile. It is worked on cross-stitch canvas in fairly thick wool.

First embroider the surface with cross stitches worked in the usual way in rows. Then, a row at a time, cover a line of cross stitches with a narrow strip of paper. Now work a second line of cross stitches over the paper and right through the canvas. Then with small, sharp scissors snip through the stitches above the paper (the paper is to prevent the scissors catching in the first row of work). You now have a line of cross stitches with a line of fluffy wool-ends on either side of it. At the back is a double line of stitches, very strong.

Cut-Wool Work

Cut-wool work is sometimes found on tea-cosies, cushion covers, and even bags for shopping or needlework, but it is perhaps best of all on children's dressing-gowns, cot covers, and blankets, because it gives them so much pleasure. It is very easy to do, because it is worked in ordinary back stitch, but loops are left. Some people use a cardboard gauge to keep the loops even, but this is hardly necessary. When the space is completely covered in this way, cut through the loops and trim to shape, fluffing up the ends of the wool with a strong needle or the points of your scissors.

Ducks or chicks worked this way in yellow wool will delight children. Cut-wool work combines well with appliqué or satin stitch, for example, if you work an orange in cut-wool work you can add leaves in satin stitch.

Rug-Wool Couching

We have already dealt with couching in Chapter VII., but here we want to say a special word about the use of wool in couching.

Rug-wool couching was often done with the odds and ends left over from rug-making. But now one can buy very thick 8-ply wool that is quite useful as a laid thread and gives a soft effect, but not quite so striking as though rug wool were used.

Rug-wool couching, of course, is only suitable for large surfaces that need very bold treatment, such as heavy curtains, bedspreads, wall panels, fire-screens, footstools, etc.

The designs must be large and clear, details should be avoided. If a really good design is chosen, nothing can be easier and speedier than this work; simply lay the rug wool or 8-ply wool over the outlines and couch it down with embroidery wool or embroidery cotton in the same colour. Different coloured wools must be chosen for different parts of the design, and as it is meant to be seen at a distance use strong colours such as scarlet, royal blue deep orange, or emerald.

It may happen that the ends of the laid wool are too thick to be put through the fabric with a rug needle, in this case poke a hole for them with scissors and secure them neatly on the wrong side.

When a heavier effect on a large piece of work is needed, the outline can be couched round twice in the same colour.

The best fabrics for rug-wool couching are Russian or Irish peasant crash, but any heavy cotton or linen material will do.

Appliqué and Wool Work

We have said a good deal about appliqué work in Chapter VIII. We want to point out here how useful wool is in appliqué work. Appliqué work is often a long task when edges have to be turned in, but if the appliqué pieces are sewn down with a woollen stitch along the outline, there is rarely any need for these turnings. The woollen stitch has body enough to hide the edges, especially if stitches such as outline stitch or chain stitch are chosen. Besides holding down the cut edges well, the wool looks very decorative. When using wool for appliqué work, the piece tc be applied should be of thin material like voile or organdie, and the foundation should be heavier, for example, coarse linen or crash. Cushion covers look most attractive made of linen with bright orange appliqué designs stitched on with black wool in buttonhole stitch.

Wool Work on Oil Baize or American Cloth

Oilcloth is very useful in the home. It is especially serviceable in the kitchen or nursery where one wants brightness and cleanliness. It forms, too, an excellent background for soft woollen designs. There is no need for the kitchen to be dull or unlovely.

Black oil baize is very serviceable, and forms a good background for wools of any colour.

Oil baize is a good choice for bathroom curtains as it is not affected by steam. Oil-baize curtains again are very suitable for the kitchen. You can have a very cheery kitchen if you choose red oil baize and embroider it with black wool.

Shabby tables can be made into quite beautiful dressing-tables by being covered with oil baize embroidered in wool at the edge. Choose good colours for baize and wool.

A desk-set in oil baize decorated with wool makes a very attractive present. It does not take long to make a blotting-pad or cover, a pen holder (a round box covered with oilcloth), and a pen wiper.

Oil baize decorated in rich colours (wool) makes beautiful runners, that look like satin at a distance. They look well even if they are simply blanket-stitched in wool. They can easily be kept clean with a damp cloth.

Oil baize decorated with wool also makes fire-screens. Screens are often necessary when there is a baby in the house or an invalid. They are expensive to buy, but they can be made at home. A fair-sized wooden clothes-horse often makes a good screen. Enamel it first, then cover it with oil baize, using drawing-pins that match.

Cushions of oil baize stand much knocking about and yet they look decorative. Other useful things that can be made from oil cloth and wool are—floor mats, book-covers, dust-bags, shoe-bags, basket covers.

But no woolwork is so pleasing as woolwork on felt, which we will now describe.

FELT WORK AND WOOL

Felt as a material for making certain articles has many qualities to recommend it. Its possibilities and attractiveness are not generally realised. It is easy to use, and being so soft it is especially pleasant to sew. Its cut edges require no trimming or hemming to keep them from fraying. It can be bought in a variety of beautiful colours. If you should by chance live near a felt factory where articles of felt are manufactured it might be possible to buy scraps and cuttings of waste material by the pound. This is a great advantage, as you get a variety of colours in small pieces at no very great expense.

There are many useful things that can be made in this delightful material, and the odd pieces left over can be used in a variety of ways.

Since felt is made of compressed wool it can be used for practically all the same purposes as decorated leather, and though it has not the durability or texture of leather it is much cheaper.

The only tools necessary for felt work are a six-way leather punch (see section on Leather Work), some pointed raffia needles and, of course, a pair of sharp scissors.

Wool is used for all sewing in felt work. Small balls of delightful colours and about the thickness of double knitting wool can be bought at any art-needlework shop. Wool and felt make a specially attractive combination, and woollen designs on soft felt backgrounds always look lovely.

There are a number of different ways of working felt, and before we describe the making of any particular thing we will give a brief summary of these.

(1) *Appliqué Work.*—Felt appliqués are very attractive. The design is first traced or drawn in crayon on the felt foundation. The various parts of the design are then cut out of different

coloured pieces of felt and laid down flat on the felt background
each in its proper place. The edges are fastened down with
long and short stitches, buttonhole stitches, etc., as already
described in the section on Appliqué Work.

(2) *Pierced Work.*—Simple but attractive openings are cut
out of the felt, these openings are backed with material of another
colour, this colour showing through the cut spaces. See the
section on Pierced Wood in the chapters on Leather Work.

(3) *Punched Holes.*—Interesting decorations can be made by
punching holes of different sizes with the six-hole punch in such
a way as to form a design. Material of a contrasting colour can
be placed under these holes.

(4) *Inlay.*—In this method pieces of felt are fitted into each
other and joined with overcast stitches so that only one thickness
is formed. See section on Inlay in the chapters on Leather Work.

(5) *Weaving.*—Slits are made in the articles to be decorated
and strips of felt are then woven in, making pretty designs. See
section on Weaving, and section on Weaving in Soft Leather Work.

Among the many useful things that can be made from felt
are—cushions (black felt cushions with bright appliqué work
and bright wool stitches are always attractive), slippers for
babies, children, and grown-ups (they are very soft and warm),
bags of every kind, under-arm purses, mats and table runners,
tea-cosies, berets and scarfs, dolls, blotters and book covers,
beads and flowers, and all sorts of pretty and useful little articles
such as iron-holders, napkin rings, pincushions, etc. There
really seems no end to the things that can be made from felt
and wool.

BAGS

Bags can be made in a great variety of ways. You can, if
you like, have a bag to match each costume or dress you wear !
They are very quickly made. You can have bags with gussets
and bags without gussets, bags with zip fasteners, bags with
draw-strings, appliqué bags, woven bags, and so on. It is well
to cut a paper pattern first of any bag that you are going to make.
The most economical bags are those made of different coloured
pieces of felt. Below we give suggestions for a bag made of
different pieces.

A bag of felt to carry slippers or needlework is extremely useful. A very pretty one can be made of eight pieces of felt in two or more colours—one bright, one dark, if possible. This is a good way of using up various pieces. The bag should be about 12 to 13 inches deep and 18 inches wide. Arrange the pieces as shown in Fig. 129 or in any other pleasing manner. Oversew the pieces together in wool of a contrasting colour.

Work some pretty stitches radiating from the meeting-point of the four pieces of felt, on each side of the bag. Fold the bag along the middle join and oversew the sides together. The top of the bag can be decorated by one of the woollen edges described in the beginning of this chapter. Punch six holes on each side of the bag or cut bars about $\frac{1}{2}$ inch wide through which a cord can be threaded. A cord can be made from several strands of the various wools used on the bag, and threaded through the holes or bars. If desired a second cord can be made and threaded through the opposite way so that by pulling the ends of the two cords the bag closes up.

For various ways of making cords and their tassels, see section on Cords, Tassels, and Fringes.

Another useful shape can be made from a piece of felt 10 inches by 18 inches, which when folded makes a bag 10 inches wide and 9 inches deep.

COSIES

Cosies are always useful, and felt cosies are warm and particularly attractive.

Cosies are easily made of four pieces (or three for a small one). Cut four pieces of felt to the pattern and size ($6\frac{1}{2} \times 8\frac{1}{4}$ inches) shown in Fig. 130. These can be of two contrasting colours. Decorate two sides with appliqué or punched holes as shown in Fig. 130. Next cut four pieces of felt for the lining ; be careful to make the lining slightly smaller than the outside cover. Seam the four lining pieces together with the same wool you use for decorating the cosy. Cut a sheet of wadding the shape of the cosy (Fig. 130) to place between the lining and the outside. Buttonhole the seams of the cosy together, then fasten the lining felt and the cosy together by buttonholing all round the bottom.

If desired, the lining can be made quite separately ; this is sometimes more economical. A less pointed shape with a round top can also be used instead of that shown in Fig. 130. Remember only to decorate two alternate sides.

Always plan your pattern first in paper to see that it fits your particular teapot. The measurements given in books and papers often need adjustments. Delightful shapes and decorations can be planned and none are tedious to carry out.

Bear in mind felt bags and cosies when you have to work for a bazaar. Here are some suggestions for the ever popular Cottage Tea-Cosy. Remember they are only suggestions for you to adapt and alter at your will, and improve.

The pretty cottage idea can also be carried out on an ordinary cosy shape in two pieces (or two pieces and a gusset) instead of cutting the felt to represent the cottage as described below. In the tea-cosy of the ordinary shape, clever stitches alone must depict the cottage.

A Cottage Tea-Cosy.—This delightful form of tea-cosy is always popular, and carried out in felt and wool is particularly attractive.

You can plan your cottage in four pieces, two oblongs for the sides and two pieces for the roof. The walls might be fawn colour and the roof red, brown, or grey according to your fancy. Be sure to make a paper pattern first to fit your teapot. It is worth taking a little trouble about this, as it may save wasting the felt by cutting it the wrong shape. The oblong pieces will probably be about 12 inches by 6 inches. These are easy to cut. The pieces for the roof must overlap the walls by about $\frac{1}{2}$ inch. To cut a pattern for this, take a piece of paper 12 inches by 5 inches. Fold it in half so that the two narrow ends meet. Mark 2 inches along the edge from the fold, and cut from this point to the opposite corner. Unfold the paper and you have the two sloping sides of the roof symmetrical. The roof is 4 inches along the top. Use this paper pattern to cut two pieces of felt for the roof.

On the wall pieces plan out the door and window, and work them in wool; add a few flowers in buttonhole stitches. See suggestions for stitches given at the beginning of this section.

The sides can be joined together by long and short buttonhole stitch. The roof can be left plain except for the running stitch

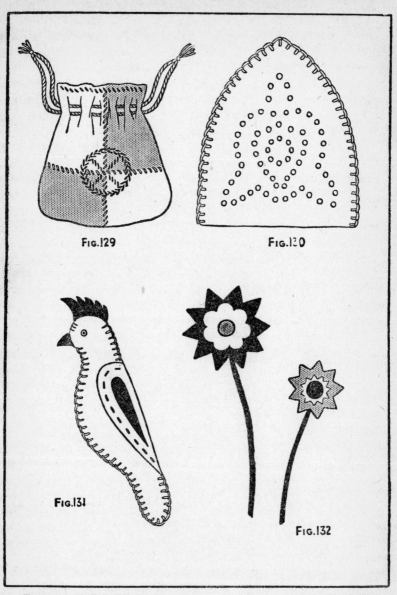

FIG. 129.—A Felt Bag in two colours. FIG. 130.—Felt Tea-Cosy.
FIG. 131.—Felt Teapot Holder. FIG. 132.—Felt Flowers.

that joins it to the walls, or stitches can be made on it to indicate thatch or tiles.

To line the cosy, lay it flat over the material to get the shape, but remember to cut it smaller than the cosy ; cut the wadding the same shape and stitch the pieces together.

SLIPPERS

Felt slippers can be made in the same way as soft leather slippers. The easiest way is to buy leather soles (with fleecy tops) from a shoe shop and make the uppers from felt. Paper patterns must be cut first to make sure that the slippers will fit. The best guide of all to correct fitting is the upper part of an old slipper. Slippers made on the moccasin pattern are described in the chapters on Leather Work. These of course do not wear well, they are only suited for bedroom use ; they are delightful, however, for babies who cannot walk much. Bought soles make a slipper that can be worn anywhere and that wears well. A pattern for the uppers is given in the chapter on Leather Work, and directions for making the slippers.

Two pieces of felt are needed for each slipper, one for the top and one for the lining.

CUSHIONS

Pretty plaited cushions can be made as described for Soft Leather Work (Chapter XXVIII.).

PURSES

Under-arm purses are very successful made of felt. The edges are generally bound together with woollen stitches to match the felt.

Little need be said about purses, because they are really only bags on a small scale. The quickest way to make a purse is to use a piece of material folded in three. If time permits it is always better to add gussets, because this means the purse will hold more and so is more useful.

All the odds and ends of felt left over from making bags, cosies, slippers, etc., can be used for pretty pen wipers, teapot holders, and felt flowers, etc.

Below we give directions for making an amusing teapot

holder and a few suggestions for flowers. These little things are very useful for bazaars.

An Attractive Teapot Holder (Fig. 131)

This can be carried out in colours to match your tea-service or it may imitate the real parrot in a brilliant colour-scheme.

Cut out the pattern on a piece of paper about $3\frac{1}{2}$ inches by $8\frac{1}{2}$ inches, making the middle part of the back of the parrot as straight as possible. Take a piece of red, blue, or orange felt 7 inches by $8\frac{1}{2}$ inches. Fold it on its long diameter. Place the pattern with the straight part of the back along the folded edge, mark round it and cut out.

The comb and beak may be red or black according to the colour chosen for the parrot. Cut two pieces for the beak and one for the comb. Cut duplicate pieces for the wings. Paste these in position. Join the cut edges with a buttonhole stitch, but leave an opening so that the parrot fits over the handle of the teapot. Sew a black or red bead in the middle of a small white circle of felt for the eye.

This parrot can also be made in suède leather (see section on Soft Leather Work). Fig. 131 shows how the different pieces of felt are arranged.

Felt Flowers (Fig. 132)

Very delightful buttonholes can be made of felt in combination with wool. Make small pompons of wool in the following way: Cut a disc of cardboard $1\frac{1}{2}$ inch in diameter with a hole in the middle $\frac{1}{2}$ inch in diameter. Place a piece of string around inner opening of the disc, and tie a loop of wool round to hold it in place. Hold the string so that the wool is wound round both it and the disc. As the opening is so small the wool should be wound round with a needle—when the disc is completely covered, take the two ends of the string and tie them in a firm knot at the centre. Put the point of the scissors under the wool at the edge of the disc and cut round, as in making the pompon described in the chapter on Cords, Tassels, and Fringes. Tear off the disc and clip the ball to make it uniform on the surface.

These balls form the centre of each flower. The petals are

cut from a piece of felt. Make a pattern of this first by folding a 2-inch paper circle into four or six parts, and round off both corners of the paper sector and unfold. You should have a flower of four or six petals, according to the number of folds you have made. If you are not satisfied with this shape experiment again until you have one that you like. Lay this pattern on the felt and cut out. Use a piece of milliners' wire for the stem about 3 inches long; bend up each end to form a loop.

Put the string with which the ball is tied through the loop of the stem and tie it firmly. Punch a hole through the centre of the piece of felt and pass the stem through it. Wind wool round the stem. Three of these flowers make a unique and charming buttonhole when worn on a coat, hat, or muff. The wide range of colours to choose from makes it possible to adapt them to different costumes. They are a great attraction at any bazaar and soon find ready buyers.

Another Way of making Felt Flowers (Fig. 132).—Make circles of various sizes and colours. The edges of some can be scalloped, others serrated. When they are finished place one upon the other and sew them together at the centre; leave ends of thread for tying to the wire stem, which can be made as already described. It is a good plan to cut paper patterns of the flowers by folding a circle of paper into four, five, or six divisions, and cutting the corners in various ways. In this way you can be sure of getting your flower forms symmetrical.

A bunch of these in a small vase will make a bright patch of colour in your room, especially in winter-time, when real flowers are scarce and expensive.

CHAPTER XVII

STENCILLING

STENCILLING has wonderful possibilities. As an art it is practically limitless in its scope. It is perhaps of special value to the home worker, and as useful to the embroideress as to the drawer or painter. Many people do not realise how effective stencilling and needlecraft can be.

Stencilling is the process of colouring a surface by painting or staining through the cut-out or perforated parts of a stencil-plate. It has, as we have said, great possibilities, though stencil-plates are most useful when one is decorating materials upon which one cannot draw an outline. They are also useful when one has to repeat a design. Excellent stencils can be bought from art shops and from all artists' colourmen. They are invaluable for those who cannot draw but who want to decorate the things around them with lovely colours.

Some home workers like to make their own stencils. The making of stencils would be an easy matter were it not for the difficulty of thinking of good and original designs and of carrying them out through the medium of heavy stencil paper. (We suggest a few simple home-made ones in the coming pages.) The beauty of stencilled work depends upon the charm and simplicity of the design, a fine colour harmony, and the ability to apply the colour in a flat tone, so that it looks as though it were woven in the material and a part of the cloth. These facts make stencilling a real craft.

Designs that are to be repeated many times should be very conventional. A continuous design, such as a border pattern (Fig. 133), may be stencilled by moving the plate along; but when using a stencil over and over again in this way, mark faint pencil-lines to keep the stencilling straight, or if the units of the design are detached, put a pin or pencil-mark at regular intervals so that they will be the same distance apart. Simple geometrical designs like that shown in Fig. 133 can be cut by oneself. One unit only need be cut. Use a sharp pen-knife or a stencil knife, and a sheet of oil-royal—the thick yellow oiled paper from which stencils are made. Trace the design on the stencil paper by means of carbon paper. It is not absolutely essential to use oil-royal for stencils; good stencils (though they will not last as long as oil-royal ones) can be cut from Whatman paper or good Cartridge paper. This paper is much easier to cut than proper stencil paper, and it can be finished with a special preparation that strengthens the paper and prevents paint from sticking to it.

To make this preparation, mix one ounce of ordinary shellac with half a pint of methylated spirits, shake the bottle well, and let it stand for some hours. This "knitting" solution, as it is called, must be painted over both sides of the paper stencil and allowed to dry before the stencil is used.

Some pleasant hours can be passed planning simple geometric patterns for borders and cutting them out as described before, but more elaborate patterns should be bought. The cutting is too difficult for the amateur.

Whether your stencils are home-made or bought, keep them carefully, as they can be used over and over again, and it takes quite a long time to get a collection of really beautiful and suitable stencils. Many stencils must be rejected as being too "fussy." Background stencils are those which have the background cut out, and the design or pattern forms the stencil-plate. Such designs are generally stencilled in one colour, and the design appears in the natural colour of the material.

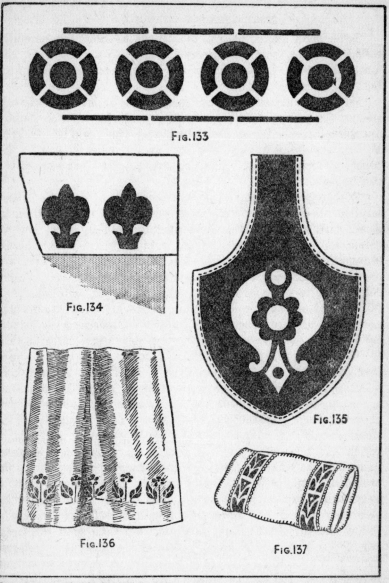

Fig. 133

Fig. 134

Fig. 135

Fig. 136

Fig. 137

Fig. 133.—A Simple Border Stencil.   Fig. 134.—Corner of a Blotting-Pad.
Fig. 135.—Black Oilcloth Work-Bag Stencilled.   Fig. 136.—Stencilled
Curtain.   Fig. 137.—Stencilled Cushion.

MATERIALS FOR STENCILLING

Some good stencil-plates—or stencils as they are generally called—brushes for applying the colour, paints suitable for the material to be decorated, and a few drawing-pins or weights for holding the material steady.

We have already said a good deal about the stencils themselves. The brushes used are generally special stubby Japanese brushes made for stencilling. They can be obtained in various sizes. For finer or more delicate work, the common bristle brush such as artists use for oil-painting can be used.

With regard to paints. (1) Oil-colours can be used on most fabrics, but these colours are more permanent if they are thinned down with a special stencilling medium sold by most artists' colourmen. (2) Washable stencil colours for fabrics can be obtained that will stand *occasional* careful washing; these are useful for cushion-covers, runners, tray-cloths, etc. (3) Water-colour paints give excellent results on paper, cardboard, or fabrics that will not require washing. Opaque water-colours and poster colours are especially suitable for stencilling on paper. (4) Printers' ink is quite suitable for stencilling on to fabrics. (5) Wax crayons, special fabric dye crayons are easy to use. (See paragraph on how to use these.) (6) Dyes. When dye is selected as the medium for stencilling, it should be prepared according to the directions on the package in which it is purchased. Then add the white-of-egg and beat until the egg is thoroughly mixed with the dye. A small portion of gum arabic, which has been dissolved beforehand in water, may be used instead of the white-of-egg. In either case add just enough gum arabic or white-of-egg to make the dye slightly heavy, like a very thin syrup. On the whole, linen fabrics should never be stencilled with dye or water-colour paints, as the moisture will follow the threads in both directions and thus spoil the clean edge. (7) Florescan colours: these are iridescent. "Florescan" is the name given to a very decorative form of stencilling in which coloured bronze powders are employed. It is particularly effective on velvet and other materials with a raised pile, but black Jap silk and satin are also very excellent materials for the work. Silks and satin are somewhat easier to use, so beginners are advised to use these materials first.

SOME GENERAL DIRECTIONS FOR STENCILLING

(1) In using oil-paints or indeed any paints, enough of each colour should be mixed, if possible, to complete the work, as it is very difficult to match the colours.

(2) The stencil brush must be clean and dry, and a separate brush used for each colour. Several colours may be used on one stencil, but a second stencil is sometimes needed when it is necessary to put one colour over another.

(3) Before beginning to stencil, always try your colours on a piece of the cloth to be stencilled, to see if it is the right colour and the right consistency. If the paint is too thin, it will run under the stencil and spoil the work, and if it is too thick, or there is too much on the brush, it will look heavy and opaque. Good stencilling, as we have said before, rarely has the appearance of being painted, it looks more like a stain. One does not want to destroy the texture of the fabric in the stencilling.

(4) Dip the brush into the paint very lightly, then wipe some of the colour off on a piece of paper or a palette, so that the brush has just the right amount of paint on it.

(5) If the cloth to be stencilled is thin, blotting paper must be placed under it before stencilling ; but if the cloth is heavy and firm, like burlap or Russian crash, newspaper can be used.

(6) The cloth you are stencilling on must be stretched as flat as possible. Use heavy weights to keep it in position or put drawing-pins in if there is a suitable margin. The stencil, too, can be kept in place by weights if necessary—drawing-pins may harm the fabric.

(7) Hold the brush in a vertical position, allowing only the ends of the bristles to touch the cloth.

(8) Always work from the edges towards the centre of the openings as much as possible, and apply the paint by a slight hammering or stippling movement.

(9) When removing the stencil, lift it up carefully to avoid it sliding off the stencil over the wet paint and spoiling the finished work.

(10) When the stencilling is finished, hang the cloth up to

dry and give it time to dry. Then place it on the ironing-board, face down, with several layers of dampened cloth and a dry cloth over it. Then press with a hot iron. This will help to set the colours, but stencilled materials should always be washed with great care.

WATER-COLOURS ON PAPER AND FABRICS

The moist water-colours that are bought in tubes are the best, they require only a few drops of water to make them the right consistency for stencilling. If the paint has a tendency to spread, add a small quantity of gum arabic that has been dis-solved in water. To make the colours lighter in tone, add Chinese white. It is often necessary to apply the colour several times, until the coating presents a flat, even effect.

Stencilling on paper is useful for (1) Making Christmas cards. (2) Photo mounts. (3) Blotter-covers and blotting-pads can be made and decorated most effectively with a simple stencil design of a repeated unit. Fig. 134 shows a design that has been cut from a piece of cartridge paper folded lengthways, and a corner of the pad with the design stencilled on it. These blotters can be made from the cardboard back of a writing-pad ; coloured blotting-paper can be used to match the colour of the stencilled design. (4) Menu cards. A pretty decoration for these is a butterfly stencil. The butterflies can always be tastefully arranged and you can be sure of a good effect. The same colour can be used throughout, or the colours may vary for each card or set of cards.

A very helpful use of water-colour stencilling is for decorating fancy-dresses, or dresses used in acting, because such dresses have to be used only a few times and the fact that the paint is not washable does not matter. For example, on a Greek costume a Greek fret can be stencilled to form a decorative border.

OIL-PAINTS OR STENCIL COLOURS ON FABRICS

Almost every kind of fabric can be stencilled on, and a rule well worth remembering is that thin materials should as a rule be stippled, while thick materials should have the colours laid on. The following fabrics are the most suitable for stencil work —net fabrics (natural undyed), Irish peasant crash, oatmeal cloth, linen, Russian crash, cotton crash, casement cloth, linen, woven Japanese grass matting (this is specially suitable for garden cushions and shopping bags), woven raffia fabric (this is ideal for stencilling purposes). Wherever possible, new materials to be stencilled should first be washed to remove the dressing. Below we give a few fabrics that need special care if they are to be stencilled successfully :

Chiffon, *ninon*, and other thin materials need careful treatment, as they are liable to slip under the plate, and should therefore be stippled.

Crash, etc., must be stippled because of its rough surface. You will need rather more paint on your brush and the paint should be somewhat thicker than that used for a thin material.

Silk.—For stencilling on silk the colour should be kept thin and the brush very dry. A Japanese brush is best, as they are soft and do not rough up the surface. The colour must be laid on with a painting movement.

Velvet and *plush* require careful treatment. Some velvets give a better effect if stencilled with the pile, but most work better *against* the pile. If the colour is used with the pile it makes it look sodden and ugly. Short-pile materials are easier to manage. In any case it is always advisable to try your colour on a small piece of the material first. Use the paint rather thick and put it on flat ; do not brush right into the pile.

We will now describe in detail some of the articles that can be made more gay and interesting by having patterns stencilled on them.

A White Ninon Scarf.—A scarf looks very effective if it has a pretty pattern stencilled at each end. Below we give detailed directions for doing this.

Pin the end of the scarf down to a flat board over which a sheet of blotting-paper has been spread. This is very necessary when stencilling on thin material, for the blotting-paper absorbs the colour which goes through the material.

Now fix the stencil-plate carefully over the material by using weights. Leave the bottom edges of the plate free so that they can be lifted from time to time to see that the colouring is correct. Another method of fixing the stencil-plate is by using small clips. Drawing-pins should not be used with thin material as the pin-holes will be visible afterwards.

For stencilling on ninon, georgette, etc., Winsor and Newton's Stencilling Medium should be used with the oil-colours, as it does not stiffen the material nor spoil the purity of the colour used. The bottle should be shaken before using the medium.

To begin stencilling : Squeeze a little of each colour you need on to a palette, and pour a little of the medium into an egg-cup. You need only a very small quantity of colour, as a little goes a long way, and only a little of the medium should be poured out at a time, as it hardens or evaporates when exposed to the air. Mix a very little of the medium with the colour. To do this, dip your brush in the medium and squeeze out against the edge of the egg-cup, then mix it with the colour to the right consistency. For ninon, the colour must never be too thick, but on the other hand it must not be too thin, as it is liable to run under the stencil-plate and cause ragged edges and blotches.

A little practice is necessary to get the right consistency, therefore it is wise to try the colour first on a scrap of the material. Be very careful not to put too much colour on the brush ; a piece of rag or blotting-paper should be kept near to rub the brush on every time you dip it in the colour. Hold the brush vertically and dab downwards. This movement we have described before. It is known as " stippling."

Black Oilcloth Work-Bag (Fig. 135).—Cut a paper pattern for the bag. Place it on the wrong side of the oilcloth, draw around it and cut out. Stencil the design in oil-paints, going over the design lightly—just enough to get a good outline. Then remove the stencil and paint over the design, making a smooth finish. A thin coat of varnish may be applied to the design when it is thoroughly dry. This gives a high gloss.

When the paint is thoroughly dry, cut a lining the size of the bag. Baste the lining and oilcloth together. Baste the two parts of the bag together and bind the edges with ribbon. The edges can, if desired, be buttonholed instead of bound with ribbon.

Casement Curtains, Silk Curtains, etc. (Fig. 136).—All kinds of curtains can be stencilled. In stencilling curtains it is well to begin in the corner—one can often arrange and space the

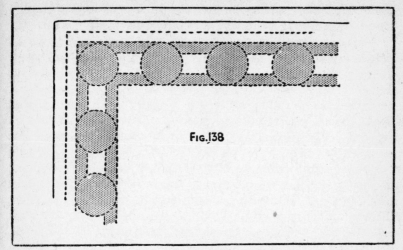

FIG. 138.—Tea-Cloth Border Stencilling encircled with Embroidery.

design better. The pattern should lie well inside the hem. It is a good plan to use the hem as a guide and fit the edge of the stencil-plate to it, provided the edges of the stencil-plate are true and equal. If you have a skirt-board use this for stencilling curtains, so that you can get as much as possible pinned down at a time.

Any colour-scheme can be used, but perhaps plain colours, such as brown, green, blue, etc., to tone with the room in which they are used, are best. Use oil-paints or Florescan colours. Florescan colours are in powder form ; they are mixed with a special medium when they are applied. This medium is supposed to make them washable. The process of Florescan stencilling consists more in laying the colours *on* the material than in working them in. Too much pressure makes the work look laboured.

All brushes used for Florescan colours must be cleaned at once with turpentine—clean the stencil, too. It is well to keep different brushes for the different kinds of paints used. Florescan colours are iridescent and scintillate in the light. To make the work more permanent it may be sprayed with Florescan fixative, using an ordinary spray.

Whether you use oil-paints or Florescan colours or any other stencilling colours, remember that with curtains thick stencilling should be avoided, as no thin material will hang well if too much colour is used.

As soon as possible after the stencilling is finished, cover it with a slightly damp cloth, and iron carefully first on the right side, and then on the wrong side. This tends to fix the colours and makes them more washable. Fig. 137 shows an example of a stencilled cushion.

STENCILLING AND EMBROIDERY COMBINED ON A TEA-CLOTH
(Fig. 138)

This cloth is made from white wash satin. Oil-paints are used as the stencil medium. It is stencilled in light blue, the outlines are a running stitch of dark blue yarn. The tints and shades of red, green, violet, and orange can be used if desired instead of blue. Be sure that the blue yarn is really the same blue as the paint, only darker—*i.e.* a shade.

Using a Stencil as a Transfer for Embroidery.—Place the stencil on the material and rub through the holes very lightly to transfer the design to the material. Use the brush as dry as possible ; the colour you employ must be a pale tint of the colour you intend to use to embroider your design later. If you are going to have white embroidery, use the palest blue, as this does not spoil the colour of the white. You must not attempt any shading, but merely apply a flat wash. Water-colours in pans are best for this purpose, and a small Japanese stencil brush must be used.

If the stencil is a simple one, you can trace round the design with a pencil on the material. This saves ironing a pattern on the material or drawing one, but if the pattern is a large one, it is rather a laborious method.

Little trifles, like pincushions, look pretty stencilled in bright colours and then enriched with some silk embroidery—something after the manner of the tea-cloth we have described. Many pretty things can be made in this way, especially cushion covers, etc.

We will now describe something quite new in stencilling.

A NOVEL METHOD OF STENCILLING

Here is something new in stencilling that has great possibilities. Look about the house for some odd pieces of lace, or perhaps you have an old lace curtain. The cheapest lace curtain if its pattern is graceful and well proportioned can be prepared as *a stencil*, and the design applied through it. Strips of lace that have become frail from long use can be sewed together with the pattern matching to form a stencil pattern. You can make a large lace stencil or a small one, a border or a central design.

Begin by choosing a piece of lace that will make a pattern for a table runner. The coarser the lace is woven the better. Stretch the lace on a wooden frame carefully, and securely fasten it with tacks or drawing-pins. (An old picture-frame often makes a good frame.) Take care not to stretch the lace too much to spoil the pattern.

When the lace is tacked down, a coat of shellac is applied. To do this, lay the frame on a piece of paper, lace side down. Stand the frame up and let the shellac dry. Then give the stencil a thin coat of paint over the shellac. (The coat of paint can be omitted for small stencils.) The lace becomes rather stiff from its coat of shellac and paint, and forms a good stencil.

Use of the Lace Stencil.—A most out-of-the-common and attractive effect is obtained by applying the lace stencil to walls. Lovely decorative panels can be made on walls by using large portions of lace curtains and outlining the finished stencil with a straight line of black or brown, or whatever colour is needed for the particular room.

The ingenious worker will find all sorts of possibilities in this stencil. Bed-spreads, borders for curtains and table covers and draperies of all sorts, decorative motifs for cushions and painted furniture, dinner sets, runners, and even garments can be ornamented by applying designs to them through these prepared lace stencils.

One advantage of this method is that the *same* stencil can be used in a variety of ways—for example, the full stencil can be used on a wall panel or a cupboard panel ; the border only can be used for bed-spreads or curtains ; just the edge of the stencil is useful for a border across the bottom of curtains ; single motifs may be selected from the lace to be painted through to decorate chairs or tables so that they match the other stencilled articles in the room.

Using the Stencil in Practice.—If the frame on which the piece of lace is stretched is the exact size and shape of the panel that is to receive the pattern, the stencil need not be removed from the frame—for example, it can be hung against the wall to be stencilled, or placed over the material to be stencilled. But as a rule the lace must be removed from the frame and pinned over the surface to be covered, or fastened to a rod and hung (in the case of a wall).

The paint used for stencilling depends on the material to be stencilled on. We have already described these paints and dyes. (For a good dye for material, see the section on Potato Printing.)

When using oil-paints or paint for walls (there are many varieties of paint for walls, and each is intended for a certain surface, so explain your wants to a paint dealer and name the surface to be covered), be careful that the paint is the right consistency or the work will be ruined. Experiment first, because the right consistency can only be learned from experience, as surfaces differ greatly. Remember whatever paint or dye you are using you must *stipple* it on. Stippling will *not* produce a rough surface, and paint *must* be stippled through a lace stencil. Use a small round stippling-brush, and apply the paint thinly.

Lace stencils have many advantages. They can easily be rolled round sticks of wood, and put away when not in use. Paper stencils must be kept flat.

Lace stencils do not deteriorate with constant use, they even seem to improve. Paper stencils weaken because the ties (the technical term for the narrow strips of paper that hold the design together) tend to tear and break. Also the sharp edges of the paper-cut stencil are more liable to blur if the brush contains too much paint. The lace stencil is of course made of round threads, so there are no sharp edges.

For really successful work, choose a good pattern of lace and good colour-scheme. This stencilling always looks well if the paint that is applied is a few shades darker than the background colour or paint.

Try a lace stencil on the ninon scarf already described.

Spray Stencilling

This is a particularly effective way of stencilling many fabrics. (See section on Potato Printing for some suitable dyes to use.)

Place the dye or ink (waterproof ink) in a bottle and use a spray such as is employed for spraying fixatives, or put the dye in a small spraying bottle with a rubber bulb and tube such as is used for perfume sprays. One spray can be used for several different bottles if it is well cleaned each time that the colours are changed. A stencil should be cut for each colour used. If you use two or more stencils, make marks on them so that they will fit over each other accurately. Another method is to put shields (pieces of paper) over the holes that you do not want the colour to be sprayed through. These paper shields can be kept in place with drawing-pins.

The material to be stencilled must be stretched and fastened to a board as in ordinary stencilling, but place it in an upright position and see that everything around is protected, because the spraying cannot be confined to a small space.

The sprayed colour penetrates the material but will not spoil its texture. The finer the spray the more satisfactory, as a rule, is the result. The depth of the colour varies with the position of the sprayer. The nearer you stand to the stencil, the darker the colour is ; the farther you stand from the stencil, the lighter the colour is. If the colour runs, you are probably standing too near the stencil and using too much colour. The safest way to deepen the colour is to spray again when the colour is dry. Be sure the colours are thoroughly dry before you press the material.

Another method of spray stencilling is to use a resist paste instead of dye in the openings of the stencil. This is a little like batik. (See the section on Batik Work.) To make a resist paste, make a thick paste by adding flour to a strong solution of salt and water. Place the stencil over the material to be decorated and fasten it in place. Then cover the openings in the stencil with paste and let the paste dry. When it is dry, remove the stencil and spray the surface of the material. In this method you have to be careful to get an *even* tone over the whole surface. In the other method you are only spraying the pattern, not the background.

The paste is removed by washing in cold water. This will leave the design or pattern the colour of the material, and the background will be coloured. This has the same effect as a background stencil. You will be delighted with the result, for it looks more out of the common than the ordinary method of stencilling.

CRAYON STENCILLING

This is on the whole an easy method of stencilling and not at all messy, so it appeals to many home workers. Crayons that are to be used for stencilling must contain a small amount of wax. Special crayons for decorative dyeing can be bought from such firms as Dryad Handicrafts, Leicester. They are 2d. each or 1s. 6d. a dozen, so they are not expensive. They provide a means of permanently decorating any smooth absorbent surface such as silk or cotton fabrics, paper, leather, wood, and cork, without using a liquid. If you like you can experiment with wax crayons of several makes and find out which best suits your needs. Then lay in your stock of colours. Crayons about the size of a lead-pencil are useful for general work, larger crayons are especially valuable for covering large spaces in a design. Many people find a piece of wire screening more satisfactory for sharpening crayons than a knife.

Crayon stencilling is delightfully easy work. You can even decorate the walls of your rooms or make a frieze over your dresser or on your cupboard with them.

To stencil a border or frieze in any part of your room or on a cupboard, fireplace, or screen, etc., hold the stencil firmly against the wall with the left hand, then draw around the openings in the stencil, remove the stencil, and fill in the pattern with the desired colours. One colour may be used to some extent over another colour to produce various tones or tints. Fine lines and darker touches can be added with the crayon used free-hand.

But probably the most practical work and the easiest is to use these crayons on fabrics—canvas or burlap. Pretty screens can be made. In this case the crass or canvas must be stencilled and have the colours set before they are fastened into the frame of the screen. Thin materials such as silk, voile, crêpe, or chiffon are also suitable for crayon stencilling.

Fabrics that are to be stencilled with wax crayons are treated in this way. First pin the fabric to a drawing-board, over which two thicknesses of paper have been laid, or one thick sheet of paper. Place the stencil over and pin it in position, put weights on it if drawing-pins will harm the fabric. Then take the smallest pieces of crayon of the correct colour and trace around the openings in the stencil. Hold the crayon fairly upright and do not press too heavily, as you do not want a hard outline around the design. When the pattern has been outlined in this way, remove the stencil paper and fill in the pattern with the desired colours, using the broad sides of the crayon. One colour, as we have said before, can to some extent be worked over another to get a variety of tints or shades.

When the design is crayoned in this way, as evenly as possible, except for any specially accented lines, use a soft hat-brush to remove any small particles of crayon that may cling to the cloth. This is very important that all small particles of crayon are removed, because they will appear as small spots when the hot iron is placed over them.

To set the colours, the fabric must be pressed with a very hot iron. Do not push the iron over the cloth, but set it down carefully on the design ; then lift the iron and place it down again over another part of the design. If this method is not followed, and the iron is pushed over the design, the edges will become blurred. The iron should be cleaned each time in case any particles adhere and spoil the work. If desired, a piece of thin cheese-cloth can be placed over the design to protect it while it is being pressed. The pressing causes the colours to sink into the cloth and gives a very pleasing effect.

Try to decorate the ends of a silk scarf in this way and see the effect.

Stencilling on Wood, China, Glass, and Lampshades

Wood Work.—Stencilling can be done very effectively on painted wood or upon bare wood.

Unpainted wooden articles must be sand-papered first. Use No. 1 or No. 0 glass-paper. Work with the grain of the wood, never against it. When the wood is perfectly clean and smooth, it can be stained, painted, or coated with lacquer. When this is dry the design is stencilled on in some contrasting colours. Wood-work stains can be used instead of paint, and an interesting inlaid effect can be produced. Oil-paints and enamels look well on wood. If a box is painted black with dull lacquer, the colours that are stencilled on it must be used fairly thickly.

There are many ways in which stencilling on wood can be

used to decorate and beautify the home. Often old pieces of furniture can be so changed as to look quite new. It may take some time to prepare the wood by a good deal of rubbing down, but the lovely soft finish that can be obtained is well worth the trouble. If the piece of furniture to be decorated is soiled or dis-coloured in any way, it must be well rubbed with coarse sandpaper before applying the enamel. The design can be worked in oil-colours. Small articles of furniture for children's use, such as a little stool or chair, will look especially attractive when treated in this way. A very handsome effect can be obtained by painting a small piece of furniture in black lacquer and stencilling on it.

A teapot-stand of white wood stained to match the tea-set and decorated with a stencil pattern looks most effective. If the stand is wax-polished afterwards, it can be cleaned with a damp cloth and polished again.

There are all kinds of useful wooden boxes, such as a string-box, powder-box, trinket-case, match-box cover, that can be decorated. Little children will love a pencil-box with gay Noah's ark animals, or rabbits or ducks stencilled on it.

If the white wooden article has a good finish there is no need to colour the background, as the woodwork looks quite effective.

Stencilling on China and Glass.—Few people realise how possible this is and what delightful results can be obtained. The colours will not wash off if properly applied, and with care will last quite a long time. They can always be touched up again and made to look as good as new.

Preparation of the China or Glass.—First, any article to be stencilled must be thoroughly cleaned to remove all grease and finger-marks, otherwise the colours will not go on evenly nor will they be permanent. Place the china in a large pan of cold water, add a pinch of washing powder, put the pan on the stove and bring to the boiling point as slowly as possible. This process removes all dirt and tempers the china, making it less liable to crack. Leave it in the water until cold. Then dry thoroughly and polish with a soft linen cloth moistened with a few drops of methylated spirit. Do not handle the surface after polishing.

Fitting and transferring the Design.—If you are stencilling on a curved surface such as a teapot, you must snip the stencil-plate along the top and bottom to allow it to follow the curve.

It is sometimes best to arrange for the join to come at the back of the teapot near the handle, or you can work from the back on either side and arrange some detail of the pattern so that it will fill any space left. Be very careful about the joins, because the work looks very uneven and disjointed if the stencil-plates do not meet correctly. A curved surface is more difficult, so it is well for a beginner to choose an object having flat sides. The stencil can be fastened down by using stamp paper.

Colouring the Design.—Suppose you are going to use ordinary oil-colours. These can be bought at about 5d. per tube. You will need a bottle of stencilling medium, about 1s. 3d., and Japanese brushes varying in price according to the size. They are not expensive.

Use the colours as dry as possible and thick enough to cover the surface. Keep the brush upright and stipple the paint, as the stencil-plate is less likely to move. When you have finished, remove the plate and wipe off any colour that has spread with a clean rag. Before you begin stencilling any portion of the china, clean it again with a rag dipped in methylated spirit, as the slightest finger-mark will prevent the colour going on evenly. It will help to fix the colours if you hold the china in the steam of a boiling kettle for a minute or two, turning it so that each part is held in the steam.

Stencilled china must always be washed very carefully and *never* left to soak in the water, as otherwise the colour may come off.

Stencilling Lampshades.—In this work you have to remember that your colours must show to the best advantage when the light is shining through. Any unevenness in colouring which might not be noticeable in ordinary stencilling would be seen at once. Again, the light will alter the tone of the colours, or make them lighter than they really appear. Therefore it is wise to try first on a piece of odd material and hold it up to the light to judge the effect.

If you are using vellum, stains used for woodwork are quite suitable for this material, and they go on very freely. Other suitable paints to use are waterproof drawing-inks.

If silk is to be used, see the section on Stencilling on Fabrics. Special paints can be bought for stencilling on lampshades.

Stencilling on leather, see Chapter XXIX.

Stencilling on cork mats, see Chapter XXX.

CHAPTER XVIII

THE CRAFT OF HOME-MADE RUGS FROM WASTE MATERIAL

Some Old-Time Rugs. Braided or Plaited Rugs. The Scalloped Rug. The Knitted Rug. The Crocheted Rug. Hooked Rugs—Materials for them ; Transferring the Design on the Burlap by Drawing or Stencilling. Hooking the Rug, using Cotton or Woollen Strips. Rugs woven on a *Frame Loom*—Setting up the Warp, Weaving the Rug, The Navajo Pattern.

IN this chapter we are going to describe some of the interesting and economical ways of making rugs in the olden days, in the hope that some people will copy them to-day. Many of these rugs will suggest ideas for pretty table mats. See what novel mats and rugs you can make after reading this section and what ideas you can get for designs.

Few articles of home furnishing are more useful or decorative than a well-made and attractive rug. Handsome rugs come to us from the past, and the old-time craft of rug-making is still popular and has left us an interesting technique.

For some years past there has been a great zest in the United States and in Canada for collecting old examples of rugs—the braided rug, the scalloped rug, the knitted rug, the crocheted rug, the hooked rug, the needle-woven rug, and the Colonial rag rug. We will say a word about some of these old-time rugs and then describe the methods of making rugs at home to-day.

In studying some of the old ways of making rugs one learns a good deal about design, for decoration must develop as an integral part of technique.

BRAIDED RUGS OR PLAITED RUGS (see also Plaited Raffia, Chapter XXI.)

The most distinctive feature of the braided rug is developed from the manner in which the three strands that are braided

246

or plaited are arranged ; for by braiding (or plaiting) together two strands of a darker colour with one of a very much lighter colour a characteristic pattern develops when the braids are sewed together in circular rows. By emphasising this feature in the design the rug gets a charm peculiarly its own and becomes, through a technical feature, a rug distinctive in appearance.

The really old braided rugs were made of cotton rags, or cotton and woollen mixed, in fact of anything old or new which came in handy. As they were so economical they were the ones most frequently seen in the farmhouses in New England and Middle States. They wear well and lie flatter than most rag carpets.

The cotton material is torn into strips about 1 yard or $1\frac{1}{2}$ yards long, and $3\frac{1}{2}$ inches wide. If the strips are too long they are apt to tangle. Fold in the torn edges of each strip for $\frac{1}{2}$ inch on each side, then fold these turned-in edges equally to meet in the middle. The strip should measure about $1\frac{1}{4}$ inch when finished. The width can vary a little, but it should never be narrower than 1 inch. After all the strands are folded, iron them and wind them around a heavy piece of cardboard to keep them smooth and to keep the fold along the edge in place. Take three strands of the colours needed, sew them at one end, and plait them until within 3 inches of their ends, then pin or tie these ends so that they will not unravel. Begin to make the mat by sewing the braid together, sew along the inside edges of the braids (overhand), and for a round mat begin to turn the braid at once.

The method of work is something the same as that used in making raffia mats from plaited raffia (see the chapter on Raffia Work).

Beautiful mats can be made to-day from good coloured cottons by those who like home crafts. Remember always in selecting and preparing material for braiding that stiff materials do not crush up nicely in the braids, and as the braided rug is a washable rug, all likelihood of the colours running must be done away with by giving the materials a thorough washing before they are made up.

These make delightful mats for the nursery.

THE SCALLOPED MAT OR TONGUE MAT

This gets its name from the shape of the piece of cloth from which it is built up. It is another example of a needle-made rug. It is not so frequently seen as the other mats we are describing here. It takes longer to make, but it has great decorative possibilities. The tongue-shaped units are cut out of odds and ends of woollen cloth and sewed on a burlap foundation, cotton will not wear well for this mat. The more closely woven the fabric is the better it is for a scalloped mat. Felt is excellent, or odd pieces of broad cloth (see chapter on Wool and Felt Work). The scalloped or tongue-shaped units are sewed on the burlap foundation in exactly the same way in which shingles are laid on the roof of a house. That is, they begin at the outside edge and work in towards the middle. One might also compare the construction of the scalloped door-mat to the overlapping scales of the pine-cone. Indeed the prettiest shape for the scallop and the most practical is the elongated form rounded at the edge which resembles the scale of the pine cone. Each scallop must be finished all around with a buttonhole stitch before it is sewed down on the burlap foundation. After the scallops are all sewn on, they are held in place on the foundation by a star-shaped stitch. Try a small scalloped mat for the table. Felt is very suitable, as it need not be buttonholed and thus time is saved.

THE KNITTED RUG

In old Colonial days the materials used for making knitted rugs were old rags of either wool or cotton. Square or oblong rugs were made in bands from 8 to 10 inches in width and then sewn together. This made the work easier to handle, for the strips were heavy to knit, since they were about $\frac{3}{4}$ inch in width and 4 yards long. Large knitting-needles are used for this work, 15 inches long and $\frac{1}{4}$ inch thick and a large crochet hook of the same size.

Round rugs are more difficult to make in this way than square. As the technical problem of the knitted rug is so simple, the design should be made an important feature in order to lift it out of the commonplace and into the rank of dignified handicraft. A round mat can be knitted in twelve wedge-shaped sections, and by emphasising certain parts of these sections its ornamental features can be made interesting ; for example, broad bands of dark colour can be used at intervals in the sections, while the rest of the section is knitted in a shaded thread. In a round mat after the first and last sections are sewn together, crochet a narrower border around the whole rug. Go twice around, first with the plain chain stitch and then with a scallop stitch. It is this border which gives a finished edge to the rug.

A mat for the bathroom can be made of strips of unbleached muslin. The colours chosen may be medium blue and cream-white. If a blue and white scheme is chosen, the blue can be dyed in the indigo vat (see section on Dyeing), or a commercially dyed blue calico can be used. The cream-white is the usual un-bleached muslin.

Begin the rug by setting up fifteen stitches in the blue or in the coloured thread (strip of material) selected for the dark tone of the pattern and knit sufficient length to form a square of dark (about twenty-two rows of knitting). The exact number of rows cannot be exactly estimated because different workers knit more or less closely. (See chapter on Knitting and section on Tension.) The number given is for rather close knitting and is roughly correct. Now change the thread (strip) to the cream-white by sewing this on the blue, and knit a square of it. Continue alternating with blue and white squares until seven in all are completed. This makes a strip of knitting about 6 inches wide and 42 inches long.

Begin the next strip with a cream-white square and continue in the same way alternating squares of blue and white until the desired number is produced.

Five strips of knitting are needed to complete the rug : three beginning with the blue and ending with the blue, and two beginning with the white and ending with the white. These five must be sewn together to carry out the pattern. They form the body of the rug ; the borders are added later.

The strips that form the borders are made with the blue strips of material and nine stitches are set up. Two knitted strips are needed for the sides of the rug and they must be about 42 inches in length. Two knitted strips of the same width are needed for the two ends of the rug and these must be about 36 inches in length. These four strips sewed on each side form a complete border around the rug. The size of the finished rug is about 30 by 48 inches, including borders. The middle portion measures about 30 by 42 inches. The rug can easily be enlarged in proportion by adding squares to the length and breadth.

For more about knitting, see the chapter on Knitting.

THE CROCHETED RUG

Crocheting is easy (see chapter on Crochet). Any one can crochet even if she cannot knit, but such a simple craft as crocheting can be made worth while if combined with thought and design.

Design.—The crocheted rug is related to the knitted rug because they are both needle-made rugs, but the crocheted rug is more closely related to the braided rug in actual similarity of construction. Though the braided rug is made with a different kind of needle, its coiled construction resembles the crocheted rug. The stitch of the crocheted rug which, decoratively speaking, is its unit of construction, has a line of action similar to that of the braided rug and also controls its design. Beautiful patterns and suggestions for beautiful designs can be found in the coiled basketry of the Navajo Indians (see the chapter on Coiled Basketry or Indian Basketry). Designs for crocheted rugs must be abstract in character, for the stitch of the crocheted rug suggests a formal type of ornament. It is in fact almost geometrical.

The most successful plans for any kind of handicraft are those which have a tendency to weld together surface ornament and structure. Almost every technique soon develops two styles of design, one which is structural and one which appears in various forms of surface pattern. The one can best be interpreted by line, the other by spots of tone or colour value. The structural features can be ornamented through the repetition of tone or colour value on carefully selected prints of the line action. (The chapter on Crochet Work will say more about crochet work and its characteristic designs.) Crocheted table mats can be made in round, oval, and hexagonal forms and the crocheted rug can be made in these shapes also.

Suggestions for making crocheted mats of wool for the bath-

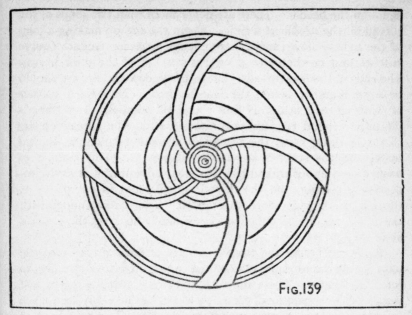

FIG. 139.—Crocheted Rug.

room, etc., will be given in the chapter on Crochet Work, here we are considering more rugs made of rags, though of course wool can be used.

Making a Crocheted Rug of Rags (Fig 139).—The rug is a round one about 38 inches in diameter. The colours used should be sharply contrasting tones, say of brown and yellow. Sharply contrasting tones are necessary in order to carry out the pattern effectively. If the rug is made for a sitting-room, bedroom, or bathroom, it must match the walls or furnishings of these rooms. A wooden crochet needle can be used, and about 20 yards of un-bleached cotton muslin if one is going to dye one's own material. Tear the material into strips before it is dyed, this makes dyeing easier. The strips must be about 1 inch wide.

Crocheting the Rug.—The stitch used in crocheting this rug is plain crochet stitch. It looks more like cross stitch when done, than any other of the crocheted stitches. Make one loop on the needle and then form a second by taking off the thread, then crochet both loops which are on the needle, leaving one loop again on the needle. There are never more than two loops of the thread on the needle at a time. Begin the rug by making a loop of the light yellow thread large enough to accommodate twelve stitches and crochet into it twelve stitches of the dark brown. The ends of the two threads, that is, the yellow and brown, should be sewn together before the loop is made. Now tie a marker of white thread into this first round of stitches. The threads in the crocheted rug are continuous; while the thread of one colour is being used, the thread of the other colour is slipped under and the stitches are crocheted over it. This manner of using a continuous thread has two great advantages, it saves unnecessary piecing, and the thread which is not in use pads out the rug, making it more substantial. The thread underneath the stitch should be pulled up occasionally to keep the stitches firm.

After crocheting the twelve stitches of dark thread into the loop, proceed and make nine or ten rounds of brown stitches, to form the centre. There must be sixty-four stitches in the last round. The beginning of each new round can be easily seen when indicated by the marker which was tied in the first round of twelve stitches. Double the stitches occasionally in these first rounds, just enough to keep the centre of the rug from " capping," but not enough to make it " fill up." When counting the stitches do not count the chain on the top but the stitches that have already been crocheted into the round below.

After the pattern begins, the doubling takes place at regular intervals and always comes in the longest count of each round. For example, in the first count of the first round make four stitches, then double in fourth stitch, then make four more, making the nine stitches of the count. It is wiser to have the doubling take place at the same points in the count as it has an effect on the shape of the rug.

Counting the Pattern.—In counting the pattern the capital L represents the yellow stitches or the lightest tone of the pattern. The capital D represents the brown or the darkest tone in the pattern. The first row of the pattern comes after the nine or ten rows of solid brown of the centre.

First Round of Pattern : 9L, 2D, 1L, 1D, 1L, 2D, 9L, 2D, 1L, 1D, 1L, 2D, 9L, 2D, 1L, 1D, 1L, 2D, 9L, 2D, 1L, 1D, 1L, 3D.

Second Round : 11L, 2D, 1L, 1D, 1L, 2D, 11L, 2D, 1L, 1D, 1L, 2D, 11L, 2D, 1L, 1D, 1L, 2D, 11L, 2D, 1L, 1D, 1L, 3D.

Third Round : 13D, 1L, 1D, 1L, 16D, 1L, 1D, 1L, 16D, 1L, 1D, 1L, 16D, 1L, 1D, 1L, 3D.

Fourth Round : 12L, 2D, 1L, 1D, 1L, 2D, 12L, 2D, 1L, 1D, 1L, 2D, 12L, 2D, 1L, 1D, 1L, 2D, 12L, 2D, 1L, 1D, 1L, 3D.

Fifth Round : 13L, 2D, 1L, 1D, 1L, 2D, 13L, 2D, 1L, 1D, 1L, 2D, 13L, 2D, 1L, 1D, 1L, 2D, 13L, 2D, 1L, 1D, 1L, 3D.

Sixth Round : 16D, 1L, 1D, 1L, 18D, 1L, 1D, 1L, 18D, 1L, 1D, 1L, 18D, 1L, 1D, 1L, 3D.

Seventh Round : 15L, 2D, 1L, 1D, 1L, 2D, 15L, 2D, 1L, 1D, 1L, 2D, 15L, 2D, 1L, 1D, 1L, 2D, 15L, 2D, 1L, 1D, 1L, 3D.

Eighth Round : 16L, 2D, 1L, 1D, 1L, 2D, 16L, 2D, 1L, 1D, 1L, 2D, 16L, 2D, 1L, 1D, 1L, 2D, 16L, 2D, 1L, 1D, 1L, 3D.

Ninth Round : 19D, 1L, 1D, 1L, 21D, 1L, 1D, 1L, 21D, 1L, 1D, 1L, 21D, 1L, 1D, 1L, 3D.

Tenth Round : 18L, 2D, 1L, 1D, 1L, 2D, 18L, 2D, 1L, 1D, 1L, 2D, 18L, 2D, 1L, 1D, 1L, 2D, 18L, 2D, 1L, 1D, 1L, 3D.

Eleventh Round : 19L, 2D, 1L, 1D, 1L, 2D, 19L, 2D, 1L, 1D, 1L, 2D, 19L, 2D, 1L, 1D, 1L, 2D, 19L, 2D, 1L, 1D, 1L, 3D.

Twelfth Round : 20L, 2D, 1L, 1D, 1L, 2D, 20L, 2D, 1L, 1D, 1L, 2D, 20L, 2D, 1L, 1D, 1L, 2D, 20L, 2D, 1L, 1D, 1L, 3D.

Thirteenth Round : 23D, 2L, 1D, 2L, 25D, 2L, 1D, 2L, 25D, 2L, 1D, 2L, 25D, 2L, 1D, 2L, 3D.

Fourteenth Round : 24D, 2L, 1D, 2L, 26D, 2L, 1D, 2L, 26D, 2L, 1D, 2L, 26D, 2L, 1D, 2L, 3D.

Fifteenth Round : 23L, 2D, 2L, 1D, 2L, 2D, 23L, 2D, 2L, 1D, 2L, 2D, 23L, 2D, 2L, 1D, 2L, 2D, 23L, 2D, 2L, 1D, 2L, 3D.

Sixteenth Round : 24L, 2D, 2L, 1D, 2L, 2D, 24L, 2D, 2L, 1D, 2L, 2D, 24L, 2D, 2L, 1D, 2L, 2D, 24L, 2D, 2L, 1D, 2L, 3D.

Seventeenth Round : 25L, 2D, 2L, 1D, 2L, 2D, 25L, 2D, 2L, 1D, 2L, 2D, 25L, 2D, 2L, 1D, 2L, 2D, 25L, 2D, 2L, 1D, 2L, 3D.

Eighteenth Round : 29D, 2L, 2D, 2L, 31D, 2L, 2D, 2L, 31D, 2L, 2D, 2L, 31D, 2L, 2D, 2L, 3D.

Nineteenth Round : 30D, 2L, 2D, 2L, 33D, 2L, 2D, 2L, 33D, 2L, 2D, 2L, 33D, 2L, 2D, 2L, 3D.

Twentieth Round : 28L, 2D, 2L, 2D, 2L, 2D, 28L, 2D, 2L, 2D, 2L, 2D, 28L, 2D, 2L, 2D, 2L, 2D, 28L, 2D, 2L, 2D, 2L, 3D.

Twenty-first Round : 29L, 2D, 2L, 2D, 2L, 2D, 29L, 2D, 2L,

2D, 2L, 2D, 29L, 2D, 2L, 2D, 2L, 2D, 29L, 2D, 2L, 2D
2L, 3D.

Twenty-second Round : 30L, 2D, 2L, 2D, 2L, 2D, 30L, 2D, 2L,
2D, 2L, 2D, 30L, 2D, 2L, 2D, 2L, 2D, 30L, 2D, 2L, 2D, 2L, 3D.

Twenty-third Round : 33D, 3L, 2D, 3L, 36D, 3L, 2D, 3L,
36D, 3L, 2D, 3L, 36D, 3L, 2D, 3L, 3D.

Twenty-fourth Round : 36D, 3L, 2D, 3L, 39D, 3L, 2D, 3L,
39D, 3L, 2D, 3L, 39D, 3L, 2D, 3L, 3D.

Twenty-fifth Round : 39D, 3L, 2D, 3L, 42D, 3L, 2D, 3L,
42D, 3L, 2D, 3L, 42D, 3L, 2D, 3L, 3D.

Finish the edge of the rug by winding it over and over with
a strip of the brown to suggest the finish on the edge of a basket.
The strip of brown can be threaded into a bodkin and be worked
in and out through the chain of stitches on the edge of the rug.
This finish emphasises the general effect of basketry in the design.

This is one of the most attractive hand-made rugs. To make
it successfully the pattern must be carried out with the greatest
exactitude.

As soon as the pattern begins to develop and you can see its
effect, the work becomes easier, but the first few rounds of the
pattern must be followed very carefully. It is most important
to remember that the last round of brown in the middle of the
rug must contain sixty-four stitches. Try this pattern in wool
of the same colours or choose dark and light shades of another
colour. Fig. 139 shows the pretty pattern that you will get.
Many readers will perhaps prefer wool because it seems easier
to handle than the strips of material. Strips of material,
however, make the stronger mat.

The above pattern will be found in *The Craft of Hand-Made
Rugs*, by Amy Mali Hicks (R. M. McBride), a book which I fear
is now out of print.

THE HOOKED RUGS

Probably the hooked rugs or the " pulled rugs " are the most
important of hand-made rugs and are more universally known
than any others.

One can often see examples of them in the showrooms of
many Arts and Crafts Societies.

Collectors in the United States and Canada are always looking out for fine examples of these fine old rugs. The women of the New England farms have been associated with this style of rug and its traditions for several generations. In our own islands the " Hookie " rug is made in the north of Britain, from Wales to the Shetlands. The rug is very popular among the mining and fishing folk of our country, and if it is made of old materials as the braided rugs and the other rugs described, it is a " Thrift rug." Perhaps it is a heritage from the ancient Scandinavian settlers in the British Isles.

First, we will describe the making of the old mats, and then show how they are made to-day. The process has hardly changed at all.

Hooked rugs are made from either cotton or woollen materials. The same tools are used for both kinds, for there are only slight differences in their technique. The main point of difference being in the way in which the loops of material are pulled up through the foundation on which the rug is made.

The foundation is first stretched on a wooden frame. It is made of burlap (a raw jute, as it is often called commercially). The principal characteristic feature of this rug is the hooking of the strips of material into the foundation, where the collective loops form the textile. The loops are crowded in between the meshes of the burlap and held by pressing one against the other.

In rugs made of cotton strips the loops are pulled up evenly ; but in rugs made of woollen strips they can be uneven, because the woollen rug is clipped after it is hooked. Clipping improves the pile, for the colour of the flannel loop deepens when it is cut, and becomes velvety in texture. The cut ends of the loops in the woollen rug also tend to meet together and this makes the pile more uniform.

Cotton rugs are not clipped because the cotton strip has no tendency to felt, it only frays, and fraying weakens the texture of the rug. Cotton rugs, however, can be washed. These rugs can be made in large sizes, as they can be hooked in sections and sewed carefully together afterwards ; the seams do not show.

Materials for the Rug.—Hooked rugs can of course be made of odds and ends of material. New material lasts longer, and beautiful designs can be made. If cotton material is being used, tear it into strips about $\frac{1}{2}$ inch wide ; for wool rugs use flannel, and *cut* the flannel strips ¼ inch wide and as evenly as possible. This is how it can be cut. Divide it into single yards, roll each yard into a tight roll, and tie the roll 4 inches from the selvedge and in the middle firmly with a cord. Cut the flannel strips off the rolls with a very sharp knife just as if you were slicing a loaf of bread ! (Do you think this is possible ? Try it and see.)

The hook used to be made at home, but now it is bought. It was made from a large wire nail bent to form a suitable hook and then fastened in a handle.

Before beginning to work it is wise to make a hem of single thickness all round the burlap and stitch it down on a sewing-machine, the line of stitches being one-quarter of an inch from the edge. (Most workers turn under 2 inches of burlap.) The stitching strengthens the edge of the rug. The extra thickness of burlap at the corners, where the hem is turned under double, is cut away and the raw edges over-handed. The loose flap of the hem is caught down and held in place by loops of material when the rug is hooked. The old-fashioned method of finishing a hooked rug was to hem it after all the hooking was done. Then the hem of burlap was sewed down on top of the under-side of the rug over a hooked portion. This left the burlap outside exposed to rubbing on the floor. Some burlap is apt to fray out, by hemming the foundation before it is hooked, this is prevented, and the underside of the rug has a neater appearance, because it is uniform to the very edge. There is little difficulty in hooking the strips through two thicknesses of burlap.

Transferring the Design to the Burlap Foundation.—The design can be drawn on the burlap or printed with a stencil. If the rug design is to be repeated several times, it is more convenient to use a stencil. If, on the other hand, the design is only to be used once, it is more convenient to draw it on the foundation.

To draw it on the foundation : first divide the foundation into a suitable number of squares, say twelve ; use white chalk for making these divisions. Number them from one to twelve so that they correspond exactly to similar cross-lines drawn on the pattern being copied. The scale for the drawing may be something like 1 inch to 1 foot.

Now copy into each square with the marking chalk, that

Shopping or work bag, with top border cut from cretonne and appliquéd on.

[To face p. 256

Tea cloth and cosy in check gingham, with plain appliqué.

Detail of hemmed or blind appliqué.

Appliqué traycloth, with contrasting hem faggoted on.

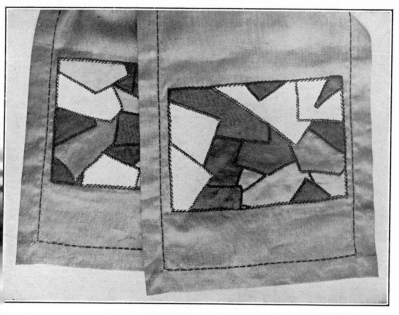

Crazy patchwork panels on linen runner.

Cushion in American block patchwork, in the old " Little Red Schoolhouse " design.

Quilted linen tea-cosy.

Nightdress case in Italian quilting in white organdie.

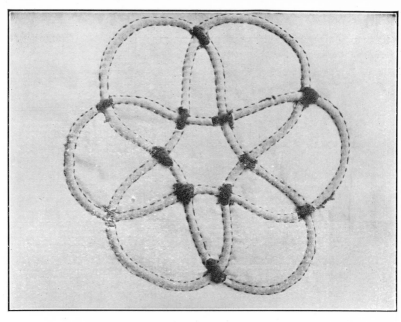

Italian quilting, wrong side of nightdress case design,
showing how the wool padding is inserted.

Chair back of crash embroidered in wool.

Chinese pagoda tea-cosy, embroidered felt.

Sachet made up quilting round the design of a floral handkerchief.

Making Artificial Flowers. *Stage* 1.—Leaves cut and arranged on circle of stuff for a felt posy.

Stage 2.—Felt posy finished.   Flowers are small circles pinched up at the centre.

piece of the design which falls into that particular square. Thus section by section the pattern can be copied and enlarged. With a medium-sized paint brush and liquid blueing trace over all the chalk marks of the design, omitting the lines of the squares which were only used for the enlargement. After the blueing has dried, brush off the remaining chalk and the foundation is ready to be stitched on a frame of some kind. The frame can rest, as embroidery frames do, on the back of two chairs or on a table. Each rug-maker must adjust the height of the frame to suit herself.

Hooking the Rug, using Cotton Strips or Wool.—Take a strip of material and hold it under the foundation with the left hand. With the right hand take the rug hook very much in the same manner as one would a crochet hook. Push the hook through the meshes of the burlap and pull up the strip by drawing an end through first. Hold on to this end from underneath so that it will not slip back again. Then put the hook down again through the foundation, draw up the strip which will this time be a loop, make the loops $\frac{3}{8}$ inch high. Hook in all directions, and for the cotton rug pull the loops up just as evenly as possible. When beginning a new strip, draw the end up into the same hole occupied by the end of some other strip. Leave from two to three meshes of the burlap between each loop, and be sure not to split the threads of the foundation, as this weakens the fabric of the rug.

It is a good plan to begin hooking the rug pattern by first outlining the design. Outlining is easier than filling in and it gives one a clearer idea of the design to first outline it. After the outlining is completed fill in all the spaces of the design with the colours required. Always hook from the edges towards each frameful. The most central spot should be the last to be filled in. Change from colour to colour as the design requires, but do not leave the background the last to be filled in. When changing the colour of the strip and going from one part of the design to another, do not double the strips on the under side of the rug. Cut them and begin again. Overlapping the strips makes a clumsy lump on the underside that is apt to cut through the rest of the rug. Hooking the rug from the sides towards the centre prevents the edges of the rug from ruffling up. There

9

is always a certain amount of fullness which comes from the stretching of the burlap. This extra fullness may be pushed by the hooking towards the centre of the rug where it is taken up, and the edges of the rug remain flat. When hooking, push the new row of loops against the rows already hooked. This method prevents wide spaces from coming in between the rows. After one frameful has been hooked, it can be rolled up and another frameful tied on. The rug is hooked frameful by frameful ; in this way the frame need not be too large and so take up too much room in a small house.

Stencilling Patterns on Burlap.—Choose a suitable pattern. Enlarge the pattern by dividing it into squares, but instead of drawing it direct on the burlap, first draw it on a piece of tough wrapping-paper or stencil paper. Lay it on a hard substance, and cut out the stencil by following the lines marked on the paper. (See chapter on Stencilling.) Do not cut into the background of the design, and do not pull out the cut parts until all the cutting is finished. Pulling out these cut parts weakens the stencil, makes it buckle up and therefore more difficult to cut. Cut well down into the corners of the design, else the pieces are apt to stick when they come to be pulled out. Be careful to leave the ties that hold the design together. Get a fairly large brush (a cheap shaving-brush, cut until it measures 1 inch long will do) ; lay the burlap on a large table, place the stencil on it, and press it down firmly with dressmakers' pins. (Dressmakers' pins are steel and do not bend.) Then take the brush and some liquid blueing and brush over the holes in the pattern ; rub the colour well in, but be careful not to shift the stencil. After the pattern has been printed in this way, let it dry thoroughly.

Hooking the Rug, using Woollen Strips.—The process is the same as already described for cotton strips, except that the loops in the wool rug are pulled up unevenly and clipped. Draw every three loops up to a height of a $\frac{1}{4}$ inch and one loop to $\frac{3}{8}$ inch. Thus when the rug is clipped, only every one in four loops is cut off.

After each frameful has been hooked, clip the rug until it is completed. Use a strong pair of shears, and holding the left hand under the rug, lift up that portion of the surface which is to be clipped. Clipping the rug improves the texture and the pile. The very old-fashioned hooked rugs were not clipped and consequently were not so attractive as these made by the method described above.

For still more modern methods of making hooked rugs, see Chapter XIX.

Those interested in the history of rugs may like to know that these are minor rugs, the rag-bit rug, and the ravelled rug, which might be called forerunners of the hooked rug. These rugs are chiefly interesting because they show how a real technique may grow out of small beginnings. They are mentioned here for the sake of interest, not to be copied, their methods are far too crude to suggest constructive designs.

The rag-bit rug is the most primitive. It is made by sewing small bits of woollen cloth on to a foundation. Odds and ends of cloth of all shapes and kinds are used so that no effect of texture or design is produced.

The ravelled rug is made from thread ravelled from old pieces of carpet. These threads are drawn through the meshes of a loosely woven foundation with a crochet hook. The crowding of the threads between the meshes of the cloth holds them as in the hooked rug.

There is an interesting book published in America but now out of print called *The Craft of Hand-made Rugs*. It tells a good deal about the old-time methods of handicraft, and though much of this work is not possible now, the book makes pleasant reading for those who are interested in the patient work of long ago. We have given in this chapter all the rugs that are possible to-day, when time seems to pass more quickly and people have less leisure.

Another way of making rugs from waste material, is to weave them on frames. This coarse weaving is interesting, for it teaches one a good deal about pattern making, and it is much more possible than weaving on complicated looms. Although we are going to describe weaving with strips of materials, wool can also be used. Coarse weaving on small frame looms makes useful dish cloths, dusters, and floor cloths as well as small mats. It is a very pleasant occupation for those whose sight is not good. All sorts of odds and ends of material (if it can be cut into strips) can be used to weave the useful articles mentioned above.

Rugs woven on a Loom (Fig. 140)

Rugs woven on a simple loom with a needle are an interesting example of craft-work, because they stand between the rugs of the needle and the rugs of the loom.

The rugs of the needle are really the hooked, the knitted, crocheted, and braided rugs that we have already described, and they are made with a single tool.

The needle-woven rug bridges the gap between the strictly hand-made rugs and the fabric which though hand-made is still mechanically produced on a primitive machine. The needle-woven rug is a combination of the needle and the loom, and is therefore the simplest form of weaving. It is still practised among primitive people to-day. The Navajo Indians of Arizona weave in this way the beautiful rugs, known and sold commercially as Navajo blankets, using the most primitive kind of a loom and a needle made of bone.

The rude frame which is used to make this loom is really the forerunner of all looms.

Those who want to try a needle-woven rug should use as their first loom, a strong wooden frame like a picture-frame, and a large wooden needle such as is used in netting hammocks.

A rug can be made of the well-known cotton cloth torn into very fine strips. This will be found quite effective, for the ravelled edges of the torn strips make a delightful and varied surface because they felt and mat together. A rug made in this way can be used in the bathroom. For the warp or the threads which make the foundation hammock twine can be used. Warp threads must always be strong to hold the rug together for the warp is really the framework of the rug. Hammock twine is very firmly twisted cord and is suitable to use as warp. The cotton strips and the twine are all that are needed in making the needle-woven rug.

The Loom or Rug Frame.—This primitive loom or frame is like the frame used in making the hooked rug. It is a rectangular frame made of four wooden bars (1 by 2 inches in thickness). For a large rug the frame should be 53 inches by 32 inches. The broad side of the bars, which is the 2-inch dimension, should form the face of the frame, and along this surface on the 32-inch

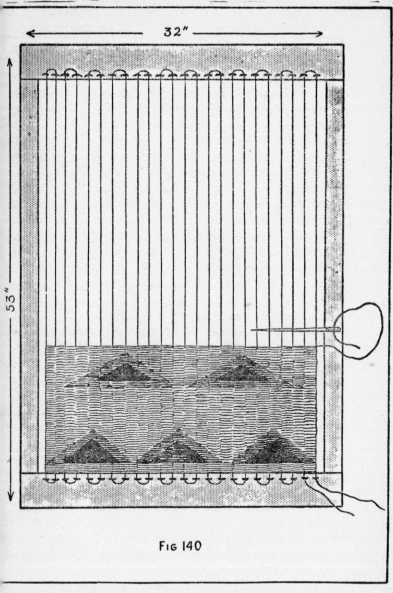

FIG 140

FIG. 140.—Weaving a rug on a frame loom, Navajo pattern.

pieces double-headed carpet tacks are driven; these make the eyelets which hold the warp threads. These double-headed tacks, forty-nine in number, are placed in a single row along the horizontal bars. They begin 2 inches from the edge of the upright bars with $\frac{1}{2}$ inch between the point of one and the point of the next. The warp thread is run through these little eyelets which are formed in this way by the tacks.

You can perhaps get some one to make a frame loom for you. Begin with a small one and weave a small mat. You will find weaving very fascinating. A picture-frame makes a good loom if the corners are strengthened. Old picture-frames can often be adapted in this way.

You can, if you like, do without the eyelets and wind the string round and round; then if you weave both sides you will have a long strip of carpet, or you can if you like tie each warp thread on separately. We will now describe in detail—

The Setting-up of the Warp.—Use for your warp something strong, as we have said before, such as hammock twine for a large mat. Probably the best warp for general work is a strong cotton yarn. Knitting cottons of various sizes can also be used. The collection of warp threads fastened on the loom, which form the structure or framework of the rug, is called in weaving *the warp.*

The warp in the rug frame that we have just described is one continuous thread and runs without interruption up and down through the metal eyelets which are used for carrying it.

To thread this loom, wind about 100 yards of warp thread on a large reel or piece of wood. After it is wound, take the end and thread it through eyelet No. 1 on the lower bar of the frame. Then carry it up and thread it through eyelet No. 1 on the upper bar. Carry it from eyelet No. 1 on the upper bar to eyelet No. 2 on the same bar. Thread it through this eyelet and bring it down to eyelet No. 2 on the lower bar. Carry it then to No. 3 on the lower bar and then to No. 3 on the upper bar; carry it from No. 3 on the upper bar to No. 4 and down again. Continue in this way, always passing from each eyelet to the next, threading two eyelets at a time on the same bar until the last two are reached, one on the upper bar and one on the lower bar.

Now unwind what remains of the thread and pull the continuous warp thread through all the eyelets until a free end of about $2\frac{1}{4}$

yards is left over at eyelet No. 1. Carry this end to No. 1 on the upper bar, then wind the end of the warp around the frame and fasten it securely by tying it. After it is tied pull all the slack out towards the other end, as the thread must be double through the last eyelets as it was through the first two. Tighten up the warp again and tie this end to the frame. If the warp threads are too slack, the rug will be found uneven in the weaving. The double warp threads at the side of the rug strengthen the rug on the edges where it gets most wear.

The warp is now set up and we are ready to put in the cross-threads or weft, or in other words, to weave the rug. The warp holds together the cross-threads which are collectively called the *woof*, or *weft*.

Weaving the Rug.—The process of weaving with a needle is exactly like darning a stocking (see also Chapter VI., Swedish Weaving or Darning). The space between the warp threads is filled by weaving cross-threads in and out among them. A raffia needle can be used for small mats and a bodkin for the large loom that we have described. A large loom is quickly worked with strips of unbleached calico.

Choose three tones to make a pretty design—a pale yellow, a soft brown, and a buff. The lightest colour can be used in the largest proportion and in the background. The buff (a deep buff) and the brown are the colours used in the pattern, which thus stands out in darker tones against the lighter ones. Any other colour combination can of course be chosen, but tints and shades of the *same* colour are always successful.

Begin the weaving at the bottom of the frame, and with the needle threaded with a piece of pale yellow calico weave across in and out the warp three times, then pack these rows firmly down with a comb (a coarse bone comb) by putting its teeth between the strands of the warp and combing hard down against the warp just as if you were combing hair. Continue to weave and pack down the woof threads until a space measuring 3 inches is filled. These 3 inches will be unravelled when the rug-weaving is finished. It is put in in order to pack the other woof threads down against it and make a straight edge. (If the space filled is exactly 3 inches all the way along, you know you will have a mat with a beautifully straight edge.) When these weft threads are

unravelled the ends of the warp threads that are thus left free
are knotted to form a fringe.

Weave with the different coloured strips as desired.
(Pattern-weaving is described more fully in the chapter on
Weaving.) When half the warp is woven, turn the loom around
and begin the whole process as before, by filling in against the
frame 3 inches of weaving that is afterwards to be unravelled.

To prevent the middle of the rug contracting as it is woven,
tie the outside warp threads at intervals to the frame. It is
always difficult for beginners to keep the selvedge sides straight.
When the rug is finished unravel the extra 3 inches each side, cut
the thread at the top of each eyelet, and knot each two warp
threads together. Push the knots up close to the weaving
so that it shall be held very firmly. The loose ends of these
threads form the fringe at the end of the rug. Do not cut all the
warp threads at once but only two at a time, as they are needed
for tying together. Lay the rug on the floor and comb out the
fringe and make it even by cutting off any longer ends.

The surface of a mat made like this improves with wear, for it
mats and felts together very prettily. Fig. 140 shows a rug being
woven on a frame loom. The pattern is that of a Navajo blanket.
The colours most used are white, grey, black, a bright yellow,
scarlet, and sometimes blue. Separate balls of wool of different
colours are used for carrying out this pattern.

In the chapter on Weaving, some simple looms are described
that can be used on the table or when you are sitting by the fireside, and suggestions for simple, useful things that can be made on
them. Pattern-weaving will also be dealt with more fully. In this
chapter we have been more concerned with the making of rugs.

In Chapter XIX. you will read about the most popular of all
home-made rugs to-day, those made from rug wool and canvas
with the crochet hook.

CHAPTER XIX

MODERN HOOKED RUGS MADE FROM WOOL AND CANVAS

Modern Hooked Rugs. Knotted Pile Rugs. The Lichfield Method. Locker-Stitch Rugs. The Short Pile Method or Knotted Rugs made with the Needle. Another Way of making a Knotted Rug. A Third Way. Chenille Rugs. Knitting a Wool Rug. Choosing Designs.

RUG-MAKING is as popular at the present time as in the olden days, though life is less leisurely.

The materials used most frequently to-day are wool and canvas, and the methods vary only in details. The most popular methods are those that produce the knotted pile rugs.

As a rule it is best to buy the wool and canvas made by the same firm, as the manufacturers arrange the canvas and wool to suit each other. Special rug canvas and wool are made by several well-known firms.

The selection of canvas and wool must, of course, depend largely on the methods employed. We will wherever necessary mention the particular canvas needed, as we describe the different processes.

The Swiss use a very strong jute canvas or coarse linen made of broad flat strands of jute, the warp and weft being of different colours. This arrangement makes it easy to count the loops or knots, though there are no apparent holes as in our canvas. This material forms a very firm backing to the rugs. A material called " Panmure " cloth can be bought in our country, which is rather finer than the Swiss. The heavy material called " Hellyn " canvas is a new material for rugs that may become very popular. Its use is described in the first method of rug-making given below.

With regard to wools—*Axminster* or *Turkey* rug wools produce
the best results. They are made in sixfold, fourfold, and two
fold. Two strands of twofold worked into one stitch makes a
good texture. Waste wool, known as " Thrums," can be used
for the sake of economy, but two or three threads are generally
needed for each stitch. This waste wool never gives so firm and
even an appearance as the better wool. *Cable* wool is less useful
and should never be used for any kind of design. It is only
possible for plain rugs. Below are some of the most interesting
modern ways of making rugs. These modern rugs are perhaps
more conventional and less interesting than the rugs of long ago.
    We will begin with the hooked rugs because they are the
oldest, and we have already said a good deal about them in
Chapter XVIII. on " The Craft of Home-Made Rugs from Waste
Material."

HOOKED RUGS—THE ORIGINAL METHOD

These, as we have shown, have come to us from the past.
To-day there are two ways of making these rugs.
    (1) In the first method a sharp hook is used, and the strip
of material or wool pulled through as already described in
Chapter XVIII. Indeed we have said so much about the making
of this kind of rug that there is little further to add. To-day
wool is more often used than torn strips of material, and the
loops are often ½ inch to ¾ inch deep. A jute canvas or coarse
linen must be used. Canvas with large holes is no use.
    (2) In the second method a prodder is used to prod the wool
through the canvas. This prodder has a sharp point and an
eye like an ordinary needle. The wool is threaded into the eye
of the prodder and pushed through the *back* of the canvas. (In
this method the canvas is put on the frame face downwards and
the pattern is traced on the *back*.) As each loop is prodded
through it is caught and held in position by the left hand (which
is under the canvas) while the prodder is withdrawn to make
the next stitch alongside the first. The special needle called
the prodder can be bought. There are indeed two or three tools
of slightly different type that can be bought for making hooked
rugs, and the worker should choose the one that suits her best.
Probably the old-fashioned hook is the best. Hessian, a very

coarse linen, is used for the foundation ; as we have said before, canvas with large holes is not suitable.

These rugs often have to be lined so that nothing can catch the wool from the back and pull out the loops. The linings should be of strong material. Stitch it on here and there so that it will not bag. The backing used in some old examples of hooked rugs was often a heavy linen material called Harden or Harn. Hessian and burlap can be used, however, to-day.

A newer way to make these hooked rugs is to use Helvellyn canvas as a backing. No frame need be used for this as it is such a heavy material. Thinner qualities of wool can also be used on it, such as Persian, Straight, Shetland, and various " Thrums ' yarns. The cut and torn strips of material described in Chapter XVIII. can also be used on this. Helvellyn is not an expensive canvas, and many workers seem to like it.

With regard to lining mats—most of the mats we are now going to describe need no lining. If the work is done neatly and correctly, the backs are often as pretty as the fronts. To add a lining to some of the *pile mats* that you will now read about has two disadvantages : (1) It is very difficult to make a lined rug lie flat ; (2) Dust must collect between the rug and the lining Rugs made on good strong canvas wear quite well without lining, it is only when softer, lighter materials are used that a lining is necessary to bear the weight of the wool.

We will now describe the most popular and perhaps the most successful way of making modern rugs.

KNOTTED PILE RUGS OR HOOKED RUGS

Rugs made by this method have a rich thick pile and are infinitely softer to the feet than any machine-made rug. They are perhaps the handsomest of home-made rugs and are easy to make.

They are made on a background of coarse canvas which may be obtained in various widths ranging from 12 inches to 45 inches. Some canvases are checked with a coloured thread in squares of eight holes to correspond with charts upon which designs have been worked out, thus making it easy to follow and count the different stitches.

It is economical to buy the best canvas, for on the canvas depends the life of the rug.

When the canvas is cut out ready for making the rug, an inch turning should be left at each *end* if the sides are selvedges ; if not, turnings must be left all round. Next count the holes of the canvas and the stitches of the design, so as to place the design correctly on the canvas. The turning can be firmly hemmed on the right side with cotton, after which it can be worked over in wool with crochet or blanket buttonhole stitch to form a firm edge. The buttonhole stitch is usually worked with wool of the same ground colour as the rug. A quicker method of making a good edge is to leave $1\frac{1}{2}$ to 2 inch turnings all round, then turn the rug over on its right side and work through the double thickness.

This hook method is now carried out by working with a plain crochet hook or one with a lachet attachment—the latter is thought by some very useful. Both hooks can be bought at any wool shop. A wooden gauge is also needed to help to cut the wool up into small equal pieces. The wool is wound evenly and tightly round the gauge, and then cut by running a sharp-pointed pair of scissors along the groove of the gauge. The wool must be wound with an even tension if the cut lengths are all to be the same size. The result should be a number of short lengths of wool all of equal length.

Each piece of wool is then drawn through one mesh of the canvas by its middle, the ends are then pulled through the loop so formed, and pulled tightly in place. The following is a detailed description of how to make these knots. First remember to work straight across the canvas from left to right. Take a short length of wool and double it ; then lay the loop against one of the parallel threads of the canvas, holding it with the left hand. Insert the hook under the horizontal thread of the canvas below the loop, catch the loop, and draw it under the canvas thread towards you. Now push forward the hook again and catch up the loose ends of the wool, and draw them both through the loop. Pull them tightly with the fingers so that the loop closes on them, and thus a knot is formed on the canvas, having two free ends. The next tuft is worked in the same way on to the adjoining ridge. Remember all knots must be worked in the same direction throughout the rug.

This method produces a lovely deep pile. The complete knot

formed is very strong and wears well. The only disadvantages of rugs made by this method are : they are inclined to be thick and they take up a good deal of wool and so are expensive.

Care must be taken to work in every hole of the canvas, as missed holes always give an uneven appearance. It is perhaps easiest and best to lay the rugs on a steady table and work on that, especially for large rugs, but the work can also be done on the knee—in this case care must be taken not to pull the canvas out of shape.

Rugs made in this way, as we have said before, need not be lined ; however, some people line them with Hessian, thin glazed lining, or a thin felt. Sometimes the edges are lined with a wide webbing. The advantage of this lining is it prevents the edges from curling up. If the corners persist in curling up, they should be weighted.

When the rug is finished it may be necessary to go over it with the scissors and clip off any uneven ends ; but if the ends of the wool have been kept as even as possible very little clipping is necessary.

Now rub it well and firmly with the hands to work out the loose fluff ; the more thoroughly this is done the more glossy will be the result.

The Lichfield Method

This was thought out by Mrs. Morrison of Lichfield. It is a variation of the hook or original method. The main difference is that macramé twine is passed through each little loop of wool to fix it into place instead of doubling back the wool through its own loop as in the second method. Strutt's macramé twine No. 7 is generally used. A combined hook-needle is needed for this method. The twine is threaded through the eye at one end of the needle ; the hook end is pushed through the one ridge of the canvas as in the second method described, it catches the little loop of wool, and draws it through the canvas as before. Then the hook is pushed through the loop, drawing the twine with it. The hook is now ready for the next loop. The twine passes along the line from loop to loop over the warp threads without any knot. Care must be taken not to pull the twine too tightly. With the Lichfield method it is possible to use a much shorter and, therefore, less expensive wool pile. The gauge can be $\frac{3}{8}$ inch deep, $\frac{1}{2}$ inch wide, producing a length of wool 2 inches long.

LOCKER-STITCH RUGS

This method of rug-making is very quick and economical. It is easy to do and can be used with various wools and foundations.

The tool used is a special steel needle called a Locker needle. It is something like a crochet hook, having a hook at one end and an eyelet at the other. These needles are made in various sizes for use with different kinds of canvas, such as fine sample canvas, Helvellyn canvas, or a special canvas with sixteen meshes to the inch. They cannot be used on ordinary nine-mesh rug canvas unless Cable rug wool is used.

Helvellyn canvas is perhaps the best foundation for Locker-stitch rugs ; being a strong, heavy material, it adds weight to the rug, and this is an advantage, as these rugs are economical of wool. For Turkey wool the best canvas is Locker canvas, with sixteen meshes to the inch. Rugs made by this method have a looped pile, like those described in the first method.

About 4 ounces of wool are needed to the square foot, and sometimes less, according to the thickness of the wool. Good wools to use are Persian, Shetland, or Straight rug wools. If knitting wool is used, three or four plies must be folded together.

Method of Working.—Wind the wool you are going to use into a ball. Thread one end through the eye of the Locker needle. Pass the needle from back to front through the canvas, drawing through about a yard of the wool. Catch the wool behind the canvas over the left forefinger, as in crocheting. Hold the needle in the right hand and push the hook through the hole in the canvas next to the one through which the wool is drawn, and pick up a loop from off the left forefinger, bring this back to the top of the canvas. It is essential that the hook below the canvas should be passed over the wool *away* from the worker, and back below the wool in the opposite direction to that used in crocheting, otherwise the pile looks like tubes instead of separate knots.

Now the *loops have to be locked.* To do this, continue picking up loops through each hole in turn until you have eighteen to thirty-six loops on your needle, according to the size of the canvas, the wool, and the needle. Then draw the needle right through the whole row of loops, and you will find that they are firmly held in place by the locking thread and cannot be withdrawn from the back. This is the advantage of the Locker method over the first method we described—the hooked or prodded method. The pile is also firmly and softly padded. When turning a corner or beginning a new line of loops, pass the locking thread through to the back of the canvas and out again. This does not interrupt the appearance of an even pile of loops. Moreover, loops of another colour can be quite easily pulled through these same holes should the pattern require it. It is not necessary that the locking thread match the loops, if the underwool is not of too strong a contrast in colour to that used by the loops.

Many people finish these rugs with an edging of double crochet.

No frame is needed for Locker work. On fine canvas it is much quicker than cross stitch or gros point, and gives a rich effect owing to the depth of the pile. Chair and stool seats, bags, and many other articles can be worked very quickly in this way. Those who wish to try this method will find no difficulty in using the Locker needle, as directions are generally sold with it.

THE SHORT PILE METHOD, OR RUGS MADE WITH THE NEEDLE

This method combines the advantages of both the second method—the Knotted Pile Rugs, and the third method—the Lichfield Method. It has the firm knot as in the second method, and uses less wool as in the third method. This stitch is worked with ordinary rug needles or very large crewel needles on the same canvas and with the same wool as for Knotted Pile Rugs. A gauge is also used to keep the loops even. This is a little plain slip of polished wood $\frac{1}{4}$ inch wide and 8 inches long. Thread the needle with about a yard of wool. Begin on the first row of the pattern and work across from left to right in the following manner :

Pass the needle towards you under the lower thread of the first mesh, draw the wool through leaving the free end a little longer than the width of the gauge. Hold this free end down with the thumb of the left hand below the stitch. Throw the loose wool in the needle away from you from left to right, and push the needle under the same thread of canvas, away from you and over the wool, pull it tightly towards you. You should now have the two ends fixed in a loop as in the Knotted Pile Rugs.

Now take your gauge and lay it parallel beneath the stitch, and wrap the wool in your needle once over and back, beneath the gauge, then push the needle downwards under the next thread of canvas as before. Every two stitches when pulled tight make a secure knot from which, when cut, come two equal ends of wool. Repeat these stitches along the row, and when the length of the gauge has been almost covered, slip it out and cut along the top of the loops with a large sharp pair of scissors, to get the pile as even a possible.

The appearance of the rug is exactly the same as the Knotted Pile Rug.

Some people prefer to leave the loops uncut. Very effective patterns can be made in cut loops with the background left uncut or *vice versa*.

Some workers do not use a gauge, but are able to keep the loops even by holding them down with the thumb of the left hand.

The different colours are worked in the design by the same stitch as described, a single stitch of any one colour being done like the beginning stitch of a row without the help of the gauge. When the wool is finished or the colour in the pattern changes, care must be taken to cut off the wool being used as long or a little longer than the width of the gauge.

A Second Method of making a Short Pile Rug with a Needle

This method can be used when the canvas is closely woven. It makes a rather different knot from that already described.

Pass the needle from right to left under a perpendicular or warp thread. Draw the wool through, leaving an end of about 1 inch behind the thread of the canvas. Hold this down with its end towards you. Pass the needle over it from left to right and under the horizontal or weft thread immediately below the first stitch ; then pass over the next warp thread and pick up another stitch on the third warp thread, and repeat the stitch, leaving a loop of wool between the two stitches. Repeat this from left to right until the row is finished. Then cut each loop with the scissors.

A gauge may be used as in the first method to keep the loops even, or you can use the end of the little finger. The next row must be worked above the first.

When working on closely woven canvas it is better to pick up the stitches on *every other* warp thread as described above. When working the next row, the knotted stitches are made on the alternate threads from those used in the first row. About 2 inches of wool or even less is needed for each knot, so this is a very economical method of working.

A Third Way of making a Knotted Rug

Two successive back stitches are taken over two successive threads of canvas. The thread is then wound round a piece of narrow cardboard, which must be as narrow or wide as the depth of the pile required. When the thread has been wound round the gauge the two back stitches are repeated. When the gauge is covered with stitches it must be slipped out and placed farther along the canvas. The work may be done from right to left or from left to right. The loops may be left as they are or cut to form the pile.

This knot is rather like the Ghiordes or Turkish knot, which is the most common knot found in the woven pile carpets of the East.

A Chenille Rug

Cotton and wool chenilles which are the waste products of carpet factories make admirable materials for rug-making. They can be bought from carpet factories by weight. It is not easy to plan any definite patterns with chenille, as a great proportion of it is in mixed colours, unless a quantity of plain colour is also used.

The strand of chenille is stitched on to the canvas backing with strong linen thread, the needle catching up the woven portion of the chenille strand.

For chenille rugs it is important to have a very strong backing. Remember to hem the chenille on in the direction of the warp or weft of the canvas, not diagonally, as otherwise the canvas will not lie flat. Care must be taken over finishing off the stitches. Insert the ends of the chenille through the canvas, fray off the wool, and fasten off firmly. See that the chenille is very accurately turned when another row is laid in place. The rug must be lined. The finished rug has a very deep pile and a very handsome appearance. It should have a long life if due care has been taken in finishing off the stitching.

· KNITTING A WOOL RUG

The following knitted rug may interest some rug-makers. Two long steel knitting-needles are required, strong crochet cotton or thread, and wool cut into short lengths as used in making the other rugs described in this chapter. The rug should be knitted in strips, each strip as long as the rug is wide. The strips are then sewn together.

Begin by casting on thirty-one to forty-one stitches according to the width required, but always an uneven number. Knit the first row plain. Then begin the second row with one stitch plain ; take a piece of wool, knit it in with the next stitch, so that one half of it is at the front and the other half at the back of the work. Knit one plain again, put the half of the wool that is at the back round to the front and continue in this way alternately to the end of the row. Now knit one row of plain, then a row knitting in the wool, and so on.

CHOOSING DESIGNS

The best designs for these rugs on the whole are geometrical patterns. It is wise to buy enough wool at a time for the entire rug, as sometimes it is difficult to get exactly the same shade again, as one dye of the same intended shade often differs from another.

Beautiful effects can be obtained by using several tones of the same colour mingled together to give a broken background, which is often more pleasing than a one-toned colour. In all designs much depends upon individual taste. There is ample scope for experiment, and to many this adds great charm to the work. For those who do not wish to work out their own designs and colour-schemes, colour charts can be bought, and many find great pleasure in working these out.

But the best help in choosing colours and designs will be

FIG. 141

FIG. 141.—A Kiz-Kilim Rug.

275

found in a study of good Oriental rugs. These rugs can be studied in interesting books such as *The Practical Book of Oriental Rugs*, by Dr. Griffin Lewis (Lippincott), or *Oriental Rugs*, by J. K. Mumford. These books are expensive, but they can be consulted at libraries and notes made there of colours and designs. Beautiful rugs can also be seen in private houses and art exhibitions ; but perhaps the best place of all is the Victoria and Albert Museum. Here one can learn a great deal about beautiful designs and lovely colours. These lovely colours are produced by vegetable dyes, and we have nothing in our modern dyes to compare with them.

Oriental rugs take their names from the countries or provinces in which they are made. Bokhara rugs are made in mountainous districts in Turkestan ; they have never been successfully imitated, because the dyes used are made from a plant grown only in that district. The designs are geometrical and the colours deep maroon or blue.

The patterns of all Turkish rugs are of geometrical or arabesque designs—an edict from the Koran having prohibited the reproduction of living things. The Persians, however, weave animals and birds as their ancestors did in days gone by.

Khiva rugs, sometimes called Afghan rugs, are made in Turkestan. Some Khivas have a small pattern in red Mosaic over the surface with a circle in the middle. One often sees a rug made of a rich golden yellow with a background of dark red.

Fig. 141 shows a Kiz-Kilim rug. These are woven with the needle (for needle-woven rugs, see Chapter XVIII.), and are almost alike on both sides. They are made by the Armenians and Turks in Anatolia (the land of sunrise, the Greek name for Asia Minor). The Kiz-Kilim rug in the illustration was copied from a genuine rug. The filling is a deep blue and the borders are in Oriental colours. The centre figure is white, with red, brown, and yellow inside. This rug can be copied when making rugs in the ways described in this chapter. Much interesting and valuable information can be found in Mumford's *Oriental Rugs*, where directions for weaving Kiz-Kilims, Khivas, and Bokharas are given, with a few patterns.

More about woven rugs will be found in Chapter XVIII. See also the chapter on Weaving.

CHAPTER XX

WEAVING AT HOME ON SMALL LOOMS

Cardboard Looms. Board Looms: Warping, Weaving. Box Looms with Heddles: Use of Heddle. Weaving Patterns. Twill Effects and Tapestry Weaving. Articles that can be made. Tablet Weaving. Threading and Turning the Tablets. Weaving Coloured Patterns.

WEAVING is one of the pleasantest and most restful occupations if one uses the simple looms described here. It is, as we said in the chapter on " The Craft of Home-made Rugs from Waste Materials," especially suited for those whose eyesight is not good.

Large and complicated looms are no use in a small house, apart from their expense, so we will confine ourselves in this chapter to such looms as can be made at home or bought for a small sum of money.

CARDBOARD LOOMS

The simplest looms to use are cardboard looms. A cardboard loom for a small handbag or purse can be made from a piece of cardboard with a row of holes bored along each end. It is thus very much like the wooden frame loom described in Chapter XVIII. Rule a line at each end of the cardboard to get the holes on a level, mark them a $\frac{1}{4}$ inch apart, and pierce them with a stiletto. If you think the holes may break and run together, rule two lines very close together and mark half inches along one, and half inches along the other, but so arranged that the beginning of every half-inch in one row lies in the middle of the half-inch on the other row, you thus have holes a $\frac{1}{4}$ inch apart but at slightly different levels, so that there is no fear of their breaking as the weaving proceeds. Thread this loom with wool in the way described for the frame loom in Chapter XVIII. The warp is a continuous length of wool tied at the beginning and end of the threading. As weaving always tends to pull inwards towards the middle by its even weight and tension, counteract this by fixing a bar stitch at intervals across the outside warp thread on each side to keep it vertical all the way down.

For the weft, thread a blunt raffia needle with wool and weave in and out the warp threads as already described until the whole of the loom is covered. Tie on a new length of wool where needed and hide the knot in the weaving. Striped effects can easily be obtained by weaving with different coloured wools.

When the warp is completely covered, tear away the card, double the weaving in half across, and make up in the usual way.

Some interesting cardboard looms are described in Chapter XXI., " Raffia Work." With these looms the actual shape of the article to be made is woven. Full directions are given for making these looms in Chapter XXI.

For making and using cardboard looms one needs—(1) a piercer ; (2) weaving needles ; (3) small brass rings, these are indispensable when using weaving cards to make raffia bags, tea-cosies, slippers, etc. ; (4) raffia, W83 4-ply wool on K182 cotton yarn. All these materials can be obtained from Dryad Handicrafts, Leicester.

Board Looms (Fig. 142)

These are *permanent* wooden apparatus which can be used for needle-weaving in the same way as the card looms. They can be bought or easily made. Any flat piece of board from 12 to 18 inches long, 5½ to 7 inches wide, and ½ inch thick can be used. A strip of wood an inch wide and ½ inch thick must be nailed on each end to raise the warp off the board. It is wise to round the corners of these pieces to prevent them from cutting the warp. If made at home, the loom should be rubbed with glass-paper until it is as smooth as possible.

One can weave on this loom with a needle as though darning (as with cardboard looms) or use a shuttle.

If you use a shuttle you need a shed stick. This is a thin

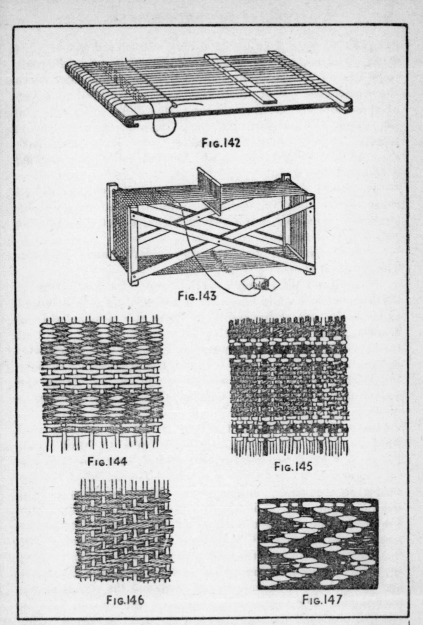

FIG.142

FIG.143

FIG.144

FIG.145

FIG.146

FIG.147

FIG. 142.—A Board Loom. FIG. 143.—A Braid Loom with Heddle.
FIG. 144.—Pattern in Weaving. FIG. 145.—Plaid. FIG. 146.—Twill.
FIG. 147.—Twill.

flat piece of wood 8 or 9 inches long and shaped like a paper knife. It is used to open the shed wide, that is, to lift up alternate rows of warp threads, thus making a sloping roof under which the shuttle goes. It can also be used to beat up the weft. Two of these are very useful and save time. An ordinary comb (see Chapter XX.) is a great help in pressing the weaving together. Ordinary knitting needles 7 or 8 inches long make good shuttles for carrying the weft through the sheds. Packing needles are also useful.

The board loom produces strips of material one and a half times the length of the loom, and 4 inches or so wide. Wider strips can be woven, but the board loom is not very suitable for really wide strips.

It is an excellent loom for working out suitable patterns. This is how it is used—

Warping.—Wind the warp carefully round the board, keeping the tension even. Any knots that are needed must be arranged as far as possible at the end of the loom at which the weaving begins. Small nails or screw eyes are put in the loom so that the beginning and end of the warp can be safely tied. Be careful not to wind the warp threads too tightly, as it is difficult to move the work round the loom when weaving begins. Space the warp threads carefully ; it is wise to work to a given number to the inch.

Weaving.—It is important to keep the threads evenly spaced while weaving. To do this, it is a good plan to insert a thin flat piece of wood between the warp threads instead of weft and thus form a firm line to weave against. The spacing will show clearly on the wood ; any irregularities can be adjusted with the knitting needle. It is a good plan to weave a few lines with a weft of stout thread in order to get the spacing as correct as possible, as described in Chapter XXI. on the frame loom. The first shed is opened with the shed stick and the shuttle containing the weft is passed through. The shed stick is then taken out and put in again to make a second shed, and the weft is passed back again. The shuttle is passed from right to left through the first shed and from left to right through the second. This is repeated throughout the weaving. This weaving sounds easy, but much care must be taken to keep the weft and warp spacing even. This is essential for good pattern weaving. The edges need much care or there will be a series of dents. It is wise to hold the edges of the warp when the weft is turned.

The strength of a piece of cloth depends not only on the strength of the threads used but on the number of times the warp and weft intersect in a given area. There should be the same number of weft threads in every inch woven.

Box Looms with Heddles (Fig. 143)

Weaving on these looms is very quick. They are stocked at most Arts and Crafts shops, or can be bought from the Dryad Works at about 3s. 6d. upwards. A small loom such as that shown in Fig. 143 will only weave braids, like the board looms, but these braids can be joined together with simple embroidery stitches, and made into bags, tea-cosies, pochettes, egg-cosies, belts, etc. They can also be used as decorations for cushions or dresses.

Some small looms slightly more expensive than that shown in Fig. 143 have rollers each side on which the work can be wound as it proceeds. This enables you to weave any length you like, without having to stop when the circuit of the loom has been made. Scarves, table runners, cushion covers, etc., can be woven on these looms, or the lengths joined together will make skirts and jumpers. Indeed, there is no end to the things that you can make on your loom.

Looms with rigid heddles like that shown in Fig. 143 are threaded in the following way : Measure right around it to find the length of each warp thread needed. (In these looms each warp thread has to be put on separately.) Add 3 or 4 inches to this measurement, and cut out the required number of warp threads.

Now look at the heddle. It is a framework containing vertical bars. A space separates each bar from the next, and there is a hole like the eye of a needle through the centre of each bar. Pass the first thread through the leftmost space of the heddle and right round the loom, double-knot the ends of the thread under the loom as shown in Fig. 143. Next thread the last hole or space at the right of the heddle, in order that the heddle will hang evenly while you are threading. Then continue threading each hole and space in turn from left to right, knotting each thread underneath. If you want a narrower braid than the heddle will weave, you must leave a certain amount unthreaded at each side of the heddle.

Now you are ready to weave. Wind your shuttle with enough of the coloured thread you require. There is no need to buy a shuttle; make one at home from a piece of cardboard 4½ inches long by about 1½ inch wide, rounding off the edges. Your thread that you wind on your shuttle can be thick mercerised embroidery cotton or 2-ply, 3-ply, or 4-ply wool.

Tie one end of the shuttle thread to the outside left warp thread near the end of the loom near you. See that the heddle is half-way between the back and the front. Now press the heddle *down* with the left hand so as to make a shed, and with the left hand slide the shuttle through the opening (known as the downward shed). Pull the thread through and beat it up with a comb or by bringing the heddle up.

Next pull the heddle *up* with the left hand, and with the right pass the shuttle through from right to left. Beat the thread up. Continue in this way till the braid extends almost all round the loom. The beating up works it round the loom, so that you will find that you are always weaving in the same position.

When the two ends of your weaving come near together, the shed becomes too small for your shuttle to go through. Cut the remaining warp threads, thus releasing the weaving from the loom, and with needle and thread overcast the first and last rows so that they will not unravel.

The shuttle will often have to be filled during the weaving; join the new thread by putting it again through the shed used for the last of the old thread. Beat this row up very carefully. Never (except for raffia work) knot your weft when weaving, because you want both sides to be neat; break your wool, do not cut it, the broken end felts with the old end. Cut ends tend to stick up through the weaving.

Now you know a little about the working of very simple looms, we can consider the patterns that can be woven on them. We will give the well-known ones, but you will soon make other discoveries for yourself, for the charm of weaving will soon possess you and you will want to try all sorts of interesting experiments with different colours, widths, and threads.

WEAVING PATTERNS (Figs. 144, 145, 146, 147)

Interesting effects can be obtained by changing the colours of the various threads.

(1) *Changing the Colour of the Warp.*—The warp can be threaded in blocks of two colours ; this will give vertical stripes.

(2) *Changing the Colour of the Weft.*—Horizontal strips can be made by weaving a band with one colour, then altering the weft and weaving a band of another colour. It saves trouble to have a separate shuttle for each weaving colour used.

(3) *Changing the Colour of both Warp and Weft.*—This is the method that gives the most varied effect. To form checks, say for the border of a runner, arrange the warp threads in stripes, each stripe being the width of the check required. Weave with one of the warp colours as many rows as correspond in width to a stripe, then change to the other colour, weave the same amount with this, and so on throughout.

You will get a more striking effect with a two-colour check if you set up the warp with a single black thread between every two stripes and weave a single black line each time before changing the weaving colour.

Plaids (Fig. 145) are obtained by stringing the warp at regular intervals with the colours used in the weft, and in similar order ; thus in Fig. 145 there are 6 greys, 1 white, 1 scarlet, 1 white, etc. The weft is woven across, forming stripes corresponding in width to the various warp colours.

In Fig. 144 the effect has been obtained by weaving alternately one row of one colour and one of another for as many rows as desired.

Other effects can be obtained by making variations in the sizes of the warp and weft threads—silk and cotton, cotton and jute, etc. Any combinations give scope for experiment.

Twill Effects (Figs. 146 and 147) can be obtained by weaving under and over two or more warp threads step fashion : 1st row, over two, under two ; 2nd row, under one, over two, under two ; 3rd row, under two, over two ; 4th row, over one, under two, over two, etc. Various patterns can be woven by using two colours for alternate rows and breaking and reversing the steps, as in Fig. 147. For this kind of weaving you must do without the heddle, which only lifts alternate threads.

The twill weave is a great favourite among Eastern races for matting, etc. You can see in Fig. 147, which is very loosely woven, the diagonal stripes it makes. Most of the weaving we have described (except the twill) is known as Plain or Tabby Weaving. In this type the weft goes over and under consecutive threads and both warp and weft show nearly equally on the surface of the cloth. The weft, of course, is always slightly more prominent.

Tapestry Weaving (see also Chapter XV., " Tapestry and Needlework Rugs ").—Tapestry weaving differs from most other forms of weaving in that the warp is entirely covered by the weft. To do this, the weft is passed from right to left through the first shed and from left to right through the second shed, and then pressed up to form *one* line of weaving. All the patterns must be made with the weft.

Tapestry weaving can be done by needle weaving and very beautiful designs worked out.

The pattern is generally woven in first, then the background. When weaving the background up and down to the pattern a slit will be left. The older tapestry weavers frankly accepted this slit and sewed it up after the work was removed from the loom. It is easy to join the background weaving to the woven centre if a needle is used, because the new thread can be linked in the threads already woven as it reaches them. (See Chapter XVIII., " Rugs Woven on a Frame.") Tapestry weaving takes much longer than ordinary weaving, though it is very interesting.

Interesting Articles made on Small Looms

Scarves.—These can be finished with their own fringe. At the end of the weaving overcast the last row and cut the warp threads evenly to make the fringe. If necessary, damp and iron it to straighten it.

Handbags can be woven in one piece if the loom is wide enough. If you have a small loom and have to join two pieces, take care that the warp striping is effective and symmetrical when the two strips are joined. You may have to weave half a pattern on each strip.

Woven cushion strip trimmings are very effective, especially down the middle of the cushion. The best way of attaching the strip is to buttonhole it on with an open stitch. Woven bands in bright colours are especially suitable for round bolster cushions. Chair-backs look best in tapestry weaving if you have time, but gay vertical stripes are very effective. Woven braids are also useful as trimmings and borders for curtains or screens.

Ties can also be successfully woven, and they do not stretch like knitted ones.

Other uses for narrow braid are : comb-cases, tie-backs for curtains, collars, cuffs, strips for dress trimmings, hair bandeaux, hatbands, etc.

We will now describe another interesting way of making braids by

Tablet Weaving

Tablet weaving is not only one of the oldest methods of weaving, but it is thought by many to be the beginning of all weaving. In the museum at Copenhagen there are the remains of a woman's dress which dates back to the Bronze Period. Around the dress is a belt which is woven by this method, a proof that it was used many thousands of years before the birth of Christ.

Traces of it are found in Iceland, Jutland, Lithuania, the Caucasus, and from Turkestan to Burmah. It is believed to have been brought by the Huns from the East to Europe.

It is most suitable for making braids and bands for various purposes. The bridles for Eastern animals were generally woven in this way. Camel harness to-day is so woven. It was also used for sword belts. In the Wallace Collection there are two Eastern sword belts made by tablet weaving.

Various useful things can be made, such as hatbands, napkin rings, and belts or girdles. From braids woven on small looms it is possible to make needle-books, pincushion, kettle-holder, egg-cosy, shoe polisher, etc. From braids woven on larger looms such articles as a tea-cosy, traycloth, pochette, table runner, etc., can be made.

The Tablets.—The tablets used in early times were made of different materials, such as thin polished wood, or tortoiseshell. Roman examples of thin bone have been found.

Tablets can quite well be made at home from stout cardboard

or leatherboard. The usual shape is a square, sides about 2 inches. For larger braids tablets can be made with sides $3\frac{1}{2}$ to 5 inches.

The edges and corners must be slightly rounded and smoothed with fine sandpaper and finally polished with a bone paper-knife, so that the tablets can be turned more easily without tangling the threads. In each corner about $\frac{1}{4}$ inch along the diagonals, holes are punched. The edges of these must be smoothed to prevent the threads from fraying.

Threads.—The most suitable threads for tablet weaving are strong fine threads such as cotton or silk. It is better to have the weft thread a little finer than the warp thread. If wool is used it must be tightly spun and if many tablets are used it is somewhat bulky. The weft thread is not seen except a very little at the edges of the weaving, hence all the colour is in the warp.

Shuttle.—This can be a small stick about as thin and long as a pencil.

The Beater.—A bone paper-knife makes a very suitable beater.

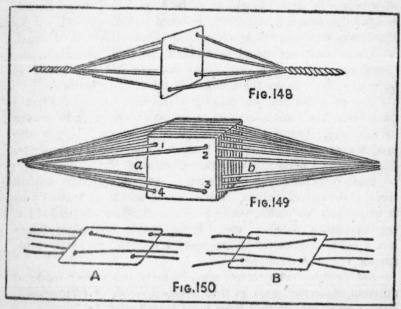

FIG. 148.—Method of threading the tablet. of Fig.). FIG. 150 A (see p. 288).

FIG. 149.—The Sheds (on right FIG. 150 B (see p. 288).

Threading and Turning the Tablets.—Four threads are needed for each tablet, one being passed through each hole, as in Fig. 148. It is convenient to number the holes as in the diagram. Begin with one tablet first, so that you can have a little practice in turning the tablet and be able to see more clearly the different sheds that are formed. Thread your tablet, tie the ends of the threads together, and pass the knot over the knob of a chair and hold the other end in one hand.

Now take hold of the tablet and turn it so that hole No. 1 is in the position of hole No. 2, and No. 2 in No. 3's place, and so on. Notice that the thread passing through hole 2 is lowered and that passing through hole 4 is raised. Turn the tablet continuously in this direction and you will see that a twist of four ply is made at both ends. If you had four tablets placed together and turned as described, the four threads of each would become four strong twists lying side by side.

We shall now see how by weaving through the different sheds (*a* in Fig. 149) the weft thread will bind these twists together in a firm ribbed band.

How the Weaving is done.—The weaving can be done without a loom or apparatus of any kind, and was so done in early times. One end of the warp can be fastened over a hook, door handle, or the knob of a chair. The other end is looped round the waist if a long braid is required, or fastened by a pin to a belt round the waist. This method is still used in the northern parts of Europe. It is a simple method and has this advantage : that by bending backwards and forwards the weaver can regulate the tension of the warp.

Shepherds in Germany, Finland, and Iceland occasionally still practise this craft. They fasten the end of the warp to the branch of a tree.

We will now suppose you have threaded four or six tablets all one way, and the ends are secured all ready for weaving.

Hold the tablets together as in Fig. 149, pass the shuttle through the shed *a*. Now turn the tablets to the right so that hole 1 is in the position of hole 2 (this is called a quarter-turn) as already described, and pass the shuttle through the new shed. Make another quarter-turn, and pass the shuttle through, then another, and do the same. Hole No. 1 is back in its first position.

After each quarter-turn the shuttle is passed through the shed, the weft is drawn tight, and the threads beaten back. The weft is seen only as a tiny stitch at the end of the braid.

You can tie the weft thread to one of the warp threads at the beginning, or you can leave a long end and weave it into the braid with a needle afterwards.

So far we have spoken of threading the tablets all the same way, but there can be a slight difference.

For example, in Fig 150 A, we might describe the threads as being put through the holes from underneath the tablet from left to right; in Fig 150 B, they are put through the holes from the top of the tablet from left to right.

If the tablets are all threaded the same way, the weaving will have a twisted or spiral pattern with the twists all running the same way; but if they are threaded in pairs one from underneath and one from on top, or two from underneath and two from on top, the twists will alternate with each other, producing a plait-like or chain effect in the weaving.

By twisting the tablets continually in the same direction, for example from left to right, the sheds in Fig. 149 become so small that it is impossible to turn them any further. In early times this difficulty was overcome by the weavers turning their tablets in the opposite direction from right to left. Thus the threads that tightened up on the left became untwisted. For beginners it is simpler to untie the threads, untwist them, and begin again.

WEAVING COLOURED PATTERNS

(1) *A Braid White on one side and Green on the other.*—Perhaps one of the best ways to learn to weave is to begin with some simple pattern. Here we have chosen what is often called the two-way weaving, in which the tablets are threaded in such a way that a band is woven with one colour, say, green on one side, and another colour, white, on the other.

Thread eight or ten tablets with two threads of green through holes 1 and 2 and two threads of white through 3 and 4. Arrange the tablets so that all the green threads are above and the white threads below. Pass the weft thread through the shed. Now turn the tablets one quarter-turn *to the left* and pass the weft through ; then another quarter-turn *to the left* and pass the weft through ; now turn them one quarter-turn *to the right* and pass the weft through, then another quarter-turn *to the right* and pass the weft through.   Beat the rows of weaving close together with the beater.   A bone paper-knife makes a very satisfactory beater.

If this weaving is continued, the band will be green on one side and white on the other.

Remember the process is first two quarter-turns *to the left*, then two quarter-turns *to the right*, and after each quarter-turn pass the weft through the shed.

To make the colours change places, you must, when the tablets are back in their original position, reverse the turnings, taking two quarter-turns *to the right* and then two *to the left*.

Examine the weaving carefully and you will notice that only one of the four threads passing through the four holes of each tablet can be seen on the surface of the woven braid.

This shows that each tablet produces *one* warp thread in the width of the braid, so that if ten tablets are used the braid would show ten warp threads.   Hence the width of the braid depends upon the number of tablets.

This two-coloured warping gives unlimited variety of patterns, and it is interesting to make experiments by turning the tablets in different ways.

(2) *A Striped Braid.*—This is made with eight tablets. Nos. 1, 2, 7, and 8 are threaded with dark threads, Nos. 3, 4, 5, and 6 with light threads.

(3) *A Striped and Chequered Braid with Twenty Tablets.*— Tablets 1, 2, 19, and 20 have four white threads each.   Nos. 3, 4, 10, 11, 17, and 18 have four red each.   Nos. 5, 6, 7, 8, 9, 12, 13, 14, 15, and 16 have two white and two red.

Tablets 5, 6, 7, 8, 9, 12, 13, 14, 15, and 16 give the white and red oblongs.   These are obtained by seeing that the red threads are up for two weaves, then the white for two weaves.   For such a wide braid as this it is best to knot each pair of warp-threads round a rod for the beginning and fasten the rod to the back of a chair.   The tablets need not be turned all together ; so many tablets may have a quarter-turn and so many a half-turn, according to the colour needed for the pattern.

CHAPTER XXI

RAFFIA WORK

Raffia—Raffia Winding. Raffia Plaiting. Raffia Weaving on Cardboard Looms. Loom for Bag and Tea-Cosy. Raffia and Canvas Work. A Blotting-Pad. Purse. Bag embroidered in Raffia. Hessian and Raffia Cloth. Raffia Millinery. Raffia Knitting and Crochet.

RAFFIA work is perhaps the most adaptable of all crafts and lends itself to a variety of uses. It is very fascinating and easy to do. Almost everything from hats and jumpers to household articles such as screens, cushions, table runners, etc., may be decorated with raffia, and indeed many things are made entirely of it. A very wide range of raffia work can be undertaken in combination with other materials. Any one with artistic knowledge and instinctive taste will find endless opportunities of making novel and attractive articles which would be very expensive to buy and yet cost comparatively little to make, for raffia has the advantage of being cheap. It can be bought ready dyed in a variety of charming colours, or in its natural tone and dyed at home.

The best quality raffia is that known as Majunga. Good quality raffia can be bought from about 1s. to 1s. 3d. per lb. There are other inferior varieties and substitutes, but although they are cheaper their use should be avoided, as the work produced will be disappointing.

It is best to buy the dry-dyed coloured raffia, and not the glycerine dyed. This latter is much too soft and splits to ribbons almost the first time it is drawn through the canvas. The dry-dyed is a little stiffer, but it is far better, as it lasts much longer. It can be softened by being rolled up in a damp towel. Another method is to draw the strand to be used two or three times round the square leg of a chair or table.

The following list gives some idea of its various uses : (1) Raffia Winding ; (2) Raffia Plaiting ; (3) Raffia Weaving ; (4) Raffia and Canvas Work ; (5) Coiled Raffia Work (see chapter on Coiled or Indian Basketry) ; (6) Raffia Millinery ; (7) Raffia Knotting and Crochet.

(1) Raffia Winding

In this method, which is one of the simplest, the raffia is wound on foundations of various shapes, usually of cardboard. A great variety of articles can be made, such as napkin rings, table mats, and other forms, by using foundations such as gas-mantle boxes, match boxes, old pestal tubes, etc.

A charming set of round or oval mats can be quickly and easily made. These look attractive on the dining-table, and are most useful for putting under vases that stand on polished surfaces.

To make an Oval Mat.—Make a cardboard foundation of the size required. Cut out a much smaller oval in the middle of the cardboard.

Cover the cardboard with raffia by winding it round and round from the inside of the oval outwards. The raffia must be laid as flat as possible when winding, and the strands must overlap well. Blank spaces will be left after the first winding. These must be covered completely by winding round a second time. To finish off, thread a raffia needle with the end and pass it under the wound strands.

A pretty decorative effect can be obtained by using a strand of raffia of contrasting colour to darn over and under the strands close to the outer edge of the mat ; going round two or three times.

A favourite way of making a round mat is to wind it in contrasting sections. Orange, blue, and dark purple make an attractive colour-scheme. Make a round cardboard disc and cut out a hole in the middle about $\frac{3}{4}$ inch in diameter. You can have six or eight sections according to the size of the mat. It is wise to estimate the width of each on the outer edge so that the sections will be even.

The centre can be filled with a few raffia stitches or left empty. If you oversew the edge with purple raffia at regular intervals, taking the needle through the raffia and cardboard, a very pretty border is made.

Many useful articles such as egg-stands, vases for artificial flowers, letter racks, etc., can be bought in framework form for raffia winding.

(2) Raffia Plaiting

Raffia is plaited in the usual way with the desired number of strands, which may be double, treble, or any multiple according to the thickness of the plait required. In this form it can be made up into such articles as floor and table mats by coiling the plait round and stitching it together as the work proceeds.

There are two ways of coiling the plait. It can be coiled round and the edges of the coil sewn together so that a fairly thin mat is made, as the plait is quite flat ; or it can be coiled round and sewn through the middle of the plait so that the plait stands on its edge, and the mat is as thick as the plait is wide.

Hats and baskets can be made by sewing plaits together according to the first method.

Broad plaits can be sewn together to make bags, handkerchief sachets, etc.

It is easier to plait with an odd number of strands, five, seven, eleven, thirteen, etc. Here is the method. Suppose you are plaiting with seven strands :

(1) Separate the strands into two groups, grasping four in one hand and three in the other. (2) Take the outside strand of the four group, and weave to the middle, thus making four on the opposite side. (3) Now again take the outside strand of the four and weave to the middle, so that there are four again on the side you began. (4) Repeat, always weaving to the middle and always using the outside strand of the group that has the larger number. In this way you will get a *straight* even plait.

To join new strands, either knot the raffia and keep the knot at the back, or place the new strand over the old and plait the two together. Avoid all the joins coming together, so begin with strands of *unequal* length.

A pretty plaited mat can be made as follows : Take five or seven strands of natural raffia and make a plait. Press it with a warm iron ; then coil it around and sew together with a fine

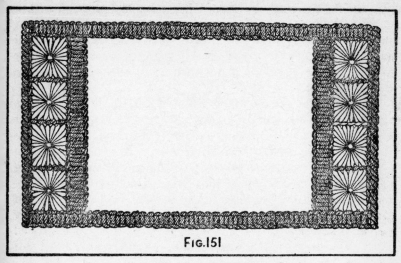

FIG. 151.—Blotting-Pad of Canvas and Raffia.

piece of raffia so that the stitches are not noticeable. Plait some strands of coloured raffia and sew on two rows to make a border. The finished mat is about 5½ to 6 inches in diameter.

For plaited or braided mats, see also Chapter XVIII., " The Craft of Home-made Rugs from Waste Material."

(3) RAFFIA WEAVING ON CARDBOARD LOOMS (Fig. 153)

Raffia may be woven on very simple and inexpensive looms which can be made at home from stiff cardboard, or bought in a variety of shapes for weaving a great variety of articles such as bags of different shapes, tea-cosies, table mats, book covers, calendars, and slippers.

Fig. 153 shows a cardboard loom for making a small shield-shape bag. It is a good example of this form of raffia weaving.

On a piece of cardboard plan out the shape of the bag. Make dots with a pencil ¼ inch apart, where the holes are to be made, and pierce through them. On each side of the card sew a small curtain ring in the position shown in Fig. 153. Sew it at the top and on each side so that it does not pull to one side and spoil the shape of the bag.

To thread the loom use a long piece of white string. Tie

one end to the ring and thread the other end through a raffia needle. Pass the needle through the top hole on the left, up through the ring at the back, then out through the second hole, as shown in Fig. 153. Take the string through the ring and then through the third hole, and so on, on each side alternately until the whole card is threaded.

To begin the weaving tie a thread of raffia to the ring close to the outer right hand warp string. Thread the raffia through a raffia needle and weave under and over the string at the top of the bag. (See Chapter XX. on Weaving.)

Weave backwards and forwards until one side of the loom is covered. Leave out the shorter strings as they become filled, and begin weaving a string lower on each side. Join all new strands with as flat a knot as possible, and push the knot underneath.

Weave the other side in the same way. The cardboard loom must be torn away to leave the bag free. The edges of the string that have passed through the cardboard will be loose, and they must now be filled in with two or three rows of weaving. The rings are covered with raffia worked with a buttonhole stitch.

A long handle can be made of plaited raffia as described, or a raffia twist can be made. (For directions for making a twisted cord, see Chapter XIII., " Cords, Tassels, and Fringes.")

Tassels of raffia make good decorations for the handle, and one can hang from the lowest point of the bag.

If an interesting colour-scheme is worked out by varying the colours of the raffia used, the bag will look most effective.

The bag may be lined.

In a similar manner a loom can be made for working a tea-cosy. Again the rings must be sewed on exactly opposite each other, but half-way between the two lowest holes.

Instead of using brass rings, rings can be made of raffia by twisting several strands of raffia round one or two fingers and overcasting them.

When the cosy is finished, the lower parts, rings and all, must be turned in neatly so as to make the bottom edge straight. This can be done when the cosy is being padded and lined.

It is wise to buy one cardboard loom for a pattern, then you can make your own looms quite easily.

The bought cardboard looms are only a few pence, and they can be obtained in great variety from the Dryad Handicrafts, Leicester.

Remember when weaving the upper parts of slippers that weaving does not stretch and adapt itself to any shape like knitting. If your slippers are too tight, they will always be too tight.

(4) RAFFIA AND CANVAS WORK

Canvas forms an excellent material for raffia work, as the raffia passes so easily through the meshes. Such work is really another form of embroiderery and the same principles of design can be employed and the same stitches used, with these modifications : there are fewer stitches, the technique is simpler, and the stitches can be longer than embroidery stitches, the greatest length being about 1 inch. The most useful stitches are running, hemming, oversewing, slanting stitch, herringbone, cross stitch, feather stitch, chain stitch, back stitch, buttonhole stitches, satin stitches.

As raffia is often uneven in thickness, it is sometimes necessary to work with several strands together if the raffia is too thin ; if it is too thick it can be split. As you work the design, flatten down the stitches with the thumb to get rid of any unevenness that may occur.

It is possible to buy the canvas already stamped with the design in the colours to be used, and in this way attractive and useful articles can be easily made. Some people may prefer to work out their own designs and colour schemes.

Excellent handbags and pochettes can be made. Other articles which lend themselves to this form of work are shopping bags, tea-cosies, table runners, table mats, sachets, blotting-pads, fancy braids, etc.

Raffia cushions are very attractive and suitable for use in the garden, or on the river, as they are light and do not soil easily, and harmonise well with their surroundings.

When making small articles such as pochettes, mats, etc., fold over the edges of the canvas and secure them, then take an overcast stitch in raffia completely over this turning. When the work is finished, press with a hot iron.

A Novel and Attractive Blotting-Pad made of Raffia and Canvas.
—Cut a piece of canvas 18½ by 9 inches ; this will allow for all
necessary turnings. Fold the canvas over at each end to make
the pockets to hold the blotting-paper. These pockets should be
about 2 to 2½ inches wide. Having decided on the width of the
pockets, work a design on them. A row of stars well filled in
(Fig. 151) looks very effective. Fill in the spaces all round the
stars as shown. Turn down the edges of the flaps and buttonhole
them ; turn down the long edges and buttonhole them all along,
sewing down the flaps or pockets at the same time. The colours
used for this design are red and brown.

Cut a piece of thin cardboard the size of the pad, and slip it
in ; cut sheets of red or pink blotting-paper and place them over
the cardboard, and the pad is finished.

Raffia Purses.—These are useful and attractive. They can
be made to match any costume. Make a rectangle of paper
twice the size of the purse you want when closed (allow an extra
amount if a flap is to be used). The purse itself can be made of

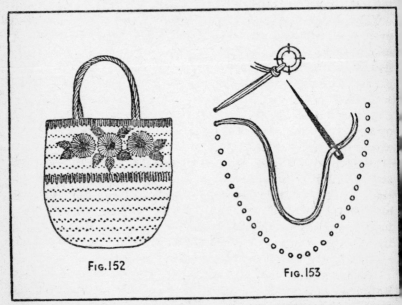

Fig.152

Fig.153

FIG. 152.—Bag embroidered with Raffia.   FIG. 153.—Raffia-weaving on cardboard looms.

wide-meshed canvas or burlap. Put the paper pattern on the burlap and cut the purse, making it 2 inches longer and 2 inches wider than the paper to allow for turnings.

Turn in the edges and work the raffia stitches ; straight stitches look well always ; no stitch should be longer than 1 inch. Arrange the lines of stitches either horizontally straight across the purse or in zig-zags. Choose good colour-schemes. Line the purse neatly, sew up the sides, and add a zip-fastening to the top.

A Bag embroidered with Raffia (Fig. 152).—A pretty and attractive bag can be made in the following way. Cut two pieces of cross-stitch canvas each 11 by 10 inches.

Draw a line on each piece parallel to and 1 inch from each edge, leaving an oblong of canvas, 9 by 8 inches. A pattern can be cut from paper for the shape of the bag ; if the paper is folded in the middle vertically the corners can be shaped so that the pattern is symmetrical. Fold each piece of canvas in the same way ; lay the pattern on each and draw a line around the corners for the shape of the bag, but do not cut the line.

The design can be planned out on the paper pattern or on a piece of squared paper. The colours used for this bag are as follows : border bands and handles are a deep violet ; the flowers, a deep rose with black centres ; the leaves, a soft dark green. The natural coloured raffia forming the background is a soft ecru.

To embroider the design use a blunt tapestry needle No. 18, or a raffia needle. The needle should be large enough for the eye to take the strand of raffia without roughing it.

Sometimes the raffia is hard and stiff. To soften it draw each strand through a damp cloth before threading the needle. See that the strands are as far as possible of uniform size. If some are too wide, tear a strip from the edge. As you work, slip the needle along the strand to keep the eye from cutting it, and see that the strand does not become twisted.

The flower centres are composed of French knots.

After the design is embroidered on the two sides of the bag, work the background. The stitches of raffia each cover five meshes. The stitches can be arranged alternately to give a zigzag effect, or in straight lines or in a checker-board effect where horizontal and vertical stitches are used to form alternating squares.

When the embroidery is finished, cut the top corners of the bag, turn in and baste the margins. Pin the two parts of the bag together. Sew the sides and lower parts together with raffia, using overhand stitches.

To line the bag : Make a fitted lining of silk, allowing ½-inch margins for French seams on the sides and bottom. Pin the lining in the bag and sew it to the canvas with short stitches. Now turn in and baste the edge of the top row of the lining. After the lining is sewed into place, make a row of short blanket or buttonhole stitches with raffia around the top edge.

To make the handle : Take sufficient strands of raffia to make a tight bunch about ¼ inch thick. First wrap it round with a single strand ; then buttonhole or blanket-stitch over this foundation ; each completed handle should be about 11½ inches long. Fasten a handle to the outside of each side of the bag by sewing each end with over-and-over stitches for about ¾ inch. Leave about 5 inches between the ends of each handle.

Hessian.—On this material the design can be of a freer type than on canvas ; but be careful to choose a design that is not too small or too detailed, as a clumsy effect may be produced. Suitable stitches are satin stitch, chain, herringbone, and Cretan stitch. Work the stitches as lightly as possible, as if they are too close together they may tend to pull the threads of the hessian apart.

Raffia Cloth.—This is an African fabric made from dried grass. It is sometimes called Madagascar matting. On this cloth satin stitch, stroke stitch, and French knots look effective.

A pretty and practical shopping bag can be made from a piece of hessian embroidered with coloured raffia. A good size for the bag is about 16 inches deep and 14 inches wide. Cut a piece of hessian the required size, long and broad enough to make the two sides when doubled.

A very effective pattern is a long satin stitch worked in rows about 1 inch wide. It is important to keep the work straight and even, so that it is a good plan to cut a strip of cardboard the right width and sew the stitches over it, drawing it out when the row is finished.

An interesting colour-scheme can be worked out, for example : the first three rows might be dark brown, kingfisher-blue, and champagne ; after the third row make a slanting stitch in dark violet and fill in the rest of the bag with natural, champagne, or dark brown. Sew the sides of the bag together and stitch round the edges with a double strand of raffia in any of the colours used.

There are various ways of making the handles. They can be made of cord wrapped round with the blue raffia, or a simple plait. Stitch in the handles firmly, and line the bag with un-bleached calico.

(5) Coiled Raffia Work

(See chapter on Indian Basketry.)

(6) Raffia Millinery

Sprays of fruit, flowers, and foliage may be made from coloured raffia for the decoration of garden hats, boxes, fancy baskets, cushions, tea-cosies, waste-paper baskets, etc.

Quite artistic effects can be obtained by using raffia dyed as near as possible to the colour of the object to be made.

The work is not difficult, but it needs a skilful use of colour, and to any one with talent in design it offers considerable scope.

Flowers can be made in various ways. One method is to use a circle of buckram, about 2 inches in diameter, as a foundation. Make the petals by overcasting thickly from the centre of the circle over the edge and back to the centre underneath. The stitches should be left quite loose in even loops that project beyond the edge of the buckram disc. Stitch the loops all round so that the buckram is completely hidden. Now make a round centre of satin stitch in the middle. To make leaves, cut out the shapes in buckram and buttonhole them in green raffia from a middle line outwards both ways.

Another Method of making Flowers.—Wind a strand of coloured raffia several times round the first finger of the left hand. Tie the ends round the loops at the bottom. Slip them off the finger. With the remaining long end make another set of loops, and then two more. Join all the loops together by tying the raffia to the end at the starting-point. If the four sets of loops are rather too loose, thread the raffia through the bottom of each, before tying it to the end.

When several flowers have been made, thread a wire through each and wrap them together with green raffia to make a stem.

(7) Raffia Knotting and Crochet

There are a few useful things that can be made by knotting raffia, such as bags for holding tennis balls or string, flower-pot holders, etc.

A crochet raffia mat is very suitable for a summer-house or greenhouse floor. It can be made on canvas; it is very lasting and quite simple to make. First join suitable strands together and wind into a ball ready for crocheting. Cut the canvas the desired shape, fold over the end and secure it. Crochet into the first mesh, making 5, 6, or 7 chain, make a double crochet into the next, then 7 chain and a double crochet, and so on.

The chains must be long enough to let the loops lap well over each other so that the canvas may be well covered.

Some Hints for Crochet Work.—All the strands needed for any article must be of the same thickness as far as possible. The secret of success for raffia crochet is to work very loosely, but it is important that, while each loop is sufficiently large for the next one to be easily pulled through, all should be uniform, or the result will be uneven and untidy.

To prepare Raffia for Crochet.—Dip the raffia in a bath of warm (not hot) water, shake it well, and if possible hang it up to dry in a draught. This makes it soft. When dry, wind it into a loose ball.

Many attractive and useful articles can be crocheted in raffia—dinner mats and small trays, and bath slippers.

Hairpin crochet can be done with raffia, and quite effective mats can be made by this method. See Chapter XXIV. on Hairpin Crochet.

CHAPTER XXII

SOME INTERESTING METHODS OF DYEING IN CONNECTION WITH NEEDLEWORK

Potato Printing, on Paper and on Fabrics. Tie-and-Dyed Work: Pretty
Cushion Covers. Japanese Tie-and-Dyed Work. Stick Printing
on Fabrics. Batik Work.

IT is very interesting when doing needlework of any kind
—embroidery or plain sewing—to be able to print one's
own patterns on the fabrics used. It adds novelty and zest
to one's work.

Perhaps few have thought that the potato can help them !
A potato helping to make a beautiful scarf seems incredible,
but read how it is done ; you will not be able to resist carrying
out these experiments—they cost practically nothing and they
are so interesting and have such practical results.

POTATO PRINTING

Potato printing is best thought of as patterns created through
the use of potatoes. The patterns can be printed either on
paper, using water-colour paint or an easily made dye as medium,
or on thin material, using dye as medium.

Some possible uses for patterns printed on paper are :
  (1) Book jackets.
  (2) Hard book covers.
  (3) Catalogue covers.

Some uses for patterns printed on material are :
  (1) Curtain lengths.
  (2) Dress lengths.

The minimum of materials necessary for experimental
purpose is :
  (1) A fair-sized potato.
  (2) A medium-sized knife or penknife.

(3) Cheap wrapping-paper, or a large sheet of ordinary paper which should be slightly absorbent and non-greasy, to prevent the pattern having a hard metallic quality. Any shop might supply cheap wrapping-paper, but it is certainly stocked by Kettles, New Oxford Street, London, at 3d. per quire.

(4) A whole newspaper or piece of felt to serve as a printing-pad.

(5) One or two tubes of water-colour paint and a paint-brush, which should be large.

A firm kitchen table is admirable to work on.

To prepare for Printing.—(1) First fold the newspaper into a pad and put the paper on which you are going to print on top of it. The wrapping-paper is best used double as it is fairly thin.

(2) Prepare a thick mixture of paint sufficient to complete a pattern on the sheet.

(3) Then with a large knife cut a potato cleanly in half broadways on.

(4) The half potato yields a block with an oval surface which can be used as it is for the pattern unit, or can be trimmed to any shape desired. The trimming is done most efficiently by placing the potato face downwards and by chopping off *downwards* the absolute minimum of potato necessary to alter the oval face to the required shape.

Use one half of the potato for purely experimental purposes, so that you need not trouble about any mistakes you make. You will find that by tilting the knife at an angle to the face of the potato you can in two cuts make a V-shaped channel on the oval face, and after a little practice you will find it easy to cut curved channels. All channels should be very shallow and cleanly cut. After cutting one or two channels, take a brushful of paint and lay it on the surface—not into the channels—of the potato face, and firmly press down the potato on to a piece of scrap paper. You will find that the spaces between the channels print and that any part that is cut away does not print.

Remembering that the parts of the potato cut away do not print, take the other half potato and on it cut channels in such positions as you feel would result in a beautiful and interesting pattern. Lay paint on the channel cut face, and then press it on the top left-hand corner of the printing paper.

After the potato has made contact with the paper it is advisable to press down firmly first to the left and then to the right with a rhythmic motion that is similar for each separate print. Lay on paint a second time and press down the potato so that its imprint either touches the first impression or is a little apart from it. Continue printing, working from left to right, allowing each print to touch the top of the paper. When the line of impressions is finished, start on the second line, again working from left to right. In this and the following lines the impressions can be directly under one another either touching or just not touching, or the spacing can be as bricks in a wall.

When you have printed a whole sheet, pin it on the wall and stand back from it to consider the beauty or possible lack of beauty in the pattern you have created. The first two or three times it is often difficult to get the feeling of a flow of line and interest from one imprint to another. Often it is necessary consciously to cut the potato in such a way that at least one part of the imprint will connect with the one adjoining it and with the one below it. This connecting of the pattern unit is usually needed to make the finished printed sheet a complete and satisfying whole instead of being a sheet on which one little pattern is printed again and again. The channels cut on the potato face need not make a pattern in themselves, for they are only the means whereby a beautiful, continuous, and rhythmic pattern is printed. If a printed sheet seems incomplete, the addition of a spot or curve of colour may create a rhythm, or link each imprint. For the addition, cut a block the required shape and either charge it with the same printing colour or any suitable one. A two-colour effect can be obtained in two other ways. Firstly, by using two colours on one block. If the colours are laid on " carelessly," the natural mingling often gives a glorious quality to the pattern. Secondly, by the deliberate division of the pattern unit, so that two blocks are cut and each printed in a different colour.

Things that help are :

(1) Two notches or V-shaped channels cut either side and towards the top of the potato form a waist which serves as a

kind of handle and makes much easier the actual printing of the pattern.

(2) The use of an inconspicuous colour for the first few printings allows the mind to be more concerned with the pattern, and rhythm of the pattern, than with the colour. Black is a good colour to use, and usually the stronger and darker the colour the more satisfactory the printing, which partly depends for its success on the contrast between the dark printed area and the colour of the paper. As a general rule there should be a marked contrast between the tone of the paper and the tone of the printing colour.

(3) After the first or second experiment always make a pattern for a definite purpose. A book-jacket or the cover of a sale catalogue are always interesting to decorate.

(4) A piece of felt makes a much better pad than a newspaper. Felt can be bought at 2s. a square yard, and cheaper than that if a remnant is bought at a carpet shop.

(5) Better than water-colour paint are printing colours, easily made from certain aniline dyes. Aniline dyes and Dextrine can be bought at many chemists, and certainly at Cooper's, Greek Street, off Soho Square, London.

Potato Printing, using Dye in place of Water-Colour Paint. —Printing with dye previously prepared allows you to concentrate more on beauty and rhythm of pattern, and certainly makes printing speedier. The materials needed to make Congo Red dye are—

(1) 1 ounce of Congo Red (1s. an oz.).
(2) 1 lb. of Dextrine (8d. per lb.).
(3) A large glass bottle (about twice the size of a full-sized medicine bottle; there is a very large-sized bottle of Glyco-Thymolene).
(4) A 2-lb. jam jar.
(5) A pan.
(6) A teaspoonful of acetic acid.

The strength of the colour naturally depends on how much dye is used, and on the actual size of the bottle. For a truly large-sized bottle pour into the bottle enough dye to occupy about one-fourteenth of its height. On top of this pour hot water so that the mixture occupies one-half of the bottle. Stir the mixture with a thin stick. Half fill the jam jar with Dextrine, and liberally cover it with water. Place the jar in a pan of water and boil for twenty minutes, stirring at intervals. When the Dextrine has cooled off, add it to the dye in the bottle, stirring it together when the mixture is reasonably cool. Stir in a teaspoonful of acetic acid. This large bottle holds sufficient dye for many printings.

A piece of felt fitted into an empty shoe-polish tin or any shallow tin makes a very good dye pad. Pour a small quantity of dye on the felt and allow it to soak in before pressing the potato on the felt, from which it will pick up sufficient colour for perhaps two imprints. A slight and almost unavoidable difference in the strength of colour of the impression often adds to the beauty of the pattern. You will find the felt pad can only absorb so much dye at a time, so that at regular intervals the pad must be resaturated. The dye pad must be removed from the tin after use to prevent the tin rusting.

By using dye, which makes printing very much quicker, possibly two or three sheets of patterns can be printed in half an hour. One set of cuts on a potato block can make several patterns, and it is interesting to try for four different results with one block. When a simple printing has proved unsatisfactory, a brick arrangement of the imprints might be better, or half-drop printing might produce a more beautiful result.

Printing on Materials.—This is very similar to printing on paper. The material is best thin and soft with no dressing in it, though organdie is quite suitable. For experimental purposes a soft cotton length is excellent.

Smooth out the material over the felt printing-pad and keep it in place by means of drawing-pins pressed through the selvedge. The material must not be stretched.

Water-colour paint is useless on a material that has to be laundered, but the made-up dyes are fast if steamed before washing. The steaming can be done by rolling the printed fabric in a spare piece of material so that no part of the print touches another part and no part is exposed to the steam. This can best be managed by having a piece of stuff twice the size of the printed fabric so that the latter can be placed between the material as the filling of a sandwich. Then the three layers of material can be *lightly* pressed together so that steam has free access to the unprinted and protective material. A small improvised line on the clothes-line system could be used to suspend the materials above the steam for about half an hour. Afterwards the printed fabric should be carefully washed in warm soapy water and smoothed on the wrong side with a cool iron. It may be found necessary to steam fabric with a large printed area longer than half an hour. After steaming and first washing, the colouring is a little lighter, so the printing colour should be darker than is finally required.

TIE-AND-DYED WORK (Figs. 154, 155)

There is always a great pleasure in producing beautiful gradations of colour, tints, hues, and various delightful blendings in a piece of fabric. To any one who has ever attempted to do this, colour will always appeal with a greater fascination than before and will give added pleasure. Again a knowledge of using dyes is a most valuable asset in planning decorations for the house and in designing costumes.

The tie-and-dyed method is a most interesting one and is particularly attractive when applied to the decoration of children's dresses. When once the simple technique of the process is mastered, you can begin to invent shapes and decorations of your own.

By this method patterns are made on materials by a series of knots so tied as to make a design. The knots prevent the dyes from penetrating through to the material, so that when after dyeing they are removed, a lighter-ringed outline is left against the darker background.

Thin materials are best suited to this process, such as unbleached muslins, cotton voile, cotton crêpe, cotton georgette, or silk.

Waste scraps of material can be used for experimenting in tying the knots and testing the dies. Many different designs can be made by different methods of tying, as will be explained when describing the dyeing of various articles.

A very effective cushion cover can be made from a piece of unbleached muslin about 18 inches square. Place a marble in the centre and draw the muslin down smoothly on all sides.

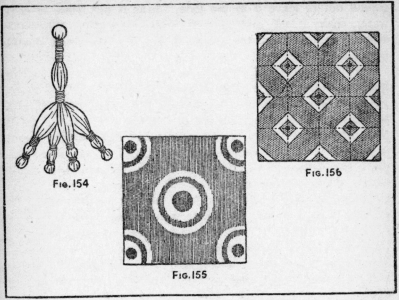

Fig. 154

Fig. 156

Fig. 155

FIG. 154.—Muslin Square tied and ready for dipping.   FIG. 155.—Muslin shaken out.   FIG. 156.—An attractive Cushion Cover.

Tie the muslin by winding a piece of string round it close up to the marble, then continue winding the string round until you have covered a space about 1½ to 2 inches wide. The winding must be done tightly, but it need not completely cover the muslin, for if there are spaces between, the dye can penetrate the material and the result is very effective—little patches of colour appearing in the space that would otherwise be quite white. Now wind string around the muslin about 1½ or 2 inches below the first winding. This second winding can be narrower than the first, say about 1 inch. Now tie a marble into each corner of the square with two bands of winding. Fig. 154 shows the square of muslin tied and ready for dyeing.

There are many good dyes on the market to choose from, but whatever dye is used be careful to follow closely the directions on the packet or bottle.

First soak the muslin in clear water, until all the folds are well saturated. It should be soaked for quite ten minutes. Then dip it into the dye, hot or cold as the directions state. Be careful not to leave it in too long. Take it out, rinse in cold water, shake it out, and hang up until nearly dry. When the string is removed and the muslin shaken out, the result should be similar to Fig. 155.

Another method of obtaining a similar design is the sewing method. Many people prefer this way. This is how it is done. Fold the four corners of the square to the centre, being careful to see that all four sections are of uniform size. Lay a small plate or saucer exactly in the middle and draw lightly round it with a piece of coloured chalk or pencil. Take away the plate, and with a needle and strong thread sew around the circle with running stitches about half an inch long. Draw in the thread and fasten it securely. Now see that all the gathers lie evenly, as in a ruffle. Begin to wind round with thread or fine string, starting at the gathering thread and winding until the desired width is obtained. Leave a space and wind again. Then soak in water as before, and dye. Remove the string and gathering thread, and a design similar to Fig. 155 should appear.

Dye a square of plain muslin for the back of the cushion at the same time as the tied muslin.

The Twist-and-Dye Method.—There is another method which is simpler and often more effective in producing closer colour harmony and a greater variety of pattern. It is also a quicker process. It is the twist-and-dye method.

To make a Handkerchief in Three Shades.—Take a 9-inch square of white cotton voile. The edges may be hemmed, or treated in a more decorative way. Prepare three basins of dyes : No. 1 pink, No. 2 blue, No. 3 dark pink. Have plenty of cold water at hand to rinse the piece after each dip in the dye.

Now fold the piece while dry in half so as to make an oblong ; fold this again to form a square, fold the square along the long diagonal so that the corners all hang down. Hold it by the centre and dip in clear water, then dip it in the pink dye so that the colour penetrates the fabric. Take it out and rinse in clear cold water. Then, still holding it loosely by the centre, dip it into the blue tint so that the dye covers the edges. Take out and rinse again. You will find that the blue tint over the pink has made a lavender for the edge and corners. Now comes the twist. Take the edges and centre of the piece in each hand and twist the middle. Dip the middle part into the dark pink. Rinse again, shake out and dry. The twist will produce mottlings of darker colour round the middle of the piece. The tighter the twist the more distinct are the markings. If the twist is loosened while dipping in the dye the colours will be softly blended. You can get lovely pastel colours by overlapping the tints.

Other Designs in Tie-and-Dyed Work.—A different method of tying will produce oblong bands of white across the dyed background. A very pretty table runner can be made in this way :

Take a yard of white cotton crêpe. This makes a good proportion for a table runner. Decide upon the position of the white band for the border—how far it will be from the end and its width ?

Now pleat each end of the runner, the pleats being about $1\frac{1}{4}$ or $1\frac{1}{2}$ inch wide. Fold them as you would fold pleats in paper when making a fan.

Begin to wind round the pleats at the point where you mean the white border to start from the edge of the runner. Continue winding to the required width of the border. Any little spaces left between the windings will allow the dye to penetrate through and produce a most attractive stencil-like effect in the border.

When both ends of the runner have been tied, soak the whole thoroughly in water so that you are sure the folded portions outside the tied bands are wet.

Now wring out the water and dip it into the dye. Leave it in the dye as long as the instructions tell you, then take it out, rinse in cold water, wring out and hang it up until it is partly dry ; then remove the strings and shake until dry.

Turn in the edges and finish with a running stitch of mercerised knitting cotton of a colour that harmonises with the dye chosen.

A pretty finish to the corners is made by small balls of cotton attached to a cord. The balls can be made on small cardboard discs as described for making pompons.

Fig. 156 shows a very attractive cushion, and is an example of a pattern in which a unit has been evenly distributed over a surface.

This is an interesting design to work out in the " tie-and-dyed " method.

Fold an 18-inch square of unbleached muslin into sixteen small squares, and crease the folds. In Fig. 156 the dotted lines represent the folds. Cut from stiff paper a 4-inch square and cut from its middle a hollow 1-inch square. Place this over the centre of the muslin and mark its position by four dots. Then place it in the positions shown. Use half the pattern in the middle of each side and a quarter of the pattern for the four corners. Now take a running stitch of thread around each of these squares and parts of squares. Leave two ends of the thread in each case, draw in the stitches and tie tightly.

Now start from the sewing and wind round towards the centre of each shape for the width of about an inch. The muslin is now ready for dyeing by the processes already described. When untied and shaken out, the result should be as shown in Fig. 156.

It is better not to press articles dyed in this way in order to dry them completely, but shake them until they are dry. The slightly wrinkled effect that results from this method is quite attractive.

The design can be enriched by adding, after dyeing, a few stitches of wool of a deep contrasting colour in the middle of each small square.

Other units such as circles, diamonds, or ovals could be worked out in the same way.

The cushion cover can be decorated with a cord. For various ways of making cords, see Chapter XIII.

To make a Wave Design in Tie-and-Dyed Work.—This is a pretty design for the end of a table runner. First decide upon the position of the wave. Then draw across the end of the runner two parallel lines the right distance from the edge, using a piece of charcoal with a sharp point.

Between these draw an undulating line representing waves. Sew along this line with running stitches and rub off all charcoal marks. Draw in this thread and tie it securely to prevent it slipping. See that the folds of the muslin are adjusted evenly. Wind string round the muslin beginning at the line of sewing and continuing above it as far as the width of the wave required. Now leave a space smaller than the width of the wave, and wind round a second and narrower band of string.

Do the same with the other end of the muslin. When it is dyed, for example a deep green, there will be two wave-like bands, one broad and one narrow, across each end, both attractively speckled with the dye where it has entered any little spaces between the string.

The sides and ends can be turned in a broad hem and sewn with buttonhole stitch in a wool of a darker shade. Tassels can be made for each corner. (See Chapter XIII., " Cords, Tassels, or Fringes.")

JAPANESE TIED-DYEING

This is a very ancient craft, only practised in Japan by women of aristocratic families. It is a highly skilled art, needing considerable dexterity. The pattern is made on thin materials such as silk, georgette, etc., by a series of knots tied in order to make a design in dotted outline. The knots are tied very closely together, sometimes at every eighth of an inch, and only once, so that the pattern consists of tiny white rings with dark centres.

STICK PRINTING ON FABRICS

This is somehat similar to potato printing, but variety and experiment are less possible with sticks than potatoes. The tools consist of small pieces of wood with a simple shape cut in one end. This end is charged with colour and pressed on the material with the hand. Almost any material can be decorated. The decoration of cork mats is described in Chapter XXX. Smooth surfaced linens, cottons, and silks for handkerchiefs, scarves, and table mats or cloths are all suitable.

Printers' ink or dyes must be used for printing on fabrics. This is the method of work—spread the colour on a pad made of two or three pieces of felt as already described for potato printing. Lay the fabric on a flat surface over a folded newspaper or piece of felt, and pin it down with drawing-pins. Press the stick on the pad containing the right colour and then press it firmly on the surface to be decorated so that a good impression is made. The sticks must be cleaned for each new colour (with turpentine for printers' ink).

Patterns made by stick printing tend to be stiff. Fine

effects can often be obtained by enriching the stick printing with beautiful stitches.

BATIKS AND HOW TO MAKE THEM

As we have implied before, hand-decorated textiles are perhaps the most satisfactory form of applied art. To be able to dye fabrics at home for interior decorations or costumes that will be exactly fitting is very possible when one knows how.

By the batik process wonderful results can be obtained amd very elaborate pictorial designs printed. It is not so limited as the tie-and-dyed work just described. All that is needed for batik work is beeswax, dye, and a little skill. The beeswax is used as a resist to protect the fabric from the dye.

The process came originally from Java, where batik has been the native method of decorating materials for many hundreds of years. From Java it came to Holland, then to America and England.

Materials for batik work can be bought from most artists' colourmen, for example, Reeves & Sons. One can of course prepare one's own wax at home, but this is rather a messy process. White crêpe de Chine is the easiest material for beginners to use, but batiks can be done on all kinds of woven material such as cotton, silk, velvet, wool, mixed goods, or leather. Silk is an easy fabric to work as the wax penetrates easily and it takes colour well. This applies to chiffon and similar sheer materials.

The first step in the batik process is to prepare the material. In some cases it is wise to give the material a thorough washing, which will result in freeing the goods from any artificial loading and will shrink the piece. If one is using " dyed-in-the-piece goods " (that is, material already dyed one colour), it is a good plan to boil it for ten minutes, in order to remove any loose colour, and to make sure that no unexpected colour will run and mix itself with the dye in which the fabric is being dipped. The drying and ironing of the material makes it ready for the design.

Stretch the material on the table (it is well to cover the table with a piece of white paper), and pin it with drawing-pins. Have the design prepared upon paper. This design can be transferred to the material in one of the two following ways :

(1) By lightly drawing the design in pencil upon the fabric.

(In using transparent material the design can, of course, be placed underneath it, and the pattern traced directly through.)

(2) By the method known as " pouncing." This is the most satisfactory method. Draw the design upon tracing paper, and carefully trace over the whole of the drawing with a tracing wheel. Place the perforated paper on the fabric and rub charcoal through the holes. Many, however, prefer to use pouncing powder. In this case, with a small pad made of cotton-wool rub the powder in so that it penetrates the little holes made in the tracing paper and reaches the material below, then carefully remove the tracing paper.

If the pricking has left a jagged edge to the holes in the paper, rub the perforations lightly with sandpaper in order that the powder may go through cleanly and easily. When the finished work is to be in more than one colour it is advisable to strengthen the charcoal outline with pencil or Conté Crayon No. 2, otherwise it is washed off in the first dipping. The pouncing powder can be fixed by placing a piece of tissue paper over the material and ironing with a fairly hot iron.

Waxing.—Having traced or pounced the design on to the material, the next operation is to wax over those parts of the fabric which are to remain the original colour of the material. Heat a little wax in the saucepan over a spirit stove, taking care that the wax *does not boil*, and with a fairly stiff brush (Reeves' Fitch-Hair Brushes, Series No. 180) paint the wax on the material. It is wise to place stencil paper or thin smooth paper under the material being waxed.

Dyeing.—There are two methods of dyeing, either by dipping or painting on the colour with a brush. The brush is useful for small details and small articles or where many colours are being used. The brush is perhaps easier for beginners. We will describe the first method first.

Dipping.—Having covered up with wax all the parts of the design which are to remain white or the original colour of the fabric, it is now ready for the first dye bath.

Select the lightest shade in the colour-scheme for the first dyeing. To be sure of getting the desired shade it is well to test a sample of the fabric. The simplest batiks are, of course, those in which only one colour is used and consequently only one dipping is required. After dipping, the material should be rinsed thoroughly in lukewarm water. Avoid the use of cold water, especially when another dyeing is to follow, as the cold will cause the wax to become brittle and crack, and unintentional crackling is a sign of poor craftsmanship.

If a marbled effect is required, the wax can be cracked. In this case the material should be placed in cold water to harden the wax, and should be dyed while wet. The marbled effect is best upon large surfaces, and is obtained by rubbing the material between the hands after the wax has become hard.

Removing the Wax.—If the batik is to be in only one colour, it is now ready for the removal of the wax. This is a simple business. Experts generally rinse the fabric very thoroughly in gasoline or Carbona. In small work another method of removing the wax is by ironing over the material when dry, first placing the fabric between sheets of blotting-paper or newspaper. The iron should not be too hot and the process repeated with fresh paper until no wax comes from the material. If, after ironing, faint traces of wax are left in the material, they can be removed by placing the fabric upon blotting-paper and rubbing carefully with a clean rag dipped in petrol, or by submerging the whole article in petrol for a few minutes. If pouncing powder has been used, rubbing with petrol is necessary to remove the design, but the wax must be removed first. Remember never to use petrol near a naked light.

A word might be said here about the misuse of gasoline. When doing large work, a work you hope to sell, remember the gasolining should be done very thoroughly ; one of the faults of most amateurs is insufficient rinsing, and the fabric still stiff with wax is offered as a finished product. Often the lovely softness of a drapery is lost and a papery quality substituted because there have not been a sufficient number of gasoline baths.

When possible, gasoline should be used out of doors and in an earthenware vessel. It is quite economical because it can be used over and over again. The last baths for one batik, containing only a small amount of dissolved wax, can be used for the first bath next time. It is quite easy to run off the dissolved wax and save only the clear fluid.

More elaborate colour-schemes are produced by a repetition

of the process, simply covering up with fresh wax the parts one wishes to retain in the shade of the last-dyed colour. This re-waxing, dipping, and rinsing is continued until all the colours that the scheme demands are obtained, and then the wax is removed as described.

Painting with a Brush.—This is an easy method for amateurs. Pretty handkerchiefs and the borders of scarfs can be decorated in this way. When designing and waxing it must be remembered that the parts of the material which are intended to be of different colours must be separated by a waxed portion to prevent the dyes running into each other (unless it is intended to produce this effect). Pour a little of each dye to be used into a separate china saucer, diluting with water to obtain lighter shades when required. Take a soft brush (for example, Reeves' Squirrel-Hair, Series No. 208), and after dipping it into the first dye, paint over that part of the design which is to be of that colour, and use in a similar way the second dye and as many other dyes as are required. Rinse the material in lukewarm water (not absolutely cold or the wax will crack) after all dyeing has been completed, and after dabbing it with a clean rag to absorb some of the moisture, hang it up to dry.

In small articles like this, the wax can be ironed off with a fairly hot iron as already described.

If you cannot make your own designs for batik work, sheets of assorted designs can be bought at about 9d. each.

Here are a few hints for successful dyeing :

(1) Dyeing by dipping produces much more satisfactory results than the painting-in process, so it is worth while trying to dye successfully in this way, although it is more trouble.

(2) Don't use too much dye. To avoid any waste, it is a good plan to prepare a concentrated solution in a small pan and use it with care. Do not add it all at once to the water in a large vessel, but rather make a weak bath into which the piece is put, after being rinsed in clear water and squeezed out. When the colour is all taken up from the bath, remove the fabric and add more of the concentrated solution. Do this several times rather than pour in the whole strength at once. When the desired colour is reached, it will be found that the dyes are faster and a good deal less colour has been used. If care has been

taken, the water will be practically clear at the end of the proceedings.

Another good reason for not using too strong a bath is that with a weaker solution it is much easier to avoid streaks that so often annoy the inexperienced worker.

(3) The use of too small a vessel is another cause of uneven dyeing. The material must really swim in the tub so that no dye can possibly settle in the folds; for this same reason it is essential to keep the materials stirred the whole time they are in the dye.

(4) After the material has been removed from the dye-bath, it should be rinsed *very thoroughly* and dried. Do not wring it on any account, or the wax will be broken. Wrap the rinsed material in old sheets and towels and so blot up most of the moisture. When thus treated it soon dries. If it is hung up and allowed to drain, there will be streaks.

(5) The material should be thoroughly dry before the second waxing is applied. This is essential.

(6) A crackle effect can be produced all over the design by crushing the fabric, more or less gently, according to the amount of colour that one wishes to be allowed to penetrate to the material, just before the last dipping.

(7) The simplest colour-scheme consists of an arrangement of yellow, green, and blue. Always begin dyeing the lightest colour first and work through the colour-scheme to the darkest shade; for example, if you want to use the colours yellow, red, and black, the dye-baths must be arranged in the same order.

(8) Be careful to follow the directions on your packet of dye, but remember that the dyeing of a batik depends on the temperature of the dye-bath, for hot water will of course melt the wax and a too cold bath will make it so brittle that it will crack in unexpected and undesired places.

(9) When painting colours in with a brush, remember: (*a*) Painted-in colours stand out, and are useful for very bright effects; they do not harmonise with the general scheme in the way that colours do that have been dyed over each other. When colours are dyed over each other the darker tones are a composite of the colours dyed previously, and the whole effect is almost sure to show a pleasing relationship of colour. (*b*) If you have

to paint in a large surface with the brush, the colour tends to be uneven. This is because the moment the silk is touched with the brush, that particular spot gets the full strength of the dye, which fades out towards the edges. Any touching up fails to produce such a perfectly even surface such as can be obtained by dipping. (c) The dye, when painted in, is cool and the colours will naturally not be as fast as when the fibres of the material slowly absorb a hot dye. (d) The patterns or spots that have to be coloured always have to be first outlined in wax to prevent the dye from spreading ; this gives a light outline round a dark surface. This is not always an advantage.

(10) When dyeing a batik with one colour over the other, the second colour dyed will always be affected by the tone of the first dipping ; for example, if the material is first waxed and dyed yellow, then waxed again and dyed blue, the fabric will not come out as a true blue but, according to the strength of the blue dye, will be either light green, green blue, or blue green. This is always pleasing. (An odd spot of red or other unrelated colour must be painted in finally—if a conspicuous touch is required.)

If red is dyed over yellow one can get shades of orange, and so on. Batiks in one or two colours are always simpler than those in which a variety of tones are required, but with a little thought and practice many colours can be used together on the same piece.

CHAPTER XXIII

KNITTING

Materials and Tools. Methods of Casting on. Plain Knitting, Purling. Methods of Casting Off, Joining Wool, Increasing and Decreasing, Tension, Grafting. Stitches and Patterns in Knitting: Plain Knitting or Garter Stitch, Stocking Stitch, Ribbed Knitting, Cable Stitch, Moss Stitch, Block Stitch or Dice Stitch, Basket Stitch, A Pretty Basket Pattern, Barred Stripe Stitch, Lace Stitch. Knitting Charts. Picking up Stitches on an Edge ; Making Holes for Ribbons ; Seaming ; Buttonholes ; Sewing on Buttons ; Double Knitting ; Knitting in Several Colours. A " Tartan " Plaid.

SOCKS AND STOCKINGS.—General Directions ; The " Seam " Stitch ; Making the Round ; Welts ; Shaping ; The Heels ; Two Methods of turning the Heel ; Instep and Toe ; Two Methods of shaping the Toe ; Knitting a New Heel into a Sock ; Strengthening a Heel ; Baby's Boots ; A Knitted Sock on Two Needles.

COATS, CARDIGANS, AND JUMPERS.—Vests ; Caps and Berets ; Baby's Knitted Gloves ; Knitted Lace Patterns.

SOME GOOD IDEAS AND HINTS ON KNITTING.—Embroidery on Knitting ; How to use up Odds and Ends of Wool ; Useful Hints ; Glossary of Words used in Knitting.

KNITTING is really producing a fabric by making a number of loops that are passed backwards and forwards on two long pointed needles. Like crochet it is a delightful occupation for spare time and for long winter evenings. It can also be done almost anywhere—at home, in the train, in the park, and by the seaside. There is little strain on the eyes in knitting and really useful and lovely things can be made— jumpers, school sweaters for the children, stockings, socks, coats, cardigans, vests, gloves, scarves, and so on, down to the humble square kettle-holder or iron-holder which is always so useful. It is said that those who can knit or crochet are never lonely or discontented, and perhaps this is true.

MATERIALS AND TOOLS

Needles.—These were formerly always made of wood, bone, or steel, but now you can also get celluloid and light metal ones. Steel needles are always best for the finer sorts of work. The size of the needles depends upon the material employed, whether thread, cotton, silk, 3-ply or 4-ply wool, etc. As the size of the needles depends upon that of the cotton, a knitting gauge is used. The range of needles is from 1 to 24, 1 being the coarsest and 24 the finest. Steel needles are generally made in numbers from about 10 to 24, while the larger ones are more often found in sizes from 1 to 12. Sometimes the needles have their numbers clearly marked on them, but this is not always so. It is well to test one's needles by a reliable gauge, *e.g.* the Bell, to be sure all of a set are true to size.

Straight knitting is usually done with two needles only ; for round knitting three, four, or five needles are used. Circular or round knitting can also be done on one flexible needle with two firm ends. Use specially short needles (in sets of four) for glove fingers. Pins, *i.e.* needles with a knob at one end, are useful for loose, heavy work liable to slip off the ordinary needle. These can only be used for flat knitting, not circular.

An average-sized needle for a man's sock is 13, while quite a usual size for a lady's jumper is 8 or 9.

For knitting pure silk garments, coarse needles should not be used ; a tight knitter could use No. 8, and a loose knitter No. 9. These needles will give a soft yet close fabric. For artificial silk, use Nos. 8 and 7, for if finer needles be used a very heavy garment would be made.

Wool.—Plain fingering wools vary in thickness from 2 to 6 ply, while thicker wools of sports type are good for beginners to use. Fingering (often called Scotch Fingering) is suitable for all general purposes, especially for socks and stockings. Then there are many fancy wools and silk and wool mixtures for pretty garments of all descriptions. It pays to buy good wool.

Silk.—Pure silk and artificial silk.

Cotton.—Many good cottons can now be bought.

Besides needles and wool, silk, or cotton, the worker may

find a wool or cotton holder and a wool-winder useful. These are described in the section on Crochet Work.

Stitch Holders.—These are often useful in knitting. They are like very large safety-pins from 3 to 6 inches long, with blunt points. Stitches are transferred to a holder of this kind and the pin fastened, while another portion of the work is being done. This is specially useful when two sides of a jumper have to be divided for the neck.

HOW TO KNIT

Casting on.—There are two methods :

(1) *A Loose Edge* (German Method).—With two needles (Fig. 157). First make a slip knot and do not pull it too tight. Take right-hand needle between forefinger and thumb and insert it also into the loop. Place the wool over the forefinger of right hand (an effective way of regulating what is known as the tension of the yarn is to pass it under the two middle fingers and over the fourth finger) and round the right-hand needle ; this will give a thread which has to be drawn through the first loop, thus forming a second one. Slip this loop on to the left-hand needle and you will have two loops instead of one. Repeat this until you have the required number of stitches on the left-hand needle.

This method gives a very elastic edge and is very useful where a good deal of stretching is required, as at the top of socks or stockings or the edge of vests.

(2) *A Firm Edge* (another method of casting on).—In this method of casting on *one* needle only is used. Take enough wool from the ball for the number of stitches required (about 1 inch to a stitch is a good allowance). Make a slip-loop at the end farthest from the ball ; hold the needle in the right hand. Hold the left hand close to the needle with wool (loose end) held through the hand and over the thumb ; pass the wool (near the needle) round the thumb, forming a loop ; pass the point of the needle through the loop. Pass the wool (from ball) round the point of the needle and draw it through the loop, draw cut end close, and so complete another stitch.

This gives a firm edging for the rim of a beret or the bottom of a sweater, jumper, or cardigan.

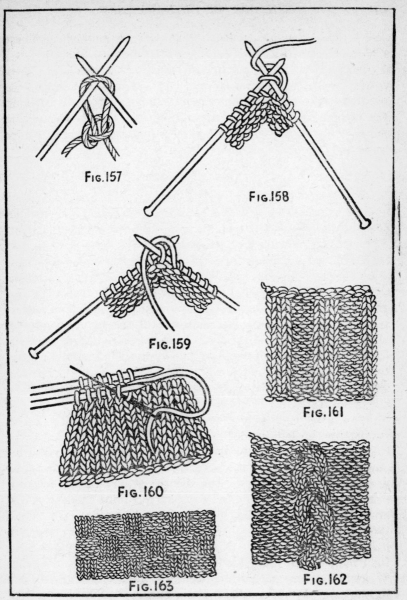

FIG. 157.—Position of needles for casting on.   FIG. 158.—Plain Knitting.
FIG. 159.—Purl Stitch.   FIG. 160.—Grafting being done on front needle.
FIG. 161.—Ribbed Knitting.   FIG. 162.—Cable Stitch.   FIG. 163.—Basket
Pattern.

(3) *Casting on for a Circle.*—Use the first method, and cast a third of the total number of stitches required on the first needle, then one more, but do not transfer it to needle 1. Drop needle 1, take up 3rd needle and cast on another third of the stitches. As before, knit one stitch too many and do not transfer. Take 4th needle to complete the casting on. Arrange the needles to make a triangle, and see that the work is not twisted before continuing the knitting.

BEGINNING TO KNIT

(1) *Plain Knitting* (Fig. 158).—After you have the necessary number of stitches on the left-hand needle insert the right-hand needle through the first loop, pass the wool, which should be at the back of the work, round the point of the right-hand needle, and with the first finger pass the point of the needle under the stitch so as to form a new stitch with the wool passed round, as in " casting on " ; only, instead of placing the newly formed stitch on the left-hand needle, leave it on the right-hand needle, and let the stitch drop off the point of the left-hand needle. Repeat this until all the stitches are passed on to the right needle.

Repeat this row as required, but always slip 1st stitch (after 1st row) on to the right needle without knitting it. Passing a stitch from one needle to the other without knitting it is called " slipping a stitch." This gives a neat, close edge.

(2) *Purling* (Fig. 159).—Cast on as usual, and hold the cast-on stitches in the left hand. Slip the first stitch, then bring the wool forward between the needles. For purling, the wool must always be *at the front* of the work. Now, instead of inserting the needle in the same way as you did for plain knitting, insert it from the back to the front, so that the right-hand needle is always in front of the left-hand needle, as in Fig. 159. Twist the wool round the front needle and knit the stitch off the left-hand needle on to the right in a backward direction, passing the right-hand needle under the stitch and behind the left-hand needle.

Plain knitting and purling are the foundations of all patterns in knitting. When you have learned these two and had a little practice in working them, you will be able to follow out the instructions found in any book, and what is more, perhaps invent your own designs.

Casting Off.—To finish off your garment and get rid of all the stitches, the following methods are employed :

First of all, knit two stitches plain as usual. Now there are two stitches only on the needle. Miss the last stitch made, insert the left-hand needle from left to right through the next one, lift it over the missed stitch and over the point of the needle, and withdraw the left-hand needle, leaving one stitch only on the right-hand needle ; knit the next stitch, insert the left-hand needle again from left to right through the previous stitch, and lift it over the stitch just knitted, withdraw the left needle and again there is only one stitch on the right-hand needle. Continue in the same way until all the stitches except one are cast off. Break off the wool from the ball and pass the end through the last stitch on the needle, pulling it lightly. The end of wool is afterwards darned into the work.

Be careful not to cast off the stitches too tightly, as the work becomes contracted. Beginners often make this mistake. The casting off should be loose enough to afford each stitch its usual tension.

Loose Casting-off.—Convey stitches to a crochet hook with hook at ball end. Hold hook in right hand, wool in left. Draw through one stitch, then through two, alternately, till all are cast off.

To join Wool.—Do it if possible at the end of a row. If the wool is thin, lay the two ends of wool, the new and the old, by the side of each other, overlapping about 3 inches, and knit five or six stitches with the double thread. The loose ends can afterwards be threaded into the garment on the wrong side, where they will be completely hidden.

Another way to join thick wool is to unravel the ends for 3 or 4 inches according to looseness of knitting, and cut out half the strands from each. Place ends overlapping, slightly damp them, and roll between fingers on palms of the hand.

To Increase.—Increasing is usually done at the beginning or end of a row. However, adding to the number of stitches can be done at almost any point, if required. There are two methods :

(1) Increasing without making a hole. (*a*) Knit first into the front and then into the back of the same stitch ; or (*b*) kint into stitch of row below.

(2) Increasing, making a hole. Pass the wool round the end of the right-hand needle without knitting a stitch. This increases. To make a hole without increasing the number of stitches, first knit two together, then pass thread round needle without knitting. Several rows worked in this manner give a series of little holes in the fabric, these can be used for forming a design or to emphasise a special line of garment.

It will thus be seen that there are various methods of increasing, and as a rule the instructions belonging to the garment being knitted will state where, when, and in what way such increase is to be made. Increasing rarely occurs in stocking knitting.

To Decrease.—To narrow a garment, or when finishing off, decreasing must be done. There are two methods of doing this—

(1) With decrease turned to the right : knit two stitches together, or if it is a purl row, purl them together.

(2) With decrease turned to the left : slip a stitch, knit the next, then pass the slipped over the knitted one, letting it drop off the needle. A slipped stitch should always be transferred from one needle to another, with the needle in position, as for plain knitting, not purling. This decrease slopes from right to left.

By using the two methods described above, decreasings are paired, and correct lines are given when following shapings of garments such as the two edges of cardigans, jumpers, etc.

Stockings are decreased down the back of the leg and also at the gussets and toes. Such decreasings are also called " intakes."

Tension.—It is very important to have the same tension to your knitting as there is in the pattern you are copying. This is regulated by the number of stitches to the inch ; the size of the finished garment depends absolutely on getting the right tension. One way to ensure this is to knit a sample about 4 or 5 inches square, press it with a hot iron and a damp cloth, then measure how many stitches there are to the inch. If this does not agree with the pattern, you can alter the size of your needles —for example, if your knitting shows too few stitches to the inch, you must use coarser needles, but if too many, finer ones must be employed.

Many directions give the exact thickness of wool and the size of needles to be used, but even if you follow these instructions exactly you must make allowance for the fact that you may be either a loose or a tight knitter. Most patterns are given for medium tension.

On the whole, garments are best made from instructions which give measurements, not number of stitches or rows. To knit on this plan you must know exactly how tightly you knit with the wool and needles in question. Knit a trial piece as suggested above. By this calculate the number of stitches to cast on and the number of rows to knit, to obtain the required measurements given in the pattern.

Grafting (Fig. 160).—This method is used for joining together stitches on two separate needles to make a seam without an uncomfortable ridge, as in the toe of a stocking or the shoulder of a sweater or jumper.

Have the same number of stitches on each needle and fold the knitted fabric, with the wrong sides facing together and the two knitting needles parallel (Fig. 160). Break off the wool, leaving a foot or so, and thread the wool into a darning needle. Pass the point of the needle through the first stitch of the front needle knitways (that is as for plain knitting), and pass the stitch on to darning needle, then pass the darning needle purlways through second stitch on front needle ; leave stitch on needle, but draw wool through both stitches. Bring the wool round under the front needle to the back one, and pass the point of the darning needle purlways into stitch of *back* needle, and pass the stitch on to the darning needle. Then pass the point of the darning needle into second stitch and leave on the needle, drawing the wool through both stitches. Bring the wool forward again under the needles to the front needle and repeat as before until all the stitches are worked off. Fasten the wool securely at the end.

This grafting makes the work look exactly as if there were no join at all, if you have pulled the wool through evenly.

This is the method used when working in stocking stitch (see heading, Stocking Stitch), but if the garment is in garter stitch (see heading, Garter Stitch) you must work in the same way as described above on the front needle, but instead of reversing the directions for the back needle, repeat the instructions for the front needle. In brief, both the front and back stitches are worked in the same way.

Stitches and Patterns in Knitting

There are only two stitches really used in knitting (1) *plain*, which is generally referred to as " knitting," and (2) *purl*, which is always so called. Every pattern is made up of these stitches worked in different ways. Groups of stitches called by certain names such as Garter Stitch or Stocking Stitch are really not new stitches, they are patterns made by a certain way of grouping plain and purl, and no new stitch is involved. All the stitches we are now going to describe would be more correctly called patterns, but we keep the word " stitch " because it is so commonly used. It is wise when trying a " stitch " (pattern) for the first time to practise on odd bits of wool. It is worth while spending some time over this.

Plain Knitting or Garter Stitch.—Any number of stitches, odd or even, may be used.

To work.—Simply do plain knitting on *two* needles. This is the easiest of all stitches. It is very useful for babies' bonnets, coats, socks, children's jumpers, berets, and collars and cuffs.

Stocking Stitch, or Stocking-web Knitting.—This stitch is so called because it has the smooth effect necessary for a stocking or sock.

To work.—On two needles this stitch is made by knitting one row and purling the next. Continue alternately in this way. On four needles, continuous knitting, without any purling, will produce stocking stitch.

This stitch gives an ideal fabric. It will be quickly seen that the *smooth front* of the knitted rows and the *smooth back* of the purled rows gives a good appearance to the work, for every stitch and row is clearly defined. This stitch is very suitable for almost any garment where a flat surface is desirable.

Ribbed Knitting (Fig. 161).—This is used where the material will receive a certain amount of stretching, for ribbed knitting is very elastic and keeps its shape in spite of a good deal of tension. It is often used at the tops of stockings and socks, at the bottom of jumpers, and for the cuffs of sweaters. It is also most valuable for vests.

The ribs can be knitted any size, knit 2 and purl 2, or knit 3 and purl 3 ; or you can have uneven ribs and knit 3 and purl 1, and so on.

To work.—Take care in casting on that the number of stitches is some multiple of the total number of stitches in the rib that has to be repeated. For example, if you are using knit 2, purl 2, there are 4 stitches in the repeated portion ; therefore your full number of stitches must be a multiple of 4 (that is, a number divisible by 4). Knit 2 stitches, purl 2, and repeat this to the end of the row.

Cable Stitch (Fig. 162).—This stitch is often used for men's sweaters and pullovers. In appearance the pattern looks like a twisted rope at intervals. It makes a strong, hard-wearing garment, but it is a little more difficult than some of the stitches we are describing.

To work.—An extra needle of the same size is needed. Choose a fairly broad-ribbed pattern, say, 6 plain and 1 purl. After a few rows, say five or six, a twist is worked in each broad smooth rib as follows : Slip first 3 stitches (half a rib) of rib on to the extra needle and push it to the back of the work ; knit the next 3 stitches, then knit the 3 stitches on the spare needle. (This gives the crossed-over effect.) Each twist is made in this way across the row, then several ribbed rows are worked again before the next row of twists. A very small cable can be made by purling 4 and knitting 4 for five rows.

For the 6th row—slip 1, purl 4, slip the next 2 stitches off on to a spare needle, knit the next 2 stitches, then knit the 2 stitches on the spare needle. Repeat this to end of row and finish with knit 1. Six rows must be knitted in this way. When once you have memorised these six rows you will find the work very easy. Small cables are suitable for children's garments.

Moss Stitch (see chart for Moss Stitch, Fig. 165).—This makes a decorative pattern. It is suitable for entire jumpers and also for borders.

To work.—An odd number of stitches is best if possible. Knit 1 and purl 1 to the end of the row. On the return row a smooth stitch (knitted stitch) is worked over the rough stitch (purl) facing you, and a rough over a smooth, this gives the " moss " effect. It will be clear when you realise that it is just the opposite to ribbing (see Fig. 164). A variation can be made by forming double moss stitch. In the first row, knit 2, purl 2 to the end. In the second row, knit 2 (if you ended with knit 2 in the previous row), purl 2, and so on. If you finished with purl, start also with purl.

Block Stitch or Dice Stitch (Fig. 166).—This fancy pattern is suitable for jumpers, children's coats, and other garments. It produces a raised effect and looks a little like plaiting. Each block (called dice if small) may be almost any size, from 2 inches square to 9 or 10 inches square. The larger patterns are specially useful for pram covers and for sweaters.

You must begin with a number of stitches that are some multiple of twice the number you have in one block. Thus if each block has 7 stitches, your total number of stitches must be a number divisible by 14.

The chart shown in Fig. 166 will tell you clearly how it is worked. Suppose you are working a 5-stitch block, proceed as follows : in the *first five* rows, knit 5, purl 5 to the end of each row.

For the next five rows, purl 5, knit 5 to the end of each row (Fig. 166).

Basket Stitch (Fig. 163) is only a slight variation of the above. Below we give the pretty basket stitch. It is set out very clearly, and when it has been mastered, all sorts of variations will suggest themselves. Basket stitch can be used for all the articles already mentioned under Block Stitch. It is especially suitable for coverlets.

A Pretty Basket Pattern (Fig. 163).—Cast on 30 stitches.
First row : Plain.
Second Row : * Knit 7 plain, purl 3, repeat from *.
Third Row : * Knit 3 plain, purl 7, repeat from *.
Fourth Row : * Knit 7 plain, purl 3, repeat from *.
Fifth Row : Plain.
Sixth Row : Knit 2, * purl 3, knit 7, repeat from *, and end the row by knitting 5.
Seventh Row : Purl 5, * knit 3, purl 7, repeat from *, ending row with purl 2.
Eighth Row is the same as the sixth.
Ninth Row : Plain.

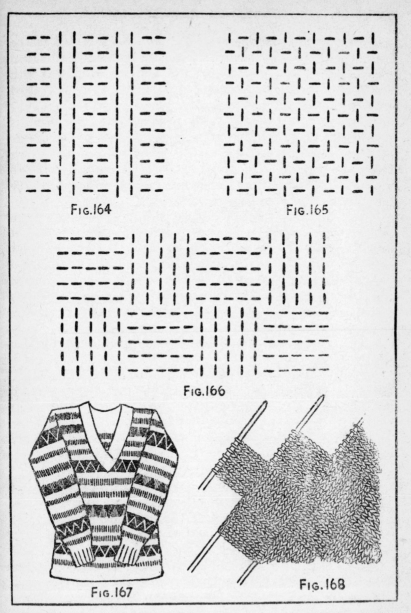

FIG. 164.

FIG. 165.

FIG. 166.

FIG. 167.

FIG. 168.

FIG. 164.—A Chart for Ribbed Knitting. FIG. 165.—Chart for Moss Pattern.
FIG. 166.—Chart for Block Pattern. FIG. 167.—Fair Isle Pullover.
FIG. 168.—A Tartan Plaid.

This pattern can be made larger or smaller to suit the size of the garment ; for example, for a smaller one, 8 stitches to the pattern would be enough, that is 5 plain and 3 purl ; if larger, 12 stitches, that is 7 plain and 5 purl, would be needed. The number of the stitches must always be divisible by the size of the pattern necessary.

Barred Stripe Stitch.—This is a very definite pattern, and it looks well on golf stockings. It is also suitable for boys' jerseys and for jumpers. It makes a fairly elastic garment. The width of the stripe can of course be varied according to taste, so too can the distance between the bars.

For stockings you must knit as follows : In the first six rows, knit 4, purl 1 to the end of each row. In the seventh row, purl every stitch. Repeat the seven rows.

Lace Stitch.—There are a number of patterns that give an open-work lacy appearance to the knitting. These are most useful for decorations and for shawls. These lace stitches need close attention until the pattern is learned.

A well-known pattern of lace stitch in knitting is that known as Feather Pattern. It is most suitable for a border, because it gives the appearance of a scalloped edge. Little dresses for small children might be knitted in this stitch.

To work.—Cast on 32 stitches (or more, according to the size of the work. It is best to have a multiple of 15 and 2 extra stitches).

First Row : Knit 1, * knit 2 together three times, bring wool forward, knit 1 five times, knit 2 together twice. Repeat from * to the end of the row, finish with knit 1.

Second Row : Knit 1, purl to the end of the row, finish with knit 1.

Repeat these two rows for the length required.

This pattern can easily be varied. When altering the pattern remember that the number of stitches reduced by the knitting together of stitches must be made up for by the number of times the wool is brought forward, as this results in an extra stitch being formed each time. Always begin and end with a knit 1 ; that is why two extra stitches must be cast on. (For explanation of " bring wool forward," see Glossary at end.)

KNITTING CHARTS (Figs. 164, 165, 166)

Many knitters like to use knitting charts for patterns and find these easier to follow than written instruction. It is interesting for the knitter to arrange the stitches according to her own design on squared paper. For very complicated designs, of course, fuller instructions are needed than these only given on charts.

SOME MORE METHODS IN KNITTING THAT YOU MUST KNOW

We will now give some processes that the knitter will find useful whatever garment she is making, and then proceed to give directions for making some of the most needed articles of clothing.

Picking up Stitches on an Edge, or Knitting-up Stitches.—In some garments and at stocking heels it is necessary to " knit up " stitches in order to add an extra piece, for example, the side of a heel flap on a sock or a sleeve knitted on to a shoulder instead of seamed.

An even edge is already made by slipping the first stitch in each row—plain in a purl row, and purl in a plain. Pick up the absolute edge from the wrong side with a spare needle ; when knitting the first row off this needle, knit into the short side of the stitch. On a sock the back of the stitch will be short on one side of the heel flap, and the front will be short on the other side. This twists the stitches of the first row and prevents holes occurring. (See paragraphs on Heels.)

Another method is to hold the edge, where the stitches require knitting up, in the left hand, pass the point of the needle through the first loop, put the wool round the needle as for knitting, and draw a loop through the loop of the fabric ; continue into each loop until sufficient stitches are " knitted up."

Making Holes for Ribbons.—To make one hole, bring the wool forward between the needles and knit two stitches together, taking the wool back over the needle. Knit as many stitches between each side as required.

Seaming.—Hold the two parts of the garment with edges even and right sides facing, and crochet the two together, *i.e.* draw wool through two loops, one from each side of the garment, then through one.

To make Buttonholes.—It is very important to have a button-hole that will not stretch and pull out of shape. Therefore they need to be carefully made and strengthened afterwards.

The simplest method is to cast off four stitches or more according to the size of the hole required. In the next row cast on loosely the same number of stitches opposite those cast off.

When knitting these, cast on stitches (in the next row), insert the needle from the back, which makes the second edge as firm as the first. Sometimes the hole is too big ; the remedy in this case is to run several threads of wool round the opening, on the wrong side, to reinforce it and pull it together. If necessary, a line of buttonhole stitch can be done as well.

For little children's and babies' garments crocheted loops are frequently used. They are quickly made, and simply consist of a line of chain worked on a fine hook. (See section on Crochet Work.)

With crocheted garments, one can often use holes in the pattern itself. These should be buttonholed round to prevent their stretching and pulling out of shape.

Sewing on Buttons.—When sewing buttons on knitted or crocheted clothes, take care that they have a good foundation by placing on the underside a small piece of material of the same colour and sewing through on to that. This applies especially to children's cardigans or coats, because they are so often roughly pulled.

Double Knitting.—This is very useful for belts and scarves, etc. Cast on an even number of stitches and twice as many as required for the width. Slip the first stitch of every row purlwise. Then alternately knit 1 and slip 1 purlwise. The slipped stitch of one row is knitted in the next.

Knitting in Several Colours.—This is suitable for stocking tops, jumper borders, etc. Coloured pattern work looks best done in stocking stitch, as the smooth nature of the surface shows the pattern well.

While knitting in one colour the threads of the others lie along the back until needed. To prevent the formation of long loops which catch and break, these are twisted. Indeed the whole success of this particular form of knitting lies in keeping your balls of wool in a definite order, by twisting the colour which is being worked under and over the colour or colours not in use. To do this by crossing over the balls each time is so long a process that multi-colour knitting of the amateur has been largely restricted to jumper borders and stocking tops. All-over patterns can be knitted fairly quickly in several colours (bringing flecked, small lozenge, and diaper designs within reach of the hand knitter) by knitting either into the left hand or right as desired. Fair Isle jumpers show an elaboration of this kind of knitting.

Before beginning knitting of this kind try a small sample in different colours, so as to get used to managing the wools. On the wrong side the strands of wool should lie flat without being in loops, but they should not be so tight that they drag the work. Fig. 167 shows a Fair Isle pullover in five different wools.

Below we give a suggestion for colour work. This method makes delightful quilts and rugs, and it is not wasteful. Further on, you will read how to make pram covers, blankets, etc., by using up oddments of wool, and you will want to try your hand at this patch-work knitting.

A " Tartan " Plaid (Fig. 168)

This coloured block pattern recalls the various tartans and devices from Scotland, but here, to prevent the extra thickness gained by carrying the wool across at the back, each check is made separately on the bias and deftly knitted together. Hence while the Scotch mode rather tightens the material, this new slantwise way gives it a great deal of elasticity, so much so, that when used for stockings, one-third of the ordinary stitches may be suppressed.

In the diagram (Fig. 168) the blocks are eight stitches square and of two colours, but when selected as borders for quilts much larger squares can be obtained by having from twelve to sixteen or twenty stitches and using coarser wool. Also more diversity may be introduced into the colouring by the blending of several contrasting hues, or the artistic shading of one colour from the lightest to the darkest shade, and *vice versa*. Even when knitted in one colour the blocks can be varied by intermingling with the plainly knitted checks, others of purl, ribbing, moss stitch, etc.

To work the pattern take any number divisible by eight, according to the size required. For the four checks shown, cast on 32 stitches, and set them, if for large work, by one plain and one purled row.

Half Squares.—1st Row : Knit plain with the darkest colour 8 stitches ; leave the remaining 24 a side, turn the work, and with a third needle purl back, taking the last 2 stitches together. Repeat this at every alternate row till there is but 1 stitch left on the needle. Thus in the 3rd row you will knit 7, in the 5th row 6, in the 7th row 5, in the 9th row 4, in the 11th row 3, in the 13th row 2, in the 15th row 1. Your reductions have been made on one side only. Now, with the needle that has the one stitch only, pick up and knit 7 stitches along the opposite side, which will bring you back to the 24 stitches. In raising the loops, take up the *back* part of every stitch. Leave this needle untouched. The first triangle is complete ; go on to the next by knitting off eight more loops and decreasing them as before ; pick up the stitches of the straight side again, leave them on the needle, and continue in the same way to make two more triangles with the sixteen remaining stitches.

The Complete Squares.—2nd Row : The first row has produced 4 triangles, on each of which has been left a needle holding 8 loops. These sets of loops form the foundation of squares which, sloping in a reverse direction, fill up the spaces between the triangles. They are likewise made separately and joined to the side of the half-squares whilst working. Proceed as follows : With contrasting wool purl the 8 loops of either the first or the third triangle, it does not matter at which end you begin. Knit back 7 of the stitches ; then slip the last loop off on to the needle already full. With the needle now free, lift up the back part of the first stitch on the decreased side of the next triangle ; pass the eighth or unknitted loop on to its own needle again, and knit the two together, but *from the back*, for the last loop of the square being made always falls *over* the picked-up stitch.

Return by purling, and continue in each knitted line to raise a stitch from the side. As eight are to be picked up, every alternate loop will, of course, be taken. Remember to seize the front part of the side loops to avoid showing any ridge. When the first square is completed, leave the eight loops, as before, on the needle, and proceed to work on the loops of the following triangles in the same way.

3rd Row : Here we have another series of squares or diamonds fitting into those below ; they are worked on a like principle, but in a contrary direction, their slope corresponding to that of the triangles.

Raise 8 loops with the dark wool again ; this time on the right instead of on the left side of a block ; purl them, turn, and knit together in the ordinary way the last loop of the light square and the first loop of the fresh one, taking care that the latter falls well over. Take two together thus at the beginning of every knitted line, and when the block is made, leave the loops on the needle, and pass to the next square.

The second and third rows comprise the whole work, and having repeated them as often as desired, make the top straight by introducing triangles, as at the lower edge.

The numerous needles will be found rather troublesome, especially at the beginning of the work. To get over this difficulty each square may be cast off as it is finished. This does not prevent the stitches from being picked up, just as if the needle were there.

SOCKS AND STOCKINGS

General Directions for knitting Socks and Stockings.—Socks and stockings are generally knitted in " rounds " of plain knitting, using four steel knitting needles. When worked in rounds, the plain knitting has a " smooth " appearance on the right side of the pattern and a " ridged " appearance on the wrong side, so that it is not the same on both sides as when using two needles.

It is the easiest possible work to do.

For men's socks and stockings, 4-ply fingering is suitable. Heather mixture 4-ply fingering is best for ordinary wear, and yarn, which is harsher, for heavy wear. Five ounces of 4-ply fingering makes one pair of socks and supplies mending. The needles used can be Nos. 11 or 12, or even 15.

For children's or babies' garments use 2- or 3-ply wool with Nos. 15 or 16 needles.

Socks have a ribbing at the top, which is called a " welt," and consists generally of 2 plain and 2 purl stitches worked alternately all round, which gives elasticity to the upper portion. The purl stitches must always be made over the purl stitches, and the plain over the plain stitches. The " welt " is made 3 or 4 inches deep, according to fancy.

Remember you have to decide whether the ribbing at the top of the sock (the welt) is to be fine or coarse, and regulate your number of stitches accordingly. The total number of stitches must be a multiple of the number in each complete rib (see paragraph on Ribbed Knitting).

When changing from one sort of knitting to another during the making of a sock, always finish the round, the beginning of the round can be seen if an end of wool is left when making the first stitch in casting on.

The first few stitches on each needle are apt to be looser than the others, so special care must be taken to knit them tightly, otherwise an unwanted seam is produced that looks like a " ladder."

When working in rounds four needles are used until the heel is reached, then only two needles are required, and the knitting proceeds in rows backwards and forwards, in alternate rows of plain and purl, to continue the smooth surface of the work. After the heel-shaping is finished four needles are again used, and the work continues in rounds to the end of the foot.

The " seam " stitch in a stocking is generally purled to form a perpendicular line from the top of a stocking down to the heel ; it denotes the back of the leg, and is a guide to the place where decreasings (or intakes) are made.

There are all these parts to consider in the making of a sock : (1) beginning or making the round ; (2) knitting the welt or ribbed top ; (3) legs and shaping ; (4) making the heel ; (5) the foot and toe. We will say a word about each of these parts.

(1) *Beginning or making the Round.*—To join round, cast on the full number of stitches on to one needle for the beginning of a sock or stocking, and then divide them on to three needles, according to directions for numbers. When you have arranged the required number of stitches on three needles, the end of the third needle with the ball of wool attached to it is put to the beginning of the first needle beside the tag end of the wool, making a triangle, and the first needle is held uppermost. Arrange

all the cast-on stitches evenly on their respective needles, without twisting ; insert the fourth needle into the first cast-on stitch beside the tag end of the wool on the first needle, and knit all the stitches from the first needle on to the empty fourth needle. The wool must be drawn tightly after knitting the first stitch, so that there is no gap between the stitches. If there is a gap produced by joining into round, close this by working as follows : *Second round* : Knit in pattern along half the stitches on the 1st needle, pass these on to the end of the 3rd needle. Finish 1st needle. Knit 2nd needle half-way, and pass the stitches just knitted to the 1st needle. Finish 2nd needle. Knit along 3rd needle for corresponding number of stitches taken from the 2nd needle, and pass them on to 2nd needle. The joining tag will now be midway on the 3rd needle. Work one more round. *Fourth round* : Repeat 2nd round, and " tag " will be once more in position as at the beginning of 1st round. Knit on in pattern, always drawing the wool tightly at the beginning of each needle.

(2) *Welts.*—These are knitted in any size of rib or any depth according to the taste of the knitter. They vary from a welt of 1 plain and 1 purl, 2 to 3 inches deep for babies' socks and children's stockings, to a welt of 3 plain and 3 purl, 4 to 5 inches deep for boys and men. In boys' and men's three-quarter hose the welt is usually covered by patterned stocking tops. In these cases the fancy top is worked first, then this is turned inside out and the welt continued from this point. The ribbed welt makes the top of the sock more elastic. Many pretty patterns for turn-back tops (or turnover tops) will be found in most Practical Needlework books.

Here are directions for knitting a welt of 2 plain and 2 purl.

Cast on the required number of stitches, join in a round as already described, and knit plain the first two stitches ; bring the wool to the front (between the two needles) and purl the 2 stitches next following ; pass the wool to the back (between the needles) and knit 2 ; again bring the wool to the front, between the needles, and purl 2, and again pass the wool to the back, continue in this manner, knitting 2 and purling 2, to the end of the round.

(3) *Legs and Shaping.*—The leg portion of socks needs no shaping. It is usually worked in plain knitting to the required

length, or if preferred the rib used in the welt can be continued. In stockings and three-quarter stockings when the required length has been knitted after the welt, a series of shapings must be made. Some workers make a seam stitch down the back of the stocking by purling the last stitch of every round, thus helping to emphasise the shapings each side of the leg. Many knitters, however, prefer the plain stitch—marking the start of the round by a tag or by the end of wool left from the casting-on. This is perhaps best for children's stockings ; because stockings put on crookedly or pulled in wear do not look quite so tidy. *To decrease :* In men's socks begin to decrease after 2 inches of plain knitting after the welt (welt = 3 inches of ribbing). You need to make about five decreasings, do these on every tenth row thus—knit two together immediately before and after the seam stitch. When the necessary decreasings have been made, continue without shaping for the ankle until the heel is reached.

(4) *The Heels—Turning the Heels.*—There are several methods of doing this. Perhaps this is the favourite and simplest :

The heel is, of course, worked on half the number of stitches in the round with two needles.

Divide the stitches as follows : put half on to the heel needle, which will have the seam stitch as its middle. The remaining stitches will be on the other two needles, where they must remain for the time.

Now purl the stitches on the heel needle off on the empty fourth needle and work the heel by knitting one row and purling the next on these two needles, until it measures $2\frac{1}{2}$ inches. Always slip the first stitch in every row.

Now turn the heel as follows : Start with a plain row and knit, say, 28 stitches, leaving 9 stitches unknitted ; turn, purl 19, knit 19, taking up with the 19th stitch the first of the 9 previously left unknitted. Turn, purl back, taking up with the 10th stitch from the end the first of the unknitted stitches. Continue to knit in this way until all 9 stitches that were left each end have been taken up. If you had 37 stitches on the heel needle to begin, you will now have 19 left, and the heel is finished.

Another Heel (Oblique Heel).—Divide the stitches as before so that half the number in the round are on the heel needle (or back needle) with the seam stitch in the middle (if you are not working with a seam stitch the middle of your needle must correspond with the middle of the decreasings of the leg). Place the remaining stitches on the other two needles evenly divided and leave them for the instep.

Now knit and purl alternate rows, always leaving the last stitch of the previous row untouched, until 10 stitches are left each side. The last row is a purl row if you started your heel with a plain row. Now continue knitting and purling, taking up one of the rejected stitches each row, but before picking it up, pick up a loop from the side so as to make an extra stitch. Do this until all the side stitches are worked off and are on one row again, which should be a purl row.

Knit back half the stitches, thus leaving the heel complete and ready for the instep.

(5) *Instep and Toe.*—Put the stitches left on the two instep needles on one needle again.

With a needle knit the remaining heel stitches and knit up one stitch to each loop down the side of the heel ; with another needle knit the instep stitches ; with a " third " needle knit up one stitch to each loop along the other side of the heel stitches, and the following half of the heel stitches. In this way the work is in a complete round again ready for the shaping that brings the foot to its correct size. Decrease for the instep by carrying out alternate rounds of plain and decreasing. When the instep is finished, continue without shaping to the toe.

Shaping the Toe.—There are two good methods : 1st Method.—The toe is always worked in plain knitting throughout, shaping as follows : divide the stitches so that there are half the total number on the instep needle, a quarter on the second, and a quarter on the third needle. 1st Round : knit to the last three stitches on the first needle, knit 2 together, knit 1. On the second needle knit 1, knit 2 together, knit to the last 3 stitches, knit 2 together, knit 1. On the third needle, knit 1, knit 2 together, knit to the end of the needle. Knit 2 rounds without shaping (*i.e.* decreasing). Repeat from the first round until the toe measures about $1\frac{1}{2}$ inch (or until there are 24 stitches left). Now knit the stitches from the first needle on to the third needle and graft off the stitches. (See section on Grafting.)

This is thought by many to be the best shaped toe. It is the favourite toe for children's wear.

Second Method.—On each needle, in every alternate round, decrease at the beginning and end, by knitting together the second and third stitches, and the last but two with the last but one. Continue until you have four stitches on each needle. Remove two stitches from the third needle on to the first, and the other two on to the second, giving six stitches on each of two needles.

Taking another needle, and holding the first and second parallel, knit a stitch of each simultaneously. Knit one of each again, drawing the first over the second as in casting-off, until one loop is left. Thread the wool through this and fasten off.

Many think this toe is more easily made than the first.

How to knit a New Heel into a Sock or Stocking.—First get the wool to match the sock in colour and texture, and choose four needles which will give a similar tension. Now unravel the old heel. Great care must be taken not to unpick one stitch of the leg below the instep level. Pick up on two knitting needles the stitches across the sole of the foot from one side of the instep to the other so that they will not slip. Next pick up the stitches for the heel-flap on one needle ; join in the wool and knit to the last stitch on the heel needle, and slip one stitch off the side needle on to the heel needle, and take these two together.

Turn and purl to the last stitch of the heel needle, and, once again, slip one off from the side needle and take two together. Continue doing this at the end of each row until the heel flap is long enough. Count the stitches left at the centre of the sole of the sock, put them on one needle, then *turn* the heel by the same method that was used in the original knitting. There should then be left on the heel needle as many stitches as were counted on the sole. Now place the two needles side by side, take a wool needle and graft the heel and foot together. Darn in all ends of wool, both new and old, very neatly and securely, especially near the instep parts and at the end of the grafting. (See paragraph on Grafting.)

Strengthening a Heel.—To strengthen a heel use a 2-ply

fingering or a reel of Star Sylko or No. 8 D.M.C., the colour of your stocking. Join this to your work when beginning the heel flap, and knit it together with the stocking wool for the heel flap and the turning of the heel. This can also be done for the toe, if joined on when the decreasings are begun. This method is of great value as it lengthens the life of a stocking considerably.

Baby's Boots.—The material required is one ounce of fingering and three needles. Cast on 49 stitches.

First Row : Purl.

Second Row : Plain.

Third Row : Purl.

Fourth Row : Slip 1, make 1, knit 4, take 3 together * knit 4, make 1, knit 1, make 1, knit 4, take three together, repeat from *, knit 4, make 1, knit 1.

Fifth Row : Plain, repeat 3rd and 4th rows 12 times.

Thirtieth Row : Plain.

Thirty-first Row.—Purl.

Thirty-second Row : Slip 1, * make 1, take two together, repeat from * to the end of the row. This row is for the ribbon.

Thirty-third Row : Purl.

Now do 4 plain rows and break off the wool, divide the stitches for the foot, 16 for one side, 17 for the top of the foot, and 16 for the other side, using three needles. Take the 17 stitches for the top of the foot, and knit 20 rows plain, then begin to knit the first 16 slipped stitches ; when you have done this, lift 12 stitches up to the side of front and take 8 of the stitches at the end of front, which will take you half across your piece of knitting. Begin with another needle and repeat the same on the other side ; you have now the work on two needles only. Now knit 10 rows.

For 11th row, take the first 2 stitches together and the last 2 of each row.

For 12th row do the same. Put the two needles together and cast off in the same way as you would for a stocking. Sew up where required.

A Knitted Sock for a Child (on Two Needles).—This sock fits well and is easy to make. Materials required : one ounce of fingering. It is knitted on two needles, backwards and forwards.

Cast on 22 stitches and knit 22 rows, but increase once at the end of every other row on the right side of the work, so that there are 33 stitches in the 22nd row.

Now cast off 28 stitches and knit 12 rows, increasing 1 stitch at the end of every other row. Now 12 more rows, decreasing 1 stitch at the end of every other row; this forms the toe.

Cast on 28 stitches on the same needle, and knit 22 rows, decreasing 1 stitch at the end of every other row, and cast off.

Pick up the 68 stitches on the upper part of the shoe and knit 20 rows, 2 plain and 2 purl rows alternately, decreasing 1 stitch in each side of the 12 stitches in every other row, which forms the toe and front of the sock. Knit 14 rows of 2 plain, 2 purl stitches alternately, then 3 open rows with 1 plain row between. The open rows are worked as follows: * Purl 2 together, purl 1, make 1, repeat from *; 3 plain rows, one open row, 1 plain row, and cast off. The sock is sewn together down the back of the leg, centre of sole, and the point joined like a gusset to form the toe.

COATS, CARDIGANS, AND JUMPERS

For all garments of this type two needles only are used. An average-sized needle for this work is No. 8.

They can be knitted in stocking stitch, moss stitch, or garter stitch (garter stitch is most often used for children's wear, it is less effective for grown-ups).

Cardigans with sleeves are generally knitted in five pieces—the back, the right front, the left front, and the two sleeves. Of course the back and the two fronts may, if wished, be knitted in one piece, but the drawback to this (unless the garment is very small) is that the work becomes cumbersome and heavy on the needles.

Many jumpers are made in six pieces—front, back, two sleeves, two cuffs.

Work is begun at the *bottom* of the articles in all cases; this is especially important in sleeves, which usually have a few inches of ribbing at the cuff to grip the wrist. If you were to finish at the cuffs you would find that it is not easy to cast off at just the right tension to give the ribbing the necessary amount of elasticity.

Of course all seams joining the pieces together must be neatly sewn with the same wool, and not stretched in any way as they are sewn.

Knitted coats and jumpers adapt themselves to the figure and do not need to be shaped in the same way as those made of material, so that one can easily make one's own patterns. However, one must not trade too much on this fact.

Pockets.—There are two recognised ways of making pockets in knitting :

(1) *A Patch Pocket.* This is the easiest method. You knit a pocket and then sew it neatly on the garment with the same coloured wool.

(2) You may knit the pocket into your garment as though it were part of it.

One of the great dangers of pocket-making is that they become loose with continual stretching. On the whole it is well to avoid pockets. They rarely add to the beauty of the garment, and if they are used they quickly become unsightly. To put them on merely for the sake of ornament seems waste of time.

VESTS

It is really worth while to knit one's own underwear. It is much cheaper and the garments can be fitted to one's own measurements. A good quality of wool, however, is essential. It must be soft if it is to go next to the skin, and it must stand washing.

Vests are knitted in very much the same way as jumpers, but of course without sleeves. They are generally formed of two pieces, the front and the back. These are worked separately and afterwards sewn together. Sometimes the whole garment is knitted on four needles, then no seam is necessary.

CAPS AND BERETS

Caps and hoods of all kinds are easily knitted and easily adapted to the prevailing fashion.

Below we give directions for knitting a cap, but it is quite easy to invent simple caps oneself for little children.

A CHILD'S KNITTED CAP

This cap is suitable for a child of about two years. You will need $1\frac{1}{2}$ ounces of 4-ply Scotch fingering, white or any colour desired, two No. 10 needles and two No. 12.

Begin by casting on 76 stitches, using No. 10 needles. **Knit** a rib of knit 1 and purl 1 for 3 inches.

Take No. 12 needles and knit a plain row and a purl row alternately for 9 inches. Then work another rib of knit 1 and purl 1 on No. 10 needles for 3 inches, and cast off.

Now double the work in half, and sew up the seams neatly on the wrong side. Turn up the ribbed piece, and fold over the two corners to the rib and fasten down with a crochet button.

To make the button, work 3 chain and join into a ring. Now work double crochet for several rounds. Increase every few stitches to keep the work flat. Work one round with no increasings, and then begin to decrease every few stitches in order to draw the work in for the under-side of the button. Fill the button with cotton-wool, and sew it on to the cap.

Baby's Knitted Glove

One ounce of 2-ply fingering will be needed. Use No. 15 needles. Cast on 41 stitches.

First Row : Make 1, slip 1, as if about to purl, but instead of doing so slip it on to the right-hand needle, knit 1, and repeat to the end of the row.

Second Row : Make 1, slip 1 purlways, knit the next stitch and the stitch that lies over it together, and repeat the same to the end of the row. Work 36 more rows the same as the second row. This should be sufficient for the depth of the gauntlet.

Thirty-ninth Row : For the wrist—knit 1, purl 2 together, and repeat.

Fortieth Row : Work in ribbing, knit 1, purl 1 alternately to the end, continue this ribbing for 10 more rows.

Fifty-first Row : For the hand—work the same as the first row.

Fifty-second Row : Knit as for the second row, and go on until 30 rows are done.

Next row for the thumb : Work 8 ridges of pattern as in second row, and leave the other stitches on the left-hand needle, turn, and knit on 8 ridges for 20 rows, then make a row of knit 1, knit 2 together, followed by 4 rows of ribbing, the same as at the wrist, break off the wool and with a worsted needle draw the wool through the stitches and sew up the top of the thumb. Begin again where you divided for the thumb, and work for the finger part 30 rows as in the second row.

Thirty-first Row : Knit 1, knit 2 together to the end of the row. Then 4 rows of ribbing, and gather up the top of the finger part, fastening it firmly, then join up the thumb, also the sides of the glove.

Knit the other glove in the same way, only begin the thumb at the beginning of the thirtieth row instead of the thirty-first.

Crochet an edge at the top of the gauntlet by working 1 double crochet in one of the ribs of the knitting, * 4 chain, 1 double crochet in the same rib, repeat from * twice more in the same stitch, then 1 double crochet in the next rib, and 1 double crochet in the next row following and repeat from the first * ; do this all round and fasten off at the end of the round. Tie a piece of ribbon round each wrist with a bow at the back of the hand : tack the ribbon to the glove.

KNITTED LACE

For those who like knitting better than crocheting, knitted lace will appeal. Knitted lace can be used for all the purposes that crocheted lace is used. One cannot, however, have such varied patterns in knitting as in crochet.

Below is a knitted edge and two patterns of knitted lace that will be found useful.

A Useful Knitted Edge.—This is an easy and yet extremely effective pattern. It looks best made of a smooth twisted thread which shows up the pattern clearly. Cast on 9 stitches.

First Row : Slip 1, knit 2, 1 over, 1 plain intake, knit 2, 1 double over, knit 2.

Second Row : Slip 1, knit 2, purl 1, knit 4, 1 over, 1 plain intake, knit 1.

Third Row : Slip 1, knit 2, 1 over, 1 plain intake, knit 6.

Fourth Row : Make a chain of 2 stitches, knit 5, 1 over, 1 plain intake, knit 1.

Repeat from the first row.

Knitted Lace Pattern.—Cast on 22 stitches.

First Row : Plain.

Second Row : Slip 1, knit 17, make 1, knit 2 together, make 1, knit 2.

Third Row : Knit 7, purl 12, leave 4, turn the work.

Fourth Row : Knit 15, make 1, knit 2 together, make 1, knit 2.

Fifth Row : Knit 8, purl 12, leave 4, turn the work.

Sixth Row : Knit 16, make 1, knit 2 together, make 1, knit 2.

Seventh Row : Plain.

Eighth Row : Slip 1, knit 3, purl 12, knit 5, make 1, knit 2 together, make 1, knit 2.

Ninth Row : Knit 7, make 1, knit 2 together to the end of the row, and if there is 1 stitch left, knit it.

Tenth Row : Slip 1, knit 3, purl 12, knit 5, make 1, knit 2 together, make 1, knit 2.

Eleventh Row : Cast off 5 stitches, knit to the end of the line, and begin the pattern again.

Another Lace Pattern.—This makes a narrower lace. Cast on 7 stitches.

First Row : Plain.

Second Row : Slip 1, knit 1, make 1, knit 2 together, make 2, knit 3.

Third Row : Knit 4, purl 1, knit 1, make 1, knit 2 together, knit 1.

Fourth Row : Slip 1, knit 1, make 1, knit 2 together, knit 5.

Fifth Row : Knit 6, make 1, knit 2 together, knit 1.

Sixth Row : Slip 1, knit 1, make 1, knit 2 together, knit 5.

Seventh Row : Cast on 2 stitches, knit 3, make 1, knit 2 together, knit 1.

SOME GOOD IDEAS AND HINTS ON KNITTING

Embroidery on Knitting.—Few people realise perhaps how effective a little well-chosen embroidery is on knitting. It is much easier to do a little embroidery on a garment when it is finished than to work in different colours while the making is going on.

The result is, of course, a little different, the application of stitches afterwards gives a raised effect, which one does not see when the wool is knitted in different colours. On the whole it is better to use wool on wool and silk on silk. A pattern carried out in cross stitch makes a pretty border to a jumper.

One of the advantages of this work is, that if you get tired of the pattern you can easily pick it out and start a new one.

Pretty pram rugs can be made of double knitting and decorated in bright colours. Children indeed love a few bright colours worked into their frocks or coats.

How to use up Odds and Ends of Wool.—If one does a good deal of knitting or crocheting in wool one gets a number of odds and ends left, but not enough of any one colour to complete a garment. There are a number of ways in which these odds and ends can be used up.

(1) Making knitted balls. (See section on Some Ideas for Gifts and Bazaars.)

(2) Making fringes, tassels, and pompons. (See section on Cords, Tassels, and Fringes.) Scarves can be finished off with a fringe of a contrasting colour, tassels are decorated on cushions, girdles, and berets. Pompons are ideal for tiny children's clothing, either on little caps or at the end of a crochet chain used for a neck or waist string.

(3) Making fancy tops for children's stockings and socks. Children, as we have said before, love bright colours. As well as fancy tops for stockings, remnants of wool make pretty little collars and cuffs for finishing off children's jumpers and coats, also buttons for these garments.

(4) Many articles can be finished off with a row of chain stitches or a more elaborate crochet edging in coloured wool of a contrasting colour, for example, mats, cushion covers, etc. (See section on Some Practical and Modern Uses of Crochet.)

(5) Don't forget that some odds and ends must be kept for mending ! Socks need refooting, and all garments whether of children or grown-ups need mending sooner or later, so some wool must be kept for this. It is almost impossible to buy the right shade to mend a garment.

(6) But perhaps the easiest way to use up odds and ends of wool is to do some patchwork knitting. Such small lengths of wool can be used for this that practically any remnant comes in handy.

Knit all your patches the same size, the finished effect will be better, and it is easier to see them together. So first decide on the size of your patch and shape—square or oblong. Then think out your colour-scheme if your odds and ends allow you to have a colour-scheme. However, one can always have a riot of colour on the rug for a little child's cot. Use your thick wool for pram blankets, warm scarves, etc., and your thin wool for cushion covers, work-bags, etc. What you make will, of course, depend a little upon the coloured wools you have. The patches can be knitted in garter stitch or moss stitch. Garter stitch is perhaps best, because the work lies so flat.

The joining of the patches can be carried out in suitable wool or by fancy stitches worked in silk or cotton ; for example, feather-stitching, cross stitch, etc. A border can be made of crochet if desired.

A bright coloured rug made in this way is a delightful gift for an invalid who has to lie out of doors a good deal.

Some more Useful Hints on Knitting

(1) Never leave off knitting in the middle of a row, it makes your work uneven, as the stitches get pulled out of shape. But lay aside your work at the end of a row. Put the spare needle through the ball of wool, not through the work already done.

(2) *Advice about Ribbing.*—Ribbing may easily get drawn out of shape ; to avoid this—(a) When beginning with ribbing, knit the first row into the *back of each stitch*, this has the effect of forming a firmer edge. (b) Carry out the ribbing on needles one or even two sizes smaller than those used for the rest of the garment. Smaller stitches have less power of stretching than larger ones, and so the shape is preserved better. When ribbing is cast off, the edge tends to be too tight, because the cast-off edge has less power of stretching than the ribbing itself, so remember to cast off *rather loosely*—to do this it is a good plan to use needles one size larger than the rest of the knitting.

(3) Never wind your wool into a hard ball. Wind it loosely over three fingers, changing their position frequently, and a soft, loose ball will be the result.

(4) *Brushing the Surface.*—Sometimes a raised surface is necessary, as in the case of babies' clothes and cuffs of jumpers. A teasel brush should be used, and the wool lightly brushed up

to produce a " fluffy " surface.   Be careful not to tear or damage the material, and see that the brush is clean.   If teasel or rabbits' wool is used, however, the surface will be raised of its own accord, and little or no brushing is needed.

For finishing off Crochet Work in Knitting and Washing, see the next chapter.

A Useful Glossary of Terms used in Knitting

This will be found very helpful when working at the different recipes given in books and magazines.

Brackets, thus (——).   Portion between, to be worked number of times stated.

Casting off.   Finishing off stitches at the end of a piece of work.

Casting on (or setting in).   Making the first row of loops in knitting.

Decrease.   Knit two stitches together.

Double over (or two increases).   Throw the thread twice round the right needle.   See Overs.

Fingering, also called Scotch Fingering.   A suitable yarn for all general purposes, especially for socks and stockings.

Grafting.   A method used for joining together stitches on two separate needles, as in the toe of a sock or the shoulder seams of a jumper.

Increase (or increasing).   When it is necessary to add to the number of stitches, knit into a stitch in the ordinary way, but before slipping it off the needle, knit also into the back of the loop.   See also Overs and Make.

Intakes (or decrease).   See Decrease.

Knitting in rounds.   Applied to the use of three needles, a fourth being used to work with.   One round = 3 rows.

Knitting, plain (k.).   Making the ordinary knit stitch, with the wool behind the right-hand needle.

Make.   By bringing wool forward between needles and over right-hand needle.   See Overs.

Making a stitch.   The taking up of an extra loop from the back of a stitch to make one more.   See Overs.

Overs.   These form holes in plain knitting and are used for open-work patterns and for increasing.   To make an over, bring the wool forward and lay it over the right-hand needle, and in the next row knit this loop like any over-stitch. Each over adds a stitch to the preceding number of stitches. In cases, therefore, where the number is to remain the same you have to take as many intakes as overs. Overs can only be made in connection with other stitches.

Plain intake (or decrease). Knit two stitches together plain. This is done when intake is from left to right.

Pulling over. This means slipping a stitch from the left needle to the right one without knitting it, knitting the next stitch plain, and pulling the slipped stitch over the knitted one. In this manner two or three stitches can be pulled over a knitted one.

Purled intake (or decrease). Purl two stitches together. This is done when the intake is to be visible and when on the wrong side it is to incline to the right.

Purling (p.). Making a stitch with the wool forward, and the needle inserted into stitch to be knitted from above.

Ribbing. Alternate sections of plain and purl, such as 2 plain, 2 purl, or 4 plain, 4 purl.

Seam stitch. A seam or line produced by making, in each row, one purl stitch in otherwise plain knitting. Used chiefly in socks and stockings.

Single over (or increase). Throw the thread once over the right needle. See Overs.

Slipping a stitch (or not knitting a stitch). Passing a stitch from the left needle to the right one without knitting it.

Welt. The ribbing at the top of socks.

Wool forward (wfd.). See Overs.

CHAPTER XXIV

CROCHET WORK

Materials and Tools. First Attempts. Foundation Stitches—Chain Stitch, Single Crochet, Double Crochet. Trebles—Half Treble, Treble, Double Treble, etc. Increasing. Decreasing. Tension. Patterns—Rose Stitch, Ribbed Stitch, Knitting Pattern, Treble Pattern, Bullion Stitch, Blanket Pattern, Close Shell Stitch ; Picots of different Kinds. Open Squares on Spaces, Solid Squares, Filet Crochet. Copying Tapestry Patterns in Crochet, using various colours. Shadow Crochet. Crochet Lace.

MAKING FINISHED ARTICLES—A Square Shawl ; A Pretty Shoulder Shawl ; A Tea-Cosy ; Coats ; Bath Mats.

SOME MODERN USES OF CROCHET—Crocheted Seams, the use of the Crocheted Chain.

FINISHING OFF WORK IN KNITTING OR CROCHET—Ironing, Sewing the different parts together ; Washing Knitting or Crochet ; Drying.

Hairpin Crochet or Fork Work. Glossary of Terms used in Crochet.

CROCHET work is easy, as we said in Chapter XVIII. when speaking about crocheted rugs, but although easy, intricate and beautiful designs can be made. The foundation stitch on which even the most elaborate crochet is based can be managed by any one, and all the work is done on a single hook of a size appropriate to the work. The materials required for crochet are similar to those used for knitting, the difference in the finished fabric being due to the use of a hook for the crochet work and knitting needles for the knitted fabric. Crocheting produces a more bulky type of fabric than knitting ; also it is not so elastic, but on the other hand so many varied patterns are possible, and the work grows so quickly, that " to crochet " is always a favourite occupation.

MATERIALS OR EQUIPMENT

These are very simple and not expensive.

(1) *Wool*, or for finer work, *cotton*.—When buying wool, it

351

pays to buy the best wool. In the cheaper wools the colours run, and they have a " tickly " surface which is very irritating if the finished crochet work is worn next to the skin. For fine lace effects use one of the many crochet cottons that can now be bought.

(2) *Hooks.*—You can now obtain celluloid or light metal ones and these are, on the whole, better than hooks made of wood or bone. Wood or bone needles are inclined to splinter and have a rough surface, in which the stitches catch. Steel hooks are best for fine work, but you must be careful that they do not rust, so keep them in a dry place.

(3) *Wool or Cotton Holders.* — These are not absolutely necessary, as strips of cardboard or folded strips of paper can be used. A popular holder is made of celluloid or wood in the shape of a Maltese Cross, about three inches long. The wool is loosely wound around this and the arms prevent it from escaping too quickly and becoming tangled. Another holder consists of a shuttle that revolves on a pivot which is attached to a stand.

(4) *Wool Winders.*—These make the winding of a ball of wool from a skein easier. The wool winder has four wooden arms, like a windmill, and the skein is stretched over these. The arms revolve on a stand so that one person alone can wind the wool without asking any one to hold the skein.

(5) *Ball Holders.*—These are little bags hanging on the wrist to hold a ball of wool. They have a hole at the top for the thread to come through and can be bought or easily made.

General Advice on Buying Hooks and Wool or Cotton.—As a rule the home worker copies the printed designs given in so many excellent papers and magazines on crochet work. In this case it is essential to use a crochet hook of the exact size specified and to get wool of the same thickness.

Crochet-hook sizes are difficult sometimes to determine, as different makes are graded in various ways, but the best firms number them in accordance with the knitting sizes so that the lower numbers are the coarsest. Sometimes the hook has its number marked clearly on it, but very often this is not so. When the number is not clearly marked the only sure way of finding it is to measure the hook in a gauge which can be bought quite cheaply, or to ask them to do it for you at the shop. The range of numbers is from 1 to 24—1 being the coarsest. Where wool and the heavy type of pure and art silks are used a No. 7 or 8 hook is suitable.

Abbreviations

In crochet directions many abbreviations are used. Here are the most common ones that it is useful to know :

Ch.=chain ; d.c.=double crochet ; tr.=treble ; d.tr.= double treble ; t.tr.=triple treble ; s.c.=single crochet ; sl.= slip ; sp.=space ; rep.=repeat.

When you come to an asterisk, it means that the directions immediately following it are to be repeated, for when you get to the end of these directions, it will say " repeat from *."

First Attempts and How to hold the Work

When you are first beginning, practise the stitches in wool with a No. 8 hook until you are quite used to the stitches and the tension. The wool and work are both held in the left hand. Hold the first stitch (and later the fabric) between the 1st finger and thumb, pass the wool from the ball over the 1st and 2nd fingers, under the 3rd, and round the 4th finger. Hold the hook between the 1st finger and thumb of the right hand and out over the hand as a pencil is held. Keep the middle finger on the loops of the different stitches as they are formed on the hook—this helps to keep the work even.

Foundation Stitches

(1) *Chain Stitch* (Fig. 169).—This is the beginning of all crochet and nothing could be simpler. It can be worked to any length and it is often used to thread through waists, necks, and so on, instead of ribbon. If the chain is used in this way it must be finished off with a tassel. To make the chain, make a slip loop on the hook, pass the hook from left to right under the wool (from the ball), catch this wool on to the hook, and draw it through the loop already there. Repeat until you have the length of chain you need.

Notice carefully in Fig. 169 how the wool is caught up by the needle. This is the correct way for every stitch, but it is described differently in different books—some say " place the

hook under the thread or wool," others, " pass the wool round
the point of the hook," and others, " place wool over hook,"
but the meaning is the same, and Figs. 169, 170, and 171 show
exactly how the wool goes round the needle ; " place wool over
hook " is perhaps the most usual phrase, or simply " over."

Be careful not to pull the stitches too tight ; keep the tension
even. In most good crochet instructions you will find the
tension of the work stated. It will say so many stitches to the
inch, and sometimes the number of rows to an inch in depth.
(See the section on Tension in the chapter on Knitting.) Tension
is very important when doing crochet that must be exact, for
example, well fitting garments. Practise your stitches until you
find that your crochet also makes that number of stitches to
the inch. Check your tension now and again as you work, to
make sure that you are not tightening up or loosening your
stitch. After a while your tension should become automatic.

As you make your chain, move your left hand along it every
three or four stitches, so that you are always holding your work
fairly close to the hook. When working a row of chain for a
foundation, many people make a few more stitches than are
actually wanted. The superfluous chain can be cut away
afterwards.

Single Crochet or Slip Stitch, or Small Close Stitch (Fig. 170).—
First work a length of chain. Insert your hook through the
chain loop next but one to the hook ; this gives you two loops
on your hook. Pass the wool (from the ball) round the point
of the hook, as for chain, and draw it through both loops. Continue to the end of your row. When you turn to come back
make one chain, which counts as the first single crochet in the
next row. Put your hook through the next stitch to this, and
draw the wool through both loops. When you come to the end,
turn as before with one chain.

When you work in rows, you can put your hook through
both the loops of the previous edge, or just through one, but
always do the same, otherwise the surface will be very uneven.
Single crochet is used for making a very narrow row, joining at
the end of rounds, or slip-stitching along a piece of fabric to
continue the pattern on another portion of the fabric.

Double Crochet or Plain Stitch, or Close Stitch (Fig. 171).—

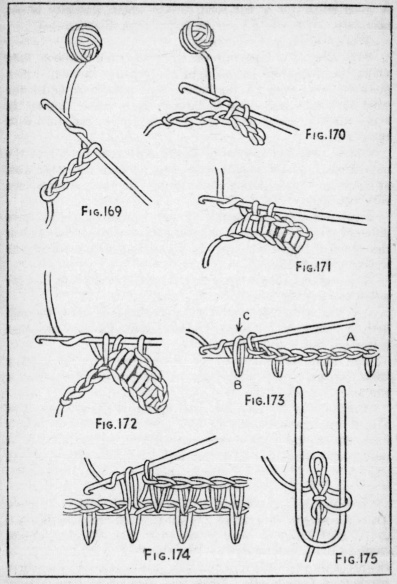

FIG. 169.

FIG. 170.

FIG. 171.

FIG. 172.

FIG. 173.

FIG. 174.

FIG. 175.

FIG. 169.—Chain Stitch.   FIG. 170.—Single Crochet or Slip Stitch.   FIG. 171.
—Double Crochet Stitch.   FIG. 172.—Half Treble.   FIGS. 173 and 174.—
          Crocheted Seams.   FIG. 175.—Hairpin Crochet.

A good stitch for a flat solid surface where elasticity is not necessary. It is a loop longer in height than single crochet.

Work a length of chain stitch.

First Row : Put hook into the third loop from the hook, then under the wool from left to right and draw it through, which gives you two loops on the hook. Pass your hook under the wool as before, and draw it through both loops. Repeat in every stitch (or loop), and when you come to the end, turn with two chain.

Second Row and subsequent Rows : Put your hook into the next stitch, draw the wool through, pass the hook under the wool as before, and draw through both loops. Repeat. Always turn with two chain.

Double crochet is capable of two variations, which give different effects. In one case a *flat* surface is produced, and in the other a ridged surface. It depends on the taste of the worker which is chosen.

The beginner should try both and see which she likes best, or which will suit her work best.

The *flat surface* is produced by placing the hook through both the loops which form the top edge of the previous row, that is through both sides of every stitch.

The *ridged surface* is made by placing the hook through the back loop only of the top edge of the previous row, that is through the back of the stitch only.

The first way gives a rather more open pattern, and is perhaps a little easier and quicker to work, but the second method is more ornamental. Whichever method you choose, keep to it until your work is finished or the surface will look very muddled.

TREBLE STITCH

Trebles are little columns or bars made of loops or stitches. There are several varieties of this stitch which are given below :

(1) *Half Treble or Short Treble* (Fig. 172).—Work a line of chain to the length required. Pass the wool round the point of the needle in the usual way and then insert hook into the fourth stitch from your needle. Draw wool through to form a loop, which will make three loops on the hook. Pass the needle under the wool as usual and draw it through the *three* loops.

Second Row: When you turn at the end of the row, work three chain (which represents the first stitch); then pass the hook under the wool and into the stitch next to the back and continue as before. Work the rest of the rows in the same way, always turning with three chain.

As for single and double crochet the effect of the surface may be varied by putting the needle through both loops or one only of the chain-stitch edge. When taking up one only, this should be the highest loop. In one row this will be the loop nearest you, in the next it will be the farthest away. The results are very different and it is interesting to work samples of both.

Treble or Ordinary Treble, or Plain Treble.—When treble is mentioned in any directions for crocheting it is this stitch which is meant.

Make the length of chain required.

First Row: Pass the hook under the wool as in the other stitches, then put it into the fourth stitch from the hook. Pass the hook under the wool again and draw it through two of the loops; pass the hook again under the wool and pass it through the other two loops. Repeat to the end.

Second Row: Turn with three chain (the three chain represent the first stitch) and work one treble into each remaining stitch either ridged or plain as required.

Long Treble or Double Treble, or Long Stitch.—In this variety of treble, you wind the wool twice round the hook (or in other words you place the hook under the wool twice in succession before inserting it in the stitch below), then draw the loops through just as in the ordinary treble.

Triple Treble.—This is worked in the same way as double treble, except that the needle is put three times under the wool (or the wool is wound three times around the needle), miss the first five stitches instead of four, and then draw the wool through two loops at a time until you have just one left on the hook. Turn with five chain. Begin again in the stitch next to the five chain.

It is of course possible to have Quadruple Treble or even Treble of a greater number, by increasing the number of times the hook is placed under the wool at the beginning of the stitch.

INCREASING

Increasing is quite simple, and consists of working two stitches into one loop, instead of one stitch. It can be carried out in almost any part of the work, but it is best done at the beginning or end of a row, if the work is being crocheted in rows.

DECREASING

The method is to miss a stitch of the previous row, thus shortening the length of the work. Do this as near the beginning or end of the row as possible, so that it is not too obvious.

TENSION

As in knitting, it is necessary to know at what tension you are working. The best way to check your tension with that of the pattern you are copying is to measure how many stitches you are crocheting to an inch and compare it with the instructions. Quite a large piece should be worked with the required wool and hook. It is more difficult to arrive at correct measurements in crochet than in knitted fabric, for in crochet the work expands with the first few rows and gradually " takes up " as the work extends, thus making it very difficult to plan out the work to a special size. Whenever possible allow that a border or edging may be added if necessary, to give any extra size that may be needed. The more solid the pattern, the more it " takes up."

When beginning it is easy to work too loosely or too tightly, but if you are careful to use the size of hook recommended when you are working from directions, a little practice will probably soon give you the right tension.

PATTERNS

When once the simple stitches have been learned a great variety of patterns can be made up. We will describe some of the easy and well-known patterns, but the clever worker will soon learn how to make patterns to suit her own requirements.

Rose Stitch.—This is used for making bedroom slippers, shawls, mufflers, children's vests, etc. It consists of rows of double crochet worked to and fro, the hook being placed each time under both loops of the previous row of stitches. It is simple and the work looks fairly compact. (See paragraph on Double Crochet—flat surface.)

Ribbed Stitch.—Worked to and fro as for the rose stitch, but the hook is passed through the back part only of the stitches of the preceding row. (See paragraphs on Double Crochet— ribbed surface.) This stitch is used for shawls, slippers, mufflers, vests, etc.

Knitting Pattern or Afghan Pattern.—This is so called because you are working most of the time with a number of stitches on the hook as in knitting. It produces a smooth effect. It can be done in narrow strips, which are afterwards joined. It is suitable for any plain garment.

Make a length of chain.

First Row : Miss a stitch, then draw a loop through each of the remaining chain, leaving all the loops on the hook as for knitting.

Second Row : Work back by placing wool round hook and drawing a loop through two loops every time until all the stitches are finished.

Third Row : Draw a loop through each stitch of the previous row, leaving them on the hook, and working back the same as before. Repeat the second and third rows as required. Finish the work by making one double crochet into each upright stitch of the last row.

Blanket Pattern.—This stitch is very suitable for any type of blanket or counterpane. Work it on rather a small hook and it will form a compact piece of work which is very warm.

Make a length of chain.

First Row : Put hook under wool, draw a loop through the 4th chain from the hook three times to make seven loops or stitches on the hook, then with hook under wool, draw a loop through all the stitches. Next, one chain, * miss one chain, with wool over hook, draw a loop through the next chain three times to make seven stitches, draw loop through all the stitches on hook, one chain. Repeat from * to the end of the row and finish with three chain.

Second Row : * With wool over hook, draw a loop three times through the space between the first and second groups of the

previous row to make seven stitches, one chain. Repeat from *
to the end of the row, finishing with three chain.

Repeat the second row as often as necessary.

Treble Patterns.—When you have worked the different treble
stitches, you will notice the effects of single, double, and triple
trebles. These stitches are especially used in insertion and lace
and as decorations for jumpers and children's garments. The
result of treble, as you will soon learn, is to form columns or
bars, and these can be increased in height almost indefinitely
by adding to the number of times the wool is wound round the
hook at the beginning of the stitch. It needs a good deal of
practice, however, to work well anything greater than triple
treble.

When working trebles to and fro, and not just an odd stitch
or two in a pattern, you must be careful to make some chain
stitches at the beginning of each row, and pass over the first
treble below, which is replaced by the chain.

Bullion Stitch.—For bullion stitch choose a needle which is
a little thicker towards the handle and finer at the other end
than one you would take for any other crochet stitches. Do
not use *wool* for this stitch.

All forms of this stitch consist of a series of coils either long
or short according to the number of times the thread is wound
round the hook.

Begin by a chain of very loose stitches, then wind the thread
very evenly round the needle several times (or the stated number
of times), put the hook into a loop of the chain, draw the thread
through and then draw it with another over (pass the wool *over*
needle) through all the other loops, except two, these last being
drawn through with a new loop.

In bullion stitch the thread is generally wound ten or twelve
times round the needle.

Close Shell Stitch.—This is a well-known and effective design.
It can be used for almost any purpose, but it is especially suited
for shawls and children's garments. It produces a closely woven
surface if worked on a small hook. It can also be used as a
border to a cover for a child's bed or perambulator.

This stitch can only be worked in rows all one way and with
a very loose thread. It is very easy and it has the additional

advantage of being very quickly done. It can be finished off at the end of each row.

Make a length of chain.

First Row : 1 chain stitch, 7 trebles in the first stitch of the row beneath, * 1 chain, 7 trebles in the fifth stitch, and repeat from *.

Second Row : * * 7 trebles in the chain stitch of the last row which separates 7 trebles, 1 plain in the 4th of the 7 trebles of the 1st row, and repeat from * *.

In the third row, set the trebles in the plain stitch of the second row.

PICOTS

The last row of most crochet work is ornamented with picots, that is, small points of various shapes and sizes : there are closed picots, chain picots, and lace picots.

The size of the picots varies according to the number of stitches used : generally the number of chain required for each is stated in the directions. When making a five-chain picot you work five chain, and then work a slip stitch into the first of them ; also when working a picot edge make single crochets into the stitches between the picots—leave, of course, an even number between them all.

Below we give some well-known picots :

Small Rounded Picots.—You can make these separately and then sew them on, or you can make them at once on to a crochet border. In the first case you make 1 plain stitch in the edge, * 3 chain, then coming back over these stitches : 1 plain stitch on the 2nd chain and 1 on the 1st chain stitch, skip 1 or 2 stitches of the row beneath, 1 single ; repeat from *.

Large Rounded Picots.—5 chain, skip 3 stitches, 1 treble on the 2nd and 1 on the 1st chain stitch. When you want to fasten these picots to a piece of work, fasten them by 1 single stitch missing 3 or 4 stitches, instead of 1 or 2 as directed above for the small picots.

Pointed Picots.—To crochet these, cast on 6 chain, when returning and skipping the 6th stitch : 1 single, 1 plain, 1 half treble, 1 single treble, 1 double treble.

Picots with Leaves.—Crochet * 4 chain, 3 plain treble in the

1st chain, 1 single in the same stitch with the trebles, 2 or 3 chain, and repeat from *.

If you wish to use these picots to finish off a straight edge make single stitches in the preceding row instead of chain stitches.

Chain Picots.—To crochet small chain picots make : 5 chain, 1 plain in the 1st of the 5 chain. For large chain picots make 5 chain and 1 treble in the first.

Picots in Bullion Stitch.—Make 5 chain, 1 treble in bullion stitch drawn up into a ring and joined to the 5th chain stitch, 5 chain, and continue in the same way.

Drooping Picots.—Make 5 chain, drop the loop, put the needle into the 2nd of the 5 chain, take up the dropped loop and draw it through the stitch.

Lace Picots.—These are formed of chain stitches worked in the following way : 2 chain, put the needle into the 1st, 1 over, bring the thread back to the front, 2 chain, * bring the needle out through the 2 loops, put the needle into the 2nd loop and into the 1st chain at the same time, draw the thread through in a loop, make 2 chain and repeat from *.

These lace picots will be much more firm and even if you make them over a coarse knitting-needle or over a mesh.

They may be attached to the edge of a finished piece of work in the following way :

Make 1 plain, draw out the loop to the proper length for a picot and slip it on to a mesh, put the needle into the horizontal parts of the last stitch, turn the thread round the needle, draw it through a loop, make 1 plain stitch in the next stitch and continue in this way.

Picots with an Edging of Trebles.—Make 7 chain, 1 plain on the 4th chain, 1 triple treble on the 1st of the 7 chain, * 1 picot of 4 chain closed by 1 plain stitch, 1 triple treble set in the 2nd of the 3 overs of the triple treble, and repeat from *.

All these make useful edgings. Before describing any more well-known patterns and methods in crochet work, we ought to say a word about joining threads.

Joining Thread or Wool.—As for knitting, it is always better to do it as far as possible at the beginning of a row. Lay the two ends together as for knitting and crochet a few stitches with the double thread.

OPEN SQUARES OR SPACES

These are very useful, for they can be worked in rows to form a net-work. They are used in filet crochet, combined with blocks or solid squares.

Spaces are made in this way : first make your length of chain, with five chain extra. Make 1 treble in the ninth chain from the hook, make 2 chain, then 1 treble in the third stitch from the previous treble. Repeat. If you are working in rows turn with 5 chain, and work 1 treble into the next treble, make 2 chain and work 1 treble into the next treble. Repeat. Effective lace or insertion can be made in this way after the style of darned filet net (see Chapter VI.). In this case the crochet or insertion is selected for the purpose of allowing for the darning, which is done with coloured cotton or silk.

BLOCKS OR SOLID SQUARES

Solid squares are made by working 4 treble, and for every extra block add 3 treble; therefore for two blocks you work 7 treble.

A "*hole*" is made with 2 chain, miss two stitches, 1 treble on next stitch.

Filet crochet, as we have already said, is made up of spaces and solid squares. Pattern charts for filet crochet are very easy to follow. Each square represents an open space of 2 chain and 1 treble stitch following 1 treble already worked (see the "hole" above), and each open space should come exactly over another space or over a block of trebles. Further necessary directions are always given with charts. Some charts give colour-schemes and then, as a rule, each square represents one stitch. The different colours are marked by numbers or signs and detailed on the chart.

COPYING TAPESTRY PATTERNS IN CROCHET WORK AND COLOURS

From what has been said above, it will be seen that tapestry patterns can be copied in crochet. Printed cross stitch and many embroidery patterns are easy to copy, especially if they are only in two colours, or rather are drawn in one colour on a plain ground. To reproduce these patterns in crochet you make nothing but rows of chain stitches and trebles, one above the other, thus forming a surface of little squares. Remember for every square marked on the pattern you count for the crochet grounding 1 treble and 2 chain stitches; for the solid squares, 3 trebles.

The squares formed by the chain stitches should always begin and end with a treble.

You should begin each row with 3 chain stitches and finish with a treble.

When a solid square comes between open squares, count 4 treble for the solid square, because the last treble of the last open square touches the three trebles of the solid square. Thus for two squares, side by side, you must have 7 trebles, and for three squares, 10 trebles.

Embroidery patterns worked in *several colours* are reproduced in crochet either by trebles and rows worked *one way only*, cutting off the thread at the end of each row, or by plain stitches worked in rows to and fro.

If you are using not more than three colours you can pass two threads under the same stitches; but if you use more colours, you must leave the ones not in use for the moment on the wrong side of the work and only bring them to the right side as they are wanted, leaving the one you have been working with on the wrong side in its turn. The threads can only be disposed of in this way if there is a right and a wrong side to the work, otherwise they must be carried along under the stitches.

The colours will alternate according to the pattern being copied. Notice that the last stitch before a change of colour cannot be finished with the same colour it was begun with, the new colour must be drawn through the last loop, which must be drawn up with the new thread.

Shadow Crochet

This is a pleasing change from ordinary crochet. It is especially useful for household linen. In general it differs from the ordinary crochet, for the pattern or solid part is always worked as four treble into the same chain loop, and the chain loop is worked into the centre of the four treble ; they are thus divided two on each side.

CROCHET LACE

From what has been said it is clear that crochet lace is easy and pretty. Lace-work indeed is much more suitably done in crochet than in knitting, more varieties are possible, and it is easier to work with a fine crochet hook than with fine knitting needles.

Crochet lace is most used to-day for household linen, afternoon tablecloths, d'oyleys, and towels.

CROCHET EDGING

Many articles can be finished off prettily with a row of chain stitch, or a more elaborate edging of several rows of treble. Wool or silk of a different colour often looks effective. This is especially the case when making cushion covers, mats, and table centres where some sort of border is a real necessity.

A Narrow Crochet Lace Edging.—This can be worked on the material itself by making a row of trebles with 1 chain stitch between each. If you do not want to work on the material, make a chain first, then a row of trebles with one chain between each. To work the lace, proceed in the following way :

First Row : 1 treble on one of the trebles of the row before, * 5 chain, 1 treble on the stitch in which the 1st treble is placed, 5 chain, skip 3 trebles of the row beneath, 1 treble on the 4th treble of the row beneath, and repeat as often as is necessary from *.

Second Row : ** 1 treble on the 3rd of the chain stitches between the two trebles placed in the one stitch of the first row, 3 chain, 1 treble in the same stitch, 3 chain, 1 treble in the same stitch, 3 chain, 1 plain in the 3rd of the next 5 chain stitches, 3 chain, and repeat from * *.

MAKING FINISHED ARTICLES AND GARMENTS IN CROCHET

A number of good cheap magazines and papers can be bought at most needlework shops containing useful recipes for making lace, shawls, garments, or other suitable articles according to the fashion of the day. When once the stitches we have described are mastered, the reader will find no difficulty and much pleasure in following the directions given in these books and seeing what delightful articles they can produce.

We are going to give a few easy recipes in this book for practice, so that later on you can with confidence attempt something more ambitious. But you need to get your tension right first. The work of any one person should be uniform throughout, that is, the tension should be the same, provided the same sized needles and the same thickness of wool is used. Good durable knitting or crochet is fairly tight, but the stitches should run readily along the needles without being inclined to stick.

Get into the way of doing your work evenly and more than half your difficulties are over.

The first article we give a recipe for, is an easy shawl, because shawls are always useful and no fitting is needed. Wool, too, is the best material for a beginner to work with. This is a particularly easy shawl.

A Square Crocheted Shawl.—This is a pretty shawl and most suitable for a beginner.

To make this shawl use fingering, a fine soft wool like Shetland.

For a shawl of fair size about three-quarters of a pound of wool is needed.

The stitch is quite simple, for it consists only of chain, trebles, and a few doubles when you come to the border, combined in different ways.

But a word of warning : see that the treble stitch is long in the loop, and the whole loosely worked, for a tightly crocheted woollen shawl mats and becomes hard after washing.

Begin by making 6 chain, and join the ends to form a ring by drawing the wool through the first loop. Next crochet 3 chain, which will in future mark the starting-point for a round. Now work 15 trebles into the ring, draw the wool through the third stitch in the little chain of three and so complete the *first* round. To start the *second* round, make as before a chain of three, then, passing by the chain below, make 8 trebles between that chain, which really represents the first of 16 trebles, and the 1st treble you made. Pass by 4 trebles below, and make 8 trebles into the spaces between the 4th and 5th trebles below.

Pass by 4 more trebles, and again make 8 trebles, this time between the 8th and 9th trebles, and repeat this once more between the 12th and 13th trebles.

The groups of 8 trebles are the starting-points for the corners of the shawl, and it is from the centre of each 8 that you will have to increase the stitches as you proceed. You can now see the tiny centre of the shawl, and even at this early stage it is wise to form it into a square with the fingers. Join up to finish the round and make 3 chain as before.

In the *third* round you simply crochet 4 trebles between the 2nd and 3rd, the 4th and 5th, the 6th and 7th trebles of each of the 4 groups of 8 trebles.

In the *fourth* round do the same thing with one change. At each corner there are now 4 trebles—not 8 as in the previous round—and by working 8 trebles into the middle of the 4 you increase the size.

In the *fifth* round you make 3 sets of 4 trebles at each corner just as you did for the third round. Thus every *alternate row* has 8 trebles at a corner.

You must be careful about the corners, as it is easy to forget whether it is the turn for the 4 or 8 trebles, and a mistake here will cause the shawl to get out of shape and pucker.

As the shawl progresses notice how far a skein of wool goes and how large you will be able to make the shawl with the wool at your disposal. Allow a generous amount of wool for the border, which consists of seven rounds, the last with an edging and the first three alike. Make the border as follows:

First Round : 4 trebles between 2nd and 3rd trebles below, 2 chain, 1 double between 2nd and 3rd trebles below, 2 chain. Repeat to end.

Second and Third Rows: As above, but making double through double below.

Fourth Round : 1 treble between 1st and 2nd trebles, 4 trebles between 2nd and 3rd trebles, 1 treble between 3rd and 4th trebles, 2 chain, 1 double through the double below, 2 chain. Repeat to the end.

Fifth Round : 1 treble, 1 treble, 4 trebles, 1 treble, 1 treble, 2 chain, 1 double, 2 chain. Repeat to end.

Sixth Round : 1 treble, 1 treble, 1 treble, 4 trebles, 1 treble,

1 treble, 1 treble, 2 chain, 1 double, 2 chain. Repeat to end.

Seventh Round : This needs care, for it has only 3 trebles at the point of the scallop, and an edging along it. You proceed in this way : 1 treble, 3 chain, 1 double into the last 2 loops of the treble just made. This forms a pointed edge. 1 treble, 3 chain, 1 double, 1 treble, 3 chain, 1 double, 1 treble, 3 chain, 1 double, 3 trebles, each with 3 chain, and 1 double for the edge. The other side of the scallop is a repetition of the first. You then proceed as in previous rounds—2 chain, 1 double, 2 chain.

The corners of the border should present no difficulty, the scallops being worked exactly as they come, whether one happens to fall just at a corner or not.

After completing the above shawl you will be ready for the following one, which although more difficult is very decorative.

A More Difficult Shawl.—This makes a delightful wrap for the shoulders or a very cosy shawl for a baby. It is best made of fine soft Shetland wool. Remember to let the treble stitch be long in the loop and the whole be loosely worked.

Begin by making 8 chain and join the end to make a ring by drawing the wool through the first loop.

First Row : 6 chain which will mark the starting-place for a round ; then work 14 treble into the ring, 1 chain between each treble.

Second Row : 6 chain into the first space, the 6 chain count for 1 treble, 1 chain and 1 treble in the same space. Repeat the 2 treble in each space with 1 chain between each treble to the end of the row. You will now have 28 trebles.

Third Row : 6 chain and 1 treble into the next space, 1 treble into the next space, 2 treble into the next, and 1 treble into the next ; repeat the 2 treble and the 1 treble to the end. Always have 1 chain between each treble.

Fourth Row : 6 chain and 1 treble into the first space, 2 treble into the next two spaces, 2 treble into the next space. Repeat to the end of the row.

Fifth Row : 6 chain and 1 treble into the first space, 3 treble into the next 3 spaces, 2 treble into the next space, and 3 treble into the next 3 spaces. Repeat to the end of the row.

Sixth Row : 6 chain and 1 treble into the first space, 4 treble into the next 4 spaces. Repeat to the end. Every row you will increase 1 treble until you have 19 trebles between the double trebles.

Now for the Border.—*First Row :* 6 chain into the first space, and 1 treble in the same space, 2 double trebles in the next 2 spaces, miss 1 space, double treble into the next, 1 treble into the next, miss 1 space, double treble into the next 3 spaces, miss 1 space, double treble into the next, 1 treble into the next. Repeat to the end of the row.

Second Row : 6 chain into the first space, 1 treble into the same space, 1 treble into the next 2 spaces, miss a space, 2 treble into the next space, 3 chain and 2 treble into the same space, 2 treble into the next 2 spaces, miss 1 space, 2 treble into the next 2 spaces, miss 1 space, 2 treble into the next space, 3 chain, 2 treble into the same space, 2 treble into the next 2 spaces, miss 1 space, 2 treble into the next space. Repeat to the end of the row.

Third Row : 6 chain, 1 treble into the first space, 1 treble into the next space, miss 1 space, 1 treble into the next space, miss 2 treble, and put 3 treble into the 3 chain, 3 chain and 3 more treble in the same 3 chain, miss 2 treble, 1 treble in the next space, 1 treble in the next space, miss a space and 2 treble into the next space. Repeat to the end of the row.

Fourth Row : 6 chain, 1 treble into the first space, 1 treble into the next space, miss a space, 1 treble into the next space, miss a space, 1 treble between the 2 treble, 3 treble into the 3 chain, 3 chain, 3 more treble into the same 3 chain, 1 treble between the 2 treble, miss a space, 1 treble in the next space, miss a space, 1 treble in the next space, 2 treble in the next space with 2 chain between. Repeat to the end of the row.

Fifth Row : 6 chain, 1 treble into the first space, 1 treble into the next space, miss a space, 1 treble in the next, 2 treble between the first and second of the 3 trebles, and 3 treble into the 3 chain, 3 chain, 3 more chain into the same space, 1 treble into the first of the 3 treble, miss the other 2 treble, 1 treble into the next space, miss a space, 2 treble into the next 2 spaces, 2 treble into the next space with 2 chain between. Repeat to the end of the row.

Sixth Row : 6 chain, 1 treble in the first space, 1 treble in the next space, miss a space, 1 treble in the next space, miss a space, 1 treble between the second and third treble, 3 treble in the 3 chain, 3 chain, 3 treble into the same 3 chain, 1 treble between the first and second treble, miss 2 treble, 1 treble into the next space, 2 more treble, missing a space between each, 2 treble into the next space with 2 chain between. Repeat to the end of the row.

Seventh Row : 6 chain, 1 treble in the first space, 1 treble in the next space, 2 more treble with a space between, 1 treble between the 3 treble, 3 treble in the 3 chain, 3 chain, 3 more treble into the same chain, 1 treble into the 3 treble, 1 treble into the next space, miss a space, 1 treble, miss a space, 1 treble. Repeat to the end of the row.

Eighth Row : 6 chain, 1 treble in the first space, 1 treble into the next space, miss a space, 1 treble into the next, miss a space, 1 treble into the 3 treble, 3 treble into the 3 chain, 3 chain, and 3 chain into the same 3 chain, 1 treble into the 3 treble, 1 treble into the next space, miss a space, 1 treble, miss a space, 1 treble, 2 treble into the next space with 2 chain between. Repeat to the end of the row.

Ninth Row : 6 chain, 1 treble into the first space, 1 treble into the next space, miss a space, 1 treble, miss a space, 1 treble, 1 treble into the 3 treble, 5 treble into the 3 chain, 1 treble into the 3 treble, 1 treble into the next space, miss a space, 1 treble, miss a space, 1 treble, 2 treble into the next space with 2 chain between.

Begin in the middle of the last 2 chain, double crochet, 7 chain, miss a space, double crochet into the next space, 7 chain, miss a space, another 7 chain, miss a space, 7 chain into the first treble of the 5 treble, 7 chain, miss 2 treble, 7 chain, double crochet into the last treble, 7 chain, miss a space, working this all round until you come to the 5 treble. Then double crochet, 7 chain between each treble.

The next two rows are the same, 7 chain, double crochet into the middle of the 7 chain.

This shawl takes rather a long time to do, but it is worth doing and it is not difficult, as one soon sees how the pattern goes. But we will follow with directions for making something smaller—a tea-cosy.

Tea-cosies are always wanted, and as they soon wear out many people will be grateful for directions for making pretty cosies quickly, so that they can be made for home use, for bazaars, and for presents. The one we are going to describe is especially convenient because there are openings for the handle and the spout.

An easily made Tea-Cosy.—This is a very pretty tea-cosy. It is simple and easy to make. It is made so that it can be kept on the teapot when pouring out the tea, as there is an opening on one side for the handle and one for the spout on the other. Three ounces of four-ply fingering is required. Three shades of one colour can be used to match the tea-set or tablecloth. About double the quantity of the second shade will be required. With a large crochet hook make a chain of 40 stitches and join. Use a medium-sized hook for the rest of the work. It is done in tufts as follows :

First Round : 3 chain for the first stitch, * 4 treble into the next loop ; take out the hook and place it in the first of these trebles and then draw through the loop of the fourth (the tufts are all made in this manner) ; 1 treble in the next loop ; repeat from *, making 20 tufts in the round, joining the round with a single between the three chains which began the round and the first tuft.

Second Round : Again 3 chain, * make a tuft in the stitch, between the tuft and the single treble, 1 treble between the single treble and the next tuft, repeat from * all round, and join with a single as last row.

Third Round : Cut off the wool and join the next shade. Repeat the second round, but at the end do not join, but break off the wool again, as now an opening is left for the handle.

Fourth Round : Join the same shade and work as before for 10 tufts, cut off the wool, and now begin the opening for the spout. Join the wool and make 10 more tufts, and again break off the wool Next work two divided rounds with the lightest shade, then join the second shade, and work a row for a cord by making 1 treble in each space before and after each tuft. For the edge, * work 5 double crochets very loosely in the top of 1 treble, miss 2 trebles, 1 double crochet in the next, miss 2 and repeat from * ; continue all round and join with a single. Make a

cord in one of the ways described in Chapter XIII with tassels, and
run it in. This ties above the handle of the teapot and fastens
the ends of the wool. Ribbon may be used instead of a cord.

Coats that are warm and light can be crocheted for little
babies. They can be worked in double crochet (rose stitch). It
is easiest to make them in three pieces, the body and the two
sleeves. The pieces are easily sewn together. Little fitting is
needed. (See section on Finishing-off Work in Crochet and
Knitting.)

Bath Mats.—Bath mats crocheted in colours to match your
bathroom have lately become popular. Two colours are most
effective. Use 8-ply wool, a No. 10 bone crochet hook, and a
flat bone netting mesh 1 inch wide and about 6 inches long.
(A ruler or a strip of stiff cardboard will also do.) It must be
worked in alternate rounds of double crochet and extra long
trebles worked over the mesh or gauge. All stitches are worked
through both loops at the top of the stitch on previous round,
after the first round, and all rounds are joined with a slip stitch
to the top of the first stitch.

Mats of various sizes can be made. If you begin with 84 chain
for the middle of the mat you will make quite a good-sized mat.
Work down each side of this chain with double crochet. Don't
begin to work over the gauge until the third row.

We have now described several very different ways in which
crochet is useful, and we have left to the last one of its most
modern and decorative uses.

SOME PRACTICAL AND MODERN USES FOR CROCHET

Crocheted Seams (Figs. 173 and 174).—In Chapter V. we
dealt very fully with insertion stitches, but crocheted seams
executed in wool of contrasting or harmonising colours make
most effective joinings. Ornamental ends can be attached to
curtains in this way. It is an economical way of making
curtains fit different windows. Strips of material can be joined
by wide crocheted seams of bright beautiful colours to make
curtains that many will envy.

Crocheted seams can also be used on sport dresses and blouses
and dressing wraps of different kinds. Indeed, there is no end
to the uses of these decorative seams. This is how they are

worked : Fold under each edge to be joined $\frac{3}{8}$ inch or more, and crease. Tacking is unnecessary, because the crocheting holds the edges in. On each edge to be joined a border of single crochet is worked, taking two chain stitches between each two fastening stitches so that a space of about a quarter of an inch is left, as shown at A in Fig. 173. For every fastening stitch insert the hook a quarter of an inch or more down into the cloth as at B in Fig. 173, pull a loop through (this loop is called C in Fig. 173). There are now two loops on the needle ; put the wool around the needle and draw it through both these loops as in Fig. 173. Make two more chain stitches and then another fastening stitch in the same way. Continue crocheting all along the folded-down edge until it is covered. You will be delighted at the pretty edge.

Now cover the edge of the second piece of material in the same way.

Along one of the edges thus crocheted put a row of crochet in a good contrasting colour, using either plain, double, or treble crochet. To do this take a stitch into the top of every deep stitch (or joining stitch) of the first row, and also between each of the two chain stitches (that lie between the joining stitches) as in Fig. 174.

Next place the edge of the material that has only the single row of crochet opposite to this edge and sew them together with needle and wool, using over and over stitches. The extra row, being of another colour, is now framed between the two simply crocheted edges.

Double or treble crochet can be used, then the seam is wider and more effective. All sorts of possibilities will suggest themselves from this simple border. Three or more colours can be combined in a very ornamental seam.

By means of these decorated seams small pieces of beautiful or expensive material can often be used that would otherwise be thrown away.

The Use of the Crocheted Chain.—A crocheted chain can be used for insertion work. Crochet a chain of wool in a contrasting colour to the fabrics to be joined. Press it flat and sew this between the two pieces of material.

Another use of the crocheted chain is to sew it or appliqué

it along a stamped pattern. If chains are crocheted of many different colours they can be stitched (by hand or machine) along the lines of a pattern on a cushion cover or curtain. Very effective designs can be made in this way. It is a much quicker form of decoration than embroidery.

A Double Chain Stitch.—Here is another useful idea for an insertion. To make a double chain, begin with two slip loops. Put the hook through both and draw a loop through. There is now one loop on the needle. To continue, put the hook in the left loop (or left part of the stitch) and pull a loop through, there are now two loops on the needle ; put the hook under the wool and pull a loop through the two loops, and so on. Remember always to put the hook in the left part of the stitch just made and pull a loop through to get two loops on the needle again.

Work as evenly as possible and loosely so that the double chain can be seen. The chain must be pressed flat under a damp cloth with a hot iron.

A jumper or sweater can easily be enlarged by having this chain seam (in a contrasting colour) between the sleeves and the main part of the sweater. Sew it with wool and a needle so that it looks decorative.

Finishing off Work in Knitting or Crochet

Ironing.—When making knitted or crocheted garments they have to be very carefully put together. Before any attempt is made to sew up the finished pieces of any garment they should first be carefully pressed separately. Lay a damp clean cloth on the wrong side of the work. Press gently but firmly with a moderately hot iron, not *too* hot.

Stocking stitch can be ironed on both sides if desired, because the more it is pressed the better it looks, but the same of course does not apply to the more raised types of knitting and crochet— for example, moss stitch, garter stitch, treble stitch.

These must be pressed quite lightly on the wrong side *only*. This applies also to fancy patterns ; if these are made too flat it will take all the character out of the work.

Ribbing must *not* be ironed. Ironing will not improve it and may take away its elasticity.

Sewing Different Parts Together.—Before sewing up any finished work, see that all the ends of silk or wool are neatly darned in on the wrong side. Lay the two edges to be sewn side by side, and carefully draw the loops of each together, using silk or wool that matches. This sewing must be done rather loosely to allow for the stretching of the finished garment. Press all the seams after they are joined.

The way in which a seam is sewed up is of vital importance to a finished garment. Shoulder seams and seams that show need of course the greatest attention of all. Never sew knitting or crochet as you would a seam in needlework, the correct method has already been described above. Sometimes, when sewing the side seams of a jumper or cardigan, the two edges do not exactly correspond, although one knows that they each have the same number of rows. In this case, one side must be eased in a little in order to make it the same size as the other. It is fairly easy to do this, only take care to make the easing very gradual so as to avoid puckers.

Washing Knitting or Crochet. — This is a very important subject, especially in the case of woollen articles.

The first washing done carelessly often means the ruin of all one's work. If the first washing is done badly, no amount of further washing, however well done, will make up for it.

Some people try to shrink wool while it is in the skein to prevent any decrease in size when it is washed. This, on the whole, is not wise, it must spoil the look of the finished article. Garments made from wool shrunk before use never look fresh.

But supposing before knitting your wool it has a " crinkly " appearance, because large quantities perhaps have been unwound. In this case you must do something to the wool. Wind it first around your elbow and hand into a skein again, lay the skein flat on an ironing-board, and press it with a damp cloth. This should produce a straight thread again. Never knit up crinkled wool and try to make it straight afterwards.

In washing crochet or knitting, remember *white garments* or articles must be treated rather differently from coloured. There is always the danger of white garments losing their whiteness and becoming yellow in tint. This is generally caused by having the water *too* hot. Water too hot will also shrink woollen garments, though it leaves cotton ones unaffected.

The best method of washing white work of the above kind is to make a good soapy lather of warm water (the temperature of the water should be such that the hands will feel quite comfortable in it) and add a teaspoonful of ammonia. Move the garments gently about in the suds, avoid rubbing them, merely squeeze them carefully. Take care that each portion has equal treatment. Leave the garments in for several minutes, squeezing all the time. Rinse in clean warm water about the same temperature. Be very careful, in the case of garments especially, never to hold one up in its length or width when it is full of water, but keep it in a close heap.

Coloured Garments.—These must have no ammonia in the water, and if anything have the water a shade cooler, as there is always the danger of the colours running. This can often be prevented by giving the articles an extra rinse in water to which about a tablespoonful of vinegar has been added.

Never use soda when washing any type of knitted or crocheted articles. It not only spoils the colours but also destroys the surface and " mats " the wool.

Drying.—Drying must be very carefully done as the shape of a garment is very easily ruined. Squeeze out the water with the hands and partly dry the garment in a heap placed on a clean towel near a fire which is moderately hot. Some remove the garment from the water at once, place it in a clean dry cloth and squeeze dry by twisting the ends of the cloth until most of the water is gone. Never wring hard, as this is very bad for the texture of the wool. Woollen things must never be hung up to dry, even on a wooden hanger, as the weight of the water in the material pulls it out of shape for ever. The best way, as we have said before, is to lay it out on a clean piece of cloth or paper and let it dry in the sun or before a fire which is only moderately hot.

When nearly dry the garment can be patted or pressed into its correct shape and size and dried off over an airing rack.

Woollen garments especially should not be left to lie about in a damp condition ; they must be dried as soon as possible or shrinkage will occur and colours will be inclined to run.

Of course the success of washing knitting or crochet partly depends on the way in which the article has been worked. It is more difficult to wash a loosely knitted garment well, as it stretches much more easily than a tightly woven one. But the latter has the disadvantage of being liable to " mat " or " felt," and therefore lose some of its surface. Some of the best varieties of wool are guaranteed not to shrink, the cheaper wools tend both to stretch easily as the wool is less elastic and to shrink.

Hairpin Crochet or Forkwork (Fig. 175)

Many years ago this was called " Maltese Lace " and was worked with fine cotton upon an ordinary hairpin ; though it was pretty and interesting as a lace it lacked variety. Now that special forks can be bought for this work, many beautiful patterns are possible. Especially pretty mats can be made, and dainty lace for trimmings and insertions. Good fringes are also possible.

Hairpin crochet is delightfully quick and easy work for those who have learned how to crochet.

Method of Working.—The two-pronged forks can be bought in various sizes from about $\frac{3}{4}$ to $1\frac{1}{2}$ inch, and very charming effects can be produced by making use of the different sizes, as well as by grouping the loops in various ways.

Fine crochet cotton should be used and a steel crochet needle.

To begin.—Hold the crochet needle in the right hand and make a stitch as if about to begin crocheting. Take the fork in the left hand and hold it between the thumb and first finger with the round part downwards in the palm of the hand. Slip the end of the cotton between the prongs and hold it in the hollow of the hand while you insert the crochet needle between the prongs, holding it exactly midway between them by the pressure of the thumb ; pass the working thread over the right-hand prong and carry it between the second and third fingers of the left hand ; pass the hook round this thread and draw it through the stitch on the needle. This is the first movement (Fig. 175).

* Bring the hook to the front with the stitch that is now on it in such a way that you can rest it for the moment across the fork horizontally ; keep the hook in front and pass the handle downwards through the space between the prongs and at the same time *turn* the fork from right to left, so restoring the needle to its original position, handle in front and the hook at the back.

Now pass the hook round the cotton that is still held between the second and third fingers of the left hand, and draw it through the stitch on the needle (like a chain stitch). Now insert the needle to take up the top thread of the loop on the left-hand prong and draw the cotton through; then cotton over the needle and draw it through the 2 stitches on the needle (double crochet stitch). Repeat from * continuously, and you will find that by every " turn " of the fork you will produce a loop upon a prong, first one prong and then the other alternately; and after every " turn " you will work first a chain stitch and then a double crochet stitch upon the crochet braid that runs up the middle of the fork. As you become accustomed to the work you will find it proceed very quickly. Some people can work so rapidly that you can scarcely see the movement of the needle as the fork turns from side to side.

Always draw the double crochet stitches tightly. Keep the crochet plait or braid as nearly as possible in the middle of the space between the prongs so that the loops are the same size on each side. Uneven loops spoil the effect of the work.

As the fork gets full, press the work downwards closely, and when there is no room for more, take it all off except the last three loops; these are needed to form a firm renewed hold; then go on as described until a sufficient length of trimming is made.

These stitches can be doubled, or you can make several trebles in each loop, or arrange the plain stitches in different ways.

Methods of joining Two Pieces of Hairpin Work.—(1) This method is the same as that used for joining two strips of wool crochet in which you work a stitch right and left alternately and join the pieces by forming a series of slip stitches running up between them. Make a stitch on the crochet needle and then take up the two pieces of hairpin work and hold them side by side. Insert the hook in the first loop of the piece to the right and draw the cotton through the loop and also through the stitch on the needle; now insert the hook in the first loop of the piece on the left and draw the cotton through the loop and through the stitch on the needle, and continue in this manner to the end.

You must use your judgment in gauging the length of the slip stitches; if they are too short the work will be puckered, and if too long it will hang untidily and look stretched. Any number of pieces may be joined in this way, which is the simplest method of joining.

(2) Two pieces of hairpin work can also be joined together by a zigzag of chain-stitch crochet. This is a very popular method of joining and any number of lengths can be so joined. By a clever arrangement of hairpin work and crochet handsome insertions and borders can be made, also shawls and scarves.

Hairpin Insertion.—This is an old recipe for making a pretty insertion. Make first three stripes with the fork, covering each thread with two plain stitches. The stripes are joined by the loops by skipping a left loop over a right, then a right one over the next left.

At the end of the stripe you fasten off the last loop by a few stitches. To strengthen the edges join two loops together by 1 plain, 2 chain, 1 plain, and so on.

Hairpin Lace.—Make two sufficiently long stripes of hairpin crochet with 2 treble in each loop; join the loops two and two with a thread, if desired, of a colour to contrast with the rest of the work: 1 plain stitch joining two loops on the right; 2 chain, 1 plain, joining two loops on the left; 2 chain, return to the right, and so on until you have taken up all the loops. This forms a zigzag line in the middle.

A scalloped edge to the lace is made in two rows:

First Row : Join three loops by 1 plain and 5 chain.

Second Row : On the 5 chain stitches 1 plain, 1 half-treble, 3 treble, 1 picot with 5 chain, 3 treble, 1 half-treble, 1 plain.

The footing of this lace is made by joining two loops together by 1 plain, 2 chain, 1 plain, and so on.

GLOSSARY OF WORDS USED IN CROCHET

This glossary arranged in alphabetical order will help the reader to understand any recipe.

Chain (ch.). A series of loops forming a chain, used at the beginning of most crochet patterns.

Close Stitch. The same as Double Crochet.

Decrease. Miss a stitch; do not put the hook under a stitch.

Double Crochet (d.c.). A stitch made by a double action of the crochet hook. Put the hook (with the loop already on it) under a stitch, place the wool over it and draw the wool through to make two loops, put the wool over the hook again and draw it through both loops.

Double Treble (d.tr.). A more elaborate form of treble, the thread being wound twice round the hook instead of once.

Half Treble or Short Treble. Wind the wool around the needle in the usual way, insert hook into stitch and draw wool through to form a loop, this makes three loops on the needle, put wool around the needle and draw it through all three loops.

Hole (h.). A " hole " is made with 2 chain, miss two stitches, 1 treble on the next stitch. Used for ribbons.

Long Stitch. The same as Double Treble.

Long Treble. The same as Double Treble.

Making a Stitch. The taking up of an extra loop from the back of a stitch to make one more.

Picots. Small points of various shapes and sizes.

Plain Crochet. The same as Double Crochet.

Short Treble. See Half Treble.

Single Crochet (s.c.). Made by passing the hook through a stitch and drawing the wool through both loops on the hook.

Slip Loop or Slip Knot. A loop that can be drawn to any size ; used as the first stitch in crochet.

Slip Stitch (sl.st.). The same as Single Crochet.

Space (sp.) is 2 chain following a treble, and 1 treble in the 3rd stitch from the previous treble.

Tension. How tightly or loosely you crochet or knit. To find your tension count the number of stitches you knit to an inch.

Treble (tr.). Ordinary treble stitch made by winding thread once round the hook before inserting it into the stitch of the preceding row ; then pull a loop through, which makes three loops on the needle ; pass hook under the wool and draw it through two loops, pass hook under again and draw it through the other two.

Triple Treble (t.tr.). A still more elaborate treble, the thread being wound three times round the hook instead of once or twice.

CHAPTER XXV

HOME DRESSMAKING

Introduction. Stitches used in Dressmaking: Tacking—Crêpe Tacking, Even Tacking, Tailor's Tacking, Diagonal Tacking, Slip Stitching, Top Hemming, Fly Running, etc., Arrow-head, Tailor's Tack. Using and altering Paper Patterns. Taking your own Measurements. Directions for Cutting Out Different Materials: Cutting Double; Turnings. Using the Scissors. Marking the Fitting Lines. Tacking Up. Fitting. Method of Making Seams—An Open Seam, a Welt Seam, a Tucked Seam, a Stitched Seam, a Strapped Seam. Darts. Plackets. Facings. How to make a Plain Skirt. Skirts with Pleats. A Skirt with a Shaped Yoke. How to make a Shirt Blouse. A Sleeveless Tennis Frock. Jumpers. Various Kinds of Sleeves. Collars.

IT is the duty of every woman to look her best, and she cannot do this unless she knows that she is well dressed.

This does not necessarily mean that she must be extravagant. To be dressed suitably for the occasion is to be well dressed. Remember it is far better to be under than over dressed.

A happy outing or party can be ruined for the sensitive woman if she realises that she has overdressed for the occasion, whereas, when suitably clothed, she is able to make the best of herself.

There are very few women who have a complete disregard for clothes and fashion, and it is only the rich who can afford to look poor.

When planning to buy an addition to your wardrobe, give it due consideration and thought. It is a good idea to put out all the articles that will probably be worn at some time or another with the new article. This ought to suggest to you the colour and also the style of thing that is wanted.

A colour-scheme is usually very economical, so that hat, scarf, shoes, and stockings can be worn with more than one outfit.

Good materials are usually cheaper in the end, for poor ones never look well, even when new, and soon lose their shape and look shabby. It is very much better to have a few good clothes than a great many cheap, shoddy ones, when you will always be in that unhappy state of having nothing fit to wear.

The latest fashion in the cut of a garment should be avoided ; try to get the same effect with small details, such as collar, cuffs, belt, and so on. As fashion changes so quickly, a perfectly good frock may have to be discarded unless you are content to go on wearing it long after the fashion is past history. Small accessories can soon be changed, and the garment is up to date again.

To-day the choice one has of materials is overwhelming, and the colourful, shimmering beauty of the fabric halls in the modern store is a joy for the eyes.

When you go to the shop to buy a dress length, go with an open mind, tell the assistant the kind of thing you want, and allow him to advise you. Remember that most woollen materials are made in two weights and widths. A heavy one, 54 inches wide, for the coat, and a lighter weight to match, 40 inches wide, for the frock or cardigan suit.

Silk materials of the cheaper kind are often weighted with tin or lead, to give them substance, and to make them appear thicker than they really are. The great disadvantage of artificial silk has now disappeared, and uncrushable fabrics can be bought in an amazing variety.

Great care must be taken in the washing of these silks, as the threads stretch and break very easily when they are wet, although they are quite strong when they are dry.

STYLE

Study your figure and choose a style that will make the most of your good points and hide weak ones.

If you have ever had a frock that you feel happy in wearing and one that other people tell you suits you, discover what it is that has given the good result, and try to achieve the same in a new garment.

Stout people usually look well in dresses cut on trim lines. A skirt should be made with a panel or with a seam running diagonally across the figure, in order to cut up a broad width and deceive the eye. The same applies to a bodice.

Remember trimmings usually stand away from the figure and appear to add to its width.

Buckles, medallions, etc., should be very carefully placed, especially if they are a complete contrast to the material of the dress.

Stripes, unless they are broad ones, generally help to make the stout woman look slimmer, if they are well arranged.

The tall, slim girl will find frills and flounces improve her appearance. Frilly jabots, puff sleeves, or ruches on the skirt all tend to make the figure look more becoming.

A shaped yoke on the bodice or the skirt will tend to shorten it, and so take from the length of the figure.

STITCHES USED IN DRESSMAKING

(1) TACKING.—For tacking as an embroidery stitch, see Chapter VI.

(a) *Crêpe Tacking* (Fig. 176).—Use this stitch for tacking springy fabrics such as georgette, jap silk, and wool crêpe. Fasten on with a back stitch, take up two small pieces of material on the needle, leave a big space, about $\frac{1}{2}$ to 1 inch, work two more small stitches, and so on, as in Fig. 176.

(b) *Even Tacking.*—This is used for seams, hems, and marking fitting lines on single material. For directions for working see the stitches in Chapter IX., " Plain Sewing."

(c) *Double or Tailor's Tacking* (Fig. 177).—This is used for marking the fitting lines on double material, or when chalk or the tracing-wheel is not suitable. Use double cotton, threading a long strand at a time. Work the stitch in the same way as crêpe tacking, but leave long loops, as in Fig. 177, after making each set of two small stitches. When the tacking is complete, pull the two pieces of material gently apart, as far as the stitches will let them come. Then cut through the middle of the stitches, between the layers. This will leave a clearly followed outline of tack-ends on each piece of material. When it comes to picking out these tack-threads you will find small tweezers useful.

(d) *Diagonal Tacking or Basting* (Fig. 178).—This is used to hold together two large pieces of material, such as a coat and its lining. Always work the stitch when the material is flat on the table. Place one piece on the table, smooth it out with the hands, from the middle to the sides, then place the other piece on top, pin at the corners, and if it is a very long strip like the facing of a coat, put pins in at short intervals.

Begin on the part farthest away from you, make a big stitch from right to left through both thicknesses of material, make another the same size exactly under the last, and continue in this way down the length of the garment, pushing the work away from you as you proceed. The size of the stitch and the distance between each depends on the size of the article being tacked.

(2) JOINING STITCHES.

(a) *Slip Stitching* (Fig. 179).—This is an invisible stitch which is constantly used in dressmaking to join together two folded edges. The stitches are worked on the turnings of the two pieces of material. Fold in the turnings of the two pieces to be joined and tack them together with the edges quite level. Fasten on the cotton between the two thicknesses of material at the right-hand side, and work towards the left.

Take up a small piece of material on the turning just below the fold, draw the needle through, and put it in again on the fold exactly opposite where the cotton came out in the last stitch and bring it out a short distance to the left.

Pull the cotton as tight as possible without puckering the material.

(b) *Hemming.*—The method for working this stitch will be found in Chapter IX., " Plain Sewing." It is not worked so finely or so close together in dressmaking.

(c) *Tailor's Hemming, or Top Hemming* (Fig. 180).—This is worked in a similar way to hemming, but the folded edge is held away from the worker, as in Fig. 180.

It is used when a facing is being attached to a garment, as, for example, round the bottom of a tight-fitting sleeve, or in any case when it is easier to hold the edge away from you instead of towards you. Top hemming is always used to sew a lining into a garment.

(d) *Invisible Hemming.*—See a slip-stitched hem in Chapter IX., " Plain Sewing and Trimmings for Plain Sewing."

(e) *Stitching.*—This is used to make a strong join in materials that are too thick for the machine.

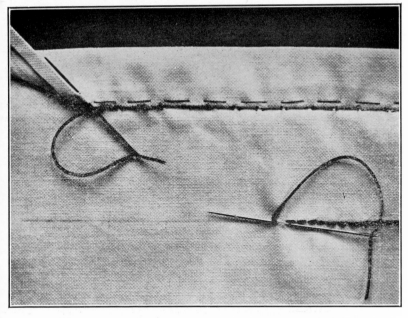

Above: Slip stitching.   *Below:* Back stitch.

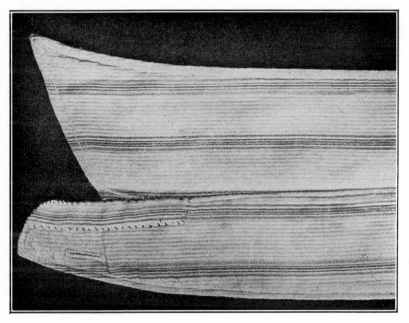

Matched patch on man's soft collar.

[*To face p.* 384

Overcasting lace to raw edges of garments (underwear).

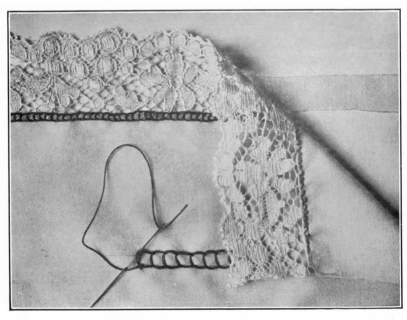

Lace attached with Roman or ladder stitch.
Below : How to make the stitch.

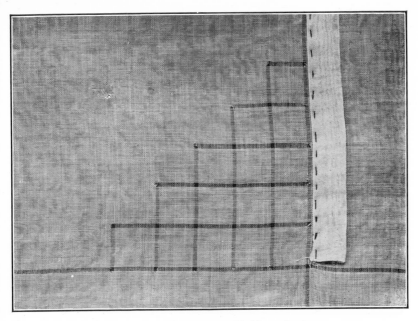

Stage 1.—Drawn-thread and added lace-edge hem.

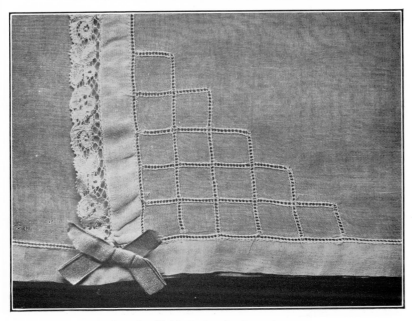

Stage 2.—Finished trimming for underwear.

How to fold material for cutting bias strips.

Cutting bias strips in finishing material.

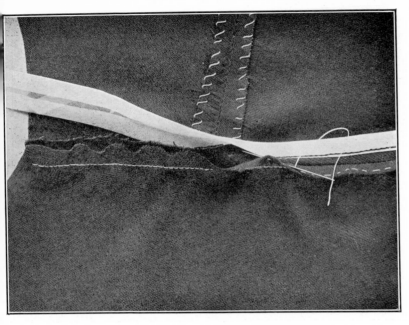

Plain seam neatened *above* with binding, and *below* with turned-in stitched edges.

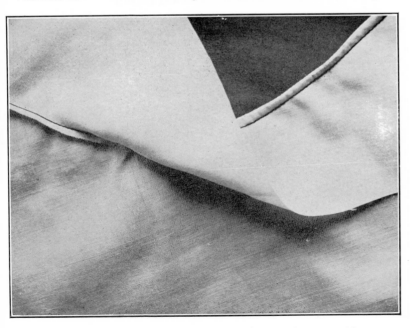

Plain seam : *on the left*, the right side ; *on the right*, the wrong side.

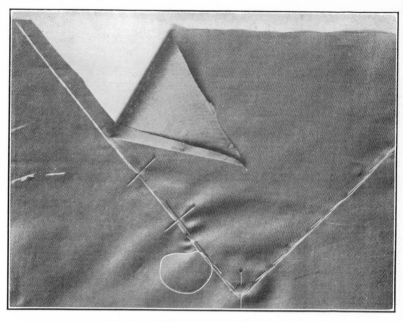

Tacking a lapped seam.

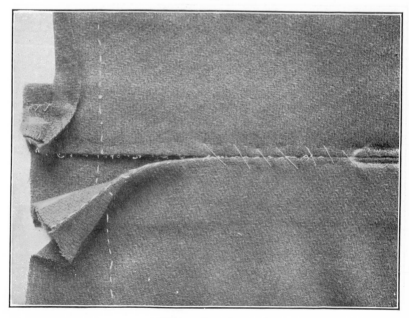

Making a box pleat.

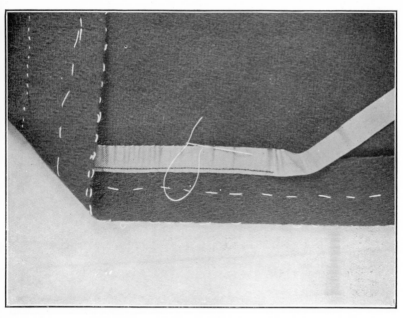

Turning up wool hem with prussian binding.

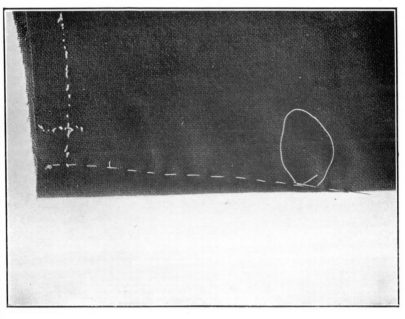

Tapering off a dart to nothing.

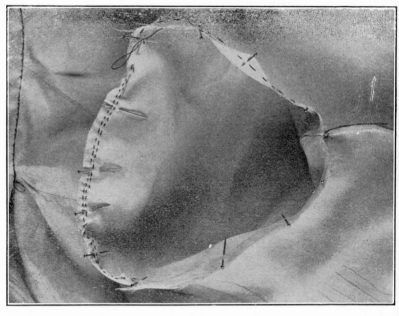

Setting in a sleeve

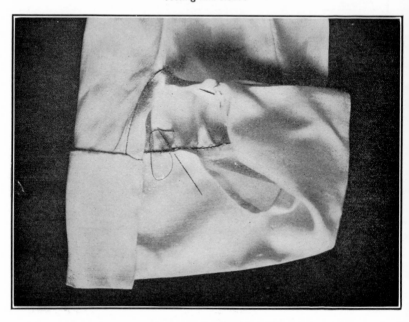

Hemming down cuff to inside of blouse sleeve.

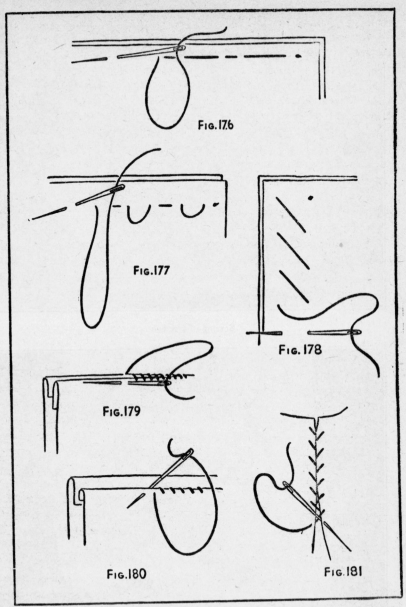

FIG. 176.—Crêpe Tacking.   FIG. 177.—Double or Tailor's Tacking.   FIG. 178.
—Diagonal Tacking.   FIG. 179.—Slip-Stitching.   FIG. 180.—Top-hemming.
FIG. 181.—Fishbone Stitch.

Suppose a seam has been made by the machine, but part of it is too thick to pass under the foot of the machine without breaking the needle, in this case you must continue the line of stitching by hand in the following way : Slip the needle between the folds of the material, fasten on with a back stitch, and work from right to left. Put the needle in as if to make a second back stitch, but bring it out a few threads to the left of the last stitch. Work back over this space and bring the needle out the same distance to the left as in the last stitch. Continue in this way so that there are no spaces left between the stitches.

Small pieces of stitching, such as that made at the end of a sleeve opening, are very much more easily worked by hand than by machine.

When very thick material is being stitched, or more than two thicknesses are being joined together, bring the needle out first on one side of the material and then on the other. This is generally called " stab stitching."

(3) GATHERING STITCHES.

(*a*) The ordinary gathering stitch is described in Chapter IX., " Plain Needlework." In dressmaking it is worked in the same way, except that the gathers are not stroked.

(*b*) *Fly Running.*—This is the quickest way of gathering thin material such as georgette or any thin silk. Hold the edge of the material between the thumb and finger of both hands and the needle under the right thumb. Push the needle along with the thimble, and at the same time move the material in the left hand quickly up and down. This action of the left hand puts a fold on the point of the needle, while that of the right picks up with the needle. The action is slight and quick, so that you seem to be shaking the needle through the material. This will make very small, even stitches. This is an exceedingly difficult process until you have gained the knack of doing it.

If you cannot manage it, hold the material rather tightly across the first and second fingers of the left hand. Now quickly lift the material up and down with the needle, at the same time pushing it along with the thimble. The result should be the same as the first method.

(4) STITCHES TO NEATEN EDGES, ETC.—Many of these have already been dealt with in the Embroidery Section and Plain

Sewing Sections. We will mention here the stitches most usefu
in dressmaking :

(a) *Overcasting*.—This is a very quick and easy way of neatening the raw edges of flat seams, especially used on frocks of
marocain and crêpe de Chine, etc. Use cotton of the same
colour as the dress, and work the stitch loosely. See Chapter IX.,
" Plain Sewing." It is worked something like oversewing, but
from left to right and with needle well sloped.

(b) *Catch Stitch* (see Chapter IX., " Plain Sewing," and
Chapter XIV.).—This is used for holding hems and turnings in
places which will be covered later.

(c) *Herringboning*.—See Chapter III., " The Herringbone
Group of Stitches."

(d) *Loop Stitch or Blanket Stitch*.—For the method of working
this stitch see Chapter II., " Simple Modern Embroidery."
When it is used for neatening a raw edge it must be worked very
loosely, the spaces between each stitch depending upon the
material on which it is worked. The more likely a material is
to fray, the closer must be the stitches. This way of neatening
a raw edge is more decorative than overcasting, and gives a
firmer edge. It is more suitable for the seams on a dressing-gown
than a frock.

(e) *Buttonholing*.—See " Buttonholes " in the section on
Fastenings, and in Chapter II.

(f) *Fishbone Stitch* (Fig. 181).—This is often used when two
raw edges meet without overlapping. The needle is inserted
between them and picks up first one edge and then the other as
in Fig. 181, moving a pace ahead each time. (See also the
Fishbone Stitch used in embroidery in Chapter III.)

(5) ORNAMENTAL STITCHES.

(a) *Arrow-head or Sprat's Head* (Fig. 182).—These are used
to finish the end of a seam at the head of an inverted pleat on a
skirt, at the ends of a bound buttonhole or pocket in a coat, or
anywhere when a neat, smart finish is needed. On a coat or
skirt they should be worked with buttonhole twist, but on a
frock embroidery silk is often used.

First mark the position of the arrow-head by working a
triangle of small running stitches in tacking cotton (Fig. 182, a).
Fasten on with a back stitch on the wrong side, and then bring

the needle out at the bottom left-hand corner. Take all the stitches from right to left. Make the first stitch at the apex of the triangle by taking up a tiny piece of material, about two threads.

For the next stitch, put the needle in at the bottom right-hand corner and bring it out just to the right of the cotton already there.

Continue to work a stitch above and then one below until the space is filled. Each stitch at the top is made outside the triangle and so is a little larger each time, and the one at the bottom is made inside and so is a little smaller each time. See Fig. 182.

(*b*) *Tailor's Tack* (Fig. 183).—This is made the same shape as the arrow-head, but it gives a firmer and stronger finish to a seam. Tack out the shape as before, and a line from the apex of the triangle straight down to the base. Each stitch must be stabbed through from one side to the other. Bring the needle out exactly at the apex, put the needle in at the bottom left-hand corner, and bring it through to the wrong side of the garment. Bring the cotton up to the right side as close as possible to the last stitch, and down again at the apex.

There are now two stitches across the left side of the triangle ; work two in the same way on the right side.

Continue to work in this way until the space inside the triangle is filled. Put the needle each time as close as possible to the previous stitch and pull the cotton firmly but not enough to pucker the material.

The tacking thread down the middle of the triangle will help you to keep the stitches on each side exactly the same length. If they are uneven, the whole appearance of the tailor's tack is spoilt. See Fig. 183.

(*c*) *Cross Stitch.*—Directions for working this stitch will be found in the Embroidery Section, Chapter VI.

Three or four cross stitches are usually worked on the petersham of a skirt to make the centre front. Sometimes a large cross is used. To work this, make a knot in a length of buttonhole twist, and bring the needle out on to the right side, $\frac{1}{8}$ inch to the left of the centre front. Put it in $\frac{1}{8}$ inch to the right and $\frac{3}{4}$ inch lower down and make a stitch $\frac{1}{4}$ inch in length. Complete the cross stitch, bringing the needle out at the starting-point.

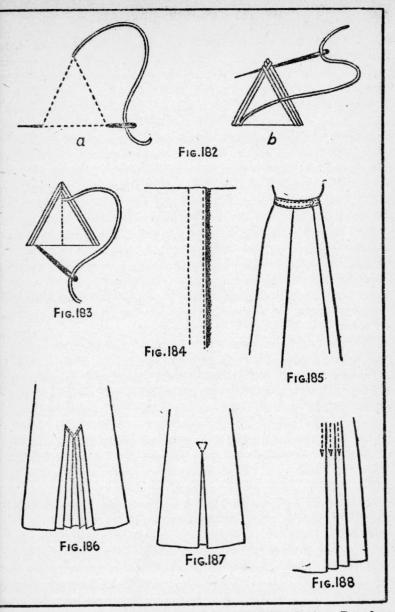

FIG. 182.—Arrowhead or Sprat's Head.   FIG. 183.—Tailor's Tack.   FIG. 184.
—A Welt Seam.   FIG. 185.—Plain Skirt.   FIG. 186.—Skirt with pleats.
FIG. 187.—Inverted Pleats finished with a triangle of stitching.   FIG. 188.—
Pleats finished with tailor's tacks.

Work over the same stitches two or three times, and then fasten them down tightly in the middle, where they cross each other. Fasten off on the wrong side with a back stitch taken over the embroidery cotton.

USING AND ALTERING PAPER PATTERNS

However well your garment may be stitched and finished off, if your pattern is not a well-cut one the result will probably be dowdy and have that terrible " home-made " look about it.

Some of the patterns sold to-day are excellent, and are cut by expert dressmakers. Instructions for making the garment are also given, and each step should be followed in the order in which it is given. If you have not tried your hand at dress-making, then this book will help you to understand and follow the instructions given with a pattern, which necessarily have to be rather short and concise.

Patterns of French models can be bought from some pattern-makers, but do not be tempted to make your first effort with one of these. A skirt made of a firm and rather thick material is a good choice, or if you do not want to spend so much money, make a blouse or summer frock in plain cotton material. Striped, checked, and patterned materials are always a little more difficult to make up, as they must be matched at the seams, and the same pattern or check must appear on the left and right sleeves.

Before going to buy a pattern, take your bust measurement round the fullest part of the figure, and your hip measurement 7 inches below the waist, then buy one as nearly as possible agreeing with your own measurement. Having bought your pattern, study the measurements given on the envelope, length of skirt, length of sleeve, width of bust and hips, and compare them with your own measurements. Then write down the number of inches that must be added or taken off the pattern.

Patterns are cut to stock sizes, and if your measurements are not the same, then the garment made from them will not fit you.

Remember that only half of the pattern is given, so that when there is a difference of 2 inches in the bust measurement, for instance, make a 1-inch alteration on the pattern.

To make a Blouse or Bodice Pattern Smaller.—Pin a tuck

down both pattern pieces from the middle of the shoulder to the waist. Both tucks must be the same size and together equal the amount of the necessary alteration.

To make a Blouse or Bodice Pattern Larger.—Cut the blouse front into two pieces, from the middle of the shoulder, straight down to the waist line. Pin the two pieces on to a sheet of paper, keeping them the same distance apart all the way down, and the cut edges on the same level.

Now do the same to the back of the blouse pattern. The alteration on the back of the pattern must be the same as on the front, and together must equal the amount of the necessary enlargement. Draw a line from the neck edge of the shoulder to the armhole. This will be your new shoulder line. Now cut round the pattern.

When the blouse is too short or too long from neck to waist, cut the front and back across half-way between the armhole and the waist, and make the necessary alterations as described above.

To alter Sleeve Patterns.—When the pattern is too narrow, cut it down the middle, and make a new pattern by pinning it on to paper, as described for the front of the blouse.

Make the pattern narrower by a tuck straight down the middle of the sleeve.

Length alterations must be made midway between the shoulder and the wrist of the sleeve, unless it is a tight fitting one. In this case the alterations must be made equally in the middle of the top half of the sleeve and the middle of the lower half.

To alter Skirt Patterns.—Never buy a skirt pattern which is too small for you. If you have to make use of one too small round the hips, add an equal amount on each side of all pattern pieces except a front or back panel.

When the difference is more than 1 inch, especially if there are only two pieces in the skirt, it is better to cut the pattern down the middle from the waist to the hem line and insert a piece of paper the necessary width.

If the skirt pattern is less than 2 inches too short for you, cut off the difference at the bottom, but when it is more than 2 inches it is better to make a tuck about half-way down each piece of the pattern, otherwise the skirt will be made too narrow.

When the skirt is too short, cut the pattern across half-way down and insert strips of paper. Then straighten off the sides of the pattern.

Special Alterations.—When making garments for a figure which is not quite normal, some special alterations must be made.

A very upright figure needs a long bodice front and a short back. In this case cut off the necessary amount on the back shoulder and neck, then pin the bodice front on to paper, and add to the shoulder and neck.

A stooping figure needs the front of the bodice lowered and the back lengthened.

If the back is cut short at the neck line, any collar that is attached will stand away from the figure and be very uncomfortable.

When the figure has a prominent abdomen, add a certain amount to the front of the skirt, gradually taking it off to nothing at the side seams ; and if the figure is very flat at the back as well, then take off a little at the back in the same way as you have added it in the front. If this is not done, the skirt will stand out in the front, and little can be done to improve matters when the skirt is fitted.

As You Progress.—When you have made a simple frock or skirt, you will probably want to make one in a more elaborate design.

For this you must take more measurements from the figure, and use them carefully when testing a pattern.

Below will be found the measurements that you will require, and how to take them.

Preparation of the Figure

1. Define the waist line by pinning a tape measure tightly round, pushing it down as far as the hips will allow. All length measures must be taken to the bottom of the tape.

2. See that the person is standing straight in her normal attitude.

3. Find the nape point, the lower of the two prominent bones at the back of the neck.

To take the Measurements

Write down in a book, so that it will not get mislaid, a list of all the measurements that you are going to take. Then get a friend to measure you, and write down each measure as it is taken. The full-length measures should be written down, but only half the width.

The right side of the figure should be measured, unless there is any noticeable difference, then it is wise to measure both sides.

The Bodice

1. Length of back . Taken from nape of neck to the waist.
2. Length of front. . From the nape over the shoulder to the centre front rather tightly.
3. Underarm . . . From the muscle under the arm straight down to the waist.
4. Width of back . . Taken at quarter of the length of back from the nape, across the shoulder from armhole to armhole.
5. Width of front . . Taken at the same level as the back. Never take this measure tightly.
6. Width of bust . . Pass the tape round the fullest part of the figure under the arms.
7. Width of waist . . Tightly round the waist.
8. Over the shoulder . From the centre waist at the back, over the shoulder, passing 1 inch above the armhole, across the figure, to the centre waist in front.

When taking the bust measurement, pass the hand under the tape, backwards and forwards, so that it is quite loose.

Sleeve Measurements

1. Armhole . . . Pass the tape under the arm and bring it up to meet on the shoulder. Take this rather tightly.
2. Armhole to elbow . Taken from the centre back to the elbow —deduct from this the half width of the back.

3. Elbow to wrist . . . Continue the tape to the wrist and from this deduct measurement 2.

4. Wrist . . . . Loosely.

5. Upper muscle . . Taken half-way between armhole and elbow.

6. The bend . . . Pass the tape round the elbow when the arm is bent.

7. Lower muscle . . Taken half-way between elbow and wrist.

When taking the length measurements for the sleeve, raise the arm in a line with the back, and bend the elbow so that the fingers touch the chest.

If the sleeve is to slip over the hand without an opening, place the thumb on the palm of the hand, and take the wrist measurement round the knuckles.

Skirt Measurements

1. Width of waist . . Taken not too tightly.

2. Width of hips . . Taken 7 inches below the waist quite loosely.

3. Front length . . Taken from the bottom of waist tape to the ground and then deduct the number of inches the skirt is to be off the ground.

4. Side length . . . Taken over the hip bone to the ground in the same way as No. 3.

5. Back length . . . Taken from centre back to the ground in the same way as No. 3.

Some of these measurements may seem to you unnecessary, but if they are taken and used when making alterations in your pattern, and again when the garment is being made, you will find that the hang and fit of it will be greatly improved.

DIRECTIONS FOR CUTTING OUT DIFFERENT MATERIALS

Use a large uncovered table. The kitchen table is the best ; as it is not shiny there is no fear of the material slipping, nor need you be afraid of spoiling its surface by sticking pins into it or scratching it with scissors.

If the table is very low, the cutting out can be a back-aching business, so it is worth while to raise it with equal-sized blocks of wood.

You will also need scissors or shears, a tape measure, a ruler, some tailor's chalk, needles, and tacking cotton, pins, and if there is any tracing to be done, a tracing-wheel and a piece of thick cardboard.

First open out the pattern pieces and study the lay-out in the diagram which is usually given with patterns.

The Way of the Material.—This is very important as some materials are a lighter shade one way than they are the other.

All fabrics, except stockinet, are made with two sets of threads, the warp and the weft. The warp threads, which run parallel with the selvedge, are stronger and do not stretch so easily as the weft threads.

So when fitting the different parts of the pattern on to your material, see that the selvedge threads run down each piece from neck to hem. This is the general rule which must be followed if the hang of the garment is to be good.

There are exceptions, as, for instance, when stripes are placed diagonally across a dress, or a part of a garment is designed to be cut on the cross. But these instructions are always printed on the pattern and must be followed exactly.

It is the fashion at present to cut whole dresses on the cross ; in this case each piece of the pattern must be cut on the true bias. Study the lay-out very carefully before cutting any part.

Materials with Nap.—The nap on cloth should always run down a garment. Take great care when cutting out a garment in material with a nap, for if a piece is cut the wrong way the garment is spoilt. Before pinning on the pattern pass your hand over the surface of the material and then make arrows in chalk the way the nap runs. It is very easy to make a mistake, especially when contriving to fit in the patterns in an economical way.

You will therefore need more material when using a cloth with a nap.

Velvet and Velveteen.—The pile should run upward on each piece of the pattern.

Many people make up a velvet frock with the pile running downwards, but the appearance is not so good, and it is not so dark or so rich-looking as when made the correct way.

Use fine needles for pinning the pattern to the material, or lead weights, 1d. per dozen, are better still.

Velvet is usually narrow, so it is advisable to choose a skirt having several parts rather than one with only a back and front which would necessitate joins.

Patterned Materials.—Conventional designs can sometimes be cut either one way or the other, but when working cn a material with a flowered design, all pieces of the pattern must be placed one way, as with cloth that has a pile. If it is a large design, make sure that the same pattern comes on each sleeve, and down the middle of the skirt back and front.

Stripes.—Small stripes are easy to handle, as they can practically be disregarded, but large ones must be carefully planned. Put one stripe down the middle of the skirt front, sleeve, and so on. When a bodice and skirt are cut separately, see that the same stripe is continuous in both.

Checks.—The same rules must be followed as when cutting out flowered designs. The checks must be matched at the seams. It is a good plan to arrange for each pattern piece—then cut out the front of the garment and place it along the edge of the back of the pattern to make quite sure that the checks match before cutting both pieces. Material is bound to be wasted in doing this, but scraps of checked material are often useful for trimming plain garments.

The Right and Wrong Side of Materials.—It is sometimes very difficult to distinguish between the right and wrong side of a material. When it has a diagonal rib, hold the cloth up against you ; if the rib runs from left shoulder to the right foot you are holding it with the right side outward. Mark this with a pin. The selvedge is usually a little smoother on the right side.

Woollens and silks are folded right side inside, and cottons and artificial silks right side outside.

Cutting Double.—Do not begin to cut until all the pieces have been pinned on or allowed for. It is best to cut all parts in double material so that the two sides are cut together. When this is not possible, make sure that you cut the two pieces for *opposite* sides. A good plan is to cut out one sleeve, for instance, and place this, with the pattern, on the space you have left for the second sleeve, with the right sides together. Then cut the second sleeve.

The Turnings.—Many patterns are cut with allowance for turnings. When this is not the case, you must leave extra material all round the pattern. The amount will depend upon the garment and the material. It is well to allow large turnings on materials that are inclined to fray out quickly.

The width of a skirt hem depends on fashion and on your own individual taste.

If you find, when planning a frock, that you have not enough material for a big hem, a facing of lining can be used or the raw edge neatened with binding. This is not advisable for children's frocks, which will probably need to be let down in the future.

USING THE SCISSORS

Put your thumb into the round hole and two or three fingers into the oval one. You may find it easier, when cutting out, to hold the first finger under the scissors in front of the oval handle.

Keep the left hand quite flat on the pattern, only a few inches to the left of the edge you are going to cut.

Open the blades wide, slip the pointed end under the material, and make long clean cuts, carrying the scissors well up into the corners.

Try not to raise the pattern more than you can help.

Darts, either in a bodice or a skirt, must not be cut out.

Leave the pattern of each piece on the material.

MARKING THE FITTING LINES

1. *On Cotton Materials.*—Take each piece in turn, lay it on a thick piece of cardboard, and mark the fitting lines with a tracing-wheel. Work with a backward and forward movement, pressing heavily and only lifting the wheel at the points in the pattern.

Keep as close to the pattern as possible, but carry the tracing-wheel to the extreme edge of the turnings, so that the two lines cross and there will be no difficulty in finding the point of the pattern later on.

Be sure to mark any notches with a straight line at right angles to the pattern, and trace the darts carefully.

A tracing-wheel can be bought for a few pence, and when once you have got used to it, you will find that you can use it quite quickly. A lining is very easily and accurately fitted into a coat if the fitting lines have been traced.

2. *On Cloth.*—Sharpen the edge of the tailor's chalk, and mark as close as you can to the paper with fine, clear lines.

This only marks one side, so you must take off the pattern, and fold the material with the wrong sides together, and the chalked piece on the top. Now tap the edges smartly, and you will find that the under side has become faintly marked with the chalk. Open out the material, and if both lines are not quite clear, re-chalk them.

3. *On Velvet and Fine Materials.*—On silks and fine woollen materials, both the tracing-wheel and chalk are unsuitable.

In order that the garment can be accurately tacked and stitched up, the fitting lines must be marked before the pattern is removed from the material.

Mark out all fitting lines and darts in tailor's tacking, using fine cotton. Be sure to make a stitch at each point of the pattern. See " Stitches used in Dressmaking."

TACKING UP

Before taking the pattern off the material, look at each piece carefully, read all the directions that are printed thereon, and then pick up two pieces which are to be joined together and begin on those.

Place one piece flat on the table right side up, now put the piece to which it has to be joined on top, with the right side down.

When one edge is cut on the straight and the other on the bias, put the biased edge on top, and be careful not to stretch it.

Pin the two edges together, putting the pin through the two fitting lines and bringing it out on the turnings. Use plenty of pins.

Now tack the seam, still keeping it quite flat on the table. Use cotton of different colour from that used for marking the fitting lines, so that you will not be confused.

Use ordinary tacking stitches, unless the material is springy or loose, then long and short tacking is better. (See Fig. 176.)

Pin and tack each seam in this way. Do not be tempted to pin all the seams of the garment to get an idea of what it will be like when it is finished, for you will find it more difficult to get each piece flat on the table, and the material will get creased.

Do not be in a hurry over the tacking up. Match all the fitting lines carefully, using small stitches for short seams.

So many people think when they begin to make their frocks that it is quite enough to pin the seams before machining. If you attempt to do this, the seams of your garments will be puckered, however well you press them later on, apart from the fact that pins get in the way of the machine needle and will probably break it.

Expert dressmakers and tailors are most particular about their tacking, as they realise that the fit of a garment depends so much on good tacking, since the stitching is made on the tacking lines.

If you are not sure of the pattern, pin the underarm and shoulder seams with the turnings on the right side, so that any alterations can be made during the fitting of the garment. Put the pins in along the fitting lines in this case.

FITTING

A dress should be fitted twice. The first time is to test the correctness of all the seams that have been tacked and to judge the general hang of the garment. The second fitting is for testing the length of the skirt, seeing that the sleeves and collar are in the right place, and that the garment is thoroughly comfortable to wear.

If the garment has been cut from a pattern tested by your own measurements, there should be very few alterations to make.

Before altering any part, examine the whole fit of the garment, for an alteration in one seam generally affects another seam, which must be attended to, and if you are not careful the lines of the pattern will be spoilt.

The right side of a person is generally fitted first, and the left side is made to agree afterwards. If the figure is unsymmetrical, both right and left sides must be fitted. Avoid over-fitting and remember that tightness is not fit.

When the right side has been fitted correctly, unpin the left shoulder and underarm seams; fold the garment down the centre front and back, and pin the two thicknesses of material together along the new fitting line. With chalk or tacking thread mark the alteration on both sides of the garment, then remove the pins.

METHOD OF MAKING SEAMS

Whichever way you make your seams, they must be neat, flat, and strong.

Use silk for all materials except cotton or linen, as it is more elastic than cotton and so not likely to snap when the seam is pressed.

An Open Seam.—This is the seam that is most generally used in dressmaking. Machine the two edges together exactly on the fitting line, cut the turnings down to an even width. Open out the seam and press it on the wrong side over a roller (see Chapter XXVI. on " Pressing," etc.). The raw edges are usually neatened by overcasting.

If the material is thin but firm, the edges may be turned under and stitched close to the fold.

The turnings on an unlined coat are generally bound with prussian binding, ribbon, or a strip of lining of the same colour as the coat. Fold the binding in half, then hem it first on one side and then on the other. Bias binding, already folded, is useful for this purpose.

A quick way of finishing the edges of cloth that does not fray easily is to " pink " it—that is, to cut triangular pieces out all along the edge.

A Welt Seam (Fig. 184).—This kind of seam is often used on a blazer, a little boy's coat or knickers.

Stitch the seam in the ordinary way, cut one turning to $\frac{1}{4}$ inch, fold the other turning over it, and pin here and there. On the right side run a line of tacking $\frac{3}{8}$ inch from the seam. Press well and then stitch, following the tacking thread. The seam may be made narrower if you like, or two lines of stitching can be worked—one close to the edge, and the second as before (Fig. 176).

In this seam the turnings must fold towards the front, unless there is a panel in the back of the skirt, in which case the turnings must fall towards the back.

A piqué tennis frock looks well if the seams are stitched in this way.

A Tuck Seam.—This seam looks well on each side of a panel of a skirt, or when one part of a pattern is lapped over another. Tack the seam in the ordinary way and then fold back the edges as described for a welt seam. Then stitch $\frac{1}{4}$ inch from the edge, take out the tackings and press. Sometimes this tuck is made $\frac{3}{4}$ inch wide on each side of a panel of a skirt.

A Stitched Seam.—This seam is used on coats and skirts, and on tweed and linen hats.

Make and press a flat seam. Then work a line of stitching on each side of the seam. On hats the stitching is sometimes $\frac{1}{4}$ inch from the seam, but on coats usually not more than $\frac{1}{8}$ inch.

A binding is sometimes tacked on the wrong side before the stitching is worked.

A Strapped Seam.—This is not very fashionable at present. It is a strong seam and is often used on children's leggings.

Make an ordinary flat seam ; the turnings can be brought to the right side instead of to the wrong if you like, and this method will save neatening the raw edges later on. Press the seam over a roller. If the strapping is to be of silk, it must be cut on the bias, but if of cloth, cut it across the width of the material. Any curved seam is better strapped with bias material.

Cut it twice the width it is wanted when finished, fold the edges to the middle of the strip, and catch them together with fish-bone stitch. Press the strap on the wrong side and then tack it over the middle of the seam. Stitch along both edges and press again.

Other Seams.—Washing fabrics and overalls are usually seamed so that all the turnings are hidden. Mantua-maker's, French, and run-and-fell seams are suitable. The method for working these will be found in Chapter IX., " Plain Needlework and Trimmings for Plain Needlework."

DARTS

Darts are a very flat and neat way of disposing of surplus fullness in the interior of a garment, where it cannot be taken up by a seam, and where gathers would be too bulky.

Skirts.—In plain skirts, the fullness at the waist is taken out in the form of darts. They are usually about 5 inches long.

Pin them at the point and at the waist, then down and up to the waist line, taking care that the fitting lines come together. Tack them on the fitting line, shaping them nicely at the end. Stitch from the waist downwards, carrying the stitching about $\frac{1}{2}$ inch beyond the tacking, catching up only a mere thread. This should prevent the dart from " poking " at the end. In thick material a dart must be shrunk ; you will find the method of doing this in Chapter XXVI. Cut the dart open to within 1 inch from the end. Cut down the turnings and oversew them. Press over a roller. (For the roller, see Chapter XXVI.)

Underwear.—Darts are used to make a brassière fit the figure. These are made in the same way as skirt darts, then one edge is cut away nearly to the line of stitching, and the other turned under and felled down over it.

On a lace brassière the turnings are cut to within $\frac{1}{4}$ inch or even less of the stitching, and then buttonholed.

Bodice.—A dress will sometimes be cut with a dart at the underarm or front shoulder. Make these in the usual way, but do not cut them open, merely fold the tuck to one side.

If several are made at the shoulder, they are generally stitched on the right side to form a trimming.

Coats.—Darts, pointed at each end, are often made at the waist of coats, to take up the fullness under a belt. Taper both ends off to a thread, and tie the ends of the machine cotton together.

PLACKETS

These are openings, usually in a seam, to enable a garment to take on and off easily. They are provided with fastenings to close them in wear. They must be very neatly made. For making plackets, see the coming section on " How to make a Plain Skirt."

FACINGS

A facing is really a hem made of an added piece of material instead of by double-folding in the edge of the garment. Facings are straight-cut for straight edges, bias-cut for bias edges, and sometimes cut to shape by the pattern used for the garment. Front facings to coats and blouses are too wide to be classed as hems. However, they serve as hems for centre-front openings, but also provide the material which shows when revers are turned back, and give a double thickness for fastenings. See the coming section on " A Sleeveless Tennis Frock."

How to make a Plain Skirt (Fig. 185)

A plain skirt is just as easy to make as a blouse, although people do not always realise this.

If you want to make a skirt of a medium weight tweed, and the pattern you have chosen has a panel down the front, seams at the side, and the fullness at the back taken up in the form of darts, you proceed in this way :

Cutting Out.—As the material has no " up " or " down," you can fit the top of one piece into the bottom of another.

Take the pattern and place the centre front of the panel to a fold, and the front edge of the side gore to the selvedge on one width of the material, and the centre back to the fold on the material below the front panel.

Pin the selvedge edges first, then pass the hands over the pattern, and pin the corners. A few more pins will be necessary down each side.

Be sure to allow for the hem and turnings all round the pattern, except the centre front and back.

If a high waist is required, decide on the amount you want above the waist, and allow this on each piece of the pattern.

Before cutting out, read the instructions given at the beginning of this chapter. Do not forget that the darts must not be cut out.

Fitting Lines.—Mark the fitting lines with tailor's tacking, not forgetting the darts.

If chalk shows up sufficiently, you can mark the fitting lines in this way ; but chalk is inclined to rub off, so that it is wiser, if you are a beginner, to use the tailor's tackings.

Tacking Up.—Open the front panel and back portion of the skirt, and run a tacking thread from the waist to the hem, on both pieces, to mark the centre back and front. Put the front panel flat on the table with the right side up, place one of the two side pieces on top, right side downwards, with the selvedge edge over the edge of the panel.

Pin from the waist downwards, matching the fitting lines exactly. Tack the seam carefully, making the stitches quite small over the hips, but longer for the end of the skirt. Pin and tack the other side piece to the panel in the same way.

Tack up the darts in the back of the skirt. Pin the back to the front with the turnings on the right side ready for fitting.

The Fitting.—Slip the skirt over the dummy or on to the person for whom it is intended.

Fasten the skirt opening and pin the waist line into position at the front and back. First notice the general hang of the garment, and whether the seams take a proper line. They should appear to be in a straight line from the waist to the hem.

If the skirt falls away from the feet in front, unpin the side seam and lift the front piece a little above the back. This may correct the trouble ; if it does not, make the side gore a little narrower at the foot.

If the skirt seems generally loose all round, it is a good plan to stitch each seam $\frac{1}{8}$ inch inside the fitting line ; but remember that on a skirt with four seams this will tighten the width by 1 inch. The skirt can be made wider in the same way.

Make the darts taper to a fine point. Never alter the waist to fit tightly ; it should be loose. Then the fullness is eased into the waist band and the skirt hangs more gracefully.

Take off the skirt and make any alterations on the fitting lines.

Remember that the skirt will be slightly tighter after the seams have been stitched, as tacking always " gives," and so makes the skirt appear to be looser than it really is.

A skirt should be comfortable and not wrinkle badly when you sit down. If you fit your skirt too tightly, it will soon look shabby and will not wear well.

Stitching the Seams and Darts.—Stitch the seams from the waist downwards. A flat seam with the edges oversewn on the wrong side is quite suitable for a tweed skirt. A welt seam makes a nice finish on tweed and gives it a very professional air.

Use silk on the machine, and remember that it always looks a little lighter after it is worked than it does on the reel.

Leave the left-hand side of the panel unstitched for 10 to 12 inches from the waist downwards. This is for the placket. Cut down the turnings to an even width.

Pressing and Neatening the Seams.—Press the seams over a roller, as described under " Pressing " in Chapter XXVI. Overcast the turnings on the wrong side, or neaten them in any other way you prefer. See methods explained under " An Open Seam."

The Placket.—This should be just long enough to enable the wearer to slip the skirt off and on easily.

When the placket is finished, it should be quite invisible, and should continue the line of the seam. One side of the placket, and in some cases both sides, are cut on the cross, so take care not to stretch them or they will not set flat.

A Placket in an Open Seam.—Turn in the right side of the opening exactly on the fitting line, and press. Catch-stitch the turnings to the skirt, being careful that no stitches show through on to the right side.

If the material is very thin, put a strip of linen or lining under the fold before you fasten it down.

Now cut two strips of material 1 inch longer than the opening ; one piece $2\frac{1}{2}$ inches, and the other $1\frac{1}{2}$ inch wide. On the narrow piece turn under $\frac{1}{4}$ inch on each side and at one end. Pin it over the turning $\frac{1}{4}$ inch in from the fitting line on the right side of the opening, with the raw edge level with the waist. Fell it neatly into place.

Put the right side of the wide strip to the right side of the left edge of the opening, $\frac{1}{4}$ inch in from the fitting line, and the extra length at the bottom. Stitch by machine and press. Turn in the wrong side of the wrap, and fell over the raw edges. Oversew the end of the wrap.

Pin the placket as it will be when the skirt is worn and mark the position for the stud fasteners with pins exactly over each other, on the under and upper sides of the opening. They should be $1\frac{1}{4}$ inch to $1\frac{1}{2}$ inch apart and sewn to the lining.

Work a small loop (explained under " Fastenings " in Chapter XXVI.) across the seam at the bottom of the opening.

A Placket in a Welt Seam.—This placket is also suitable for a skirt with tucked seams.

Snip across the turnings of both thicknesses at the bottom of the opening very nearly to the stitching.

Cut a strip of material $2\frac{1}{2}$ inches wide and twice the length of the opening. Place the wrong side of this strip to the wrong side of the under part of the placket and $\frac{1}{4}$ inch outside the fitting line. Tack and stitch the two edges together, with the extra length at the bottom of the opening. Turn in the upper part of the placket to the fitting line and lay the other part of the strip under the raw edge. Tack and then stitch on the right side to match the seam. Take care to make it a continuous line, so that the placket will not show. Press on the right side. Now neaten the edges with prussian binding or ribbon, and sew on stud fasteners about $1\frac{1}{2}$ inch apart. Taped fasteners can be bought and sewn on over the raw edges if preferred.

The outer edge of the strip must be neatened by pinking, overcasting, or loop-stitching.

This is a quickly worked, neat fastening, and there is no chance of the seam splitting, as the strip of material is continuous on both sides of the opening.

Finishing the Waist.—Cut a piece of petersham that will fit the waist, *after* the hems at each end have been worked.

Pin one end of the petersham to the edge of the wrap on the under side of the placket. Fasten the opening and pin the other end of the petersham to the upper side of the placket, so that the two edges of the petersham exactly meet. Keep the skirt $\frac{1}{4}$ inch above the petersham, and tack the two together, arranging any fullness evenly.

Do not go any farther than this until the skirt has been fitted again, as you may not have arranged the fullness in a satisfactory manner.

After fitting, turn down a $\frac{1}{4}$ inch of the skirt over the edge of the petersham. Tack prussian binding over the turnings, carrying it beyond the petersham to cover the raw edges at the top of the upper side of the placket.

Stitch the binding at both edges. Sew two hooks and eyes on the petersham, and one at the top of the placket $\frac{1}{8}$ inch inside the fitting line. A buttonholed loop is better here than a metal eye.

The Second Fitting.—If you think that the fitting line at the bottom of your skirt is probably correct, pin it up to that line and try the skirt on for the second fitting.

Take a piece of cardboard and measure from one edge the

number of inches you want your skirt to be off the ground. Make
a notch. Now hold this on the ground and test the length of the
skirt all round. Make any alterations that are necessary.
Instead of the cardboard a ruler can be used, and chalk marks
made about 2 inches apart all round the skirt.

Before taking off the skirt, notice whether the darts taper
off nicely, the placket is quite flat, and the fastenings are invisible. If the seams are at all puckered, they probably want
a little more pressing.

Finishing the Hem.—Turn the material on to the wrong side
at the new fitting line, and tack ¼ inch from the edge. Press
under a cloth. Suppose your hem is to be 2 inches wide, then
make a notch on a post card 2¼ inches from one edge.

Place the edge of the card at the bottom of the skirt, and
mark the turning at the notch every 2 inches or so, with chalk
or pins. Now cut down the turning on the line that you have
just made. Turn under ¼ inch, press with an iron, and then
tack down firmly. Slip-stitch the hem to the back of the threads
of the skirt (see Dressmaking Stitches).

A hem is sometimes stitched by machine, but this is not
considered to be a good method.

A Hem on Thick Material.—Turn up the skirt at the fitting
line, tack it, and then cut it down to an even depth, as described
in the above method. Now, instead of turning under ¼ inch,
tack prussian binding to the raw edges, and stitch it by machine.
Hem the binding to the skirt by invisible stitches (see Dressmaking Stitches).

A Hem on a Wide Skirt.—On a very wide skirt the hem will
not set quite flat if it is treated in either of the above methods, as
the skirt is so much wider at the foot than it is where the hem
is sewn down.

Prepare the hem as described, but before adding the binding,
gather the raw edge so that it fits the skirt quite easily. Then
tack on the binding, stitch it, and finish in the same way as
before.

If the skirt is made of a thick cloth, it is better to take out
the fullness in pleats. Remember to make several small pleats,
rather than one large one.

A False Hem.—If you have not enough material to allow for

a wide hem, or if the cloth is thick and you do not want to make the skirt any heavier by a hem, add a false hem of lining.

Cut strips of material on the cross 3 inches wide, or narrower if you prefer a smaller hem. Join them until you have a piece long enough to go round the skirt ; press the seams.

Turn up the skirt to the fitting line and press. Cut the turnings down to an even width.

Place the right side of the strip to the right side of the skirt edge, and stitch by machine $\frac{1}{4}$ inch down. Press the turnings out over a roller ; then turn under the top edge and tack the false hem quite flat. Hem it down with invisible stitches.

A false hem can be made with cross-way strips of cloth to match the skirt, in which case finish the hem with prussian binding as described under " A Hem on Thick Material."

Never cut a false hem from material on the straight. It will make the hem of the skirt hang badly.

Finishing off the Skirt.—(1) Sew two loops to the petersham at the side seams of the skirt. To make these, cut two pieces of prussian binding 4 inches long. Turn down the ends and then fold each in half lengthways. Oversew the edges all round.

(2) Mark the centre front of the skirt with three or four cross stitches.

(3) Look the skirt over, inside and out, remove the tacking cottons, and make sure the seams are all neatened and hooks and eyes sewn on.

(4) Give the skirt a final pressing.

SKIRTS WITH PLEATS (Figs. 186, 187, 188)

In most bought patterns the exact position of pleats is marked by perforations (trace lines), making pleating an easy matter. After cutting out, tailor-tack the perforated lines. Then when you are ready to put in the pleats, all you have to do is to fold and tack them along the tailor-tacked lines and they are ready for pressing.

Side pleats are folded to lie all one way, usually facing out-wards from the centre front.

A *box-pleat* is a pair of pleats placed so that they just touch, each pleat facing outwards away from the other.

An *inverted pleat* is the exact opposite of a box-pleat—that is, a pair of touching pleats which face inwards towards each other.

Snip the turnings of the skirt before folding them under and stitching on the right side. An inverted pleat is often trimmed with a tailor's tack or a triangle of stitching. (See Figs. 186, 187, and 188.)

A Skirt with a Shaped Yoke

The skirts of nearly all dresses of to-day have a yoke of some kind. Turn under the lower edge of the front yoke to the fitting line, and tack close to the fold. Place the skirt flat on the table with right side up, pin the yoke in position first at the centre front, then outwards to the side seams, and tack it firmly with small stitches. Pin and tack the back yoke in the same way.

Pin up the side seams with the turnings on the right side, fit the skirt, and make any necessary alterations. Take out the pins and the tacking thread joining the yoke to the skirt. Snip the turnings of the lower edge of the yoke and press thoroughly on the wrong side.

Now join the back and front of the skirt and the back and front of the yoke. Press and neaten the seams. Fix and tack the yoke over the skirt in the same way as before, placing a piece of cardboard inside, so that the two layers will not be pinned together. Stitch as close to the folded edge of the yoke as possible, and neaten the turnings on the wrong side.

Finish the skirt in the same way as described for a plain skirt.

How to make a Shirt Blouse (Fig. 189)

This is a type of blouse that is always fashionable, although the style of the collar and the amount of fullness at the top of the sleeve changes from year to year. For morning wear with a trim tailor-made coat and skirt, a shirt blouse is excellent. Its success depends on a good fit and a neat finish, so that it must be made carefully, step by step.

Suitable Materials.—Plain coloured or striped materials are more suitable for the style of the blouse than patterned or fancy ones. Narrow stripes are generally more becoming than wide ones.

Any kinds of washing silk such as satin, jap silk, or tussore can be used. Striped crêpe de Chine or Macclesfield silks make very smart and serviceable blouses. Two yards of 36 inches wide material will be needed for the normal-sized figure.

The Pattern.—Buy a good pattern, adapt it to your own measurements, and keep it for future use. There will probably be six parts to the pattern—the back, front, sleeves, yoke, collar, and cuff.

Cutting Out.—Place the back to the fold of the material and the straight edge of the yoke to the selvedges on the same level. Open out the rest of the material and fold it in half weft way. Now place the sleeve and the front on the double material, with the selvedge threads running from the top to the bottom of each piece.

Arrange the patterns of the cuff and collar to the best advantage, but remember that the selvedge threads must run round the cuffs and along the length of the collar.

The yoke, collar, and cuffs must be lined with either the same material or a thin lining.

When cutting out a blouse in striped silk, see that the same

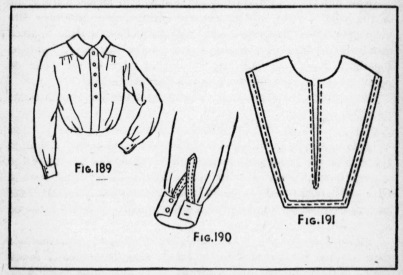

FIG. 189.—A Shirt Blouse.   FIG. 190.—Opening in a Shirt Blouse Sleeve.
FIG. 191.—Wrong Side, Tennis Frock.

coloured stripe comes to the edge of each cuff. Sometimes a blouse is cut in striped material with the front and back on the cross. In this case see that the stripes meet on each side, and that one stripe just comes to the waistline in the middle of the back and the front.

Allow 3 inches on the right front of the blouse and $1\frac{1}{2}$ inch on the left; $\frac{1}{2}$ inch on all other edges except the collar and cuffs, which need only $\frac{1}{4}$ inch.

Mark the fitting lines with tailor's tacking.

Making the Blouse.—The opening of the shirt blouse is worked in the same way as that of a man's shirt, except that the box-pleat is made on the right side instead of on the left. On the right-hand side of the blouse, fold over 2 inches on to the wrong side. This is the width of the box-pleat. Again, fold over 2 inches to form a solid hem.

Put a tacking line $\frac{1}{4}$ inch in from the second folded edge, and then fold back the front, and you will see that you have made the box-pleat. Run another tacking thread $\frac{1}{4}$ inch in from the folded edge.

Stitch the pleat on the tacking lines, using silk on the machine. On the left-hand side of the blouse turn a 1-inch hem, tack and stitch it.

Fastenings.—Buttons and buttonholes should be used as fastenings on a shirt blouse. Hooks and eyes or stud fasteners are most unsuitable and spoil the style of the garment.

Work the buttonholes down the pleat and not across, with two barred ends. Sew on the buttons in the middle of the hem on the left side of the blouse. Pearl buttons with pierced holes are generally used. The first buttonhole should be 3 inches down from the top.

The Yoke.—Gather the fronts along the shoulders, once on the fitting line and again $\frac{1}{4}$ inch below it. Gather the back in the same way. Turn under the edge of the yoke the necessary turnings, and press with a warm iron.

Place the lining of the yoke flat on the table with the right side uppermost. Put the back of the blouse on top, with the wrong side downwards, and the edges that are to be joined together quite level. Draw up the gathering threads to fit the yoke, and then tack on the fitting line. Again put the lining of the yoke on the table with the right side uppermost, and fix the front gathers in the same way, leaving about 1½ inch plain at each end.

Pin up the underarm seam and try the blouse on. Notice if the fullness hangs well, and whether the armhole is too tight or too loose. It is most important to make the armhole fit well, as on it depends the success of your sleeve.

If the armhole is too tight, let out the underarm seam just a little at the top, and snip the turnings of the armhole. The wrinkle that is made will guide you as to the depth of the snips. Do not be tempted to cut away any material.

If the armhole is too big, take a little out at the underarm seam and lift the back and front. The armhole should not be fitted too tightly or the blouse will be uncomfortable to wear.

Take off the blouse and make the alterations on the unfitted side, then stitch the yoke lining by machine.

Now pin the yoke itself in position over the gathers, tack and then stitch on the right side as close to the edge as possible.

The Seams.—Tack and stitch the underarm and the seams of the sleeves. A mantua-maker's or a French seam is suitable for thin materials. See the seams already described and decide which one is best for your blouse.

The Sleeve Opening (Fig. 190).—The position for this is probably marked on your pattern, but if it is not, cut it 3 inches long, on the under side of the sleeve 1 inch from the folded edge opposite the seam.

The Under Side.—Cut a strip of material 1 inch wide. Place the right side of the strip to the wrong side of the sleeve, edge to edge. Tack and then stitch the two together ¼ inch from the edge. Fold the strip of material on to the right side, turn under the raw edge, and machine into position over the first line of the stitching.

The Upper Side.—Cut a strip of material 2½ inches wide and 1 inch longer than the opening. Place the strip in the same way as before, with the extra length at the top of the opening. Tack and stitch the two together ; then fold the strip over, and machine on the first line of stitching.

Fold the extra length at the top of the opening into a point, and cut away the under part of it if it seems bulky. Wrap the upper over the under side and tack the point down to the **sleeve**. Stitch across the base of the point and all round it.

Other Ways of Working the Sleeve Opening.—(*a*) The **under** side is neatened in the same way as the first method, or a narrow hem, tapering off to nothing, may be worked instead. On the upper side put a false hem turned on to the wrong side of the opening. (For making a false hem, see Chapter IX., on " Plain Needlework.") Wrap the upper over the under side, making a small pleat at the top of the opening. Tack firmly and then work two rows of stitching to prevent the opening tearing down. This is an easier way than the first.

(*b*) A quick way is to snip the end of the opening for $\frac{1}{8}$ inch. Turn down, tack, and stitch a hem on both sides $\frac{1}{4}$ inch in width. Now fold the upper side over the under, which, you may find, needs to be snipped a little more. Pin securely and then work by hand two rows of stitching across the hems to prevent the opening tearing.

(*c*) Another quick way is to turn down narrow hems on each side of the opening, tapering them off to a thread at the top. Fold the upper over the under side and work a buttonholed loop through both thicknesses to secure them together and to make the opening strong.

The Cuffs (Fig. 190).—If the cuff has been cut in one piece, fold it in half lengthways, right sides together, and machine up the ends. Snip tiny pieces off the upper corners, so that when the cuff is turned on to the right side the corners can be made quite sharp.

Sometimes the cuff is stiffened with muslin. In this case cut the cuff out in two pieces. Tack the muslin and one side of the cuff together, and turn them both down for $\frac{1}{4}$ inch on to the wrong side. The turnings are catch-stitched on to the muslin, if the material is fairly thick.

Turn in the edges of the other side of the cuff for $\frac{1}{4}$ inch and tack into place, edge to edge, leaving one end open for inserting the sleeve. Gather the sleeve and draw it up to the size of the cuff.

Pin the cuff into place, putting most of the gathers on the upper part of the sleeve. Tack first on the right side, turn under the edge on the wrong side, and tack again. Press the cuff thoroughly.

Now stitch the cuff on the right side all round, as close to the edge as possible, and again $\frac{1}{4}$ inch farther in. Work two buttonholes on the upper side, and sew on two pearl buttons on the under side of the cuff.

A Quick Way of joining Cuff and Sleeve.—Leave the seam of the sleeve open and make the cuff long enough to slip over the hand without an opening.

Gather the edge of the sleeve and place the right side of the cuff to the right side of the sleeve. Regulate the fullness and then stitch the two together $\frac{1}{4}$ inch from the raw edges. Now join the sleeve from the armhole to the end of the cuff by placing the right sides together and machining $\frac{1}{4}$ inch from the raw edges.

Press the seam and overcast the turnings on the wrong side. Turn under the raw edge of the cuff, fold it over, and fell it down over the line of stitching.

Setting in the Blouse Sleeve.—Gather the top of the sleeve twice, leaving about 4 inches plain on either side of the seam. If on your pattern the seam of the sleeve is to be put 3 inches in front of the underarm seam, then leave 6 inches plain on the underside of the sleeve and $1\frac{1}{2}$ inch on the top part.

Turn the sleeve right side out and put it into the armhole while holding the wrong side of the blouse towards you. Pin in the sleeve, beginning at the seam, matching the notches carefully. Pin the plain part first, easing the sleeve into the armhole, rather than stretching it. Tack the sleeve into position, holding the sleeve towards you. If you do not want the fullness to be noticeable at the top of the sleeve, hold the work over the fingers and at each stitch ease in a little of the fullness. Now try the blouse on.

Notice whether the straight of the material runs down the middle of the arm, from the armhole to the elbow, and if the arm can be moved easily without dragging the blouse.

Alter the position of the gathers until the sleeve is quite satisfactory.

Take off the blouse and stitch the sleeve into position by hand, holding the sleeve towards you.

Cut down the turnings to an even width and bind them with a piece of the material cut on the cross, if it is not too thick. Bias binding can be used or the edges may be oversewn.

The Collar.—Put the right sides of the collar and lining together, tack and stitch ¼ inch from the raw edges. Cut tiny pieces of the corners, turn inside out, and press, making good sharp corners. Put the lining to the right side of the blouse, with one end of the collar to the middle of the box-pleat and the other end to the middle of the hem. Pin it in position. Fasten the blouse and see that the two ends of the collar exactly meet in the middle of the box-pleat. If it is correct, tack, and then stitch by machine.

Turn in the edges of the box-pleat and the hem not covered by the collar, and oversew them. Trim the turnings of the blouse and the collar, then turn under the edge of the collar, tack and stitch exactly over the first stitching. The outer edges of the collar must now be stitched to match the cuffs. Sew on a small hook and eye to fasten under the left side of the collar.

The Lower Edge of the Blouse.—Turn up a hem ½ inch in width all round the lower edge of the blouse, press it, and stitch as close to the edge as possible. Work another line of stitching ⅛ inch from the fold of the hem.

Run an elastic between the two lines of machining and sew the ends to the inside edge of the hem on the left side and the box-pleat on the right side of the blouse. Oversew the ends of the hem. Sew on hooks and eyes. Give the blouse a final pressing.

A SLEEVELESS TENNIS FROCK

A tennis frock is generally made quite simply, with revers, plain collar, and a skirt with pleats of some kind.

It is advisable to buy a good material for a tennis frock, as the fashion does not change very much in this kind of garment, and so they can be used for many years.

Read the directions that are given under the heading of " Cutting Out " before pinning the pattern on to the material.

Pin and tack up the bodice and skirt in the same way as is described for the making of a blouse and skirt, but leave the shoulder and underarm seams open.

The Neck Opening.—With Revers (Fig. 191).—Turn down narrow hems on the sides and lower edge of the facing. Tack and stitch them. If the material is thick, like piqué, turn the edge once only on to the wrong side and then stitch close to the fold.

Place the facing in position on the bodice with the right sides together, and tack down the middle to mark the opening. Stitch ⅛ inch from the tacking, on either side of it, making a point at the end. Cut down the opening as far as possible to the stitching, and turn the facing on to the wrong side. Press thoroughly, making the join come at the extreme edge. Work a buttonholed bar at the end of the opening to prevent its tearing down. The top of the facing is joined in with the shoulder seam.

Without Revers.—This is made in very much the same way as the opening in the sleeve of the shirt blouse, and it looks exactly the same when it is finished. Neaten the left side with a strip of material 2 inches wide. Cut a strip 3½ inches wide and 1 inch longer than the opening. Stitch this to the other side as in making the sleeve opening, fold the strip to the right side of the blouse, turn under the edge and tack it down about ¾ inch beyond the join, so that the middle of the pleat comes in the middle of the opening. Stitch the left side of the pleat ¼ inch from the edge. Wrap over the opening as it will be when it is fastened, and pin it together. Form the end of the pleat into a point, and then complete the stitching all round it.

Buttonhole the raw edges on the wrong side, and sew on the fastenings.

The Fitting.—Pin the shoulders from the neck to the armhole, stretching the front when necessary, and pin the underarm seams, both with the turnings on the right side. Tack the bodice to the skirt with centre front of each exactly together, and seams matching at the sides.

Try on the frock, and notice the general hang of it, in order to decide where alterations are necessary.

If there are wrinkles across the shoulder, stretch the front a little, or lower the front shoulder. The seam should fall towards the back rather than to the front. Let out the underarm seam (the front part only) if the frock is too tight across the bust.

If the armhole is tight, let out the top of the underarm seam, and snip the material where it is necessary. The wrinkle will generally guide you as to the depth of the snips. Slight fullness is unavoidable at the armhole, and should not be fitted away. When it is very big, make the alteration at the underarm and the shoulder seams. See that the seam at the waist is in the right position, and fit the skirt in the same way as is described under the making of a skirt.

Take off the garment by unpinning the left shoulder and underarm seams, and make the same alterations on the left side as have been made on the right, after having untacked the waist seam. Tack the shoulder and underarm seams with the turnings on the wrong side.

Stitch all the seams in the bodice and the skirt, press and neaten them.

To join the Bodice and Skirt.—Turn under the edge of the skirt for ¼ inch and snip the turnings. Pin the skirt over the bodice at the centre front, centre back, and at the side seams. Gather any fullness in the bodice, and arrange it evenly, and then tack the skirt to the bodice. Stitch close to the fold and neaten the edges on the wrong side by oversewing. A petersham is sometimes used on thick frocks to keep the waist line in the proper place. The seam should be made to come to the middle of the petersham.

The Side Opening.—This can be made in the same way as described for the placket of a skirt. For a thin frock a continuous bind is generally used, so that no stitches show on the right side. Cut a strip of material 2½ inches wide and long enough to go all round the opening, with an allowance for turnings. Place the strip in a line with the side seam with the right sides together, and stitch up one side and down the other. Turn under the loose edge and fell it down over the turnings.

Allow both false pieces to fold towards the right, and then work a buttonholed bar at each end of the opening to keep them in position. Sew on the fastenings.

The Neck and Armholes.—Make up the collar, pin it to the neck of the frock at the centre back and in the front, then attach it in the same way as described for the shirt blouse.

Bind the armholes with a French hem or a false hem. (See " Bindings.")

The Hem.—Pin up the hem of the dress at the fitting line, try it on, and make any necessary alterations in the length.

Finish the hem in the most suitable way, and make a belt. (See " Fastenings.")

As each part of the bodice and skirt is worked, you will find

14

it a great help if you refer back to what has been written about that particular part in the making of the blouse and the skirt.

Take out all the tackings, and give the frock a final pressing.

JUMPERS

The upper part of these are made in very much the same way as a blouse, but often they are cut in at the waist and the blouse is gathered into the lower part that fits the hips tightly. To do this neatly, cut a crossway strip of material 1¼ inch wide, and 1 inch longer than the edge of the hip yoke. Tack and stitch it in position on the right side ⅛ inch from the edge, and then turn it back on to the wrong side and press. Gather the upper edge and draw it up to fit the lower one. Tack the lower over the upper and stitch close to the edge.

Turn the crossway strip over the gathers on the wrong side and fell down neatly.

The lower edge of the jumper is usually hemmed up with prussian binding. Stitch the binding over the raw edge on the right side, then turn up the bottom once and press with a moderately hot iron. Slip-stitch the binding to the jumper, so that no stitches show on the right side.

Another way without using binding is to turn a narrow fold on to the wrong side, stitch it close to the edge, and press thoroughly. Then turn up the edge a second time, press again, and slip-stitch it down invisibly.

The opening is generally made in the left side, above and below the waist line. It is better to finish the seam and then unpick the necessary amount for the opening, as the marks of the stitches will help you to keep it in a continuous line with the seam. Sew hooks and eyes at the waist line and not stud fasteners.

VARIOUS KINDS OF SLEEVES

Some frocks have loose sleeves gathered into a cuff like those described in the making of a shirt blouse, but a great many have fitted or semi-fitted sleeves. These are either made in two pieces or one piece, shaped by means of a dart at the elbow or wrist. Sometimes a sleeve has a join between the shoulder and the wrist. When this occurs, the seam in the upper and the lower sleeves must be made before the two are joined together, in the same way as a yoked skirt is made.

When fitting any sleeve to its armhole, remember that the sleeve is always bigger, to allow for ease in wear. Ease this fullness in carefully around the top half of the sleeve. See the method described in " Making a Shirt Blouse," and how to shrink away fullness in the section on " Pressing."

A One-Piece Sleeve.—Pin and tack up the dart, first shaping it carefully to a point (see Darts), and then tack the seam of the sleeve. When the frock is being fitted, turn in the armhole of the sleeve to the fitting line and pin it to the front of the frock according to the notches, and then to the back in the same way. Put plenty of pins in over the top of the armhole across the seam and not alongside it.

Notice the general hang of the sleeve first, then if it does not look quite right, decide whether it is wrong at the top or lower part before you begin to make any alterations. If the top of the sleeve appears to twist, arrange the gathers differently. If this does not correct matters, the whole sleeve will have to be moved round a little, either towards the back or the front. This very rarely happens when the notches in the sleeve and frock have been carefully matched. The straight of the material ought to be exactly in the middle of the top part of the arm.

Before making any width alterations, move the arm to be certain whether the width is needed in movement. Take great care not to make the sleeve too short, as when it has been worn for some little time it wrinkles and tends to become shorter.

If less fullness is wanted at the top, turn under the head of the sleeve the required amount, and when it is removed see that there is a good curve there.

A kilted frill is sometimes put into the dart of this kind of sleeve. For the method of making the frill, see Chapter XXVI.

A Two-Piece Sleeve.—Place the larger or upper piece flat on the table with the right side up, and the smaller one on the top, right side down. Make snips in the turnings, once at the elbow, once below, and twice above. Have the front seam, the shorter one, away from you, and begin to pin at the wrist, bringing the upper part to meet the under. In this way the turning will be standing up. For the back seam, turn the sleeve round and pin the seam in the same way, beginning at the elbow notch to the armhole, and then from the wrist to the lower elbow notch. Gather the fullness in the upper sleeve until it fits the under, and pin the seam at the elbow ; keep it flat on the table all the time.

Tack very carefully on the fitting lines, taking out the pins as you go along.

Fit the sleeve in the same way as the one-piece sleeve, making any width alterations in the back seam.

Stitch, press, and neaten the seams as before.

Finishing off the Wrists of Sleeves (Fig. 192).—If stiffening is required, use a crossway strip of muslin or canvas 1 inch wide. Place it to the fitting line at the wrist, then fold the sleeve turnings on to the muslin and catch-stitch them into position. Face it with a crossway strip of material or a narrow ribbon. The opening should be from 2 to 3 inches long, left in the outer seam. Turn in the wrist edge of the sleeve to the fitting line, and the edge of the upper sleeve in a line with the seam. Tack and press on the roller. The turning of the seam on the under part of the sleeve forms a wrap, and may be oversewn or bound (Fig. 192).

If hooks and eyes or buttons and loops are going to be used to fasten the opening, sew them on now. Cut a crossway strip of silk 1 inch wide, turn the edges on to the wrong side under a warm iron. Sew it on to cover the turnings round the wrist and along the upper side of the opening. Use top hemming when sewing it to the turnings of the sleeve, and invisible hemming at the other side.

For sleeves of thin material a continuous placket worked in the same way as the skirt placket is more suitable, so that no stitches show on the right side.

A French hem is a good finish for the wrist edge, a double crossway fold being used if the material is very thin. (See " Bindings.")

If a shaped cuff is to be added, neaten the wrist edge by a hem, turned up on to the right or wrong side of the sleeve, but leave the opening unworked. Make up the cuff and press it thoroughly on a roller, leaving the same length of opening as in the sleeve. Tack the cuff into position and fold in the turnings at the opening, edge to edge, and then slip-stitch it all round. Press again on the roller.

A velvet sleeve is generally pointed over the hand. The best way to neaten this is to cut a facing the exact shape of the sleeve about 3 to 4 inches deep. Put the two right sides together edge to edge, and stitch them. Snip the turnings and cut them very narrow at the point, then turn the facing on to the wrong side. Arrange the opening by turning in the edges of the facing and the sleeve, and slip-stitching them together. Catch-stitch the lower edge of the facing and sew on the fastenings.

Sometimes a hem is made at the wrist and hidden by a French fold of self material. (See Chapter XXVI.)

Collars

The usual double collar and the method of attaching it has already been described in the making of the shirt blouse.

Unlined collars, or single collars, are generally of a trimmed or fancy type. Finish its outer edges with plain hems, hem-stitched hems, a frill of lace, etc., or with binding or machine picoting. To apply a single collar you need a bias tape or bias strip of self-material about 2 inches longer than the neckline measurement. Pin together the exact centres of both the collar and the neckline, right sides touching. Over these place a bias strip wrong side uppermost. Tack all three layers together from the centre both ways, then stitch them. Lastly, hem down the free edge of the bias strip to the inside of the neckline.

Detachable collars are generally light-coloured ones on a dark dress. As a rule they are the unlined ones described above. Slip the neck edge of the collar into a double bias tape or crossway bind, machine-stitch it in place. Face in the neck edge of the dress with a matching bias strip.

CHAPTER XXVI

HOME DRESSMAKING (*continued*)

PRESSING—Appliances necessary for Pressing, Pressing Hems, Seams, Darts, Pile Fabrics, Fancy Material. *Shrinking*—Canvas, Cotton, Woollen Materials, etc. *Trimmings*—Frills of all Kinds, Box-Pleated Edging, A Box-Pleated Ruche, Ruches of different Kinds. Methods of Finishing the Edges of Frills, Ruches, etc.: Picot Edging, a Whipped Edge, Plain Hem, Machine Edge, Hemstitched Edge, a French Hem. Folds. Shirring: Tucked and Corded Shirring. Shell Trimming, Shell Hemming, Tucking. Stitching. Embroidery, Bead Embroidery, Appliqué, Crochet Trimmings, Crochet Buttons.

FASTENINGS—Buttonholes, Working a Buttonhole cut on the Cross and on Thick Material; Bound Buttonholes; Sewing on Buttons; Buttonholed Loops and Bars. To cover Button Moulds. Loop Fastening. Eyelet Holes. Hooks and Eyes. Stud Fasteners. Zip Fasteners. Belts.

Pockets. Bound Pockets. Welt Pockets.

YOU know a great deal about dressmaking if you can make a simple blouse and skirt well. This chapter adds some further important details that will make your work more interesting and successful. We will begin with directions about pressing, because pressing plays a larger part in dressmaking than most people realise, and requires special care and attention. Garments that have been well cut, carefully made, and neatly finished can be quite spoiled by insufficient use of the iron.

It is a good plan to have your ironing-table ready, and the iron warm, all the time that you are working, then you will not be tempted to hurry on to the next piece of stitching before pressing the last.

A tailor is constantly using the iron, a very heavy one, called a tailor's " goose "; this is the reason why there is such a great deal of difference between a garment made by a dressmaker and that made by a tailor.

If you try to carry out the rules given in this chapter, you will be surprised at the professional finish that your garments will have.

Appliances necessary for Pressing

(1) *A Table.*—This should be covered with a sheet only, not a blanket and sheet which is usual for ordinary ironing. The reason for this is that a soft-padded surface throws the impression of the turnings through on to the right side. A blanket is occasionally needed (see section on Pressing).

(2) *A Roller.*—This is made by covering a rolling-pin or broom handle with one layer of thin material, generally thin flannel. Wrap it round the roller so that the edges just meet, and sew them together with fishbone stitch. In this way there will be no ridge to mark the material while it is being pressed.

(3) *Skirt Board.*—This board makes the pressing of skirts easier, but you can quite well do without it. Cover it in the same way as the broom handle.

(4) *Irons.*—These should be from 4 to 8 lb. in weight. A tailor's " goose " should be used for long seams or very thick materials. It is heavy, about 12 lb., so less personal strength is needed when using it.

Irons should not be too hot, as the material will scorch more quickly than when ironing a damp article in laundry work. If the iron is too cool, it will not do the work properly.

Remember when doing pressing of any kind, it is pressure rather than heat that is necessary.

(5) *An Iron Stand and Holder.*

(6) *A Bowl of Water and a Cloth.*—Nearly all dressmaker's materials have enough moisture in them to serve the purpose of damping, but very thick cloths and some serges must be damped before pressing in order to get a flat surface.

Use as little water as possible, and only damp a small piece of material at a time and press it at once until it is quite dry.

(7) *Soap.*—A little yellow soap is rubbed on both sides of the turnings of a seam in very thick materials. The heat of the

iron melts the soap, sticks the turnings to the garment, and makes the seam flat.

PRESSING

Pressing Hems.—For thick materials, such as tweed and serge, cover the table with a cotton cloth only, so that you get a good sharp edge to the fold. Place the garment flat on the table, with the right side down, and press with a heavy iron. If this does not give a satisfactory result, damp an odd piece of material and pass it over the hem, then press again. Hems on thin materials should be pressed over a blanket and sheet.

Do not let the iron touch the material, and do not use any water, or you may spoil the surface of woollens and make silks stiff and papery.

Pressing Seams.—Turn the garment on to the wrong side and slip the roller inside under one of the seams. See that the seam is straight down the length of the roller. Now with the left hand pull the material away from the seam, and hold it firmly on each side of the roller. Press the seam firmly, then move the left hand along and press the next piece, and so on until the length of the seam is finished. In this way the seam is pressed, the stitching stretched, and there is no fear of the turnings being pressed down to leave ugly marks on the right side.

On very thin materials, the seams may be pressed quite satisfactorily on the table with a sheet, but no blanket.

If you find that you cannot flatten the seam as well as you would like, and you decide to damp it, use the water very sparingly. Pass a damp cloth down the seam ; *never* put a wet cloth on it, and press, or you may find you have shrunk the cloth, and your garment will be pulled up at the seams.

Pressing Darts.—Press these in the same way as a seam. The material at the point of the dart should be shrunk, if you are quite sure that water will not spoil the fabric. First take an odd piece of the material, put a damp cloth over it, and press. Notice the result. If there is no difference in the appearance, you can safely proceed. Place the garment flat on the table right side down, damp a small piece of the material, and place it over the point of the dart. Now take a hot iron and hold it ust a fraction of an inch away from the cloth. When no more team arises, examine the dart carefully, and if there still seems o be a little fullness, run a gathering thread in a circle round the oint. Put the roller under the dart and a damp cloth over it. Hold the iron on top, and wait until all the moisture has dried.

Pile Fabrics.—Velvets, velveteens, and fur fabrics must not be pressed as other materials, or the pile side will be crushed and the appearance spoiled.

Professional dressmakers have a special ironing-board for the purpose which looks and feels something like a wire brush. Velvet can be pressed on such a board with no harmful results, as the pile sinks between the wire bristles. Two wire brushes placed on a board and screwed down firmly from the back make a very good substitute for the professional article.

The usual way of pressing hems and seams in velvet is to pull them across an inverted iron. The fabric must be held firmly between the fingers to do this ; so to avoid making permanent marks, make yourself little velvet finger-stalls.

Long seams are best held out straight by two people while one passes the iron over the turnings.

To raise the Pile.—Sometimes a velvet garment becomes creased in the making, or the pile is flattened accidentally. To restore the appearance, try this simple process. Place a hot iron on its heel on a stand and put a wet cloth over it. Now hold the velvet close to the steam, and the pile will be raised. Face-cloth can be treated in the same way.

Pressing Fancy Materials.—Take great care when you are pressing artificial silks. They will not stand very much dry heat, and are inclined to shrivel up and become hard, like the wood pulp from which they are made.

Metal brocades quickly turn black and tarnish, so it is not wise to press them with a hot iron. It is a good plan to test scraps of material left over after cutting out to find out whether dry or wet pressing is the better treatment for them.

To remove the Glaze caused by an Iron.—If an iron has been left too long on one piece of material, or a cloth has not been placed between the material and the iron, a shiny patch is the result. This can usually be removed in the same way as described for raising the pile of velvet.

SHRINKING

(1) *Canvas*.—This is used to stiffen a collar or cuff of a coat. Before using canvas it must be shrunk, or the garment will lose its shape the first time it is damped by the rain.

Open out the canvas and damp a strip of it with a cloth wrung out of cold water. Then rub yellow soap over the damped portion. With a very hot iron run very lightly and quickly over the canvas, then press more heavily until it is quite dry.

(2) *Cotton Materials*.—Some cotton materials, especially piqué, drill, and linen, shrink a great deal in the first washing. It is a very simple matter to shrink such materials before cutting out a garment, and so save expense and disappointment later on.

Open out the material over the ironing sheet and blanket, tear off the selvedge, and place it face downwards on the table. Wring a piece of clean old sheet out of cold water and place it quite smoothly over the wrong side of the material. Then iron quickly and lightly over the damped cloth with a very hot iron. Iron more heavily until all the moisture has dried. Proceed in this way until the whole length has been shrunk.

Another way is to lay the cloth right side downwards on the damp cloth and then iron on the wrong side. Care must be taken not to scorch the material.

(3) *Woollen Materials*.—Nearly all woollen materials are shrunk before they are sold. It is not advisable for any home dressmaker to attempt to do this herself, as so many materials in these days depend on their surface for their novelty and charm. This could very easily be ruined by inexpert shrinking.

When a woollen garment is damped by the rain and shrinks, it can usually be put right again by careful pressing on the wrong side with not too hot an iron.

If you wish to shrink woollen material, it should be done in the same way as for cotton goods.

Fullness at the Top of a Sleeve or Skirt.—At the top of a sleeve a certain amount of fullness is required for freedom in movement, but it is not always the fashion for this fullness to be noticeable. The same applies to the fullness at the top of the skirt.

In each case run a gathering thread along the fitting line,

and snip the turnings. Dip your fingers into a bowl of water, shake off the drops, and then run them over the material, a little above and below the gathering thread. Have the gathers towards you at the edge of the table, and hold the iron over the damped material. If the material is very thick, damp and press again until the material shrinks sufficiently. Only damp a small piece of the top of the skirt at one time, and press that at once until it is dry.

Final Pressing.—This is the pressing that is done when the garment is finished. Carefully smooth away all creases with a moderately hot iron. The skirt can be pressed more easily if the garment is right side out. Put it flat on the table, lift up the top piece, and press the under piece on the wrong side.

A cloth must be placed over serge or any other material that is likely to become shiny in the pressing. Look the garment well over and notice whether any of the seams, facings, or hems need any further pressing.

TRIMMINGS

Frills.—These are always fashionable in some form or another. A gathered frill is generally cut on the bias to make it hang more gracefully, but a pleated or kilted frill must be cut with the selvedge threads running across the width of the flounce ; this means that the joins will be made parallel with the selvedge.

The strip of material for a frill is cut half as long again as the space it is to occupy, so that if a child's frock is 2 yards wide, the frill must be 3 yards long.

Frills of organdie and other thin materials can be made very full. If the frill is required to stand out from the garment, cut it two or three times as long as the space it will occupy.

The bottom of the frill can be picoted at a shop for about 2d. or 3d. a yard, or it can be finished by hand in any of the ways described at the end of this chapter.

A Gathered Frill.—First decide how wide you wish the frill to be, add to this amount an allowance for the heading at the top of the frill, and also for neatening the bottom edge. For instance, if the frill is to be 2 inches wide, allow ½ inch for a heading and ½ inch for a narrow hem at the bottom—that is, 3 inches altogether.

See Chapter IX., " Plain Sewing," for directions how to cut a strip of material on the bias and how to join such strips.

If the frill is long for gathering, fold it into four, six, or eight divisions according to its length, and mark them with pins or a tacking thread. Divide the space where the frill is to be fixed in the same way. This will help you to arrange the gathers quickly and evenly. If it is a short frill this will not be necessary.

The usual way of treating the top of a frill is to turn under about $\frac{1}{2}$ inch on to the wrong side, or $\frac{1}{4}$ inch of a narrow frill. Then run a gathering thread a short distance from the fold ; the amount depends on your own individual taste. Sometimes two, three, or even more gathering threads are used, especially in taffeta frills on an evening frock.

To attach the frill, first tack it into position, division mark to division mark, and back-stitch it invisibly. To do this, bring the needle out on to the right side between one of the folds, then put it in behind and bring it out farther on between another fold. In this way the folds will hide the stitches.

A net frill is sometimes cut on the straight, the edges top and bottom are left unneatened and attached to the garment by a row of machining worked over the gathering thread. Take great care in fixing such a frill, for it depends for its beauty on a crisp, new appearance ; the less it is handled the better.

A Gathered Frill on a Cuff or Collar.—Cut the frill as described before, but allow for only a small turning at the top. Neaten the bottom edge, and run two gathering threads $\frac{1}{4}$ inch from the top.

Place the collar or the cuff flat on the table, right side uppermost. Put the frill right side down, with the edges level with those of the collar. Pin them together at each end, and then pull up the gathering threads to the required size. Arrange the gathers evenly.

The frill and collar should be equally divided by pins or creases, if you think you cannot manage to arrange the gathers evenly.

If there is a corner on the collar, push plenty of fullness there, so that the frill edge will not be straightened out.

Tack the collar and the frill together, and then pin and tack the lining into position over the frill. Stitch by machine $\frac{1}{4}$ inch from the edge.   Snip the turnings and fold the collar on the right side.

Press the join on both sides, placing the collar flat and the frill standing out over the edge of the table.

A Frill attached to Single Material.—First Method : Sometimes a frill is needed at the edge of a single collar or short sleeve or jabot.   Prepare the frill in the usual way, and attach it to the edge as described for the double collar.   Now instead of placing the lining over the frill, use a crossway strip of material instead, and tack it into position with the raw edges quite level. Stitch the three thicknesses together.   Cut down the turnings, fold the strip over them, turn under the edge, and tack down the hem.   This hem can be made very narrow and stitched by machine from the right side, or a row of tiny French knots or stem stitch can be worked instead.

Second Method : Turn under the edge of the sleeve or collar, and place the fold to the first gathering thread of the frill.   Arrange the gathers evenly and tack securely.   Stitch by machine as close to the fold as possible.   Cut down the turnings and oversew them.

Another way to finish the wrong side is to turn under the raw edges of the sleeve for $\frac{3}{4}$ inch, or more if the material is not very thin.   Stitch as before, and then turn under the edge of the sleeve and fell it over the turnings.

A Kilted Frill.—Cut the frill on the straight with an allowance for neatening the bottom edge and $\frac{1}{4}$ inch for turnings at the top.   The frill must be three times as long as the space it is to occupy, as no space is left between the pleats, and each pleat takes up three times its own width—the top of the pleat, the under part, and the material the pleat rests on.

Finish off the lower edge of the frill, then place it flat on the table, with the edges to the left and right.   Now make the pleats, keeping each one straight to a thread, and pin them at the ends and in the middle.

It is a good plan to make notches on a card to guide you to get all the pleats exactly the same width.

When about 12 inches have been worked, tack the pleats with diagonal tacking, putting one stitch on each pleat, first at one side and then the other.   If the frill is wide, it must be tacked once or twice in the middle.

Remove the pins and proceed with the pleating. When it is complete, press the frill on the wrong side, under a damp cloth, if the material will stand damping. Otherwise, use a dry cloth, for the iron must be held for some time on each pleat.

Narrow frills that need fine pleating should be sent to the shop for kilting. Finish off the lower edge first.

Attach the frill in any of the ways previously described in this chapter.

A Frill joined into a Seam of a Dress.—A kilted frill is sometimes used as a trimming across the front of the bodice of a dress or down the sides or back of the skirt.

To attach the frill to the bodice, turn under the right-hand side to the fitting line and tack it over the edge of the frill. Pin the left side of the bodice in position under the frill, with the raw edges level. Tack and then stitch on the right side, as close to the fold as possible.

When the material is somewhat thick, it is not advisable to stitch through both sides of the bodice in this way. Attach the frill to the right-hand side, and then back-stitch the left into position by hand.

Frills on a skirt are usually joined into the seams. To do this, follow the directions given for attaching a frill to a collar, earlier in this chapter.

Box-Pleated Frill.—The same amount of material is needed for this as for a kilted frill.

Proceed in exactly the same way as before, but fold one pleat away from you and the next toward you, and so on alternately along the length of the frill. Use plenty of pins and then tack with diagonal tacking. Mark the width of the box-pleat by notches on a card, and use this to guide you to keep the pleat the same width the whole of its length.

A Simulated Box-Pleat.—Sometimes there is not enough material to make the pleats touch each other, and a space must be left between them, usually the same as the width of the pleats.

In this case notch the card for measuring the width the pleat is to be made, and again at the width of the whole box-pleat.

Make one pleat to fold away from you, using the first notch on the card ; now measure by the second notch, and make the second pleat the same width as the first, but folding toward you.

To make this kind of pleat, cut the material about one and a third times as long as the space it is to occupy.

The frills at the bottom of loose covers are generally made in this way.

A Box-Pleated Edging

Cut strips of material on the straight, twice as wide as the edging is to be when it is finished, with an allowance for turnings.

Join the strips together until it is three times as long as the edge to be trimmed. Open the seams and press them. Fold the strip in half lengthways and press with a warm iron.

Now make the pleats, first one towards you and then one away from you alternately. Use plenty of pins, and when the material is all pleated, tack it just above the raw edges with crêpe tacking.

Evening gowns are sometimes trimmed at the foot with a box-pleated edging.

It is a very usual trimming for a baby's bonnet.

A Box-Pleated Ruche

At present these are very fashionable, especially on evening frocks of taffeta or net.

The net should be cut on the straight, and the edges either left raw or turned down once and secured with a fancy stitch, or worked in embroidery cotton of matching or contrasting colour.

Sometimes, when the edges are left raw, a tinsel thread of gold or silver is run in and out of the net about two threads down from the edge of the ruche.

A taffeta ruche is often frayed at the edges. Cut the silk on the cross, and with a strong needle, or with the points of small scissors, fray out the edges.

A ribbon box-pleated ruche is being worn a great deal on hats.

Decide the width the ruche is to be, remembering that it always looks a little narrower when it is fastened down the middle. Cut it three times as long as required for the finished ruching. Make the box-pleat from $\frac{3}{4}$ inch to $1\frac{1}{2}$ inch wide, and allow the pleats to meet on the wrong side in the same way as described for a box-pleated frill. Tack down the middle of the ruche.

To attach the ruching, pin it into position on the frock, and then either work a row of fancy stitches down the middle, or secure it on the wrong side by small running stitches.

A Double Box-Pleated Ruche

Cut the strips of material five times as long as the finished ruche. Neaten the edges, and then pleat it. Make one pleat away from you, another the same width exactly on top, and then pleat towards you in the same way.

A double or treble box-pleated ruche should be used for net or very thin silk materials. To give the ruche a more dainty appearance the top pleat on each side is often sewn together at the edge. This is a very popular way of outlining the neck of a backless evening gown.

To avoid the necessity for neatening the edge of the ruche, the material may be used double, provided it will not give a clumsy appearance. Cut the material on the straight and twice the width the ruche is to be, and a little extra for turnings. Fold the sides of the material over to the middle to slightly overlap, and press with an iron. Make the pleats in the usual way, pin and tack them down the middle.

Tack them in position on the garment, and stitch by machine or in any other way that has been previously described.

A Gathered Ruche

This is more easily made than a pleated ruche. Cut out the material for a taffeta ruche on the cross if the edges are to be frayed, as straight edges that are frayed are too stiff to be dainty.

When the edges are to be neatened in any other way, cut them on the straight to simplify matters.

The ruche should be made as full as possible and not too wide, or the sides will fall down instead of standing up.

A narrow, full ruche can be gathered just once, down the middle, and sewn on to the garment by invisible stitches placed between the gathers, but wide ruches must be treated differently.

A very dainty way to gather a ruche is to work three tiny

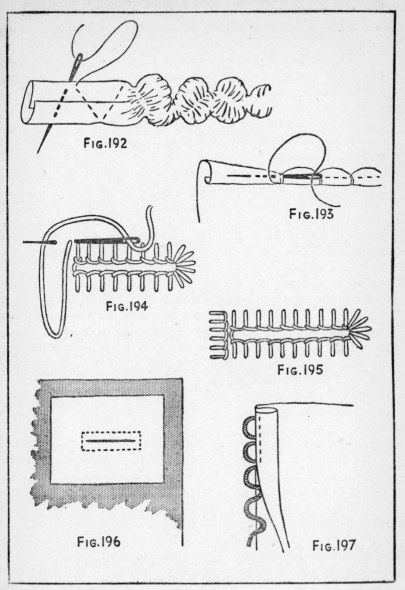

FIG. 192.—Shell Edging.   FIG. 193.—Shell Hemming.   FIG. 194.—Buttonhole with needle in position for working the square end.   FIG. 195.—Buttonhole.   FIG. 196.—Working bound buttonhole.   FIG. 197.—Loop Fastening
for blouse.

tucks down the middle, and then pull them up to the required length.

Cut out the ruche, making an allowance for turnings at the edges and for the tucks in the middle. Neaten the outside edges of the ruche, then fold it in half, right side outside. Now run in the first tuck about $\frac{1}{8}$ inch in width, then two more, one each side of the first, of the same width. Draw up the threads to the required length and fasten them off on the wrong side.

Occasionally a ruche is drawn up by means of a piping cord. Use a very fine one for evening frocks; a fine white string will often serve the purpose.

Run the tucks as described above, but instead of drawing them up, insert the piping cord and draw up the ruche to the required length. Wider tucks must be worked if a thick piping cord is to be used. Attach the ruche to the garment down the two outside edges of the cords.

Sometimes only one cord is used in the middle to draw up the ruche. In this case attach it to the garment on the right side, by taking a stitch first on one side of the cord and then one on the other.

A Ruched Band of Trimming

This is seldom used except on net or taffeta frocks, when it is a very popular form of trimming.

It is used round the neck and sleeves of frocks and sometimes round the hem, where loops of the trimming are formed at regular intervals.

In silk dressing-jackets and dressing-gowns it is an ideal trimming. There are two ways of making it.

The first is quick and easy. Cut the material on the cross as wide as the band is required, with 1 inch extra for turnings. Turn under $\frac{1}{2}$ inch on each side and press with an iron. Gather both sides $\frac{1}{4}$ inch from the edge, and draw it up to the required size. Run two tacking threads on the garment where the edges of the ruche are to be sewn. If this is not done, it is difficult to keep the trimming the same width along its length, especially when it is formed into loops or any other pattern on the skirt of an evening frock. For a neck or sleeve, the amount of trimming must be cut off and joined into a round before beginning to fix it to the garment.

In the second method the sides of the ruche are piped. First cover the piping cord with a crossway strip of material, as described in the Plain Needlework Section. Gather the ruche $\frac{1}{4}$ inch from the raw edges and then tack the cord on top, with all the turnings level. Stitch into place by hand or by machine. Prepare the garment in the same way as in the first method and tack the ruche into position, with the turnings tucked under it. Secure it by slip stitches on the right side or running stitches on the wrong side.

When this ruche is made narrow, say 1 inch in width, it makes a very pretty trimming for children's party frocks.

A ruched band of trimming put across the corners of an eiderdown, or a large circle put in the middle, is very effective.

METHODS OF FINISHING THE EDGES OF FRILLS, RUCHES, AND OTHER ARTICLES

(*a*) *Picot Edging*.—This is done by most cleaning agents and fancy-work shops. Hemstitching costs a little less, so if you wish to economise ask the shop to hemstitch the material and then cut off one side of it yourself, when the result will be the same as a picot edge. Run a tacking thread $\frac{1}{4}$ inch from the edge that you want hemstitched before taking it to the shop. Be sure to get this quite straight, as it is used as a guiding thread when the work is executed.

A picot edge is only suitable for thin materials such as georgette, wool or silk, crêpe de Chine, or organdie.

A smart finish is often given to an edging if it is picoted with silk of contrasting colour—a white or yellow frill edged with black or red, a black frill edged with white, and so on.

(*b*) *A Whipped Edge*.—If there are more than a few yards to be finished, do not start to whip the edges, for it will take you too long. When the material is thin, whipping is quite a good way of neatening the edges, unless it is cut on the cross. In this case do not attempt whipping, as it is very difficult to prevent the edge from stretching, and to make a neat, tight roll. The directions for whipping will be found in Chapter IX., " Plain Needlework."

Silk of contrasting colour may be used for sewing the roll, and often gives a smart finish. The edges of net frills can be oversewn as in whipping, without first rolling the edge. A contrasting silk or tinsel thread is always used in this case.

(*c*) *Plain Hem.*—Fold, tack, and press this in the usual way and then stitch it on the right side with matching silk. This method is only suitable for a pleated frill of fine woollen material, such as would be attached to the front of a bodice.

A very narrow hem turned down with a warm iron and then secured with running stitches about $\frac{1}{8}$ inch long is suitable for thin materials. Use embroidery silk for the running, and take care to make the stitches of equal length.

(*d*) *Machine Edge.*—This is suitable for thin wool or silk materials that do not fray easily. Turn down about $\frac{1}{8}$ inch on to the wrong side, using a warm iron. Stitch by machine on the right side, as close to the edge as possible, and then cut away any loose ends of the material at the back.

(*e*) *Hemstitched Edge.*—This is a very pretty way of finishing the edge of a georgette frill down the front of a dress. For working the hemstitching by hand, see Chapter V., " Embroidery Stitches." The more usual way is to have the work done at a shop, in the same way as the picoting. For this method, prepare the hem in the ordinary way, and tack it securely, close to the edge. Machine-worked hemstitching in contrasting colour is very effective.

(*f*) *A French Hem.*—This is suitable for a narrow velvet frill that is sometimes sewn on to an evening cloak. Directions for the hem will be found in Chapter IX., " Plain Sewing and Trimmings for Plain Sewing."

FOLDS

A fold of material is sometimes used as a means of finishing and trimming the wrist of a tight-fitting sleeve, the edge of a velvet evening cape, or anywhere when gathers are joined to a straight part of a garment, in order to hide the seam.

Sometimes a bodice is cut into various pieces, according to the fashion ; a fold of the material is often stitched over the seam of such pieces in order to accentuate the lines.

To prepare such a fold, cut crossways strips of material twice the width of the fold and $\frac{1}{4}$ inch extra for turnings. Turn down this $\frac{1}{4}$ inch on to the wrong side, then slip the other edge under it and tack it into place.

Press the fold lightly on the wrong side. Place the tacked edge just over the seam and no farther. Hold the seam over the left hand and tack the fold down, easing it, but not gathering it, over the rounded parts of the seam.

Stitch by machine as close to the edge as possible. Stretch the outer edges of the fold where it is necessary, in order to make it lie flat. Press under a cloth on the wrong side.

A French Fold.—This is generally made of velvet. Cut strips of material $1\frac{1}{2}$ inch wide, on the cross, join them and press open the seams. Make sure that the pile of the velvet is running in the same direction. Pull the strip lengthways to stretch it. This helps to make the fold set flat when it is finished.

Fold both edges on the wrong side and the upper one again like a hem. Slip-stitch this fold down, taking up a tiny piece of the lower edge and a long stitch in the fold of the upper edge.

Do not tack the fold to the garment or it will become flattened, and the whole beauty of it is spoilt. Slip-stitch it into position on the right side or by running stitches on the wrong side.

A French fold is often used as a slot to keep a belt in position, or to hold down the ends of a scarf. Sometimes two or three folds are joined together by faggoting to form a trimming for the neck of a blouse or edge of a cuff.

Never cut a fold from material on the straight, or the edges will poke out and look very ugly.

SHIRRING (see also Chapter XI. for Italian Smocking or Shirring)

This is rows of gathering made at equal distances. It is often used at the top of a full sleeve of thin material, or on the collar of a velvet coatee.

The beauty of shirring depends on its being worked evenly ; so decide on the depth of the space between the rows of gathering and notch a card to guide you.

Fasten on firmly with a back stitch, and make sure that you have enough cotton to finish the row. The cotton should be strong so that it will not break when the gathers are pulled up.

If the material is thin, the work can be easily and quickly done with fly-running. (See " Stitches.")

The gathering can be done with the machine, but it never looks so dainty as when done by hand.

Use a large stitch, and loosen the tension and work rows of machining at equal distances. When all the rows have been worked, pull up the under thread slowly and carefully, and then pull up the upper thread. If one should break, the ones that have already been pulled up must be flattened as much as possible, before the row is machined in again. The ends of the cotton can be tied together or fastened off with a back stitch.

Tucked Shirring. — This is only worked on thin, dainty materials. The fullness of hanging draperies on evening frocks is often taken up by tucked shirring, and it gives a very pretty effect.

Run tacking threads at equal distances across the material to be shirred, not forgetting to allow for the tuck. Fold the material on the tacking line and run the tuck at the desired depth. Draw up and secure the threads in the same way as before.

Corded Shirring.—This is used for the same purposes in dressmaking as tucked shirring.

Prepare the material in the same way, and then run the tucks. Thread a bodkin with strong cotton and attach it to the end of the piping cord. Now run the bodkin through the tucks, and pull the material carefully over the cord. Arrange the fullness evenly on each cord, so that the material is not twisted between the rows.

When the corded shirring is to be used as a trimming and not as a means of gathering part of a garment, the material should be cut on the cross. The fullness between each cord will then be more puffed and will not lie flat.

Use fine cord or string for a frock, and space the tucks not more than ½ inch apart. A group of two or three and then a space is effective.

For puffed or ruched cushions the cords may be quite thick, and the tucks run at any distance apart, in groups or otherwise.

When a round cushion is being made, join the material before working the tucks. At the end of each one, unthread the needle and leave 1 inch open for inserting the cord. Then, when all the tucks are finished, put in the cords, pull them up to the desired length, and sew them together end to end with strong oversewing stitches. Re-thread the needle, finish the tuck, and fasten off.

Some people find it easier to run the tuck and at the same time insert the cord. To do this, put in the tacking lines for guiding, in the same way. Then put the piping cord on the wrong side, underneath the tacking thread, and run the tuck as close up to it as possible.

The danger in this is that it is difficult not to catch up a thread or two of the piping cord; in which case the cord will pull the sewing cotton and break it, and the tuck must be run again.

Shell Trimming or Edging (Fig. 192)

This is not used on dresses, but it can be put on almost anything else.

These are some of its uses : to edge the lining of a fur coat, an evening cloak, or a fur tie ; to finish the edge of a coat pocket, or the inside lining of a silk bag. It is a charming little trimming for a wool or silk dressing-jacket. It can be made any width, but it must be cut on the cross.

For an edging for a coat lining, cut the strips $1\frac{1}{2}$ inch wide and join them by the selvedge until you have a long length. Turn the two edges over to the middle of the wrong side. A warm iron will do this very quickly and easily.

Use silk to exactly match the material, and work from right to left.

Fasten on with a back stitch at the top of the fold, work small running stitches across the strip in a slanting direction ; now work to the top in the same way, and so on, up and down along the entire length.

When you come to the end of a thread, draw it up carefully, arrange the gathers evenly, and fasten off with a back stitch. A little shell-shaped edge is thus formed. To attach it to the garment, pin it into position and then secure it by invisible back stitches placed between the folds of the material.

Shell Hemming (Fig. 193)

This has very much the same appearance as shell binding (see Chapter IX.). It is useful for quickly finishing off the edges of an organdie collar or cuff of a cotton frock, or the neck and sleeves of a silk nightgown or any other lingerie.

Turn down a narrow hem, not more than $\frac{1}{4}$ inch, and tack it. Fasten on by making a back stitch right over the hem, make small running stitches for about $\frac{1}{2}$ inch ; then again make two more stitches over the hem, pulling the cotton tightly, and so on along the entire length.

The distance between the back stitches depends on the material and on your own personal taste.

Shell Tucking

This is only suitable for thin materials. Sometimes a thick frock, say of velvet, has an inset or shaped yoke of georgette. The effect is charming if the whole of it is shell-tucked.

Work the tucks before cutting out the shape of the inset.

There are two ways of making the tucks. The first way is to run the tucks in curved lines. Begin about $\frac{1}{4}$ inch from the top of the fold, make about four running stitches in a curve, to bring the needle to the edge of the fold. Now make four more in a curve, the last one $\frac{1}{4}$ inch down from the fold. Continue in this way along the length, making each scallop about $\frac{1}{2}$ to $\frac{3}{4}$ inch in width. The running cotton is pulled up a very little to give the edge a scalloped appearance. It is easier to work all the tucks before drawing them up.

The second way is more simple, and is similar to the working of shell hemming. Work four or five running stitches in a tuck not more than $\frac{1}{4}$ inch in width, then make a back stitch pulled tightly over the tuck, and continue working the running and back stitches alternately. The size of the scallop depends on the width of the tuck, and they will look more dainty when worked on the cross of the material.

Stitching

Rows of stitching, worked at equal distances, gives a garment a smart, neat finish, whether it is worked in matching or contrasting colour to the material.

The collar, cuff, or belt to be stitched should be made and thoroughly pressed beforehand. Begin at the outside edge and machine as close as possible to it. Lift the foot at each angle or corner, turn the work to the correct position, and proceed with the stitching. Unless this is done, the corners will probably become rounded and the appearance quite spoilt, as the beauty of stitching depends on its regularity.

The space between each row of stitching is usually $\frac{1}{4}$ inch, and this can be gauged by the foot of the machine. If it is a very narrow belt or collar, it is advisable to work the rows of stitching $\frac{1}{8}$ inch apart.

A skirt made of a heavy tweed or cloth for country wear is often finished at the foot with rows of stitching. Turn the hem up once, the required depth, press on the wrong side under a cloth, then work the stitching, beginning at the fold.

A quickly worked trimming, suitable for a child's winter frock, can be made by filling the spool of the machine with embroidery cotton or buttonhole twist instead of the ordinary cotton. Slightly loosen the tension and work the stitching on the wrong side of the garment. A large stitch gives a bolder effect than a small one.

Another way is to work the stitching with matching cotton, but rather loosely and with a large stitch. Now thread a needle with thick embroidery silk, and work over every other stitch of the machining, always putting the needle in at the same side and bringing it out at the other. It is easier to put the eye of the needle in first, so that threads of the material are not caught up.

Simple outlines of animals on rompers, feeders, and so on, can be quickly worked in this way.

Diamond or oval shapes stitched three or four times, $\frac{1}{4}$ inch apart, make good trimmings for a coat for a little boy, while a triangular shape, partly or wholly filled with stitching, is a neat trimming for a pocket on any frock or suit.

Stitching, placed $\frac{1}{4}$ inch apart and worked over a space of 6 or 7 inches, makes a smart yet cheap trimming for the present fashionable puff sleeves. In this case work the stitching before setting in the sleeve and before the cuff is attached.

EMBROIDERY

Embroidery in some form or another is generally fashionable. It gives the individuality, that so many people appreciate, to the dress made at home, and to the ready-made dress the worker can add a finish that will make it very different from the original.

Simple designs and stitches, if worked in the right colour-schemes, can be as effective as elaborate embroideries.

When choosing a design, make sure that it suits the style and material of the dress. A stiff geometrical design, however beautiful, would spoil a pretty frock, and a flower design would ruin a smart one.

Cross-stitch embroidery can be worked by any one, even if they have very little skill. Transfers can be bought, with the crosses marked, for working on materials where the threads are too fine to be counted.

Full directions for working the cross stitches and all embroidery stitches will be found in Chapters II., III., IV., V., VI., VII., and VIII.

BEAD EMBROIDERY

This is another kind of embroidery that does not require skill. It is more often worked on transparent materials than on thick ones.

Tack the transfer on to the wrong side, and sew on the beads through the material and the paper. When the work is complete, pull the transfer gently away.

There are two ways of attaching the beads. In the first, bring the needle out on to the right side and fasten on strongly ; thread a bead on the cotton, make a back stitch, and bring the cotton out $\frac{1}{4}$ inch farther along the design, and so on.

In the second way, the beads are threaded on a strong cotton, and caught down to the material with a stitch taken between the beads, as in couching a thread.

APPLIQUÉ

This is not much used on frocks in fancy designs, but geometrical-shaped pieces are very effective on cuffs, collar, or scarf ends to give a touch of colour.

Small round pieces of felt in different sizes and colours, arranged as your fancy dictates, and sewn on with a cross stitch in the middle, are gay and unusual.

The method of working the appliqué will be found in Chapter VIII.

Usually the best results are obtained, not by buying a transfer design, but by " cutting your garment according to your cloth " —that is, getting out all the scraps of material you have that tone with or are in contrast to the frock, then picking out the ones that you like best, and cutting them into shapes suitable for the parts they are to adorn.

As to the shapes, the simpler they are the better. A great deal can be done with triangles. Three cut out in different coloured materials, and sewn to the garment, each one slightly overlapping the other, is one idea. The same can be done with circles, half-circles, squares, or oblongs.

Once you have started arranging pieces for appliqué, you will realise its endless possibilities.

Triangles placed with the base of each in a straight line, or the base and apex in a straight line, makes a good border to go round such places as the full part of a sleeve.

Here are some other ideas. An oblong, with a smaller one on each side ; a square and a circle placed alternately ; a half-circle and a triangle alternately.

For children's frocks, scarves, and other articles of thin materials, conventional flowers are generally used. These can be cut out as quickly and easily as the geometrical patterns, even if you are not an artist.

A flower border for a child's frock can be made in the following way :

Cut out circles of material with an eggcup or coffee-cup. Several can be cut at the same time if the material is not too thick. Fold the circle into four, shape the edges, cutting off a tiny piece along the folds, and then cut off a piece in the centre of the circle. Open it out and you will find you have a flower shape. Stick the flowers with paste round the hem of the frock, leaving $\frac{1}{4}$ inch between each one.

Secure the flowers in any of the methods described in the Embroidery Section.

The centre of the flower can be filled with French knots to resemble stamens, or a few lazy-daisy stitches worked in a circle.

A design of this description looks equally well round the neck of a georgette frock or on the end of a crêpe de Chine scarf. In the latter case, the flowers should not be in straight lines but in any way that seems pleasing.

After you have worked such a design as this you will realise your own capabilities, and probably begin something much more ambitious.

An original design of your own will give you more joy in the working of it and in the wearing of the garment than one bought at the shop, and it will cost you nothing.

Crochet Trimmings

To most people this probably sounds very dull, as they begin to remember the crochet mats and antimacassars they have seen in the homes of their grandmothers.

Crochet trimmings can be very smart if they are worked in the right colour and in a style to suit the frock, and they are hard wearing and wash well.

Medallions, not necessarily round ones, worked in gold or silver thread, look well let into the sleeve of a transparent frock.

A child's school frock, say of navy blue, can be brightened by the addition of a crochet edging on the cuffs and collars, worked in different colours.

To do this, turn under the raw edge of the collar, and stitch by machine close to the fold. Cut down the turnings and then, with a fine steel hook, work over them with double crochet. Work several more rows, each one in a different colour or all alike, just as you please. Of course, if you are a good worker, you will prefer to make an elaborate edging, but the simple double crochet is very smart.

If the material is too thick to enable you to make the first row of double crochet, the edge must be blanket-stitched or knot-stitched, and the crochet worked into the loops.

For the method of working the crochet and the stitches, see Chapter XXIV., " Crochet," and Chapter XVI., " Wool Craft."

CROCHET BUTTONS

Any one who can work a chain and a double crochet can make crochet buttons. It is very much cheaper to make them than to buy fancy buttons to trim a frock.

When you cannot find the right shade of button for your dress, let a crochet button come to the rescue.

A chain joined into a circle and worked round with double crochet, until it is large enough to cover the button, is the simplest way of covering a button mould, but any small medallion pattern could be used instead.

It is generally necessary to cover the mould with a piece of material first, then slip over the crochet and draw the edges together tightly.

Round buttons can be stuffed with balls of cotton-wool.

If a crochet chain is used to join two buttons together, a pretty link fastening is made suitable for a front opening of a dress or for the sleeves of a fancy blouse.

FASTENINGS

BUTTONHOLES (Fig. 194)

Work buttonholes on double material. If one is required on single material, a piece of tape or small piece of material must be felled on the wrong side.

Cut the slit carefully. If it has jagged edges you cannot work a good buttonhole. Make a clean cut with buttonhole scissors about ⅛ inch longer than the button.

If you have not any proper scissors, scratch the position of the buttonhole with a needle straight to a thread. Put a pin in at one end and bring it out at the other, and then fold the buttonhole in half. Keep the pin in the material so that one-half of the slit is exactly over the other, and then with sharp scissors make a small snip. Take out the pin, put the scissors into the hole that you have made, and cut first to one end and then to the other end of the scratch.

Use stronger cotton for buttonholes than you use for ordinary sewing. Buttonhole twist is best for flannel and woollen garments.

Some people find it a help to work a few oversewing stitches down each side of the slip before buttonholing it. This should be done with material that frays easily.

Take enough cotton to work round the slit : 1 yard is sufficient for a 1-inch buttonhole, ¾ yard is sufficient for a ¾-inch hole, and so on.

The working of the buttonhole stitch has been already described in Chapter II.

Fig. 194 shows an ordinary horizontal buttonhole with the round end towards the edge of the garment. The method of working it is as follows : Work from left to right, with the edge away from the worker. Begin by inserting the needle between the layers about 1 inch from the hole. (The end of the thread will be cut off against the surface.) Take a back stitch or two quite near the hole. Work the stitch with the thread from the eye passing under the point of the needle in the direction of working. Draw the knot home ; grip the stitches already worked under the left thumb and pull against this grip. When you come to the round end (Fig. 194), work this with plain over-and-over stitches and *no knot*. Be careful to radiate all the stitches evenly from one point. Nine stitches are generally needed, sometimes only seven. Work the second side the same as the first, then get the needle into position for working the square end (Fig. 195). A bar can be made here, if desired, for extra strength ; to make a bar, make one or two stitches from one end of the buttonholing to the other, and buttonhole over this bar, but catching up the material as well.

A buttonhole in the front of a shirt or nightgown is usually made with two square or barred ends. To do this, work one edge of the slit, turn the work round and work the second edge, and the bar as described above, then slip the needle to the opposite end, and work a second buttonholed bar, then fasten off.

If the cotton should break while making a buttonhole, cut off the old thread, leaving about ¼ inch. Slip the needle with the new thread through the folds of the material and bring it out in the knot of the last stitch. Work on in the usual way, keeping the old end of cotton at the top of the raw edges.

Making a Buttonhole cut on the Cross.—On rompers and on the yokes of children's frocks a buttonhole has often to be cut across the threads (that is, on the bias). In this case the hole must be stranded or strengthened. To do this, lay a couching thread along each edge of the slit, quite near the edge, securing it from pulling up by a tiny back stitch. Then to hold the couched thread and prevent fraying of the cut edges, without cutting off the stranding thread, use the rest of it to take a few widely spaced overcasting stitches over both slit and stranding thread. Then work the buttonhole stitches as already described.

Working a Buttonhole in Thick Material.—Holes on thick material are shaped at the round end. Cut the slit in the usual way and then at the end nearest the edge of the garment make two little snips at right angles to the slit. Now cut off these small corners of material and you will have an enlarged end which will enable the hole to set properly over the button.

If there are three thicknesses of material where a buttonhole has to be made, take a fine but strong cotton or silk and oversew them together all round the slit. Work the stitches close to one another and be sure that all the edges are quite level. Then work the buttonholing as before, using buttonhole twist or waxed thread ; but in buttonholing only take up as much material as is necessary to make a firm edge. When the slits are covered put two strands of thread across the end and buttonhole over them, only taking up the material which lies under the threads. Buttonholes worked on thick materials over very little depth of stitch are called *Tailor Buttonholes*. The stitches are generally taken over a waxed thread. If these are too difficult for the average home dressmaker, a working tailor will do them for a few pence when they are in fashion for coats or tailored dresses.

Bound Buttonholes

These are slits bound with self or contrasting material. The bind is usually on the straight thread. They are useful in silk or wool materials that fray very quickly. They are quick and easy to make. There are two methods.

First Method.—Carefully mark the position of the hole with a tacking thread, and do not cut it. Now cut a crossway strip of binding material 1 inch longer than the hole and 1½ inch wide. Place this strip over the buttonhole mark, *right* sides together ; from the wrong side tack the position of the buttonhole on to the strip. Now frame all round the buttonhole mark with

back-stitching or machine-stitching; keep as close to the tacking
thread as possible, $\frac{1}{16}$ inch in the case of thick material, but $\frac{1}{8}$ inch
if the threads are likely to fray (some workers make this back
stitched border $\frac{1}{4}$ inch away). Fig. 196 shows the buttonhole
slit marked on the binding material and a frame of back stitches
worked around it.

Cut the slit exactly on the tacking thread through both
thicknesses of material, and then make snips at each corner
very nearly to the line of stitching. Bring the binding material
through the slit to the wrong side, so that the raw edges of the
slit are covered as in a bind. Trim away any surplus material
turn in the raw edges, and hem them down. At each end
arrange the corners neatly in a tiny pleat. This bound button
hole is always made on a double thickness.

Second Method.—A bound buttonhole for decorative purposes
only, or as a slit through which a scarf is pulled, is sometimes
needed on thin materials, such as georgette, organdie, or crêpe
de Chine. The first method is unsuitable, as the turnings would
show through on the right side.

For this method, mark the position of the slit as before with
a tacking thread. Cut a crossway strip 1 inch wide, fold it in
half right side out, and stretch it under a warm iron. Now cut
two pieces off $\frac{1}{2}$ inch longer than the slit, and tack them one on
each side of the tacking thread, raw edges meeting. Stitch by
hand, or machine, each side of the slit represented by the tacking
thread and $\frac{1}{8}$ inch (or more) from the raw edges. Cut the buttonhole on the tacking thread, push the turnings through to the
wrong side, and fell the folded edge exactly over the stitching
Press carefully. The turnings at each end of the hole must be
cut down and overcast or buttonholed. While doing this, make
a few invisible stitches from one side to the other to protect the
ends of the slits.

SEWING ON BUTTONS

Buttons may actually fasten some part of a garment or be
merely ornamental. Space them carefully; the only way to do
this is to mark the position of each beforehand with chalk or a
pin.

Buttons that are for use must be attached to a double thickness of material. Provide the second, if necessary, by putting a small square of stuff behind the spot where the button will be sewn, or, where a long line of buttons are to be attached, tack a strip of tape on the wrong side, and then when the buttons are all secured, remove the tacking stitches. When there is to be a great deal of strain on the button, sew a small button on the wrong side of the garment at the same time as the one on the right. This small button will take the strain, and so prevent the garment from being pulled out of shape.

Remember when sewing on buttons that you must leave room between the button and the material to which it is sewn to allow for the thickness of the buttonhole—the amount of room depends on the buttonhole. So give your button a shank or stalk of suitable length. When sewing buttons on thin fabrics hold a pin across the button and take your stitches over it. Draw out the pin, and gently pull the button away from the material, then pass your cotton firmly round and round the strands until you have made a strong little stalk or shank. For a longer shank use a match-stick instead of a pin. You need this on boys' clothes, coats, etc. When the shank is made, take the needle to the wrong side and finish off with two or three back stitches. When sewing on buttons that serve as trimming, carry the cotton from one to the other on the wrong side, instead of fastening off each time. It is quicker and just as strong.

When sewing on buttons with shanks, let the flat way of the shank be parallel with the bottom hem of the garment and the stitches parallel with centre front or back.

BUTTONHOLED LOOPS

On dainty blouses, at the openings at wrist and neck, and on babies' robes, a buttonhole makes a clumsy fastening, so buttonholed loops are worked.

Use sewing cotton or buttonhole twist when working on wool or silk materials, and embroidery thread for cotton materials.

Fasten the thread with a back stitch on the wrong side, and bring the needle out at the edge of the garment. Put it in again a short distance to the right ($\frac{3}{8}$ inch for a $\frac{1}{4}$-inch button), and bring it out at the starting-place. Make this loop of cotton slack enough to pass easily over the button. Make two or three more

15

loops in the same way, and then buttonhole over them, making the stitches close together and pulling the cotton tight. To fasten off, take the needle to the wrong side, make a back stitch, and then run the needle between the folds.

In working a row of loops, carry straight on from one to the next with the same thread. To make the second exactly the same size as the first, cut a slip of cardboard that will go through the first and make the loop stitches of the second over this, or work them over a pencil.

Buttonholed Bars

These are used instead of sewn-on eyes. Work the bar in the same way as the loop, but keep the strands quite flat to the garment. Use the eye of the needle when working over the strands and take care not to pick up any of the threads of the material, as the bar must be quite free. A bar like this can be worked at the waist of a frock or coat, large enough for a belt to be slipped through. For buttonholed bars, see also Chapter V.

To Cover Button Moulds

Wooden moulds can be bought in sizes and shapes, and are very useful when a particular colour is wanted to match a dress.

They can be covered with scraps of ribbon, silk, or velvet. The best parts of old white kid gloves (if they are clean) make very smart and unusual button coverings for a navy blue or black frock.

Cut the material large enough to cover the whole button, oversew the edge, and draw it up loosely. Slip in the button, draw up very closely, put in a stitch or two to secure it, and fasten off. Fell a small round of material over the raw edges.

The button may be embroidered with very striking results. A few brightly coloured French knots in a circle, square, or star are easily worked, or a flower in daisy stitch is very dainty and effective.

When using kid or any thin material to cover the button, use a lining, or the shape of the mould will show through.

Loop Fastening (Fig. 197)

This is very fashionable at present, especially for the back opening for blouses or dresses.

First make a tubing of the same material as the dress. Cut a strip on the cross, ⅜ inch wide (the width depends on the size of the button). It is wise, perhaps, to practise first on strips twice this width. Double the strip lengthwise, with the right side inside, and machine along the edges with the narrowest possible turnings. Now turn the tube so formed right side out in this way : slip a bodkin into one end of the tube, with its eye end sticking out a little. With needle and cotton sew the eye rather loosely to the end of the tube. Then push the bodkin straight through the tube. It will draw the attached end with it as it goes, and so turn the whole tube right side out. Belts and shoulder straps are made in this way (see section on Belts).

Turn down the back of the blouse for 1 inch on to the wrong side, and then tack the tubing into position to form loops, as in Fig. 197. (If the material is thick, it is better to cut each loop the required length and attach it separately.) Stitch on the right side ⅛ inch from the edge, then on the wrong side, fold the turnings over the raw edges and fell down neatly, as in Fig. 197. The loops may be made of fine cord instead of material.

Fine tubes of cross-cut material, called rouleaux, are made in the above way to decorate dresses.

EYELET HOLES

These are used for an outlet for a draw-string in babies' clothes, so that the garment can be wrapped over and fastened neatly. In ready-made garments the tape is very often brought out at the ends of the band ; this makes an untidy fastening. If the garment wraps over for an inch, make the eyelets ½ inch in from the edge on the single material, one on the upper and one on the under side, so that when the tape is tied it is quite invisible.

These eyelet holes are very much better than metal eyes for making a fastening with hooks on shoulder or wrist openings of dresses. The fastenings set flatter, and there is less chance of the hooks showing.

The making of eyelet holes has already been described in Chapter IV., when writing about broderie anglaise. Make the hole with a stiletto, bring the needle between the folds of the material to the edge of the hole, and then oversew the edge, making the stitches close together and very tight. Fasten off with a back stitch on the wrong side. Use buttonhole twist if the eyelet is to receive a hook, and embroidery cotton for other purposes.

HOOKS AND EYES

There are many ways of sewing on these fastenings, and strength and neatness must be considered.

Use buttonhole twist or cotton to match the material. Mark the positions of all the hooks and eyes to be sewn on. A hook must not be seen when the opening is fastened, so put the end at least $\frac{1}{8}$ inch inside the edge. Fasten on with a back stitch, make two or three stitches over the shank, and two or three at the top of the hook. Now buttonhole the rings of wire on to the material. Some people prefer to buttonhole all round the eye, so that no metal shows at all.

Never sew hooks and eyes on to single material. When this is necessary, put a piece of tape on to the wrong side of the material, and sew them to this at the same time.

STUD FASTENERS

Sew these on by making several stitches through each hole, over the edge, and through the material. Always sew them to double material in the same way as hooks and eyes.

ZIP FASTENERS

These are very useful in making an edge-to-edge fastening in thick materials. Close the zip and put the metal tag at the end of the opening. Sandwich the braid between the garment and its lining, and stitch as close to the metal as possible.

Loop several strands of wool through the tag or make a neat loop of material and attach it to the tag.

BELTS

Decide on the width and length of the belt. The length of the belt must always be cut selvedge way, so that it will not stretch.

Cut a strip of material the length of the belt, plus an allowance for wrap-over and turnings; the width must be double that desired for the belt plus turnings. Fold the strip in half engthways, right sides together, and stitch ¼ inch from the raw edges. Turn it right side out, as described for "Looped Fastening," and fold it so that the join comes at one edge or ¼ inch in from he edge. On the left-hand side of the belt (the under part), fold in the turnings and slip-stitch them together. The other end that overlaps is usually mitred. The easiest way to do this s to fold the belt in half lengthways, right side inside, and back-stitch it ¼ inch from the raw edges. Open the material and turn out the corner. Use the scissors or a bodkin to push the corner into a sharp point. Hem down the straight edge.

Work eyelet holes with buttonhole twist at regular intervals. Press the belt, and attach the buckle.

If the belt is to be trimmed by rows of stitching, work it after the mitre has been made and the pressing done.

Belts are often piped, and directions for this will be found in the Plain Needlework Section. Stitch the piping round the edge of the belt, and then top-hem the lining into place.

A belt is sometimes fastened with hooks and eyes or stud fasteners, and then the pointed end is slipped under a loop of material, made in the same way as the tubing (see "Loop Fastening").

POCKETS

Only the simplest are given here, for the more elaborate ones are used only on tailored garments, and are not wanted by the average home dressmaker.

Slot or Bound Pocket or Jumper Pocket.—This simple pocket is suitable for children's wear and washing garments, for plain jumpers, and little boys' rompers, etc. It is made very much like the bound buttonholes.

Mark the position of the mouth of the pocket with a line of tacking or with chalk. Centre over it a strip of self-material about 10 inches long and 1½ inch wider than the pocket opening. Be careful to put strip right side downwards. Mark the mouth on this exactly over the mark on the garment. Tack the strip to the garment well outside the marked line. Machine-stitch round in a long oval curve, as in Fig. 198. Begin machining at the lower centre, not at a corner. Begin from the middle, and cut each way along the mouth line to within two or three threads of the stitching. Pull the two halves of the strip through the slit to the wrong side as for a bound buttonhole, and tack them twice to the edges of the slit, once close to the edge and again $\frac{1}{4}$ inch away. Machine-stitch all round the opening $\frac{1}{16}$ inch from the edge. Machine-stitch along the outer line of tacking. Turn the work over on the wrong side. Form the pouch by pressing the upper half of the strip well downwards over the lower half, fit the two halves properly, round the corners, and seam them. Overcast the raw edges.

Figs. 199 and 200 show another bound pocket. Notice how the cuts go to the corners of the stitching in Fig. 199.

A Welt Pocket (Figs. 201 and 202).—Cut two pieces of material 1 inch wider than mouth of pocket ; length of one piece equal to depth of bag + turnings + twice depth of welt, length of the other equal to depth of bag + turnings. Mark mouth on garment.

Tack a $2\frac{1}{2}$-inch-wide strip of neatening and strengthening material (linen or some firm thin material) to the wrong side, with its lower edge $\frac{1}{2}$ inch below line of mouth. Place the two pocket pieces right side down and edges meeting at mouth and seam. Make the upper seam a little shorter than the lower.

Mark required width of welt from line of stitching as shown by arrow in Fig. 201. Fold back on this line and tack. Snip each side at level of pocket mouth, as in Fig. 202, the snips long enough to reach ends of stitching.

Cut mouth the length of shorter stitching. Snip turnings on short side only. Open seams and pull both pieces through mouth. Turn under ends of welt ; press, and secure by machining or hemming (invisible on top).

On the wrong side turn under the ends of the neatening strip, then fold down to cover all raw edges, and hem to back of pocket. Turn the edges of the pouch to face each other and machine twice, the raw edges being thus neatened between stitchings.

Patch Pocket.—This is the simplest of all pockets, as it is just a more or less square patch of stuff with its top edge hemmed, bound, or faced, with its other three edges turned in singly and stitched to the garment. The lower corners are often rounded, or the bottom edge shaped to a point. Jumper pockets can be prettily decorated.

Side Pockets in Little Boy's Knickers.—It is easier to put

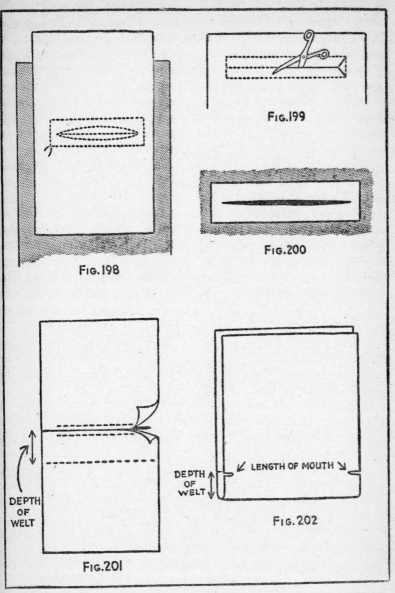

FIG.199

FIG.200

FIG.198

DEPTH
OF
WELT

FIG.201

DEPTH
OF
WELT

LENGTH OF MOUTH

FIG. 202

FIG. 198.—Bound Pocket.   FIG. 199.—Cutting Mouth for Bound Pocket.
FIG. 200.—Finished Bound Pocket.   FIG. 201.—Welt Pocket.   FIG. 202.—
Welt Pocket.

these pockets in before the trouser seams are sewn. The position for them will be marked on the pattern by notches. Mark the length of the pocket opening with chalk on the front and back of trousers and on the two pocket pieces, which are probably squares and are usually cut in strong lining. Place one square of lining to the front of the trousers on the wrong side, and a crossway strip of material 2 inches wide on the right side, all edges level. Stitch the three thicknesses together for the length of the pocket opening. Turn the strip of cloth over on to the pocket, so that the seam is exactly on the edge, press well, and then stitch it $\frac{1}{8}$ inch from the fold. Stitch the other end of the strip of material to the pocket.

Join the second square of lining to the back of the trousers in the same way. The two pieces can be joined together now or later on after the side seam is made. Snip the turnings of the trousers above and below the pocket opening before making the seam, and work buttonholed bars afterwards, to prevent the opening from tearing.

CHAPTER XXVII

INDIAN BASKETRY, OR COILED BASKETRY

Introduction. Materials. The Different Stitches—The Navajo or Figure
Eight Stitch or Weave, the Lazy Squaw Stitch, the Peruvian
Stitch, the Mariposa Stitch, the Samoan or Double-Knot Stitch,
the Syrian Stitch, Fuegian Stitch, West African Stitch, Toas
Stitch, Shilo Stitch. How to begin Round and Oval Bases; In-
creasing the Stitches in Round and Oval Bases. Joining New
Strands of Raffia and Changing the Colour. Joining the Cane.
Arranging Designs. Making Mats and Baskets.

INDIAN Basketry, or Coiled Basketry, is a great craft. It
appeals to all who love sewing, because it is designed and
shaped with the needle. The number of different stitches that
can be used, the different patterns that can be thought out, and
the great variety of basket forms that can be made, make it a
craft of infinite interest.

We have already mentioned the beautiful designs of the
Indian in coiled basketry in writing of the braided or plaited
rug in Chapter XVIII. One craft always helps another. The
coil is the favourite weave of the best basket-makers in the
world, namely, the Indians of the West and South-West (North
America). The material of the coil may be almost anything
capable of being coiled, such as string, cane, raffia, grass, straw,
etc. Taking a length of the coil material, it is tightly wrapped
with raffia or whatever is to be used for sewing, and then sewn
round and round in the manner described for the plaited rugs
in Chapter XVIII. That is coiled basketry in its simplest
form.

It can be very delicate work or very bold. In form, the
coiled ware may be perfectly flat, as in a table mat, or built up
into the most exquisite jar shape; in design, the upright

stitches lend themselves to the greatest variety of intricate patterns.

You can therefore make for yourself lovely table mats and baskets. Make a basket for your embroidery in the colours that you like ; it will add to the pleasure of your work. You will find directions for doing it here. We will first describe the materials used to-day, then the interesting stitches used, and the actual making of mats and baskets.

MATERIALS

The material generally used is round cane worked over with raffia. The cane can be bought in several sizes or thicknesses, depending upon the size of the basket or mat to be made. Thick cane can never be used for small baskets, but thin cane is sometimes used to make quite large baskets.

The cane used for coiled basketry should be of good quality. No. 4 cane is used for fine work, No. 6 for ordinary work, while for fairly coarse work No. 8 is a good size. No. 6 is a very suitable size for a beginner, as it is not too coarse to make the starting of the coil difficult, and it is fine enough to be pliable.

For baskets about 6 inches in diameter No. 6 or No. 8 cane could be used. For large baskets such as a waste-paper basket you would need No. 12. It is best for beginners to start with making small articles.

Substitutes for Cane.—(1) Thick string or fine cord makes a very good coil. It has several advantages over cane. No joins are needed, and it makes a very regular mat or basket. It is easier to handle than cane.

(2) Bunches of raffia made from pieces that are too thin to use. This soft coil needs constant watching and feeding to ensure a regular and even appearance.

(3) Thick rushes may also be used, but all soft materials need special care if the basket is to be a good shape.

The best of all these, however, is cane or string.

Raffia Needles.—For sewn basketry, wool or tapestry needles may be used, but as the raffia is hard for the eyes of these needles they sometimes break. The special raffia needle known as the J raffia needle is very satisfactory.

THE DIFFERENT STITCHES OR WEAVES USED IN COILED OR INDIAN BASKETRY

There are really two main stitches used—the Lazy Squaw and the Figure Eight stitch or the Navajo weave; all the other stitches are variations of these two. Each has its own particular form, merits, and effects, which should be thoroughly understood by the worker. These stitches are quite easy to learn, and the fascination of coiled basketry lies in the charming effects produced by the introduction of different stitches. The work becomes more and more interesting as you master the various stitches. It is work that needs care and accuracy and a certain love for beauty of form and design.

We will now describe the most important and useful stitches.

(1) *The Navajo or Navaho Stitch* (Fig. 203), sometimes called *The Figure Eight Stitch.*—This is decidedly one of the most useful stitches, it is the strongest of all weaves and the most popular. It will make a strong beginning for any of the other stitches. In its actual formation, this stitch is a series of repetitions in raffia of the figure 8, the upper half of the figure encircling the unworked cane and the lower half encircling the cane used for the last row, thus holding the two rows together. Fig. 203 shows the details of the working.

In oversewing the centre ring it is easier to bring the needle *up* through the hole than to take it *down*, and when it is time to start the second row, instead of taking the raffia round over the *outside* of the cane, as before, bring it over the ring only and *under* the cane to be covered, right round it (which will bring the needle downwards again) and up through the middle hole, having completed one Navajo stitch.

(2) *The Lazy Squaw Stitch*, or *The Long and Short Weave.*— This stitch is more quickly made than the Navajo stitch and is perhaps the easiest, but more care is needed to make it firm and compact. If the stitches are loosely made, the rows will be uneven and an irregular surface is the result when the basket or mat is finished.

Fig. 204 shows how this stitch is worked, where it will be seen to consist of a short and long stitch in alternation. Notice that it is winding the raffia round *the new* coil *only* which gives the appearance of a *short* stitch, while taking the needle and raffia down below the two coils makes the long stitch which holds them both together.

(3) *The Peruvian Weave.*—This stitch is merely a variation of the Lazy Squaw. It is very dainty in appearance, but it does not make a very strong basket.

Begin as for the Lazy Squaw, the only difference afterwards being in the number of wraps around the single coil. The long stitches make the pattern either singly or in pairs, separated by a number of short stitches. The number of wrappings must be increased with each round or the effect of the pattern will not be attained. Only the strand for the long stitch requires a needle ; the wrapping may be done with the fingers only.

There are many varieties of patterns, single or double diamonds, single or double lines, straight or slanting, or a combination of both.

It is not a very strong stitch, and if worked slackly the basket is very unstable and gets out of shape. It would be well to work the base in Lazy Squaw and introduce a single or double row of the same stitch to give more strength to the basket.

(4) *The Mariposa Stitch* (Fig. 205).—This is perhaps the most beautiful of all the variations of the Lazy Squaw stitch.

The first part of the stitch is exactly like the Lazy Squaw, a short stitch formed by taking the raffia round the new coil only, and then a long stitch over the new coil and the last row together ; but now comes an addition which entirely changes the character of the stitch. After the long stitch has been taken through under the last row in the usual way, the needle is brought up on the left of the stitch, between the new coil and the last row, and taken down again on the right, leaving the raffia across the stitch and so forming a kind of knot, hence it is sometimes known as the Knot Stitch. Fig. 205 shows the details of the working.

This stitch is very effective, and looks extremely well, used in bands as an insertion between other weaves. The cane does not lie so closely as in the Lazy Squaw weave.

(5) *The Samoan or Double-Knot Stitch.*—This weave is very similar to the last. Begin in exactly the same way, but repeat the knotting process twice and wind the raffia several times

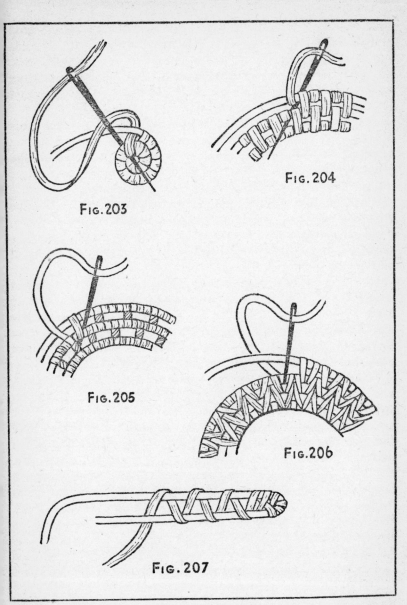

FIG. 203.—Navajo Stitch.   FIG. 204.—Lazy Squaw.   FIG. 205.—Mariposa or
Knot Stitch.   FIG. 206.—V-shaped Stitch.   FIG. 207.—Oval Base in Navajo
Stitch.

round the cane between the knot stitches. This gives an open-work effect.

To increase the size of the coil more winds of the raffia must be made between the knot stitches. If they get too far apart and the work ceases to be firm, make new long stitches at regular intervals.

(6) *The Syrian Stitch.*—This is another variation of the Lazy Squaw. Here the long stitch is made *into* the lower coil instead of under it. This is a very suitable stitch when the coil is composed of raffia.

(7) *The Fuegian Stitch.*—This is really a buttonhole stitch.

(8) *The West African Stitch* (Fig. 206), sometimes called the *V Stitch.*—This is again a variety of the Lazy Squaw, and is a very effective stitch ; but it is not well suited to elaborate pattern design. You can get very pretty effects by using bands of different colours.

Begin as in Lazy Squaw. In the second row put a second long stitch into the first hole (separated from the first by a short stitch). Then make a long, a short, and a long stitch for the next hole, thus putting two long stitches separated by a short stitch into each hole, and passing to the next hole with a long stitch—not separated from the last stitch by a short stitch as in Lazy Squaw. To increase, make an occasional long, short, and long stitch into the space between the two long stitches in the previous row.

(9) *The Toas Stitch.*—This stitch is really a combination of the Navajo and the Mariposa stitches. The centre is divided into four sections, having the two stitches worked alternately. The Mariposa stitch must be very tightly made, or the work will soon become an oval instead of a round ; but if a slightly oval form is required, then this is a very suitable way of making one. Here the distance between the canes should be a little wider in the middle of the knotted sections than where they join the Navajo stitch. There is a long stitch which goes over two canes together to form a dividing line between each section.

(10) *The Shilo Stitch.*—This is a very effective corrugated stitch, and is not difficult. The corrugation is produced by the use of a fine and thick cane alternately ; the greater the contrast in the size of the canes the more striking the corrugation.

How to begin Round and Oval Bases

The Round Base.—Before any definite working stitch can be used a centre ring must be made and oversewn to keep it in position. This rule holds good for all the stitches that have been described.

Take a No. 5 or No. 6 cane. Wind it loosely round the hand to form a coil, leaving about 1½ foot uncoiled with which to begin working. Tie the coil round with raffia in two or three places to keep it in position while you are making the centre. As more cane is required, the tie can be slipped farther round the coiled cane.

With a sharp penknife shave the end of the loose length of cane for about 2 inches to as flat a point as possible. This pointed end is used to form the tiny ring for the beginning of the base, and from this ring the cane is carried round and round.

The cane will need a little coaxing, and it is best to dip the end for 5 or 6 inches in boiling water, hold it there for a minute or two, and then wipe it dry. Now curl the cane twice round a thin pencil. The curled end must be held securely or it will slip undone. Take a blunt tapestry needle or raffia needle, threaded with a strand of raffia, and insert it from the front, holding the short end of raffia in place with the left hand. Continue to insert the needle from the front, working from right to left.

Fig. 203 shows clearly how the ring is made. It is well to work a few rounds with the Navajo stitch first and then continue with the Lazy Squaw or any other stitch decided upon. This is a particularly good method for the beginner.

As the curving for beginning of the ring is necessarily sharp, the most difficult part of the work is over when the ring is made.

How to begin an Oval Base

(1) *The Oval Base in Navajo Stitch* (Fig. 207).—The proportionate length and breadth of any oval mat will depend on the length of the cane from its point to the first sharp bend; this length we will call the "first row." A simple device will

enable any one to produce the desired oval. Suppose you want to make an oval for a small dinner mat 8½ inches long by 6 inches wide. Cut a piece of paper to this size. Fold it lengthways, and measure across the fold. This fold shows that half the width of the paper is 3 inches. Open the paper out and make a mark on the folded line 3 inches from each end. The unmeasured space between the marks is the required length for the " first row " of working.

If the cane is hard or of a coarse size, it should be left for a minute or two in boiling water, before bending it. If it should crack, the roughness can be shaved off and a little more raffia wound round to keep the size of the coil even.

Hold the cane in the left hand with the sharp bend to the right. The raffia is started by winding it two or three times round the bend and then lacing the two rows together, using the Navajo stitch. The canes must be close together, but the winding need not be too close, as the next round will put a second covering on both.

When the cut end is reached, the cane must be bent sharply round it. A few extra windings are needed here, as there is no hold for the needle ; but as soon as you have turned the corner, begin the Navajo stitch again, and it can be continued for the rest of the work.

(2) *Making an Oval Base in Lazy Squaw Stitch.*—An oval base is more quickly and easily started in this stitch than in the Navajo. The cane is bent in exactly the same way, and the raffia is started by being wound round the end in the same way, but instead of lacing the two canes together they are only bound, the raffia going round both until the cut end is reached. Here the second sharp bend must be covered with raffia, as described for the Navajo. It is important to notice one special point when binding the canes together : the raffia on the right side of the work must be *straight* across the canes, or the beauty of the work will be spoilt.

Of course the raffia must slant somewhere, but this must be on the *wrong* side where it will not be seen. Even if done very carefully, the raffia may still slant a little. This can be put right in the *second* row by using the needle to draw the bindings back into position before the next stitch is taken through.

Increasing the Stitches in Round and Oval Bases

When working a round base the number of stitches must be increased in every row. In an oval base you must increase the stitches only at the ends, each of which is in reality half a round, the length of the oval being determined by the straight section between them.

Joining New Strands of Raffia

When a new strand of raffia is needed, lay it along the cane and work over it for about five or six stitches. Gently pull the new piece until the short end disappears. Then thread the needle with the new raffia and work it over the old end and the cane together for about six stitches and cut away the old end.

Coloured raffia is laid on in the same way—the strand of raffia which is not needed for the immediate stitch being carried along with the cane and covered with stitches.

Joining the Cane

Pare off the upper part of the old cane for about $1\frac{1}{2}$ inch; do the same to the under part of the new. Put the two together (splicing). One or two stitches may be taken through both ends with a fine needle to hold them together while they are being covered.

Design in Basketry

This is a most interesting and fascinating part of the work. It is well worth while to study the many specimens of native work in the British Museum. Many of these show a wonderful power of design and are examples of beautiful work produced with a very limited range of material. Among the American Indians the women did most of the work, and the patterns they wove into the baskets had a meaning and expressed their hopes and fears, their love and aspirations, so that their baskets were to them " their poems, their paintings, their sculpture, their cathedral, their music."

All the Indian designs are symbolical and have been handed down through many generations. A very much used design is the zigzag, which among some tribes meant the lightning;

among others, a flowing stream or steps up a mountain, or a mountain chain with peaks and valleys. Another frequent design is a star shape that was suggested by the top view of the calyx of a flower, and so the number of rays varies. Some Indian designs show four sections that radiate from a centre, representing north, south, east, and west.

Working in Coloured Raffia and Arranging Designs

A design in concentric circles in two colours, using the figure eight or Navajo stitch, is a simple one. The first bit of the design will be one row of colour, showing on one cane only, the others being covered by the natural coloured raffia.

There is a break where the coloured circle begins and ends. This is seen in all Indian baskets, but it is not so apparent when isolated patterns are used. There is no need to finish off one colour before starting the next ; the best plan is to carry each colour in turn along the under side of the cane, exchanging one for the other as needed. The same thing is done when several colours are used.

Fig. 208 shows a typical Indian basket design, perhaps the oldest. It is the characteristic design of a Navajo basket. This makes an excellent pattern for a mat. In all these patterns it will be noticed that the forms are bounded by two classes of lines, vertical and horizontal, the lines of the warp and the weft. Oblique bands of colour are always made up by a series of rectangles, giving a stepped outline.

How to arrange Designs on Round Mats

A skeleton coil can be made, or bought, and the design arranged on this (Fig. 209).

Many people trust to their eye to tell them when to begin or end any pattern, and this is perhaps the best way. Others count the stitches to see where to begin the design ; this is only possible if the stitches are easy to count.

One difficulty in making a uniform design lies in the fact that the number of stitches increases in each round ; therefore all increasings should be made if possible in the groundwork, so that the patterns themselves are uniform.

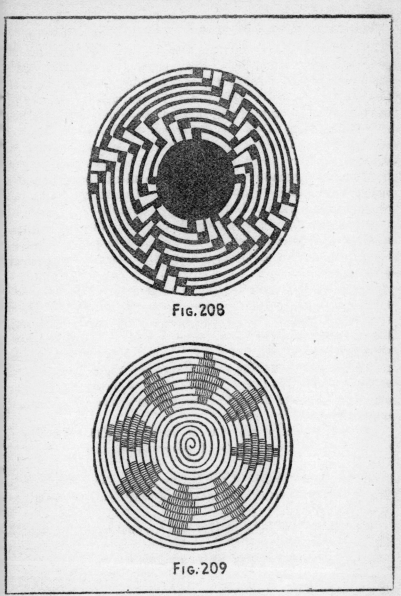

FIG. 208

FIG. 209

FIG. 208.—Characteristic design of a Navajo Stitch.
planning out the design.

FIG. 209.—Coil for

SOME SUGGESTIONS FOR INTERESTING ARTICLES TO MAKE

(1) *Table Mats in Mariposa Weave.*—A very pretty set of plate mats can be made in the following way. Choose two shades of blue and violet that go well together. For the foundation use No. 8 cane or thick string. A particularly strong and useful mat is made by using the cane and the string together as a double coil. Bind the string and cane together at one end with a strand of violet raffia for about an inch, then bend it round to make a small ring and to start the spiral coil. When beginning the second row, catch in the end and bind the raffia round the coil three times. Now make a long stitch, taking the needle through the hole in the centre of the mat.

Now take the needle through between the first and second coils and across the long stitch to form a Mariposa or knot stitch. Go on winding round the coil, making the long stitches about ½ inch apart.

Begin working with the blue strand when you have made a circle of about 3 inches diameter. Insert the end of a blue strand and bind it four or five times to the cane and string. Lay the violet strand alongside the cane and continue to work with the blue raffia for one row. Violet should now take the place of the blue for the next five rows; the last row of all should be worked in blue. To finish, cut off the end of the cane and string. Shave the end of the cane to a tapering point and bind it securely.

To make a set of six of these mats you would need about 6 ounces of No. 8 cane, ¾ lb. of coloured raffia, and 43 yards of thick string.

(2) *A Basket in the Lazy Squaw Stitch.*—For this basket you need the ring centre, the making of which has been described already (Fig. 203).

Remember the Navajo stitch is the actual beginning needed for the Lazy Squaw stitch, and for the beginner it is always wise to start with the ring centre and one row in Navajo before beginning the Lazy Squaw. Then make the Lazy Squaw stitches as already described.

No definite rule can be given for increasing the number of stitches when a centre is being made. It may be enough to put an extra stitch in *every other* short one in the row beneath, instead of into every one. The object is to keep the work as uniform as possible, while taking care that all stitches point to the centre. Stitches which slant out of position spoil the effect of the work. The shape of the basket develops with the work, and must be done by the eye.

If it is to have upright sides, the base must be kept quite flat, and when it is large enough the cane must be gradually raised till it is exactly above the last row. This gradual raising of the cane should be done in less than 3 inches of length, otherwise the sides will slope.

When shaping a basket the work must be carefully watched and the cane adjusted if necessary after every 2 inches have been sewn. In this way it is easy to keep any shape true to the design or model. If too much cane is covered in a wrong position, nothing can be done to remedy it.

A Work-Basket with a Lid.—Use No. 6 cane, and begin the coil as already described. Make the base about 8 inches in diameter, and then gradually pull the cane over to form the sides. Watch the shape of your basket carefully and adjust it as you work. The sides should be about 5 to 6 inches deep, roughly about 20 rounds.

To finish off the basket, slice the end of the cane as thin as possible, pull it down under the row beneath, and cover both together, so making a strong and tidy finish.

Make the lid a little larger than the basket, so that it may go on easily. It is generally enough to make one extra row, but if the winding is light, two are sometimes needed. As you work the round, pull it down gradually to form the lid ; then to make the edge of the lid, sew the cane down almost at right angles. Five rows would be sufficient for the edge.

To make a ring for the handle of the lid, use No. 9 cane. Shave one end very thin, bend the cane to make an oval ring, bind the thin end firmly to the other piece, using a long stitch for every fifth or sixth stitch. Shape the ring as you work—when finished, stitch it to the lid of the basket.

This basket could be made most attractive by working it in natural raffia, with a slantwise design in two contrasting colours for the sides and the lid.

CHAPTER XXVIII

SOFT OR SUÈDE LEATHER WORK

Different Kinds of Leather. Tools for Soft Leather Work. Punching the Holes. Ways of Thonging. Joining Thongs. Beginning and Finishing Off. Sewing Leather. The Fixing of Press-Buttons. Articles made from Velvet Persian. Making Hats and Coats of Leather. Glove-Making. Moccasins and Slippers. Tea-Cosies. A Book Carrier. Leather Cushion Covers. Interlaced or Woven Cushion Covers. Woven Seats for Stools.

HERE is another craft for those who like sewing. It is such interesting sewing, too, with bold, decorative stitchery. Many of the embroidery stitches given in Chapters II. and III. can be used in soft leather work, and many of the different ideas found in this book can be worked out in leather.

Indeed, leather is one of the most beautiful materials to work with, and the work generally becomes a fascinating hobby. The simplest form of leather work is perhaps that done with soft leather or suèdes. It is this type of leather work that especially appeals to the needle-woman and embroideress. There is a wide choice of skins to be had in lovely colours. Soft leathers are dressed on what is known as the flesh side, so that they have a soft, velvety surface. Here are the names of some soft or suède leather :

(1) *Velvet Persians.*—These are beautiful leathers made from the skins of the finest Persian sheep. They have a fine silky pile like velvet, hence their name. They can be bought in a wide range of colours. Their beautiful shades and the softness and suppleness of their texture make them delightful to handle. You will fall quickly under the spell of leather, and find in its work a new and absorbing interest.

(2) *Velvet Sheep.*—These leathers are made from the skins of English sheep, and are about twice the substance of Persians. They are cheaper, but they cannot be dyed in such delicate shades nor is the pile so good as that of the Persians. The skins vary in size from about 5 to 7 square feet. The grain side is generally very free from imperfections, so that the leather may be used with equal advantage on one side as on the other. They are very useful.

(3) *Lacing Persians.*—These are thinner than the velvet Persians, and they are used for cutting into laces or thongs. They are also used for linings and for making gussets.

(4) *Suède Fleshes.*—These skins have a velvet finish on both sides. They are economical in use, and are particularly suitable for moccasins, motor cushions, etc.

(5) *Gloving Leathers.*—These are chamois, white washable doe, and suède Cape, a beautifully soft and supple leather.

There is another very useful skin used for soft leather work. This is *sheepskin*, dressed on the hair side to retain the natural grain, and has a brown antique finish. This leather is very suitable for making bags, blotters, book covers, and is much used for making cushions to go with dark oak furniture.

In a great deal of work with soft leathers the articles are thonged, that is, put together with thongs or strips of leather. These strips are cut very narrow, and are threaded or laced through holes which have first been punched round the edge at regular intervals of about $\frac{1}{4}$ inch.

A very large number of beautiful and useful things can be made, such as bags and pochettes of various kinds and sizes; articles of dress, such as belts, ties, collars, waistcoats, and jackets; cushion covers, seats for stools, blotters, pocket-books, purses, etc.

TOOLS FOR SOFT LEATHER WORK

These are very few, and are not expensive. The most necessary tool is a six-hole spring punch for punching holes for the thongs to go through. This punch cuts holes of six different sizes. Other useful tools are a press-button set, a pair of scissors, a sharp knife, and a light hammer to use with the press-button set. Other tools can be added as the need arises.

PUNCHING THE HOLES

For this purpose the six-hole punch is used. This is very useful, as it gives six different sized holes for thonging. It is a matter of taste how far apart or how far from the edge of the leather the holes should be punched, but $\frac{1}{4}$ inch apart and $\frac{1}{8}$ inch from the edge is quite a good rule. The spacing will, of course, vary slightly according to the size of the work.

It is well to put a small piece of cardboard or solid leather under the work where it is desired to punch a hole, so that the edge of the punch does not come in contact with the hard surface behind the leather. The advantage of doing this is that only half the pressure is needed to punch the holes, and the punch will keep an edge as keen as when new.

Some workers prefer slit holes for thonging. These are made by using a three-pronged tool or a fine carving chisel kept for the purpose. The leather should be laid on a piece of linoleum while the slits are being made. If two or more surfaces are to be joined together, the holes should be made through all the pieces of leather at the same time. They may be opened for threading by using an awl or the tracer.

By varying the size and grouping of the holes made by punching, a variety of simple and effective designs can be made.

WAYS OF THONGING

(1) The most effective way is to thong over the edges like oversewing ; the thong should be taken twice through the holes at the corners, as this gives them a neater finish.

(2) Other stitches copied from needlework may be used in thonging, such as cross stitch, buttonholing, etc. (See chapters on Embroidery Stitches.)

(3) The running stitch is often effective as a decoration, but is not so satisfactory for joining leather as the oversewing.

The threading of the thong or lace is made much easier by " tagging "—that is, wrapping a piece of sheet brass or other metal round the end of the thong.

A simpler method of pointing a thong is to dip it in seccotine or strong glue and then allow it to dry stiff.

Cutting Thongs.—Although it is best generally to buy thongs already cut, for some purposes one can cut one's own. Thongs may be cut very economically from odd pieces of leather. First cut the piece into the shape of a circle, then cut carefully and continuously round and round. This is a good way to use up small pieces of leather, and the result is a much longer thong. Any little irregularities in the cutting are not noticeable when the thonging is finished. The thong can be straightened by very gentle pulling; but you must not pull too tightly, especially when lacing.

JOINING THONGS TOGETHER

Skive or bevel the ends of the thongs to be joined with a sharp penknife. Rub a minute quantity of seccotine on the under side of one and the upper side of the other, and press the two surfaces firmly together. The join should be long enough to go through at least two holes. Let it dry well before going on with the thonging.

BEGINNING THONGING

When joining two pieces of leather together, begin at the top left-hand corner by threading the thong through the first hole, but only through the top layer of leather, and leave a tail end of about $1\frac{1}{2}$ inch inside. This must be to the left, flat between the two layers of leather, and parallel to the edge, as in seaming. It is advisable to place a tiny touch of seccotine on this tail end, and then press it sandwich-like between the two leathers. Now thread the thong over the edge through the first hole at the back, and into the corresponding hole at the front again. This makes a very secure beginning. The tail end of the thong lies parallel to and between the edges and holes, and is gripped fast in the thonging and cannot be seen. This is the neatest way of beginning the work.

FINISHING OFF

Thread the end of the thong through a rug needle and bring it between the two edges on the inside, work the needle down through several stitches, drawing the thong through firmly. This is a possible method when making fairly large bags, as it is necessary to have the bag well opened and to be able to look inside while doing it. Another method of fastening off is to thong the last few stitches loosely at first, thread the end of the thong back under them, and pull the stitches up tightly one at a time, finally pulling up the end and trimming off what is left. This is quite a secure method.

Thonging, well done, is a decoration in itself. For successful results the following points should be noticed :

(1) The holes must be regularly spaced. For edges the distance between the holes should be the same as the width of the thong.

(2) The holes should be in a line with each other and be parallel to the edge.

(3) The thongs should be of uniform thickness; the most useful width is $\frac{1}{8}$ inch.

(4) Do not draw the thongs too tightly in soft leather, otherwise the leather will pucker.

(5) The best length for a thong is no more than 3 feet. If it is too long, much time is wasted in drawing it through the holes, and the thong becomes somewhat frayed.

SEWING LEATHER

For making up many leather articles sewing can be used. There are three ways of sewing leather :

(1) *A Running Stitch* can be used ; then the needle is taken back into the same holes so that the thread goes over the space where the first time it went under. This gives a continuous stitch on both sides of a join or seam, and if it is evenly done it looks like a machine stitch.

(2) *The Cobbler's Stitch.*—Here two needles are required. They are put through the same holes but in opposite directions. This method is used for sewing thick leathers together, and the holes have to be pierced first ; it is not a method that need be used by the home worker.

(3) Leathers, such as Velvet Persians, etc., may be stitched quite well on a sewing machine. You must use a long loose stitch. It is a good plan to put a piece of thin paper between the leather and the needle when stitching ; this will protect the leather from any marks. You can easily remove the paper when the work is finished.

All the ordinary needlework stitches, as well as the embroidery stitches, can be used when working with very soft flexible leathers, and such decorative stitches can be used with delightful effects in making up various leather articles. Further advice is given on sewing leather when describing the making of hats, coats, gloves, etc.

Hand-sewing is generally used for grouping and binding inside pockets. Saddlers' silk, or well-twisted silk of moderate weight, is perhaps best for all light and pliable skins. As a contrast, wool or cotton in various shades may be used.

For certain skins, such as lamb, kid, doeskin, suède, fine cotton thread is better than silk.

Linen thread tends to cut the leather. If it is necessary to use it because of its strength, pass it across a piece of yellow or white beeswax, or resin, and so lessen its tendency to cut the leather. Another good hint when sewing leather is to dust the thread lightly with French chalk ; this prevents it from feeling sticky.

Before stitching two pieces of leather together it is sometimes necessary to stain the white raw edges. A faint guide-line drawn on the leather is sometimes a great help in spacing the stitches.

When beginning a new thread, always sew back for several holes ; loose ends of threads at joinings should be frayed out, hammered flat, and slipped in between the two leathers. A tiny touch of seccotine will secure the parts.

Further advice on sewing leather is given when describing the making up of coats, hats, and gloves.

The Fixing of Press-Buttons

The press-button is the most convenient and popular way of fastening a bag or purse.

A press-button consists of a " cap " and a " spring stud." These are held in position by eyelets, which pass through from the *under* side of the leather—hence there are four parts in all.

(1) *The " cap."*—This is usually covered with celluloid. Many colours can be obtained. It will be found that those colours which closely match the work look best.

(2) *The cap eyelet*, a component part of the cap.

(3) The *spring*, or spring stud.

(4) The *spring eyelet*, a component part of the spring.

When making up the work it is generally best to put the press-buttons on last.

Suppose you have made a bag with a deep flap, and want to put a press-button in each corner. You must first fix the position of the buttons on the flap. This should be quite easy if their position was thought out when the decoration of the flap was planned.

Bend the flap over in its correct position, and put under it a stout piece of cardboard. Place the buttons in the right position and press them firmly down so that they make a slight impression on the leather. Now put them aside and prick a hole with a pin or needle through the centre of the mark made by the cap. The cardboard will prevent it going through to the back.

Remove the cardboard, set the flap truly with sides and bottom edge. Insert pins into the holes you have already made in the flap, and push them through perpendicularly until they penetrate the front of the bag. The pinholes in the flap and the pinholes in the bag should now coincide, and will represent the centres of the respective parts of the button.

If the buttons are placed near the edge of the flap, punch a round hole with the punch pliers exactly over the pinhole. This hole should be just large enough for the cap eyelet to pass through it to the front of the work. It is better to have the hole too small than too large. For inelastic leather, such as calf, the cap eyelet should be about $\frac{5}{16}$ inch in diameter, but for soft leathers, such as velvet Persian, $\frac{3}{16}$ is quite large enough.

Sometimes the position of the button makes it impossible to use the punch pliers ; then the hole must be hammered out with a round cutting punch of suitable size.

If the hole is too small, it can be slightly enlarged with a tapering punch, by putting it through the hole and moving it about until the leather stretches a little.

Now a press-button tool and die is needed. This is a convenient little set of tools made of brass, consisting of two punches and a round die with a recess into which the cap fits.

Place the die upon the work-table and place the cap upside down in the recess. Pass the cap eyelet through the hole in the flap from the under side, and lay it exactly over the cap. The under side of the flap is now uppermost. Insert the punch with the projecting end in the cap eyelet. It should fit easily. Hold the punch upright, and with a smart light blow of the hammer drive the two parts of the button together. This should secure the upper part of the press-button.

Now you have to fix the bottom part of the button, the " spring."

Punch a smaller hole over the prick which was made in the front of the bag. It should be just large enough to allow the tapered eyelet to be fixed through from the inside of the bag.

Put the cardboard inside the bag, and on this place the die so that the back of the eyelet rests upon the flat surface of the die. Place the spring over the projecting point of the eyelet. Take up the other punch and place its hollow end over the spring, and with a smart light blow from the hammer drive the two parts of the spring together.

A Point worth Remembering.—The larger holes for the cap eyelet are always in the flap ; the small holes for the spring eyelet are always in the body of the bag.

How to regulate the Resistance of the Spring.—The top of the spring is divided into six little sections. If the press-button is difficult to fasten, close two sections against the barrel by gently nipping them between the jaws of a pair of pincers. This will reduce the resistance by one-third. If two more are closed up, the resistance is reduced by two-thirds. If you find the button is now too loose, a gentle tap or two with the hammer will spread the sections, and so increase their grip.

Some leather is so elastic it will hardly hold the press-button parts. It is important then to plan the article so as to avoid having the " stretchy " part of the leather in that part that will have to bear the strain of the press-buttons. If this cannot be done, it is advisable to paste another piece of leather under the part where the holes have to be cut. This will also help to preserve the shape of the bag.

ARTICLES MADE FROM VELVET PERSIANS

The variety of dainty, beautiful, and useful things that can be made from velvet Persians is very great indeed. The work is interesting and need not be expensive, and the results are eminently satisfactory. We give here a list of some of the things that can be made. A study of this will show you what a very wide field of fascinating work leathercraft opens up.

If the amateur wants to begin with small articles easily made, there are : comb-cases, scissors-cases, stamp-cases, season-ticket holders, fountainpen holders, shopping-list covers, spectacle cleaners, bookmarkers, note-cases, serviette rings, note-book covers, purses, vanity bags, pochettes, book carriers, calendars, etc. Many of these require very small pieces of leather, and so for a trifling cost delightful and artistic gifts can be made. As you plan and execute these, many new ideas will come to you as your knowledge and skill increase.

Then there are many articles of wearing apparel that can be made : hats, waistcoats, gloves, coats, moccasins, baby's shoes, etc.

Besides those mentioned above, many other pretty articles can be made for household use, such as : table runners, table mats, cushion covers, table centres, tea-cosies.

Then there are shopping-bags of infinite variety, hand-bags, under-arms (the latter can be made with pockets), blotters, writing-pads, and writing-cases. All these lovely and durable things can be made at much less cost than they can be bought, and there is added to them the pleasure of making.

We shall now give some general directions about the making up of some of the articles suggested.

MAKING HATS AND COATS OF LEATHER

There is no great difficulty in making up delightful leather hats and coats. Indeed the velvet Persian leather is so beautifully soft and pliable that it is a pleasure to work with, and quite easy to use in a sewing-machine. Soft suède is principally used, and can be obtained dyed in all the most fashionable and beautiful colours. Another interesting point about working in leather is that not a scrap of leather need be wasted. Pieces left over can be made into small purses, floral trimmings for hats, and, cut into small circles or squares or other suitable shapes, can be used for appliqué designs.

Patterns for hats or coats of fashionable shapes can be bought, and with the pattern the number of skins necessary to make the article is given.

No special tools are required for making up the leather, as it can be stitched by machine, as already described. It is well to experiment on a small piece of leather first, so that you may regulate the machine stitch and the tension to suit.

For sewing leather by hand, use a gloving needle, as it can be passed through the leather more easily than an ordinary one, though many workers use ordinary needles. A punch is also useful for punching small eyelet holes to take a buckle fastening or for lacings.

For directions for cutting out the patterns, see the section on Cutting Out in Chapter XXV., " Dressmaking."

Seaming.—Here again you will find that leather is, in fact, very little trouble to make up. It is a simple matter to make an edge look neat by just turning it in once to the wrong side and stitching down flat. Another method is to bind the edge with a strip of leather. To do this, lay a strip of leather along the edge of the garment, on the right side, so that the edges come level, and stitch along just below these edges ; then turn the other edge of the strip over to the wrong side, and stitch it down flat.

Raw edges can be pinked out with the scissors, but this is not necessary, as the edges of leather will not fray out as do those of material. If you wish to sew down a turned-in edge by hand instead of by machining, use a large stitch such as herringboning or catch-stitching.

Trimming and Lining.—If strap trimmings are used they are simply laid over the leather article and stitched down raw-edged, the edges being cut away quite close up to the stitching afterwards. If desired, embroidery may be done on leather by using a running stitch or couching. For couching, a strand or two of wool is laid over the leather following the lines of any particular design, and oversewn or couched down at regular intervals with silk.

Linings for a coat are hemmed to the turned-in edges of the leather in the usual manner adopted for coat linings. Press all seams in the usual way, but use only a warm iron. A hot iron will ruin the leather.

Buttonholes are generally bound with leather, or worked

with buttonhole twist. If you are using very strong leather simply cut a slit and machine round it just outside the cut. Work eyelet holes with twist in the usual way.

A few points to remember when making up leather :

(1) Use needles, not pins, for pinning, as the latter mark the suède.

(2) For the same reason, use Sylko, or sewing silk, for tacking instead of cotton.

(3) Be careful to take out tackings by cutting each stitch and drawing it out separately.

(4) Leather requires careful handling to preserve its velvety finish and to prevent marking and splitting.

Cleaning Leather.—A weak solution of oxalic acid (a teaspoonful to a cup of water) should be made. Dip a soft rag in the solution and rub it over the leather. This will improve the appearance of the leather.

A Word about Glove-Making

Gloves are not difficult to make, but they need the greatest accuracy in both cutting and stitching. They well repay any time and care spent in the making, as good quality home-made gloves last about twice as long as factory-made ones, while costing about half the price. Decorated hand-made gloves are very expensive to buy.

Gloving Leathers.—Gloving leathers are chamois, white washable doe, and suède Cape sheep, in greys, fawns, and browns. This last is a beautifully soft and supple leather. It has a pile surface very much like real antelope. Other leathers are oak tan Cape, or red Cape and chrome leathers.

Choice of Leather and Tools.—This will depend chiefly on the use for which the glove is intended. For ordinary wear chamois or a heavier suède is very serviceable. Chrome-tanned sheep skin can be used for motoring gloves, while for special occasions a fine gloving suède would be suitable.

When buying a skin for gloves it is better to buy a small one, as such skins are tougher and do not stretch so much either in the making or the washing.

The only tools necessary are a pair of sharp scissors and ordinary needles. Some people prefer to use gloving needles.

Cutting the Pattern.—Glove patterns can be bought of various kinds, with instructions for making up the gloves, or an old but well-fitting glove may be taken to pieces and used as a pattern.

When buying a pattern there is no need to choose one having an elaborate series of different-sized forgettes or fourchettes, with " quirk " pieces. The forgettes are the inside finger parts, and the quirk pieces triangular pieces inset at the base of the fingers. A quite satisfactory fit can be obtained from a glove pattern which consists of the main part of the glove, the thumb, and forgettes all cut to one shape.

Of all kinds of gloves perhaps the long gauntlet shape without buttons is the most elegant, and these gloves are decidedly the least troublesome to make.

It is important to find a pattern that fits your hand, as it is a difficult matter to alter it.

Before cutting out the pattern, hold the skin up to the light with the wrong side towards you, and look carefully for any thin places or tiny holes. Mark them with pencil or chalk, and try to avoid them when cutting out, or see that they come on that part of the glove where there is least strain.

Next, it is most important to test the skin for stretching. As a rule skins dressed for making into gloves are far less elastic when stretched from neck to tail, than from flank to flank ; but this is not always the case, hence the need for stretching. In the case of chamois and all leathers called fleshes (that is, skins which have had the " grain " side removed) the material must be well stretched in both directions before marking and cutting out the pattern. It is most important to remember this, as some chamois will stretch to at least half as wide again.

The pattern must be arranged so that the stretch comes across the hand. It is wise to avoid the edge of the skin, as this sometimes stretches both ways. The strongest part of the glove should be at the gauntlet, as this is the part that takes all the strain of pulling on.

When a good pattern has been found, it saves a great deal of time if the pattern is cut out in thin " Vulmos " board, which is a firm and tough material well suited for cutting out patterns which are frequently needed. It can be obtained from Messrs. Mosses & Mitchell, Golden Acre, London.

16

Lay the skin out smoothly, wrong side up, on a drawing-board or flat table, and secure it with drawing-pins ; place the patterns on it, and with a pencil sharpened to a fine point draw closely round the main part of the glove, taking care to be very accurate ; do the same with the other parts. Do not forget to reverse the patterns for the second glove.

Sewing up the Glove.—There are so many different kinds of patterns, each with their particular instructions, that it is only necessary here to give a few words of general advice.

It is a great help to have by you a well-made glove, so that you can more easily see the shapes and sort out the pieces belonging to each glove.

To sew the gloves, buttonhole twist or strong mercerised cotton is most suitable for chamois and other soft suèdes. Some workers use Sylko, size 8, or Lister's silk, wound on cardboard. It can be the same colour as the leather, or black.

Stab-stitching is the most usual method for hand-sewn gloves. The two raw edges are placed evenly together, wrong sides facing each other, and are joined by stab-stitching (see " Running " in section on Sewing Leather). The sewing should be regular, the stitches being placed $\frac{1}{16}$ inch in from the edge. The stitches should not be made very small, as they only tend to weaken the leather.

Decorating the Glove.—The use of coloured thonging, or simple embroidery in strong threads, adds to the attractiveness of a glove. The gauntlets may be embroidered, or pieces of different-coloured leather may be put on in straps or vandykes, fringes or scallops. Fur or laced edgings may be used.

The three lines of stitching running up the back of the glove are called points or nips. These must be sewn before making the side seam from the little finger to the wrist. They can consist of a row or two of chain stitch, or more elaborate patterns can be worked out, using some of the many embroidery stitches.

It is important to remember that stitches on leather must be very elastic, and must not be massed too close together.

MOCCASINS AND SLIPPERS

Moccasins (Fig. 210).—Moccasins of soft suède lined with fur, or some fleecy material if fur is too expensive, make delightful

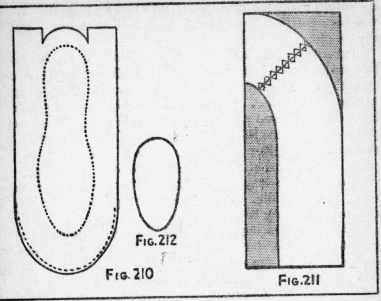

FIG. 210.—Pattern for Moccasins.   FIG. 211.—Slipper Pattern.
FIG. 212.—Toe-piece.

gifts for birthdays or for Christmas-time. They are simpler to make than slippers, and wear better because there is no seam between the uppers and the sole to come undone. They are not expensive to make, if you compare their cost with shop prices.

There are various ways of making them. You can, if you wish, buy a pattern, or make your own. The pattern is in two pieces only—the slipper proper and the toe-piece. To make your own pattern, proceed as follows :

First get the shape of your foot. Place under it a piece of paper, and draw the shape of the sole, keeping both sides approximately symmetrical. Next draw another line about 1 inch from the toe all round the front part of the sole. Draw a straight line from each end of the curve round the front of the sole to meet a line drawn about 1 inch away from the heel (Fig. 210). Make a small semicircle with its base exactly the width of the heel. This bends up to form a lappet over the heel. Cut out this paper pattern, and from it cut the leather for the moccasins. Now cut from paper an oval shape to lie about ½ inch in from the outline of the sole, and to extend as far as the instep. When you have got the shape correct, cut it out in leather. This is the toe-piece (Fig. 212).

The sole portion is to be finely gathered in round the lower half of this oval. Make the gathering stitches very regular, but do not pull too tightly, for the toe-piece should lie flat and evenly between the gathers. It should be stitched in for a short distance beyond the gathered part, so that the loose portion or tongue is about one-third the length of the toe-piece. The back seam and the lappet must be neatly hemmed over. Then bind the free edges of the tongue and the ankle and the back of the shoe.

The toe-piece may be embroidered in various ways, using raffia, beads, or silk. A pretty appliqué pattern in leather of another colour may be used.

Slippers.—To make slippers that will really last, buy leather soles from a shoe shop. Cut out a pattern of the uppers, as shown in Fig. 211 (an old slipper upper is a good guide in cutting this pattern). It is impossible in a book to give measurements for all sizes, but it is quite easy to make a pattern like that shown in Fig. 211 that will fit you. If you like, the toe can be cut separately and have a join, as shown in Fig. 211. This is worth remembering, because you can often use up odd pieces of leather. Sometimes you have enough leather to make a shoe, if you can fit the pattern on *in pieces*.

To make a warm shoe, cut four pieces of suède or velvet Persian, two for the outside and two for lining. Choose contrasting colours. Keep the cheaper leather for the lining. Buttonhole the two pieces (lining and top) together with a thick thread of cotton or artificial silk (Clark's flex thread is useful). Next take the soles—on each a piece of material will be found protruding from the edge; buttonhole around this, also using a strong needle. This buttonholing is, of course, quite decorative.

Now overcast the backs of the slippers together, and sew them on to the soles in the same way. Take care that all the fullness comes round the toe. Most people begin stitching from the middle of the toe. The middle of the upper must be placed over the middle of the toe exactly.

All slippers are made more or less in this way. Felt uppers are buttonholed and seamed in wool (see section on Wool and Felt Work).

We have given no suggestions for decorating these slippers. The pretty suède and silk is itself decorative. If desired, the toes can be ornamented with beads or appliqué work. Any decoration like this must be done before the slippers are lined and sewn to the soles.

TEA-COSIES

There are various ways of making these.

A Tea-Cosy in Four Sections.—Cut four sections so that their circumference gives plenty of room round the tea-pot at the base. The height of each section should be about one-sixth more than its width at the base. The angle at the apex of each section must be either a right angle or just a little less than a right angle, otherwise the top of the cosy tends to sink inward. It is a good plan to cut a pattern of one section out of paper first ; then this pattern can be placed on the leather, and the sections cut out with very little waste of the leather.

If the cosy is decorated with appliqué work, the designs should be pasted on before punching the holes.

For more details about the making of cosies, see section on Felt Work and Wool.

A BOOK CARRIER

This is an article that is always acceptable as a present, or finds a very ready sale at a bazaar. Made in a pleasing shade of velvet Persian and well thonged, it really requires no further decoration. But those who wish can ornament it in appliqué work, or decorate it with pierced work, or with a stencil. These methods are described in the section on Various Ways of Decorating Leather.

It should be made to fit the ordinary library edition. For this you will need a piece of leather $\frac{1}{4}$ inch bigger all round than the book when opened flat, two strips 2 inches wide and the same depth as the book, and two strips 11 inches long and $\frac{3}{4}$ inch wide for the handles.

Place the narrow strips at each side of the larger piece on the inside, with the wrong sides of the leather facing each other. They can be held in position by slip-over paper fasteners, loosely slipped over so as not to mark the leather. Punch holes round the double edges only ; insert the ends of the handles about 2 inches from each end, and thong the pockets in.

If you decide to decorate the leather, it must be done before the pieces are thonged together.

LEATHER CUSHION COVERS : CUSHIONS OF MANY COLOURS

There are many interesting ways of making cushion covers of velvet Persian. Perhaps the most economical method is to use up the accumulation of small pieces which you are bound to get if you do a great deal of leather work, and make a patchwork cushion.

You can regard patchwork as a form of inlay, and it is quite good practice as a preparation for the more elaborate forms (see section on Other Ways of Decorating Leather).

Patchwork is not difficult if you use great accuracy in cutting out the patches all the same size. You should make a cardboard template of the pattern you decide upon, and use this for cutting the pieces. There are a variety of shapes to choose from—square, diamond, triangle, hexagon (six-sided figure). The square is the easiest shape to use, and a useful size is from 3 inches to 4 inches, according to the pieces of leather at your disposal. Smaller squares can be used, but of course they involve more time and work. The most interesting and perhaps effective patterns are those made from triangles (half a square) and hexagons. (See section on Patchwork.) A very attractive arrangement of these shapes is to have two strongly contrasting colours, one light and one dark.

If you are making your cushion from waste pieces and odd scraps you will be limited in your colour scheme. You will probably have five or six different colours, and they will have to be arranged judiciously to form a pleasing whole. Sometimes a large square can form the middle of the cushion and the pieces be fitted round it. Again, the size of your cushion will depend upon the number of the pieces.

A good size for a square cushion is 15 inches by 15 inches.

The pieces can be joined together in three ways. You can oversew them together on the wrong side, or machine them on the wrong side, or the pieces can be joined together by cross stitch. This last method is very decorative. You can use thongs or silk. An *even* number of holes must be punched in each side of the patch, and it is best to punch through two pieces placed one over the other, in order to get the holes in corresponding positions on each piece. Join up at once, being very careful to keep the joined sides quite flat.

INTERLACED OR WOVEN CUSHIONS

Very delightful cushion covers can be made by cutting slits in the leather and weaving through strips of contrasting colour. This is a very quick method. There are various ways of arranging the weaving. Slits can be cut right across the leather from within an inch or $1\frac{1}{2}$ inch from each end. The slits can be from 1 to $1\frac{1}{2}$ inch wide, or wider according to taste. Strips of leather of a contrasting colour must be cut for the weavers. If these are the same width, the pattern will be in squares, but all sorts of interesting variations in pattern can be made by varying the width of the strips.

Another design in weaving, a little more difficult to carry out, but with very effective results, is to weave a strip 1 to 2 inches wide along each side of the cushion about 1 or 2 inches in from the edge. The middle could be woven to show a chequered square. It is wise to plan out the slits first on a piece of paper the size of the cushion, so that the corners may be symmetrical.

AN INTERLACED OR WOVEN SEAT FOR A STOOL

This makes quite a good seat. On the whole it is quickly made, and has a fine appearance. An ordinary white-wood stool lacquered in black and so treated would become a very handsome piece of furniture.

Measure the stool carefully, and decide on the width and number of the strips of leather. It is wise to allow a little space between each strip, as the weaving of the last few rows becomes very difficult.

The strips should be cut from the thickest parts of the skin. They need not be of the same width, provided you cut two pairs of each kind for both warp and weft strips.

The ends of the strips can be nailed to the inner side of the top rails of the stool.

Stool frames for this purpose can be obtained from The Dryad Works, Leicester—price from about 5s. to 6s. Any one whose hobby is carpentry would be able to make one very cheaply.

CHAPTER XXIX

MODELLED AND STAINED LEATHER WORK

Materials. Tools. Choosing the Design. Transferring the Design.
Modelling the Design. Staining or Colouring Leather—Different
Methods. Purses. A Purse with Gussets. Modelling and Staining
a Scissors-Case. Cut or Incised Work. Punched or Hammered
Leather. Other Ways of Decorating Leather—Blind Tooling,
Embossing, Stencilling, Pierced Leather Work, Inlay, Appliqué,
Poker Work, Cloutage.

L EATHER is a fascinating material to work with, because
it lends itself to such a variety of ways of decorative
treatment. It is easy to model, and lovely effects can be obtained
with *one* simple modelling tool. Those who rather fear staining
leather will find much pleasure in modelling on leather already
stained. Some examples of modelled and stained leather will
be seen in Figs. 215 and 216. Those who like colour-work can
produce wonderful results in leather. Then there is blind tooling
for those who like arranging geometrical patterns, and so on.

We will now describe in detail some of this varied and pleasant
work, beginning with some account of the leather and tools used.

MATERIALS

The following are the chief leathers used for modelling (see
also section on Staining).

(1) *Calf.*—This *must* be used for all fine work. It is the
most suitable of all leathers for modelling. It is mellow in
texture and has a very fine grain. The most delicate modelling
can be done on it, and it retains the work put into it. The best
English calf is about 3s. per square foot.

(2) *Cowhide.*—This is a thicker leather, and will be found
useful for all larger articles.

(3) *Indian Calf.*—This is very much more reasonable in price, and is excellent for beginners. It models quite well and is most suitable for geometrical designs.

(4) *Sheepskin* or *Natural Basil.*—This is a very much cheaper leather, costing about 10d. to 1s. 6d. per square foot. It has a smooth surface and, being a soft leather, it does not retain the pattern very well, but it is useful for practice work.

English calf and Indian calf can be bought already coloured : the stock colours being tan, medium brown, and dark brown.

Besides modelling leather, you will also need the following for making up various articles :

Lacing Calf.—This is a thinner leather excellent for making pockets and gussets.

Skivers are used for lining all articles, and can be obtained in an almost infinite variety of shades. They are the grain or hair side of sheepskins, and are very thin, so offering very little resistance to a tearing strain. They vary in price from about 9d. to 1s. per square foot.

TOOLS

Very few tools are needed. The essential ones are a tracer, a modeller with fine and broad points, and one or two matting punches. These tools are better when made of brass or nickelled. Steel tends to cause black stains on the leather if the latter is a little too damp.

Modelled work may be produced with an incised line, which helps to give a greater relief, or by a traced line strengthened with the edge of the modelling tool. We will take the latter method first, and deal afterwards with incising.

CHOOSING THE DESIGN

The best designs are those that have no unnecessary ornamentation, but are clearly and simply defined in as few lines as possible.

No definite rules can be laid down as regards subjects for designs, as so much depends upon the individual taste of the worker, but on the whole conventional designs of animals such as dragons, snakes, Egyptian scarabs, and interlaced geometrical patterns, particularly Celtic patterns of various kinds of knots, are perhaps more suitable than flowers, fruit, or other natural forms. The former designs are more difficult to carry out, hence a simple design of acorns and leaves, etc., is often best for a beginner.

TRANSFERRING THE DESIGN

Whatever method of decorating the leather is decided on, a suitable design must be chosen and transferred to the surface of the leather ; and the process of transferring the design on to the leather is the same whatever form of decoration you choose. So we will describe it here at the beginning, once for all.

If you are a beginner, it is wise to choose a piece of basil because of its cheapness, as the first attempt may not be very successful, and it is a pity to spoil expensive leather such as calf.

Having chosen a simple design with bold, clear outlines, draw it on a thin, strong sheet of cartridge paper. Some prefer to trace the design on a sheet of tough tracing paper or, better still, architects' tracing linen.

Place the leather on a drawing-board face upwards and damp the *entire* surface with a sponge, using clean, cold water. It is essential to damp the whole surface, not just the part where the design is to appear, as in the latter case a distinct halo would be formed around the work. The surface must also be damped *evenly*, as otherwise ugly patches may be left which will *not* come out afterwards. After the first moistening, portions of the surface may be damped without injury.

Place the traced design on the leather. If it is on transparent paper you can easily see that it is straight and exactly centred, so that it is the same distance from all four sides.

The tracing must not shift, so a weight should be provided to hold it down, or you can clip both leather and tracing paper with drawing-pins, so that the heads of the pins hold them tightly without letting the pins go through the leather. Another method of holding the tracing steady during the transfer of the design is to fold the edge of the tracing to the back of the leather and fix it with a little adhesive ; or the tracing and the leather can be held together with wire paper clips close to the edge so that they cannot become displaced. These methods will allow the tracing to be partly lifted when required for examination of the work, to see if you have reproduced all the lines.

Now take the tracing tool and, using it as you would a pencil, go over every line of the design with a firm, even pressure. This process should result in a clearly seen impression of the design. If the outline is lighter than the leather, or too faint, it is a proof that the leather requires moistening again, or that the pressure on the tracer is insufficient. Lift the tracing occasionally to see that the design is well defined. It is better to avoid going over a line twice.

MODELLING THE DESIGN

We will now suppose you have chosen your design, and transferred it to the leather as directed.

You are now ready to begin the modelling.

Place the leather on a drawing-board or a sheet of thick glass. Damp it all over with a sponge ; do not make it too wet ; you can always damp it again and keep it just moist enough to make it plastic so as to take the modelling.

Now study your design carefully, and make up your mind which are the more prominent parts that you would like to stand out in strong relief, and which would be best left unobtrusive. If the lines of the tracing are not clear, deepen these first with the tracer. Take the modelling tool and, using the broad end, press down the edges on the outside of the design, holding the tool as flat as possible. This will accentuate the design. Always keep the leather damp. Press down the parts that should be low, and keep the raised parts high. Keep before your mind a picture of what the finished design should be like, and use every action of the modelling tool to represent this.

Each design, of course, requires slightly different treatment, so we will give some general directions that should prove helpful to a beginner.

Fig. 213 shows a leaf that makes an interesting piece of work for a first attempt. First make the outline of the leaf quite clear with the modelling tool ; then depress the inner parts a, keep b as high as possible, round off the part c where the leaf curves.

Notice the part of the leaf that is curled over ; here the part immediately beside the curled-over part must be pressed down very firmly so as to give the effect of being underneath. Veins and markings should be put in, as it is wonderful what a difference a few markings will make in the general effect.

Fig. 214 shows a scroll which is another good exercise for a beginner to try. Depress the parts *a* and *b* to give the correct impression of turning under ; let *c* stand as high as possible ; *e* must be lower than *c*, but not so low as *b*, and so on ; *d* should be a little lower than *c*.

Try to make all lines with one movement of the tracer. Do not go backwards and forwards over the same line. Keep the tracing tool as upright as possible. Modelling tools should be held as flat as possible, otherwise they make grooves in the leather. Do not press too hard with the modeller, as you may bruise the leather and so make it look dirty and shiny.

Flat modelling is the easiest. It consists only in laying down the background by rubbing its surface with the flat broad modelling tool, working in all directions, but being careful to work *up* to the line of the design, but not over it. The leather must, of course, be kept moist during this process by damping it on the under side with a sponge. If the leather wrinkles when being rubbed, the direction of the rubbing should be changed.

Excellent effects can be obtained in flat modelling by the simple arrangement of straight lines.

STAINING OR COLOURING LEATHER

Leathers suitable for staining are English calf, Indian calf, cowhide, and basil in their natural colour.

Calf is the best of all leathers for staining. It is of a light tannage, and so the stains are very little affected by the natural colour of the leather. Cowhide is more difficult, as it is not so easy to get a uniform surface. Basil is useful for practice work, but the stains do not show to the best advantage as the natural colour is not so pale as the other leathers. Leather already coloured can be improved by staining.

Stains.—There are two kinds of stains most generally used— spirit stains and water stains.

Spirit stains are easy to manage, and the very best results can be obtained with them. They deeply penetrate the surface of the leather, so that the resultant shade has plenty of " body." They have two disadvantages :

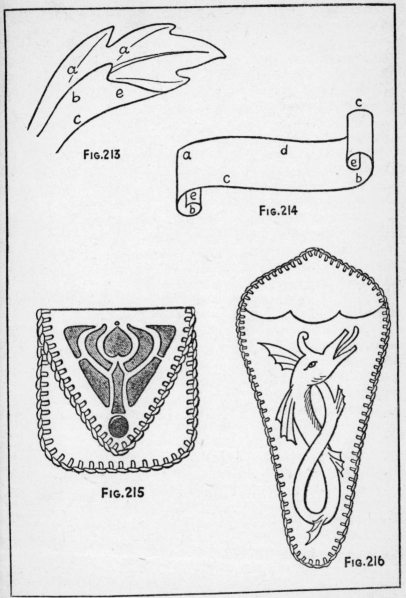

FIG. 213.—Modelling a Leaf.   FIG. 214.—Scroll.   FIG. 215.—A Small Coin Purse.
FIG. 216.—A Scissors-Case, stained and modelled.

(1) They " strike " very quickly, and unless one has considerable practice in staining backgrounds, or unless the background colour is a very dark one, it is difficult to get a regular tone, and " streakiness " resulting from bad colouring spoils the work. To avoid this, do not apply the colour in a backwards and forwards motion in a more or less straight line.

(2) The methylated spirit in the stain tends to harden the leather and to render it somewhat brittle. The expert application of stain is to get the desired tint without hardening the leather.

Spirit stains dry out more quickly than water stains, hence the results obtained with them are quickly apparent ; and so, where several colours are being used, work can be proceeded with almost at once.

Stains may be obtained in liquid form, ready mixed, or in small boxes or tubes and mixed as required.

The powders must be thoroughly dissolved in methylated spirit. The proportion of colour to spirit is soon found by trial on a piece of waste leather, according to the depth of tone required. It is possible to blend the colours *after* dissolving, by mixing one with another, and so obtain a great variety of tones.

Water stains lend themselves to soft colouring well, and as they do not penetrate the leather so deeply as spirit stains, it is easier to get an even tone, therefore many people prefer them for colouring large surfaces. As the water darkens the leather and takes longer to dry, the effect of the colouring is not so quickly seen, and you must wait until the leather is dry before proceeding with the work.

Water stains can be bought in either liquid or powdered form. The powders must be dissolved in hot water. A tube, costing 6d., is sufficient for about 8 liquid ounces (that is, an ordinary medicine bottle full). Test the stain on a piece of leather first. If, when dry, it has a metallic lustre, then the stain is too strong, and more water should be added.

Before beginning the actual staining it is well to make sure that the surface of the leather is free from all greasy marks. It can be cleaned by using rectified benzine with a piece of clean rag or a little pad of cotton-wool. Rectified benzine can be obtained from any local chemist. It is very highly inflammable, and must never be used near an open flame.

We will now suppose the design has been modelled on a piece of natural coloured leather and it is all ready for staining.

Method of applying the Stain.—Make a solution of the colour much lighter than the finished tint, and see that you have a sufficient supply of this. The next step is to damp the surface of the leather all over with a sponge dipped in water. It should be well and uniformly damped. It should be remembered that the desired tone is not to be produced by a single application of the stain, but by several repetitions, so that the first wash should be quite pale and not of the full tone required.

You may feel a little nervous about putting on the first wash in your anxiety to get a good uniform colour, but if you follow the directions carefully and have patience and confidence, you will soon overcome all difficulties.

All being ready, a camel-hair brush (large if the background is being stained) is well filled with the liquid, and rapidly and evenly passed over the part to be coloured *with a circular motion*. Gently wipe off any superfluous colour with a piece of soft linen or old washing silk in order to prevent hard lines from forming. Do not apply a second wash of colour until the first is dry (or nearly so, in the case of a gradation of colour). Apply further washes until the required tone is reached.

In staining very large surfaces a soft sponge may be used or a small pad of cotton-wool wrapped in soft linen. Having stained the background, the design itself can be begun. For this a smaller brush must be used, not too full, as it is important to avoid any colour going on to the background. As each brushful is put on, quickly and gently wipe with the rag to remove any excess of the fluid. Of course it is not necessary to begin with the background ; any order can be taken, and it may be necessary to go from design to background over and over again until a perfect result is obtained. It is sometimes effective when the whole of the staining is done to brush a very pale wash of the background tint over the entire surface of the work ; this brings the whole together. Some may prefer to colour the design only, and leave the background the natural colour of the leather. It is well to try the strength of the colour on a piece of waste leather before applying it to the design.

Other Methods of Colouring Leather

(1) *Waterproof Inks.*—These are cheaper and the results produced are very bright and shiny, and therefore, perhaps, not quite so artistic as the softer effects produced by the spirit or water stains already mentioned.

(2) Another method of colouring a smooth leather, such as russian calf or cowhide, is to use a very thin wash of dye made by mixing oil-paints and turpentine. This must be wiped off immediately with a soft cloth, and then allowed to dry thoroughly before polishing, which is done by rubbing with the hand or a piece of chamois skin. This method of colouring shows the grain or pores of the skin in the colour of the dye applied, and is to be used on coloured leather.

(3) For use of ordinary water-colours and oils, see section on Stencilling on Leather.

(4) For staining small articles or for drawing features on toys made of leather, hat dyes are quite effective and most economical. Almost any shade can be obtained from a chemist. The dye should be well shaken, poured into a saucer, and spread over the article with a sponge. For making fine markings, a small brush must be used.

(5) When the design is coloured it can be outlined with a pen, using indian ink or a dark dye.

There are various methods of producing special effects, such as sprinkling, marbling, and shading.

Sprinkling is done with a long narrow brush and a metal sprinkler ; the brush is filled with stain and rubbed backwards and forwards over the sprinkler, an inch or two above the leather surface, scattering on it a fine shower of colour.

For marbling, a sponge with large holes is used. The sponge is filled with stain and lightly dabbed over the leather so that parts are left untouched.

Shading is produced by working the colour on with a circular motion and with different shades of stain.

We will now consider the actual making of some useful and attractive articles in modelled and stained leather.

PURSES

A Small Coin Purse (Fig. 215).—Two pieces of light brown calf are used for this purse. Cut a full-sized pattern in paper and plan the design in outline. Decide what spaces are to be tooled. The tooling darkens the leather. The background may be tooled, making the design appear raised and light, or the design may be tooled, making the background light. Lay the pattern on the leather and mark round it with the tracer, and cut out the purse. Cut the pocket to fit. If the cut edges of the two pieces of the purse show a white line owing to the exposure of the inner substance of the leather, they can be stained with a fine brush.

When the purse has been modelled, cut pieces of skiver of a suitable colour for lining it.

Directions for Lining.—These directions apply to the lining of all leather articles, whether large or small.

You want a fairly liquid paste so that you can cover the surface quickly, otherwise, if it is a large surface, the paste dries in parts before the skiver is put on. Flour paste is good for large surfaces and for continuous edges.

The following recipe will make a strong adhesive : 3 ounces of the best flour, $\frac{1}{2}$ a teaspoonful of alum, and 1 pint of cold water. Mix these ingredients together in an enamelled saucepan to a very fine paste, getting rid of all the lumps. Boil very slowly and stir all the time. Lastly add a little seccotine to the paste. It can be thinned, if necessary, by adding boiling water.

Place the leather face downwards and damp it slightly. Paste the back, taking care that the paste covers the entire surface smoothly, leaving no parts out, and no small lumps anywhere.

Now put the skiver on and press it down, using a soft rag. Always press from the centre outwards and take great care that the edges are well stuck together. Place it under a drawing-board slightly weighted, and leave it until perfectly dry, otherwise the skiver tends to wrinkle and come apart.

Making Up and Thonging.—Place the two pieces of the purse together and secure them with a wire paper-clip, not too tightly pressed in, otherwise it may mark the leather. In making up small articles this is hardly necessary, but for large pochettes and bags, etc., it is a wise precaution.

For making holes, use the smallest size on a six-way punch, and do not make the holes farther apart than $\frac{1}{8}$ inch. Many amateurs spoil their work by making holes that are too big and too far apart, thus making their work look coarse and clumsy.

Begin punching from the top left-hand corner of the pocket, and punch all round the double edges and the flap. The purse in Fig. 215 is thonged in the buttonhole stitch. This is a very effective way, and wears longer than plain thonging. The thongs may be drawn more tightly when lacing calf than when lacing velvet Persian. Now put the press-buttons on as already described. Polish the purse with a piece of soft silk.

A Small Oblong Purse in Brown Leather.—This can be made from one piece of leather $8\frac{1}{2}$ by $4\frac{1}{2}$ inches. Cut the pattern from stiff brown paper or cardboard, lay this on the leather and trace round as a guide for cutting. The cutting may be done with a sharp knife or a pair of scissors. Round the corners of the flap of the purse. Trace and model the design on the flap. Line it with skiver to harmonise with the colour of the leather. Fold up the part to form the pocket, secure carefully with paper clips, and punch through both edges and round the flap. Thong the edges together, and fix two press-studs at the corner.

A Purse with Gussets.—Cut two pieces of thinner or lacing leather as long as the purse is deep, and about $1\frac{1}{2}$ inch wide. Shape them to a rounded point at the base. They can be lined, but it is not always necessary. Fold the gusset lengthways, and punch a hole at the bottom. Fold the purse over, and punch a hole in the centre of the bottom fold ; punch one in exactly the same place on the other side of the bag. Get the correct position by measuring the distance of the first hole from the top. It is most important that both holes should be accurate, otherwise the purse will be one-sided. Fit the front edge of each gusset to the edge of the purse and punch holes through, $\frac{1}{8}$ inch apart. Secure these edges by tying them together with string. Fit the back edges in the same way, and punch holes as before. Begin thonging on the left-hand side of the pocket ; go round the gusset, flap, and the second gusset. The gusset can be made more secure by making a stitch over the top. Always put three stitches into each corner of the flap.

When the purse is finished, polish with a soft piece of silk. Wax-polish may be used if desired.

Under-Arm Purses.—These are very simple to make. A piece of leather about 10 by 15 inches is a good size. A design is modelled on the flap. When folded, the purse is about 10 by 6 inches. Gussets can be put in if desired.

We will now describe the modelling and staining of an article in natural colour calf.

A Scissors-Case (Fig. 216)

First choose a suitable piece of leather without any marks or blemishes. Transfer to this the shape and design of the front piece of the case, but do not cut out the shape until the modelling and staining is done.

To model the design, start with the head, and with the fine end of your modeller make a little round in the centre of the eye, mark the oval of the eyeball, and draw a tiny line to mark an eyelid. Press down the leather round the eye so that the cheeks stand out ; the body should be made rounded at the thickest part. Notice the interlacing of the tail and body of the animal. Here you must be careful to make the top lines stand above those they are crossing ; the under lines should be pressed down *each* side of the crossing one. Little lines of shading will help this effect. All the parts outside the design should be smoothed down so that the original tracing lines do not show as grooves.

In staining the leather you may begin with the design first, and then colour the background, or *vice versa.* Many people like to work the two together, so that they can see the effect of one against the other.

Suppose you decide to colour the dragon red and the background brown. This would be a wise choice, as brown is the easiest colour to stain.

See that you have everything ready. You will want small brushes for this small article. Ox-hair are quite good and not so expensive as sable. As far as possible, keep each brush for the same colour : a brush for red stain should not be used for any other colour.

Now damp the leather all over. Begin with the design. Colour the dragon red; do not be afraid to make the colour too bright, but be careful not to let it dry with hard edges. Always let your work dry between washes of colour, as it is not possible to see what the finished shade will be while it is still wet. If the colour is too light, then another coat may be added.

When you have finished the design, the *whole* of the leather should be damped, and a wash of *pale* brown, very much diluted, should be quickly taken over the whole. Use a larger brush for this, and work quickly with plenty of stain on the brush. With a silk rag gently remove any superfluous stain. You must now let your work dry thoroughly, and while you are waiting you can stain the back piece of the scissors-case with the same diluted solution.

When the work is dry, deepen any parts of the dragon that look too pale. Now have ready a saucer of a much deeper tint of brown, and go over the background only. Let the work dry, and if you are not satisfied with the colour, put on another coat. It should not be necessary to put on more than three coats.

When the staining is finished, be sure to go round the outline again with the modelling tool and mark in any details, such as markings on the tail or wings that may have become blurred. The staining and damping tend to make the modelling less distinct, so these finishing touches are very necessary. You should now have a very pleasing result.

For those who are more ambitious, a more elaborate colour-scheme might be worked out, for example, in blue and green. This combination is one of the most effective colourings and is not difficult to produce. If you want the head and upper part of the animal to be green and the lower parts blue, begin by colouring the top of the head yellow, with a little patch on the cheek. Colour the jaws too; leave some of the head unstained where it is going to be blue. Colour the tongue red. The upper side of the body down to the tail should be yellow, leaving the other part unstained. Look at your design carefully; wherever you have put yellow it will become green when the blue is put on, so that plenty of unstained leather should be left. Now damp the leather, and put on an " all-over " wash of pale blue, covering the whole of the leather.

When the work is dry, add any darker shades on the dragon.

Cut a piece of leather for the back of the case, and stain it to match the front. Cut out the front piece, and thong the two together.

Before thonging the pieces together, the back of the scissors-case could be lined with a piece of brown skiven, to match the brown stain.

CUT OR INCISED WORK

The outline of modelled work may be emphasised by cutting into the leather with a sharp pointed knife to about one-third of the thickness of the leather. This is called incised or cut work, and it is very frequently used in conjunction with modelling, with the result that the design appears as if raised on the surface of the leather. The leather used must not be too thin.

Incising is not a difficult process, and gives most effective results.

We will now describe the various steps in this work.

Cutting the Lines.—The leather, with the design clearly traced upon it, should rest upon a slab of marble or other hard material. Take the knife in the right hand, and place the forefinger well down the back of the blade, while the left hand rests upon the leather. Insert the point of the knife into the line to be cut, and draw it along the line, keeping the knife vertical ; an inclination to the right or left will produce a slant-cut edge, which will tend to curl when the background is pressed down. The result should be a clean, sharp incision, absolutely vertical and plainly visible to the eye. The depth of the incision will depend upon the effect to be produced by modelling, but it should never be deeper than one-third of the thickness of the leather.

When curved lines are being cut, the leather must be gently turned by the left hand so that it is always in the best position for the knife. The knife itself should not be turned.

Two lines that meet or cross each other must not be cut right up to the point of meeting or intersecting, but a small space left, and the line afterwards continued with the modelling tool; otherwise the piece of leather between the intersecting lines will curl up and spoil the appearance of the work.

Opening the Cut.—For this purpose a special tool called an opener may be used, but many workers prefer to use only the edge of a fine modeller. Before using the opener on the leather, moisten the leather with a sponge dipped in water; allow a few seconds for the water to sink into the surface. Now insert the thin end of the tool into the cut, holding the modeller between the thumbs and two fingers, with two fingers of the left hand also on the end for additional pressure. Press gently forward with a slight gliding motion, with the edge of the modeller against the outline, and the broad or round part of the tool outwards so as to press down the background.

Although you must move the tool *forward* as you open the cut, it is easier to work the tool to and fro to ensure that the edges are well and evenly parted.

The width of the opening will depend upon the design and the nature and size of the work, but in any case it is necessary to work the tool along the cut several times. The background is now sunk by pressing the modelling tool upon it, while sliding it over the surface. Keep the tip of the tool close against the outline, so that the outer edge of the cut may be smoothed into the ground.

If the incisions are too deeply cut they are likely, when the work is finished, to show a white line between the modelled part and the background, owing to the exposure of the inner substance of the leather; this also happens if the incisions are opened too widely. The only thing to do is to stain the line to match the surface of the leather. When the opening has been done, the next step is the modelling. This has already been described.

Incising may be made very attractive, without modelling, by adding colour or punching, or both; a cut outline indeed always adds considerable emphasis to the ornament.

There are in Salzburg and also in the Vienna Museum old volumes, the covers of which are decorated with dragons and ornaments in cut leather, while the background is slightly stamped. So beautiful are these cut-leather covers considered that facsimiles of them will be found in most European museums.

PUNCHED OR HAMMERED LEATHER

This form of decoration is generally done on calf-skin or cowhide, but it can quite well be done on the cheaper leather called basil. Leather decorated entirely by means of punches is called hammered leather. Punched work is often used in conjunction with modelled and incised leather. Punching should always be done after the leather has been stained.

Backgrounds ornamented by steel punches give greater beauty to the work, giving texture to the background and rendering the raised parts more distinctive. Punching also makes the leather more durable, as the more you hammer leather the stronger it becomes.

The matting punches used are steel or brass, with the design cut at the point either in relief or in intaglia. Punches are made in many different forms, and an infinite variety of patterns can be produced with their aid, either singly or in combination. (See section on Blind Tooling.)

If steel punches are used, they must be kept bright and clean or a bluish mark is sometimes made by them on the leather when it is damp. The punch can either be pressed on the leather by the hand alone, or (and this is the better way) tapped gently but sharply with a small hammer flat on the head. You must be careful to hold the punch perfectly upright, as if it slopes ever so slightly the impression left on the leather will be blurred and unsatisfactory, one part of the pattern being almost invisible while the other part will be forced too deeply into the leather.

For hand pressure only the punches should be fixed in wooden handles to afford greater grip and power. They may be used hot, and then the punch-mark on the leather is darkened. In working, the punch must be placed against the outline of the design, but on no account must it rest on the outline itself. First punch all round the design and then over the complete background, using the same force with each blow of the hammer.

The impressions need not be made in any regular order, and it does not matter if the pattern of the punch overlaps in places, as long as the whole background is well covered, but not so even as to look machine-like. For background purposes the most useful punches are those which produce a small check or powdered design. Punches with patterns of dots, pearls, stars, leaves, etc., are used in Mexican decoration for accentuating part of the design. If the punched depressions are varnished and then painted with bronze or gouache (water-colours so mixed as to present a dead opaque surface), or gold or silver powder, a very pleasing effect is produced.

Where punches cannot be obtained, the blunt point of an iron nail produces quite good effects, and screw heads can be shaped into useful punches by filing.

FURTHER SUGGESTIONS FOR DECORATING LEATHER

There are other interesting ways of decorating leather such as the following : (1) Blind Tooling, (2) Embossing, (3) Stencilling, (4) Pierced Leather Work, (5) Inlay, (6) Appliqué, (7) Poker Work or Pyrography, (8) Cloutage.

(1) BLIND TOOLING.—This is a process of decorating leather by pressing patterns on it by means of the punches already described. A beginner is astonished to see the infinite number of designs or patterns which may be evolved from the geometrical and other forms embodied in the ends of the punches. There are circles, curve lines, dots, simple leaf and flower forms of all kinds. These can be judiciously ranged so that they blend into one harmonious whole. By repeating geometric patterns, interesting border designs can be made.

The punches may be used cold, but if heated the impression they make is more permanent.

Directions for using Heated Punches.—First prepare a pattern on paper according to the shapes and sizes of the tools you have available. Clip the design down on the leather (see section on Transferring the Design). Heat the tool in a gas flame. It is wise to ascertain the correct temperature by trying the tool on a piece of waste leather. The tool should leave a clear impression when pressed on the leather ; if too hot, it may scorch the surface of the skin. You can reduce the heat of the tool by laying it on a piece of damp rag. When you have got the correct heat, press the tool on the lines of the paper design until it is all transferred. Now remove the paper and go over the design once more on the leather to deepen and sharpen the pattern. You must be careful to apply the right tools to the corresponding impression. The paper can be removed and the design printed directly on the leather.

For blind tooling nothing further is required except to varnish lightly with a pad of cotton-wool dipped in light French varnish, or to polish with a soft rag followed by a brisk rubbing with the hand. If you decide to varnish the leather, you should apply starch size to it first, but there is no need to varnish ; simple polishing is quite effective.

(2) EMBOSSING is raising parts of the design from behind, using either a ball-nosed tool or modeller ; the latter is quite suitable. Trace the pattern on the leather in the usual way. On the back of the leather place a piece of carbon paper with the carbon side against the back, and trace over the part of the design you want to raise, and the lines will appear on the back of the leather. You can now see the parts that are going to be raised. Damp with a sponge all the parts to be embossed. Now lay the leather face downward upon some soft pad of rubber or felt. Press the modeller into the pattern on the back of the leather, and as the soft pad gives way the leather is forced out. Do not press the leather out too much, as there is a danger of making the work look lumpy and inartistic ; it is delicate rather than bold treatment that is to be desired.

The parts of the design that are forced into high relief must be supported, otherwise they will sink back again, so the hollows must be filled with a mixture of paste and paper or cotton-wool. Then paste a piece of paper over the back and proceed with the modelling. The outline of the pattern may be pressed in with the modeller to intensify it, or it may be incised and the background pressed down and punched, as already described.

A matted background is very effective, as it forms a marked contrast to the smooth surface of the modelled portion.

Embossing is an interesting process to try, and most charming effects can be obtained by keeping the main part of the work delicate and low, and raising a few spots in higher relief. The contrast between the delicate modelling and the bolder appearance of the embossed portions is very delightful.

(3) STENCILLING ON LEATHER (for advice about Stencilling, see Chapter XVII.).—You can use stencilled patterns with excellent results upon any kind of leather. It is a quick and

effective way of colouring leather—quick because it does away with the necessity of tracing the design.

We will deal first with stencilling on calf or basil. Choose a good clear piece of leather, and cut it the right size. Fix the leather to a drawing-board as already described, and lay the stencil over it. Colour carefully, using either spirit or water stains. Aim at getting a good clean colouring; do not attempt a great deal of shading. Apply the colour very sparingly.

When you have stencilled the design and the colour is quite dry, damp the leather very carefully, and outline the design with a modeller; then press all the background down flat with the modeller.

For stencilling on soft leathers, oil colour thinned with turpentine is suitable. Use the colour very sparingly, and be very careful that it does not spread beneath the stencil plate; for the whole effect of the stencil depends upon clear-cut edges and well-defined shapes, and if your brush is too full of colour it will ooze under the plate and ruin the article. When dry, the nap of the velvet can be restored by scraping it with the back of a knife.

(4) PIERCED LEATHER.—This form of decoration is perhaps most suitable for suède, velvet calf, or other thin leathers. It is very similar to stencilling. A pattern is cut out of the leather, and a different coloured leather is placed on the under side so that it shows through the interstices.

It is most important that the shapes cut out should be pleasing in form and well arranged. As in stencilling, the ties play a most important part, because they knit the whole design together.

It is wise to plan the design on paper first. Then it can be transferred to the leather by tracing over it with a steel point. Whether carbon paper is used or not depends upon the surface of the leather. Now cut out the shapes with a sharp knife that pierces right through the leather so that a neat edge is made. A sheet of glass forms a good surface for cutting on, but it tends to blunt the edge of the knife; cardboard can be used instead. The cut edge may be stained if it shows too white.

Hints on cutting the Leather.—Do not draw the knife in a forward movement over the design, but aim at feeding in the leather towards the knife with the left hand.

To do good work in pierced leather requires considerable skill in cutting stencils, and this can be acquired with practice. Wood-carving tools are very useful when doing bold openwork. They make clean, direct cuts as compared with the knife, which tends to drag the leather.

Now lay the leather face downwards on a drawing-board and spread over it a thin layer of paste. Place a piece of leather of suitable size and colour over it so that it shows through the spaces in the pattern. Put weights upon it, and let it dry.

This form of decoration is most effective when used for a monogram on a card-case.

A very simple form of pierced leather work can be done by punching holes, varying the size and spacing of the holes so that they make a pretty design, and then pasting leather of a contrasting colour behind the design. In this way initials or monograms look very effective on book covers, bags, or notebooks. If the design is to be in the corner, then the punch pliers can be used, but if it is to form the centre of a cushion cover or other large piece of work, it is better to use a single punch and a hammer.

An attractive Blotter decorated with Pierced Work.—This is not a difficult blotter to make. Choose a piece of velvet Persian in some deep shade, about 19½ by 12½ inches. Lay it out very flat on a drawing-board and secure it round the edges with drawing-pins. As this outer edge is going to be cut off, it does not matter if the pins mark the leather.

Select a simple bold stencil design, place it in position at one end of the leather, and go over the outlines with a tracer. Any straight lines can be drawn with the help of a ruler. Take the knife and cut (as already described) along the lines of the pattern. Transfer the design to the other end of the leather and do the same. Unpin the leather. Now cut another piece of a contrasting colour and the same size. Pin this on the board, suède side upwards. Turn the cut piece of leather suède side downwards, and paste over the glazed side, then turn it over and lay it on top of the other piece. When pasting be very careful not to put too much paste near the cut edges, so that there is no danger of the paste coming out. Place a board over the two pieces, weight it heavily, and leave until dry.

Then cut off about ½ inch of leather all the way round, having first ruled a line with the tracer. Take care to see that the corners are square. Punch holes all round about ¼ inch from the edge, and thong with thongs of the darker leather.

Before beginning the thonging, cut a strip of leather about ⅓ inch wide, punch holes each end to correspond with the holes in the fold of the blotter, and thong it down the middle to hold the blotting-paper in place.

(5) INLAY.—This form of decoration is similar to inlay in woodwork. It consists of letting one piece of leather into another. The two leathers must be of the same thickness, and it is more suitable for thick leathers. It is a suitable decoration for table mats of all kinds. It is a difficult process to fit the pattern exactly into the space cut out, and can only be done with patterns of bold simple outline.

(6) APPLIQUÉ.—In this process shapes of leather of a different colour or texture are pasted on the leather to be decorated. (See chapter on Appliqué Work.)

(i) *Appliqué Work with Calf* is used more particularly for book-covers of good quality, as otherwise its place is usually taken by staining, which is much simpler. The piece of leather to be applied must be damped and pared very thin. When it is dry, cut it the right shape, pare the edges to a uniform thickness, paste the back, and put it in the right position. It must be allowed to dry under pressure. The edges can be tooled or decorated with an incised pattern.

(ii) *Appliqué Work with Soft Leathers, Velvet Persians, Suèdes, etc.*—A great many of the suggestions already given in the chapter on Appliqué Work can be carried out in soft leathers. These are particularly suited to this type of work, as the edges do not fray.

It is a good plan to save up the countless scraps of leather left over after making up suède articles, as they are invaluable for making all kinds of delightful designs. You can also buy bundles of coloured leather for this purpose. Address books, writing-cases, notebooks, bags, almost anything can be decorated with this work.

Many of the suggestions in the chapter on Appliqué can be worked out in leather.

Monograms and initials can be cut from leather and used for decorating card-cases, book-covers, purses, etc.

Grip-Fix is a good paste to use, as it does not soil the leather so easily as seccotine. It must be put on sparingly, so that it does not ooze out and spoil the design. Instead of using paste, appliqué patterns of soft velvet Persians can be sewn on with silk. (See Chapter VIII., "Appliqué Work.")

(7) PYROGRAPHY, OR POKER WORK.—Poker work can be done on leather with quite effective results, and it can be combined with staining and colouring.

The design is transferred to the leather in the manner already described. Then fasten the leather on a drawing-board with drawing-pins, and go over the outline with the tracer. The outline is then ready for poker work.

Heat the point and outline the design, burning *only* the surface of the leather. This makes a brown outline round the design. Tones of brown may be given to the design or background if desired.

(8) CLOUTAGE.—This is a method of decorating leather by using the heads of special nails, which may be either plain or of fancy design.

There are two kinds of nails : those for decorating leather-covered boxes, and those used for decorating articles of soft leather such as bags, pochettes, etc.

Decorating Leather-covered Wooden Boxes.—Boxes decorated in this way are most artistic objects, and their enduring and serviceable character well repays the time and cost spent in making them. There is no need to buy special boxes for the purpose. Cigar or similar boxes are quite suitable. The leather used for covering them must be thin. Specially prepared thin calf gives the best results. It can be left plain or modelled and coloured.

To cover the Box.—Cut a piece for the top of the lid, leaving $\frac{1}{8}$ inch margin all round. Pare the edges evenly with a sharp knife. Paste the back of the leather, and after leaving it for a few minutes, lay it carefully over the lid of the box. Smooth out all wrinkles, and be especially careful to see that the edges stick well to the box. Now cut a band of leather for the sides long enough to overlap a little when placed tightly round the box, and as broad as the depth of the box from the upper edge of the lid when shut to the bottom of the box. Carefully thin or pare the ends of the leather that overlap, and the top of the band where it will cover the leather on the lid. Paste it and put it round the box so that the join comes in the middle of the back. Let it dry thoroughly. Then run a sharp knife along the joint between lid and box at sides and front only. The " V " groove at the hinge will give you the point of insertion of knife. The box is now ready for decoration with the nails. You must first decide where the nails are to go. Then with a fine pointed awl, held perpendicular, prick deeply through the leather and the wood of the box. This hole will prevent the nail slipping sideways and so being hammered in aslant, and makes it unnecessary to hold the nail for hammering.

Use a ruler as a guide if the holes are to be in a straight line.

If the nails are to be very close together in the design, great care must be taken to see that each nail rests exactly beside the next. It is best, therefore, to measure the diameter of the nail head and then arrange the holes so that the distance between them is equal to the diameter of the nail head. Another way to fix the position of the nails is to prick through the paper pattern of the design after you have traced the main lines.

Decorating Soft Leather.—For soft leathers the nails used have double shanks, which are put through holes in the leather, then turned back and hammered flat. When the nails have been put, for example, in the flap of a bag or pochette, it is advisable to line the flap with brown paper to about $\frac{1}{4}$ inch of the edges before putting on the skiver, as otherwise the shanks of the nails may show through and spoil the lining.

Those who are interested in this form of leatherwork (or indeed leatherwork of all kinds) will find the catalogue called *Better Leathercraft*, issued free by Messrs. George & Co., Noel Street, London, most helpful. It gives the uses of the various leathers, their prices, tools, and hints on using them, and all the various accessories needed for leatherwork.

CHAPTER XXX

SOME USEFUL IDEAS FOR GIFTS, BAZAARS, AND THE HOME

Cheap and Pretty Bags. Mats for the Verandah, Motor, or Garden. Calico Christmas Calendars. Billie Socks and How to make Him. A Child's Knitted Ball. Knitted Reins. Decorating and Colouring Cork Mats. Chair-Back and Arms. Some Pretty Border Designs. A Table Runner.

CHEAP AND PRETTY BAGS (Fig. 217)

THESE bags are very inexpensive to make and yet look very attractive. They will be welcome gifts at any time, and are specially useful for bazaars.

The materials required for a bag are: a small dishcloth of loose but even weave; woollen yarn in two or three contrasting colours; a crewel needle or a darning needle, with an eye large enough to be easily threaded; cotton thread, needle, and scissors.

The dishcloth will make a bag 7½ by 9 inches; this is a useful work-bag. The design can be planned on squared paper, but many suggestions for patterns will be found in the section on Embroidery upon Counted Threads.

The patterns may be arranged on the bags either vertically or horizontally. (The dishcloths may, of course, be dyed before use with cold-water dyes.)

After the design is planned, weave it with a double thread of woollen yarn. Do not break the yarn, but cut it with scissors. Draw the yarn through the meshes very carefully and slowly, to prevent the dishcloth from puckering. Lay the work flat on the table now and then, to test its smoothness.

If several adjoining rows of yarn are to be made the same colour, cut a piece of yarn long enough for at least two rows.

511

The stitches at the edges between the rows will be hidden by the seam. Begin each row of stitches about four meshes from a selvedge, and weave the thread across the dishcloth to within two meshes of the opposite edge. No knot or fastening of the stitches in the ends of the yarn is necessary, since the seam which joins the edges together holds the yarn in place.

After the design is woven on the dishcloth, put the two long edges together, allowing two meshes of the edge which has four empty meshes to project beyond the other edge. Sew them together with cotton thread, using back stitches. Bring the wider edge over the other edge, and sew it down with overhand stitches. Tuck in the edges of the yarn as you sew. Finish the top edge of the bag with blanket stitch, using the yarn double.

Since the dishcloth ravels easily, the first row of stitches for a French seam at the bottom of the bag should be sewed before the extra cloth is cut off. Overhand the edges of the cut cloth before reversing the bag and making the second row of stitches.

Crochet the draw-strings, using single chain stitch.

To make a tassel, first cut a piece of cardboard 2 by 4 inches, and wind the yarn around it. Clip the yarn along one edge, and place it folded over the draw-string. Wind a piece of wool (yarn) around the bunch of yarn, just below the draw-string. Tie this with a hard knot, leaving 2-inch ends to mix with the other cut ends. Trim the ends of the tassel evenly. For further suggestions for cords and tassels, see Chapter XIII. When finished, put a cloth over the bag and press it with a hot iron.

A white dishcloth bag decorated in blue and black wool looks attractive.

Mats for the Verandah, or Motor, or Garden

Pretty light mats can easily be made. They are convenient to carry about, and look decorative. They have the additional advantage of being soft and cushiony, so that they are pleasant to sit upon.

To make these mats one needs two pieces of grass matting. The best matting for the purpose is fibre matting or Japanese matting that can be bought in most big shops. One can sometimes get a plain matting given to one, because it is used to wrap up certain commercial products and is often thrown aside as a

Loose covers: method of measuring chair for quantities of materials needed.

[To face p. 512

Easy-chair in cretonne loose cover.

Part of couch with loose cover piped in contrasting shade,
showing how loose cushion covers are made.

Arm-chair in loose cover with box-pleated frill.

Cretonne cover completed.

Velour curtains and pelmet, voile glass curtains.

Knitting garter stitch.

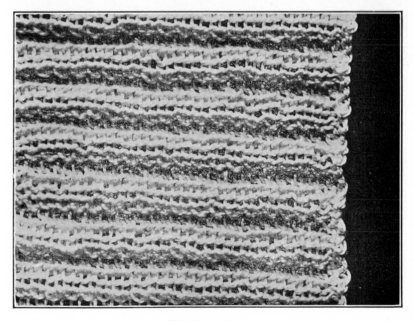

Knitting—ribbing

Double crochet or rose stitch.

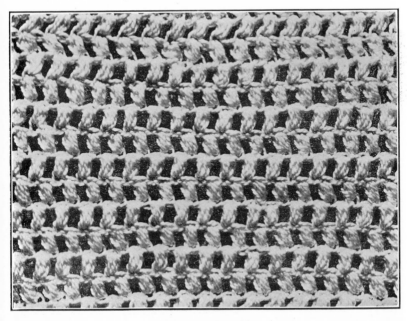

Crochet, single treble.

Tray cloth edged with crochet lace.

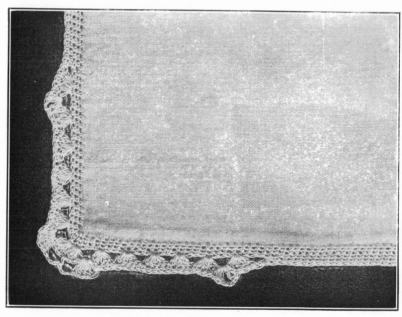

Detail of crochet-lace edging to tray cloth.

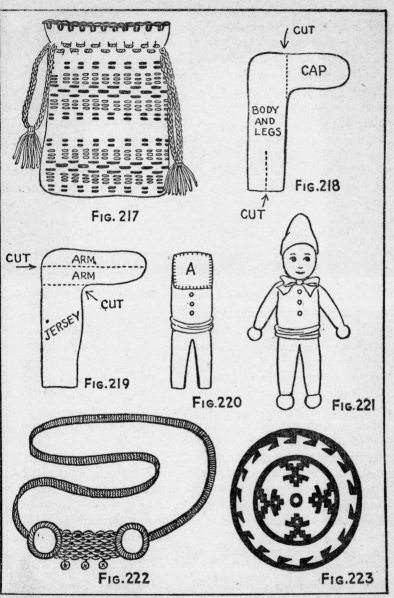

FIG. 217.—Dishcloth Bag.   FIGS. 218, 219, 220, and 221.—Billie Socks.
FIG. 222.—A Child's Reins.   FIG. 223.—Painted Cork Mat.

waste material. However, unless one knows the right kind of shops that use this material, one must buy it. The bought kind, of course, looks the best and is not torn, soiled, or broken in any way, so that every bit can be used.

The mats can be round, square, or oblong. Two pieces of matting are needed for each mat. Cut them the actual size the mat is to be when finished. To make a round mat it is best to draw round a large round utensil—the lid of the copper, etc. To keep the edges from fraying, it is wise to stitch around them with a sewing machine.

Over this a band of fancy braid or bright tape can be sewn, but this is not essential except perhaps for round mats. Instead of binding square or oblong mats in this way, the edges can be turned under. In this case 2 inches extra must be allowed on all sides for turning under. Cut away a little of the turned-down edges at the corners, or mitre them to avoid bulkiness. Baste the edges down with strong thread. (The edges of both pieces of matting are later sewn together with wool.)

Having prepared the two pieces of matting in this way, the next step is to think of a design. A design can be applied to both pieces of matting or to the top piece only. Stencils may be used (see Chapter XVII., " Stencilling ") or transfer designs may perhaps be obtained. Some people, who can draw well, draw a simple pattern freehand with chalk on to the matting.

There are now several ways of working up the design. It can be outlined with woollen stitches and some parts entirely filled in with stitches. There are plenty of suitable stitches to be found in the different sections about embroidery—a simple running stitch is easily worked on this matting, and a back stitch makes a very effective outline. Stitches like the stem stitch or the outline stitch are a little difficult if the matting is stiff. For parts that have to be filled in, use plain over-and-over stitches. When the two pieces of matting for the top and bottom are ready, the next thing to do is to make the padding or cushion for the middle of the mat. To do this, cut two pieces of un-bleached muslin about $\frac{1}{2}$ inch larger than the matting all round. Sew these together and stuff it—any odd pieces of material torn or cut up into small bits will do for stuffing. It is wise to tack through the cushion at intervals to keep the stuffing evenly distributed. The cushion should be at least 2 inches thick when it is stuffed, because it soon presses or mats down to less than this.

Now put the padding or cushion between the two pieces of matting, and sew the matting together. There are several ways of doing this :

(1) If the edges have been turned under, they look best if they are held together by woollen stitches. First stitch around the mat edges with evenly spaced diagonal stitches ; then turn the mat over and go around again in the opposite direction, crossing the first stitches so that the edge looks prettily cross-stitched.

(2) If the two pieces of matting have been edged with braid, the edges can be drawn together by oversewing them with a strong piece of yarn. The stitches need not be too close together.

(3) Another method, if the matting has been turned up and no braid is used, is to join the pieces together with a buttonhole stitch. Turn the mat so that the edge of the buttonholing will be on the upper side when it is finished. The advantage of this method and the first method described is that the inner pad or cushion shows through the woollen stitching, and if the pad is covered with a bright material it looks very effective showing through stitches of a contrasting colour.

A very decorative mat can be made by painting the design on the matting in oil colours, letting it dry, and then outlining it with bright-coloured wool.

Two finished mats fastened together along one long side make a very comfortable seat, one mat for the back to rest against, and one to sit upon. Try this on a hard garden seat, or for an extra seat in the car.

Calico Christmas Calendars

These are attractive novelties for a bazaar or a Christmas gift. They are quick and economical to make ; all sorts of coloured scraps of material, or sample patterns may be used. Cut a piece of cardboard the required size—3 by 4½ inches makes a pretty little calendar. Cut the scraps into triangular pieces of various sizes ; trim the frayed edges very closely. Arrange them in a pretty combination on the cardboard, so that no two pieces of the same material are next to each other. Now paste them in position, covering the surface and the four edges. The back of the cardboard can be covered in the same way, or another piece of cardboard of the same size can be pasted over, hiding the turnover edges of the pieces of material. Cover a strip of cardboard, 1 inch by 3½ inches, with the scraps, and paste it to the back of the calendar to act as a support.

Outline each triangle of cloth with black crayon. Give the whole calendar a coat of white shellac. This will preserve the cloth and give the surface a smooth finish. Add a tiny calendar.

A pretty way of outlining the triangles is to make a row of stitches round each, taking the needle right through the thin cardboard and back again. The back can be covered with cardboard or a piece of material.

BILLIE SOCKS AND HOW TO MAKE HIM (Fig. 221)

This amusing little doll is easily made from a pair of men's socks or from two odd socks of different colours.

Cut one sock as shown in Fig. 218. Sew up the legs and the open part at the side. Stuff with cotton-wool, bits of wool, or soft rags, and sew up the top. The second sock makes the jersey and the arms, and is cut as shown in Fig. 219. Slip the jersey part over the body and roll up the end. Sew a piece of white cloth over the part parked A, Fig. 220, for the face. Embroider the eyes, nose, and mouth ; two buttons could be used for the eyes. Tie a piece of ribbon round the neck and put on the foot of the first sock for the cap. Make arms from the foot of the second sock. Tie a piece of strong thread around the arms and legs to form hands and feet respectively (Fig. 221).

A CHILD'S KNITTED BALL

This is an easily made toy that delights little children. It can be knitted from any odd lengths of wool of medium thickness. It may be made in two colours. It is formed of eight sections knitted in one piece. The directions for making the ball are as follows : Use two needles, No. 14. Cast on forty loops.

First Row : Knit to within *one* loop of the end of the needle, turn the work round ; although the wool seems in the wrong place to continue the knitting, take no notice of this.

Second Row : Slip off the first loop (keeping a firm hold of the wool), and knit to within *one* loop of the end.   Turn the work.

Third and Fourth Rows : Knit to within *two* loops of the end.

Fifth and Sixth Rows : Knit to within *three* loops of the end. Continue knitting until there are ten loops remaining unused at the end and beginning of the row.   Knit to the end of the row, and join on as invisibly as possible with the other colour.

The same process is repeated till the eight sections are completed.   Cast off, leaving an end long enough to finish sewing the circle.

Put into a pill-box or other small box a few beads or small buttons to rattle.   Wind any odd pieces of wool or frayings of wool round the box to make it the right shape to fill the knitting. Sew up the case, leaving all ends inside the ball, and press it into a good shape.

KNITTED REINS (Fig. 222)

To make these reins, you need 3 ounces of fingering in red or blue or a combination of two bright colours, No. 9 needles, and four little bells.

For the reins, cast on eight stitches in plain knitting, slipping the first stitch in every row, and knit a length of $2\frac{1}{2}$ yards.

For the armholes, cast on ten stitches, and knit two pieces about $\frac{1}{2}$ yard long.   Get some cord and cover it with any material the colour of the wool ; sew the knitted piece round it, and sew to the reins.

For the breast-piece, cast on eighteen stitches, knit a length of about 10 inches, and join it to the armholes at the front. Finally sew on the bells.

THE DECORATION OF CORK MATS

Table mats are always useful about the house wherever the protection of a polished surface is necessary, and they are extremely decorative if you choose colours that harmonise with your room and crockery.   Cork mats are not expensive to buy ; they can be decorated in a variety of ways, using such materials as beads and embroidery cotton, raffia and cane, or they can have simple patterns stencilled on them.   These mats are particularly useful for the dinner-table, as they do not allow the heat to penetrate through them.

To decorate a Set of Mats with Raffia.—You will require a needle with an eye large enough to take a strand of raffia, but it must not be too coarse as it will break the cork. There are a variety of stitches to use—buttonhole, oversewing, etc., and by using two different coloured strands of raffia many interesting borders can be worked out.

(1) Suppose you choose blue and orange for the raffia, and decide to oversew the edges of the mats. Turn the mat over and draw a pencil-line round the mat about $\frac{1}{4}$ inch from the edge. This will be a guide-line for your stitches. Divide it into spaces about $\frac{3}{10}$ inch.

Begin with the blue raffia, and pass the needle through one of the pencil marks, leaving an end for joining. Take the raffia over the edge of the mat, and bring the needle up through the next hole, and so on all round the mat. Tie the two ends of raffia in a reef knot on the wrong side of the mat. Sew round the mat again with the orange raffia, but work in the opposite direction, taking the needle into the same holes. You will now have a pretty V-shaped border.

(2) Another pretty border can be worked in the following way. Mark out the stitches in pencil as before, but this time make a pencil mark on the right side of the mat, above every alternate pencil mark on the under side.

Bring the needle up through one of the pencil marks, leaving an end for fastening off ; take the raffia over the edge and bring the needle up through the same hole again. Now push the needle down through the next pencil mark on top of the mat, bring the raffia back over the edge and down through the same hole again, then up through the next pencil mark, and so on all round the mat. Now thread your needle with a strand of raffia of contrasting colour and, using a running stitch, fill up the spaces that have been left. This is the same stitch that the Japanese use in sewing together the pages of their books.

Join all new strands where necessary with a reef knot, and see that the knots come on the wrong side of the mat.

(3) Another variety of raffia border is to lay strands of raffia along the edge of the mat, and hold them in position by

oversewing with raffia of a contrasting colour. Mark the position of the stitches as already described. Blue and orange raffia would look bright and effective. Lay the strands of orange raffia around the edge of the mat, and let them overlap the top to the depth marked out for the stitches. Oversew them in position with a strand of blue raffia. To finish off, let the ends of the orange raffia overlap for about an inch, and sew over them.

(4) A cork mat with a border of string and raffia may be made, using the Mariposa stitch.

Choose a cord about the thickness of the mat, measure a length of it round the mat, and mark the joining-point—allow about an inch for joining ; fray out both ends, and thin them slightly so that they will join together neatly.

Mark the position of the stitches around the mat about $\frac{1}{2}$ inch from the edge and about $\frac{1}{2}$ inch apart. There should be an even number of stitches. Place the cord on the edge of the mat and insert the needle through one of the pencil marks. Take the raffia round the cord four or five times, and insert the needle in the same hole. You will now have made a long V-shaped stitch. Continue in this way all round the mat.

When the joining-point is reached, work over the ends and secure the end of the raffia strand by threading it along the cord under the raffia for a short distance.

Now measure off the cord for the next row, and prepare the ends in the same way. Work as before, but take the stitches in between the stitches of the first row, not into the mat, and connect the rows by a long stitch as used in the Lazy Squaw.

A third row can be added in the same way, or as many more as desired.

No. 8 cane, or a foundation of several strands of raffia, could be used instead of cord.

A bright colour scheme for three rows would be green, red, and green, or orange, green, and orange.

Square wooden beads of contrasting colours make a pretty edging. They should be sewn to the mat with buttonhole stitches of mercerised embroidery cotton of a colour to harmonise with the beads.

The stitches must be carefully spaced and marked out around a pencilled circle about $\frac{1}{4}$ inch in from the edge of the mat. If you are using two or more colours of beads, you must count the spaces to see if the colours fit in correctly.

In sewing on the beads use a double thread of the mercerised cotton to thread the needle. Insert the needle vertically so that the stitches will be the same size on both sides of the mat. Begin by making a buttonhole stitch, leaving an end for fastening off ; take one, or for quickness two, beads on the needle, and take the needle through the next pencil mark. Draw the threads tight so that the beads are firm against the edge of the mat. When joining on another length of cotton, arrange for the knot to come inside one of the beads. To finish, tie the last threads to the ends left, then thread each double end, one to the left and one to the right, through the beads, and cut off closely.

Colouring Cork Mats

A really novel and attractive set of mats can be made in fine colour schemes, using designs from Indian basketry, weaving, or pottery.

Before painting the mats, they can be given a coat of size if desired, thus obtaining an even surface more easily, as the cork is somewhat porous. But this is not necessary.

Various paints can be used, such as the following :

Enamel.—A special enamel can be obtained from the Dryad Works, Leicester. This is not readily marked by moderately hot plates and dishes. It dries very quickly, so that if you are painting the whole surface of the mat it must be applied with a fairly large brush, and as swiftly as possible.

Do not work it about with the brush or the surface will be spoilt. Two coats of enamel give a good surface. Each coat takes about twenty minutes to dry. For decoration on the enamel, use a fine brush and choose a simple border pattern, as very fine work cannot be done with enamel.

Artists' Oil Paints.—These, with the exception of black, should be mixed with just enough white enamel to give them a gloss.

Opaque Water-colours or poster paints and indian ink for the black portions can be used.

Ordinary Water-colours may be used. When these are dry the mat must be painted with a coat of white shellac.

The whole mat may be coloured a suitable background colour, and the design painted round the edge, or the middle can be left showing the plain cork.

The Design for the Mat.—Many beautiful designs can be found by studying the basketry, weaving, beadwork, and pottery made by the American Indians. Specimens of this work can be seen in the British Museum, from which designs can be worked out. For designs in Indian Basketry, see the section on Coiled Basketry.

The design must be worked out on a piece of paper the size of the mat, and may be transferred to the mat by means of carbon paper. If the design is a bold simple one (and these are best) it can be marked on the mat with a pencil to make sure it will fit in. Apply the paint with as free a movement of the brush as possible, so that it does not have a laboured effect.

Fig. 223 shows a very effective pattern in tan and black; the design is built up on concentric circles and is taken from a basket decoration.

Stencilling with washable Stencil Paints is another effective method of decoration, and is particularly useful where a number of mats have to be decorated. For a round mat it is necessary to cut only a quarter of the stencil, and for an oval mat only half, as the stencil can be cleaned, turned over, and used for the rest of the mat. You must be very careful to see that the joined portions of the pattern are correct (see Chapter XVII., ' Stencilling ").

Stick-Printing.—This is an interesting way of making designs, and simple border patterns for mats can be carried out most effectively. It is really a process of printing, for the colour is applied to the end of a small stick and stamped on the material. The sticks are of various shapes—square, circular, triangular, semicircular, oblong, etc., while some are cut in simple designs. All these various shapes and designs can be combined in a great many ways to form very attractive patterns.

The paint used can be special stencil paint, or printers' ink. Enamel is not quite so good, as it does not give such a clear impression.

To print the designs on the mats, you can use either pads of felt as already described (see Chapter XXII., " Potato-Printing "), or you can paint the colour on the end of the stick with a brush. Some people prefer the latter method, and obtain excellent results with it.

The sticks should be cleaned with turpentine very thoroughly after use, so that when used again they will print good clean patterns.

A very good leaflet on the decoration of cork mats, with many suggestions for patterns, is published by the Dryad Handicrafts, 42 St. Nicholas Street, Leicester.

CHAIR-BACK AND ARMS (Fig. 224)

The design for these can be drawn by any one, and only two simple stitches are used in the working of it. It depends for its effect on the colour scheme chosen. It is worked on natural-coloured, loosely woven linen with " Anchor " Flox embroidery cotton, which is thick and so fills the design very quickly. Dark cyclamen colour is chosen for the double line of back stitches, and green for the daisy stitches.

Cut out the chair-back to the size required, and the arms, to about 17 by 13 inches. Make hems ⅜ inch in width on three sides of each piece, and ¾ inch across the front.

Now draw the design above the wide hem. Mark the middle of the chair-back by a crease, then make two more in the opposite direction, one 3 inches up from the front edge and parallel with it, and another 1 inch up. Using the edge of a small plate, pencil a curve 2 inches deep and 6 inches across, exactly in the middle of the chair-back. The crease marks will help you to do this quickly. Now pencil more scallops on each side of the first, each one overlapping the last one for 2 inches, as in Fig. 224. Connect the scallops together with a loop (Fig. 224). Draw a second set of scallops and loops ¾ inch inside the first (Fig. 224). Continue the design to the extreme edge of the chair-back. It is immaterial if a scallop is incomplete when both sides are alike, which they should be, if you began to draw exactly in the middle. Begin at the left-hand side with the dark cyclamen, by working a few running stitches between the two pencil-lines and bringing the needle out on the lower one. Work the stitches on the inner curve quite close together, but a fraction of an inch apart on the outer one. This does not mean that the material may

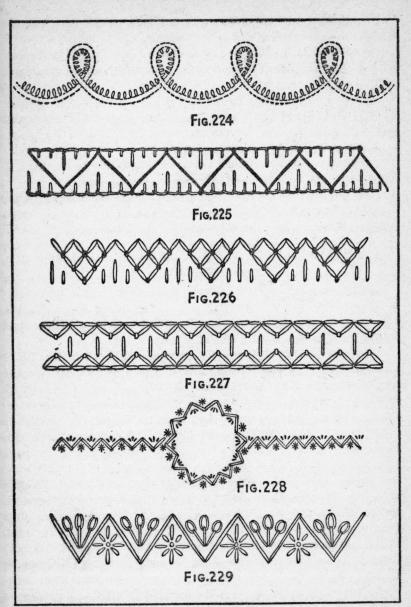

Fig. 224

Fig. 225

Fig. 226

Fig. 227

Fig. 228

Fig. 229

FIGS. 224, 225, 226, 227, 228, and 229.—Pretty Border Designs for Household Articles.

show between the stitches, for the effect would be spoilt if it did.

(A method of working a double line of back stitches is shown in Fig. 77, Chapter VI., under the section about Roumanian Embroidery.)

When you have worked as far as the loop, slip the needle to the other side of the lines that cross each other, and continue working, so that when the embroidery is finished, it will appear as if one piece is looped over the other.

Work green daisy stitches along the inner side of the loops. Press the work on a thick blanket on the wrong side.

The covers for the arms are worked with the same design on a smaller scale. Make the scallops 1 inch in depth and 3 inches across, half the size of those on the chair-back.

Some Pretty Border Designs for Household Articles and Presents

These designs can be used on household articles made of loosely woven linen and worked in wools or Anchor Flox. They can also be used effectively on children's frocks ; for dresses or frocks use stranded cotton or silk.

First Border (Fig. 225).—Draw two parallel lines $\frac{3}{4}$ inch apart, and then mark off the top line into divisions of 1 inch. Work any stitches that meet diagonally in a point, as in Fig. 225 in rust-red Anchor Flox, making the lower stitch half-way between the stitches made at the inch marks on the top line. Work the blanket stitch in dark brown along the two parallel lines, making each stitch the same distance apart and all the same length except the middle one, which is longer.

Second Border (Fig. 226).—Draw parallel lines 1 inch apart and work six fly stitches in groups to form pyramid shapes as shown in Fig. 226. Leaf-brown is suggested and emerald green for the straight stitches. A French knot may be made in the middle of each fly stitch to introduce a unit of another colour if desired. A 2-inch border can be made by working the design twice to form a diamond shape.

Third Border (Fig. 227).—In this border, back, fly, and straight stitches are used. The back stitches are worked in blue, the fly stitch in green, and the straight stitches in orange.

A TABLE RUNNER (Figs. 228 and 229)

A pretty one for a gift can be made in " Old Glamis " Strathmore Linen, which has a shot effect, is loosely but strongly woven, and is 50 inches wide. " Old Bleach " Linen or any kind of linen crash can also be used.

Cut out a strip of linen 50 inches by 16 inches, turn down and tack small hems at the sides and ¾-inch hem at each end.

Draw a circle 3 inches wide, using a glass or cup, 2 inches up from the end, and exactly in the middle of the runner. Mark it off into divisions of ¾ inch.

Begin at one division point and work feather stitch round the circle, as shown in Fig. 228, the outer stitches half-way between the inner ones and about 1 inch apart, as shown in Fig. 228. Use jade-green wool or Anchor Flox. Work a flower to fill the outer space in daisy stitch with mauve thread, and a green French knot for the centre. The inner space is filled with three tail chain in blue (a chain stitch with a tail, as shown in Fig. 229). This combination of colours is very attractive, but they must be altered if they do not fit the colour scheme of the room. Fig. 229 will help in spacing the stitches.

Fasten down the hems with magic chain, using the blue and green threads.

To work the Magic Chain.—Thread the needle with the two threads, and work a chain stitch, holding the blue thread only under the thumb ; pull the needle through in the ordinary way, and then hold the green thread under the thumb, and so on alternately.

CHAPTER XXXI

FURTHER HINTS ON MENDING, REPAIRING, AND PRESERVING GARMENTS

Combined Patch and Darn for Trousers, etc. Swiss Darning, Filling a Hole with Swiss Darning, Fine Drawing, Stoating. Gusset Patches, Square Patch for Knicker Fork, Oval Patch on Magyar Garment, Adhesive Patches. A Quick Way to mend Lace Curtains. Mending with Tape. Mending Men's Shirts. Frayed Cuffs and Collars. Reinforcing—Boys' Trousers, Knickers, Forks of Trousers, Pyjamas, Skirts. Some Miscellaneous Hints on Mending.

WE have already given some directions for mending and patching in Chapter X. There you will find the well-known cross-cut darn and hedge-tear darn. The hints we are now going to give are perhaps less well known and therefore more valuable.

COMBINED PATCH AND DARN

This is used where darning is less visible than a patch would be, for example, on the exposed parts of an outer garment of plain material. Strength is given by placing material that matches the garment, or nearly so, behind the darn. It is especially useful for *boys' coats and trousers*.

It is worked in this way. First place the patch to the wrong side with way of thread following that of garment. Then darn the frayed ends of the tear on to the material with ravellings or fine silk. Darn from the right side, but at the ends of the rows take the needle to the back and bring to the right side again in position for the next row, leaving a loop on the wrong side. If the tear is not complete—that is, if only one set of the threads is broken—it is not usually necessary to cross. Lastly, trim down the turnings and round off the corners at the back, and neaten the edge of the " patch " with loop stitch or overcasting on thin and medium materials, or lightly hem on the wrong side of heavy materials.

(On transparent materials such as voile, trim away close to the darn (which is made as small as possible) on the wrong side.)

The combined patch and darn is most useful for—

(*a*) Elbows of frocks or boys' coats.

(*b*) Seat of trousers.

(*c*) Back of frock torn out from armhole seam.

(*d*) Torn buttonholes can be darned on to material (on tape on under-garments) and the hole reworked, at least at the end.

(*e*) For household articles, for example, slits in sheets, etc., can be darned on to tape. Large worn areas on turkey towels, etc., can be darned preferably by machine on to *net*, which gives strength without bulk. (Machine darning is done with a special machine attachment. Directions for using it are supplied with the machine. It is a great time-saver. It is not difficult on treadle or electric machines.)

(*f*) For stocking knees. Tack net the same colour as the stocking to the wrong side. Darn as already described, but fill the hole with chain stitch worked in close rows to the foundation of net—*or* darn across in the ordinary way.

Swiss Darning (Fig. 230)

This is a method of joining two pieces of web by imitating the knitting-stitch with ordinary needle and thread. Take the needle into a loop and out of its neighbour on one side, as in Fig. 230. Repeat on the opposite side. Return to the first side and go into the loop already containing a thread and out of its neighbour (without one), as in Fig. 230. Repeat. Sometimes a thin place on a garment of coarse knitting is strengthened by following the original weave in the same manner.

Filling a Hole with Swiss Darning (Fig. 231).—First unravel the sides to obtain a square or rectangular hole. Strand with cotton going into one loop and out of its neighbour, first at the top then at the bottom, but always go into a hole containing a strand and out of one without, as in Fig. 231.

Next do the filling with thread to match the garment. Go into the loop from which the thread comes, and out of its neighbour. Take needle and thread round the back of the two strands which run into this loop, before reinserting needle in the same loop and out at the next, as in Fig. 231.

Fine Drawing (Fig. 232).—This is very useful on a straight slit or to let in a cloth patch of thick material. It is worked as described for a patch for thick cloth.

Stoating (Fig. 233).—Darn across the slit with fine silk or ravellings. The rows are not side by side exactly, but cross each other in figures of eight and are very uneven in length. The stitches are taken in the thickness of the material and do not show through to the right side.

GUSSET PATCHES

These are very important. A gusset is a piece of material (usually square or triangular) used at the *angles* of seams for the purpose of strengthening and also of neatening. *Patches* of this type are used where the damage to be repaired has been caused by *strain* rather than ordinary wear. The gusset patch replaces worn material, but often adds to the size of the garment as well.

Square Patch for Knicker Fork (Fig. 234).—This is generally double for strength.

First cut a sufficiently large square and fix the turnings to the wrong side. Next place the square on the right side of the garment with a point to each of the four seams which meet at the fork (as shown in Fig. 234), so that the edges of the patch lie smoothly on the garment. The distance from the fold to A may be larger on the patch than the distance from the fork to A on the garment, which will therefore pucker behind the patch until cut away. But the *edge* of the patch must lie smoothly from the beginning. Cut away the worn material, leaving ¼-in. turnings. Place the second patch on the inside. The inside patch is generally hemmed, the outside patch may be machined or oversewn.

Oval Patch on Magyar Garment (Fig. 235 (*a*) and (*b*)).—In some garments not too well cut, a sharp angle at A would cause splitting in the underarm seam. An oval patch, B C, will make the curve less sharp and provide bias material in the direction of the greatest strain as well as replacing the torn part of the garment.

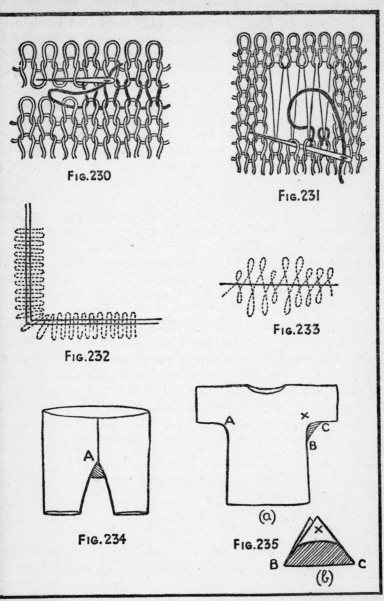

FIG. 230.—Swiss Darning.
FIG. 231.—Filling a hole with Swiss Darning.
FIG. 232.—Fine Drawing.   FIG. 233.—Stoating.   FIG. 234.—Square Patch
   for Knicker Fork.
FIG. 235.—Oval Patch on Magyar Garment.

529

Cut a square of a suitable size and straight by the thread. Fold diagonally, and round off the corners opposite the fold B C (Fig. 235 (*b*)). Unpick the seam of the garment. Mark the middle of the hollow on both back and front of the garment, and middle of both curves on patch (X in Fig. 235 (*a*) and (*b*)). Seam one side of the patch to the front of the garment, with marked centres matching. A seam to match that of the garment is usually used. It must be made sufficiently far in on the garment (by cutting away worn material), but turnings must be left. Cut away a similar amount on the back. Finally, do up the whole seam unpicked, which will now include the patch.

Adhesive Patches.—These patches are very quickly put on, but their use is limited. Materials of various colours are now sold so prepared that pieces of them can be stuck on a garment to fill up a hole. The general method is to place the patch with right side to wrong side, and with the hole closed up as much as possible, then pass a slightly warm iron over—this melts the gummy preparation on the patch ; leave a few minutes to set. Of course the particular instructions sold with the patch should be carefully studied. They may differ slightly from those that we have given. Examples of these adhesive patches are " Mend-a-tear " for mackintoshes, cloth, motor-car hoods, and so on, and " Lustru " for the heels of stockings ; *but good stockings should always be darned*.

Compare these adhesive patches with the " Emergency Patch " described in Chapter X.

Mending Lace Curtains

This is a good hint for mending lace curtains. Starch a patch when starching the damaged curtain. Then, when ironing, place the *damp* patch over the hole and it will stick by means of the starch. The edges must not be turned under.

Mending with Tape

Tape is invaluable for mending, because its sides can be hemmed without turning in as for material. Cotton, linen, and French tape of all widths can be used, according to the texture needed.

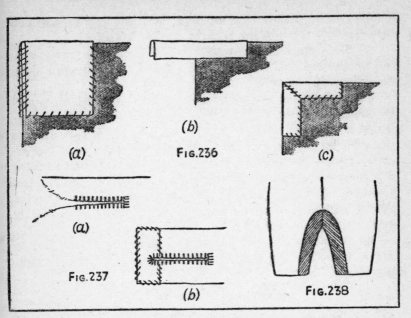

FIG. 236.—How tape can be attached to corners to strengthen them.   FIG. 237.
—Use of tape in mending a buttonhole.   FIG. 238.—Reinforcing knickers.

Tape is especially useful—

(1) To strengthen and mend the torn corners of sheets, towels, tablecloths, etc. If the corners of sheets get weak where they are pegged on a line, an angle of tape can be fixed on, as in Fig. 236.

(2) For mending buttonholes, it forms a backing for reworking part of a hole. If buttonholes tear out at the ends of pillow-cases, etc., as in Fig. 237, fell on a narrow piece of tape, as in Fig. 237, on the right side, and tidy the wrong by buttonholing.

(3) If buttons tear off pillow-cases, etc., taking the material with them, fell tabs of linen tape on both sides to neaten and make strong for new button.

(4) It is used for new ends on bands of aprons, etc.

(5) As a backing for darning slits. On underclothing ribbon should be used. Cash's tape is good ; it is soft cotton, and this is stronger and generally preferred to silk.

(6) A straight slit in a sheet or garment may be covered by

a tape patch. Either hem on from right side and turn in and hem the torn edges to the tape, or reverse the sides.

(7) Short cracks in selvedge edges of sheets and towels, etc., can be checked and repaired by a strip of tape oversewn along the edges and hemmed.

Fig. 236 (*a*), (*b*), (*c*) shows how tape is attached to corners to strengthen them. Fig. 236 (*a*) shows a wide piece of tape folded in half and set to a corner. On one side of the corner is the fold, on the other side the edges are oversewn. The remaining edges are hemmed. You must be careful when mending a pillow-case not to catch more than one of its layers when hemming. Fig. 236 (*b*) and (*c*) shows a narrow tape set to a corner. Fold in half lengthwise and set in position. Mitre at the corner by folding (do not cut away surplus inside), and hem.

Men's soft collars can be patched with tape if the tear or fray is where it will not show when worn, as near the right-hand buttonhole.

MENDING MEN'S SHIRTS

" Topping and tailing " is a special variety of patching used to mend men's shirts when the edge of the collar rubs a little hole through in front while the rest of the shirt is in good condition. As the patch needed will show, it must be of the same material and large enough for its *edges* not to be visible in wear. Therefore from the shirt tails cut a piece large enough to extend right up to the shoulder seam and collar band, and far enough down for its join to be covered by the waistcoat.

The damaged tail can easily be made good with pieces that do not exactly match, cut from a shirt past repair or from an old pillow-slip.

FRAYED CUFFS, COLLARS, ETC.

Cloth.—The frayed edge is a fold, therefore cut through the fold right round the cuff and trim away any long frayed ends. Turn the edges in to face each other but with inner layer slightly lower. Press under a damp cloth and secure with top hemming (tailors' hemming).

A *fold-back cuff*, as on a shirt or blouse. If the inside is good the whole cuff can be turned ; if this is not possible, cut through and seam together again through all layers. Herringbone the turnings closely to one layer. That the seam may be just under the edge of the cuff when turned back, make the distance from the upper edge to the seam only a little less than from the lower buttonhole, or the buttonholes will not match sufficiently well for links. In the case of striped material the seam must be very accurately fixed.

Straight Cuff (Cotton).—This can be treated as for cloth. On a shirt, and, if suitable, on a blouse or frock, secure by machine edge stitching from the right side instead of hemming on the wrong side.

Collar.—If a collar is worn at the edge of the roll, the best plan is to make an ornamental laid-on strap of similar or contrasting material.

Wear at Base of Shirt Neckband.—This is often due to rubbing by a stiff collar. Unpick the neckband and let in a dress patch. This can be done so that it is a very invisible repair, and it is worth doing unless the garment is very old. In the case of an old garment, fishbone the slit together and darn on to tape.

Reinforcing

Some parts of a garment receive special strain, and it is often wise to strengthen these parts before use. This applies especially to boys' trousers. Below we give some methods of reinforcing that are most useful.

Boys' Trousers.—Place a patch at the seat on the right side. When this wears through it can be removed, and the garment is good underneath. If the garment is not made at home, tailors are quite prepared to do this ; with some it is a matter of course.

Knickers (Fig. 238).—Many women are so heavy on these that they find it worth while to follow a somewhat similar practice. If two pairs of the same material and colour are bought, then, when one pair is worn, its good parts can be used to reinforce the second pair. The chief wear is not at the seat, but either side of the leg seams, and mostly to the front. Fig. 238 shows the shape of the pieces. The thread follows that of the garment. Take the pattern as for shaped facings. The width on the front is about 5 to 7 inches, and on the back about 4 to 6 inches.

Forks of Trousers.—These are reinforced by 2- or 3-inch triangles of interlining.

Pyjamas.—Men often split the coat down the middle of the back, others at back of armholes. On home-made garments it is wise to reinforce either the outside or inside ; on bought garments match the material as nearly as possible and reinforce the inside.

Skirts.—If skirts bag at the knee, line the front breadth only. If they bag at the seat, make a ¾-length lining a little smaller than the skirt and hanging free from the waist to take the strain.

Some Miscellaneous Suggestions for Mending

(1) When running new elastic or tape through a seam, sew one end of the new elastic to one end of the old. Then as the old elastic is pulled out, the new is pulled in.

(2) *Table-Linen Mending.*—Table linen is best mended with embroidery cotton of a number to correspond with the quality of the cloth. Under the ragged edges of the tear tack a piece of stiff paper, and make a network of fine stitches backwards and forwards over its edges, carrying the stitches about an inch beyond the tear. Thin places and breaks in linen may be run with flax or embroidery floss.

(3) *Slits on Under-Garments.*—Whip together edges of slit on the wrong side, thus giving the appearance of a seam on the right side. This method is most suitable for dainty underwear not subject to heavy wear, and where darning would be too noticeable. It is also used as a quick method on garments which are not worth the time or trouble involved in patching or darning. It is also a method that can be applied to ladders *at the back* of cheap stockings.

(4) *Gloves.*—Wool and fabric gloves are darned. Slits in skin gloves can be drawn together with fishbone stitch worked in silk. Holes can be mended by obtaining a small piece of skin by shortening the wrist. Cut it to the exact size and shape of the hole and graft it in with fishbone stitch. Seams in gloves are most easily re-sewn with a curved glove needle. See also the sections on " To Mend Leather Gloves " and " To Patch Leather Gloves."

CHAPTER XXXII

SOME MORE USEFUL IDEAS FOR GIFTS, BAZAARS, AND THE HOME

A Waste-Paper Basket. A Telephone Cover. A Blotter. Book-Ends. A Pretty Cushion. Some Easily-made Gifts: Lingerie — trimmed with Braid Edging Stitch, Braid Stitch, and Hemstitch, "Sham." Embroidered Gloves. A Stool-Top in Jacobean Embroidery. A Fan-shaped Cushion. Ribbon Work: A Square Cushion decorated with Ribbon, A Handkerchief-Sachet made of Ribbon, Ribbon Flowers, A Tea-Cosy decorated with Ribbon Flowers, How to tie Ribbon Bows. A Simple and Dainty Luncheon Set. A Pair of Appliqué Curtains. A Cross-Stitch Lady. A Dainty Set of Tea-Napkins. Pretty Calendars. The Use of Circles in Embroidery. Some Pretty Hot-Plate Mats. An Umbrella Shawl.

SOME interesting and suggestive ideas will be found in this chapter which, it is hoped, will lead to many happy hours of work. Experimenting, contriving, and making are always a source of pleasure and sometimes of profit.

Some of the ideas in this chapter are worked out completely, some are meant to be suggestive only. There should be sufficient choice here to suit every taste.

A Waste-Paper Basket (Fig. 239)

For this you need cardboard, linen (a rosy shade of Old Glamis, Strathmore or Beavie Cloth is suitable, as they are both strong and yet loosely woven), and "Anchor" Flox in green, nigger brown, and blue.

Cut four pieces of cardboard 10½ inches by 7 inches, and one piece 6¾ inches square for the bottom. Cut out the linen, using the cardboard as a pattern, and allowing 1-inch turnings all round.

Next place the cardboard on the right side of each piece of linen, pencil round the edges, and mark the middle of each side. Then draw the lines shown in Fig. 239—the curved lines are drawn round the edge of a saucer.

Buttonhole the edge in nigger brown, as shown.

Run a tacking thread ¾ inch in from the curved lines to make an oval shape ; mark this oval off in divisions of an inch. Work a flower in daisy stitch with the blue thread at each mark, then work the leaves and a knot in each flower with green thread. The details of the design are shown in Fig. 239.

When all the embroidery is finished, press it on the wrong side and cover the cardboard with the linen, catching the edges together with long stitches taken from side to side and from top to bottom on the wrong side. Line each piece with the same material or any remnant of silk that tones with the embroidery. Work buttonhole stitching all round the edges with the brown thread, then sew the stitches together down the sides to join them. Sew the bottom on in the same way—use green or blue thread for this. Any suitable stitches can, of course, be used for the edges, if they can be whipped over to join the sections.

A TELEPHONE COVER (Fig. 240)

This is made with " Old Glamis " fine undyed linen, No. 494–30100. Cut out three pieces of cardboard according to the measurements shown in Fig. 240. Cut out three pieces of linen, using the cardboard as a pattern and allowing 1-inch turning all round. Cut a lining for each piece without any allowance for turnings. The lining may be linen or a remnant of silk. Cut out leaves in green or brown linen, using an oak or rose leaf as a pattern. Stick them with paste to form a border at the base of the large piece of linen, or in any other way you prefer. Stick one leaf on each of the smaller pieces of linen. Work the embroidery in stranded cotton. The colour of the stranded cotton will depend on the colour of the leaves. F100 Oak Brown is suggested for some leaves and F153 Reseda Green for others. Work the veins and stalks first in stem stitch and the outlines in blanket stitch, either even or uneven. Sew the linen to the cardboard as described for the waste-paper basket, and line it. Finish off the edges in the same way as each piece of the waste-

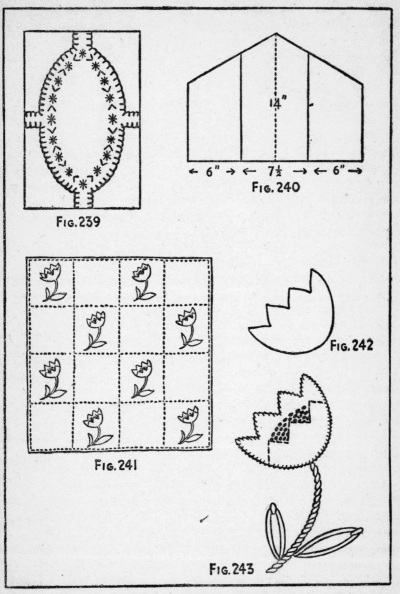

FIG. 239.

FIG. 240.

14"

← 6" → ← 7½ → ← 6" →

FIG. 241.

FIG. 242.

FIG. 243.

FIG. 239.—Waste-Paper Basket.   FIG. 240.—Telephone Cover.   FIG. 241.—
Cushion Design.   FIG. 242.—Detail for Design.   FIG. 243.—Flower-Top.

paper basket. Use F20 Maize Gold for the buttonhole stitch. Join the two side pieces to the front section by whipping over the buttonhole stitches in brown thread.

The waste-paper basket and telephone cover can be made of the same material and embroidered to match each other.

A BLOTTER

This costs less than a shilling, but it makes a very elegant blotter. You need ½ yard of coarse canvas (27 inches wide), some purple and green raffia, gold paint, a piece of green sateen, and three or four sheets of mauve and green blotting-paper.

Cut off 14½ inches of the canvas. Turn down 1 inch along two sides and 2½ inches along the selvedges, then fold in half and press with a warm iron. Work a border around each side of the cover in this way—with the purple raffia work stitches 1 inch deep, two threads down from the folded edges ; work a cross stitch between each long stitch.

Work all round the blotter and along the fold on the left-hand side.

Work a bunch of violets in the middle of the blotter. Make the violets with loosely worked French knots quite close together, make the leaves with small straight stitches of green raffia grouped together, and the stalks of long stitches (some stalks can be made with green raffia and some with purple). In each corner work a triangle of purple outlined with green.

Paint the canvas all over with gold paint, using a small brush so that the raffia is not smeared.

Slip-stitch the green sateen lining inside the cover, and tack the blotting-paper into position.

BOOK-ENDS

Wooden book-ends can be bought with the iron parts that go under the books loose and ready to be screwed on. These cost from 1s. 6d. to 2s. a pair. These book-ends can be covered with almost anything from quilted taffeta to tapestry or leather.

Here is one way to cover them. Buy ¼ yard of dark brown velvet or furnishing velour, ¼ yard of silk for lining, beige-coloured embroidery silk, and 1 yard of ½-inch petersham ribbon of the same colour.

Mark the shape of the book-ends with chalk on the wrong side of the velvet, and cut out, allowing about 1½-inch turning all round. Work a border of stitches with the beige silk 1 inch in from the chalk mark, using a tacking thread to keep the work straight. Lay the velvet on the table wrong side up, put a thin layer of cotton-wool over it and then the book-end on top. Draw the edges of the velvet across the back with long stitches from side to side, or fasten it down with small nails. Line the back with silk and slip-stitch the ribbon over the join, to lie quite flat on the edge of the book-end. Screw the metal stand into position.

A Pretty Cushion (Figs. 241, 242, and 243)

A little square cushion to fit the seat of a wooden Windsor chair is always useful.

Cut a piece of warm brown linen 14 inches square for the top of the cushion ; the under piece of casement-cloth may be a darker brown or orange if a very decorative effect is required.

Measure half an inch in from each of the edges of the linen and darn along each side with orange. Now divide the square into sixteen squares, as shown in Fig. 241. Darn along the dividing lines with orange, as shown in Fig. 241.

If desired, the squares can first be marked out by drawing two threads ; measure 3¼ inches between each set of drawn threads. You must then darn along the drawn-thread lines with orange wool, going over three threads and under one.

Now cut four shapes like that shown in Fig. 242 in red felt and four in yellow. Sew these in alternate squares, as shown in Fig. 241, having the red flowers in the top row, then the yellow, then the orange, and finally yellow once more.

Work a circle of brown French knots in the centre of each flower. The details of the embroidery are shown in Fig. 243. The flower-top is appliquéd to the cushion cover with tiny hemming stitches. The stem is worked in stem stitch, orange wool being used, and the leaves are lazy-daisy loops also worked in orange wool.

When the embroidery is finished, press the work well under a damp cloth, sew the linen to the casement-cloth on three sides, and slip the cushion-pad inside. Then sew up the remaining side.

Other colours can be chosen than those given. It is best to choose colours that go well with the room for which the cushion is intended. A black cushion with orange and lemon yellow flowers looks effective. In this case the squares can be outlined in green.

A more difficult colour scheme can be worked out in blue. Choose a deep butcher blue for the background and embroider the flowers in magenta, mauve, and purple.

Some Easily-made Gifts

There are many people who have not the time to make their gifts and yet would like to give that touch of personal work which is so much appreciated, because the receiver of the gift knows that trouble has been taken beyond the mere buying of the article.

For people in this position it is often possible to buy an article ready-made, and then work a little embroidery on it to enhance its value.

(1) *Lingerie.* Buy a perfectly plain garment, which is generally of better quality than a trimmed one, and trim it yourself with net edging or embroidery. If it is made of satin or crêpe de Chine, stamp small sprays of broderie anglaise here and there and work them in matching or contrasting silk. An artificial silk stockinet garment must not be worked with eyelets, or the material will ladder.

For a nightdress or petticoat, cover the machine-stitching with a thread of embroidery cotton couched over it, and sew lace to the edge. Another easy way is to work a border of simple stitches along the hems. Make dots with a ruler 1 inch apart along the hem. Work three daisy stitches at each mark, then, using a darker shade of thread, work three French knots between each group and a straight stitch inside each daisy stitch, as shown in Fig. 244.

Contrasting colours give a charming effect—pink or green on blue garments or yellow on brown ones. Use stranded cotton—three strands at a time is generally thick enough. This decoration only adds a few pence to the cost of the gift, and it is very quickly worked.

Lace can be used to cover the hem, and the best way to

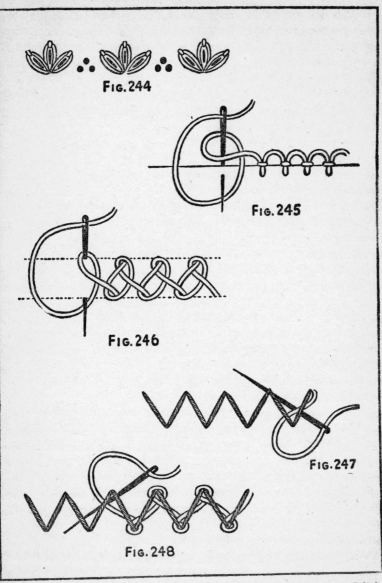

FIG. 244.—Border for Nightdress Pattern.   FIG. 245.—Braid Edging Stitch.
FIG. 246.—Braid Stitch.   FIG. 247.—Hemstitch, " Sham."   FIG. 248.—Hemstitch, " Sham."

secure it is by French knots worked in one or two colours in groups or in a straight line. The lace must be fastened to the top of the hem here and there from the wrong side.

Here are some suggestions for some quickly worked and rather uncommon borders—

(a) *Braid Edging Stitch* (Fig. 245).—This stitch is worked from right to left along a hem or turned-in edge, the latter being held away from the worker. The thread is brought through from underneath the edge, as shown on the right of Fig. 245. Loop the thread as shown, take the needle through this loop and insert it behind the material, bring it out again a short distance below the edge and *over* the working thread, as shown by the needle in Fig. 245. The thread is then pulled through but not quite tight, as at this stage it may be necessary to adjust the loop.

It is important that all the loops should be the same size, to ensure a good effect. When the loop is the right size the thread is pulled tight *away* from the worker, and a firm knot will thus be formed against the edge. This stitch needs a little practice to get it regular in appearance, as at first the loops tend to vary in size. This edging can be used for *any* embroidered article.

(b) *Braid Stitch* (Fig. 246).—This stitch, although called by the same name as that described in Chapter III. and shown in Fig. 31, is very different.

The braid stitch shown in Fig. 246 is best worked in a rather coarse thread and makes an *attractive border*. It is worked from right to left. It is wise for the beginner to rule two lines, as shown in the diagram. Bring the thread through on the lower line and loop it as shown in Fig. 246. Hold the loop down on the material with the left thumb, insert the needle through the loop and into the material at the top of the line, and bring it out on the lower line immediately beneath, as shown by the needle in Fig. 246. Before drawing the needle through, pull the loop on it tight. Then draw the needle through over the working thread and the stitch is completed.

(c) *Hemstitch, " Sham "* (Fig. 247).—This is a useful stitch to work over a run-and-fell seam in lingerie or any similar articles in fine material. It makes an effective covering for the seam line, at the same time imitating the effect of a hemstitched seam. It also makes a good border stitch.

FIG. 249.—Stool-Top in Jacobean Embroidery.

The zigzag foundation line is worked first from right to left as in Fig. 247. The second thread is then laced over this foundation, as shown in Fig. 248, without piercing the fabric except at the beginning and the end of the line.

(2) *Gloves*. Embroider the edge of the gauntlet with a narrow border of daisy stitches worked with " Sylko " Mouliné in shades of beige and brown for dark gloves and natural colours for light ones.

Tan cape gauntlets are improved if the edges are thonged with a suède leather of a lighter shade than the glove.

Small cross stitches can be worked at equal distances over the stitching on the backs of yellow chamois gloves, and several rows of cross stitches worked from the wrist upwards at the side of the gloves.

A STOOL-TOP IN JACOBEAN EMBROIDERY (Fig. 249)

Jacobean embroidery has been described in general terms in Chapter XV., " Tapestry and Needlework Rugs," but no patterns or detailed decorations for working this kind of embroidery were given. Fig. 249 shows a typical Jacobean design. This will make a beautiful stool-top or cushion cover, and look a thing of real worth. It makes a really valuable gift and will convert a plain deal stool into a fine piece of furniture.

The design shown fits a stool about 11 inches by 16½ inches, or any similar size. It will fit a larger stool with advantage, for a plain margin can be left all round. It will also make a fine cushion cover; in cutting the material for the cushion keep the proportion 2 to 3.

For those who want a fireside stool, an inexpensive deal stool can easily be made or bought and then stained. Make a pad to fit the top. Next cut a piece of brown linen 16½ inches by 11 inches for the top and a strip 55 inches long by 2½ inches wide for the sides. You will want some yards of tapestry wools in mixed colours. If you buy tapestry wool from a good maker you can get all sorts of colours that blend together beautifully, such as terra-cotta, salmon pink, jade green, and so on. Excellent wools can be bought from Robert Cullen, Knitting Wool Specialist, 181–182 Tottenham Court Road, London, W.1. They will willingly send samples and price-lists.

Next you must choose your pattern. The pattern shown in Fig. 249 can easily be enlarged and drawn. Methods of transferring one's own design are given in Chapter I. and also in Chapter XVIII., where very detailed directions are given for drawing or stencilling designs on burlap.

Suitable transfers for Jacobean work can also be bought and ironed off on the linen.

Now suppose we have the pattern shown in Fig. 249 suitably transferred, we can choose our colours and begin. Notice the stitches used. Leaves, petals, and scrolls are often outlined in chain stitch. All the solid parts are in long-and-short stitch or satin stitch, as can be seen in Fig. 249. The veins of the smaller leaves are in stem stitch. Keep the darker shades of wool for the scroll and inside of the leaves. Notice how the space marked A in Fig. 249 is filled in. The filling-in is shown on the opposite side. It is very characteristic of Jacobean embroidery and is known as *Back Stitch Trellis*. It is ordinary back stitch arranged as a trellis pattern, and it makes an attractive and easily-worked

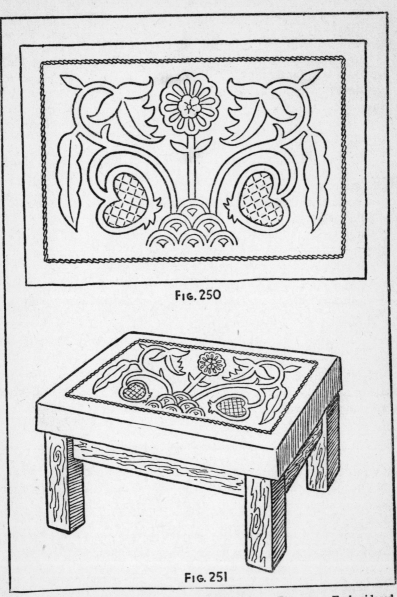

FIG. 250

FIG. 251

FIG. 250.—How design is spaced on the material. FIG. 251.—Embroidered Cover for Wooden Stool.

filling. Notice the squares are decorated here and there with small French knots. Tiny cross stitches or single cross stitches can be used with good effect at the corners or also in the middle of the squares instead of French knots. When working this trellis, it will be found quickest to work all the parallel lines in one direction, going down one line and up the next. The parallel lines lying at right angles are then completed in the same way. This is an excellent pattern not only for Jacobean work but for any light filling.

All the other stitches used have been dealt with in other parts of this book. Notice the leaves are good examples of gradation in embroidery.

Work a containing border as shown in Fig. 250. Use dark wool and the chain stitch. When the chain stitch is finished all the way round, work over it with large oversewing stitches so as to give a corded effect. For this oversewing use a contrasting colour.

When the embroidery is finished and pressed, sew the plain strip of linen round the sides of the oblong. It is an excellent plan to put elastic in the lower hem to keep the stool-top in position. Fig. 251 shows clearly how the cover is put on. The pad fits the top exactly and is underneath the cover.

It is, of course, necessary to cut the brown material for the cover carefully, so that it fits the top. We have given only rough measurements. Measure your own stool before cutting out and make any adjustments. The pattern must be well spaced, as shown in Fig. 250.

A FAN-SHAPED CUSHION (Figs. 252, 253, 254, 255)

Directions for making cushions are given in Chapter XIV., but it has been rightly said that one cannot have too many fashions. Fig. 255 shows a modern fan-shaped cushion, especially comfortable because it fits the back so well. Figs. 252, 253, 254, 255 show the dimensions necessary for cutting out a cover for this fashionable cushion. The measurements given are for the usual fan-shaped cushions seen so often in shop windows. They can be adjusted to one's own particular needs.

To make the cushion cover shown in Fig. 255, you will need—
(1) About 1½ yards of 36-inch-wide taffeta or repp.

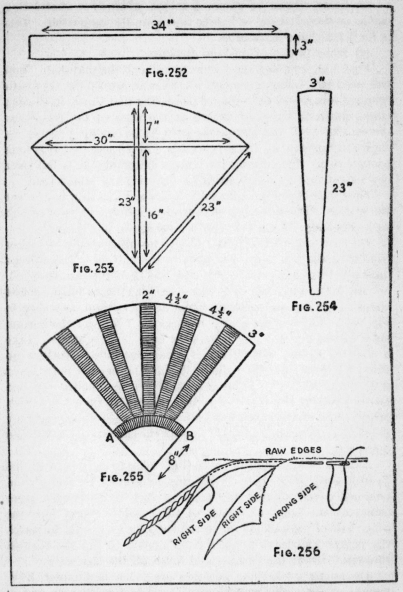

FIGS. 252, 253, and 254.—Pattern for cutting out material. Fig. 255.—Modern
Fan-shaped Cushion. FIG. 256.—Method of stitching.

(2) Some ribbon or galon, 2 inches wide, of a contrasting colour or deeper shade or lighter tone than the repp itself. This is for a fan-shape decoration.

(3) Some piping of medium thickness.

Figs. 252, 253, 254 show how to cut out the material. You will need two triangular pieces like that shown in Fig. 253 with rounded tops, two wedge-shaped pieces like that shown in Fig 254 (these must be the same length as the sides of the triangular pieces, Fig. 253), and lastly, *one* strip 34 inches by 3 inches, as shown in Fig. 252, for the curving top. Make sure that it is long enough to fit this curving top. Any material that is left over can be cut into crossway strips for covering the piping cord.

Now take one of the triangular pieces and fold it in half to get the middle. Down the crease thus made stitch a piece of ribbon 14 inches long; this is the middle strip shown in Fig. 255.

On each side of this strip, stitch two other strips 4½ inches from it at the top and touching it at the bottom. These strips must also be 14 inches long. Fig. 255 shows how they are arranged.

Stitch two more pieces of ribbon each 4½ inches from the last strips at the top and touching them at the bottom, as shown in Fig. 255. These strips are 13¾ inches long. Now for the bottom strip A B in Fig. 255 that covers the ends of these strips. Take a strip of ribbon and gather it along one side. Measure up about 8 inches from the point each side and lay the ungathered side of the ribbon in a curve parallel to the rounded top and neatly covering the strips of ribbon just where they touch each other. Pull up the gathers and stitch the curved ribbon carefully in place, as shown in Fig. 255. Be sure the curved edge is stitched down flat.

Seam a wedge-shaped piece (Fig. 254) to each end of the 34-inch strip (Fig. 252). Pipe this long strip to the ribbon-trimmed cover, so that the point of each wedge-shaped piece comes at the point or corner of the cushion. Next pipe the other half of the cushion on to the strip, being careful to match the points, and leave a space large enough to slip the cushion through. Insert the cushion and finish off the last seam.

Directions for stuffing cushions are given in Chapter XIV. Directions for piping will be also found in this chapter and in Chapter IX., " Plain Sewing and Trimmings for Plain Sewing."

These are the methods to follow in piping this cushion—

Double the crossway strips (which have been cut and joined as described under " Binding " in the Dressmaking Section) lengthwise over shrunk piping cord of medium thickness and tack them together with cotton that matches, so that the cord is closely enclosed. To apply this prepared piping, lay it along the right side of the edge of the cushion cover, cord inwards, and the cut edges lying flush with and over the cut edges of the material. Pin it in position, nicking the piping cover almost to the cord at the corners or curves so that it will lie flat. Now pin the long strip over this, right side downwards and edge flush with the other raw edges, tack, and then stitch together as shown in Fig. 256.

Here is a good hint to remember when making cushions to go inside covers—

If you want to make your own cushion to go inside this fan-shaped cover or any cover, make it the same shape but *larger*, not smaller. It is a general rule that the soft stuffing for cushion covers should be larger than the cover itself.

Of course cushions can be bought ready for covering, and a square cushion will fit all sorts of shapes.

RIBBON WORK

PRETTY GIFTS AND ARTICLES FOR THE HOME MADE WITH RIBBON OR DECORATED WITH RIBBON TRIMMING

Ribbon is a pretty and quick way of decorating many articles. We have already shown how it can be used to decorate a fan-shaped cushion.

Fig. 257 shows a square garden cushion trimmed with ribbon.

Very pretty cushion covers can be made from broad strips of ribbon sewn together. Glove-sachets and handkerchief-sachets can also be made of narrow strips sewn together by means of some of the pretty insertion stitches or faggoting stitches given in Chapter V., for example, the stack stitch (Fig. 59).

A Pretty Handkerchief-Sachet made from Ribbon.—Fig. 258 shows a pretty handkerchief-sachet. To make this, first cut the ribbons the right length—the length depends on the size of the sachet and the width of the ribbon. Three lengths of ribbon only are used for the sachet in Fig. 258. Notice the middle strip is the longest. Mitre the ends as shown. Mitring is referred to in Chapter XXVI. under the heading of Making Belts. Turn up the other ends and pin the ribbons to a piece of brown paper ready to be joined with a faggoting or insertion stitch (for directions for working this stitch, see Chapter V.). The stack stitch has been used for this sachet. When the ribbons have been joined, unpin them from the brown paper. Now line the sachet (a padded lining can be used), sew up the sides, and buttonhole the points as shown.

Many pretty things can be made on the model of this sachet. Different effects are obtained by joining together narrow strips or broad strips and using different insertion stitches. It is often wise to line each piece of ribbon by slip-stitching another piece to the back. This gives more substance to the finished article. On the whole it is best to make small things of ribbon—table runners are generally successful.

Ribbon or tape appliqué has already been described in Chapter VIII.

Ribbon Flowers (Figs. 259, 260).—Pretty ribbon flowers of different shapes can be made. This is a good method of using up odd pieces of ribbon. Cushions and cosies are pretty, decorated with ribbon flowers of different colours. Fig. 261 shows a pretty cosy; the flowers are made of ribbon and the leaves are embroidery stitches.

The flowers are very easily made. Pretty little flowers can be made from ribbon 1 inch wide. Gather along one edge of a length of ribbon and pull it up tightly to make a circle, as in Fig. 259. Cut off any that is not needed and join the two ends neatly together. A piece of ribbon about $9\frac{1}{2}$ inches long will make a good flower. Notice the hollow circle left in the middle. Make another little flower in exactly the same way from a piece of baby ribbon so that it exactly fits this hollow, as in Fig. 260, and forms the centre of the flower. Needless to say, the centre flower must be a different colour—yellow or brown is appropriate.

A Pretty Tea-Cosy decorated with Ribbon Flowers (Fig. 261).— Fig. 261 shows how flowers of different colours can be arranged to decorate a tea-cosy. This tea-cosy is 14 inches by 10 inches (turnings must be allowed). The cosy in Fig. 261 has been drawn

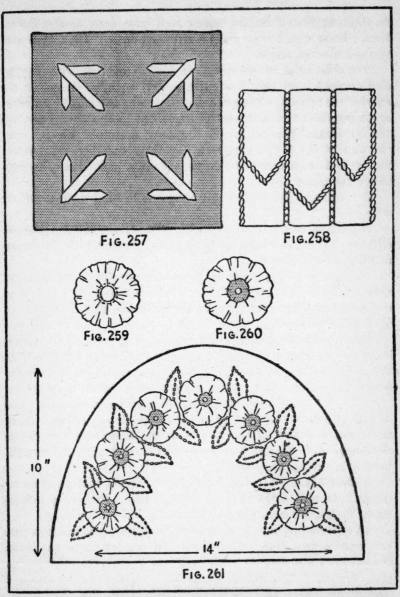

FIG. 257.

FIG. 258.

FIG. 259.

FIG. 260.

10"

14"

FIG. 261.

FIG. 257.—Square Garden Cushion trimmed with ribbon.   FIG. 258.—Handkerchief-Sachet.   FIGS. 259 and 260.—Ribbon Flowers.   FIG. 261.—Tea-Cosy
decorated with Ribbon Flowers.

to scale, so that it can be clearly seen how many flowers made from ribbon 1 inch wide can be arranged on it. The leaves are worked in stem stitch.

The two sides of the cosy are joined together with piping and covered with ribbon or with material similar in colour to some of the flowers. The method of attaching two edges by means of piping cord has been clearly explained in the description of the fan-shaped cushion in this chapter. A simpler way to join the two halves of the cosy is to lay them together, right sides facing, and seam round the curve. Make a padded cosy to slip inside the cover.

A third way to join the cosy shapes is to bind them together with galon.

A garland of flower rings looks very attractive on a square cushion. There is indeed no limit to the decorative possibilities of these dainty shapes.

How to tie Ribbon Bows on Boxes.—A present looks of more value if it is tied up daintily. At Christmas-time it is very necessary to pack one's gifts in pretty boxes and tie them up with gay ribbons.

Some people find it very difficult to tie a good bow. There is, of course, a right way and a wrong way of tying a bow. The best method is to begin as shown in Fig. 262, which shows a ribbon being tied round a box. First one end is twisted over the other —that is, a " single knot " is made. Turn the box as in Fig. 262 so that one loose end goes up and the other hangs down. Then make the *first loop* of the bow with the lower end and bring the upper end *over* the loop as in Fig. 263, slotting it through behind in the ordinary way.

A Double Bow (Fig. 264).—A beautiful double bow needs more ribbon. It also looks best in wide ribbon. Ribbon 4 inches broad makes a decorative bow for a box.

To tie a double bow, first of all tie an ordinary ribbon bow (do not make a knot first). Then tuck first one end under the same knot at the back, then the other end, thus making two more loops.

A SIMPLE AND DAINTY LUNCHEON SET (Figs. 265, 266, 267)

These suggestions for simple mats and napkin-rings will be useful when making gifts, and they are of special value to the

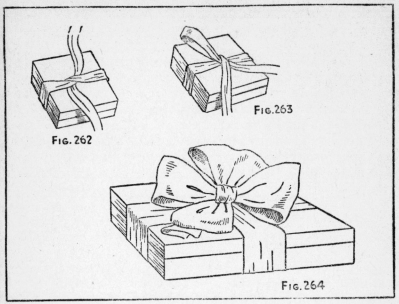

FIGS. 262 and 263.—Steps in tying a Ribbon Bow.   FIG. 264.—A Double Bow.

home worker who wants a pretty modern home.   These luncheon mats look well on a dark polished table ; two or even three can be used on the long narrow tables now so fashionable.

The mats and napkin-rings are made of buff linen decorated with needle-weaving in green thread—twisted mercerised thread is very suitable.

Cut the luncheon mats the size that you require—16 inches by 10 inches is a common size.   Now turn up and tack very narrow hems round each side.   Make holes at regular intervals ($\frac{3}{8}$ inch apart) all round, just inside the edge.   This is for crocheting a border.   Take a crochet-hook and the green thread and make three double crochet into a hole, work one chain, and then make three double crochet into the next hole.   Continue in this way round every edge.   Directions for working these crochet stitches will be found in Chapter XXIV., " Crochet."   Next we have to decorate the mats.

Mark out a square (sides $1\frac{3}{4}$ inch) in running-stitch in green thread in each corner, as shown in Fig. 265, and two smaller

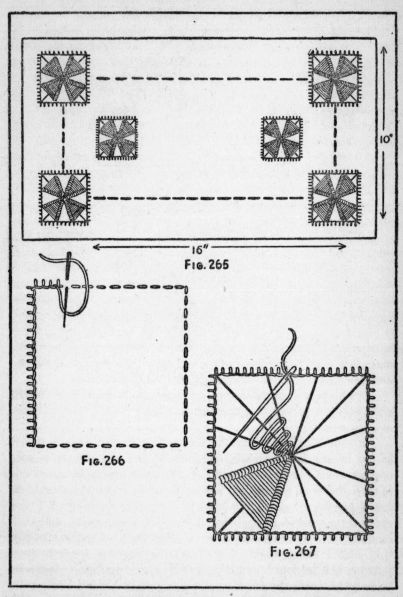

FIG. 265.—Mat for the table.   FIG. 266.—Outline of Buttonhole Stitch.
FIG. 267.—Criss-Cross Design.

squares (sides $1\frac{1}{2}$ inch) in the middle, as shown in Fig. 265. Cover
the running stitched outline with buttonhole stitch, as shown
in Fig. 266. Within the square make a criss-cross design from
corner to corner—the supporting threads for this come from
along the sides of the square, as shown in Fig. 267. When working
these supporting threads, carry the needle along the *back* of
the buttonhole stitch to reach the required position for crossing
the square. Directions for this kind of weaving and further
patterns will be found in Chapter VI., " Embroideries Done upon
Counted Threads.''

For the weaving shown in Fig. 265, begin in the centre of the
web with two over stitches to gather the threads into a centre.
From this centre work the stitches in and out over three strands,
as in darning (Fig. 267). When enough weaving or darning has
been done on three strands, slip the needle under the weaving
at the back and up to the centre again. Then work over the
next three strands. When all the threads have been worked
over and the square finished, cut away the linen from behind
the weaving, close up to the knotted edge of the buttonhole
stitch. Work straight lines in running stitch or back stitches
from square to square along the edge, as shown in Fig. 265.

If you do not want the polished table to show through the
open squares, the mats must be lined. If green does not suit
your dining-room, you must choose another colour—orange on
cream is always pretty.

How to make the Napkin-Rings (Fig. 268).—Cut a strip of the
buff-coloured linen $2\frac{1}{4}$ inches by $6\frac{1}{2}$ inches. Turn up and tack
very narrow hems round each edge and work a crochet border
as already described for the mat. Mark out the three squares,
as shown in Fig. 268, in running stitch, the side of each square
being $\frac{3}{4}$ inch. Buttonhole these squares and work a needle-
weaving pattern in them in the same way as already described.
Cut away the linen from behind the weaving as before. Cut a
piece of lining of brown (choose a pretty golden brown) casement-
cloth or sateen and slip-stitch it on. At one end make a buttonhole-stitched loop, and at the other stitch a pearl button.

If you are making a set of napkin-rings for home use, each
should be worked in a different colour and have a differently
coloured lining.

Probably the ingenious worker will think of better ways of arranging the squares than that shown in Fig. 265. A good effect can be obtained by making the corner squares the smaller ones, the two middle squares bigger. Peri-Lusta mercerised cotton is a good thread to use for the above work.

A Pair of Appliqué Curtains

These curtains are suitable for a bedroom or a dining-room. They are made of blue Bolton sheeting and the design is carried out in casement-cloth of primrose yellow. Although it is a very simple design and easy to carry out, it is most effective.

For the actual making of the curtains, see Chapter XIV., "Making the Home Beautiful."

To make the Design.—From the yellow material cut out 3-inch squares. Measure from one corner 2 inches along each side, and make a tiny mark. Join these two points and cut off the corner (Fig. 269). Hold one of the sharp points of the triangle in the left hand, round off the corners, and shape it to make a leaf (Fig. 270). The larger piece makes the flower. You will need two leaves to every flower, so cut out some 2-inch squares ; cut them across diagonally and shape each half.

Pin the flowers in position 5 inches apart down the sides of the curtains. Put the first flower 2 inches in from the edge and the second $5\frac{1}{2}$ inches, and so on, so that two short edges of the flowers are in a straight line (Fig. 271). Mark the stalk with pencil or chalk to come from the middle of one flower to the top of the next. Pin the leaves in position with the shorter side towards the stalk.

Begin at the top of the curtain and unpin each flower and leaf in turn. Brush each over lightly with paste on the wrong side and put it in position again. Use as little paste as possible, so that the material is not stained. Press each piece from the middle outward with a wad of cotton-wool or a piece of rag.

Hold the edge of the flower or leaf towards you and work blanket stitch in primrose yellow stranded cotton all round. It can be worked in long and short stitches, or the stitches can be all the same length. Work the stems in chain stitch and the veins on the leaves and flowers in outline stitch, using three strands of the cotton.

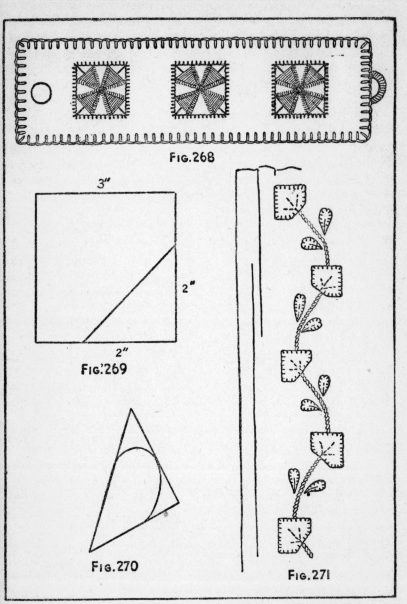

FIG. 268.

3"

2"

2"

FIG. 269

FIG. 270

FIG. 271

FIG. 268.—Design for Napkin-Ring. Appliqué Curtains.

FIGS. 269 and 270.—Details for Design for
FIG. 271.—Pattern for Design.

There are many other pretty colour combinations that may be used. Old Glamis, No. 2 Bloom Linen 16313, which is a flamingo and grey woven mixture, would be charming, with the appliqué patterns cut from a plain flamingo-coloured linen.

A Cross-Stitch Lady (Fig. 272)

A good deal about the ever popular cross stitch will be found in Chapters VI. and XV.

It is very amusing to plan out cross-stitch pictures. Many like to do this and frame their most pleasing results. Cross-stitch pictures indeed look very quaint and effective in narrow black frames. Fig. 272 shows a cross-stitch lady. She can be easily drawn on paper and then worked in cross stitch. Plan her dress in different ways until you get used to making pictures in cross stitch. Notice some parts have to be outlined in back stitch. Work the lower part of the skirt and the bands on the bonnet in mauve, and the upper part of the skirt in blue, and the bow in blue. Outline the arms, etc., in dark mauve, using back stitches.

Firm linen of a biscuit shade makes a good background. Work the tree in brown.

This cross-stitch lady looks very decorative on a tea-cosy or a table runner. Remember the rules for working cross stitch. Cross every stitch in the same direction, and when working two or more stitches side by side, work the under part of each first, then return and cross them.

Although bought transfers of pretty crinoline ladies with all the stitches clearly marked out can be bought, it is more interesting to plan your own lady and dress her to suit your own taste.

If you ever wish to frame your cross-work design, after carefully pressing it, you must cut a piece of cardboard to fit it. Then strain the work over it, lacing the edges of the linen together at the back. Then frame it as you would an ordinary picture. It is always wise to plan your pictures on squared paper and mark out the groups of different coloured stitches in crayon, then tack the paper on to your linen.

Following will be found further suggestions for the use of the cross stitch.

Fig 272

FIG. 272.—Design for Picture of a Lady in Cross Stitch.

A Set of Dainty and Quickly-made Tea-Napkins

A dozen of these tea-napkins will make a most acceptable gift. From 1 yard of cotton crêpe 27 inches wide, twelve napkins can be cut, each 9 inches square. Fringe the edges to a depth of ¼ inch, and decorate each with a design in cross stitch.

Tack a piece of Penelope canvas to the crêpe to form a diagram upon which the cross stitches may be worked. When the pattern is finished, the tacking stitches and the threads of the canvas can be drawn out, leaving the cross stitches on the crêpe. (See Chapters VI. and XV. for Cross Stitches.)

There are many sheets and books of cross-stitch patterns from which you can get ideas for these designs. The same design might be carried out in a different colour scheme in each mat. The colour scheme is most important, as a good design can be spoilt by badly chosen colours. Be careful to select designs that make no attempt to express realism.

Pretty Calendars (Figs. 273, 274)

Pretty calendars can be worked in cross stitch or in any of the many stitches given in this book. Fig. 273 shows a pretty pattern.

The actual method of making the calendars is very much the same, whatever the design may be. Figs. 273, 274 show two types of calendars, one with a frame and one without a frame.

Cut a piece of cardboard the size of the calendar required. This size will depend on the little printed calendar you are going to sew on. It must be well spaced with regard to the design, as shown in Fig. 273. If a cross-stitch design is desired, use a piece of cross-stitch canvas or single thread canvas half an inch larger all round (24 squares to the inch). Decide where you will place the little calendar and mark its position. Work a border of cross stitches as shown, and a pretty geometrical design above. Any single lines can be worked in back stitch. Sew the little calendar on with two or three stitches. Mount the canvas on the cardboard, fastening it with long stitches across both ways, as already described under the heading " A Cross-Stitch Lady," where the framing of cross-stitch work is discussed. The frame is made of strips of cardboard, ¼ inch broad or more, according to the size of the calendar. Cover these strips with gold or black paper, but be careful to leave a good $\frac{1}{2}$ inch of paper along each edge, so that there are wide flanges on each side of all the strips. Paste one flange to the back of each cardboard strip, but leave the other for the time. Cut the ends of each strip diagonally so that the strips fit together, as shown in Fig. 273. Now take each strip and glue it neatly and firmly to the edge of the canvas, taking care that the flange left unpasted is outside. Now take each flange, bend it over to the back, and paste it. Finish off the calendar neatly with a backing of white paper. The calendar shown in Fig. 274 is made in very much the same way, but it has no frame. In this case the design is worked on linen in simple stitches. The flowers are in lazy-daisy stitch, with French knots in the middle ; the outline of the basket, the handle, and the stems are in stem stitch, and the leaves in stroke stitch. When the embroidery is finished, stretch the linen neatly over the cardboard and secure it tightly with long stitches taken both ways across, as for the first calendar. Sew a little piece of ribbon to the back for hanging the calendar, neaten the back by gluing on a piece of thick white paper slightly smaller than the cardboard.

The little bought calendar is glued in place underneath the embroidery.

THE USE OF CIRCLES IN EMBROIDERY

Bold and effective designs can be made from circles without the help of any transfers.

Fig. 275 shows an arrangement of circles drawn from cups, saucers, and egg-cups, suitable for a cushion. These can be worked in chain stitch ; an outline of herringboning also looks well. It is very effective when the cushion is made of shot silk or linen and the circles worked in shaded stranded cotton of the same colour.

Fig 276 shows an arrangement for half-circles for the end of a runner. Make the runner of linen 36 inches by 15 inches. Turn down and tack a narrow hem at the sides and $\frac{3}{4}$-inch hem at the ends. Cut out ten circles of cretonne to tone with the linen and the colour-scheme of the room, using a cup or glass $3\frac{1}{2}$ inches across. Each circle must be cut in half and hollowed out, as shown in Fig. 276. Place four pieces of cretonne across the ends of the runner, the straight edges to the edge of the linen. Pin them in place and then pin three, two, and one above.

Now take off one at a time and stick it down with paste. Buttonhole round the outside and inside of each piece, beginning at the top one and working downwards. Look at the methods of working appliqué in Chapter VIII., if you wish to choose another way of fastening down the cretonne.

This arrangement of circles is often found in Jacobean embroidery (notice the Jacobean covering for a footstool given in this chapter). Circles like those shown in Fig. 276 can be marked out on coarse linen and worked in tapestry wool.

Fig. 277 shows an arrangement of two circles drawn so as to appear as if they were linked together. Draw them with a basin or jar in the middle of a cushion, chairback, or runner. Embroider the circles in one colour or several, using any of the border designs given in this chapter or any one stitch such as chain or outline, worked closely together.

SOME PRETTY HOT-PLATE MATS

Hot-plate mats are always needed for the dinner or tea table, or wherever it is necessary to protect a polished surface.

Here is a way to provide a set that would be extremely decorative and an attractive item on any table.

You can buy, sometimes quite cheaply, mats made of cardboard wrapped with raffia which is stitched to the cardboard. This raffia, neutral in tone, makes a fine background for any colour-scheme you choose for your decoration.

The decoration used consists of circles of coloured felt, their number and size depending on the size of the mat. Mark out the circles on the felt by drawing round a coin of the right size, and cut them out. Space them well round the mat, paste them on, and secure them firmly with a single stitch through the centre. The white stitching on the mat can be covered with similar or any suitable stitches in black wool. The mat can be lined with felt, or if there is not enough felt, a piece of paper of the right colour should be pasted to the under side.

If a good colour-scheme is used, you will be delighted with the result.

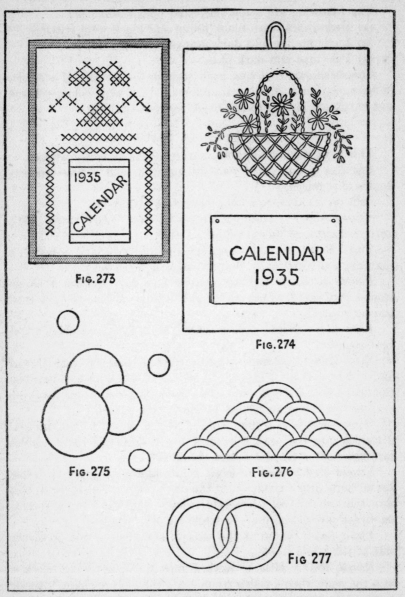

FIG. 273.—Calendar in Cross-Stitch.   FIG. 274.—Embroidered Calendar.
FIGS. 275, 276, and 277.—Use of circles in embroidery design.

The following are some suggested colour-schemes :
(1) Red circles, with black lining and black wool stitches.
(2) Light orange and dark orange.
(3) Pale blue and dark blue.
Choose colours that tone each other down, and are, if possible, in harmony with their surroundings. Whatever colour-scheme you choose, it is wise to use black for the stitching.

An Umbrella Shawl

This is an uncommon and interesting shawl, easily worked.

For this 5 ounces of two-ply fingering and a fine crochet-hook are required.

Cast on 4 chain, join, put 14 trebles into circle.

Second Row : 4 chain, 2 trebles between every treble, with chain between, 28 inches round.

Third Row : 2 trebles between the first two, and 1 between the next two alternately round, with chain between.

Fourth Row : 2 trebles between first two trebles, 2 single trebles into separate spaces, then 2 trebles on top of next two. Repeat round.

Fifth Row : Begin with 2 trebles, then 3 single trebles. Repeat round.

Sixth Row : 4 chain, 2 triple trebles—namely, cast thread and pull over three times on top of two—4 single trebles between the next raised part on top of two on the preceding row, working on until there are 19 trebles between each group.

Border.—Miss 1, treble, work 2 trebles into the next, miss 1, 2 trebles into the next, 2 trebles into the next, 2 triple trebles into the next. Repeat round the shawl.

Second Row : Miss 1, work 1 into the next space, 1 treble again, do 2 single trebles into the next, 2 chain, 2 single trebles into the same place, 2 separate trebles—making 2 single trebles on either side of the four—2 triple trebles. Repeat.

Third Row : Same as the second, but missing one on either side of the triple treble.

Fourth Row : Miss 1, work 1 into the next space, work 1 into the next, then 3 single trebles into the next, 2 chain, 3 single trebles into the same place, 2 single trebles, making 2 on either side of the six ; now work 2 triple trebles, and repeat.

Fifth Row : Miss 1, work 1, miss 1, work 1, miss 1, work 1, 2 trebles into the next, 2 chain, 3 trebles into the same place, 3 separate trebles—making 3 single trebles on either side of four—2 triple trebles, and repeat.

Sixth Row : Miss 1, work 1, miss 1, work 1, miss 1, work 1, 3 trebles into the next, 2 chain, 3 trebles into the same place, 3 separate trebles as on other side of six—that is, making 3 separate trebles on either side of six—2 triple trebles, and repeat.

Seventh Row : 1 treble, 3 chain, fasten on first of 3 chain, 1 treble into the next ; repeat round the shawl, always working triple treble on top of the same pattern of the previous row.

CHAPTER XXXIII

A FEW HINTS ON MILLINERY

Materials for Millinery. Equipment Needed. Suggestions for Hat Blocks. Hats of Different Materials. Felt Hats : Altering their Size and Shape ; Fastening on the Brim ; Fitting the Crown and Brim. Making a Beret. Leather Hats. Hints for Cleaning Leather Hats. Tweed and Cloth Hats. Taking Correct Head Measurements. Hints on Making Brims. More Berets. Straw Hats. Making Hats from Plaits and Braids. Pleated Raffia Hats. Crêpe Paper Hats. Buckram, Esparto, and Canvas Shapes. Covering Buckram, Esparto, and Canvas Shapes. Lining Hats. Trimmings for Hats : Self Material ; Ribbons ; Raffia and Straw ; Cut Felt ; Feathers ; Pompoms ; Organdie ; Lace ; Velvet ; Trimmings as a Means of Altering Shapes.

A NUMBER of people enjoy retrimming hats and altering and adapting them. It is a pretty occupation that appeals to all who love dainty things. Some indeed seem to have magical fingers when they begin to handle and alter hats. The fashion in hats changes quickly, and the hats we write about here will be old-fashioned in a year's time, but the *methods* of altering hats, shaping them, and making them remain. Whoever reads through this chapter carefully will gain ideas that will help them in the art of millinery whatever the fashion is.

Just at present the beret is the most popular hat, made of velvet or cloth or very fine felt. It is large and floppy. It dips over one eye and leaves most of the back of the hair uncovered. The smaller berets are, however, the more comfortable to wear, and some ideas for making them will be found in this chapter.

Tricornes are going to be popular. They are three-cornered hats that skilful fingers can make from old-fashioned beaver or hatter's plush.

FIG. 278.—Head Block. FIG. 279.—Wire Frame. FIG. 280.—Wire for a "round" crown. FIG. 281.—Wire for a "square" crown. FIG. 282.— Wire shape assembled. FIG. 282A.—Shaping a felt hat with tucks. FIG. 282B.—Stab Stitching. FIG. 283.—Horizontal Tucks. FIG. 284.— Pattern shape for four-piece hat.

If one has a little knowledge as to how to shape a hat, every new fashion becomes possible. The Russian toques and hats that are now worn with winter coats are shaped from velvet with wide bands of fur. When it is the fashion, as now, for hats to be made of the same material or colour as the coat, it is very helpful to be able to fashion one's own hat from a piece of surplus material, or if this is not possible, from felts, velours, or velvets which are dyed to tone.

Then again if the actual making of hats is too difficult, trimming is possible. A great many chapters in this book contain ideas that will help one to trim hats. It is wonderful how one art or craft helps another. For example, when trimmings are simple, as at present, and so often consist of cords and strands of vivid-coloured wool with tiny matching felt flowers, then the ideas found in Chapter XIII., "Cords, Tassels, and Fringes," and Chapter XVI., "Wool Craft and Felt Work," will be found useful.

Some general suggestions for trimmings will be found in the coming pages.

EQUIPMENT

The equipment needed for home millinery is small and very much the same as that required for home dressmaking, namely :

(1) A tape measure, cutting-out scissors, small sharp embroidery scissors, milliners' pliers, a small iron, a kettle.

(2) For sewing—needles ("straws" and "sharps"), fine steel pins, a bodkin, a stiletto, a thimble, and, of course, silk and cotton threads to match the materials being used.

(3) For those who want to plan and cut out their own patterns —brown or plain pattern paper, drawing-pins, and compasses will probably be needed.

(4) The machine is occasionally needed—especially for decorative lines of stitching on felt.

(5) A hat block. This is the one most expensive item. It is only necessary if one wants to make hats or completely reshape old ones. It is obviously essential for foundation work and for moulding hats from soft fabrics.

SUGGESTIONS FOR HAT BLOCKS

(1) Since hat crowns vary so greatly in shape, and fashions alter so quickly, it is a pity for the home worker to buy an expensive block made to a certain shape. This can be bought, of course, but they are rather for the professional workers.

(2) Head blocks can be made from the hat-stands in metal or wood that are used for display in milliners' showrooms. These are about 12 inches high, and the head of the stand must be padded to the shape and size required. Cotton-wool is useful for padding. Each layer of padding must, of course, be carefully moulded and fitted so that it lies flat, for the finished block must be solid and smooth, with the head of the stand embedded in it. When the mould is the correct size it is covered with fine linen or lawn. The covering must fit smoothly over the mould, and it is sewn neatly and flatly through the cotton-wool. The lower edges must be gathered underneath the blocked shape and sewn firmly.

It is a great help to use two rings of broad elastic, one around the top and one near the bottom of the mould, to keep the material in place whilst it is being moulded, as in Fig. 278.

(3) The crown of a bowler hat makes a very good temporary block.

(4) A wire shape may be made and padded to the correct size. Copper wire covered with white cotton is generally used, as it does not rust. Fig. 279 shows a wire foundation with round crown. Notice the closeness of the wire in building it up. Large spaces cause ridges. The first ring of wire must be cut to the head measurement, plus 1 inch. It is joined into a ring by wrapping the ends closely with strong cotton or by slipping the ends into a ferrule of white metal made for this purpose. Mark off the ring into eight equal parts.

Now cut the four cross wires that go over the top of the crown. These wires must equal the " over crown " measurement from back to front of the block, and they will vary in length according to the shape desired. A " square " crown, as in Fig. 281, will need a longer length than a " round " crown (Fig. 280). An extra inch must be allowed on each piece of cross wire for the hook at each end for joining, as shown in Figs. 280 and 281.

Bend one of the cross wires as shown in Fig. 280.   Hook it on
to the head ring as shown in Fig. 282, and press back the little
hooks until they grip around the ring quite firmly.   You will
need a pair of pliers for this.   Use the nose of the pliers when
pressing, and cut off any projecting ends when the wire is fixed.
Bend and attach the other three wires in the same way, leaving
even spaces between them.   The eight divisions marked on the
first ring help the spacing.   Tie each cross wire to the other at
the centre.

For the wiring round the sides shown in Fig. 279, many joined
rings of wire are needed.   These must be cut to fit over the
frame of cross wires in Fig. 282, and then joined.   When each
wire ring is made it is tied to each cross wire and secured by
knotting.   The size and position of each wire ring will depend
on the outline of the block being made.   They must be so arranged
that the final shape is sharply outlined.

These wire blocks are very useful for lace hats and also for
fancy-dress purposes.

HATS OF DIFFERENT MATERIALS

Hats are made of many different materials, and each material
needs its own special treatment.   It will be perhaps helpful if
we discuss hats under the headings of the materials from which
they are generally made.   Fashions change so quickly that even
if one does not want to make one's own hat, it is a great advantage
to be able to alter a hat.

FELT HATS

Felt hats are always popular, and as they last so long it is
well to be able to alter them and adapt them to the fashion.
We will discuss both the altering of old hats and the making
of new ones.

Felt hats, as most people know, are beaten, steamed, and
moulded from the flat.   They can therefore be easily remoulded.

*Stretching Felt Hats that are Too Tight or have become Too
Tight.*—Damp often causes shrinkage in the head size of a felt
hat.   It is therefore important to put it on the block to dry
after it has been in a shower of rain, and leave it until quite dry.
If this is not possible and the hat has been allowed to dry so that

it contracts, steaming, stretching, and warming combined, if done carefully, will generally soften the felt so that the size around the head part where it binds the head most uncomfortably can be enlarged.

Steaming, it must be remembered, tends to soften felt so that it can be *stretched*.

The following is the correct method of stretching felt hats : First remove the lining and any bands or trimming around the crown. Then prepare a kettle half full of fast boiling water. The fingers are then placed inside the hat crown, and the hat held in the steam and carefully stretched around the tight places until it is comfortable.

Decreasing the Size of a Felt Hat, or altering its Shape.—Head sizes of felt hats may be *decreased* slightly by shrinking in the steam of fast boiling water.

Tucking is another method of decreasing the size or altering the shape of a felt hat. If the tucks are to be on the crown or head part, it is necessary to cut either the whole or a section of the crown and brim apart.

Tucks can be vertical, as in Fig. 282 *a*, to shape the crown or make it tighter ; or horizontal, as in Fig. 283, to shape the crown or lower it.

Tucking must be very neatly done if it is to look professional when finished.

For the first tuck it is wise to run a coloured tacking thread along the line to be followed. To work the tuck, use a short strong needle and either silk or cotton that exactly matches the felt. Be sure the silk or cotton is strong enough to stand constant tugging. Use either *stab stitching*, as shown in Fig. 282 *b*, working it close to the fold of the felt or machine stitching. If the hat tends to look " thick " or heavy after tucking, place it on the block, pull each tuck along its length, and steam well. It is sometimes necessary to steam, brush, and block the whole crown, moulding it to the shape required.

Fastening on the Brim of a Felt Hat that has been cut off.— When the brims of felt hats have been cut off and cut across their width at the back so that the crown can be tucked at the back to fit the head more closely (as already described), they are sewn on again in the following way :

First, the brim must be made to fit the reduced size of the crown, so steam it and pull it so that the inner curve fits the head part of the crown. To make a neat, flat join lay the felt edge to edge, and pull together with fishbone stitch (see Fig. 181, Chapter XXV., " Home Dressmaking "), then press under a cloth.

A large felt hat can have the brim cut off, a band can be cut from the base of the crown for trimming, and the crown itself then cut into four pieces, each shaped as in Fig. 284, so that they fit together. They are then overlapped at the seams and machine-stitched five times. The brim is fitted as already described and five rows of stitching are added to the edge of the brim for decoration. *The join between the crown* and the brim is made neat by the 1-inch band cut from the crown. This is decorated by five rows of stitching before it is fastened to the hat.

Fashions vary greatly, but although shapes alter, it must be remembered that methods of work remain the same, so that if you can alter a hat to suit one style you can alter it to suit another newer style. The alterations suggested above are merely to show *methods of work.*

Further Hints on fitting the Crown and Brim.—The brim must always be fitted to the crown on the *head of the person* for whom the hat is intended. It is a much safer method than fitting the hat on a head block, unless it is a very good head block.

When making a soft felt hat, most milliners bind the join between the crown and brim, on the inside, with a piece of narrow petersham ribbon, this ribbon being cut to the exact head measurement. This naturally keeps the fit of the hat exact and prevents stretching.

MAKING A BERET (Fig. 285)

Berets have been found so useful that they will probably never go wholly out of fashion. Delightful berets can be made from felt, with scarf and bag to match if you wish.

A good deal has been said about felt work and wool in Chapter XVI., and those who have read that chapter will be better prepared to make this beret. The colour-scheme must

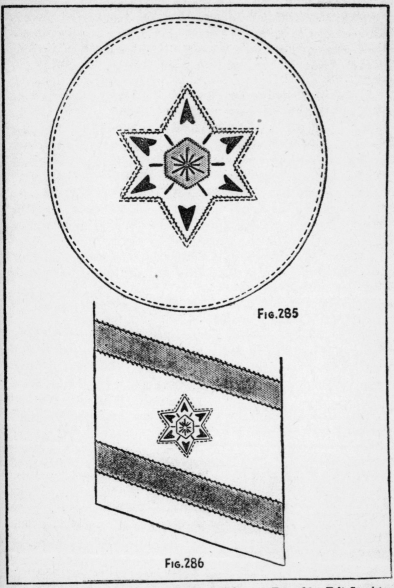

FIG.285

FIG.286

depend upon individual taste and on what the beret is intended to match. On the whole it is wise to choose a dark colour, especially if a design is to be applied, as in Fig. 285. The design shown in Fig. 285 is an example of inlay (for the method of working inlay, see Chapter XVI. on Felt Work, and Chapter XXIX. on Leather Work). The advantage of inlay as a decoration for a felt hat is that as the felt is cut away and another piece let in, there is never more than one thickness of felt, so that the beret is not heavy or clumsy. Appliqué work adds to the weight of the hat. For the top of the beret, cut out a circle of black, dark blue, or nigger felt. This circle should be about 10½ to 11 inches in diameter. The underneath part consists of a circle the same size, but from the centre of this a circle about 6½ inches in diameter is cut. This will leave a ring all round 2 inches broad. Whatever size you cut your beret, be sure that the breadth of the ring underneath is never less than 2 inches. Some may need the circle for the head to be 7 inches in diameter.

Draw the design on paper first and cut out the pieces as required. Cut the large six-pointed star first and place it on a piece of pale blue felt. Cut the blue felt carefully. Inlay the hexagon into it before fixing it in the beret. Cut the hexagon of darker blue and place it on the pale blue star-shape, draw round the shape with a sharp pencil. Cut slightly within this drawn line with a sharp penknife. Insert the hexagon and seam it over with small firm stitches. Next insert the six small dark blue wedge-shaped pieces in the same way. Be careful not to cut the place for more than one of these pieces at a time or the felt may tend to stretch and get out of shape. When the six-pointed star is finished, press it well on the wrong side until it lies quite flat and is the proper shape. Then cut out the place in the beret into which it fits in the manner already described, and seam it in. The decorative stitching shown in Fig. 285 is done in wool of a contrasting tone or shade. This adds a finish to the design. A row of running stitch in pale blue is worked ¼ inch from the edge of the star all the way round, and another row is worked about ¼ inch from the outer edge of the circle. If this design is too elaborate, a simpler one can be chosen. The one given above merely illustrates a method of work.

As soon as the decoration of the top is completed it can

be seamed to the underneath part. Next cut a piece of pale blue felt the length of the headpiece (probably about 21 inches) and 1½ inch broad. Decide which is the back of the beret and begin binding there. The binding must be put on fairly tightly, so that it fits to the head. Begin on the right side, and sew with blue hemming stitches about ¼ inch over the edge of the black or dark blue felt (or whatever colour the beret is). Turn the binding over and hem again on the other side; be careful not to let the stitches show through.

If a scarf is made to go with this hat it can have the six-pointed star and hexagon inlayed at each end, and strips of light blue and dark blue felt seamed across each end. The decoration of the ends of the scarf are clearly seen in Fig. 286.

Those who find inlay difficult (though it is not really difficult, because felt is so adapted to this method of work) can make the beret of plain felt of a good decorative colour. Simple wool embroideries are also effective, and many stitches found in different parts of this book can be adapted to the decoration of hats.

LEATHER HATS

Leather hats are made in very much the same way as felt hats, but they are heavier and in some ways less adaptable. The most suitable leather for making hats has already been described in Chapter XXVIII., " Soft or Suède Leather Work," where also will be found plenty of hints on sewing and machining leather. Suède hats are very suitable for sports, country walks, and particularly motoring, as they can be made to brave any weather and keep out draughts. They can also be made so that they easily fold up. They stand rain better than felt, since they do not tend to shrink.

They are equally suited for town wear, and trimmed with silk or woollen embroidery have a charm of their own which is not easily rivalled by any other millinery. Leather pullovers will probably always be fashionable. Delightful ones are now made with eight gores (Fig. 287 shows a gore) and a pretty brim, narrow in front and broad at the sides, as it should be to protect one in all weathers. It must be remembered that if one can make a four-gore hat one can make an eight-gore hat. Remember to allow turnings on all edges of gores, generally 1 inch on straight lower edge of each gore and ⅜-inch turnings on all other edges. Pin each edge of gore to each gore. It is best to arrange them on the table, with all the points meeting at a centre, before pinning. When they are pinned, begin to stitch the seams *from the point of the gore* to the lower edge, then open the seams and stitch the turnings flat, stitching from the inside of the crown.

Excellent patterns for these " All-Weather Hats " can be bought from Weldon's.

We give below a few hints for cleaning and preserving suède hats. They should have a long life.

Hints for Cleaning Suède

A wire brush, obtainable from any shoe shop, is most useful for preserving and cleaning suède, and should be used at once when any shiny place appears on the leather.

If the leather is soiled, it should be brushed first with the wire brush. Then go over the surface carefully with a piece of sand-paper. Always change the sand-paper for a new piece as soon as it becomes soiled.

If there are any marks which the sand-paper cannot remove, rub some powdered starch on them and leave it for several hours. Then brush it off with a clean brush.

Benzine can be used for cleaning white doeskin. It should be rubbed in with a clean rag. Hang the article to dry out of doors. It must never be put near a fire.

Tweed and Cloth Hats

Tweed and cloth hats are very popular and are sure to remain popular, because tweed and cloth can now be manufactured in featherweights. This fact has really given us a new material, as it were, for hats. For sports wear they are delightful. Children can have charming little tailored hats that match their tailored coats.

Patterns for tweed hats can be bought—for example, the pattern for the " All-Weather " hat discussed under Leather Hats.

If one wants to make a cloth hat oneself it must first be planned in paper on stiff French canvas and fitted before the

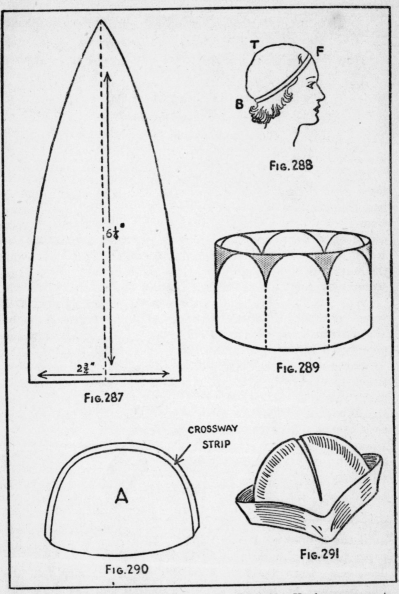

FIG. 287.

FIG. 288.

FIG. 289.

CROSSWAY STRIP

A

FIG. 290.

FIG. 291.

FIG. 287.—Gore for an eight-gore hat.
FIG. 288.—Head measurements.
FIG. 289.—Pattern for plain-fitting crown.
FIG. 290.—A close-fitting crown.
FIG. 291.—Tricorn with pleated crown.

material is cut out. One must begin, however, by getting correct head measurements.

How to get Correct Head Measurements (Fig. 288)

The easiest way to get correct measurements is to place a strip of wire ribbon round the head where the hat is to fit, and join it, as shown in Fig. 288. Then measure the distance from F in front to T at the top of the head and to B at the back, as shown in Fig. 288. Measure the length of the wire used, and use this when making the brim.

From the measurements we now have we can make a pattern for a plain fitting tweed crown. Cut a strip of paper equal in length to the wire, plus $1\frac{1}{4}$ inch more, and as wide as the distance from F to T. Join this strip into a ring, divide it equally into six or eight parts, and pin up six or eight darts to make the crown, fitting the edges as neatly as possible. Then trim away the surplus paper, as in Fig. 289. A crown can also be made in sections by cutting down to the bottom of each dart, this will provide a pattern for each of six or eight separate sections or gores on which, of course, turnings of $\frac{3}{8}$ inch extra must be allowed when cutting out the material. (See also Fig. 287, the gore for an eight-gored leather hat.)

In the case of a close-fitting crown, a crossway strip of material is cut to equal F, T, B, and moulded into shape on a block, then two sections shaped as A in Fig. 290 are cut; these fill in the spaces each side. This is often a useful method of hat-making, as it can be adapted to different purposes. Fig. 291 illustrates a way of adapting the method. It shows a three-pointed hat, a tricorne, with a pleated crown.

Hints on making Brims

Brims can either be made to turn up or turn down. Begin by cutting a flat brim, as shown in Fig. 292, and then shape it until the desired effect is obtained. It is easy to make a flat paper pattern of a brim from the wire head ring we have just described. Draw the outline of this on paper, then fold the ring carefully in halves both ways so that you can draw two intersecting lines A B and C D, as shown in Fig. 292. Draw two more through the centre as shown. Mark off on each line the

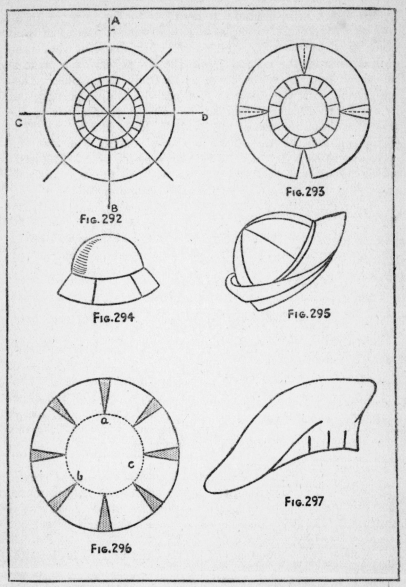

FIG. 292.
FIG. 293.
FIG. 294.
FIG. 295.
FIG. 296.
FIG. 297.

FIG. 292.—Pattern for brim.   FIG. 293.—Darts to shape brim.   FIG. 294.—
Mushroom brim.   FIG. 295.—Tweed Hat with sectional crown.   FIG. 296.—
Pattern for a beret in one piece.   FIG. 297.—Beret, showing the use of darts.

width of the brim desired; it need not be the same width all
the way round—for example, you may want it narrow in front
and broad at the sides, and so on. The shape of your brim
will depend on the fashion. Join the marks you have made in
a curved line, draw the curve as carefully as possible. Then
cut round with the scissors. Cut out the middle portion, but
allow ¾-inch turning; this can be snipped at intervals to the
line that shows the size of the head, as shown in Fig. 292. The
brim can now be shaped by means of darts. The size and
positions of each dart decides the shape of the brim. The darts
must radiate from the head part, as shown in Fig. 293, and care
must be taken not to cut or alter the outline of the head. For
a mushroom shape the darts are equal at all points, as shown
in Figs. 293 and 294. For a bonnet shape, or when protection for
the ears is needed, the brim has darts chiefly at the sides. When
the darts are cut out, their edges are neatly overlapped and pasted.
The brim pattern is now ready, cut across the back so that it
can be laid flat on the material.

Brim patterns are generally placed on the exact cross of the
material and on folded material so that the upper and under
brim are cut at once.

If the brim needs stiffening, it must be interlined with fine
French canvas, or leno muslin, or heavier canvas. The kind of
canvas depends on whether a soft or stiff brim is needed.

In joining up the different parts of a tweed hat, the directions already given for leather hats apply; for example, always
seam from centre crown to base, machine stitching decorates
and strengthens the brim, the join between the brim and crown
can be hidden by a stitched band.

Fig. 295 shows a typical tweed hat with a sectional crown.
The sectional crowns described above are always easy to make,
and are economical, as they can often be made from tweed
cuttings. The brim is rather an elaborate one, and should not
be attempted by a beginner.

A little boy's tweed hat is perhaps the best to begin with.
One can be made in five sections, with a crossway brim as described, turned down except at one side. The brim and band
should be machine stitched. A five-section hat fits well, but
four sections are generally enough for children's hats.

Berets Again (Figs. 296 and 297)

We have already described one beret in writing about felt hats, but as berets are so popular we will describe one more. They also teach a good deal about shaping hats.

The first beret was made in two pieces. The beret we are now going to describe is made in one piece. We will give no measurements, as so much depends on individual taste—some people liking very large flapping berets, and some small ones.

Fig. 296 shows the principle on which a beret is cut in one piece. A pattern is cut from a large piece of paper ; first make a circle and cut it out, then by means of darts (pleats or tucks can also be used) shape the under side. When folded under, the inner edge thus made must be cut to the correct head measure found by the wire ribbon. Bind this inner edge neatly with corded ribbon or self-material.

Darts play a very important part in shaping berets. Fig. 297 shows a smart tweed beret which illustrates the clever use of darts. It can be made in soft tweed or soft woollen material or velvet.

Straw Hats

Straw hats often need adjusting. (1) Sometimes this adjustment is needed to make them fit ; (2) sometimes because the hat has lost its shape ; and (3) sometimes to bring the shape up to date.

All hats made of plaited straw such as panama, raffia, and Yedda plaits, may be softened quite well by damping them with cold water and moulding them on a suitable head block in the same way as felt hats can be moulded. It is necessary afterwards, however, to stiffen straw hats ; this is done by spraying them with a stiffening solution. (A brush can be used if desired instead of a spray.) The solution is sold in pots or bottles with directions for use. Clear varnish is often applied to straw hats if a gloss as well as stiffening is needed, or clear brown shellac (from an oil shop) can be dissolved in methylated spirits and used.

Hats made of plaited straw can be unpicked and entirely remade, or their shape or size can be altered by plaits as the felt hats. Even a stiff hat can be pleated while it is being steamed, as the straw becomes soft and sticky. It is then fairly easy to pinch and fold it. When the pleats are made they must be pinned in position, and then fastened with strong tacking stitches.

Making Hats from Plaits and Braids

Those who have done some Indian basketry or read Chapter XXVII. on Coiled Basketry will not find it difficult to make hats from straw plaits which can be bought ready to be sewn. Plaits of different widths and kinds can be bought. The narrow, hard plaits are the most difficult for the home workers, such as pedal, tagel, and others that have sharply-turned and self-supporting edges.

The following hints on sewing straw plaits to make hats may be useful ::

(1) Crowns and brims are generally made separately. Begin the crown in the centre and the brim from the *outside edge*. In the crown each succeeding row is placed *under* its neighbour.

(2) Linen thread or strong cotton, to match the plait, and a straw needle are necessary.

(3) To make the crown, begin by unravelling an end of plait and wrapping it with cotton, then twist the plait round and stab stitch through and through while fitting each coil to shape, as shown in Fig. 298. When the top is complete it can be steamed and flattened or moulded into shape. The plait is, of course, tightened as the sides of the crown are formed, and then the work proceeds steadily down to the brim line. Constantly test the shape on a block. A buckram frame or a hat of the correct head size may be used to help shape the crown and to prevent drawing the braid while sewing. Take care not to sew the braid to the foundation.

(4) Sewing the brim. A stiff paper pattern can be prepared, as already described, and used if desired. Begin sewing the plait *at the back* and on the outside edge of the brim. The plait is worked from right to left, as in Fig. 299. Hold the right side of the plait towards you and stab-stitch through and through. Each round is sewn *above* its neighbour. As each row is smaller, the plait requires easing on its inside edge all the time, until

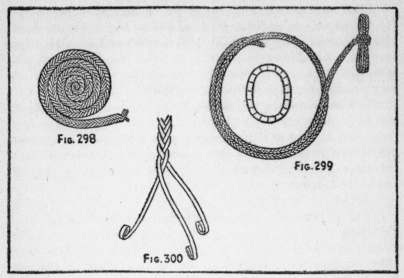

FIG. 298.—Straw plait.   FIG. 299.—Straw brim.   FIG. 300.—Method of plaiting.

the head line is reached.   Now an extra row (not eased) is added and turned upwards round the head line.   It is to this that the crown is attached.

PLAITED RAFFIA HATS

Many people like making their own plaits.   Raffia can be bought plaited, and sewn into hats.   It is, however, a heavier hat than one made of straw plaits.   Dolls' hats to amuse children can be easily made from raffia plaits.

CRÊPE PAPER HATS

Delightful hats can be made from crêpe paper.   Dennison's crêpe paper is the best.   They look exactly like those of straw, silk, or felt.   You can do every bit of the work yourself—cut the paper, plait it, and make it up.

Probably you will say, " What happens if it rains ? "   Fortunately, crêpe paper hats can be sprayed with Dennison's Water Resistant, which retards moisture and makes the hat practical. The cost of a paper hat is, moreover, very little compared with that of other hats.

There are several different ways of making paper hats.
(1) The paper can be cut in strips and sewn to a buckram shape
(see next section for buckram) ; (2) braided and sewn together
without a foundation ; (3) strips of paper may be folded and
sewn to a buckram or crêpe paper foundation ; (4) folded strips
may be sewn together without a foundation.

Hats of any style can be made—sport hats, tailored hats,
picture hats—whatever the fashion may be or your fancy wish.

To cut a strip of crêpe paper evenly when making folds or
braids, slip from the packet the required width, then cut through
the entire fold with a pair of sharp scissors, using the edge of
the folder as a guide.

The strands of paper will not tangle when they are being
plaited if the ends are rolled up and pinned as shown in Fig. 300.
The ends of the strips are joined with paste when joining is
necessary. Four, five, or six strips plaited together look very
effective, especially if more than one colour is used. Directions
for plaiting are given in Chapter XXI. on Raffia Work.

Paper plaits are sewn together as already described for straw
plaits. Paper is really a wonderful material for making hats,
because it stretches so smoothly. An interesting and useful
pamphlet can be obtained from the Dennison Manufacturing
Co. Ltd., 52 Kingsway, London, W.C. 2, which tells all about
the art of making hats with Dennison Crêpe.

BUCKRAM, ESPARTO, AND CANVAS SHAPES

Buckram is several layers of coarse leno muslin, heavily
sized and pressed. The *smooth* side is the right side. It can be
bought only in black and white.

Esparto is softer, lighter in weight, and more pliable than
buckram. It is made of a basket plaiting of shredded and
flattened esparto grass. It is cream in colour. The quality and
stiffness of esparto varies. A covering of muslin is often attached
to the right side of the plaiting and it is stiffened with size. One
must choose one's esparto according to the shape one is making.
A large brim needs a fairly stiff esparto. A small hat is best
mounted on softer esparto, and so on.

Cream and black canvas, leno muslin, and fine French canvas
are also used by milliners at different times.

All these materials can be steamed and damped and moulded into shape or cut into strips on the cross and stretched. On the whole it is not wise for the home worker to attempt to make an entirely new shape. Buckram and esparto shapes can be bought in great variety, so it is easy to find one that suits, and if one cannot it is easier to adapt a ready-made shape to one's requirements than to make an entirely new shape.

COVERING BUCKRAM, ESPARTO, AND CANVAS SHAPES

Covering materials are very varied—velvet, panne, satin, tulle, georgette, ninon, lace, and so on, including of course crêpe paper already mentioned.

Shapes may be covered in two ways :

(1) *Stretched Coverings.*—Patterns are generally cut in tissue paper and they must be true to the shape being covered. Plan each piece of the pattern so that the crossway of the covering materials is at the point where careful moulding is required.

Fig 301 shows the brim of a buckram hat being covered. The crossway seam of the covering is joined at the back, and it is carefully pulled over the brim ; the turnings are snipped as shown. Be careful not to snip too much. Stab-stitch the turnings to the crown as shown, just above the fitting line. Turn $\frac{1}{4}$ inch of material over the brim edge and neatly catch-stitch to the under side of the shape. (For catch stitch, see Chapters IX. and XIV.)

The under-brim covering is applied in very much the same way. There are many different ways of treating the brim. Two common ways are : (1) turn in a $\frac{1}{4}$ inch of the lower covering, and neatly slip-stitch it to the upper covering ; (2) bind the edges with self-material cut on the cross, or corded ribbon, etc.

For the crown probably a two-piece covering is the easiest for the amateur. This consists of a flat round piece moulded to fit the top of the crown and a side band of cross-cut material.

(2) *Gathered Coverings.*—If these are to fit well they should be cross-cut, whether for crowns or brims. Methods of tucking, cording, and shirring material have been dealt with in the chapters on Home Dressmaking.

Fashion changes the coverings of hats each year, but, as we have said before, methods remain very much the same.

When covering hats it is well to remember that the *professional milliner* always uses hidden, not surface stitching—this applies also to linings as well as covers. The slip stitch may be called the milliner's stitch. (For the slip stitch, see Chapter XXV., " Home Dressmaking.")

The exception to this is *tailored hats*, when machine stitching is used as a decoration.

Lining Hats

The main qualification of a good lining is *smoothness*, so that the hat slips easily on and off.

Sarcenet is supposed to be the best silk to use, but taffeta and jap silk are quite frequently employed. All these are expensive, and if expense is a consideration mercerised cotton and artificial silk are really good substitutes.

Transparent hats are generally lined with net or tulle.

The two most well-known ways of lining hats are :

(1) The so-called " bag shaped " lining. This is seen in many hats. First cut a circular top piece, A in Fig. 302. This is often called the " tip "; then a cross-way strip, B in Fig. 302. The crossway strip is cut to the head size and the depth of the crown. The lining and top can be joined by the machine and the edges neatly pressed. The lower edge of the lining is slip-stitched inside the crown just below the head line, so that it neatens the join.

(2) Linings made in sections. Tailored hats and hats made in sections, like many already described in this book, generally have the lining cut from the same pattern.

Trimmings for Hats

Trimmings are of infinite variety and vary with the fashion, but some because of their real beauty and fitness survive all changes. It is interesting to consider all the different materials used for trimming hats.

(1) *Trimmings made from the same Material as the Hat.*— This is the most inexpensive form of trimming, and it is always pleasing and in good taste. We have already mentioned stitched bands for felt hats or for tweed hats.

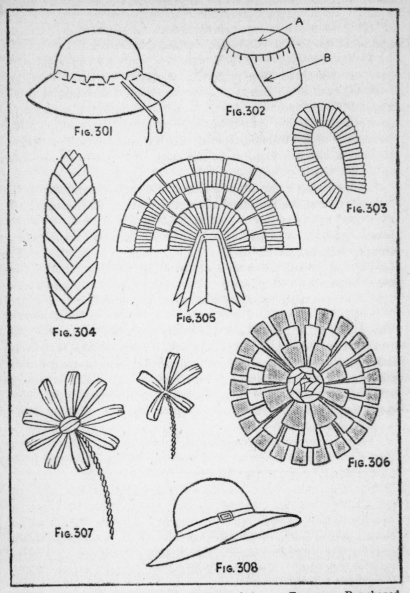

FIG. 301.—Covering the brim of a buckram hat.
lining of hat.   FIG. 303.—Cockade.   FIG. 304.—Ribbon decoration.
FIGS. 305 and 306.—Hat decoration of ribbon.   FIG. 307.—Raffia flowers.
FIG. 308.—Hat decorated with dog's collar.

(2) *Ribbon.*—Ribbon again is always an effective decoration, and most people can successfully trim a hat with it.

Ribbon makes pretty shell trimming, especially for children's hats or bonnets. (For different ways of rucking, shirring, tucking, etc., see Chapter XXVI., " Home Dressmaking (*continued*).") Ribbon can also be sewn into either a bow or a rosette ; this should always be done by hand. To make a bow, each loop is neatly folded into position and sewn flat before the end is folded over to make the knot. Large bows may have to be mounted on wire.

The wiring of hat foundations has already been described, but fine trimming materials often need wire. Mounting (used by electricians in coils) is sold on reels and can be obtained in black and white and in colours. " Lace " wire is sold in coils ; this is also used for ribbons.

For flat bows, use corded or petersham ribbon. Flat bows have loops only and no ends. Fold the loops neatly and finish off with a piece of ribbon pleated across the middle.

Cockades are made from pleated corded ribbon, as shown in Fig. 303. Fig. 304 shows another kind of cockade. Figs. 305 and 306 show two other suggestions for ribbon decorations. There is indeed no limit to the pretty shapes that can be made from ribbon, and the most beautiful ribbons the world has ever seen are offered to us in the shops to-day at quite low prices. (For more about ribbon work, see Chapter XXXII., " Some More Useful Ideas for Gifts, Bazaars, and the Home.")

To make rosettes, one decides on the size of the circle required, then the ribbon is marked off into equal lengths ; sew each ring down firmly before setting the next loop in position.

(3) *Raffia Trimmings and Straw Trimmings.*—These vary in popularity. Fig. 307 shows a raffia flower. The centre is a wooden button wound round with raffia, or better still a ball of cloth covered with raffia. The petals are loops of raffia sewn round. Fig. 307 also shows how violets or bunches of violets can be suggested. (See also Raffia Millinery in Chapter XXI., " Raffia Work.")

Narrow straw braids or raffia braids are often sewn into pretty shapes for trimming. Fancy straw hats are sometimes trimmed with raffia flowers, and hats when made of raffia canvas are decorated with raffia embroidery. All these ways of decoration depend on the fashion.

(4) *Cut Felt Trimmings and Felt Flowers.*—Felt flowers, and felt trimmings with gay woollen stitches are always attractive. Some suggestions for felt flowers are given in Chapter XVI., " Wool Craft and Felt Work." Felt flowers that match the hat are good trimming.

(5) *Feathers.*—There are many ways of trimming hats with feathers, and the kind of feathers used and the method varies greatly with the fashion. At the present day one sometimes sees an absurdity like this—a peacock feather, with the quill shaved the whole of its length and just a blot left at the end. Such is fashion ! Yet feathers are lovely things, and neat little feathers, very unobtrusive, deck serviceable hats of the tammy or beret style. It is interesting to notice that osprey and ostrich feathers are becoming fashionable for grand occasions.

The great difficulty in trimming a hat with one feather is to get that one feather just in the right position. This is a real art, or perhaps gift.

(6) *Pompons or Stiff Little Brushes.*—These are fashionable on Russian hats. For the making of pompons, see Chapter XIII.

(7) *Organdie Trimmings.*—Organdie, like ribbon, can be used in several ways—ruching, shelling, pleating, gathering, cording. It is also used for making very dainty artificial flowers.

(8) *Lace Trimmings.*—These, of course, are always mounted on thin millinery wire, covered to match the lace. The wire foundation for the shape required, say a bow or a butterfly, is made first, then the lace folded over it and stitched. The edges may be buttonholed in embroidery silk and details added in embroidery of the same colour.

(9) *Velvet* or other materials lined with a different colour or material is a good and effective trimming. Remember, if you use lining for velvet, only line the loose ends or the trimming may be too bulky.

(10) Then there are always odds and ends used for trimming that depend wholly on the fashion of the moment, like the peacock's feathers already described, or the hat shown in Fig. 308, which is decorated with a leather dog's collar. These, by the way, can be bought in pretty tones of red, blue, or green.

We have written on very general terms about the trimming of hats, because exactly how the trimmings are made depends absolutely on the fashion. The materials themselves only vary slightly. It is interesting to notice unusual trimmings and add them to one's list of possible materials.

(11) *Trimmings as a Means of altering Shape.*—To make the crown of a hat higher, cut it or unpick it away from the brim, and insert a crossway band of stiff buckram or canvas. Stitched or ribbon trimming is then used to hide the join.

A crown can be enlarged by cutting it through the middle from *front to back*, and letting in a contrasting band. To bring this into harmony with the hat as a whole, trim the brim and make a narrow hat bind of the same material. A brim may be widened by stiff corded ribbon. This is eased around the edge in a simple way. Net or organdie edges are best for straw hats, but they must be mounted on wire foundations.

CHAPTER XXXIV

FUR, FUR TRIMMINGS, RENOVATING FUR, AND SPECIAL HINTS ON DRESSMAKING FOR CHILDREN

Cutting Fur ; Seams in Fur ; Lining Fur, and sewing it on. Fur Bands for Trimming. Altering the Shape of Fur. Mending and Renovating Fur. Cleaning Fur. Preparing and sewing on Marabout. Fur Fabrics.

A Few Special Hints on Dressmaking for Children. Materials. Girls' Clothes—Suitable Trimmings. Boys' Clothes—Seams for Blouses, etc. Knickers—The Fly Opening.

FUR is always popular on coats—it is probably true to say that fur will never be out of fashion. It is very economical to be able to make one's own fur collar for a coat, because it considerably lessens the cost of the coat. As a rule it is the fur collar that sends up the price.

The amount of fur you need for a collar varies with the style, but for an average coat a yard of 8-inch fur should be ample.

Cutting Fur.—Fur must always be cut on the wrong side with a sharp knife, *so that the hair is not cut.* Never cut fur with scissors. A furrier's knife should be used if possible—failing this, a really sharp penknife is quite satisfactory.

The exact outline to be cut must be marked with pencil or indian ink on the skin first. The ideal plan is to get some one to hold the fur out taut for you while you cut along the pencil line. If this is not possible, place the fur right side down on the table, and very carefully cut through the outline without allowing your knife to go right down to the table ; in this way you may avoid cutting through the hairs of the fur.

Remember, to cut a shaped piece such as a collar from fur,

591

a complete pattern is needed, as you cannot fold fur for the two halves to be cut at once.

Seams in Fur.—Seams in fur must be made so that the hair matches in colour and runs the same way. In the case of a collar, when the hair must run over both shoulders in the same direction, the overlapping of the hairs in the centre-back seam will (especially with long-haired fur) be very clumsy, and therefore noticeable. A good way to avoid this is to cut the edges of the skins which are meeting in vandyked points, so that they fit into one another.

Joins are always necessary if you are using small pieces of fur to make your collar, so we will give detailed directions for joins or seams.

Having seen that the fur on the joined pieces smoothes the same way, take an ordinary short needle and a strong glazed thread, or No. 30 cotton. Place the two cut edges together, *skin side* uppermost, pushing down any fur that pokes up, then oversew the edges firmly together with very small stitches, being careful to sew through the skin only without catching up the hair in the cotton. Push the hair down between the edges of the opening with the needle if necessary. When the seam is finished, brush the fur gently on the right side. It is often advisable to *slightly* damp the seam on the wrong side, stretch it out smoothly on a flat board, and fasten it down with needles. Leave it to dry thoroughly for about twenty-four hours. Fasten long-haired furs to the board with the skin downwards.

Sewing on Fur.—Before sewing on fur it must be lined, and it needs an interlining as well as a lining if it is to look rich and soft, and wear really well. All fur is first mounted on dormette, which forms the interlining. Dormette is a soft material, not unlike a woolly canvas ; it can be bought in black or white from all large drapery houses. Some people use double dormette ; cotton-wool (not the absorbent cotton-wool sold by chemists) can also be used for interlining.

Cut the dormette by the pattern, and allow *no* turnings. Turnings must be allowed on the fur. The edge of the fur is turned in over the dormette and herringboned down into position, as in Fig. 309. In the case of collars and cuffs, the fur is then faced with material or lining ; turn in the outer edges of the

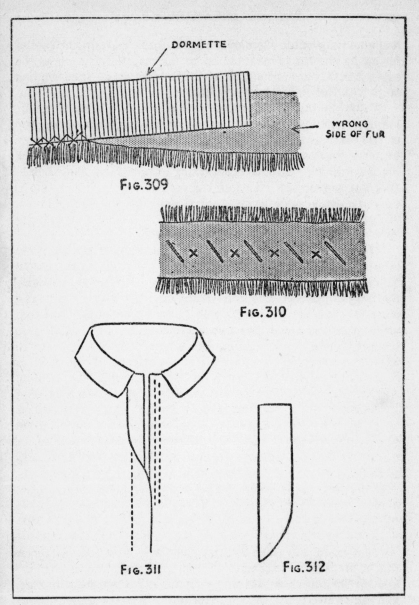

FIG. 309. — Dormette: edge of the fur being turned in over dormette and herring-boned down.   FIG. 310.—Sewing marabout on foundation before use. FIG. 311.—Blouse finished with Box-pleat Front.   FIG. 312.—Pattern for Fly-opening.

lining and slip-stitch them over the fur turnings. In the case of fur strips, the fur is mounted on to the material as soon as the edges have been turned in over the dormette. (See coming section on Fur Bands for Trimming.)

Putting on the Collar.—Having interlined and lined the collar, join and tack the inside of the coat neck against the wrong side of the coat collar (the lining pulled up safely out of the way). Turn the coat to the right side, and from the outside of the neck oversew through to the fur turning, using good sewing silk. When this oversewing is done, smooth down the collar lining, turn in its lower edge, and fell this down neatly over the join.

FUR BANDS FOR TRIMMING

If you are using fur bands for trimming, they should be interlined with dormette, and if desired the edges neatly taped. You can use strong flat bias binding, tape, or braid for neatening the edges. Smooth the hair down from the edge of the fur, place the tape along the right side, its upper edge level with that of the strip, and over the two edges together with small even stitches. Now place the interlining strip of dormette at the back of the fur, turn the tape over it, and herringbone the edge to the interlining. To stitch on your trimming, take your stitches into the taping, but be careful not to catch in the hair.

Another quicker way of sewing on fur strips is to put in the interlining, pin the strips in position on the right side of the garment, then turn to the wrong side and run the material to the fur at the upper and lower edges of the band. It is quite easy to feel with your left hand where the fur starts and finishes.

If you buy fur banding by the yard, you will have no joins to make.

ALTERING THE SHAPE OF FUR

Sometimes you want to alter the shape of a piece of fur so that it fits a collar or something that you are trimming. If only a slight shaping is needed and your fur is not too worn or thin, you can stretch it the desired shape in this way.

First remove the lining and padding, and damp the skin side with cold water. When it is soft and pliable place it (skin side upwards) on a board and very gently—for fur tears easily when wet—ease and coax it to the shape you want, securing the edges of the fur to the board with small drawing-pins. The stretching process must be very slow and gentle, as we have said before, otherwise the skins may split. The pins keep it stretched to its new shape. Leave it thus for at least twenty-four hours until it is thoroughly dry. Choose a *cool*, dry place for it, because heat will crack the skin.

It is well to remember the rule that thick fur is fastened wrong side downwards, but a thin fur can be placed hair side downwards.

Mending or Renovating Fur

The least worn parts of a fur can often be cut out and used for fur trimming. A really shabby fur coat often has enough good pieces to make a lovely collar.

First clean the fur as described in the coming section on Cleaning Fur. Then mark on the wrong side the pieces you want to cut out and cut them out as directed. Fit them together carefully, match the shading, smoothing, and thinness or thickness of the pieces to be joined. When the pieces are well matched in every way, cut their edges to fit. Fine skins, such as ermine or chinchilla, should have their edges vandyked, and the points fitted in to one another as exactly as possible. This method has already been mentioned; a join made thus is practically invisible. All fine skins must be worked carefully, as they are brittle and easily torn. It is wise before you seam the edges together to work along them with buttonhole stitch or oversewing, using good sewing silk. Directions for joining the edges have already been given. When oversewing the edges, it is a good plan to push the hairs down with a piece of thin cardboard—a thin post card will do—so that you do not catch them in.

Cleaning Fur

Old furs must be cleaned before they are used. The best way perhaps is to clean them with hot bran. Rub the bran into the fur, and put the fur into a box with more bran. Leave the fur for twelve hours, then beat and brush out the bran thoroughly.

White fur is cleaned with powdered magnesia. Rub it well in, and leave it for twelve hours before brushing and shaking it out.

If the neck is greasy, it can be cleaned with a little powdered orris root.

Preparing and Sewing on Marabout

Marabout trimming must be mounted before it can be satisfactorily stitched to a garment. It is generally sewn to a strip of thin Japanese silk in the same shade, but any thin silk or muslin will do.

To mount marabout.—Take a long strip of silk, turn in the edges, and then sew the turned-in edges together to make a perfectly neat double strip. When completed, it should be about a third the width of the marabout.

Now place the marabout flat on the table with the worst side upwards. Be sure that it is quite flat, for there must be no twist in it. Lay the folded silk over the top of the marabout, along its middle. See that the lapped edges of the folded silk are downwards. Pin it to the stem of the marabout at intervals. Now sew it into position, taking one long and one short stitch alternately, as shown in Fig. 310. The smaller stitches are for firmness. Work from right to left.

When sewing the trimming to the garment, sew both edges of the strip with running stitches, stitch from the wrong side if the material is thin enough. Be careful not to catch down the marabout itself.

Fur Fabrics

Fur fabrics are cut with scissors like ordinary material, but if it is used for collars, cuffs, trimmings, etc., it is interlined with dormette or double dormette or cotton-wool, just like real fur. If you are making a coat of a fur fabric, back it with a layer of muslin. This will strengthen it and make it last longer. Use cotton when sewing fur fabrics.

A FEW SPECIAL HINTS ON DRESSMAKING FOR CHILDREN

A great deal that has been said in the chapters on Home Dressmaking applies to children's clothes. Whether one makes one's own dresses or not depends a good deal on time and ability, but it is possible, and a *very* great economy for a mother, to make at home all the clothes for little girls up to, say, twelve, and for boys until they are six or seven.

The small, simple garments for a baby are very easy to make, and as the child grows one's work tends to improve, so that one hardly notices that garments become slightly more difficult.

Although children's clothes are made very much like adults, there are one or two special points to be considered when making them.

(1) Children are rough with their clothes—that is, buttons come off more quickly, pockets tear, and so on. Therefore, when making their clothes, remember—

> (*a*) If buttons come on single thicknesses of material, place behind the button a piece of extra stuff to take the strain.
>
> (*b*) Make them fully large enough so that there is no strain.
>
> (*c*) Strengthen the parts that get specially hard wear. Suggestions for strengthening garments have been given in Chapter XXXI.
>
> (*d*) Follow the American plan of stitching a good-sized piece of the material from which the garment is made in with the side seam on the wrong side. It is not seen, it gets washed with the garment, and when a patch is needed, it is *exactly the right colour.*

(2) Allowance must be made for rapid growth. The hem should be deep, tucks are useful, allow wide turnings to side seams, and so on.

Fortunately, fashions do not change so quickly for children as for grown-up people. This makes patching or letting out a garment more possible. As far as possible children's ordinary day clothes should be washable. This often decides one's choice of material.

Materials

The following is a list of materials for children's wear :

(1) *Outdoor and School Wear.*—Serge, face-cloth, tweed, wool rep, knitted fabrics.

(2) *Summer Materials.*—Prints, voiles, lawns, linens, and muslins all wash well.

(3) *Materials for Party Frocks or Best Frocks.*—Crêpe de Chine, jap silk, velvet, taffeta, georgette, organdie muslin.

(4) *Other Suggestions for General Wear.*—Viyella, rep, stockinette, wool crêpe de Chine, and mixtures of wool and cotton or wool and silk.

GIRLS' CLOTHES

These have simple trimmings that are not easily torn or become untidy. The following are suggested : Tucks, contrasting binding, piping, pleats. Method of working these trimmings will be found in the chapters on Plain Sewing and Home Dressmaking. Hand embroidery is always delightful on little one's frocks, and many stitches described in this book can be used. Avoid faggoting or hemstitching because children tear them quickly. Excellent stitches for children's dresses are feather stitch, fly stitch, lazy-daisy, and French knots. But perhaps the strongest and most pleasing because of its varieties is the buttonhole stitch.

BOYS' CLOTHES

A little boy up to four can have a pretty garment decorated with simple trimmings and embroideries like a little girl ; but as he gets older he wants something more manly, and therefore he will like his clothes plainer.

The straightforward-looking flat-fell seam is very suitable on little blouses, shirts, and pyjamas. To make a flat-fell seam, first make a plain seam with wide turnings. Press both turnings one way and trim one of them off narrowly. Turn in the wide one, lay it flat over the narrow one and tack down. Then stitch again from the right side along the tacking line. This seam will have a really tailored look if it is pressed twice—that is, first when the first line of seaming is done, and then again at the finish.

By the way, the flat-fell seam looks very neat and workmanlike on your overall. The side, shoulder, sleeve, and armhole seams can all be flat-felled. For more about seams, see Chapter IX., " Plain Sewing," and Chapter XXV., " Dressmaking."

The box-pleat front described in the making of a shirt blouse in Chapter XXV. is also very useful for little boys' blouses and shirts. Fig. 311 shows a blouse with a box-pleat front made by pressing out a wide hem.

When working the buttonholes on children's garments, *strand* the slit so as to give extra strength and prevent stretching and *buttonhole closely all round the slit*. Finish the inner end with a bar, made by taking several short stranding stitches across this end and buttonholing over them. The knickers should have the waist edge faced in with a strip of firm longcloth or calico about 3 inches deep.

The front-fly opening of boys' knickers must be both neat and strong. It looks an intricate piece of work, but it is not difficult to manage. It is helpful if the beginner first makes a rough fly opening of two thin pieces of material of different colours—one for the lining and one for the material. These can be partly pinned together.

You must remember that boys' clothes fasten over the opposite way to ours. In the following directions the left and right sides refer to the knickers when they are laid flat on the table, right side out, and with *the legs towards you*.

Begin by cutting the extra pieces needed—three pieces from the knicker material and two from calico or lining. The three pieces must follow the line of the fly opening, be about 2 inches wide at the top, and taper off in a curve below the bottom of the opening, as in Fig. 312. First face in the upper right side of the opening with a piece of material. After seaming the edges together, turn the facing material back to the wrong side and press it flat so that the seam comes just a very little over on the wrong side, and so cannot be seen from the front. Machine-stitch all down the opening $\frac{1}{4}$ inch in from the folded edge. Tack the inner edge of the facing material to the garment.

Next make the flap to hold the buttonholes. Lay together, right sides touching, a self-piece and a lining piece. Seam them together and turn right side out. Seam them so that the material will lie towards the front of the knickers, against the faced edge. Work three (or about three) horizontal buttonholes in the flap, treating of course the material side as the right side. Remember to work the buttonhole stitch all round the slit for strength.

Lay the finished flap in position against the faced edge of the opening so that this edge projects ⅜ inch or a little more beyond the edge of the flap. Tack the flap to the knickers along its inner curved edge, leaving the edge nearest to the opening free. From the right side, stitch over the tacking, through the facing and the flap.

Next, each buttonhole can be enclosed in a separate little pocket by running a line of hand back-stitching across the flap between the buttonholes. Back-stitch through the flap and the facing, but of course *not* through the actual knickers, as no stitches must show on the right side. Now the upper or *right* half of the fly is finished.

The left or lower side of the knickers is provided, like a frock, with a projecting piece (sometimes called a fly wrap) which fits under the right side. It is made like this—seam the last piece of material, the third piece, to the under-fly edge, and press it out so that it projects. Now seam the last lining piece to the free edge of this projection, right sides touching. Press the lining backwards over the seam to line the projection or wrap. Run it by hand down to the seam of flap and projection, then overcast the three sets of turnings together. From the right side machine-stitch ⅛ inch inside the outer curve of the projection, and also on the knickers ⅛ inch inside the fly seam.

CHAPTER XXXV

LACE AND LACE-MAKING

Materials and Tools. Various Kinds of Lace. The Making of Pillow
Lace. Winding the Bobbin. Regulating the Supply of Thread.
Movements for Making Stitches. Cloth Stitch, Half Stitch,
Twisting. Torchon and Russian Lace.

THE making of elaborate lace is a difficult task, but perhaps
no book on the Art of Needlecraft is complete without
an allusion to it. Moreover, although lace like Honiton or
Mechlin, with its five hundred bobbins, cannot be attempted by
the home-worker, there is a certain amount of lace that is both
easy and practical and forms pretty borders for lawn handkerchiefs and other dainty things.

No one quite knows the origin of that lovely fragile thing
called lace. Lace-making probably began in or near Venice,
and we hear about it in the sixteenth century and we know it
was worn in Renaissance days. It was the great lady of the
Renaissance period who often started lace-making as an industry
in the neighbourhood where she lived, and worked at it herself
as a hobby for her own leisure hours, which were perhaps more
plentiful in those days than now. Some say Catherine of Aragon
introduced lace-making into the English Midlands. In any case,
from that time lace-making has been both an industry and a
hobby. Even to-day, when like everything else hand-made lace
has been largely superseded by machine-made imitations, genuine
hand-made lace is still made, worn, and appreciated. Lace-
making is really fascinating ; it is not laborious (we refer to the
simple kinds we are going to describe), it is not unduly trying to
the sight, *but*—and there is generally a *but* to everything—it is
not easy. However, no time need be spent in experimenting, one
can begin to make a narrow simple piece of lace at once.

All the various kinds of lace may be grouped under three headings :

(1) *Pillow Lace.*—This is made on a pillow. It can be most difficult and intricate, but it can be fairly easy, and is therefore well suited for first attempts. It is the making of a simple form of pillow lace that we are going to describe.

(2) *Needle Point Lace.*—Point lace is made with the needle, as its name tells. It is too difficult and intricate for the home worker, so we are not dealing with it here.

(3) *Knitted and Crochet Lace.*—This has already been dealt with in Chapters XXIII., " Knitting," and Chapter XXIV., " Crochet."

The Making of Pillow Lace

Tools and Materials needed :

(1) A Pillow.
(2) Bobbins.
(3) Pins. Thread. Stand. The stand is not essential.

The *pillow* for yard lace, which is the easiest to make, must be bolster-shaped. A pillow 10 inches wide and about 18 inches round is a good size. The covering may be strong calico, and bran and sand make a good filling, because hard, even stuffing is necessary. The pillow can be made at home, or if this presents any difficulty, it can be bought.

The *bobbins* are for holding the supplies of thread. They can be made of bone or ivory, but they are generally made of wood. Fig. 313 shows a bobbin wound with thread and with its cover on. Fig. 314 shows a bobbin being wound with thread. A beginner needs about four dozen—that is, twenty-four pairs.

Fig. 315 shows another type of bobbin with no cover. The cover is not necessary, though it keeps the thread tidy and clean. Bobbins cost about one shilling a dozen when made of well-finished box-wood.

Pins.—The pins should be proper lace pins. They are like ordinary pins, but they are 2 inches long and rather slender. Brass lace pins cost sixpence for three hundred ; lace pins with coloured heads are fivepence per dozen.

Thread.—Linen thread is far the best. Cotton thread tends to get fluffy with washing, and then the appearance of the lace

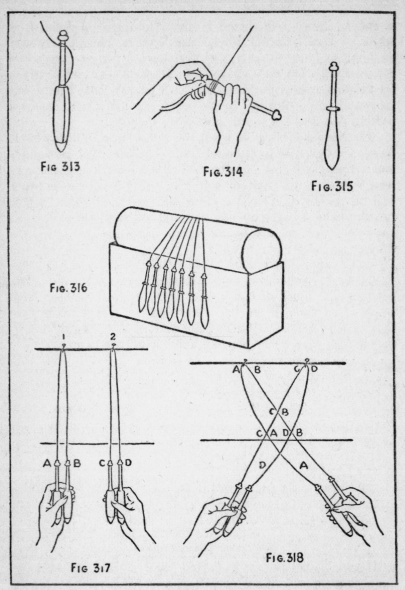

FIG. 313.—Bobbin wound with thread and with cover on.   FIG. 314.—Winding thread on bobbin.   FIG. 315.—Bobbin without cover.   FIG. 316.—Pillow in stand.   FIG. 317.—Beginning the Cloth Stitch.   FIG. 318.—Completing the Cloth Stitch.

is spoilt. Linen lace thread is about fourpence a skein, it is white or ecru. Cotton thread can also be bought for lace-making, and is suitable for beginners. Coarse mercerised coloured balls are very cheap. No absolute rule can be given for the thickness of the thread, as each pattern looks best in one particular size of thread. When beginning it is wise to choose a pattern that does not require a very fine thread.

The Stand.—This is to keep the pillow from rolling about. A wooden box without a lid will do. The box must be slightly longer than the pillow, but not too broad, so that the pillow may rest wedged firmly half in and half out. Some people work with the pillow on their lap. It is said that a very good pillow can be made quickly by one dozen straw bottle-cases, turned heads and tails, tightly bound together and covered. Fig. 316 shows a pillow in a box or stand.

To the above list can be added :

(1) Paper patterns of any lace you decide to make. The patterns are quite an important part of your outfit. They are fastened down on to the pillow and the lace is made over them. They are not a bit like the pattern in the finished lace, they merely show where the pins and stitches are to go.

(2) Cards prepared for pricking designs.

(3) Squared paper.

(4) Pricker or piercer for above.

(5) Skein-winder and bobbin-winder. These are not at all necessary, and greatly add to the expense of lace-making.

Having got together all the materials, there are three things to learn before beginning to make lace :

(1) To wind the bobbins. This is easy.

(2) Regulate the supply of thread.

(3) Know and practise the movements necessary for making the stitches used in some simple form of lace-making.

WINDING THE BOBBINS

If you do not possess a bobbin-winder, which, as we have said before, is not at all necessary, you wind your bobbin in the following way : Hold the bobbin (with cover off, if your bobbins are of the covered type) in your right hand, the head of the bobbin turned to the right. Take the end of the thread in your left hand, and put it round the bobbin at the end farthest from the head, as in Fig. 314. Hold the end in place with your right thumb, and begin to wind. You may wind either *away* from you or *toward* you, but whichever direction you choose, wind all your bobbins alike. When the bobbin is full, replace the cover, leaving an end of thread about 6 or 7 inches in length between the cover and the shaft, as in Fig. 313.

To prevent the thread from becoming unwound, a loop known as a " half-hitch " must be made close round the head of the bobbin. To make a " half-hitch," you wind the end of the thread round the left forefinger so as to form a loop. Then take your finger out of the loop, put the head of the bobbin into it, and draw the thread tight, as in Fig. 313.

Regulating the Supply of Thread

(1) *To Lengthen the Thread between the Work and the Head of the Bobbin.*—To lengthen the thread, hold the bobbin in your right hand at right angles to the line of the thread, then roll the bobbin between finger and thumb, keeping the thread taut as you do so.

(2) *To Shorten the Thread between the Work and the Head of the Bobbin.*—To shorten the thread, hold the bobbin as for lengthening ; with the left hand take hold of the thread that passes down the bobbin and pull it away from the bobbin towards you—keep it taut while you roll the bobbin from the right to the left with the finger and thumb of the right hand.

It is essential that the supply of thread between the work and the head of the bobbin should be kept even. If the bobbins are allowed to hang unevenly, they at once become twisted together, and it is wonderful the confusion they can cause !

Movements for Making Stitches

Torchon lace and Russian lace can be made with only two kinds of stitch ; moreover, neither lace requires an unmanageable number of bobbins, so that they are both suitable for the beginner.

The two stitches used in Torchon lace and Russian lace are *Cloth Stitch* and *Half Stitch*. Learn and practise these before you begin any definite piece of lace.

Cloth Stitch.—Fasten a piece of checkered paper about 3 inches square upon your pillow. Set a row of seven pins, each two squares apart, across the top of your paper. Thread fourteen bobbins and knot them together in pairs. Hang a pair of bobbins on each pin, *and see that they all hang evenly,* as in Figs. 316 and 317, with about 6 inches of thread from the pin to the bobbin head.

Start from the left, take Pair 1 (A, B) in your left hand, and Pair 2 (C, D) in your right, as shown in Fig. 317. Cross B over C ; then cross C over A, and D over B ; lastly, cross A over D. This completes the stitch as in Fig. 318.

Now stick a large pin (a hat-pin will do) in the pillow about 4 inches or 5 inches out on the left-hand side, and hang Pair 2 to the left of it to keep it out of the way. Repeat the cloth-stitch process with Pair 1 and Pair 3—Pair 3 taking the place of Pair 2. Now hang Pair 3 beside Pair 2, but to the right of it. Repeat the cloth-stitch with Pair 1 and Pair 4. Send Pair 4 to join Pair 3 and 2. Continue in this way until you have worked through all the pairs and have come to the right-hand side of the work. Next, stick in a new pin two squares below the right-hand pin, and see that Pair 1 falls to the right of it and Pair 7 to the left. Work back from right to left in exactly the same way as on the outward journey, using Pair 1 all the time and the others in the following order : 7—6—5—4—3—2. Pair 1, which are always in use, are called the " workers."

Half Stitch.—This is really incomplete cloth stitch. It can be made either by the first two movements or the last two movements of cloth stitch ; but whichever way you make it, you must keep to the same way of doing it throughout the same piece of work. Follow all the directions given for cloth stitch, but leave out the third movement—that is, the crossing of A over D, or if you like, leave out the first movement—that is, the crossing of B over C. Half stitch is worked just like cloth stitch : first from left to right, and then back again from right to left. Remember, as in working cloth stitch, to set in a new pin below the last each time you come to the end of a row.

Twisting.—In addition to the stitches given above, " twisting " is much used in making lace. " Twisting " means placing the right thread of a pair over the left of its own pair ; it is done

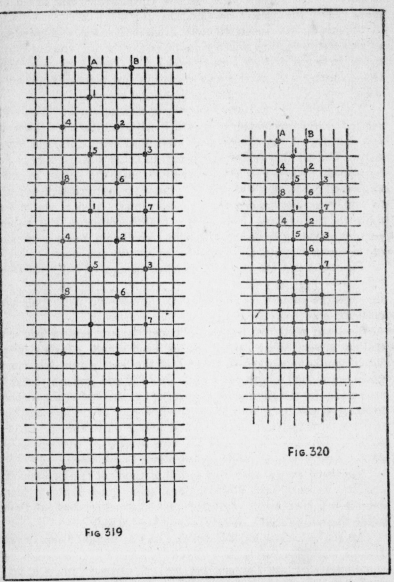

FIG. 319.—Pricked pattern for Everlasting Lace for coarse thread.   FIG. 320.—
Pricked pattern for Everlasting Lace and Edging for fine thread.

in between the stitches to make the fabric firmer and to define more clearly the lines of the design.

When you have mastered cloth stitch, half stitch, and twisting, as well as the winding and regulation of the thread, you are quite ready to begin making a piece of lace. Choose a piece of lace that is simple and narrow and needs but few pairs of bobbins— six or seven pairs is enough—for your first attempt.

First study the pattern you have chosen carefully. You will see that the paper pattern is marked with numbers for the first working out of the design, and after that with dots and lines only. The numbers show the places in order where pins are to be placed. When you have worked through the design by this numbered guide, you will probably know the pattern well enough to find your way among the dots and lines. If not, you must refer to the written instructions that accompany the paper pattern, or perhaps, better still, before you begin, make a tracing of the number guide, and keep this by you as you work.

Figs. 319 and 320 show the pricked pattern of " Everlasting Edging." Fig. 319 shows the pattern for coarse thread, and Fig. 320 the pattern for fine thread. Seven pair of bobbins are needed ; three pair are hung at A, four pair at B.

You will need two lengths of paper pattern (unless you are making a very short piece of lace), each about 3 inches long. When you have worked to the end of the first length, you must place the second length quite close up to it and proceed to work over this ; by the time you have worked to the end of the second length you will be able to unpin the first part of the lace and set free the paper pattern under it, and join it on to the end of the second. Proceed thus, using the two lengths of pattern alternately until you have made as much lace as you need.

You have now a little idea of the methods of the lace-maker, and if you only succeed in making some good Torchon lace, even if you cannot call yourself a real lace-maker, you will have made something that is pretty, useful, and strong.

All the materials for lace-making can be bought from Dryad Handicrafts, Leicester, and those interested in lace-making should get *Practical Lace-making*, by C. C. Channer, price 3s. 6d., from the same firm.

CHAPTER XXXVI

MISCELLANY

I. The Sewing Machine. Care of Machine. Its Uses. Machine Seams. Attachments. II. Making use of Waste Material—Old Jars, Tins, Reels, Clothes-pins, Bricks, Square Tins, and Cardboard Boxes. III. A Few Facts worth knowing : How to renew Old Transfers ; How to prevent Mats and Rugs from turning up ; How to keep your Scissors and Machine Needle sharp ; How to avoid Broken Buttons on a Shirt ; How to make Warm Shoes and Gloves for Baby in a Few Minutes ; The Simplest Way of crocheting a Rug. IV. Two Amusing Trifles for a Bazaar : A Doll to mind your Needles ; A Wire Gnome. V. Framing in Passe Partout.

I

THE SEWING MACHINE

THE sewing machine is indispensable if you intend to do very much dressmaking at home. Seams take a long time to work by hand, and it is difficult to keep them flat and unpuckered.

The electric sewing machine is ideal, and can be plugged in to any point in the same way as any other electric appliance, so that it can be used in any room. Near the foot there is a bulb to throw the light exactly over the work, and as both hands are free for manipulation, the machine can be worked very quickly. The hand machine takes up less room than the treadle, and can be carried from one room to another, but it is more difficult to use, as the worker has only one hand with which to arrange the material.

When you buy a machine, allow the shop assistant to show you exactly how it works, or, if you have forgotten any little detail, call in at any of the sewing-machine shops and have your memory refreshed.

20

CARE OF THE SEWING MACHINE

Your machine, if properly cared for, will last a lifetime. Many people are very neglectful of their machines. They would not dream of using a motor-car or a bicycle knowing that it had not been oiled for several months, yet they will light-heartedly leave their sewing machine unoiled and expect it to serve them just as well. This is a great mistake. If you want your machine to work well you must oil it *regularly* ; every day is not too often if you are using it a great deal.

Occasionally remove the footplate and clear any fluff from the claw or teeth, and, more rarely, take off the end plate and clean.

All moving parts of the machine that come in contact with each other must be kept covered with a thin film of oil, otherwise the friction causes the metal to wear out quickly and the machine runs stiffly. This means that the handle will need more energy to turn it, instead of the merest touch that should be necessary when all parts are working smoothly together.

Oiling the Machine.—Use only the best oil and not too much. Put one drop into each of the holes which are placed so that the oil drops on to the vital points, and into all places which your book of instructions says must be lubricated. Be careful to remove any superfluous oil, especially wiping the needle-bar, as oil collecting there stains the top thread and any part which carries the loop of the top thread over the shuttle to lock with the under thread. Now run the machine over an odd piece of stuff (without threading) so as to catch any stray drops of oil.

It is most important to use only the special oil of the best quality, as cheaper oils are heavier and tend to clog the delicate parts of the machinery and so cause the machine to work heavily. The more oil you apply to remedy the trouble the worse it becomes, so in every way it pays to use the best oil.

Cleaning the Machine.—If the machine seems to run heavily it is probably clogged with dust and fluff from woollen materials and should be cleaned at once. A suitable brush for cleaning can be bought from the manufacturers, or a soft typewriter brush can be used. To clean the machine, use paraffin, putting it into all the oil holes. Then leave it for about an hour, then

wipe the oil away and the dust and fluff will go with it. Take
out the slide and lift up the machine to get at all the under parts.
Then proceed to oil the machine in the usual way.

When you have finished with the machine, dust it, and flick
the duster to blow the fluff out of the crevices, especially if you
have been stitching a thick woollen material. If this is neglected
the fluff falls further into the machinery, and causes trouble
later on. For the same reason always keep the machine covered
to protect it from the dust.

If the room where the machine is kept is at all damp, cover
it all over with a woollen cloth, or the dampness will penetrate
and rust the needle and other parts that are not oiled.

To begin the Work.—It is advisable to learn to stitch quite
straight before beginning to make a garment. Otherwise bad
results will probably discourage you in the making of further
efforts. The foot of the machine will help to guide you when
stitching only a short distance from an edge, but at first it is a
good plan to draw lines on odd pieces of material and try to
stitch exactly over them.

Remove all pins that are likely to blunt or break the needle.

Before starting, bring up the under cotton by holding the
needle thread quite loosely in the left hand and turning the wheel
towards you until the needle moves up and down once. You
will find if you draw the needle thread a little tighter that you
can pull the under thread through the needle hole quite easily.
Now put both cottons out to the back of the presser foot. The
upper cotton should be about 5 inches long, or the needle will
come unthreaded when you begin to stitch. Keep the bulk of
the material to the left of the machine, and lower the presser
foot before turning the handle.

As you work you will notice that the machine is so constructed
that it feeds itself, so do not try to push the material under the
needle or pull it out at the back. Holding the work tightly or
pushing it through tends to disturb the action of the machine and
produces a varying size of stitch. It may even break the needle.

To keep straight, watch an edge of the foot in relation to
something on the material, such as the edge of a fold or hem, a
line of tacking or chalk.

Guide by holding lightly, the right hand well in front keeping the edge in right relation with the foot, the left hand controls the mass of material on the table. Be careful, as we have said before, not to push the material under the needle or over-guide, *merely prevent* the material from going crooked ; *but* over sudden thicknesses or round difficult corners give the machine some assistance by keeping the fingers of left hand behind the foot, and thumb in front. This is the *proper way* of guiding on a *hand machine.* Feed stretchy bias edges quickly (by pushing in the work), to counteract the stretch.

To turn Corners.—Have the needle piercing the material, raise the foot, pivot the material on the needle, drop foot and continue.

Machining Gathers.—If you are machining gathers, place the gathers against the claws. If the gathers are above, the foot is apt to force the top layer into a wave in front. However, you must break this rule so as to machine *inside* circles—for example, armholes or cuffs. It is best also to place the more stretchy of two layers against the claw.

Finishing Off.—Do not work a single stitch beyond the material, or the cotton will become entangled and form a knot in the needle hole. If this does happen, lift the machine and poke the cotton out with the small pointed instrument usually supplied with sewing-machine tools. Never attempt to remove it by working the machine needle on it, for it will probably snap quickly, and cause accidents.

When a seam or hem is finished, see that the needle is as high as it will go, then lift the presser foot and pull the work gently towards the back and left. Cut the threads with the scissors, do not try to break them with the fingers, or you will either pucker the end of the work or snap the needle.

There are three ways of finishing off :

(1) Draw both ends of cotton to the same side (the wrong side), then tie them with an overhand knot. This is not always neat enough or strong enough for the stitching on some parts of a garment. In this case it is better.

(2) To thread a needle with the cottons, make a back stitch, and run them between the folds of the material, or the ends can be simply darned in.

(3) A good strong method is to double stitch by pivoting and going back half an inch.

Points to remember when Stitching and making Seams

(1) In stitching a seam together with one side on the straight grain and one on the bias, put the bias to the teeth or claw of the machine, keeping the straight on the top. This, as we have said before, applies to fulness, the teeth of the machine easing in the under side. If the fulness comes on top, the foot of the machine is inclined to push the material forwards. Also remember when sewing seams on the bias, to use a short stitch and a loose tension so that the cotton will not easily break when the material is stretched.

(2) A piece of tissue-paper tacked to a seam in georgette or any thin material is a great help to keeping the stitching straight. Indeed, all flimsy material should be machined with paper beneath ; this is torn away afterwards.

(3) Stitch all the seams in a garment in one direction, from the neck downwards.

(4) In plain seams stitch just outside the *fitting* line, especially on tight-fitting sleeves, etc., because machining will produce a closer fit than tacking. Stitch below a gathering thread.

(5) On straight-by-the-thread seams, hold the work with one hand behind the foot and one in front, and so pass through the work stretched between the two hands.

(6) Take out the tacking threads that have been used to mark the fitting lines in case they should get entangled in the stitching. This applies chiefly to tacking threads in seams.

(7) The stitching looks better if the garment has been well pressed beforehand.

(8) To sew flannel on bias seams, use a short stitch and as light a tension as possible, so as to leave the thread loose enough to withstand the strain of stretching the goods.

Seams are always stronger and neater when machined. Here is a useful summary of machined seams you ought to know :

Machined Seams important in Dressmaking and for the Home Worker

(1) *Run-and-felled Seam or Flat-felled Seam.*—A seam for everyday garments, strong and flat for ironing. This is termed *Run and Fell* by hand and *Machine Fell* by machine. For this

seam, see Chapter IX. Machine fell is useful for any garments requiring special strength, *e.g.* overalls, shirts, etc., and also on washing frocks and blouses when double rows of stitching are fashionable.

(2) *Plain Seam, Open Seam, or Single Seam.*—The seam for outer-garments. This seam is the one most commonly used, and is very simple and well known. It is much used in dressmaking. The layers to be joined are firmly tacked together, the tacking just inside the line you are to sew along, and parallel with it. Machine the seam, press it open, and neaten the edges. How you neaten them depends on what material you use; sometimes the edges are overcast. When the edges are firm, as in flannel, it is sufficient to *pink* them—that is, to snip little V-shaped pieces out all the way along, as in Fig. 321; sometimes the edges are bound with bias binding, as in Fig. 322, and so on.

(3) *A French Seam* for dainty underwear and outer-garments of transparent material. For this seam, see Chapter IX.

(4) *A Stitched Seam.*—Make an ordinary single seam, press it open, and tack. Turn to the right side and machine down either side of the seam.

(5) *Raised Seam.*—See Machine-felled (1).

(6) *A Strapped Seam.*—See Chapter XXV.

(7) *Lapped Seams.*—Used on outer-garments wherever a line is to be accentuated or where firmness is an advantage. It is often used down the centre of a skirt, generally on tweed or similar material. Turn in one edge of the seam and tack it over the right side of the other raw edges level inside. Stitch down within the folded edge. The turning should be pressed before it is tacked down.

A quicker method of lapping a seam, which gives the effect of a genuine lapped seam, is called:

(8) *A Tuck Seam.*—Make a single seam and press both the turnings to one side. Tack them in place, then on the right side machine through the three layers just within the seam. See Chapter XXV., " Home Dressmaking."

(9) *Mantua Maker's Seam.*—Useful for washing frocks and blouses, also where one selvedge and one raw edge come together

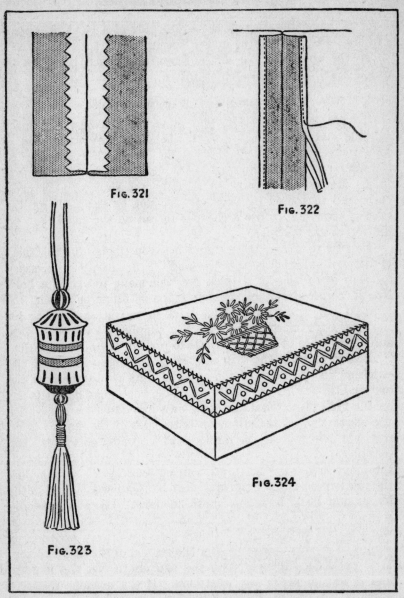

FIG. 321   FIG. 322   FIG. 323   FIG. 324

FIG. 321.—An open seam with the edges of the seam pinked out.   FIG. 322.— A bound seam.   FIG. 323.—Decorated cord for drawing curtains.   FIG. 324. —A cardboard box covered with embroidered material.   Edge of box covered with galon.

—for example, the edge of the wrong side of a pleat or among gathers. For the mantua-maker's seam, see Chapter IX.

In the above list the *Plain Seam*, also called the *Open* or *Single Seam*, is the most important.

A Few more Hints on Machining

To get the best results you must use the best and most suitable materials. Poor quality silk snaps very easily and is sometimes knotted along the length. It is always better to use silk for all woollen and silk goods and cotton for cotton goods only. Mercerised threads are usually not so strong as plain ones, and so should be avoided. Do not be tempted, for the sake of economy, to use a cheaper thread on the spool than on the top of the machine.

Be sure to change the needle when you change the thickness of material on which you are working. A fine needle is necessary for thin materials, for a thick one will make too large a hole. No. 11 needle is suitable for fine crêpe de Chine or muslin. A coarse needle must be used for thick materials, say No. 18 for tickings, boys' clothes, etc. Keep a supply of various needles, stuck in a piece of greased flannel to prevent them from rusting.

Before starting the stitching on a fresh garment, test the stitch on an odd piece of the material. As a rule, the finer the material the smaller the stitch should be, but a good deal depends on the type of material and your own individual taste. Notice the appearance of the stitch on both sides of the seam. If on the right side you can see the loops of the under cotton, the top tension is too tight, and must be loosened. If, on the other hand, the loops of the needle thread can be seen on the wrong side, the top tension is too loose and must be tightened. Read in the instruction book how this must be done. There is generally a little thumb nut over the spring, which tightens the tension when turned to the right. Unless you are a very experienced worker, it is most unwise to alter the tension of the under cotton. It is perfectly adjusted when the machine leaves the factory, and it seldom needs any alteration. If the machine misses a stitch or two, the needle has been put in too high up; lower it a little at a time, for if it is too low down it will be snapped off by the spool or shuttle.

Remember that cotton always looks a shade lighter when stitched on the material, so choose a darker rather than a lighter one.

All stitching should be done on the right side of the material, as the needle thread gives the better appearance.

This has been said before, but it is such a common fault among beginners that it may be wise to repeat it here—do not attempt to stitch anything that has only been pinned. The pins get in the way and will sooner or later break the needle. It is quite impossible to stitch a seam unless it has been neatly tacked first.

The Attachments

People are generally delighted when they first possess the little box of attachments, and become very excited when they see the wonderful things that can be achieved with them by the assistants in the sewing-machine shops. But it is seldom that the same people take the trouble to use them. It is a great pity, for so much work that is somewhat dull can be quickly done by these fascinating little gadgets.

The foot is usually taken off and the gadget screwed on in its place. Follow the instructions carefully and patiently and you will be rewarded with strong, neat work that has a very professional finish.

We will now say a few words about the different attachments. They are, it must be remembered, of *varying* value. The materials on which they can be used and the occasions on which they can be successfully applied are limited, but within these limits they can be of the *greatest value*. It is because people do not respect these limitations that they fail to get the full value from the attachments. Most of the attachments are successful on firm cotton made up in simple styles.

The Binder.—The binder attaches bias binding to a curved or a scalloped edge in less than half the time it takes to do it in the ordinary way.

It makes a quick, cheap, and easy way of finishing children's underclothing. It should be used on *cotton*—cotton frocks, nightdresses, and pyjamas. It is especially effective when the binding is in contrast to the material of the garment. The machining shows on the right side, but remember *curves* need a good deal of practice.

The Quilter.—The quilter is simple to use. It is not always necessary, of course, to work the quilting to form squares, diamond shapes can be made by stitching diagonally across the article. However, many people find the quilter less accurate than the ordinary method. It is only a little quicker.

The Tucker.—This is not of great value always. It is less accurate than the hand method and very little quicker.

The Gatherer or Ruffler.—This is very useful on *long* frills. The ruffler pleats and sews on ribbon at the same time. It can be used to trim children's party frocks, table runners, etc.

Braider.—This is very useful for applying soutache. Machine over the design on the wrong side. It is very easy to use, therefore of great value when such trimming is in fashion.

Hemmers.—These are especially useful on *long, straight edges*, such as silk scarves on the bias, frills for cretonne loose covers, but remember heavier fabrics go through the hemmer on the straight thread but rarely on the bias. The hemmers are also useful for seams and hems on cambric under-garments. Do seams *after* any hems they cross.

The small hemmer or narrow hemmer should always be used for small hems on silk scarves or handkerchiefs, and for the narrow hems that are necessary on frills and similar trimmings. Lace can be sewn on at the same time as the hemmer is used, but if you do not like machine-stitching to show on dainty garments, work an embroidery silk over the top of every other stitch. This hides it completely and adds to the decoration.

Success with the narrow hemmer depends on guiding exactly the right amount of turning into the attachment—too much is just as bad as too little. The first inch or so needs to be machined down *afterwards*, in the ordinary way.

Many workers, if they want to stitch a hem by hand, run it along with the hemmer first, leaving the needle *unthreaded*. The hem is thus turned in and marked already for hand-stitching.

The modern way of finishing edges on delicate fabrics, where it is necessary to have a light and dainty appearance, is to make a narrow single turning, and to machine it from the right side close to the fold. The raw edges are trimmed away afterwards.

Darner.—This is really an efficient and valuable time-saver. It is not difficult to use on treadle and electric machines. The machine must be clean, oiled, and in really good running condition for the use of the darner. The chief reason, perhaps, for the failure of machine-darning is that so many machines are kept in bad order. The stitch size should be reduced to nothing and the work stretched tightly in a shallow frame that will go under the needle without catching or bending it. Suitable shallow frames are supplied by Singer. Then with both arms resting on the machine, move the frame backwards and forwards while running the machine. To make the stitches closer or more scattered, change the speed of the hands moving the frame. On the whole, guiding is easiest at high speed.

On household linen and cotton under-garments use the special embroidery thread supplied for the purpose. Most people like Singer's No. 50. On woven or knitted under-garments use fine sewing silk.

It is quite an interesting process to embroider by machine.

II

MAKING USE OF WASTE MATERIALS

It is wonderful what a number of things that accumulate in a house, and are often finally thrown away, can be made into objects of real use and beauty by simple and effective decoration.

We shall give here as many suggestions as possible, and these should be of great value to all who are called upon to supply articles for bazaars and sales of work.

Jars, Pots, Bottles, Tongue-Dishes, Tins of all Kinds.—First let us think what can be done with all the varied assortment of jars, pots, honey-jars, gum bottles, tongue-dishes, etc., that are available. From these attractive vases and bowls for holding flowers and bulbs can be made, and these are always useful and will find a ready sale.

The paint used is a quick-drying enamel which can be used on earthenware, glass, and tin. Fairly soft brushes are best, large ones for painting the whole surface and fine ones for the designs.

Choose jars as far as possible that are shapely and of fine proportions. They may be painted in colour schemes that suggest certain flowers, but whatever the colour scheme the design should be simple, and suitable to the object you are decorating.

Fine work should not be attempted. It is out of place on such simple shapes, and cannot be carried out with enamel, which is a fairly thick paint. For successful effects, designs made with the free use of the brush, such as straight or wavy lines, are best, or flower patterns made by simple brush strokes. Keep the brush sufficiently full of colour so that it flows easily but does not make blobs. Keep the colours as clean and bright as possible.

Pots of natural stone colour, or red brick, make a very effective background for bright colours. If their colour is not suitable they can be enamelled first. Porous pots must first have a coating of size painted over the surface to prevent the enamel sinking through.

Tins can be adapted to various uses, according to their size. Large tins can be used for tea, coffee, etc. ; smaller tins are useful for holding pins, buttons, reels, etc., while shallow tins would make useful trays for cigarette ashes.

As tins have printed matter on them, they must be covered with two coats of enamel to hide this, before they can be decorated. Tins covered with paper often have a plain silvery surface when the paper is taken off. This makes quite an effective background for a pattern in red or black. Tins painted black and decorated with a simple all-over pattern in gold or silver have a pleasing effect.

Empty Reels (Fig. 323).—A novel use for empty reels. Here is a way of decorating reels so attractively and putting them to good use for making cords for pulling back curtains, that they will find a ready sale at any bazaar. Fig. 323 shows the finished result. The reel is painted with opaque water-colours and varnished. Two button moulds have been glued to the top and bottom of the reel and coloured beads added. (For making the tassels and cords, see Chapter XIII., " Cords, Tassels, and Fringes.") If the beads are wooden ones, they can be painted to harmonise with the reel, or glass beads of suitable colours may be used. Instead of a tassel a pendant of permanent modelling clay might be made and painted. When choosing the colour-scheme, remember that these small decorations are most effective when carried out in brilliant colours, with strong contrasts of dark and light.

Clothes-pins.—Clothes-pins that open and shut with a spring are most useful for holding back window curtains that may flap disturbingly at night, or be injured by rain or wind in the daytime. Decorate these in enamel paints or opaque water-colours and you have an interesting and useful article. They should be painted in pairs. Whatever design you apply to them must be suitable for filling a long, narrow rectangle. It is interesting to draw the rectangle on paper and then think out the design. Simple border patterns surrounded by marginal lines are very suitable. These curtain clasps make attractive items on a bazaar stall.

Bricks.—A useful and decorative weight to keep a door open can be made from a brick.

Select a brick with straight edges and an even surface and give it a coat of paint or shellac. This is very necessary, as the surface is porous and the enamel paints used would sink in.

Before marking the design on the brick, take care that the shellac is thoroughly dry. Plan out the design for the top of the brick on a piece of paper cut the same size. Choose a simple design, cut it out, place it on the brick and draw round it. When painted, apply a coat of shellac to protect the surface. Lastly, cut a piece of felt the exact size of the brick and glue it to the bottom, otherwise the brick will scratch the floor.

Large, Round, or Square Tins and Cardboard Boxes, such as can be obtained from a Grocer.—These make excellent waste-paper baskets if they are covered with natural linen and dainty wool embroideries. A round tin 8¼ inches deep and 6 or 7 inches in diameter makes a dainty waste-paper basket if it is covered with a strip of natural linen about 21 inches long and 10 inches wide. The cross-stitch lady described in Chapter XXXII. looks very gay repeated twice, with autumn flowers or trees in between. First arrange your pattern on the strip of material. You may like to have one lady only, so arrange her in the middle—the join will come behind. If you do not want to make your own design, use a bought transfer.

When the embroidery is completed, make ¼-inch turnings at the top and bottom of the linen and press with an iron. Sew up the side seam to make a tube, and slip it over the tin. Stick the linen to the base of the tin with seccotine. Turn the top edge over and stick it carefully inside, using seccotine as before. Allow this to dry, then sew galon to the top and bottom edges and inside the top of the tin.

A method of making a waste-paper basket from pieces of cardboard has been described in Chapter XXXII., but it is perhaps easier to start with the cardboard shape already made, so that it only needs to be covered with decorative material. These boxes can be covered in pretty patterned material if desired.

Very good work-baskets can be made from old cardboard boxes of a suitable shape ; sew the coverings of these boxes on, do not glue them.

Small cardboard boxes can also be covered in linen or silk, with dainty designs worked on it.

Long boxes make useful glove-boxes.

To cover the boxes, first take the measurements of the lid and the box. You will need a piece of silk or linen for the top of the cover, a piece for the base of the box, a long strip to wrap round the sides ; you must allow for turnings and cut the strip 1 inch deeper than the box. A piece of galon 1 inch wide, long enough to go round the box, will do for the edge of the cover. Cut also pieces for lining the box and lid and two pieces of wadding for padding for the lid and base of box if desired. Embroider a design on the piece for the top of the box and for the sides if desired.

Line the top piece, leaving an opening for a piece of cardboard. Insert the padding between the cardboard and the embroidered top. Sew up the opening. Now stitch galon round the lid at right angles to it. To this the padded embroidered top is sewn.

Seam the narrow ends of the strip for the sides together and stitch it to the piece of material for the base of the box. Join the pieces for the lining in the same way. Pad the bottom of the inside and then slip the lining in. Now fit the box into the cover just made, turn in the raw edges of this cover and the lining, and slip-stitch them.

Fig. 324 shows a box covered with silk or linen and embroidered.

III

A Few Facts worth Knowing

(1) *To renew Old Transfers.*—When you have used your transfers once, do not throw them away ; you may find them useful later on. Transfers may be renewed many times in the following way : Scrape half a block of washing blue into an egg-cup, add the same amount of castor sugar, and mix them together with a teaspoon. Add cold water drop by drop until it is the consistency of cream. Now mark out the lines of the pattern, using a fine paint-brush or a perfectly clean, soft nib in a pen-holder. Take care not to make blots or tear the paper by pressing too hard with the pen. When the mixture is quite dry and firm, the transfer can be used again.

This method of renewing the transfer will save your buying two designs for a pair of cushions or chairbacks. It is useful for a favourite design that you are unable to buy again.

(2) *How to prevent the Ends of Mats and Rugs from turning up.*—Many mats, particularly if they are not very expensive, turn up at the corners and so look untidy, and even shabby. It is a good plan to sew a strip of milliners' wire on the under side of each end of the mat. This will keep the ends and corners of the mats quite flat.

(3) *How to keep your Scissors sharp.*—Work the open blades of the scissors on each side of a narrow-necked bottle as though you were trying to cut off the neck. After doing this about twelve times you will find that scissors that have become slightly blunt will now cut quite well. Another method is to cut up pieces of sandpaper with the scissors.

(4) *To Sharpen a Sewing-Machine Needle.*—This can be done in a similar way to the second method of sharpening scissors. Work a few inches of stitching through a piece of sandpaper. The grit of the sandpaper sharpens the point. Then hold the needle point in the flame of a match.

(5) *How to avoid Broken Buttons on a Shirt.*—Take the buttons off the shirt front and in their place make buttonholes. Stitch the buttons on to a broad piece of tape and slip them through the buttonholes that have been made. They can be removed

when the shirt is sent to the wash, so that one set of buttons will do for every shirt.

(6) *The Most Quickly-made Baby's Shoes and Gloves* (Figs. 325 and 326).—No shoes are more easily made than these, as they consist simply of straight pieces of treble crochet.

You will need about 1 oz. of 4- or 5-ply super-fingering.

The sole is made as follows : 7 chain, 6 trebles—11 rows.

The upper part : 12 chain, 11 trebles—18 rows.

To make up the slipper, place the first treble of the last row to the side of the beginning chain of the first row (Fig. 325), and sew neatly along the sides. Pin the sole to the upper, and sew together.

A pretty decorative effect is produced by working a row of double crochet all round the sole and the upper in a contrasting colour.

For the ankle, make one row of trebles all round and then a row of double crochet with the contrasting colour. Make a chain and thread it through the trebles round the ankle, and finish at the front with two pompons.

To make the pompons, first wind the wool round three fingers forty-five times. Hold one end of the loops between thumb and finger of the left hand and tie firmly round the middle. Cut through both ends and trim into a ball.

For other methods of making chains and pompons, see Chapter XIII., " Cords, Tassels, and Fringes."

Baby's Gloves (Fig. 326) : For these you will need 3-ply super-fingering and a pair of needles, size 8.

Cast on 32 stitches.

Rib in 2 plain and 2 purl for about 18 rows.

Knit plain for 30 rows.

Rib in 1 plain and 1 purl for 12 rows. Cast off.

Fig. 326 shows finished piece. Double this, and sew up along cast-off stitches and edges to the top of the wrist. Finish with ribbon at the wrist.

(7) *The Simplest Way to Crochet a Rug.*—This is one of the quickest ways of crocheting a rug. Especially thick wool is needed.

Begin with a chain of about four, work double crochet twice into each chain, round and round, increasing the number so

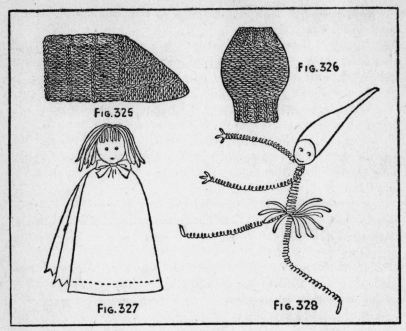

FIG. 325.—Baby's Shoe. FIG. 326.—Baby's Glove. FIG. 327.—A Doll to hold your needles. FIG. 328.—A Wire Gnome.

that the rug is quite flat. Continue until the rug is the the right size. When finished, press well under a damp cloth.

IV

Two Amusing Trifles for a Bazaar

(a) *A Little Doll that minds your Needles.*—Cover a small ball of cotton-wool with a piece of calico to form the head of the doll. Tie securely round the neck with a piece of thread and cut off the odd ends of the calico.

With pen and ink or a fine paint-brush mark in the eyes, nose, and mouth. Thread a needle with yellow, brown, or black wool and make long, straight stitches round her forehead for a fringe. Make big loops of wool on each side of a line down the middle of the head, cut the loops through, and the doll has long hair parted in the middle.

Next make the clothes, which are to hold the needles. You need two pieces of white flannel and a piece of silk for the outside, each about 2 inches wide and 8 inches long. Vandyke round the edges of the pieces of flannel and hem round the edges of the silk. Fold the three pieces in half along the width, cut a hole in the middle of the bend and push the doll's head through. Sew the head neatly to the silk and flannel. Tie a bow of narrow ribbon round the neck, and the doll is finished, as in Fig. 327.

(a) *A Wire Gnome* (Fig. 328).—Quaint and amusing little gnomes, brownies, and goblins can be made from thick wire or pipe-cleaners wrapped round with wool. The head is made of a small ball of cotton-wool covered with chamois or glove kid. Paint the features. Hat dyes are very suitable for the purpose (see Chapter XXIX., section on Other Ways of Colouring Leather). A fine brush is needed. The features could also be put in with stitches.

Bright green wool can be used for wrapping round the body and arms, and brown for the legs; the fringe round the waist might be made of various-coloured woollen ends. Make the cap of brown kid and sew it to the head.

V

FRAMING IN PASSE PARTOUT

This is quite a simple process and is certainly worth knowing, for it is a pleasant thing to be able to frame photographs or pictures in an artistic manner and at a comparatively small cost.

Materials required.—Passe-partout binding. This is made in a variety of colours, but black is the safest colour to use, as it suits almost all types of pictures. If you are mounting sepia prints, brown binding is effective. Coloured bindings are perhaps only suited for decorative panels, such as lettered quotations.

Passe-partout binding is made of especially strong paper. The underside of the paper is already gummed, so that it has only to be damped and stuck securely to the edge of the picture. There are many varieties of passe-partout binding—some are made in imitation of wood or leather—but the plain matt surface or a very finely pebbled surface is the best to use. It is sold in small rolls of 12 yards.

Instead of passe-partout binding, adhesive tape can be used. This is made of strong cotton and the underside is covered with rubber solution. It has two advantages: The rubber solution does not require damping; it need only be pressed on to the edge of the picture. Cream-coloured tape can be bought and decorated with paint to harmonise with the picture. Ordinary poster colours are used. When finished, they must have a coat of matt surface varnish.

Other materials necessary are cardboard for backing, ring-hangers, glass or cellophane (the latter is a transparent colourless material which does not break), glass-cutter if the cutting of the glass is undertaken.

To Frame a Picture.—Some pictures require mounting, especially if they are not the exact size of the glass. Many pictures look much better with a mount—for example, small pictures with a good deal of detail. Mounts can be white or coloured. In the latter case the colour should tone with the picture. The picture should be placed on the mount with an equal margin all round. This should be done very accurately. Do not trust to your eye but test your accuracy by measuring, and mark the position of the top corners of the picture on the mount with a pencil. Put a very small quantity of smooth white paste on the underside of the two top corners of the picture and place it on the mount, with the top corners to the pencil-marks. There is no need to paste the lower corners, as the glass will hold the picture in position. Grip-Fix is an excellent paste to use, as it is white and smooth, and adheres well.

Cut a piece of cardboard for the back the exact size of the mount. Use a stiff cardboard, but not too thick, for a thick cardboard makes a very clumsy edge. Special cardboard can be bought already cut in various sizes.

Now cut the glass, also, the exact size of mount. In case you would like to cut your own glass, here are a few hints on the process. It is not a difficult job. It needs a steady hand and firm pressure in using the cutter. Lay the glass on a flat surface. Place a metal ruler along the line where the glass is to be cut. Hold the cutter almost perpendicular and draw it several times along the edge of the ruler, making a deep scratch. The glass can then be snapped easily along the scratch. Cellophane can be cut with the scissors. See that the side of the glass or cellophane that comes next to the picture is thoroughly clean, as no marks can be rubbed off after the picture has been framed.

To Fasten the Hangers.—Two hangers are needed for most pictures, and their position will naturally depend on the shape and size of the picture. They must be exactly in line with each other. Make two small holes in the cardboard backing, insert the hangers through, open out each clip and knock them with a hammer. A piece of brown paper pasted over the clips will prevent them from working loose and perhaps tearing out of the cardboard.

Now fix the mounted picture to the cardboard backing with a small dab of paste in each corner. Place the glass over the picture and tie them together across their width.

To Fix the Passe-Partout Binding.—Cut from your roll four strips of binding—two for the length and two for the width of the picture—each strip being half an inch longer than the exact measurements of the glass. The two short sides are framed first. The width of the binding round the picture is usually about ¼ inch. Fold down the binding accurately for ¼ inch and make a crease along the fold. Open out and damp evenly all down the narrow side of the creased line. Lay the damp part to the glass so that the crease runs exactly along the edge of the glass and the ends of the binding project ¼ inch each way. It is most important to make the binding adhere firmly to the glass, and this can be done by pressing and rolling it with the fingers. Now damp the other part of the binding, bend it over, and press it firmly to the backing board. Do the same the other side.

To Secure the Corners.—There are two methods. The first is the easiest way. With a pair of sharp scissors cut off the ends level with the edges of the glass, then the corners of the binding are at right angles. The second method is to mitre the corners as described in making the calendar in Chapter XXXII.

The Dryad Handicrafts publish an interesting leaflet on Passe-Partout Framing, price 3d., and supply all the materials necessary for this craft.

INDEX